Protection, Patronage, or Plunder?

British Machinations and (B)uganda's Struggle for Independence

I have enjoyed reading the book. It is well researched and a welcome addition to D. A. Low and R. C. Pratt's book, *Buganda and British Overrule 1900-1955.*
—E. F. Ssempebwa S.C, Professor of Law and Former Chairman, Uganda Constitutional Review Commission.

The work is a master-piece of the forensic recovery of a critical African history. But it is not just about the past. It is also the story of the present situation and how past events created it.
—Robert Kalundi Serumaga, Writer, Political and Human Rights Activist.

A remarkable book and a worthy successor to Low and Pratt's *Buganda and British Overrule 1900-1955.* It is successful in presenting an extensive documentary account by providing original material revealing the character of the administrative relationships between the governments of Buganda Kingdom, the Protectorate and Great Britain.
—Nelson Kasfir, Professor of Political Science and Government, Dartmouth College USA and Author on Africa and Uganda's Politics.

A timely, essential and sober discussion of how best to re-build Uganda. It is a crucial contribution to our understanding how we came to where we are today and how to forge ahead. It deserves the attention of everyone who has our country at heart.
—Phares Mutibwa, Professor of History and Author of "Uganda Since Independence: A Story of Unfulfilled Hopes."

This book helps one understand what colonial Uganda was like, what drove the British to do what they did, the role and place of Buganda then and now and why Uganda and Buganda will be in a tango–until we confront the ghosts of our history. It raises many emotions - pain, sadness and anger at the way things were and how little they have changed in contemporary Uganda. Books like this propel us in the right direction in seeking ways to deal with our future from an understanding of our past.
—Jacqueline Asiimwe, Lawyer and Women Activist.

A marvelous and extremely well researched book that uses primary sources to analyse British colonial rule in Uganda. The book will be useful not only to scholars and researchers but also to politicians as well as general readers.
—Ambassador Mathias Semakula-Kiwanuka, Professor of History and Author on Africa and Uganda's History and Politics.

With the recent damning discovery of 'migrated files' on Britain's colonial past at Hanslope Park, historians are rewriting histories of the British Empire. Apollo N. Makubuya's book is a pioneering effort in this direction on British rule in Uganda. With more narratives of this kind —from all corners of the Empire— we should begin to understand the true and unsavory character of British imperialism.
—Samwiri Lwanga-Lunyiigo, Professor of History and Author of "The Colonial Roots of Internal Conflict in Uganda" and "Mwanga II: Resistance to Imposition of British Rule in Buganda, 1884-1889."

Protection, Patronage, or Plunder?

British Machinations and (B)uganda's Struggle for Independence

By

Apollo N. Makubuya

Cambridge Scholars Publishing

Protection, Patronage, or Plunder? British Machinations and (B)uganda's Struggle for Independence

By Apollo N. Makubuya

This book first published 2018. The present binding first published 2019.

Cambridge Scholars Publishing

Lady Stephenson Library, Newcastle upon Tyne, NE6 2PA, UK

British Library Cataloguing in Publication Data
A catalogue record for this book is available from the British Library

ISBN (10): 1-5275-2374-8
ISBN (13): 978-1-5275-2374-6

To my grandparents:
Ssalongo Shem Walusimbi, who in 1966, paid the ultimate price for his King and country, and
Kasalina Nakulima Walusimbi, whose love and faith in Buganda and the Kabaka are boundless.

TABLE OF CONTENTS

LIST OF ACRONYMS

ACHPR	African Charter on Human and Peoples' Rights
BIC	Buganda Independence Committee
BIS	British Interests Section
BMATT	British Military Advisory Training Team
CAT	Convention Against Torture and Other Forms of Cruel, Inhuman and Degrading Treatment
CBE	Conqueror of the British Empire (a title invented by Idi Amin, not to be confused with the British order, Commander of the British Empire)
CBS	Central Broadcasting Service
CHOGM	Commonwealth Heads of Government Meeting
CMS	Christian Missionary Society
CO	Colonial Office
CRC	Convention on the Rights of the Child
DFID	Department for International Development
DP	Democratic Party
DRC	Democratic Republic of the Congo
EAD	East Africa Department
EAF	East Africa Federation
ECGD	UK Export Credits Guarantee Department
FCO	Foreign and Commonwealth Office
FEDEMU	Federal Democratic Movement of Uganda
GCMG	Grand Cross of the Order of St Michael and St George
HM	Her Majesty
HMG	Her Majesty's Government
IBEAC	Imperial British East Africa Company
IBRD	International Bank for Reconstruction and Development
ICCPR	International Covenant on Civil and Political Rights
ICESCR	International Covenant on Economic, Social and Cultural Rights
ICJ	International Court of Justice
IMF	International Monetary Fund
KAR	King's African Rifles
KBE	Knight Commander of the Most Excellent Order of the British Empire

KCB	King's College Budo
KCMG	Order of St Michael and St George
KY	Kabaka Yekka
LEGCO	Legislative Council
MBE	Most Excellent Order of the British Empire
MNC	Mouvement National Congolais
NAC	Native African Church
NCNC	National Conference of Nigerian Citizens
NPC	Northern People's Congress
NRA/M	National Resistance Army/Movement
OAU	Organisation of African Unity
OBE	Order of the British Empire
ODA	Official Development Assistance
SAP	Structural Adjustment Programme
TNA	The National Archives (at Kew, UK)
UAU	Uganda African Union
UDHR	Universal Declaration of Human Rights
UFM	Uganda Freedom Movement
UHCP	Uganda Hereditary Chieftainship Party
UMHK	Union Miniere du Haut Katanga
UNC	Uganda National Congress
UNLF/A	Uganda National Liberation Front/Army
UNM	Uganda National Movement
UN	United Nations
UNC	Uganda National Congress
UNUC	United Nations Operations in the Congo
UPC	Uganda People's Congress
UPM	Uganda Patriotic Movement
UPU	Uganda Peoples' Union

PREFACE

Following the Berlin Conference of 1884-1885, Britain and other Western powers cajoled, conquered and ultimately colonised diverse peoples across Africa. In the scramble for minerals, land, raw materials, cheap labour and markets, they arbitrarily carved out, occupied and controlled the continent. While the conquest and plunder was often justified on the ideology of the "civilising mission" of primitive Africa, the reality was that it was largely intended to service the material interests of the West, as well as, in the case of Britain, to build and control a global Empire.

It is well known how, in setting up an exploitative imperial hegemony, Britain created new countries and, working with Christian missions, disfigured and disempowered traditional and cultural institutions. Only a handful of those institutions survived colonialism. But the survivors, like the once powerful kingdoms of Buganda in Uganda, Kwazulu in South Africa and the Ashanti in Ghana, are largely alienated in the new political order. Thus, many decades after British rule, these kingdoms struggle to find their past position and power within the new colonially-determined geographical and political boundaries.

Despite the prominence of these actors before independence, the historiography of colonial rule in Africa is dominated by narratives of the West. Furthermore, at the end of colonial rule in Africa, British, Belgian and other colonial powers destroyed, burnt or hid vast colonial records. Consequently, African perspectives on how a few men with a few guns quickly imposed imperial rule and effectively occupied a vast continent for several decades are not well documented or known.

For the kingdom of Buganda—considered an intercessor in expanding and entrenching British rule in Uganda, whose leaders believed that the coming of Christian missionaries was at their "invitation" and who had much faith in the sanctity of its treaties of "protection" with Britain—little is known of how, or why, an erstwhile ally became an adversary. Indeed, the British frustrated Buganda's aspiration for full autonomy and, instead, ensured that the kingdom remained inextricably locked in a politically problematic colonial construct called Uganda.

Relying on some hitherto unpublished and classified records at the British National Archives now at Kew and the National Records and

Archives Centre in Uganda, and with a focus on Buganda, this book unpacks and reconstructs a mostly untold history of secretive plans, events, decisions and personalities that founded, implemented or executed British imperial rule in Uganda. Central to this account is an examination of the notions of "protection"—the bait to the execution of suspect treaties between Buganda and other parts of Uganda with Britain, where Buganda lost its sovereignty and the latter, by hook or crook, acquired or imposed unbridled suzerainty. It also examines aspects of colonial plunder and patronage. Beyond the colonial epoch, the book also reflects on Anglo-Ugandan relations after Uganda was granted independence, to demonstrate both how Uganda's contemporary politics has been defined by its colonial past and how, under British and other influences, its future is bound by a neo-colonial order.

This account, which is less about grousing over the effects of colonialism and more about unmasking the machinations and politics of colonial and postcolonial Uganda, shines a new spotlight on the historical complexities and a largely shredded legacy of British imperialism. It challenges the misleading narrative on the benevolence and objectives of colonialism in (B)Uganda and elsewhere and interrogates the power relations between Britain and its former colony, and particularly how these have influenced and shaped the latter's politics and economy for over a century.

It is hoped that this historical study on the objectives and methods of British rule in Uganda will help modern African states and traditional entities—like the kingdom of Buganda—to learn from this history as they struggle to liberate themselves and thrive in a new era.

ACKNOWLEDGMENTS

This book has been a labour of love originating from a yearning for more knowledge about the (hi)story of the ancient kingdom of Buganda, particularly with the puzzle of how it grappled with the complexities presented by the forces of Christianity and, later, colonial rule starting in the late 19th century. My interest was, almost at once, both heightened and satiated by the opportunity to serve in the kingdom and thus to witness first-hand the cultural, political and other dynamics at play for many years. In writing short pieces on some aspects of the kingdom's history—including on the tribulations of Kabaka Mwanga; the coronation of Kabaka E. F. Mutesa II, his deposition and life in exile; and on other contemporary issues of the kingdom—I was encouraged to write a book. Dr Joe Oloka-Onyango, my former law professor, was at the forefront in this regard. By introducing me to the resources of the British National Archives at Kew Gardens, Prince David Wassajja set me off on a long but enjoyable voyage that has resulted in this work.

I thank the Kabaka (King) of Buganda, Ronald Muwenda Mutebi, Omumbejja (Princess) Dorothy Nasolo, Prince Kassim Nakibinge and Prince David Namugala for their encouragement and access to historic family collections. I am equally thankful to Professors Lwanga-Lunyiigo, Mathias Semakula-Kiwanuka, Edward F. Sempebwa, Phares Mutibwa, Fredrick Jjuko and Nelson Kasfir who read and made useful comments on the manuscript. I also thank Jackie Asiimwe, Robert Kalundi-Serumaga, Timothy Kalyegira, Jon Elliot and Samantha Stevens for their comments the early drafts. Jonathan Mwesigwa, Dennis Asiimwe and Francis Birikadde also helped with the early editorial work. I am particularly grateful to Dr Ginevra House for her enthusiasm and support with the manuscript. I am grateful to the editorial team at the Cambridge Scholars Publishing, who were always available and supportive.

I also thank the staff at the British National Archives at Kew in Surrey, for their help in accessing valuable historical records and Robert Kabushenga and Betty Nakabiito Musoke of the *New Vision* for their help with photographs. I thank my colleagues at MMAKS Advocates for encouraging and supporting me on this journey.

Finally, I thank Stella Mukasa, my wife, and our daughters Athena, Angela and Andrea, as well as my parents, Titus K. Walusimbi and

Monica N. Namubiru, for their comments and encouragement on the work—but mostly for enduring many days of my absence and distraction as I navigated Uganda's historical records and as I experienced the pains and joys of writing.

I hope that this work will be useful and enjoyable to those that read it. I take personal responsibility for any errors or misjudgements in opinion in the book.

Ssabasajja Kabaka Awaangale!

Apollo N. Makubuya
Kampala, May 2018

A NOTE ON THE TOPONYM (B)UGANDA

The kingdom of Buganda straddles the Equator in central Africa and borders the northern shoreline of Lake Victoria. In both geographical and political terms, it lies in the centre of present-day Uganda. Its history,[1] with an unbroken line of 36 kings, dates back to the 14th century. In that sense it predates the colonial construct called Uganda by many years. It has an estimated population of 8 million people, known as the Baganda, whose language is Luganda. The kingdom is currently headed by Kabaka (King) Ronald Muwenda Mutebi II.

Relative to other parts of Uganda, the kingdom had the earliest contact with European explorers, namely, with the explorers John Hannington Speke in 1862 and Henry M. Stanley in 1875. These two adventurers were followed by Christian missionaries starting in 1877. The explorers and missionaries found the kingdom welcoming and promoted it in Britain as a suitable colony. They wrote glowing stories about Buganda, especially about its organizational structure, willingness to embrace modernity and economic potential. Following the Berlin Conference of 1885, the kingdom instantly and unilaterally became a part of the British Empire.

To impose its rule, Britain proceeded by way of a commercial charter granted to the Imperial British East Africa Company (IBEAC) led by Captain Frederick Lugard. Once the foundations for imperial rule were set, and the Company ran into financial troubles, Britain reluctantly took the region over as a Protectorate. From that point on, the kingdom of Buganda became a foothold for the expansion and entrenchment of its rule in the other parts of the territory of today's Uganda.

Because the Arab and Swahili traders from the Indian coast referred to the kingdom of Buganda as "Uganda" and its people as "Waganda," the Europeans, who relied on Swahili porters and guides to penetrate the interior of Africa, used the same to refer to the kingdom of Buganda. In that way, the name Uganda was derived from that of the kingdom of

---

[1] On Buganda's history see, generally, M. S. M. Semakula Kiwanuka, (1972) *A history of Buganda, from the foundation of the Kingdom to 1900*, Longman; Wright, Michael (1971) *Buganda in the heroic age*, Oxford: Oxford University Press; and Low, D. A. (2009) *Fabrication of Empire: The British and the Uganda Kingdoms, 1890-1902*, Cambridge: Cambridge University Press.

Buganda. Consequently, when Sir Harry Johnston signed an agreement with the kingdom in 1900, he referred to it as the Uganda Agreement, and to its infant Kabaka, Daudi Chwa, as the King of Uganda. Later, when the rest of modern Uganda fell under British control, the entire colony was named the Uganda Protectorate. And, due to the centrality of Buganda to Uganda in both geographical and political terms, the name Uganda was sometimes used by the colonial administrators to refer to the kingdom and *vice versa*. In *The Uganda Protectorate,* Johnston writes about the kingdom of Uganda when he is in fact referring to the kingdom of Buganda.[2]

Similarly, John Roscoe, in his seminal anthropological study on the Baganda, makes reference to the kingdom of Uganda when describing the kingdom of Buganda.[3] Thus, the name Uganda was historically used synonymously with that of Buganda. For this reason, in this account, the term "(B)Uganda" is used to refer both to the interchangeable use of the two toponyms in documents from the colonial period, and to express the transition from the entity known as Buganda before and during colonial rule to one that became Uganda in the postcolonial epoch.

---

[2] See Johnston, Harry (1902) *The Uganda Protectorate*, London: Hutchison & Co. Paternoster Row, pp. 85-121.

[3] See Roscoe, John (1911) *The Baganda: An Account of their Native Customs and Beliefs*, London: Macmillan and Co., Limited St Martins Street, London, p.4.

FOREWORD

The subject of Buganda has long held a particular fascination for scholars, politicians and travelers. Such allure is not misplaced given the central role the kingdom has played throughout the recorded history of the country the British created and baptized Uganda. In revisiting the "Buganda Question," Apollo Makubuya has not been content with only the "official" story. Instead, he has undertaken a surgical re-examination of many of those facets of the chronicle and provided a fresh, exhaustive and intellectually-stimulating account of the various ways in which the British experience impacted on the kingdom in particular and on the wider territory of Uganda as a whole. Archival literature is married to legal documentation and supplemented with the accounts of some of the main actors in the drama. Indeed, the book provides a far-reaching examination of the question: was British colonial rule in Buganda designed for protection, for patronage or for plunder?

Taken together, Makubuya's account of the relationship between the British and Buganda should provide some serious cause for a reconsideration of some of the many basic questions which have surrounded this story. To what extent was the elaboration of a "protectorate" over the kingdom simply a subterfuge for what in effect was direct colonialism; how did the British deal with the vast archival material about their sojourn in the "pearl" of Africa on the eve of independence, and lastly what were the facts relating to the death of Ssekabaka Edward Mutesa and (more importantly) the reaction of both the British and Ugandan governments in its aftermath? A number of these questions have been asked before. However, Makubuya not only adds other intriguing inquisitions to the dramatic dance of politics between Britain and one of its most strategic colonial outposts, he also unearths an abundance of new archival material that will have historians, anthropologists and lawyers stimulated and engaged for decades to come.

Lest the impression be created that the book is only about events distant and arcane, Makubuya provides a succinct analysis of the implications of the history of British engagement with Uganda that extends to the present-day. While there is no doubt that the sun has set on the British empire, the ramifications of colonial rule continue until the present time, dictating political and socioeconomic developments relating to foreign affairs, resource exploitation and the overall maintenance of regime stability. Against this backdrop, Makubuya's book is not afraid to grapple with the vexed issue of Buganda's self-determination, and to ask the reader to envisage a different scenario from the centralized despotism that has been Uganda's experience since independence. Indeed, it is only by asking such hard questions that we can begin to envisage a different future from our past. *Protection, Patronage or Plunder*? sets us well on the path to a further examination of what is yet to come.

J. Oloka-Onyango

INTRODUCTION

"[I]n Africa today we are ... bringing to the dark places of the earth, the abode of barbarism and cruelty, the torch of culture and progress, while ministering to the material needs of our own civilisation ... there can be no question but that British rule has promoted the happiness and welfare of the primitive races.

Let it be admitted at the outset that European brains, capital and energy have not been, and never will be, expended in developing the resources of Africa from motives of pure philanthropy; that Europe is in Africa for the mutual benefit of her own industrial classes, and of the native races in their progress to a higher plane; that the benefit can be made reciprocal; and that it is the aim and desire of civilised administration to fulfil this dual mandate."

—The Right Hon. Sir Fredrick D. Lugard
GCMG, CB, DSO[1]

The first European explorers and missionaries that arrived at the interior of Africa in the 19th century were surprised to find a kingdom with a sophisticated cultural and traditional system of governance that they had not seen elsewhere on their journey of discovery in the "dark continent."[2] Having met stiff resistance by groups such as the Nandi and the Maasai in Kenya, their arrival and welcome in Buganda, a kingdom with a history dating back to the 14th century, was surprising. The explorers found the kingdom unrivalled in terms of its unique administration, stately leadership and economic development. Around this time, Buganda was undergoing rapid expansion, mostly at the expense of its weakening neighbours, but also because of the good trade links it had with the Arabs from the East African coast, whose supplies included guns and gunpowder.

Henry M. Stanley arrived in Buganda thirteen years after Speke and Grant, and was awestruck on arrival at the court of *Kabaka* Mutesa I, the King of Buganda.[3] On the day he arrived on the shores of the kingdom, he was welcomed by the Kabaka's ambassador, who arrived in a flotilla of large canoes to accompany him on the last stretch. The next day he was welcomed by the *Katikkiro* (prime minister) and about 2,000 excited followers, who were feasted on chicken, eggs, bananas and sweet potatoes. Ten oxen and sixteen sheep and goats were slaughtered in his honour. He was lodged in a special house. Once the Katikkiro cleared him, Stanley met the tall, 34-year-old Mutesa in a hunting village. He found Mutesa a "most intelligent, humane and distinguished prince," one with "quiet dignity" and with intelligence superior to that of the Sultan of Zanzibar.[4] In describing his environs and Buganda's capital at Mengo, he wrote:

> We viewed the capital crossing an eminence commanding a most extensive view of a picturesque and rich country teeming with gardens and plantations and beautiful pasture land … the vast collection of huts crossing the eminence were the Royal Quarters, around which ran several palisades and circular courts, between which and the city was a circular road, ranging from one hundred to two hundred feet in width, from which radiated six or seven magnificent avenues, lined with gardens and huts.[5]

Here, Stanley paints a vivid—indeed a glowing—picture of Buganda in a promising, heroic and glorious era. Winston Churchill, before he became Britain's premier, was similarly struck by the Baganda—described as the "Japanese of Africa"[6]—living in a kingdom he called a "fairy tale."[7] When he traversed the continent, he found the kingdom of Buganda distinct from "anything elsewhere to be seen in the whole range of Africa," a "complete and elaborate polity under a dynastic King with a Parliament and a powerful feudal system, an amiable, clothed, polite, and intelligent race."[8] The kingdom was equipped with a Court and a regular system of native law, and its peaceful society was characterised by discipline, industry, culture. He urged Britain, of all its East and Central African possessions, to "Concentrate upon Uganda" which had "unequalled fertility with a population of high intelligence and social quality."[9] He believed Uganda was bound to "become the most prosperous" colony and that nowhere else in Africa would the results of Britain's imperial rule "be more brilliant, more substantial or more rapidly realised."[10]

But beyond the impressionistic explorer accounts, historical and anthropological studies show that precolonial Buganda was in fact a fairly advanced African cultural and political entity with a formidable government headed by the Kabaka, a Katikkiro (Prime Minister) and a hierarchy of chiefs. It had a standing army headed by a general (*Omujasi*), a treasury headed by the *Omuwanika* (chief treasurer) and a native judicial system administered by the *Omulamuzi* (chief justice). Its traditional judicial system was well developed and structured with a mechanism for appeals from decisions made by local chiefs or clan leaders to the Kabaka's court—which was the supreme appellate organ and whose decision was final. The system also respected the rules of natural justice—similar to those recognised and applied in English law—namely the right to be heard (*audi alteram partem*) and the principle that no man can be a judge in his own cause (*nemo judex in causa sua*).[11]

Equally, in the medical field, Buganda had made remarkable strides in the diagnosis and treatment of diseases and had a body of midwives (*abazaalisa*), traditional healers and herbalists (*abasawo*) as well as orthopedics (*abayunzi*). Indeed, according to Dr Robert W. Felkin, a British medical missionary and explorer, by 1879, Baganda surgeons were already performing successful caesarean sections using African medical procedures and anaesthesia.[12]

In addition to advances in the governance, legal and medical spheres, the Baganda had made significant headway in the fields of textiles, dance, music, agriculture, trade, pottery, ironmongery, engineering and road construction, as well as in several aspects of tradition and social decorum.[13]

However, and in spite of these attributes, European observations on the natives in Uganda, and on the Baganda in particular, were not always charitable. For example, some considered that although the people in Buganda had been in earlier contact with civilisation,

> They have remained simple savages, and have not absorbed any of the civilisation, except the desire to enslave each other perhaps. The *Waganda* and *Wanyoro* have a more highly developed social system, but they have many vices which have left these people quite untouched. These people have not acquired any wants or tastes yet which render us desirable to them, and, except for a few thousand protected individuals, appear to have the profoundest mistrust of anything calling itself a government.[14]

One colonial administrator considered that although the Baganda were intelligent they were at once “a most immoral race” whose women “thought no more of sexual intercourse than [they] did of going to the rear.”[15] Another commentator considered the word Baganda to be synonymous with “sensuality, debauchery, and drunkenness.”[16] Needless-to-say these views were neither value-free nor universal.

Unsurprisingly, the power and promise that Stanley and others found in precolonial Buganda began to fade rapidly once the forerunners of British imperialism such as Captain Frederick Lugard, Gerald Portal and, later, Sir Harry Johnston arrived bearing gifts and laid the foundation for imperial rule in Uganda. Lugard arrived in Buganda in December 1890 when the kingdom, then under Kabaka Daniel B. Mwanga II, was entangled in violent religious wars and civil strife. Lugard found that an embattled Mwanga had signed a treaty of friendship with the Germans, who, led by Karl Peters, wanted to extend their East African sphere of influence into Uganda.

However, under the Anglo-German Heligoland treaty of 1890, the Germans ceded the Ugandan territory to Britain and paved the way for Lugard, under the Imperial British East Africa Company (IBEAC), to enter into a treaty with Kabaka Mwanga. In that treaty, Lugard promised, among other things, to offer “protection” to the Kabaka in return for Buganda’s sovereignty. Yet, in spite of the said treaties, Mwanga was always wary of the intentions of his new foreign allies and indeed soon revolted against Lugard’s orders. This triggered events where Lugard, with the help of Protestant converts, fought and deposed Mwanga, a development that kick-started a long and chequered relationship between the kingdom of Buganda and Britain. That relationship was sealed in the agreements of 1894[17] and 1900 under which (B)Uganda became a British Protectorate.

British colonial rule fundamentally transformed the politics and economics of the kingdom of Buganda and the rest of Uganda. Working hand-in-hand with the Christian missions, it introduced several foreign aspects of governance to the Protectorate: a British legal system, modern education and health systems, a new land tenure system, an agriculture-based economy producing cash crops such as cotton and coffee, and a new transport network (including the Uganda Railway) that opened up the interior for trade with the rest of the world. It is undisputed that these developments aided the transformation of African societies and plugged them into a global and capitalist economic order.

However, British colonial rule also came along with a dark, self-serving, exploitative and crippling side that was detrimental to the full development of the Protectorate and its peoples. As in India and elsewhere in its vast Empire, the adverse forces of British colonialism either dismantled or destroyed promising African traditional institutions to advance its imperial interests.

Given this history—and the diverse interpretations offered on it by colonial administrators, academicians and political activists—the main goal of this book is to reflect on the British colonial enterprise in (B)Uganda. The book illustrates the methods and machinations of this enterprise and how these impacted upon the colonised polity. It focuses on Britain’s colonial and postcolonial relations with the kingdom of Buganda, whose historiography has been recorded and analysed more by non-Baganda writers and considerably less by the Baganda themselves.

The dearth of literature presenting Buganda’s perspectives on British colonial rule is one of the reasons we revisit the subject using different lenses: to provide another perspective on how the British cajoled, conquered and occupied the kingdom of Buganda and other parts of Uganda and how, for over 68 years, Britain went about its imperial mission in Buganda and the roles and responses of the Baganda to colonial rule.[18]

The periodic declassification of secret correspondence and documents by the British government not only offers a new insight into the perpetration of colonialism but also helps us to better understand the powerful forces and personalities that shaped the colonial and postcolonial history of the kingdom of Buganda and Uganda.

The book is based on the hypothesis that British imperialism in Africa was founded and sustained on three principal pillars: plunder, protection, and patronage. The plunder of resources—mostly land, minerals, and African labour—was achieved either through the work of companies such as the IBEAC or by colonial governments. Plunder was perpetrated either through violence or through skewed and often dubious negotiations and treaty making with the leadership of native populations.

The second pillar—which was the real mission of colonial rule—consisted in the protection of British interests in the form cheap raw materials, cheap labour and markets for British goods and services. As we show below, protection was never about safeguarding the rights or interests of the colonized peoples. Where that happened, it was merely incidental. On this basis, we reassess and deconstruct the concept of "protection" used in the conclusion of mostly *pro forma* treaties with entities like the kingdom of Buganda, to reveal the complexity and true character of British imperialism.

The third pillar was the erection of a system of patronage under which Britain spread its prestige and influence through a paternalistic, undemocratic, unjust and a segregated regime in its colonial domains. Through patronage, Britain effectively influenced the politics and economics of its colonies to further its material and strategic interests during and long after colonial rule. To achieve this, the colonial system invariably undermined traditional leadership and institutions, often deposing and deporting what it considered the most undesirable leaders and leaving the more pliant ones as figureheads.

Original records cited in this study show how British rule, far from Lugard's narrative of "promoting the happiness and welfare of the primitive races,"[19] in reality was one of aggression and occupation. It was concerned far more with ministering to the material and strategic needs of Britain, and was executed in a manner that was ultimately antithetical to the political, social and economic development of the colonised states. The records show that colonial rule employed five methods to achieve its mission: i) suppression or replacement of traditional values and institutions with colonialist ones; ii) redrawing boundaries and borders; iii) creation of a socioeconomic system that favoured the interests of the Empire over those of the local population; iv) imposition of a discriminatory legal system that favoured the colonisers and reliance on legally dubious treaties; and v) a highly secretive regime regarding colonial strategy and official documents.

First, colonial rule in Buganda, and elsewhere, undermined and debased indigenous values and belief systems, as well as institutions and administrative structures, and replaced them with alien and paternalistic ones that were best suited to serve imperial interests. According to Captain Lugard, the essential feature of the system was that

> the native chiefs are constituted as an integral part of the machinery of the administration. There are not two sets of rulers—British and native—working either separately or in cooperation, but a single Government in which the native chiefs have well-defined duties and an acknowledged status equally with British officials. Their duties should never conflict, and should overlap as little as possible. They should be complementary to each other, and the chief himself must understand that he has no right to place and power unless he renders his proper services to the State. The ruling classes are no longer either demigods, or parasites preying on the community. They must work for the stipends and position they enjoy. They are the trusted delegates of the Governor.[20]

In the case of Buganda, colonial rule was installed and entrenched through the creation of an oligarchy of chiefs who acted as agents of imperialism in Buganda and beyond. This new class was used to subdue or entirely replace conservative traditionalists whose allegiance and loyalty lay more with the traditional order than the new one. Dominated by Christian converts (mostly Protestants), this class generally looked down upon traditional institutions and values in relation to European ones. The prominent elite members included Apolo Kagwa, Stanislas Mugwanya, Ham Mukasa, Martin Luther Nsibirwa and Sserwano Kulubya, all of whom obtained and embraced an early Christian education and looked up to the British and the church leadership.

These helped, either consciously or otherwise, to dismantle Buganda's traditional leadership and authority and facilitate the penetration of imperial rule into Buganda and Uganda. As we show further ahead, two Buganda kings—Kabaka Mwanga and Daudi Chwa—particularly suffered a great deal because of the divided loyalties of some of their most trusted chiefs. Kabaka Mwanga was in fact deposed with the help of some of his chiefs, while Kabaka Chwa narrowly survived deposition by the British working with some of his officials. The behaviour of the pro-British chiefs like Apolo Kagwa may be explained under Britain's policy that aimed at ensuring that

> [t]he personal interests of the rulers must rapidly become identified with those of the controlling Power. The forces of disorder do not distinguish between them, and the rulers soon recognise that any upheaval against the British would equally make the end of them. Once this community of interest is established, the Central Government cannot be taken by surprise, for it is impossible that the native rulers should not be aware of any disaffection.[21]

In return for their loyalty to British imperialism, many of the new chiefly class were, under a patronising colonial largess, rewarded with material gifts (including *mailo* land grants,[22] livestock and other desirable luxuries like gramophones) or, with positions, power, ceremonial titles and insignia of office such as "Your Royal Highness," the Order of the British Empire (OBE) and the Most Excellent Order of the British Empire (MBE). The use of material and other inducements to patronise and motivate African chiefs to collaborate with colonial administrators in dominating and exploiting their own people is probably the genesis of the endemic corruption in postcolonial Africa.[23]

Through the use of these local agents, which was part and parcel of the policy of indirect rule, Britain maintained the façade that the natives were in control while at once masking the aggressive character of colonialism. Indirect rule and patronage promoted the primacy of the tribe and discouraged the growth of nationalism or a common identity or awareness amongst the diverse peoples of the Protectorate.

Additionally, through African agency, both in and sometimes outside Buganda, colonial rule created a new class of subservient chiefs and landlords whose loyalties were switched from the traditional leaders to the new colonial master. As we discuss below, the resistance to pro-British agency and the resentment to imperial rule resulted in the 1945 and 1949 protests in Buganda and, relatedly, to the tragic assassination of Katikkiro Martin Luther Nsibirwa in 1945.

It is said that in the expansion of British imperial rule in Africa, the flag followed the cross.[24] In other words, that Christianity and its self-assigned mission to civilize "primitive and backward" populations in Africa often led the way and opened the doors for the imposition of colonial rule. Walter Rodney succinctly expresses this colonizing role of the missionaries: "the Christian missionaries were as much part of the colonizing forces as were the explorers, traders and soldiers," and they "were agents of colonialism in the practical sense, whether or not they saw themselves in that light."[25]

Generally, Christian missionaries approached Africa with the attitude that all things European were superior to all things African. For example, David Livingstone and Friedrick Fabri of the Rhenish Missionary Society in Namibia believed in their "civilizing" mission, which was centred as much on spreading European cultural values as on the Christian gospel. Fabri particularly viewed mission work as a "useful tool" for trade and colonial annexation.[26] The role of missionaries in Uganda was no different. Christian missions—particularly the Christian Missionary Society (CMS) and the White Fathers— acted as interested interlocutors and facilitated the fracturing of Buganda's political and social structures in order to advance both an evangelical and a colonial agenda.

Among other things, they supplied information to colonial officials which was utilized to plan how to crush local resistance and to effectively impose colonial rule; they raised funds for the IBEAC to stay in the country; they provided their stations for use as military bases from which the colonial forces launched attacks on the resisting Africans; and they lured Baganda chiefs into signing treaties they did not fully understand, which were later used by the colonialists to exert control over their territories. For example, it was Bishop Tucker who lured the Regents of Kabaka Daudi Chwa II into signing the 1900 Buganda Agreement, about which Harry Johnston wrote:

> I, Johnston, shall be bound to acknowledge the assistance offered to me by the missionaries, especially the CMS. Without their assistance on my side, I do not think Uganda's chiefs would agree to the treaty which practically places their country and land in the British hands.[27]

Prior to the Buganda Agreement, the IBEAC, under Captain Lugard, had sided with the Anglican Protestants to defeat the traditionalists and the Catholics in Buganda. Again, Johnston acknowledged the importance of this turn of events, writing that "from that point on the politics of Uganda assumed a religious character that was, for good or for worse, to perennially influence its political future."[28] It is no wonder that at the time of independence in 1962 the leading political parties—the Uganda People's Congress (UPC) and the Democratic Party (DP)—had a religious base and, perhaps more tellingly, that the country chose as its national motto the phrase "For God and My Country," a simple adaption of the British Empire's own motto "For God and the Empire."

The entrenchment of colonial rule also entailed a process of disarmament and demobilisation of all traditional defence mechanisms and their replacement with a detribalised colonial army. Native rulers were forbidden to raise or maintain an army. On this colonial policy, Lugard was categorical:

> Native rulers are not permitted to raise and control armed forces, or to grant permission to carry arms. To this in principle Great Britain stands pledged under the Brussels Act. The evils which result in Africa from an armed population were evident in Uganda before it fell under British control, and are very evident in Abyssinia today. No one with experience will deny the necessity of maintaining the strictest military discipline over armed forces or police in Africa if misuse of power is to be avoided, and they are not to become a menace and a terror to the native population and a danger in case of religious excitement—a discipline which an African ruler is incapable of appreciating or applying. For this reason native levies should never be employed in substitution for or in aid of troops.[29]

Additionally, according to David Adetayo Olusoga, a British Nigerian historian,

> for decades' colonial administrators had striven to ensure that modern weapons were kept out of the hands of their black subjects, and it was impressed upon them that the lives of white men (and more so white women) were sacrosanct. Violence against white people in the Empire elicited extra ordinary violent responses—punitive raids and exemplary punishments … black men were armed only when formed into colonial regiments (often known as *askari*) and used to fight Africans, under the guidance and watchful eyes of white officers.[30]

In line with this colonial policy, the native army in Buganda was quickly disbanded and replaced with a colonial army—the King's African Rifles (KAR)[31]—comprising mostly Sudanese troops whose fighting skills were excellent but whose general character and loyalty to the colonial government was unsatisfactory to Johnston.[32] But even then he could not rely upon black troops for unswerving fidelity to the British Protectorate. Accordingly, he relied more on Indian troops who he thought were more capable of keeping the native government "in order."[33] Accordingly, because Johnston believed that English soldiers could not be employed in the Protectorate for "climatic reasons," he depended on Indian soldiers, who represented a "core of absolutely loyal, brave, and practiced soldiers" and whose retention ensured the maintenance of Britain's "chief position."[34]

For this reason, and in order to keep the native government in check, Johnston was careful not to recruit and arm many Baganda. He recruited only 500 policemen from among them and sent the rest to other provinces where they mixed with native police comprising diverse ethnicities such as the Maasai, Swahilis, Lendus, and other negro races. This left the king and chiefs in Buganda and elsewhere vulnerable and defenceless in the face of colonial aggression. They were only allowed to employ a body of policemen who were allowed to wear starched uniforms but not to carry arms (locally called *Bamusirike*). If a situation arose that required significant force, the king and chiefs were expected to look to the colonial government for protection. According to Amone, this was a deliberate policy where

> The British did not want their colonial armies to be dominated by societies that lived near the centre of administration. This is the reason they discouraged the Kikuyu in Kenya, the Ndebele in Southern Rhodesia, and the Asante in Ghana from joining the army. Instead these societies were dominant in the civil service … the British feared an organised and large scale military resistance by members of the dominant communities in respective colonies. Since the Bantu communities especially in Buganda and the Banyoro were well organised under highly centralised societies, the British did not want to arm them. This was why the Acholi were preferred—they were not only too small in population to wage a strong military resistance, but also disunited under several chiefdoms.[35]

Colonial ethnicisation of the army and the reliance on the army to tackle political differences was partly responsible for the mayhem soon after independence and a militarist legacy in the country's governance. The majority of military coups in Uganda have been led by forces from northern Uganda, which constituted the recruiting ground for the colonial army.[36] And, as we demonstrate below, the dominance of a largely ethnicised military in the governance the country has undermined the professionalization of Ugandan forces as well as the development of strong civic and democratic institutions in Uganda.

The second method of implementing the colonial enterprise consisted of earmarking and protecting the boundaries of the imperial territory. Colonialism constructed artificial countries with arbitrary boundaries where none existed before, and brought together diverse and sometimes antagonistic tribes without common aspirations and, almost magically, branded them as "independent" and "united" nations in the dying days of the colonial enterprise. As a part of this process, and based on a policy of divide and conquer, colonial rule reconstituted tribal territorial jurisdictions within the Protectorate, taking away land from the more hostile tribes and giving it to others as a reward for their cooperation. This gave rise to tribal jealousies and enmity where none previously existed and poured oil on the flames of old rivalries, particularly between Buganda and Bunyoro. As we discuss below, the Bunyoro "lost counties" saga, for example, which took the Protectorate to a dangerous precipice on the eve of independence and beyond, was a direct result of this policy.

The question of national integration constituted a major problem once Britain contemplated decolonisation and when it began its retreat from the continent. With the pressure of African nationalism and the demand for independence, Britain, rather belatedly and half-heartedly, "attempted to arouse the national loyalties it had previously discouraged, to contain and moderate the tribalism which it had earlier encouraged, to enlist Africans more rapidly than it had ever considered necessary, and to introduce the elected institutions which it had earlier judged inappropriate."[37] It is unsurprising that these attempts met with failure and that the problems of ethnicity and the lack of national integration persist to this day. Nsibambi addresses the difficulties faced in the integration of Ugandan communities in a "united" Uganda since independence. He correctly argues that the problems of ethnocultural diversity—particularly in Buganda and Karamoja—have negated the attainment of national integration.[38]

As a third method, colonial rule engendered and prospered on a socioeconomic system that primarily served and protected colonial—and later neocolonial—interests, but also one that was incapable of spurring the kind of development needed to bring the Protectorate to the high and sustainable levels of human development seen in other parts of the world. The economy was largely agrarian, hence land ownership and control was an important aspect. The right to appropriate land for public and commercial purposes was vested in the colonial government. This explains why the land laws introduced under the 1900 Agreement were designed to consolidate colonial control over land and to create a new African society stratified between a landed gentry and a tenant peasantry.

Under a scheme of plunder, Britain, for no consideration, controlled over fifty percent of the land in the kingdom of Buganda, leaving the remainder in the hands of a few chiefs and members of the royal family. The majority of Africans thus remained as peasants and labourers at the margins of an economy dominated by Europeans and a few Asian traders. This unfair and oppressive land policy culminated in the Bataka uprisings in the 1920s and the passing of the *Busuulu* and *Envujjo* (dues and rent) laws that placed restrictions on the amount of rent landlords could charge their tenants. This problem has persisted to the present day.

The colonial economy was also supported by a tax regime exclusively imposed and controlled by the colonial government. Tax revenues were entirely in the hands of the Protectorate, which had no obligation whatsoever to account to the natives except, perhaps, to the colonial office in London.[39]

At a social level, colonialism survived on a discriminative and racially regimented order perpetuated through segregated education, housing and health systems. By 1920, there were no schools established or managed by the colonial government. Educational work among the natives was thus left entirely in the hands of the missionary societies which received annual government grants towards expenses. This demonstrates that education of the natives was not a key priority for the colonial government. With time, and as the educational facilities increased, the Protectorate operated a segregated system of education where for example, Europeans and Asians attended different schools from those attended by the Africans. Imparted mainly through Christian mission schools, colonial education was designed to educate a limited chiefly class in schools such as Namilyango, Budo, Kisubi and Gayaza, and the vast majority in other schools where their advancement was limited to the technical and vocational skills required to serve the Empire in technical and clerical roles. Similarly, colonial policy on housing reserved the more affluent and planned neighbourhoods for Europeans and Asians and the unplanned and poorer ones for the habitation of Africans. The health system was equally segregated and discriminative. These policies were all aimed to entrench a culture of racial superiority for the colonial masters, which would in turn keep the Africans at the bottom of the social pyramid and at the margins of colonial society. Under such status, Africans were incapable—beyond the provision of wage labour—of either meaningfully participating in the economic and political life of the colony or questioning colonialism itself. This racial segregation was partly responsible for the trade boycott of foreign-owned shops led by Augustine Kamya in 1959[40] and, ultimately, for the infamous expulsion of British Asians and others by Idi Amin in 1972.

The fourth method of colonial rule was to construct and entrench an exploitative, oppressive, racist and discriminative legal regime. To start with, Britain purported to enter into treaties with African leaders under which they surrendered their authority, land and labour in return for colonial protection. In reality, however, there was a lack of consensus *ad idem* on the true meaning and legal significance of these treaties. While natives, who had no knowledge or understanding of the legalese in which these treaties were shrouded, genuinely believed that they would get protection. They had no idea of the extent to which, just with their thumbprints, they had forfeited their authority and sanctioned a regime of pillage and plunder of their resources and labour. Yet, on its part and as we demonstrate, Britain did not believe in the legality and sanctity of these treaties.

With the treaties followed colonial legislation. The power to legislate was a preserve of the colonial governor and his government. This power could not be questioned. The native rulers were left to enforce customary laws as they applied to the natives. But even then, customary laws were only enforceable where, in the eyes of the Europeans rulers, they were not immoral, repugnant or contrary to the rules of natural justice. Colonial laws such as the Orders-in-Council, ordinances and proclamations defined the territorial limits of the colony and bestowed sweeping legislative, judicial and administrative powers upon the British Commissioner or Governor for the administration of Uganda. The Commissioner, for example, had power over all crown land and was vested with all mining and mineral rights. He was also vested with the prerogative of mercy and was immune from legal process. In the exercise of his powers, he was subject only to the general or special instructions of the Secretary of State in London.[41]

Under the colonial legal schema, African natives were subjects of a differentiated and prejudiced legal and judicial system that favoured Asians and Europeans over them. For example, Africans had special native courts where their disputes were handled. These courts had no powers over Europeans. Africans were also subject to draconian ordinances under which they were routinely arrested, beaten, detained or deported, often without trial. Kabalega, the *Omukama* (King) of Bunyoro, Mwanga, the Kabaka of Buganda, and other native rulers considered to be undesirable or dangerous to British rule, were deposed and summarily deported to the Seychelles and other places. These rulers were replaced by chiefs and other royals considered to be more pliant. Under the colonial tax laws, African natives were forced to pay gun and hut taxes without representation or accountability, or forced to provide hard labour on government installations if they were unable to pay.

Under these mostly draconian laws, and in order to smooth the imposition of colonial rule in Uganda, Kenya and other parts of the world, as well as to maintain law and order, British colonialists often relied on brutal and inhuman methods that, in today's parlance, would tantamount to crimes against humanity. This was in spite of Britain's avowed belief in justice and human rights as enshrined in the *Magna Carta*—a famous charter on liberties dating back to 1215. But instead of invoking the *Magna Carta* in the protection of the human rights of the colonised peoples, British imperialists used it to justify colonial rule and "sometimes to obscure the abuses that characterised the Empire."[42] For this reason, the colonial office was reluctant to popularise the *Magna Carta* or to allow Magna Carta Day to be celebrated throughout the Empire.

As the case of the Mau Mau rebellion of the 1950s illustrates, gross injustice was meted out to the people of Kenya, many of whom were beaten on the head with clubs, tortured, castrated or killed at the hands of British agents. Similar atrocities have been recorded in India and elsewhere in the Empire. However, for many years, Britain has enjoyed impunity in respect of these crimes. And, even though Britain has apologised and made reparations—after being dragged to the courts by the Mau Mau victims—there remains a general denial, a refusal to accept responsibility, and a failure to account for the injustices of colonialism.

The fifth method was that British colonialism operated and thrived under a highly covert and secretive regime that helped obscure its mission. Under this scheme, colonial personnel at all levels were sworn to secrecy and any breaches of the rules were severely punished. At the end of the empire and as Britain retreated, colonial officials methodically shredded, burnt and otherwise destroyed tons of "dirty" and potentially incriminating and/or embarrassing documents of its imperious and largely exploitative rule. Other documents, referred to as the "migrated files," were clandestinely taken back to the United Kingdom and kept in a highly secure military-like facility in Hanslope Park.

The less sensitive documents, especially those that depicted colonialism in a positive light, were kept at the National Archives at Kew for public view. For over fifty years, the cache of documents buried at Hanslope Park remained top secret and the Foreign Colonial Office (FCO) denied it had them. However, researchers on the atrocities committed during the Mau Mau rebellion exposed the massive British cover-up in which over 8,800 secret files had been hidden. The embarrassment of the discovery of the hidden trove forced the FCO to make a late and lame apology for concealing the existence of the documents and misleading the public for so long.[43] The concealment of sensitive and incriminating colonial documents served three key objectives, namely, to protect Her Majesty's Government (HMG) from legal liabilities arising out of its colonial rule; to keep away embarrassing and incriminating materials touching on the dark side of the plunder and patronage associated with it; and to help perpetuate the narrative of a clean colonial legacy representing British rule as non-aggressive, benevolent, glorious, gracious and protective of the colonised peoples.

In sum, this account shows how British colonialism in Uganda relied on a mixture of lies, force, bribery, subjugation, patronage and pillage to achieve its ends. In the case of the kingdom of Buganda, it shows how, why and when Britain, an erstwhile ally, became an adversary who frustrated its aspiration for full autonomy in the dying days of the Empire and ensured that it remained inextricably locked in a new and politically unstable entity called Uganda.

At a national level, this account shows a clear nexus between Uganda's colonial past and its present political economy. This connection makes a compelling case that the roots of political instability and economic malaise that characterize many of Britain's former colonies are deeply embedded in their colonial past. Conversely, it points to Britain's role in and responsibility for this reality and a need for accountability.

The denial or refusal by Britain, a former colonial master, to acknowledge its role in Africa's political and economic imbroglio—and its attempts to take refuge under legal and other technicalities—encourages a culture of impunity that typifies many of Africa's post-independence regimes. In this sense, this account should be seen not merely as berating colonialism but as a demand for accountability, justice and an end to impunity, especially in an era that extols the virtues of fairness, human dignity, human rights, accountability, integrity and transparency.

British colonial rule and its impacts in (B)Uganda may be broken down into five broad phases, and it is according to these that this book is structured. The first phase, between 1890 and 1939, covers the period of conquest and occupation of the colony, as well as the consolidation of imperial rule, all of which was achieved under the guise and the promise of British protection to the colonised peoples. During this era, Britain usurped Buganda's sovereignty, starting with ousting Mwanga and replacing him with his infant son, Daudi Chwa. The powerless Chwa was enthroned to "rule" together with a new class of chiefs and colonial protégées, led by Apolo Kagwa, who supported the new exploitative colonial order founded on the problematic 1900 Agreement and the 1902 Order-in-Council. The period also witnessed the emergence of conflict and inequality between a new landed gentry and chiefly class on the one hand, and the landless peasants or tenants, on the other. It also saw the erosion of traditional power at the hands and benefit of the colonial authority.

The second phase, covering the period between 1939 and 1952, witnessed the rise of resistance against the imposition of British rule and its agents. The resistance was targeted equally against the British administrators and Buganda's oligarchy of chiefs—especially those seen as colonial agents or sympathisers. This resistance contributed to and marked the beginnings of the decline in colonial authority in Buganda. But, as we will show, other factors such as the costly Second World War and a global economic recession, also contributed greatly to this decline. This period witnessed tremendous colonial exploitation of human and other resources, but, more importantly, it also saw a growing national consciousness regarding such exploitation.

Consequently, the decade from 1939 to 1949 was characterised by the rise of the Bataka movement and the protests—misleadingly characterised by the colonial regime as riots—of 1945 and 1949. Although Governor Charles Dundas introduced policy reforms aimed at empowering Africans, his replacement, Governor John Hall, reversed those reforms and set out to achieve more direct rule aimed to disempower the African leadership. As we show below, this is seen in Hall's brutal crackdown against the perceived leadership of the demonstrators both in 1945 and 1949.

The third phase covers the period between 1952 and 1960 during which there was heightened resistance against colonial rule and agitation for decolonisation. This resulted both from a rising tide of anti-colonial and nationalistic movements within Uganda and from anti-colonial pressure internationally. During this time, a new international outlook emerged—especially within the United Nations—that strongly denigrated colonialism and imperialism. This period was hence characterised by sweeping changes in colonial rule across Africa in the late 1950s and early 1960s.

In Buganda, the period witnessed a growing defiance of the British colonial order, characterised by Buganda's opposition to the concept of the East African Federation, its refusal to send representatives to the Legislative Council (LEGCO), and the series of rebellious acts leading up to the retaliatory deportation of Kabaka Mutesa II by Governor Andrew Cohen in 1953. The political and constitutional crisis that emanated from the deportation of Kabaka Mutesa precipitated the renegotiation (between a captor and a captive) of the 1900 Agreement and its replacement with the 1955 Agreement. The period also witnessed intense political activism by political parties calling for self-rule. Such was the level of agitation that in December 1960, Buganda made a unilateral and ill-timed declaration of independence, terminating its agreements of protection with Britain. The period also witnessed rapid and often acrimonious discussions (such as those regarding the lost counties) on the future relationships and constitutional framework of a new Uganda.

The fourth phase covers the period between 1960 and 1962 which marked the transition of power from the colonial administration to a government led by Ugandans. This period was notable for the constitutional conferences, held in London in 1961 and 1962, where intense negotiations were held between Buganda and the rest of the country with Britain on the future of the country. These negotiations culminated in the 1961 Agreement and, later, the 1962 Constitution under which Uganda attained independence.

The fifth phase broadly covers developments in postcolonial Uganda, from 1962 to the present. This phase highlights the problematic political relations between the leadership of the kingdom of Buganda and that of Uganda. The major events of this period include the eruption of the lost counties crisis in 1964, the blatant abrogation of the Independence Constitution in 1966, the violent coup against Mutesa in May 1966, the abolition of kingdoms in 1967, the chaotic and murderous regime of General Idi Amin, and the post-Amin politico-military dispensation that catapulted General Yoweri K. Museveni into power in 1986.

This last episode also illustrates how, over half a century since Uganda's independence, and particularly since the 1966 crisis, the kingdom of Buganda has struggled to survive and for its independence. It also shows that Britain has, through neocolonial patronage, remained intricately connected to the country's tumultuous political and constitutional history by means of military aid, trade and other covert diplomatic means. We highlight how Uganda's history over this period has been characterised by corrupt, undemocratic and tyrannical rule, militarism, and a weak civil society.

There is no doubt that the crop of Uganda's postcolonial leaders has had a lot to do with the country's dismal political and economic history over the last few decades. However, some of this reality must be attributed not only to the more than 68 years of undemocratic and paternalistic colonial rule, but also to the continuing covert neocolonial relations the country has with Britain. In other words, the woes of Africa's and Uganda's current crises are inextricably linked to the legacy of colonialism and neocolonialism. Colonialism relied more on coercion, co-option, exploitation and impunity than it did on constitutionalism, democracy and the rule of law.

Regrettably, the vicious methods of colonial rule have been replicated in modern-day Africa and Uganda, where many leaders place themselves above the laws applicable to the rest of the citizenry and where they (ab)use the law to justify oppression, discrimination and injustice. It is important to stress that a country searching for enduring peace, progress and stability needs to understand the deep forces and subtle but debilitating methods of imperialism before devising measures to confront and overcome these forces. This is the reality that is often overlooked or underrated by the political class and the general citizenry in modern Africa.

It is hoped that this account will contribute to the Ugandan literature on British rule in Buganda and, simultaneously, help the kingdom of Buganda to historicise its current struggle for rediscovery and self-determination.

Further, it is hoped that through this work, Africans in general and Ugandan's in particular will come to understand more about the powerful forces of colonialism and neocolonialism and how they impede their full economic and political emancipation. Lastly, but equally importantly, it is hoped that this account will add to the many voices that demand for justice, accountability and responsibility for British colonialism and neocolonialism in Uganda and elsewhere.

Notes

[1] See Lugard, F. D. (1922) *The Dual Mandate in British Tropical Africa*, Edinburgh/London: William Blackwood & Sons, pp. 615, 617- 618. It was Lord Lugard, an agent of the Imperial British East Africa Company (IBEAC), who paved the way for Uganda to be added to the British Empire.

[2] See Grant, J. A. (1863) *A Walk Across Africa, or Domestic Scenes From my Nile Journey.* Edinburgh/London: William Blackwood & Sons; and Speke, J. H. (1863) *Journal of the Discovery of the Source of the Nile.* Edinburgh/London: William Blackwood & Sons.

[3] He arrived on 3 April 1875. His first impressions of the kingdom are captured by Frank Mclynn, (2004) *Stanley: Dark Genius of African Exploration*, London: Pimlico, pp. 255-257.

[4] Ibid., p. 256.

[5] Ibid., p. 257.

[6] Churchill, Winston S. (1908) *My African Journey.* Hodder & Stoughton: London. p.106.

[7] Ibid., p.86.

[8] Ibid., p.210.

[9] Ibid., p.211.

[10] Ibid., p.211.

[11] These principles are encapsulated in Buganda's axioms such as *Enkima, tesala gwa kibira* (a monkey should not be an arbiter in a dispute involving the forest, meaning an interested party cannot be an arbiter in a dispute where they have a vested interest), and *tosala gwa kawala, nga tonnawulira gwa kalenzi* (one should never settle a case in favour of a girl before they listen to the boy's side, i.e., never enter judgement before you hear both sides or parties).

[12] See Felkin, Robert William (1884) *Notes on Labor in Central Africa,* Edinburgh Medical Journal, Vol. 20, pp. 922-30.

[13] See generally, Roscoe (1911) *The Baganda: An Account of their Native Customs and Beliefs* and Lule, Joseph (2006) *The Hidden Wisdom of the Baganda,* Arlington, Virginia, Humbolt & Hartman, Inc.

[14] See letter by Captain E. Delme Radcliffe, an acting sub-commissioner in the Protectorate, to Harry Johnston dated 6 July 1900 and dispatched to the Marquis of Salisbury, K. G. by Johnston on 25 August 1900 in FO 2/299, TNA.

[15] See report by F. Pordage on the inhabitants of the Busera County, Kingdom of Uganda, in FO 2/304 TNA.

[16] See Bland-Sutton, John (1933) *Men and Creatures in Uganda*, London: Hutchison & Co., p. 51.

[17] See *The London Gazette*, Tuesday 19 June 1894.

[18] Unlike earlier historical accounts quoted herein—including those by Frederick Lugard, Apolo Kagwa, Ham Mukasa, A. D. Low, Lwanga-Lunyiigo, Semakula-Kiwanuka and Phares Mutibwa—on the kingdom of Buganda and the Protectorate of Uganda we rely on new evidence to analyse and understand the history and politics of British rule in Uganda.

[19] See Lugard, F. D. (1893) *The Rise of our East African Empire: Early Efforts in Nyassaland and Uganda.* Edinburgh: W. Blackwood & Sons; and Perham, M. (1959) *The Diaries of Lord Lugard: East Africa 1889-1892*, Vols. 1-3, Evanston: North Western University Press.

[20] See Lugard, *The Dual Mandate*, p. 203.

[21] Lugard, *The Dual Mandate*, p. 210.

[22] The term *mailo land* describes the land tenure system based on allocations of squire miles of freehold land in Buganda under the 1900 Uganda Agreement.

[23] On colonialism and corruption in Africa, see Mulinge, M. M. & Lesetedi, G. N. (1998). "Interrogating Our Past: Colonialism and Corruption in Sub-Saharan Africa," *African Journal of Political Science*, 3(2), pp. 15-28.

[24] See Pakenham, T. (1999) *The Scramble for Africa 1876-1912*, England: Abascus, pp. 413-433.

[25] Rodney, W. (1972) *How Europe Underdeveloped Africa*, London: L'ouverture, p. 277. See also, Ekon, E. E. (2014). "Christian Missions and Colonial Rule in Africa: Objective and Contemporary Analysis," *European Scientific Journal*, 10 (17), pp. 192-209.

[26] Katjavivi, P. H. (1988) *A History of Resistance in Namibia*, Oxford: James Currey, p. 6.

[27] Letter from Johnston to Dr Sclater, 6 March 1900, ESA A7/6, cited in Low, D. A. and Pratt, R. C. (1960) *Buganda and British Overrule 1900-1955*, London: Oxford University Press, p. 85.

[28] Ibid.

[29] Lugard, *The Dual Mandate in British Tropical Africa*, p. 576.

[30] Olusoga, D. (2016) *Black and British: A Forgotten History*, Pan Macmillan, Basingstoke, Hampshire UK., p. 431.

[31] See generally, Lieutenant Colonel H. Moyse-Bartlett (1956) *The King's African Rifles—A study in the Military History of East and Central Africa, 1890-1945*, Volume 1, Aldershot: Gal and Polden.

[32] See letter by Harry Johnston to the Marquis of Salisbury, K.G dated 5 May 1900 in FO 2/299, TNA.

[33] Ibid.

[34] Ibid.

[35] See Amone Charles, "The Creation of Acholi Military Ethnocracy in Uganda, 1882 to 1962," *International Journal of Liberal Arts and Social Science*, 2(3), April 2014, p. 145.

[36] On the British and post-independence legacy of the military in Uganda see Tripp, Mari Aili, 2010, *Museveni's Uganda: Paradoxes of Power in a Hybrid Regime*, Lynne Rienner Publishers, London, p.133.

[37] Low and Pratt, *Buganda and British Overrule*, p. 316.

[38] Nsibambi Apolo (2014) *National Integration in Uganda 1962-2013*, Fountain Publishers, Kampala, Uganda.

[39] Lugard, *The Dual Mandate in British Tropical Africa*, p. 206.

[40] See "Uganda National Movement and Trade Boycott in Buganda," Sessional Paper FCO 141/18298, TNA.

[41] See the Uganda Order-in-Council, 1902.

[42] See Laidlaw Zoe (2015) "Empire and After," in Breay, C. & Harrison, J. (eds.) *Magna Carta: Law, Liberty, Legacy*, London: The British Library, pp. 191-207.

[43] On 6 June 2013, the then British Foreign Secretary, William Hague, expressed sincere regret for torture and abuse committed by British colonial officers against Kenyans in the 1950s. He also announced a compensation package worth £19.9 million (about $31 million), to be divided among 5,200 Kenyan victims. See "UK to compensate Kenya's Mau Mau torture victims," *The Guardian*, Thursday 6 June 2013, retrieved from https://www.theguardian.com/world/2013/jun/06/uk-compensate-kenya-mau-mau-torture (accessed 2 July 2017).

PHASE I

CONQUEST AND CONSOLIDATION OF BRITISH RULE IN UGANDA (1894-1939)

On 26 February 1885, the imperial powers of Britain, France, Italy, Germany, Portugal and Spain along with King Léopold of Belgium, concluded a treaty for the partition of Africa. Under the treaty—negotiated without the participation of any Africans—the parties "secured" free access to the interior of Africa for all nations and freedom of trade in the whole basin of the Congo. The treaty marked the start of the official "Scramble for Africa" in which the colonial powers purportedly set out to "introduce the populations to the advantages of civilisation."[1]

The conference, aimed at regulating European colonisation and trade in Africa, was held in Berlin, Germany, between 1884 and 1885. It was a grand affair where Africa was sliced up and shared between a few European powers with no regard to the views or interests of its inhabitants. By the close of the conference, nearly the entire continent and its peoples had become the property of Europe, covering "thirty new colonies and protectorates, 10 million square miles of new territory and 110 million dazed new subjects, acquired by one method or another."[2]

During the scramble, Britain, which was a pioneer in the exploration and evangelisation of Africa, "felt a proprietary right to most of the continent."[3] Indeed, on account of its earlier exploits and treaties, it took a lion's share of the territory and engulfed Nigeria, the Gold Coast, Egypt, Sudan, South Africa, Rhodesia, Botswana, Swaziland, Lesotho, Malawi, Sierra Leone, Somaliland, Kenya and Uganda. With the addition of African territories to its already vast empire, Britain emerged as the leading colonial power in the world. By 1913, British colonial power extended to "over 412 million people, 23% of the world population at the time, and by 1920, it covered 35,500,000 km^2, equivalent to 24% of the earth's total land area."[4] For this reason, the British Empire was described as one where "the sun never sets."

Captain Fredrick Lugard, a British soldier, mercenary and explorer, was the pioneering entrepreneur-cum-administrator who oversaw the establishment of British interests in Uganda under the flag of the IBEAC (Imperial British East Africa Company). The IBEAC, like the infamous British East India Company (BEIC) set up to manage India in 1600,[5] was incorporated by Royal Charter in 1888 to develop, manage and administer trade in areas claimed by the British Government. The IBEAC had wide powers, including the right to raise taxes, administer justice, make treaties and act as a government over the vast area stretching from the coast of the Indian Ocean to west of Lake Victoria. Lugard's mission was to bring this territory under the effective control of the British Government and to ensure that commercial and administrative operations were profitable.

From the outset, he was committed to permanent British occupation in Buganda, in the belief that Britain needed to beat the Germans and the French in claiming African territories, whose land and labour were necessary to support the Industrial Revolution back home. He also wanted to ensure that Britain remained an influential power in Europe and the world. Once he arrived in Buganda on 18 December 1890, Lugard immediately and ruthlessly got on with the job of controlling the new territory and would not allow anyone, including the evasive Kabaka Mwanga, to stand in his way. He wrote in his diary that he had not "come here to trifle and fool; I mean to go through with my work [in] spite of Mwanga."[6] In getting Mwanga to sign up to a treaty with the IBEAC, however, he faced one snag.

Karl Peters, well known for his sadism and ruthlessness in cutting off the heads of Maasai warriors in Kenya, had beaten him to it by signing a treaty of friendship with Mwanga on behalf of the German East Africa Company. On 29 February 1890, Peters had persuaded an embattled Mwanga to sign a treaty that would help him fight off his enemies in the Muslim camp and to handle the civil strife and conflicts between French and English religious factions fighting for new converts in Buganda. Under this treaty, Peters committed Mwanga to the principles of the Congo Act (resulting from the Berlin Conference) guaranteeing Europeans free trade, free access and the right to settle in Buganda and its tributary countries. Mwanga also agreed with the German Kaiser that he would enjoy the same rights in Germany as Mwanga had granted to Europeans in Buganda. In entering this treaty, Mwanga hoped that Peters would save him from imminent British invasion.[7]

To secure Buganda as a part of its general desire to control the source of the Nile, Britain had to find a solution to Peters' treaty with Mwanga. Accordingly, and unknown to Mwanga and Peters, Lord Salisbury, the British Prime Minister, negotiated and obtained a sphere of influence over Uganda under the Anglo-German Agreement of July 1890 (also known as the Heligoland Treaty). Under this treaty, the British surrendered the island of Heligoland to Germany, which in turn renounced its claims to Uganda and recognised the British Protectorate over Zanzibar and Pemba (previously a semi-independent Sultanate). The treaty also gave the region to the west of Lake Nyasa to Britain and allowed Britain access between Lake Tanganyika and Uganda. With the Heligoland treaty in place, Britain, acting through Lugard and the IBEAC, was ready to establish its interests in the country.

At his first audience with Mwanga on 18 December 1890, Lugard was welcomed by flute players and excited Baganda nobles. He sized up his host and was not impressed, as his face "showed irresolution and a good deal of sensuality."[8] He got straight to the point and explained that he had brought a provisional "treaty of friendship." Before taking leave, he advised Mwanga and his chiefs to sign it.[9] On 26 December 1890, Lugard returned to Mwanga's court and threatened to use a Maxim gun if the king refused to sign the treaty.[10] At this point, Mwanga signed the treaty but under duress. His chiefs, led by Katikkiro Apolo Kagwa, quickly followed suit and made crosses on the treaty to signify their "consent."[11] In effect, this provisional treaty, valid for two years, recognised Lugard and the IBEAC in Buganda and curtailed Mwanga's right to control foreign affairs and to make treaties or war as he pleased; it abolished his independence in home affairs; and it restricted the trade in arms, placing it under the control of the IBEAC as the representative of the protecting power. The treaty thus effectively usurped Mwanga's control of the kingdom's revenues. More fundamentally, it denied him the command of his own army and required him to seek the consent of the Company's representative "in all grave and serious affairs and matters connected with the state."[12]

Fifteen months after the signing of the provisional treaty, and once he was sure of his ground, Lugard procured a more permanent treaty with Mwanga reaffirming the Company's protection. The 1892 treaty was for Lugard and the IBEAC a major coup against Mwanga. Indeed, the CMS and the French priests were astonished by Lugard's success and could not believe how easily he had accomplished so much in such a short period. One of their biographers commented on Mwanga's humiliation, wondering how he had "put all the thousands of subjects and people from his vassal states under the protection of a simple commercial company."[13] Even Lugard was impressed at the success of his trickery, writing in his diary:

> No man if he understood would sign it, and to say that a savage chief has been told that he cedes all rights to the Company in exchange for nothing is an obvious untruth. If he had been told that the Company will protect him

> against his enemies, and share in his wars as an ally, he has been told a lie, for the Company have no idea of doing any such a thing and no force to do it with if they wished.[14]

Lugard knew that the agreement was legally inconsequential and unenforceable, but proceeded to pacify Buganda and to entrench both Protestant hegemony and British rule in the area. He pitched his camp at Fort Lugard, a new and parallel power base and IBEAC headquarters, at Kampala Hill (now known as old Kampala), adjacent to Mwanga's own court at Mengo. He used the fort as a garrison with many armed Sudanese and Swahili troops at his command. In fact, he housed seven Europeans and 650 troops.[15] From the beginning, Lugard was supported by Protestant converts, and many converged at Fort Lugard for protection from the Catholics (under the influence of French missionaries), who were generally hostile to him.

Mwanga at this time generally enjoyed the support of the Catholics. However, he was bewildered and angry at the turn of events and particularly with Lugard's growing influence and power in Buganda. He loathed the British and lamented the fact that they had made him sign a treaty that curtailed his power, and yet he had gained nothing at all from them in return. It must be said, though, that without Lugard's help to fight off his Muslim and Arab adversaries, Mwanga's stay in power would have been briefer.

Thus, in spite of the support afforded by Lugard, Mwanga was defiant and protested British rule. To prove his independence, he flew his own flag in a manner that dwarfed the Union Jack and refused to pull it down on Lugard's demands.[16] Mwanga also refused to hand over a Catholic man accused of murdering a Protestant believer. Lugard sent a letter to Mwanga demanding that the murderer be handed over. In reply, the self-confident Mwanga stated: "All right, I have made my decision and won't alter it. If the Captain wants war, it is his matter".[17] This angered Lugard and sparked the infamous battle of Mengo of January 1892. With the force of a Maxim gun and the help of his Protestant allies, Lugard drove Mwanga and the Catholics out of Mengo.

The vanquished king was marooned on Bulingugwe Island on Lake Victoria a few miles from Mengo, the capital of Buganda. However, this victory was not satisfactory for the thirty-four-year-old Lugard. On 30 January 1892, a week after the battle, Lugard personally attacked Mwanga's sanctuary and a massacre of hundreds of Africans ensued.[18] Mwanga, together with Bishop Hirsh, the leader of the White Fathers, was lucky to escape and lived to tell of the wrath of Lugard. He learnt the hard way the true meaning of the "protection" under his treaty with Lugard.

Bishop Hirsh best describes this bloodbath:

> It was two o'clock in the afternoon. On the road I saw fifteen boats rapidly approach the island. All of a sudden the bullets began to rain upon the royal hut, making a terrible noise in the copse that surrounded us; it was the Maxim *mitrailleuse*, which joined its fire to that of the boats loaded with soldiers. The King seized me by the hand and dragged me away. If we were not riddled it was the Lord that shielded us. A crowd of women and children fled with us. How many fell! We had soon gained the other shore of the island; the bullets could no longer reach us. But what a sight! Just a few canoes, and a crowd of 3,000 or 4,000 throwing themselves into the water to cling to them; it was heart breaking. What shrieks! What a fusillade! What deaths by drowning![19]

In Europe, the news of Lugard's incredible deeds outraged the French and the Germans but did little to move the British, who instead regarded Lugard as "a brave man, an able man, and an upright man."[20] The British press took his innocence for granted.[21] British Prime Minister Lord Salisbury expressed complete confidence in his proconsul. He set up a commission and tasked it to make an impartial report on the troubles in Uganda.[22]

In spite of his efforts at assembling the company's administration and military bases up and down in Uganda, Lugard was unable to continue the expedition because the IBEAC had run out of money and was not able to meet its expenses. Lugard's mission in Uganda was thus thrown into jeopardy once the IBEAC announced its plans to evacuate Uganda on 31 December 1892.[23] Lugard was devastated by the news. He feared that his two-and-a-half years had gone to waste. Yet, he was convinced that Britain had the right to rule and own Africa, that the African leadership had been vanquished, and that he had done all to open the door wide for British rule.

He thus quickly returned to London and started a campaign not only to "save Uganda" and have it retained as part of the British Empire, but also to defend himself against accusations that he was too harsh and that he was responsible for the massacres in the battle of Mengo. Lugard, he who had mercilessly killed hundreds in Buganda, pointed to the murder of Bishop Hannington and the killing of Christian converts by Mwanga (see p 40) to warn about a possible bloodbath if his company left Uganda.[24] He also boldly argued, in *The Times*, that

> Britain needed new tropical markets to exploit. Why reject the riches of Uganda: the coffee, wheat, cotton and gum? Britain also needed security

> for Egypt, and Egypt needed security for Uganda and the sources of the Nile. What would happen if these fell into the hands of France or Germany? British honour, too, was at risk.[25]

Furthermore, Lugard argued that he had pledged that the IBEAC would protect the natives, and the company had pledged to act in Britain's name. Finally, he asked, how could the missionaries be abandoned to their fate? And, how could Uganda be left to a civil war that the Muslim slave traders were bound to win?[26]

Lugard's appeals and petitions were not wholly persuasive to the British Establishment. However, because these appeals received wide press coverage and were greatly supported by Henry Morton Stanley and Bishop Alfred Robert Tucker (CMS missionary and Anglican Bishop of Uganda), they got Gladstone's Cabinet to send an Imperial Commissioner, Sir Gerald Portal, to inquire and report on what to do about Uganda.[27] In reality, Portal's mission was to take over the country from the IBEAC and administer it for the British Crown. The broader mission was for Britain to take over the source of the River Nile, recapture Sudan, keep out the Germans and French, and rule Egypt.[28]

On 29 May 1893, Portal entered into a provisional treaty with Buganda's Mwanga and his chiefs, Apolo Kagwa and Stanislas Mugwanya, under which the British Government inherited the rights of the IBEAC over the Protectorate. Under the agreement, Mwanga, "profoundly and sincerely desirous of securing British protection … and also assistance and guidance in the government," pledged and bound himself, inter alia:

- not to make treaties with any Europeans without the consent and approval of Her Majesty's Government;
- to recognise and be bound by all international obligations to which Britain may be a party;
- not to declare war without the consent and approval of Her Majesty's Government;
- to always obtain Her Majesty's Government's concurrence in all serious matters of state, such as the appointment of chiefs or officials, the political or religious distribution of territory, etc.;
- to allow Her Majesty's Government to assess, collect taxes and to dispose of the revenues of the country; the power provided that the property of Her Majesty's Government and of their officers, and of all servants of Her Majesty's Government shall be free from the incidence of taxes;
- to allow Her Majesty's Government to impose export and import

duties on all goods leaving or entering Uganda for its sole use and benefit (with duties to be fixed in accordance with the provisions of the General Acts of Berlin and Brussels of 1885 and 1890);
- to unreservedly place the foreign relations of Uganda in the hands of Her Majesty's Government; and
- to stop slave trading or slave raiding.[29]

In consideration of Mwanga's undertakings above, Gerald Portal, on behalf of Her Majesty's Government, agreed not to provide him with the protection, assistance and guidance sought, but to appoint and leave a British Representative with a sufficient number of staff to carry out the provisions of the agreement. With the above agreement, Portal made recommendations supporting the retention of Uganda as a Protectorate.

However, Portal's agreement with Mwanga notwithstanding, the British Government was initially reluctant to take on another "black baby."[30] But it eventually decided to adopt it and later that year appointed Colonel Henry Edward Colville as the new British Commissioner.[31] The official announcement of Buganda as a Protectorate was made in the *London Gazette* on 19 June 1894. Interestingly, this was before Colville signed a permanent treaty with Mwanga, which he later did on behalf of Britain on 27 August 1894. Under the agreement, Her Majesty the Queen "was graciously pleased to bestow on Mwanga, King of Uganda, the protection he had requested."[32] On his part, Mwanga, with the concurrence of Apolo Kagwa and Stanislas Mugwanya, once again pledged to bind himself and his heirs and successors to the following conditions:

- not to make any treaties whatsoever with any Europeans without the consent of Her Majesty;
- not to have any jurisdiction over Europeans (such jurisdiction shall lie exclusively with Her Majesty);
- to be bound by all and every international act and obligation to which Great Britain may be a party;
- not to wage war without the consent of Her Majesty, whose concurrence shall be obtained in all serious matters of state, such as the appointment of chiefs or officials, the political or religious distribution of territory, etc.;
- to assign the assessment and collection of taxes and the disposal of the revenues of the country to the control and revision of Her Majesty's Government;
- not to tax any property of Her Majesty's Government;
- to allow Her Majesty's Government the right to levy export and

import duties on all goods for its sole use or benefit;
- to place Uganda's foreign relations unreservedly in the hands of Her Majesty's Government; and
- to abolish the slave trade.

It is doubtful whether Mwanga and his ministers fully understood the meaning and significance of the agreements they signed with Portal and Colville because, like Lugard's treaty, these new agreements virtually stripped his powers and further eroded Buganda's sovereignty. Lugard had always made it clear that the usurpation of native authority was a policy of colonial rule. This policy ensured that the native authority became a *de facto* and not a *de jure* ruler over his people.[33] Had Mwanga not learnt his lessons from the Lugard era, when he was defeated and obliged to subordinate his authority to that of a British sub-commissioner? Did he not recall how, for example, he was once fined for "illegal" trafficking in ivory? Was he oblivious to the fact that, from 1895 onwards, his Royal Assembly—the *Lukiiko*—no longer met under his own control but under that of a British officer?[34]

It is equally doubtful whether there existed a *consensus ad idem* between Mwanga and Colville on the legality and scope of the agreement.[35] This is because Mwanga was immediately dissatisfied with the interpretation and implementation of the agreement and remained defiant. For that reason, on 6 July 1897, three years after his treaty with Colville, he declared a war against the British colonial authority. However, given his relatively ill-equipped force and the large arsenal and highly organised troops of the enemy, his attack was repulsed within a fortnight and he was forced to flee to German East Africa (present-day Tanzania) where he was arrested and imprisoned in Bukoba. He soon escaped from prison and returned to Buganda and once again attacked the Protectorate Government, but was again defeated on 15 January 1898 and escaped. He then went into hiding and later caught up with Kabalega, the ousted Omukama of Bunyoro, who was also on the run from the British forces. With the connivance of his former senior chiefs—namely, Semei Kakungulu, Apolo Kagwa and Andrew Luwandaga—Mwanga was arrested together with Kabalega by Indian troops in Bukedi in April 1899. Both were promptly deported, first to Kismayu in Somalia and later to the Seychelles, where Mwanga died in 1903.

Before his death, Mwanga was formally deposed by the British forces in 1897 and, with their connivance, replaced by his infant son Daudi Chwa, who ascended to the throne at the tender age of one year. The deposition and deportation of Mwanga and the enthronement of his son was a major coup and marked a new chapter in the relations between Buganda and Britain. The British established a Regency of the three leading chiefs in Buganda who effectively worked under the control of George Wilson, the new sub-commissioner in Buganda.

The summary deposition of Mwanga and other intransigent native rulers like Kabalega was in line with an established British policy under which, in the interests of good government, "the right of confirming or otherwise the choice of the people of the successor to chiefship, and of deposing any ruler for misrule or other adequate cause" was reserved for the Governor.[36]

To consolidate its new position, the British Government dispatched Henry "Harry" Hamilton Johnston as Her Majesty's Special Commissioner, Commander-in-Chief and Consul-General for the Ugandan Protectorate and the adjoining territories, whose mission was "to place the administration of the present Protectorate on a permanent and satisfactory footing."[37] Thus, with a *carte blanche*, Johnston, like Lugard before him, approached Buganda with enormous pomp and gusto. His immediate plan was to "negotiate" a new agreement with its leaders—headed by Apolo Kagwa—which would irreversibly change the social, political and economic landscape of the old kingdom of Buganda.

Sir Apolo Kagwa and the Politics of Colonial Patronage in Buganda

The establishment of British rule in Buganda and other parts of Uganda was aided by several factors, most prominent among which were the Maxim gun used to conquer or subdue resistant groups and the collaboration or co-option of its native leadership. The history of the imposition of British rule in Buganda shows that no single African aided the entrenchment of colonial rule more than Sir Apolo Gulemye Kalibala Kagwa, together with Stanislas Mugwanya and Kisingiri Kizito. It may also be said, not without controversy,[38] that no single person in Uganda benefitted from British patronage than he did.[39]

Born in 1865, Kagwa started his career in Buganda as an apprentice in the treasury of Kabaka Mutesa I's court. When Mutesa died in October 1884, Kagwa stayed in the royal court and served as the head of the treasury under Mwanga. Before the advent of colonial rule, he commanded Buganda's army and succeeded in the expansion of the frontiers of the kingdom. His legacy as a colossus in Buganda's history is thus understandable. He was an early and devout convert to Protestant

Christianity. As a court official, Kagwa influenced Mwanga to accept the Imperial British East Africa Company in preference to that of the Germans led by Karl Peters. In 1889, at the youthful age of 24 years, he was appointed Katikkiro of Buganda.

Kagwa was an imposing, knowledgeable and fearless warrior with immense influence in the Kabaka's court. He was a man of the most striking personality, with considerable education, and could read and write Luganda (the language of the Baganda). According to the report, he had undoubted loyalty to the colonial government and possessed immense influence over the natives. Working with Captain F. Lugard and other chiefs such as Gabriel Kintu and Semei Kakungulu, Kagwa actively participated in the colonial territorial and religious wars in Buganda on the side of the Protestant missionaries, an alliance that helped establish and seal a powerful British and Protestant hegemony in Buganda.

When Mwanga rebelled against the British in 1897, his Katikkiro Kagwa—with whom he had performed *Omukago,* a sacred rite of blood brotherhood—turned out to be more faithful to the British Government than to his blood brother. Alongside Andrew Luwandaga and Semei Kakungulu,[40] Kagwa participated in the capture, deposition and eventual deportation of Mwanga and Omukama Kabalega of Bunyoro in 1899.[41] He justified his actions against Mwanga on the basis that Mwanga had reneged on the agreement of protection that Buganda had with Britain and he had rebelled against the colonial master.

In the aftermath of Mwanga's deposition, Kagwa, working with the colonial authorities, installed the infant Daudi Chwa as the new Kabaka of Buganda on 9 August 1897.[42] Together with Stanislasi Mugwanya and Zakariya Kisingiri Kizito, he, with the support and patronage of the colonial government, became a Regent in charge of all the kingdom's affairs, including raising the new Kabaka. It is in this capacity that Kagwa led both the lopsided negotiations and the execution of the historic 1900 Uganda Agreement. As we show these negotiations were deeply steeped in the culture of and influenced by British colonial patronage.

Political patronage may be understood as the offering (often tacitly) of a reward, protection, prestige or other benefit to someone a public role (a client) so that they may in turn accede to or support the views or policies of the giver (the patron). Apart from outright conquest, British rule in colonial Uganda—as well as its relationships and dealings in post-colonial Uganda—was entrenched either through violence or the politics of co-option and patronage. The latter method entailed the building of networks of patronage within the native leadership. In the context of Buganda, starting with the Christian missionaries and later by colonial administrators like Johnston and Lugard, Britain ensured that native leaders such as Apolo Kagwa and Ham Mukasa were aligned to its policies and agenda—even though this sometimes meant the abandonment of their traditional or cultural allegiances. In the introduction to this book we highlighted how patronage was central to colonial policies articulated by Lugard. And, as we show below, patronage was a common strand used throughout the sixty-eight years of British rule in Uganda and beyond.

In the post-colonial period, as we show below, Britain engaged with Uganda's leaders including Obote, Amin and Museveni to perpetuate a legacy protective of its interests through patronage and other means. The politics and rewards for patronage are well illustrated in the workings of the colonial administration. These include the selective reward and promotion of conformists among native leadership, like Katikkiro Apolo Kagwa, and the punishment—including by deportation or deposition—of non-conformists like Katikkiro Samwiri Wamala. As we demonstrate below, the politics of patronage and reward underpinned the negotiations and conclusion of the 1900, 1955 and 1961 Agreements between Buganda and Britain.

Negotiating the 1900 Uganda Agreement[43]

Once Uganda had been declared a Protectorate in 1894, the next stage was to install an administrative and legal framework under which it would be governed. An ambitious Johnston set the agenda and the terms for the negotiations with a weak and vulnerable leadership in Buganda. The Agreement was negotiated at a rather difficult time for the kingdom of Buganda. Its administrative structures were weak and its population was dispersed and rudderless, as it had barely recovered from the ravages of religious and political wars.[44] It was also in the wake of Mwanga's last rebellion, carried out in a last ditch effort to save his throne. The kingdom was under the leadership of an infant king, Daudi Chwa, who depended wholly on his chiefs.

The most senior of these chiefs, led by Apolo Kagwa, had deserted for religious and political reasons and in fact fought Mwanga when he rebelled against British rule in 1897. Starting with Lugard in the heady days of the IBEAC, up to the times of Commissioner Johnston and beyond, colonial administrators worked to extend British patronage and influence by winning Kagwa to their side. For this reason, in January 1900, soon after the negotiations of the 1900 Agreement had commenced, Johnston wrote to Clement Hill, the British Principal Secretary of State for Foreign Affairs, making the case for Kagwa to visit for two months as a guest of the British Government.

According to Johnston, this was in order to fulfil Kagwa's "long cherished wish to visit England."[45] Johnston reasoned that Kagwa had "played up to us splendidly from the very beginning of the British administration here and I think useful results may be expected to follow from his being received and well treated in Britain."[46] Kagwa's visit was approved and arranged to coincide with the coronation of King Edward VII.[47] Johnston thought that "the imposing spectacle of His Majesty's coronation would greatly impress him."[48]

Because Buganda's bargaining position was weak, its new leaders could hardly resist Johnston's aggressive advances. Indeed, they were more-or-less faced with a *fait accompli* in the lopsided negotiations with him. According to Low and Pratt, they "had little choice when presented with the agreement ... they were in that exposed position in which the weaker members of an alliance often find themselves in their relation with their stronger allies."[49] Moreover, in negotiating with Johnston, they depended wholly on Christian missionaries for translation and interpretation of the terms of his proposals.

The powerlessness and vulnerability of Buganda's new leadership in relation to the colonial agents is clearly reflected in the correspondence between the Regents (Apolo Kagwa, Stanislas Mugwanya and Zakariya Kisingiri Kizito) and Johnston during the negotiations. For example, on 3 January 1900, they reverently addressed him on his proposals on taxation and land as follows:

> As concerning every "hut" to pay 3 rupees … it is not that we are refusing to pay, it is because our land has been very much devastated by the enemy and we have not recovered. Your ivory has not been prepared even, and people have not settled down to cultivation in order to get wealth.
>
> Again, Sir, we the chiefs of the land request you to give us 1 rupee out of every 3 rupees collected from each hut, and the government to get the remaining 2 rupees, for we are friends of Her Majesty the Queen as you said. It is not good for us to be poor and people laugh at us saying look at those who call themselves friends of the Queen being short of money.
>
> Again Sir, in connection with the gun licence of 4 rupees—that is all right, but we beg you to give us a period of three years in which to settle our country down. This is because our guns, together with those possessed by the *askari* in the service of the Queen are needed in defending our country. Again we are serving the Queen with those guns and we are not entirely serving ourselves. In case of emergency, we, and the *askari* of the Queen are the people who shall be first to go to the front … even now, Kakungulu is serving the Queen at Bukedi. He is trying to make the Bakedi obey the Queen.

> As for taking possession of the land, this is all in the prerogative of the Queen, and we ourselves are placed in the very positions which we hold by the Government, witness our acceptance of the Governments Orders, and also the assistance we give to the Government in ruling Buganda. Failure on our part to carry out any request is due to the immaturity of our country which is not yet used to carrying out the orders of the Queen.... For years we have been friends of the Queen, and even you yourself said so ... it is because of your kindness, and the mercy of Her Majesty the Queen, that we request you to read our letter and understand.[50]

It is not surprising that Johnston rode roughshod over the essentially powerless chiefs throughout the negotiation process, disregarding most of their pleas. Johnston's attitude towards the views in the above letter perplexed the Regents. On 16 January 1900, they wrote again grumbling but at the same time agreeing to pay three rupees as gun tax and three more rupees as hut tax.[51] In this letter, fearing for their personal status in the new order, the Regents asked Johnston several questions, including about Mwanga's fate and their own power and privileges under the new regime. They were concerned that their position in the social hierarchy not be reduced to that of *bakopi* (commoners).

They were also suspicious as to why Johnston had come up with a new agreement even though there were others that had been signed with Colville. They informed him that they had "put so much trust in these agreements" hoping that they would benefit Buganda. For this reason, they stated, they were annoyed with Mwanga for rebelling against the British and thus had abandoned, fought and captured him to ensure that they fulfilled the agreements Buganda had with Britain and against which he had rebelled.[52]

Besides taxes, position and power, the Regents were also agonised about the control and ownership of land and forests in Buganda. On this, they asked the questions: "Where shall we collect firewood in future?" "Where shall we grow crops and get pasture and clay for our pottery if you take all the wasteland?" "On what land shall our youth settle?" "Are we going to live like strangers in our country?" They added that "We would like to ask therefore that we be allowed to utilize wastelands for agricultural and pastoral purposes".[53] But it was not only the Regents who were perturbed by Sir Harry Johnston's proposals. Bishop Alfred Tucker, head of the Protestant church, was also uneasy over his speed and methods. Writing to a friend on 11 January 1900, he said:

> The new Commissioner, Sir Harry Johnston, has arrived and his first action has been to disturb the country from one end to the other by his new

> proposals … [H]e proposes on behalf of the Queen to take over the whole land of the country. The way he proposes to administer things completely turns "topsy-turvy" the whole social life of the people … the proposals are not the result of Sir Harry Johnston's investigation into the conditions of the country. He expounded them on the date of his arrival. They have been concocted in the Foreign Office in utter ignorance of the social conditions of the country.[54]

However, on the whole, Johnston was neither impressed nor changed by the Regents' submissions or the concerns of missionary interlocutors like Bishop Tucker. In fact, he thought that some of the Regents' concerns of 3 January 1900 were "peevish nonsense" or "merely sentimental," stating that:

> there is absolutely no reason for retaining any mystery about these proposals, because they are not merely my proposals but those of the Foreign Office which has sketched out their main principles in my final instructions, I only having added the details necessary to adapt these regulations to local requirements.... I shall be willing to listen to any modifications they have to suggest, but I cannot change any principle above set forth, because to do so would be to run counter to the instructions I have received.[55]

In reply to the Regents' concerns of 16 January 1900, Johnston wrote:

> The plain answer to them is that they have not the inherent strength to maintain an independent Uganda Government, which will not succumb either to some European power or to Abyssinia. That being the case, as they were forced to accept British protection and the subsidies of the British Government, they must accept the consequences, one of the consequences being that the Queen in the best interests of the country of Uganda must regularise the methods by which waste lands and forests are disposed of…. I cannot trust the chiefs and people of this country to deal with the waste land in an honest and sensible fashion … in fact as a guardian of this country I cannot permit any disposal of land to take place before a settlement of the kind I have sketched out has been arrived at.[56]

He added:

> …the Uganda people have been spoilt and the time has come for them to face the hard realities of existence in a Protectorate which does not and will not for a long time yet pay its way. Moreover, they must be made to understand distinctly that this country is described as the "Uganda Protectorate and Adjoining Territories," and that we cannot see our way to

> exempt Uganda [read Buganda] from the conditions under which the other provinces will have to be governed. If the Baganda reject us as the protectors the Germans will be very happy to step into the vacant position.[57]

On the threat of the Germans overrunning Buganda, Jackson must have been bluffing the chiefs, because by 1890 Britain had signed the Heligoland Treaty where, in exchange for the Heligoland archipelago, Germany had relinquished its interest in Uganda to Britain. Commenting on the Regents' concern that the honour and glory of Buganda would be diminished under the Agreement, Johnston was vitriolic. He wrote to Jackson:

> I think you will agree that I have managed to land one or two nice little knocks on the thick skulls of the Uganda nobility.... In spite of all they have learnt from the last 20 years they are very far from being in a position of a people able to govern themselves without European control…. What is the "honour and glory" of which they have been deprived? The honour and glory of Uganda before the missionaries returned here and the British Government took control of the country consisted in killing numbers of innocent people with the most horrible barbarities, raiding for slaves in all directions, burning each other, and holding dances and exhibitions of such a disgusting nature in Mwanga's palace that I cannot use the English language to describe such abominations. This is the honour and glory of which the chiefs imagine they are being deprived: nothing else than the right to commit these crimes has been taken from them…. [T]he Baganda are at present very nearly the bottom of the scale. If their chiefs could be carried about the world with open eyes they would realise that they are only ten years and two pieces of bark cloth ahead of the Wa-kavirondo.[58]

In February 1900, a few weeks before negotiations on the 1900 Agreement were concluded, Johnson made a verbal agreement with Buganda's chief negotiators Kagwa, Kisingiri and Mugwanya in which he promised land in further compensation for their services. Under this separate arrangement, on top of their consideration under the agreement, they would receive extra parcels of land as follows: Kagwa 20 square miles, Mugwanya 15 square miles, and Kisingiri 10 square miles. Additionally, on condition that the Agreement was signed, Johnston promised to give Kagwa 100 government cattle "whenever he is ready to send his men for them."[59] Johnston also procured gramophones to be given as presents to the negotiators on the conclusion of the important agreement.[60] After a period of three months of back-and-forth haggling over the terms of the Agreement and with the interventions of the

Protestant leadership, the two sides reached some form of compromise. There is no doubt that Johnston's presents and promises helped facilitate the early conclusion of the Agreement, whose negotiations had lasted several weeks.

Britain's colonisation of Buganda was sealed at 10 am on Saturday 10 March 1900 when Johnston, on behalf of Her Majesty the Queen of Great Britain and Ireland, Empress of India and Protectress of Uganda, signed the 1900 Agreement with the Regents and chiefs of the kingdom of Buganda on behalf of the infant king, Daudi Chwa. On this day, acting through a young Chwa represented by the influential Kagwa and several chiefs, Buganda surrendered its sovereignty to British rule. The action would lead to a struggle of many years to reclaim its status. The signing ceremony was done in the presence of 400 Sudanese troops, missionaries, colonial officials, chiefs, and a crowd of onlookers. Typically, Johnston arrived in glorious fashion and was welcomed by a 21-gun salute. He was the first to sign the Agreement, followed by the Regents and Chiefs. Only one chief, Joshua Kkaate, the *Mugema* (head of the monkey clan), refrained from signing, because he disapproved of the amount of authority left to the Kabaka. On the occasion, the infant king of Buganda was borne on the shoulders of one of his carriers in time to witness the signing.[61]

Under the Agreement, Kagwa and each of the Regents received 16 square miles of land in their private capacities and 16 square miles attached to their offices. As an indication of his wealth, it was reported that at the time, Kagwa had opened an account with the National Bank of India where he had deposited some 5,000 rupees.[62] In May 1902, in the company of his dear friend, Chief Ham Mukasa, Kagwa set off on a historic journey to Britain. He arrived in London on 13 June 1902. The British Government agreed to spend £250 on his in-land expenses and entertainment. This sum was paid out of the Protectorate's budget under the heading "Presents" to advance colonial patronage. Unsurprisingly, both Kagwa and Mukasa were greatly impressed by their hosts and the industrial and other developments in Britain. Both were to later play a crucial role in the consolidation of British rule in Buganda.

For his great services to the British Empire, in addition to square miles of land and other gifts, Kagwa was awarded with many honours and medals—the greatest being the Order of St Michael and St George (KCMG) in 1905.[63] This was unprecedented for an African at the time. For his role in the First World War, he was decorated as an honorary member of the Most Excellent Order of the British Empire (MBE). Ham Mukasa was also awarded an MBE.

Once the 1900 Agreement was concluded and British rule established and accepted amongst the Baganda natives, Apolo Kagwa, Stanislas Mugwanya and Zakaria Kisingiri, as Regents and principal intermediaries of British rule, outwardly grew even bigger in stature and authority. Their advancement, however, was largely at the expense of the young Kabaka Daudi Chwa and the unsuspecting loyal Baganda peasantry. In fact, Kabaka Chwa, who was literally born and raised in Kagwa's private court, had little or no power in the new colonial setup.[64] To the extent that they complied with the directives of the colonial administrators, the trio had the full backing of those colonial powers and their actions were unchallenged in their control of the native administration of the kingdom's government. They were the leaders of the main political factions and wielded authority within Buganda's religious structures. At a personal level, they consolidated their positions through their careful and often self-serving disposition of the mailo land grants. Their influence on appointments was usually decisive.[65]

However, and as we demonstrate below, Kagwa's power and role were to eventually diminish once he started to question or challenge colonial authority. His place or power in the colonial schema was only guaranteed whilst he served the interests of the colonial state. Once this changed his power evaporated and he was retired without ceremony.

Religion and the Politics of Colonial Rule in Buganda

A narrative on the establishment of British colonial rule in (B)Uganda cannot be complete without an account of the role of religion, religious missions and religious personalities in the propagation of a colonial and Christian patronage. Indeed, as Lugard wrote, Christian missionary work opened the way for trade and the flag in tropical Africa. In that sense, Christian missions were the pioneers of Britain's "tropical empire."[66]

The religious terrain in Buganda before the advent of Christian missionaries was dominated by native religions and Islam. Thus, the concepts of God and religion were not alien. Islam was the first foreign religion to be introduced in Buganda. Islamisation was spearheaded by Arab traders from the coast of the Indian Ocean. Islam was followed by Christianity, which was introduced by missionaries from Europe. The new religions had to contend with vibrant native religions that were negatively characterised by the Europeans as paganist.

Buganda's religious system consisted of the belief and worship of supernatural traditional spirits (*Balubaale*) like Kibuuka Omumbaale and deities (*Emisambwa*) like the Nakayima in Mubende. Traditional religious spirituality in Buganda was encompassed in the concept of *eddiini* (religion). The idea of a superior divine authority was known as *Katonda* (God). It was believed that *Katonda* resided or presided in heaven (*mu Ggulu*). *Katonda*, in various forms, was responsible for matters such as war, childbirth, family wealth or prosperity, rain and healing. Prayers and the worship of Buganda's gods were conducted by intermediaries known as *Abasamize* (high priests) in worship places known as *Amasaabo* (shrines). Praise or worship did not entail congregation and did not follow a common or written liturgy.[67]

Such was the state of religious affairs in Buganda at the time Henry Morton Stanley visited Kabaka Mutesa I and told him about Christianity, the "good news" of the Bible and the need for the salvation of lost African heathens, whose religion he considered paganistic, inferior and evil in the eyes of the God known in Europe. Mutesa I was intrigued by Stanley's idea of God and was impressed by the stories he heard about the knowledge and technology of Europe. For those reasons, he was persuaded in 1876 to write to Queen Victoria asking her, first, to send him knowledgeable experts to teach his subjects matters that would help develop his kingdom and, second, to send him teachers of Christianity and God as understood in Europe.

In inviting European experts to Buganda, Mutesa was making a strategic decision in the hope that they would help to develop his people and bolster his position in the region. On this point, Pulford has rightly argued that the aggressive and expansionist Baganda people thought "they could lever this situation to further their expansionary aims—although in the event they levered themselves into colonialism."[68]

The first Christian missionaries arrived in Uganda in 1877, with Lieutenant Shergold Smith and the Reverend C. T. Wilson of the Christian Missionary Society (CMS), locally referred to as the *Wangeleza*, leading the way. They were followed in 1879 by the Catholic White Fathers from France, locally referred to as *Wafaransa* on account of their origins. Once they had settled in, they started a competitive and aggressive campaign to recruit new converts and Christianise them.

The division between Protestantism and Catholicism was played out in the Kabaka's own court, as each side was keen to recruit the Kabaka and his pages so as to be the official or dominant religion in Buganda. However, both Mutesa and Mwanga were noncommittal and refused to be baptised, oscillating from one religion to another depending on the circumstances. The two missionary groups wasted no time in exporting the ancient doctrinal feuds of Europe into the heart of Africa. With a sea of souls to save, they "turned their fire on each other, hurling insults from their hilltop stations of Rubaga and Namirembe."[69]

The Christianisation of Buganda entailed a campaign to popularise the bible and Christianity as universal, moral and benevolent, with an emphasis that it was only those who believed in the Holy Trinity and accepted baptism—and hence received English or biblical names either in addition to or in replacement of their old African names—would qualify for salvation and a ticket to heaven, where they would encounter Jesus seated on the right hand side of his Heavenly Father. Converts were promised redemption from sin, an everlasting life and, perhaps most importantly, to be spared the horrific fires and fury of hell where Satan ruled. In addition to the heavenly promises, the Christian missions attended to the material needs of the new converts, who were taught how to read and write, how to treat common diseases using European medicine, and introduced to new technology and vocational training, including in carpentry, agriculture, mechanical and electrical sciences.

The campaign also entailed the demonization of all African religious beliefs and practices. The burning of shrines, fetishes and talismans were encouraged, as was the condemnation and ostracisation of the leaders and practitioners of African religions. On the flip side, the Christian missions rewarded and praised the converts and supported them to gain positions of power and authority within the mission structures and the kingdom—including in the Kabaka's court—from where they were encouraged to resist or challenge traditional authority over customs, practices and beliefs deemed to be evil, immoral or repugnant by the missionaries.

Bishop Tucker, who played a leading role in the establishment of British rule in Uganda, points out that "the history of the missionary work of the Church of Uganda is inseparably bound up with the political history of the Protectorate of Uganda as a development of the colonial policy of Great Britain."[70] And although he knew the Venn regulation forbidding CMS missionaries from participating in the political affairs of the country in which they were situated,[71] Bishop Tucker did not only immerse himself in Ugandan politics but worked hard to bring the whole area under a British Protectorate.[72]

With the introduction of foreign religions, Buganda's society was split in three main ways. The first division was between the Christian converts or "readers" (*abasomi*) and the non-believers or so-called "pagans". Another split was intra-Christian, between believers of Catholicism and believers of Protestantism, and third was between believers of Christianity in general and believers in Islam. The competition was not restricted to winning new converts but extended to a desire to control and dominate the politics in the kingdom through the Kabaka.

To this end, the Catholic, Protestant, Islamist and traditionalist camps all vied to gain the backing of or to control the Kabaka and his senior chiefs. Each camp developed armouries and ammunition to defend itself. The struggle that ensued resulted in violent and devastating religious wars in the kingdom of Buganda in the late 1880s and early 1890s. In this period, Mwanga was twice deposed and replaced, first by Kiweewa, who was later brutally murdered and replaced by Kalema, a Muslim convert who had the support of the Muslim camp. With the help of a combined force of the Christians, Mwanga was reinstated on the throne.

The contestation between the new religion (Christianity) and the traditional political power in Buganda reached its peak once Mwanga, in trying to reassert his authority, ordered the execution of Bishop Hannington in 1885, and later in June 1886, the young Christian "readers" (today called the Uganda martyrs) working in his court. The young men were brutally murdered because, with encouragement from their missionary leaders, they defied Mwanga and were unwavering in their newly found faith. It was a high price to pay for the young Africans but one that distinctly marked the nature and gravity of the crisis brought about by the zealous Christianisation of a deeply traditional, monarchical and conservative Buganda. Mwanga was always suspicious of the intentions and activities of missionaries. Lunyiigo explains:

> Mwanga and the missionaries were competitors for attention and service of the same people, the pages, who absented themselves from services at the Kabaka's palace to 'read' and serve at the Catholic Mission at Lubaga and the Protestant mission at Natete. Further that: "the most trusted and closest servants of Mwanga were now acting as stool pigeons for the missionaries including his own chief of intelligence, Joseph Mukasa Balikudembe. State secrets immediately passed over to missionaries. This became very clear when the fate of Bishop Hannington was being discussed. Mackay and Lourdel would immediately get the information and foolishly run to the Kabaka to remonstrate, thus betraying the source of their information … [T]herefore at some point Mwanga had to throw down the gauntlet, those for him and their country on one side and those for the Europeans on the other side.[73]

It is interesting that once the gauntlet was thrown down, the European missionaries, including Lourdel and Mackay, encouraged the Africans to become fearless martyrs, telling them not to deny the Lord Jesus and not to fear men who, as they said, were "only able to kill the body." But despite this advice, none of the missionaries followed the pages to the pyres at Namugongo where they were burnt alive. Lunyiigo poses relevant questions: "Why did these zealous missionaries not offer themselves for martyrdom along with the "readers" whom they urged to be steadfast?

Why did they just look on and not make the ultimate sacrifice in solidarity with their new converts?"[74] These questions beg for answers.

The pacification of Buganda from religious wars only came with the intervention of Lugard and the IBEAC who, in the famous Battle of Mengo, took sides with the Protestant faction (led by Apolo Kagwa) and, with the firepower of the Maxim gun and garrisons of Sudanese soldiers, succeeded in deposing Mwanga; subduing the traditionalist, Islamic and Catholic camps in Buganda; and establishing a Protestant hegemony in Buganda and later in the whole of Uganda.

However, so as not to completely alienate the Catholics, and perhaps in atonement for his atrocious deeds against them in the Battle of Mengo, Lugard offered them land and the control of Buddu County. Sir Gerald Portal, Britain's Special Commissioner to East Africa, formalised the new order once he entered an agreement with Mwanga in 1893 and hoisted the Union Jack at Mengo. But before the chiefs signed the agreement, Bishop Tucker asked the gathering to kneel and he asked God's blessing for the events which had unfolded.[75] To celebrate the formal establishment of British colonial rule, Bishop Tucker recorded that once the Union Jack was raised over Uganda, all the missionaries met for a time of "special praise and prayer" for what was considered divine providence.[76]

Portal, like Lugard before him, in consultation with Protestant Bishop Tucker and Catholic Bishop Hirth, attempted to redefine the political and religious landscape in Buganda firstly by dividing the kingdom along religious lines and allocating its counties and corresponding chieftaincies along a religious baseline. When the 1900 Agreement was concluded, the allocations of the counties along religious lines was as follows: the Catholics took Bugangazzi, Buyaga, Busujju, Buvuma, Buddu, Mawogola, Buwekula, and Mawokota; Kyagwe, Bugerere, Bulemezi, Buruli, Singo, Gomba, Kyadondo, Busiro, Sese, Kooki, and Kabula went to the Protestants; while Butambala was given to the Moslems.[77] Secondly, Portal restructured the Katikkiroship and introduced a religious split whereby the office had a Protestant (Apolo Kagwa) and a Catholic (Mugwanya).[78] The balkanisation of the politics and territory of the kingdom of Buganda along religious lines had two major effects. First, it helped in weaken the kingdom's leadership through a policy of "divide and rule," and secondly, it aided the entrenchment of religious factors in the formulation and articulation of its politics. Because of the covert and overt patronage and support rendered by British officials, the Protestant camp was the dominant player and major beneficiary.

The Catholic camp followed, leaving the Muslims and the traditionalists at the extreme margins of the new religio-political structure in Buganda. According to Griffiths, with the support of Bishop Tucker, by 1890, the "African Protestant leaders had resolved among themselves that their best option for securing the future of the church and their own position would be through seeking and retaining political power in the country."[79]

Without a doubt, the changes left the traditional power structures in disarray, more so because the kingdom had an infant as its king at this time. The major casualty of the Christian assault in Buganda was the traditional religions and their believers, who were by far the weakest and least organised contenders in the race for new converts. These became criminalised under legislation such as the Witchcraft Ordinance,[80] as a result of which many were forced underground or died.

From that point on, a triple alliance was established between the new Baganda chiefly oligarchy (mostly of the Protestant variety), the British colonial administrators and the Protestant Missionaries, all of whom joined hands to entrench a British and protestant hegemony in its bid to patronise and control politics in Buganda and the rest of the Protectorate. The convergence of interests of the alliance was crystallised in the 1900 Agreement.

When Johnston arrived in Buganda and started negotiations for the 1900 Agreement, Tucker found himself, as in 1893, with Gerald Portal, "involved in the discussion of political questions of the most far reaching character."[81] And once, when he was approached by the Baganda with concerns that Johnston's proposals were aimed at taking their land, Tucker, the politician in a cassock, according to his own account exclaimed, "Nonsense, I am quite sure the Government have no intention of doing you any injustice."[82] Once the negotiations were concluded, Tucker formed the opinion that the 1900 Agreement "from the point of view of the Baganda, was a wise one. It did much and secured much for them. It gave them fixity of tenure of their lands and secured them a large measure of self-government."[83] Clearly, on the (in)justice and effects of the 1900 Agreement, Tucker could only have been presumptuous in articulating the point of view of the Baganda and, even then, he certainly could not have been more off the mark, because as we show below, the 1900 Agreement turned out to be an unenforceable legal instrument primarily designed to foster British interests and those of the chiefly oligarchy at the expense of the majority of the African people. And, far from his assertions about stability of the regime, it did not fix the tenure of either the peasantry occupants or clan lands and it did little to secure Buganda's self-government. Instead, it undermined and eroded its sovereignty. Additionally, contrary to Tucker's claims, rather than secure

Buganda's rights over forests, minerals and land, the Agreement took away Buganda's rights over these matters and vested them in Her Majesty's Government without any consideration. On top of that, it imposed a range of taxes over the population that were used to sustain British imperial rule. This analysis shows that in the early years of colonial rule, Bishop Tucker, like other missionaries, one way or the other and under the cloak of religion, facilitated the conquest of African peoples, the imposition of colonial rule and, ultimately, the exploitation of the continent.

The Legal Framework for Colonial Rule in Uganda

The 1900 Uganda Agreement

As was feared by the Regents and the missionaries, the 1900 Uganda Agreement transformed the political and social structures of Buganda and brought about radical changes in the kingdom. Central to the revolution was, first of all, the diminution of the power and role of the Kabaka in Buganda. Under the new indirect rule scheme, the Kabaka was a ceremonial figurehead, with the real power vested in the British Commissioner and the Protectorate Government. The saying that indirect rule is direct rule by indirect means was realised in the case of Buganda. Secondly, and equally fundamental, was the great change in the control and ownership of land in Buganda. With the signing of the Agreement, Johnston had achieved his mission of establishing a colonial administration, taking control of land, and levying taxes as quickly as possible. A triumphal confidential memorandum to the Lord Salisbury, dated 12 March 1900, shows how pleased he was with himself. He wrote:

> My Lord, I have the honour to enclose for your Lordship's consideration and approval an Agreement into which I have entered on behalf of Her Majesty the Queen, with the Kabaka, Chiefs, and people of Uganda.... I believe, I do not over estimate in saying that it solves the questions of the taxation of the natives and the control of the land in the Uganda Protectorate, and, as regards the Kingdom of Uganda proper, determines once and for all its exact boundaries, rights, privileges, and obligations.... Negotiations were begun on 23 December last; but although the chiefs accepted the principle of taxation, they were averse to any control over land being ceded to the Imperial Government; and their ideas as to the amount of subsidies which should be paid to the Kabaka (King) and Chiefs in lieu of their participation in the taxation of the country were more than I could agree to.[84]

We examine some specific aspects of the major changes brought about by the Agreement in the new colonial regime, juxtaposed with Johnston's own views, below.

(i) Territorial and administrative boundaries of the kingdom—Clauses 1, 2 and 9

The Agreement defined the geographical and administrative boundaries of the kingdom, comprising twenty counties (*amasaza*) of Buganda. The Agreement controversially incorporated some areas claimed by the kingdom of Bunyoro such as Bugerere, Buruli, Bugangazzi, Buyaga and Buwekula. This was to give rise to a convoluted boundary dispute between Buganda and Bunyoro over the "lost counties" which was still ongoing when Britain granted independence to Uganda, and lasted until a problematic referendum was held on the matter in 1964. Buganda also agreed to give up its claims over adjoining provinces, particularly that of Busoga.

Under Clause 9, the appointment and dismissal of county chiefs was to be done by the Kabaka but with the prior approval of Her Majesty's Government (HMG). The chiefs would be responsible for administering justice for natives, for assessment and collection of taxes, and for the maintenance of law and order in their respective counties. In explaining to his superiors and justifying his decision on the boundaries of Buganda, Johnston commented as follows:

> The boundaries of the Kingdom of Uganda are practically those agreed after the close of the Unyoro wars ... small additions have been made by me to its area in the direction of Ankole, and as regards the large island of Buvuma and its adjacent islets. In making the addition of the districts of Kabula from out of the territories of Ankole, I but little more than recognized existing facts, because in order to suppress brigandage this Kabula district has been for some time past in the possession of Uganda soldiers under a Uganda chief. As regards the Island of Buvuma, I think for various administrative reasons it should preferably be attached to Uganda rather than to the adjoining province of Busoga. But in making these additions I have secured in return the transference from the Kingdom of Uganda to Her Majesty the Queen of all rights of suzerainty, taxation over the adjoining districts of Toru, Ankole, Busoga, or Unyoro. I shall take advantage of this transference of claims to impose on the aforesaid adjoining provinces the taxation of natives.[85]

Needless to say, in making the territorial settlement above, Johnston neither consulted with nor took into serious consideration the interests of the people whose land he was annexing to Buganda. The most important consideration for him and Britain was administrative expedience and the maximisation of tax revenues for the benefit and maintenance of the colonial government.

(ii) Incorporation of Buganda into Uganda and merging of revenues—Clauses 3, 4 and 12

Under these clauses, Buganda agreed to be administered as one of the provinces in the Uganda Protectorate and to be ranked on par with the rest. The revenues collected by the colonial government from Buganda would be merged with the general revenue of the entire Protectorate. Most notably, the agreement was silent on expenditures and accountability of these revenues. Needless to mention, although the agreement touched and bound other provinces of Uganda, the people in those parts, who in any case were not parties to the agreement, were neither consulted nor was their consent obtained.

Financial provisions: Under the agreement, the costs for the maintenance of the Protectorate were to be derived from the proceeds of the collection of taxes comprising a hut tax of three rupees, or four shillings per annum, on any house, hut or habitation used as a dwelling place; and a gun tax of three rupees, or four shillings per annum, payable by any person who possessed or used a gun, rifle or pistol. All taxes collected by the chiefs were to be handed over intact to Her Majesty's representative in Uganda as the contribution of the Ugandan province towards the general revenue of the Protectorate.

It was stipulated that in the case of i) a failure by the kingdom to pay to the Protectorate during the first two years of the Agreement an amount of native taxation equal to half that which was due in proportion to the number of inhabitants; ii) a failure at any time to pay without just cause or excuse the minimum of taxation due in proportion to the population; or iii) the pursuit by the Kabaka, his chiefs or the people of Uganda of a policy distinctly disloyal to the British Protectorate, then HMG would not consider itself bound by the terms of the Agreement and would thus withdraw its protection.

(iii) Laws applicable in Buganda and Uganda—Clause 5

The laws made by the colonial government for the general governance of Uganda, save for a few exceptions applicable to Buganda, were to be equally applicable to Buganda. The Agreement was silent on how and by whom legislative power was used. The question of democratic representation and participation by the colonised people in the making of fair and just laws did not arise.

(iv) Recognition of the Kabaka and the duty to obey and to protect—Clause 6

The Agreement was categorical and subordinated the Kabaka of Buganda to the will of, and subjected him to the laws set by, HMG. It provided that so long as the Kabaka, chiefs, and people of Uganda should conform to the laws and regulations instituted for their governance by HMG, and should cooperate loyally with HMG in the organization and administration of the kingdom, then HMG would recognize him as the Kabaka of Uganda (read Buganda) and as the native ruler of the province of Uganda under HMG's protection and overrule. The Agreement made it clear that no person would be recognized as Kabaka of Uganda without the approval of HMG.

The Kabaka was bestowed with a new English title of "His Highness," which excited the Regents despite the actual diminution of his authority in the new colonial order. Under the agreement HMG's chief representative in Uganda was at any time to have direct access to the Kabaka, and had the power of discussing matters affecting Uganda with the Kabaka alone or with others. The application and interpretation of this clause was controversial when it came to the deportation of Kabaka Mutesa in 1953 when he refused to acquiesce to Governor Andrew Cohen on the issue of the East African Federation and Buganda's participation in the Protectorate's Legislative Council (LEGCO).

Clause 6 was the cornerstone of the 1900 agreement, as it provided for the terms and conditions for British imperial rule over the Kabaka and the people of Buganda. Johnston's comments are revealing of his views on what he called "native vanity":

> As regards Clause 6, perhaps the only point to which your Lordship may feel somewhat inclined to take exception is to the application of the title and dignity of "Highness" to the native ruler of the Kingdom of Uganda. I propose, to begin with, that this ruler shall henceforth be styled "Kabaka," which is his designation in the native language. This term will sound less imposing than "King." I plead strongly, however, on behalf of the accordance of the title of "Highness," which after all, makes the native ruler of this large and populous African Kingdom no more honoured than the Sultan of Zanzibar (who rules over a territory less in area and population) or any prominent Indian prince. It is impossible in any scheme of organization which may be adopted for the administration of these East African territories to ignore the importance which is still attached by a million of black people to the native ruler of Uganda, who is represented at the present date by a little child, and I think the concession on part of the British Government of this honorific title will be amply repaid by the loyalty of the Baganda people and the support which they will give,

> financially and otherwise, to the maintenance of the British Protectorate.
>
> In considering this matter, which is after all, the hardest point of the Agreement from the Foreign Office aspect, I sincerely trust your Lordship will take into consideration the importance of an appeal to native vanity. The idea of their ruler—the Grandson of Mutesa, the descendant of a line of African Kings exceptional for its continuity, its apparent historic actuality, and the area of country subjected to its rule—being placed on the same level of importance as the Sultan of Zanzibar has done more than anything else to reconcile the Regents and chiefs of this country to surrender into the hands of the British Government the right of taxation, the control over land, and the power of life and death over the people.[86]

(v) Allowances payable to the Kabaka and the Kabaka's mother (the *Namasole)—Clauses 6 and 7*

In addition to the promise of British protection, the young Kabaka was guaranteed a yearly allowance of £500 out of the local revenue of the Uganda Protectorate. His mother was also to receive an annual allowance at the rate of £50 during her lifetime from the same source. This was not necessarily to be available to the mothers of future Kabakas.

(vi) The administration of justice—Clause 8

The Agreement introduced radical changes and segregation in the kingdom's judicial system. The jurisdiction of the native court of the Kabaka was seriously curtailed, limiting it to trying only natives, i.e. no person not a native of Uganda Province. All cases, civil or criminal, involving a mix of natives and non-natives of Uganda Province were subject to British Courts of Justice only. Although the Kabaka's courts were entitled to try natives for capital crimes, no death sentence could be carried out by the Kabaka, or his courts, without the sanction of Her Majesty's representative in Uganda.

There was a right of appeal from the native courts to the principal Court of Justice established by Her Majesty in the Kingdom of Uganda for all sentences that inflicted a term exceeding five years' imprisonment or a fine of over £100. In the case of any other sentences imposed by the Kabaka's courts which seemed to Her Majesty's Government disproportionate or inconsistent with humane principles, Her Majesty's representatives in Uganda had the right of remonstrance with the Kabaka, who was obliged, at the request of the said representative, to subject such sentence to reconsideration. It is also worth making the point that a system of prisons was introduced into the administration of justice within the Kingdom for the first time.

(vii) The Kabaka's Government and the Lukiiko—Clauses 10 and 11

While the Agreement maintained the Kabaka as the head of the kingdom, it effectively undermined his power and authority, requiring him to seek approval from Her Majesty's representative, including on the appointment of chiefs such as the Katikkiro (Prime Minister), *Omulamuzi* (Chief Justice) and *Omuwanika* (Treasurer). Similarly, although Buganda's Lukiiko (Native Council or Royal Assembly) was maintained, its power and composition were diminished and always subject to the overall authority of Her Majesty's representative. For this reason, its resolutions, which were restricted to matters of native administration, did not take effect until the Kabaka sought and obtained the approval of Her Majesty's representative.

The Lukiiko, which acted as an appellate court for decisions made by courts at the county level, had limited jurisdiction which, in any case, did not extend to claims exceeding £100, sentences of imprisonment exceeding five years, sentences of death, or matters affecting persons or property of Europeans or other non-natives. On the power, composition and role of the native council, Johnston commented that this was a subject which gave him a good deal of trouble, pointing out that "It was necessary that the powers of this body should be, to some extent, curtailed, should be accurately defined and limited, and that a reduction should be made in the number of individuals qualified to sit in this native Parliament."[87]

These clauses, as well as Johnston's comments on them, capture the real operation and effect of indirect rule. By retaining native structures in place, the impression was created that native leaders and institutions were intact and in control, whereas this was not actually the case. In reality, the policy of indirect rule disguised the extent to which native authority was eroded and how power had shifted to the colonial power to validate the view that indirect rule meant direct rule but using indirect means.

(viii) Defence and the army—Clause 13

Under Clause 13, the Kabaka was prohibited from conscripting people for military service in defence of the country without the advice of HMG's principal representative in the Protectorate. It was also considered that in times of peace, the armed forces organized by the Ugandan administration would probably be sufficient for all purposes of defence, but if Her Majesty's representative was of the opinion that the force of Uganda should be strengthened at any time, he might call upon the Kabaka to exercise, to a full or a modified degree, his claim on the Baganda people for military service. In such an event, the arming and equipping of such a force would be undertaken by the administration of the Uganda

Protectorate.

Johnston's Comments on Clause 13 show that under this clause Buganda was virtually disarmed and rendered defenceless in the face of colonial aggression. Johnston wrote that the clause "practically places in the hands of Her Majesty's principal representative in the Uganda Protectorate the power to raise an army from out of the able bodied males of the Kingdom of Uganda, and to bring this army entirely under British control."[88]

(ix) Allocation of land and payments to the Kabaka and the chiefs on the surrender of land—Clauses 15 and 18

Buganda's estimated 19,600 square miles of land was allocated under Clause 15. Under the Agreement some 10,550 square miles, including all the mineral rights and forests therein (over 54% of Buganda's land mass) went to HMG; 8,000 square miles were allocated to 1,000 chiefs and private landowners, with each getting an acreage of 8 square miles; while 350 square miles was to be the private property of His Highness the Kabaka of Uganda. The residue went to the Namasole notable princes and princesses, official estates for ministers and county chiefs, the three Regents (each getting 16 square miles), missionary societies, and government stations. As Mutesa pointed out, the *Bataka* (clan heads) were one of the biggest losers under this scheme and their "position was totally ignored by Johnston and to a great extent destroyed … [T]heir genuine grievances were to cause sporadic outbreaks of discontent for many years."[89]

Clause 18 stipulated that in return for the cession to HMG of the right of control over 10,550 square miles of what was described as waste, cultivated, uncultivated, or forest lands, HMG agreed to pay the Kabaka (upon his attaining his majority) a sum of £500, and to the three Regents collectively, £600 (i.e., to the Katikkiro £300 and the other two Regents £150 each). This, in addition to the land allocations, was a monetary payment to the Kabaka and the chiefs to entice them to sign-off on the agreement.

Johnston's comments on Clause 15 underline the coup Britain had made over the control of Buganda's land:

> It will be seen by Clause 15 that if the actual area of the Kingdom of Uganda ... be accurately estimated at 19,600 square miles, Her Majesty's Government will have acquired the exclusive control over more than half of that area, viz., of 10,550 square miles ... [T]his alone will place at the disposal of the Ugandan administration a very important source of future revenue as the country becomes developed by means of the Uganda

railway and the steamers which are to be placed on the lake. A good deal of this land handed over to Her Majesty's Government is under cultivation, but it is settled by "*abakopi*," or peasants, who up to the present have been practically serfs. These people will become, therefore, the tenants of the British Government."[90]

(x) Mineral rights and forests—Clause 17

The rights to all minerals found on private estates were granted to the owners of these estates, subject to a 10 percent *ad valorem* duty. However, for minerals on the land outside private estates, the mineral rights were to belong to the Protectorate and thus subject to control by HMG. On these waste and uncultivated lands of the Protectorate, the mineral rights were vested in HMG. In like manner, ownership of the forests which were not included within the limits of private properties, was vested in HMG. This clause underlines the reality of plunder under the guise of consent. In effect, vast mineral and forest resources were expropriated with no consideration for the native owners.

(xi) Britain not to be bound if natives fail to pay taxes or to be loyal after two years—Clause 20:

The Agreement provided that if the kingdom of Buganda should fail to pay the costs of colonial administration during the first two years of the Agreement, or if the Kabaka, chiefs or people of Uganda became distinctly disloyal to the British Protectorate, then HMG would no longer be bound by the Agreement. This clause would seem to have aimed at easing the termination and exit of colonial rule if it was apparent that the Protectorate was not economically viable or its people proved difficult to manage. However, because the Protectorate became financially viable, the clause was not invoked even though the people of Buganda showed disloyalty to HMG on several occasions, including during the 1945 and 1949 demonstrations, Mutesa's refusal to acquiesce to Governor Cohen's demands in 1953, and Buganda's unilateral declaration of independence in 1960.

In view of the blatantly unfair terms of the 1900 Agreement, a number of questions arise: Did the Baganda chiefs who signed it fully understand its terms? Did they, as Johnston suggests, sign out of vanity for titles and/or promises of rewards such as money, land and/or positions? Were they coerced into signing, given the power, arsenal and zeal of HMG's representative? Did the Lukiiko play any role and was the wider body of the Baganda constituents consulted? In *The Desecration of My Kingdom*, Edward Mutesa, Mwanga's grandson and the Kabaka of Buganda between

1942 and 1969,[91] offers a persuasive explanation:

> He [Johnston] immediately filled the chiefs with apprehension and alarm. The Kabakaship had been weakened by years of civil war and pretenders, and in particular by the failure of Mwanga's escapade in 1897. In any case, my father was still a child. The clan chiefs, the Bataka, had long been a waning influence, though one of amazing tenacity. So the men who made the treaty were the Bakungu, non-hereditary chiefs appointed by the Kabaka. These chiefs were eager to have their comparatively new ascendancy confirmed and, if possible, buttressed. Yet their bargaining position was not strong. For the first time, the British were demonstrably in control of the situation and seemed likely to remain so. They had conquered all opposition ... though not, of course, the Baganda, who had invited them into the country and shared their victories and reverses.[92]
>
> It [the Agreement] gave the most powerful group in the country a vested interest in retaining the status quo. Internationally, the Baganda felt they had won the special relationship with Britain they deserved ... internally it was a triumph for the new men, the Bakungu. Johnston was at a loss to understand the genuine pleasure he caused when he agreed that the Kabaka should be termed "His Highness"—a title taken by the Baganda as recognition of their institutions, which they had thought threatened, and their superior status in East Africa, where the only other Highness is the Sultan of Zanzibar.[93]

On 29 June 1900, three months after signing the Agreement with the kingdom of Buganda, Johnston concluded a similar one with King Kasagama, the Omukama (king) of Toro.[94] Under the terms of the Toro Agreement, the king was reduced to a "supreme ruler," but one who ironically could be deposed by HMG's principal representative in Uganda if he failed at any time to abide by any portion of the Agreement. In such event, his title and privileges would pass to any other chief that HMG's representative in Uganda may select in his place. Similarly, if the Toro king, or his chiefs, were responsible for the infringement of any part of the Agreement, it was open to HMG's principal representative in Uganda to annul the Agreement, and to substitute for it "any other methods of administering the Toro district which may seem suitable."[95] Similar agreements were to be concluded later with the kingdom of Ankole on 25 October 1901 and the kingdom of Bunyoro on 23 October 1933. The treaty with Bunyoro came much later because its people resisted colonialism and had to be beaten into submission. On the whole, this period marked a tremendous change in the power structures and relations between Britain and the colonised peoples.

For his work in further integrating Uganda into the British Empire,

Johnston received the Knight Grand Cross of the Order of St Michael and St George (GCMG) in the King's Birthday Honours list in November 1901.[96] However, in spite of Johnston's coup, the prospects of adding Uganda to the membership of the British Empire were not well received at home; in the opinion of Sir William Harcourt, who presented the policy to the House of Commons, Uganda would become a squalid, derelict place.[97]

In fact when a decision to accept it was made, *Punch Magazine* published a cartoon depicting John Bull contemplating a black foundling on his door step in Downing Street, saying "What, another? Well, I suppose I must take it in."[98] Clearly the British public was reluctant to take responsibility for what was considered to be yet another "black baby."[99] But, as we show below, in spite of the initial scepticism with which the Uganda Protectorate was received by Britain, it turned out to be the gem of the Empire. Its revenues grew and its contributions to the Protectorate's expenditure increased. Uganda also contributed to the defence and financing of the British Empire during the two world wars.

The 1902 Order-in-Council and Establishment of the Uganda Protectorate

The 1902 Order-in-Council, passed by HMG pursuant to "treaties and other lawful means," was the legal instrument that brought the entire Protectorate of Uganda under British command and control. It defined the territorial jurisdiction of the Protectorate and placed the administration of Uganda under a Commissioner appointed by HMG. The Commissioner was vested with the full—if not autocratic—powers of the Government of Uganda. He was also vested with full power over all the unclaimed land, mines and minerals across the entire country. Furthermore, he was vested with wide powers over the executive, judicial and legislative functions of the Protectorate.

In the performance of legislative duties, the Commissioner was answerable only to the Secretary of State for the Colonies in London. Under Article 12 of this law, the Commissioner had the power to make laws on the administration of justice, the raising of revenue and for the peace, order and good governance of all persons in Uganda. He was required to respect existing native laws and customs only insofar as they were not repugnant to justice or morality as understood by the British. The same standards were to be used by courts in determining all cases, civil or criminal, involving natives. The Commissioner also had the power to remove and deport from Uganda persons he considered undesirable or dangerous to the peace and order in the country. To protect him from liability, the law accorded the Commissioner personal and proprietary immunity from legal process.

The 1900 Agreement and other Agreements signed between the British and African leaders in various kingdoms in Uganda, along with the 1902 Order-in-Council, formed the legal foundation on which British colonialism was erected and thrived in Uganda for over 68 years. However, besides these instruments, there were a number of Ordinances, Rules and Regulations, Orders and Notices, as well as Emergency and Defence Regulations, that enabled the colonial regime to effectively keep the Protectorate under its grip. Specific enactments included the Deportation Ordinance, the King's African Rifles Ordinance, the Police Statute, the British Protected Persons Order, the Emergency Powers Statute, the Mining Ordinance and several Ordinances on the ownership and control of Land.

Legal Force without the Force of Law? The Legality of Treaties between Buganda and Britain

Between 1884 and 1900, the kingdom of Buganda had entered five treaties of "friendship" and "protection" with the Germans (in 1890) and the British (in 1890, 1892, 1894 and 1900). The number and sequence of the treaties is significant in illustrating the stakes involved in the transition of power from traditional to colonial rule. It also shows that treaty-making was an important tool in the entrenchment and expansion of British colonial rule. Thus, in the cases of Buganda, Toro and Ankole kingdoms, the British used treaties rather than outright conquest to entrench their rule. In the case of the resistant kingdom of Bunyoro, on the other hand, the treaty came much later than in the other kingdoms, and after violent conquest.

Two reasons explain Britain's preference for treaties over conquest in establishing colonial rule in Buganda. First of all, because Buganda was relatively organised and cooperative, it provided a strategic foothold for the colonisation of the rest of Uganda for the British.[100] Secondly, because the British administrators were few and under-resourced, treaty-making was preferred to outright military conquest. But more fundamentally, the colonial powers understood the treaties to be legally ineffective, but the natives believed in their sanctity and never questioned their legality. Colonial rule thus relied on questionable treaties to govern vast territories with only a handful of exuberant but inexperienced[101] young men[102] through the policy of indirect rule.[103]

Pakenham points out that because "the first European expeditions were too weak to challenge African rulers, it was safer to use blank treaty forms."[104] Companies like the IBEAC "equipped its agents with parcels of blank *pro formas*, which only required the inscription of the name of the relevant chief, the place, the date, the chief's mark, and—a point on which the British Foreign Office insisted—the signatures of two witnesses."[105] Lugard, the vanguard of British colonialism and "indirect rule" in Africa, describes treaty-making with African rulers as a "farce" because the treaties were "either not understood, or [referred to decisions] which the ruler had no power to make, and … rarely provided an adequate legal sanction for the powers assumed."[106]

The experiences of the Congo provide yet another insight into how colonial powers abused treaties with Africans. In expanding his empire, for example, King Léopold instructed his agent, Henry M. Stanley, to ensure that while the treaties must be as brief as possible, "they must grant us everything."[107] This wilful abuse of treaties to trick the Congolese chiefs and grab and control their resources is succinctly recounted by Adam Hochschild, who writes of how the

> chiefs signed over their land to Leopold, and they did so for almost nothing. At Isangila, near the big rapids, Stanley … was able to buy land for a station by paying some chiefs with "an ample supply of fine clothes, flunkey coats, and tinsel-braided uniforms, with a rich assortment of diverse marketable wares…. The very word *treaty* is a euphemism, for many chiefs had no idea what they were signing. Few had seen the written word before, and they were being asked to mark their X's to documents in a foreign language and in legalese. The idea of a treaty of friendship between two clans or villages was familiar; the idea of signing over one's land to someone on the other side of the ocean was inconceivable. Did the chiefs of Ngombi and Mafela, for example, have any idea of what they agreed to on April 1, 1884? In return for "one piece of cloth per month to each of the under-signed chiefs, besides a present of cloth in hand," they promised to "freely of their own accord, for themselves and their heirs and successors forever … give up to the said Association the sovereignty and all sovereign and governing rights to all their territories … and to assist by labour or otherwise, any works, improvements or expeditions which the said Association shall cause at any time to be carried out in any part of these territories…. All roads and waterways running through this country, the right of collecting tolls on the same, and all game, fishing, mining and forest rights, are to be the absolute property of the said Association.[108]

Hochschild's account represents the general dilemma of the colonised peoples of Africa, who lacked knowledge of alien western legal concepts and treaties and who confused them with traditional methods of tribal or brotherhood bonding. To them, treaties were perceived as sacrosanct and inviolable. Governor P. E. Mitchell was indeed of the same conviction. Commenting on the 1900 Uganda Agreement, for example, he observed:

> [The Agreement] is regarded by the Kabaka, the Ministers and Chiefs, and [the] Baganda generally, as having an almost spiritual authority and inviolability. In their eyes it is a document covering the relations of the parties to it, and like a Statute subject to strict verbal interpretation. The Agreement, however, considered textually, is not a satisfactory document by which to regulate the relations of the parties to it; nor could a complex and constantly changing political and administrative situation, such as exists in Buganda, be exactly regulated in every respect by the terms of such a treaty.[109]

The legality of treaties concluded between African rulers and colonial powers has historically been a subject of judicial and academic debate and consideration. In 1926, the Privy Council, in the case of *Sobhuza II v. Miller and Others*,[110] held that such agreements can never bind the British Crown even if it had, by virtue of such agreements, acquired jurisdiction in the territory from which its right to govern is challenged. In *Nyali Ltd. v. the Attorney General of Kenya*, Lord Justice Denning reaffirmed the legality and scope of the colonial power thus:

> Although the jurisdiction of the Crown in the Protectorate is in law a limited jurisdiction, nevertheless the limits may in fact be extended indefinitely so as to embrace almost the whole field of government. They may be extended so far that the Crown has jurisdiction in everything connected with the peace, order and good government of the area, leaving only the title and ceremonies of sovereignty remaining in the Sultan. The Courts themselves will not mark out the limits. They will not examine the treaty or grant under which the Crown may have extended its jurisdiction.... Once jurisdiction is exercised by the Crown the Courts will not permit it to be challenged.[111]

In Uganda, the legality of colonial treaties was tested in a case challenging the deposition and deportation of the Kabaka of Buganda by the Governor in 1953, contrary to the 1900 Agreement. The colonial government argued that "whether just or unjust, politic or impolitic, beneficial or injurious," the deportation and withdrawal of recognition "was no matter on which a court of law could give an opinion."[112] Sir John Griffin, the Chief Justice, accepted this argument on the basis of the deportation being an Act of State. In his holding, the question of deportation was not a justiciable issue, for the Crown was, by law, the judge of its own cause in such a matter.

Grace Ibingira, a leading lawyer and politician at the time of Uganda's independence, correctly observed that within Uganda and in British municipal law, colonial agreements lacked the force of law and bound the British Crown only at its pleasure.[113] He wondered how "so many treaties were concluded with literally hundreds of rulers from dependencies when there was no intention of giving them the legal force of other treaties?"[114] He also asked whether native states were competent to make treaties in international law, and if so, whether these treaties were valid. If they were not valid, or if the states were not competent, what was the purpose of making them? He concluded: "although the British were never legally bound by the agreements with African rulers, for political reasons they adhered strictly to them and departed from them only in rare cases when it seemed in the best interests of peace, good government, or imperial authority to do so."[115]

In other words, although Britain touted treaties with African rulers as serious and binding contracts, they were mostly empty ploys under which Africans not only lost their sovereignty, control and ownership of land and other natural resources, but were also deprived of their fundamental rights and freedoms. This may explain why, in signing off his secret Memorandum to senior colonial administrators in Uganda on the Relations of the Protectorate Government in Uganda with the Native Government of Uganda, Governor P. E. Mitchell warned that "it [was] important that the existence of the document itself should not become known to any except those to whom it is addressed."[116] It is interesting to note that while the British knew that treaties signed with "native" rulers had no legal basis, they tenaciously invoked them whenever it suited them in dealing with "difficult" African rulers—as was the case in the deposition of Mwanga in 1897 and later in the deportation of Mutesa in 1953.

Also, despite the fact that these treaties were hollow, the British relied on them to deny Buganda's declaration of independence in 1960. Nevertheless, as already pointed out, British colonialism did not always rely on treaties to acquire or take control of territory. In cases where it met with resistance, it resorted to forceful conflict and conquest, armed with Maxim guns. This was the case in the kingdom of Bunyoro, where Omukama Kabalega fought to defend his kingdom from colonialism.

The British were incensed by Bunyoro's resistance and particularly by Kabalega's defeat of Sir Samuel Baker's forces in the war of 1872. For that reason, they were merciless in beating Bunyoro into submission. Beyond the deaths and destitution that followed the Anglo-Bunyoro wars, Kabalega was forced to flee his throne and Bunyoro was dismembered.[117]

Much of its territory was gifted to Buganda under the 1900 Agreement, although in reality it mostly remained under British control. Kabalega—together with Mwanga, who had rebelled after signing the 1894 treaty—was arrested, one of his arms was amputated, and he was exiled to the Seychelles. Bunyoro finally entered into an agreement with the British in 1933, some thirty-three years after Buganda had signed the 1900 Agreement.

Bunyoro's history clearly demonstrates the dilemma faced by African rulers in the face of colonialism. The question was always either to resist or to cooperate. Either way, they were damned if they did and damned if they did not because the tide of colonialism was so powerful it was irreversible. It may be said, however, that for those who cooperated and submitted without resistance, the stance they took saved their populations the full wrath and devastation that was visited upon those that resisted.

(d) The Meaning of "Protection" Under the Treaties

The treaties between African rulers and European colonizers were often dubbed "treaties of protection" or "treaties of friendship." But, what did this mean in effect? Who was being protected or what were they being protected from? What was the nature of this protection? What recourse did the protected party have in the event that the protector refused, neglected or failed to protect? As we have seen above, the treaties were essentially promises without the force of law.

Accordingly, the promise to protect was largely empty. The declaration that a territory was a "Protectorate," as opposed to "a colony" or a "possession," was equally anomalous given that, in the case of the Uganda Protectorate, while Britain had treaties with the areas covered by the kingdoms of Buganda, Ankole, Toro and Bunyoro, it had none with the rest of the Protectorate's regions such as Acholi or Karamoja. These non-treaty areas were simply annexed and brought under the Protectorate. As such, they should have been colonies.

Lugard offers some guidance regarding the meaning of the terms "protectorate" and "colony." He defines a colony to be "annexed territory, and an integral part of the king's dominions, acquired either by conquest, settlement, or cession and all persons born in it have the status of British subjects."[118] He explains that the term "protectorate" gradually changed its meaning from that of "a pact with the ruler of a state, which maintained its internal but not external sovereignty, to a declaration of the territorial status of a region included in the Empire, in which not only the external, but in varying degrees the internal sovereignty also, had passed to the controlling power, in many cases … without even the 'treaty' consent of the people."[119] He states that inhabitants of a British Protectorate were styled "British protected persons and these did not enjoy the status of British subjects. While colonies were headed by a 'High Commissioner,' Protectorates were headed by a 'Governor'." Beyond these differences, Lugard argues that the distinction between the two was without practical difference. He pointed out that:

> The moment at which the civilised Powers of the world have asserted the unequivocal right and obligation of the more advanced races to assume responsibility for the backward races seems an appropriate one to brush aside these archaic and anomalous distinctions, and to abandon the farce of "acquiring" jurisdictions by treaties not understood by their signatories, and foreign to their modes of thought.[120]

Based on Lugard's explanation, the term protectorate did not in fact connote a real duty on part of the "protector" to protect the inhabitants of a protectorate. As we show below, protection under these treaties meant the protection of colonial interests, as opposed to those of the "colonised" or "protected" people. In answering the question "Who was being protected?" Professor Mahmood Mamdani correctly asserts that it was "certainly not the people of Uganda; surely not from British imperialism."[121] He elaborates:

> But the term was not quite meaningless. It meant that henceforth British interests in Uganda would be protected from the interests of rival imperialist powers. But real protection for the interests of imperialism in Uganda could not come from a paper agreement, nor from the physical presence of the British in the colony. The long term interests of imperialism in Uganda could only be protected by a socio-economic and political system that would tie Uganda up in the web of imperial interests.[122]

In view of the above analysis, it is clear that colonial treaties entered into between unequal powers—and barely understood by the native authorities—principally served the interests of the British Crown and not those of the Africans. British interests were served not only through the expropriation and control of vast native resources, including land and minerals, but also through taxation without representation by, or accountability to, the colonised peoples.

(e)The Question of Plunder

The work of the IBEAC, led by Captain Lugard—who believed in Britain's right to own and rule Africa—together with the 1900 Agreement and the 1902 Order in Council underpinned Britain's 68 years of colonial plunder, which largely consisted in the expropriation of native lands, extraction of mineral resources and forestry resources, exploitation of labour and the imposition a myriad of taxes under the guise of dodgy "protection" treaties. Under Article 15 of the 1900 Agreement, for example, over half of Buganda's land became "crown land" which, together with all the mineral rights and forests therein, was placed under the exclusive control of HM's Government. Furthermore, Britain's control of land and minerals extended beyond the kingdom of Buganda. In the 1902 Order in Council, HM's representative in Uganda was vested with full powers over all the unclaimed land, mines and minerals across the entire country.

Beyond the largely empty promise of colonial protection, there was no other justification given for Britain's taking over vast native lands, forests and minerals. Equally, there was no basis for the imposition of harsh taxes, except for the maintenance of an unrepresentative and an unaccountable colonial government. However, the legacy of colonial plunder in Uganda, and in Africa in general, is often masked by arguments about how Britain in fact helped to develop and civilize African populations through the introduction of modern technologies, education, Christianity and a cash economy that is connected to the international economy. While there is no doubt that colonialism was transformative in these areas, its objectives were not always altruistic and, thus, apologist claims that the British empire was glorious, benevolent and a gentle force in the era of imperialism need to be questioned.

Many studies on colonial history within the British Empire reveal that its pillage, patronage and plunder over the course of three centuries helped gird and sustain Britain's global political and economic power, including through the two costly world wars and much beyond.[123] George Monbiot points out that colonial plunder helped Britain to balance its resource deficits and, more fundamentally, that the economic drain from the Empire was a major factor in the impoverishment of many of Britain's former colonies such as India.[124] And, as Joseph Stiglitz, a former Chief Economist of the World Bank and a recipient of the Nobel Memorial Prize in Economic Sciences, warns, even though Britain lost its colonies, the plunder continues by other mean such as debt, trade-related investment measures, bilateral investments agreements, neocolonialism and economic colonialism.[125]

This view is consistent with the philosophy of colonial plunder that was articulated by Lugard in justifying the partitioning and controlling Africa, its resources and people:

> It is inherent in a great colonial and commercial empire like ours that we go forward or go backward. To allow other nations to develop new fields, and to refuse to do so ourselves, is to go backward; and this is the more deplorable, seeing that we have proved ourselves notably capable of dealing with native races and of developing new countries at a less expense than other nations. We owe to the instincts of colonial expansion of our ancestors those vast and noble dependencies which are our pride and the outlets of our trade today; and we are accountable to posterity that opportunities which now present themselves of extending the sphere of our industrial enterprise are not neglected, for the opportunities now offered will never recur again.[126]

The above viewpoints illustrate the fact that methods of plunder have changed with time but the underlying objectives—to promote and protect Britain's material and strategic interests—remain the same. Thus, although colonial plunder in the late 19th century was more overt, its methodology changed after the liquidation of the Empire and it became more covert and sophisticated.

Contradictions in the Transition from Traditional to Colonial Rule in Buganda

Between 1900, when the Buganda Agreement was signed, and 1914, when Kabaka Daudi Chwa came of age, the colonial administration was consolidated and the kingdom transformed and fully integrated into the British Empire. The transformation brought about by colonial rule gave rise to a tense dichotomy between the new and old perspectives on power in Buganda. In this context, the traditional and cultural order increasingly came under pressure from the new and more aggressive forces of colonial rule. And as colonial rule increased its outreach and influence, so did resistance from the traditional order. These dichotomous relations and tensions characterised British colonial rule until the country's independence and beyond.

Colonial governance was grounded and sustained on a new economic order in Uganda: coffee and cotton had been introduced to the colony. The

Uganda Railway had been completed to facilitate the movement of goods and people between Mombasa and Kampala. The story of the conception, design, financing, construction and utilisation of the Uganda Railway, also known as the "lunatic express," is one of the more fascinating aspects of British colonial rule in East Africa. The idea of the railway was first developed by the IBEAC, which intended it to facilitate the movement of ivory, timber and other commodities from the African hinterland once it was granted a Royal Charter. But when the IBEAC went bankrupt, the British Government took over the nebulous project. In Charles Miller's book *The Lunatic Express: The Magnificent Saga of the Railways Journey into Africa*, the construction of the railway was an engineering miracle. He wrote that the 600-mile route of the Mombasa-Nairobi-Lake Victoria railway

> was largely unmapped and barely explored. Behind Mombasa lay a scorched waterless desert. Beyond, a horizonless scrub country climbed towards [a] jagged volcanic region bisected by the great Rift Valley. A hundred miles of sponge-like quagmire marked the railway's last lap. The entire right of way bristled with hostile tribes, teemed with lions and breathed malaria.[127]

British rule was extended to the remotest parts of the kingdom with the help of local chiefs under the policy of indirect rule. Apolo Kagwa, who since 1889 had held the influential office of Katikkiro (until 1926) and was co-Regent of Kabaka Chwa (until 1914), was at the height of his power. Indeed, with the British administrators and Kagwa at the centre of power in Buganda, the role and authority of the young Kabaka Chwa were greatly diminished.[128] Kagwa's power was buttressed by that of a new class of chiefs who were among the main beneficiaries of the allocation of 8,000 square miles of land under the 1900 Agreement.[129] Unsurprisingly, the loyalty of many of Buganda's chiefs was shifting from the Kabaka's court to that of the colonial government.[130] The shift in the power relations within Buganda's traditional structures and between the coloniser and colonised peoples, happening as it did at a time when Daudi Chwa attained majority age, meant that he assumed kingship in a changed Buganda.

Besides looking up to the colonial authorities on administrative matters, the Regents and other senior chiefs were driven by a desire to consolidate and protect their new status and land ownership, and in this regard they created a special council of *abataka* (landlords) and *abalangira* (princes) for those chiefs and princes who held a lot of land in Buganda. Membership was to be restricted to those who held at least ten square miles of land.[131] This council was intended to give its members the right of "expressing their opinion on matters relative to land and wealth of the country."[132] Interestingly, it was proposed that the Kabaka be the nominal head of that council; but for all practical purposes the council was headed by a president elected by the majority, taking into consideration the amount of land he possessed and what he was doing on his land to promote the wealth of the country.[133] It is undisputable that the real intention of this council was to entrench the interests of the Regents and chiefs in Buganda before the young king was able to assert himself.

At his investiture on the day of his coronation, Daudi Chwa was required—as a way of acknowledging British power and patronage—to take an oath before the acting Governor in which he accepted to obey the current and future laws and directives of the British Government, as well as to fully and faithfully cooperate with it in improving the governance of the kingdom of Buganda.[134] Considering the fate of his father, who was deposed and died in exile, it is not as if the young Daudi Chwa had a real choice in the matter. And once he had signed up and agreed to pay allegiance to HMG and British hegemony in general, Daudi Chwa was accepted as the Kabaka and was later became an honorary Captain in the colonial army—the King's African Rifles (KAR)—during the First World War.[135] He was also decorated as a Knight Commander of the Order of St Michael and St George (KCMG)[136] and later with the Most Excellent Order of the British Empire (MBE). In other words, along with his kingdom, Daudi Chwa, the Kabaka of Buganda, had been subsumed in the service of the British Empire.

Daudi Chwa's reign as the Kabaka of Buganda thus started on rocky political ground, in which his senior chiefs, whose position and power had been greatly enhanced under the 1900 Agreement, had divided loyalties. With one leg in the colonial administration and another in Buganda's traditional administration, many chiefs found themselves in situations of personal and public conflict. While some wished to deal directly with HMG's representatives, as opposed to the traditional structures of the Kabaka or the Lukiiko, others—especially those who were more traditionalist and conservative in outlook—preferred to hold onto the old ways of the kingdom in which the Kabaka was the powerful sovereign.

The Regents were concerned by the disregard, on the part of some chiefs, of traditional processes and power. They complained to the Provincial Commissioner, requesting him to remind the errant chiefs that "for administrative purposes the *Ssaza* (county) chiefs should be directly responsible to the Kabaka through the Lukiiko except in the matter of collecting tax."[137] They pointed out the importance of proper recognition by all the Baganda of the power of the Lukiiko, if the Lukiiko was to maintain its proper place as the final native court and the headquarters of the native Government of Buganda. In spite of this appeal, however, the problem persisted and eventually culminated in Kagwa's falling out with the British rulers.

British colonialism impacted upon—and significantly transformed—the power relations in Buganda and beyond. In its wake, it not only created wide fissures in the traditional chain of authority, but it also debilitated traditional power centres leading, ultimately, to a power shift from traditional centres to the colonial power. Below, we highlight four case studies that illustrate the tensions and conflicts stemming from that power shift.

The Allocation of Butaka Land

Besides the difficulties of reining in his chiefs, the young Kabaka Chwa was confronted with complaints by the *abakulu b'obusolya* (clan heads) and *ab'amasiga* (sub-clan heads)[138] whose customary or clan land (*obutaka*) had been allocated to the chiefs as mailo land by the Lukiiko under the 1900 Agreement. The rights to obutaka were not recognised in the Agreement. Much of this land was in fact already held as clan land and contained clan burial grounds. In the allocation of the 8,000 square miles to the chiefs and notables in the kingdom, only a few bataka were allocated land—and then only in their private individual capacities. As such, the new landlords had to contend with and/ or confront these occupants on the land allocated to them.

Between 1900 and 1914, when the Kabaka attained majority age, the bataka and others who did not benefit from the land-sharing bonanza protested against the injustice in the allocation of their customary land and burial grounds, but were largely ignored. When one clan leader, James Miti, took the matter to court, he was told that "the court would not allow claims based on the traditional system to have precedence over the allocation," and that "the mailo system was not to be encumbered by any legal recognition of prior traditional claims."[139] In reaching this decision, the court relied on the positivist legal theory that interprets and applies the law "as it is" and not "as it ought to be." This theory disregards the morality or injustices underlying such laws. Legal positivism and the Kelsen pure theory of law—which legitimises and legalises revolutionary changes in government—were to be a hallmark of Uganda's jurisprudence, as can also be seen in the case *Uganda v. Commissioner of Prisons ex-parte Matovu.*[140]

In considering the land claims of the disaffected groups in Buganda, the Lukiiko—composed mostly of the beneficiaries under the new land order—also dismissed the batakas' claims. In addition, they rejected the Protectorate's proposals: that the areas containing ancestral clan graves should be excluded from any mailo grants; that the bataka estates should be vested in clan trustees; and that the present mailo holders of those estates should be compensated by grants of other land such as Crown land. It seems strange that the Lukiiko refused to act on the offer by the colonial government for compensation to be made from Crown lands, but this was because, as Low and Pratt put it, "throughout this whole period the ministers and chiefs were thoroughly in command of Buganda affairs and had no wish to give recognition to any others who might rival their leadership."[141]

The plight of the bataka and other peasants was aggravated by new demands to pay *Busulu* (a 10 shilling cash payment or one month's labour in lieu) and *Envujjo* (a tribute in kind from the food and/ or beer produced on the land they occupied) to the chiefs. In addition, peasants were liable to be called upon for *Luwalo* (unpaid compulsory community work, e.g. on roads) and *Kasanvu* (compulsory labour on Government projects or European plantations), and had to pay a 15 shilling poll tax to the Protectorate.

These harsh conditions gave birth to the Bataka movement that was to foment serious trouble for the chiefs and the Protectorate Government in later years. In 1921, the Bataka formed the "Bataka Association," also referred to as the "Federation of the Abataka," which questioned the validity of the allotments made under the 1900 Agreement. They appealed to the Governor to help address this question but he offered little help and instead referred them to their own traditional tribunals, asserting that the Governor could not be expected to upset or reverse the new colonial system on land ownership and control.

Dissatisfied with the Governor's stance, the bataka took their grievances to Kabaka Daudi Chwa and showed him a list of the butaka lands which they considered to have been illegally seized by the chiefs. The Kabaka returned a cautious verdict supporting their contention.[142] While acknowledging that the major estates (*obutaka bw'akasolya*) had been granted to the rightful owners, but also that many sub-clan estates (*obutaka bw'amasiga*) had been wrongly allocated to others, the Kabaka did not agree that these estates should be returned. Instead, he requested that the Lukiiko allot mailo estates to any bataka who could prove that they had lost their rightful butaka land.[143] As expected, the Lukiiko, which was dominated and headed by the beneficiaries of the land allocations, did not give the Kabaka's views serious consideration.[144]

Instead, it rejected his proposal and instead passed an obfuscatory resolution to the effect that "whenever butaka land was offered for sale by its present owner, the bataka would be given the first option on its purchase."[145] The bataka were not persuaded by the Lukiiko's measures, neither were they prepared to give up the fight. In fact, they grew more restive and appealed to the Protectorate Government once again. A special Commission of Inquiry was set up in 1924 to examine the matter and found that, in a number of cases, improper allotments resulting in the dispossession of bataka holders in favour of powerful chiefs had been made. The Commission recommended that an arbitration court be set up with powers to restore lands to their earlier owners. The Protectorate Government accepted the recommendation but passed the task of implementation over to the Lukiiko. Unsurprisingly, little came of the matter, considering the congruence of interests between the Lukiiko and the Protectorate Government. Both were reticent in addressing the batakas' concerns.

However, the incessant agitation of the bataka forced the colonial government to review the matter, and in 1926, Secretary of State L. S. Amery was asked to pronounce his position on the problem. In his despatch of 17 August 1926,[146] delivered at a special sitting of the Lukiiko with the Kabaka and his ministers in attendance, Amery, conveniently overlooking the role of the British Government in the matter, "rebuked the Regents in very strong terms for the manner in which they used their powers at the time of land allocation."[147] Interestingly, however, he too declared that he had decided not to intervene in the dispute or to interfere with the freehold titles which had been granted with the provisional or final approval of the Protectorate Government. The status quo would remain intact because, in Amery's view, "whether the ownership of large freehold estates should vest in one individual or another is, looking to the interests of the country as a whole, of less importance than the safeguarding of the interests of native tenants."[148]

The major reason that Amery let matters lie was that it was found quite impossible to deal with the compensation of persons who had suffered injustice by turning out landowners who had obtained land under the 1900 Agreement. Moreover, in 1900, there had been 3,700 new landlords, and due to the fragmentation of estates through sale and inheritance the number had grown significantly, yet there was no suitable land available in substitution. By 1939, this number had risen to 15,559.[149] Clearly, the economic, social and political cost of redressing the injustices arising out of the land allocations under the 1900 Agreement was too high for the colonial administration. Accordingly, the colonial authorities decided to kick the can down the road. Ironically, the colonial government was to face a similar, if not more difficult, dilemma in respect of the Bunyoro land it gifted to Buganda under the 1900 Agreement, which came to be known as the "lost counties."

To placate the peasants and the bataka following Amery's disappointing pronouncements, the colonial government formulated a policy that aimed to safeguard them from summary eviction by landlords and to restrict the rent payable to the latter. Under this policy, the government aimed to balance the rights of the tenants without upsetting the rights of the new landlords. In fact, as if to remedy the wrongs done under the 1900 Agreement, the British now felt that it was more important to consider and protect the interests of the tenants than to reallocate the land to the bataka. The wisdom of this policy lay in both the fact that the peasants constituted the majority of the population and would pose a security risk if they became uncontrollable but mainly because were also the biggest providers of labour and thus instrumental in supporting the colonial budget and economy that were dependent on cash-crop agriculture. The bataka were fewer in number, and since their powers in the new Buganda had been grossly undermined by the new chiefly class, they were quite dispensable.

To give effect to the new policy, the Busulu and Envujjo Law of 1927 was reluctantly passed by the Lukiiko, under great pressure from the colonial government.[150] Under this law, the size of busuulu (taxes) was fixed and the amount of envujjo (rent or tithe) was limited for any holding of three acres or less. The new law gave security of tenure to the tenants as long as they met the above conditions. For a while, the Busuulu and Envujjo Law somewhat quietened matters, but when the bataka learnt of an impending visit to Uganda by Colonel Oliver Stanley, Secretary of State for the Colonies, they wrote a letter to him in which they laid out their grievances and frustrations and resurrected their claims over the customary butaka land.[151] They pleaded with him, saying: "now since you have come to Buganda, we the Bataka of the country therefore lay [before you] this important matter which has since long been referred to the Kabaka and to the Protectorate Government."[152]

In his brief to Colonel Stanley, Governor Charles Dundas gave a historical account of the allocation of land under the 1900 Agreement and the confusion associated with it, and explained why the colonial government had decided not to intervene in the dispositions already made.[153] The Governor used the opportunity to share his opinion on the "general character" of the Buganda Government. In his words:

> That the Baganda have some talent for administration may be conceded but it is mistaken to suppose that they are markedly more enlightened or competent than other Africans. I cannot say that I am particularly impressed with their intelligence, nor have they won any reputation above others for ability either at Makerere College or in the army. A good deal of unmerited praise lavished on them from some quarters has, I fear, encouraged their conceit and they make much of their competence to manage their own affairs, but left to their own devices they show small initiative or self-reliance and their pretended self-sufficiency soon breaks down. I do not wish to decry the Baganda, but I feel it is necessary to realise that they are, after all, Africans of average African mentality and, unfortunately, of rather less than average integrity, in whom it is unsafe to repose implicit faith. With this background of character the degree of independence they have is not always advantageous to the country and there is distinct danger that Buganda will lag—if indeed it does not already lag behind the standard of general welfare attained in surrounding tribal areas.[154]

On the young Kabaka, the Governor commented:

> I had entertained hope that the youthful Kabaka might exert a good influence on his Government but I regret to say that the impression gained so far is that he is ineffective, complacent and mainly concerned for his own amusement and in the choice of his associates he has not displayed discretion.[155]

Dundas' views on the ministers (the Katikkiro, Omulamuzi and Omuwanika) and the broader membership of the Lukiiko were not charitable either; he wrote that they were only "too eager to retain popularity … and devoid of a sense of responsibility, save where their own interests are involved," and that "their manifestly rooted conception [was] that the whole land with its peasantry exists for their own enrichment and that such is the purpose of the mailo system sanctioned by the Government."[156] And on the peasantry in Buganda, perhaps more profoundly and prophetically, the Governor stated that

> they seriously resent the existing state of affairs. But equally it should not be taken for granted that they will remain quiescent indefinitely and it is possible that a more assertive spirit will make itself felt with the return of thousands of men who are in the army and have had experience of the impeccable leadership of British Officers. The danger is that if and when the awakening comes the odium for the inequities of the Buganda regime may fall on the British Government rather than on the native rulers.[157]

For that matter, Dundas concluded:

> I am compelled to recognise that the time has come for adoption of a firmer attitude on my part … so that it is not construed that [self-government] delivered the mass of the people into the hands of a privileged minority and [so] that we [do not] allow the country to fall below the standards achieved in other regions of the Protectorate.[158]

With specific reference to the foregoing batakas' petition, Governor Dundas' advice was unequivocal: "it ought to be emphasised to the petitioners that there is no intention to re-open the major question of allotment under the 1900 Agreement."[159] Unfortunately, as the 1945 and 1949 demonstrations revealed, the Governor's recognition of the problem and his perceived solution came too late.

It is quite interesting to note the sharp contrast between Governor Dundas' views when he was in charge of the Protectorate and those expressed in his book *African Crossroads,* where after leaving the scene he described Uganda as "truly the gem of the empire" and the native state of Buganda as the "exemplar" and indeed the "prototype" of British indirect rule.[160] Writing on his meetings with the Kabaka, Dundas noted: "I was at once impressed with his courteous manner, his dignity and self-possession … [and] a good sense of humour," and that "on the most solemn occasions [he] would have a little fun on the sly."[161] One possible explanation of Dundas' contrasting views on Buganda could be to justify his policy, whilst he was the Governor, of reforming colonial rule in Buganda and granting more powers to the native government—a policy which was discarded as soon as his replacement came into office.[162]

The question of ownership and alienation of butaka land after the 1900 Agreement was the subject of several legal suits, including the case of *T. Mwenge v. S. Migade.*[163] In this case, Mwenge sought a court injunction restraining Migade from obstructing the survey and sale of 300 acres of butaka land (which formed part of the ancestral burial grounds of Migade's clan) which he had purchased from one F. K. Nakatanza. Ag. Judge Gray held that in the allocation of land under the 1900 Agreement, the Lukiiko did not always allot butaka land to members of the clan and that the decisions of the Lukiiko on this matter were final and not appealable. He held further that under the 1900 Agreement,

> a Muganda landlord had been granted the unrestricted right to his alienated land—no matter of what customary tenure it may formerly have been held … [T]he plaintiff therefore has a right to this land whether it was once of butaka tenure or not.

He also held that

> in light of the new land laws, the custom on the inalienability of butaka land was so repugnant that custom must be treated as abrogated and destroyed even if the law does not expressly abrogate it in so many words.[164]

However, in what appears as a contradiction to the rule on alienation of butaka land set out in the *Mwenge* case, whereas an allottee of butaka land who was not a member of the clan had a right to alienate the land to a third party, in the case of *Fazaldin Miraneux v. Simoni Lule*,[165] the Lukiiko, under the leadership of Apolo Kagwa, Andeleya Kiwanuka and Ham Mukasa, held that

> any portion of land in Buganda which has been held as butaka of one of the clans from time immemorial and has been allotted under the Uganda Agreement [of] 1900, to a member of the clan will be regarded as subject to the customary rights of all the members of the clan and cannot be sold.

In other words, where butaka land was allocated to a member of the clan, the land remained as customary land of butaka and could not be legally sold out of the clan.

In another case, *Stanislas Mugwanya v. Lui Sensuwa*,[166] the question was whether Mugwanya—a Regent whose allocation of butaka land was discovered, after a survey, to exceed the amount specified in the certificate of allocation—had the power to sell or gift the surplus land to another party. Mugwanya argued that he had power over the surplus land and that he had subsequently obtained the grant on the surplus land from the Kabaka and Katikkiro Kagwa. When the Lukiiko (acting as a judicial body) heard this case, it decided that Mugwanya had the power to donate any surplus land found as a result of the survey. On appeal, Ag. Justice Walker ruled against Mugwanya, holding that whereas the Lukiiko (acting as an administrative/allocating body) had powers to allocate butaka land to Mugwanya under Clause 15 of the 1900 Agreement,

> an allottee of land under the Buganda Agreement has no right of ownership of, or power of disposition of that portion of an area of land so provisionally marked out which is found on survey to be in excess of the amount specified in such provisional certificate and which is accordingly excluded from the final grant made in pursuance of such provisional certificate. Such surplus land becomes a portion of the total aggregate of land remaining at the disposal of the Lukiiko for allotment to those entitled

to it under the Agreement of 1900.[167]

These cases illustrate the extent of the crisis and social distortion that resulted from the 1900 Agreement on the allocation of land in general and butaka land in particular, enacted without regard for the rights of such lands' inhabitants. There was a conflict of interest in the Lukiiko over the allocation of land and thus in their adjudication of disputes on the same, as well as a convergence of interests in the protection of the new colonial land policy between the Protectorate Government, the colonial courts and the new landed class. Needless to say, colonial self-interest and equivocation on resolving the bataka land question, not to mention the Bunyoro "lost counties," was to have dire consequences for the future of the country's land tenure and politics. The Bataka grievances and struggles over land rights were to metamorphose into political crises in Buganda, particularly in 1945 and 1949. Their pushback and resistance against colonial land policies on the one hand, as well as their fight against the native chiefly compradors on the other, marked the beginning of popular resistance against British colonial rule and, ultimately, the birth of nationalism and political activism in Uganda.

Britain's Interest in and Push for a Closer Union of Eastern Africa

Besides the dubious land allocations and Bataka agitations over the same, nothing stirred up the relations between the colonial government, the Kabaka and the kingdom of Buganda more than the Britain's interest to forge a closer union between its East African dependencies, namely, Uganda, Kenya and Tanganyika (the future Tanzania). This interest, whose real origins are traceable to the white British settlers in Kenya, was first announced by Secretary L. S. Amery at a dinner in London in 1921.[168]

The Kabaka and the Lukiiko immediately opposed a closer colonial union, saying they could never agree to the kingdom being joined up to the other colonies of East Africa.[169] It was feared that such a federation would undermine the special position Buganda enjoyed as a British Protectorate under the 1900 Agreement, amongst other concerns. But perhaps the biggest fear was the prospect that under such a federation, the Kenyan European settlers would take over and control the politics and land in Buganda as they had done in Kenya.[170] The violent imposition of colonial rule and the brutal treatment of Africans by the British settlers in Kenya must have terrified the leadership in Buganda.

The British policy to create a settler economy in Kenya meant that the settlers obtained a disproportionate share and control of land and the natives were relegated to providing cheap labour. Through expropriations, the British took over 11,000 square miles of land, most of it in the fertile regions of the Central and Rift Valley Provinces. This was in addition to outrageous policies such as the creation of reserves for ethnic groups; the banning of native Kenyans from growing cash crops; the dreaded Masters and Servants Ordinance of 1906;[171] the restriction of labourer movements; the introduction of identification passes (*ekipande*); and the forceful conscription of young men.[172]

The history and nature of atrocities by colonial authorities against the resistant native populations in Kenya were the subject of *Nditi Mutua and Four Others v. The Foreign and Commonwealth Office*.[173] In this case the British government, together with the colonial administration and individual perpetrators of the torturous assaults, were accused of having encouraged, procured, acquiesced in or otherwise been complicit in the mistreatment, ill-treatment or negligent treatment of the claimants, and were in breach of their duty of care for failing to put to a stop what they knew was the systematic use of torture and violence against the claimants.

Notwithstanding Buganda's opposition to the idea of a closer East African Union, the British Government set up a Commission in 1924 led by Ormsby-Gore to "report on measures to be taken to accelerate the general economic development of the East African dependencies together with Nyasaland and Rhodesia."[174] But in the wake of Buganda's strong opposition to the move, the work of the Commission never took off and the idea was shelved. However, another Commission, this one headed by Edward Hilton Young, was set up in 1927 to again consider and advise on a closer union of Britain's dependencies in Eastern and Central Africa.[175] Buganda, this time joined by Bunyoro, once again led the opposition to a closer union in which, it was rumoured, Kenya would automatically become the senior partner.[176] Young's report was a subject of intense debate in the House of Lords, as Britain sought to develop a long term policy for its possessions in Eastern and Central Africa.[177]

Lord Lugard, in supporting a closer union of East Africa, stated that "it is worth it for the sake of the larger interests of the Empire."[178] According to him, the whole justification for a closer union was to improve the administration and control of the East African territories and, importantly, to ensure that the holdings of the immigrant settler community were increased and their interests protected within a larger economy. In his view, this would be achieved once a system was developed where

> [the] Crown Colony government [could] be changed in these large African

> Dependencies so that the Imperial Government may retain sufficient control to enable it to fulfil its obligations of trusteeship for the native interests, while utilising to the full the political experience and capacity of the European immigrants[179]

In the end, Lugard's opinion swayed the House which backed the policy for a closer union of the East African territories.

Upon receiving Young's report and considering its recommendations supporting a closer union, a distraught kingdom of Buganda, through Governor William Gowers, wrote a long memorandum to Amery, the new Secretary of State for the Colonies, stating:

> There is no question, Sir, but this matter is causing us great anxiety, and that for many reasons which we will attempt to set forth to you in this letter. We must remind you, Sir, that when the members of that Commission arrived in Buganda, the Kabaka gave them two memoranda, and the Lukiiko also gave them a memorandum, making it clear that they could never agree to our Kingdom of Buganda being joined up to the other countries of East Africa; and they received an assurance from the Commission openly in the Lukiiko of Buganda, on the occasion of their visit to the Lukiiko, that the country would not be included in that union.[180]

As with the Ormsby-Gore Commission report before it, and in the face of Buganda's firm resistance, all involved except Kenya roundly rejected Young's report.[181] However, given the importance of a closer administration of a larger territory in East Africa to Britain's colonial agenda, Amery was not to give up on the idea. In the same year, 1929, he sent out Sir Samuel Wilson to "see what measure of agreement existed in regard to the Young Commission's recommendations."[182] Wilson met the leadership in Buganda and visited Kenya and Tanganyika. Before publication of the Wilson Report, the Kabaka and his senior ministers jointly signed a letter to Amery drawing his attention to their petition of 8 May 1929 and urging most earnestly as follows:

> In the event of the question of the closer union of Eastern Africa being definitely decided upon we most respectfully beg to be given the opportunity to send our own representatives to await on His Majesty's Secretary of State for the Colonies before the question of the inclusion of Buganda kingdom into the proposed federation is finally settled.[183]

As it turned out, Wilson found that there was no agreement whatsoever over the proposed union. He recommended the establishment of an office of a High Commissioner who would be the chief advisor to the Secretary of State on native policy. He also recommended the establishment of a Legislative Council to advise and assist the proposed High Commissioner. However, the Lukiiko rejected Wilson's recommendations and petitioned the Secretary of State to receive a delegation to put its case to him in London. The Secretary of State declined this request saying "His Highness the Kabaka may be assured that the views of himself and the native Government of Buganda are fully known to [the Secretary of State] and they need have no fear that their representations will be overlooked or that the position of the native government is in jeopardy."[184]

In 1930, the British Government published a White Paper, authored by Lord Passfield, on East Africa, in which it asserted that a closer union was necessary to promote the political development of Africans. However, it was unclear how this was to be achieved. To advance this view, a Joint Select Committee of the two Houses of the British Parliament was set up to consider and advise on the matter. The Kabaka's government was not amused with this development. In what marked the first stirrings of high level African resistance to British colonial authority in (B)Uganda since the 1900 Agreement, a perturbed Daudi Chwa wrote that "whatever native policy of the administration of these federated territories may be introduced, nothing shall be allowed to interfere with the internal native administration of Buganda Kingdom as set out in that solemn Agreement."[185]

Addressing the Joint Select Committee on the same point, he wrote that "the kingdom of Buganda should be excluded [from the proposed High Commission] and a special Commissioner appointed by His Majesty's Imperial Government to conduct the administration of [his] country who should be responsible directly to the Imperial Government at home in affairs affecting the internal administration of [his] country."[186] When the Joint Select Committee convened under the chairmanship of Lord Stanley of Alderley to consider its remit in London on 12 May 1931, Sserwano W. Kulubya, the Omuwanika (treasurer), represented the kingdom of Buganda. In his opening statement, he stated:

> We in Buganda are in a peculiar position of having an agreement with the Imperial Government whereby our interests are safeguarded and our internal independence guaranteed.... Whilst it is scarcely doubted that the terms of the agreement will be observed strictly by the Imperial Government, we cannot help showing some alarm that in all the official memoranda on the question of a closer union, the terms of the Buganda Agreement will be left entirely unimpaired. In the absence of any specified guarantee, and in view of the almost studied avoidance of such guarantee, we cannot help but feel that there are official doubts as to the possibility of bringing Buganda into closer union during the existence of the Buganda

> Agreement as it stands today. For ourselves, we cannot understand how closer union can be effected without seriously impairing our rights and privileges as provided for in the Agreement. Honourable members, we are a small community, comparatively, but we ask for fair play, we ask for a continuance of the redemption of the promise given us, we ask that the justice and the justness which has made the British Empire the mighty power it is today, be still further guaranteed to us and that we be permitted to carry on the lines which have brought us to the measure of prosperity which we enjoy today."[187]

The select committee and the British public were astounded by Kulubya's powerful and persuasive submissions. The *New Statesman and Nation* ran a story entitled "Africa has Spoken" in which it stated that "something unexpected, something portentous has arisen, marking the end of the darkest Africa and the beginning of a new dispensation. African leaders can now speak for their people; this is the startling fact with which we are confronted today, and it is a fact which must influence all our future policies."[188] Kulubya's submissions were so forceful that the Select Committee had no choice but to recommend that no form of administrative union should be introduced in East Africa, either directly or indirectly.[189]

At that time, it seemed that the troublesome chapter of a closer union of East Africa was closed—obviously much to the disdain of its supporters and to Buganda's joy. Alas, that was not to be; for as we will show, the matter was to rear its ugly head once more, twenty years later, with disastrous and far-reaching consequences for Anglo-Buganda relations. It is clear from the above that the proposal for a closer union of East Africa brought into question the respect Britain had for the 1900 Agreement, the Kabaka and the native government of Buganda. Simultaneously, it displayed not only the faith the Baganda had in the Agreement and in Britain's promise of protection, but also the overarching colonial desire to control wider state territory in total disregard of the natives' views or interests. At the same time, this episode marked the foundation of concerted resistance to British rule from the kingdom's leadership.

The Fading of Apolo Kagwa's Star and Changes in Colonial Policy after World War I

Kagwa's Regency ended when Kabaka Chwa came of age in 1914. Although he was retained as Katikkiro, his powers and clout *vis-à-vis* the Kabaka were severely diminished. This was because he was effectively divested of the supreme authority in Buganda that he had been accustomed to during the Regency. As the Katikkiro and Regent, Kagwa was in total control and command and wielded unchallenged authority for the 17 years of the Kabaka's minority. It was difficult for him and his loyalists to adjust to the change in the management of the native government required to accommodate the Kabaka. Thus in the post-Regency period, Kagwa's relationship with the Kabaka degenerated, often leading to tensions and disagreements between the two.[190]

Moreover, during the same period, Kagwa's relationship with the colonial government also sharply deteriorated as a result of the diminution of his overall authority combined with changes in colonial policy. The falling out with the Kabaka and, later, with his colonial benefactors left Kagwa without a power base and resulted in a bitter end for him. As we discuss below, he was humiliated and ultimately forced to resign the coveted office of Katikkiro which he had held for over three decades.[191]

In the same year that Kabaka Chwa attained full age and assumed office, the First World War, pitting the leading colonial powers of Britain and Germany against each other, broke out. Britain, fighting Germany alongside the Allied forces, had to call upon the resources of its Empire to support it in the prosecution of the costly four-year war. In fact, Kabaka Chwa was conscripted into the King's African Rifles (KAR) for this purpose. He also actively participated in the mobilisation of men for the war, which left severe economic and social devastation in its wake, both in Britain and in its far-flung colonies such as Uganda.

The war greatly weakened Britain's imperial power and gave more impetus to demands for autonomy and self-rule across its Empire. It thus significantly contributed to a changed perspective and methodology of British colonial rule. The end of the First World War thus ushered in considerable changes both in Buganda's leadership and in British rule—changes that seriously impacted politics and colonial relations within Buganda and the rest of the Protectorate.

In the power struggle that ensued between the Kabaka, the chiefs and the Protectorate Government, Kagwa sought to remain in control. To bolster his position in the new arrangement, Kagwa devised a devious plot to undermine the young Kabaka, designed to use the British colonial administrators to reduce the Kabaka's powers and, at the same time, enhance the power of the chiefs.[192] To achieve his ambition, Kagwa sought to work with J. R. P. Postlethwaite, then a British District Commissioner. In his autobiography, Postlethwaite recounts Kagwa's plans as follows:

> I received a visit from Apolo very early in the morning when he offered me what seemed a very unholy alliance, promising me support for my selection of chiefs and indeed for almost anything else if I would afford him my support for keeping His Highness the Kabaka as a titular nonentity

> who should in no way interfere with the Executive powers of his Katikkiro.[193]

On Kagwa's suggestion that the Kabaka should become a mere figurehead, a non-cooperative Postlethwaite commented that "apart from the injustice to the Kabaka it appeared to [him] that this policy could not possibly succeed, the Baganda being an entirely royalist tribe with great reverence and affection for their Kabaka *qua* Kabaka."[194]

Postlethwaite's refusal to accede to Kagwa's plans must have been a huge disappointment and marked a watershed in the relations between Kagwa and the colonial administration. His relationship with Postlethwaite in particular became more strained when Postlethwaite became Provincial Commissioner.[195] On Kagwa's part, it was inconceivable that a junior British official like Postlethwaite would stand in his way or deny his advice. On Postlethwaite's part, the aging Kagwa and the similarly aged Buganda leadership in general, needed to be put in their proper place.[196] In reality, given the entrenched power of British rule in Buganda at the time, there was little need for the support or influence of old-timers like Kagwa.

An incident involving the granting of beer licences in Buganda's *kibuga* (capital city) involving Kagwa and Postlethwaite vividly illustrates the shift in the power relations between Buganda's native leadership and the colonial administrations and the total breakdown of relations between Kagwa and Postlethwaite. The *Omukulu W'ekibuga* (chief in charge of Buganda's capital city) had a dispute with Kagwa on the issuance of beer licences in the kibuga.[197] To resolve the dispute, the chief made an appeal to Postlethwaite, who sided with the chief against Kagwa in the matter. A displeased Kagwa objected to the chief's conduct, particularly to his having direct dealings with officials from the Protectorate Government and not following the appropriate hierarchy within the native government of Buganda. An angry Kagwa wrote to Postlethwaite:

> It is incomprehensible why this official of the Buganda Government did not refer the matter to the Kabaka if he was not satisfied with the Lukiiko's settlement … I beg to inform you that in future the Buganda Government is not prepared to regard as right and to take consideration … matters conducted after this fashion.[198]

Kagwa argued that under the 1900 Agreement, the chief had no authority to bypass the Katikkiro and communicate directly with the provincial administration. However, Kagwa's protests did not impress or change Postlethwaite's views on the matter. In fact, he became angry and demanded an apology from Kagwa for both the tone and content of his missive.[199] In a letter to the Kabaka, Postlethwaite threatened not to have any further dealings with the Katikkiro if an apology was not tendered. Ultimately, the matter was escalated to both the Kabaka and the Governor. While the Kabaka generally supported his Katikkiro, the British Governor, Sir William F. Gowers,[200] disagreed with Kagwa's position. Gowers rejected Kagwa's thinking that all advice and instructions to the chiefs of Buganda had to be communicated through the native government hierarchy.[201]

As if to add salt to a festering wound, Postlethwaite went on to demand Kagwa's resignation, saying "at his great age his retirement with honour would bring contentment to himself and efficient harmony to the British/Buganda administration."[202] When Kagwa refused to resign following the Commissioner's demands, Postlethwaite wrote to the Kabaka asking him to force the resignation of his Katikkiro on grounds of poor health. In his letter, he went as far as naming three possible successors![203]

Kagwa was bewildered by Postlethwaite's impudence. He immediately wrote to the Governor expressing shock that His Majesty's Government would follow the unjust advice of its junior official, who had served for only sixteen years, against one of its chief officials, a native of the country, more experienced and trusted. However, in response, the Governor reaffirmed the faith he had in Postlethwaite and instead rebuked the Katikkiro for his imprudent letter—noting, however, that Kagwa was not to be forced to resign.[204] Being dissatisfied with Governor Gower's response, Kagwa appealed to L. S. Amery, the Colonial Secretary in London, on 30 March 1926:

> Sir, I would most humbly beg to point out, with all due respect, that as I contemplate retiring very soon, I considered it only right to submit the whole matter to His Majesty's Principal Secretary of State for the Colonies for his information and consideration, so that the circumstances leading up to my retirement may be placed on record. As pointed out before in this Petition, I was the Principal Agent in inviting the English people and introducing the British Government into this country; and I sacrificed the best part of my life for the good of my countrymen, as well as for the welfare and safety of the lives of the Europeans—especially the English people—who were in this country during the turbulent times of the civil wars and religious strife with the attendant unsettled condition of the country at that time; and moreover being the leading chief of His Highness the Kabaka in his native Government of Buganda Kingdom, and his principal adviser, and having held the position of principal Regent for eighteen years, I naturally expected to be treated by His Majesty's Government with special and personal consideration, having regard to my

> length of service in the Protectorate Government in my capacity as the Katikkiro of Buganda—Buganda Kingdom—a position which I have held since 1889, a period of thirty-seven years.... For the above reasons, therefore, I have decided to submit this Petition before His Majesty's Secretary of State for the Colonies for his favourable consideration, since I have not been satisfied with His Excellency the Governor's decision on the matter."[205]

Unfortunately for Kagwa, Amery declined his appeal, leaving him deeply wounded and humiliated. Kagwa also sensed insufficient or unenthusiastic support from the Kabaka, the Ssaza chiefs and his two senior colleagues, the Omuwanika (treasurer) and the Omulamuzi (chief justice).[206] Under the circumstances, he was left with no choice but to fall on his sword. He tendered his resignation as Katikkiro, effective from 31 July 1926, on the grounds of ill health. In communicating Kagwa's resignation to the Chief Secretary, the Acting Provincial Commissioner in Buganda wrote:

> The voluntary retirement from office has always been a step of peculiar difficulty to Baganda chiefs of the older school, and I feel that the Katikkiro deserves well, in that he has submitted to the inevitable with such good grace. Should His Excellency then see fit, when recording his approval, to add a few words of sympathy, it would go a long way to soften the blow and incidentally create an excellent impression.... I am sure it will readily be admitted that the indiscretions of the last few months should not be suffered to obscure the eminent services to his country which the Katikkiro has rendered in the course of his long career, more particularly his unswerving fundamental loyalty to the British connection in the troublous days of the pre-protectorate period should never be forgotten.[207]

On the occasion of Kagwa's resignation, the Acting Governor, through the Acting Chief Secretary, P. W. Perryman, wrote to the Kabaka of Buganda and asked that the letter be published "for general information." In his letter, Perryman, writing through Postlethwaite, stated:

> His Excellency, in accepting the Katikkiro's resignation, desires me to convey to you, and to the Katikkiro, an expression of his deep and sincere regret and sympathy at the cause which has necessitated this step. His Excellency hopes that Sir Apolo Kagwa will be spared to enjoy for many years the position which he has so well earned by his eminent, loyal and patriotic service in the course of his long and remarkable career, during which he has played so important a part in the history of the

Protectorate.[208]

The Archdeacon of Uganda, G. R. Blackledge, Kagwa's friend of 32 years, lamented the resignation of this pillar of the native Anglican Church, whom he admired as a warrior, leader, legislator and statesman. He wrote:

> The news of his resignation will be received with deep regret … [It] will cause feelings of consternation and dismay … after such a life of ceaseless activity on behalf of the British authority in Uganda … establishing the Christian faith in this part of Africa.… [I]t was largely because of him that the Moslem power was broken in the days of Kabaka Kalema … he was so largely instrumental in making Uganda a Christian country ... [T]hus socially, politically and from the standpoint of the Christian religion, Sir Apolo Kagwa has done great work and is worthy of that honour and praise.[209]

Based on the correspondence contained in Chwa's booklet *Why Sir Apolo Kaggwa, KCMG, MBE, Prime Minister of Buganda, Resigned*,[210] the Kabaka seemed detached regarding the matter of Kagwa's troubles and eventual resignation. He gave two reasons for the resignation: namely, Kagwa's poor health, and the clashes between Sir Apolo and the Protectorate government officials. In a chronicle narrating the history of these clashes, he did not offer an opinion on the underlying policy question of the power relations between him and the colonial government. It is unclear why he went out of his way to write a rather long missive explaining Kagwa's resignation. The Kabaka's attitude towards the colonial authority deteriorated further after this episode.

Sadly, a few months after Kagwa's resignation, death followed. At 62 years, Kagwa died a sad and dejected man. His death certificate shows that he died of heart failure at 6:10 pm on Monday 21 February 1927 in Nairobi, Kenya.[211] On the news of his death, the Governor wrote to the Kabaka sharing deep regret at the sad news, saying that Kagwa's "services to the cause of Uganda and of civilisation [would] long be remembered."[212] The Bataka, generally bitter over the land allocations under the 1900 Agreement, and especially angry about Kagwa's role in the controversial allocations, celebrated Kagwa's resignation[213] and, upon his death, they wrote:

> We the Bataka would say that God gave him a good constitution of mind when about to take him so, during his lifetime, Sir Apolo did not give due regard to or institute regulations respecting land (a) he did not respect

> Butaka land, neither did he make any law or proclamation that such land was not sellable as he did at the time of his death … (d) We therefore feel much aggrieved for the non-return of our estates and publish this article as an example to any person who may be disinclined to give us our Butaka estates, in order that such a person may realise that non-possession thereof gives us much pain, as jealousy hurts like hunger and stabs like a sharp sword.[214]

On Kagwa's fall from power, and particularly on his service to British colonial rule, Mutibwa correctly points out that:

> the crisis that led to the resignation of Apolo Kagwa as Buganda's Katikkiro was a landmark in the history of both Buganda and Uganda as a whole. First, for Buganda in particular and Uganda in general, it highlighted a central point in the concept of native administration in Uganda.… In other words, in Buganda, as elsewhere in the Protectorate, the Provincial Administration had the power to intervene, advise, instruct and supervise all the chiefs. It was a landmark that changed the relationship between the Protectorate and Buganda Governments. The crisis showed the Baganda and the rest of the people in the Protectorate the true meaning of colonial rule.… The crisis had brought into focus what had been covered under the concept: the true relationship between the ruler and the ruled when it came to Buganda; the extent to which was autonomous *vis-à-vis* the Protectorate Government.… That was it, that was all; the interests of the colonial subjects remained far behind the colonial state's wider strategic and commercial interests.[215]

Indeed, the demise of Kagwa, a long-time supporter of and warrior for the British Empire, marked the end of the era of affable colonial relations between Britain and Buganda. From this point on, as Britain sought to assert its authority in the affairs of the Protectorate, the Kabaka and Lukiiko grew in their resistance and resentment towards the colonial power. Kagwa constituted an important bridge between Buganda and Britain and his demise left the colonial administration with a big vacuum. A suitable replacement could not be identified quickly enough. Thus, filling the position of the next Katikkiro was slow and convoluted. In spite of the Kabaka having proposed the candidature of Teofiro Kisosonkole, the colonial government took considerable time to approve of the appointment. This pushed the Kabaka to appeal to the Acting Governor in November 1926, saying:

> In the old days it was the recognised native tradition on the death or dismissal of the old Katikkiro, for the Kabaka of Buganda to appoint his new Katikkiro immediately without loss of a single day, and this custom

> has been followed by all my predecessors from time immemorial.... I would have followed custom had [I] not [received] a request from the Secretary of the State to hold over the appointment until His Excellency the Governor returns from leave.... [T]his appointment ... has been vacant for five months.... [I]t would not be advisable to keep the most important post in the country vacant for an indefinite period.... I would humbly urge that the matter may be treated as urgent, and my request, that I may be allowed to appoint my new Katikkiro as soon as possible, be transmitted to the Secretary of State for the Colonies by cable to save further delay.[216]

The colonial government was not moved by the Kabaka's pleas and, after almost a fortnight's delay, to demonstrate the power of the colonial authority and, simultaneously, the powerlessness of the Kabaka and his government, it replied:

> While sympathising with your request, and while realising the difficulties of the position, he [the Governor] regrets to be unable to consider the substantive appointment of a Katikkiro prior to the return to the Protectorate of Sir William Gowers, KCMG, in about six weeks' time.... His Excellency considers that no useful purpose would be served by cabling to the Secretary of State at this stage requesting him to approve a new appointment.[217]

It was not until 11 February 1927, eight months after Kagwa's resignation and only a few days before his death, that Gowers, communicating through the Chief Secretary E. B. Jarvis, who also communicated through Postlethwaite, approved the appointment of Teofiro Kisosonkole to fill the vacant post of Katikkiro of Buganda.[218] It is not inconceivable that the imminent death of old Kagwa forced Gowers' hand in approving the appointment of the new Katikkiro. In general, the contemptuous treatment of Kagwa, as well as the chiefs of his generation, by the new crop of colonial administrators like Postlethwaite, worsened following his resignation. The old guard of chiefs was accused of inefficiency, abuse of power, and failure to keep adequate financial accounts.[219] Accordingly, they were replaced by younger chiefs.

Another measure to cut back on the power and influence of the ruling oligarchy in Buganda was the introduction of the 1927 Busulu and Envujjo Laws that forced severe limits on the rents and obligatory labour the chiefs could demand from their tenants. Thus, with this law the oligarchy of landed chiefs who had emerged with the Buganda Agreement of 1900 declined in importance, and agricultural production shifted to independent smallholders who grew cotton, and later coffee, for the export market.

The decline of Kagwa's power, his eventual demise and the changes in the colonial administration in Buganda all coincided with a change in the world order. Beyond the changes in colonial relations in Buganda, this period also marked the beginning of the decline of Britain's imperial power globally. It marked a shift in its colonial policy, following the troubles it faced in the First World War and the fermenting of resistance to its rule notably in Egypt and India. Indeed, the war was expensive to Britain. It is estimated that it cost $208 billion and that as many as 9.4 million people were killed.[220] Many more were wounded or disabled.[221] Even though Britain, alongside the Allied Forces, emerged victorious, in the end it was left with a huge debt and facing severe economic depression lasting over two decades.[222] This reality witnessed the emergence of America as the new global economic and political power.

In the First World War, Britain mobilised financial and military support from its global Empire. It recruited extensively in Africa. The King's African Rifles grew to be 30,000 men strong by the end of the war. These soldiers fought to defend and protect the Empire in the war campaign in Africa. An even larger number of Africans were recruited to serve as porters and labourers in this effort. In total British African colonies provided 62,000 troops and transport auxiliaries who fought in Africa.[223] For its part, in defending the British Empire, Uganda contributed 19,000 men as well as money.[224]

The aftermath of the war left a weakened Britain unable to effectively manage its global empire as it had before 1914. This was made more complicated by the loss of the dominions of Australia, Canada, New Zealand and South Africa, all of which had already attained autonomy.[225] At the same time, India, which had provided 1.5 million men towards the war effort, was also demanding greater self-governance, spearheaded by Mahatma Gandhi.[226] The same applied to Britain's colonies in Africa, where the seeds of resistance to colonial rule were sown and grew rapidly once Egypt was granted independence in 1922.

Overall, in the wake of the war, Britain's colonial enterprise began to unravel.[227] In this context, its outlook on its Empire began to change, with a view to reducing the cost of colonial administration and by allowing African natives to participate more in the administration of their countries.

In Uganda, these developments led to the establishment of the Uganda Legislative Council (LEGCO) in 1920, initially composed of a small number of Europeans, including the Governor as President and four officials.[228] The composition of the LEGCO changed in 1926 with the nomination of the first Indian member and another Indian member appointed in 1933. The composition and mandate of the LEGCO was of some concern to Buganda. In 1921, Chwa and Kagwa wrote to the

Governor questioning the Legislative Council's powers to make laws in Buganda. They argued that under Article 5 of the 1900 Agreement, laws made by the Governor applied to Buganda only if they did not conflict with the terms of the Agreement.

These concerns, however, did not change the colonial position on the power and composition of the LEGCO. Buganda's views were disregarded and the council continued with its work. As part of a new decolonisation policy, Africans were only admitted to the body at the end of the Second World War in 1945, some 25 years after its creation. Buganda's early resistance against the LEGCO was a foundation of major disputes between it and Britain—including the deposition and deportation of the Kabaka in 1953 and the struggle to incorporate it into a united Uganda.

Sir Daudi Chwa's Resistance to Colonialism

The relations between the Protectorate and the native leadership in Buganda and with the Kabaka in particular deteriorated further after Kagwa departed the scene. His departure left the colonial Government and Buganda in a precarious lurch. On his part, the Kabaka sought to be more assertive in his role as the supreme traditional ruler in Buganda, and to do so he needed to rein in the overly powerful chiefs and Lukiiko. At the same time, he needed to address the concerns of the Bataka, whose hostility towards the native government was on the rise.

On the part of the colonial government, the thrust was to engage younger and more compliant chiefs who would help stamp its authority over native affairs in the post-Kagwa period. It also had to grapple with and intensify the collection of taxes to support both the administration of the Protectorate and the Empire. The contradictory interests and agendas meant that there was bound to be a clash between the native and colonial administrations. It did not take long before there was a fall out between the coloniser and the colonised.

To start with, contrary to the Protectorate's policy to restrict the issuance of new leases over land, and contrary to the procedures under the 1900 Agreement—and without the consultation or approval of the Protectorate—Kabaka Chwa prepared and circulated a pamphlet on land policy in 1934, in which he strongly argued that mailo land owners held freehold land titles and should be free to lease their land to whoever they wished.[229] The Governor, Sir Bernard Bourdillion, was irate with Chwa, and after private discussions, forced the Kabaka to withdraw the offending pamphlet.[230] Then, in 1935, when the Lukiiko passed a resolution adopting the Protectorate's position, Kabaka Chwa refused to forward it to the

Governor, as was the norm. When he was pressed by the Governor, he sent it but without appending his signature. On further pressing, the Kabaka was forced to change his attitude and signed the resolution, thereby averting a crisis.[231] Mutibwa suggests that the Kabaka's signature was procured only after Bourdillion threatened to send him on a "holiday in the Seychelles"[232] where his father Mwanga had been exiled!

But besides the differences on land policy, there were other matters over which the Kabaka and the Protectorate Government clashed. Low and Pratt point out that:

> There were also divisions over appointments, over the estimates over the Kabaka's civil list, and over the upkeep of the royal enclosure, the *Lubiri*.... In 1936, the Protectorate Government offered the Buganda Government the service of a European technical officer for its *Luwalo* [public works] department. The Katikkiro and the Omuwanika agreed, but the Kabaka opposed the suggestion. The second general feature of the Kabaka's political attitude was a growing hostility to the Protectorate Government. He became less cooperative with the protecting power...He indulged in gestures of a vindictive and disruptive nature. He became progressively more obdurate towards Protectorate's advice. He even threatened abdication over one dispute.[233]

Chwa's threat to abdicate was real. In *African Afterthoughts*, former Governor Mitchell wrote that "the matter reached the stage of a threat of abdication and the court parties were certainly prepared to make as much trouble out of it as they could."[234]

Besides these acts of defiance, the Kabaka, mostly on health grounds, abstained from attending public events and largely withdrew from public life between 1937 and 1939. He was invited to but did not attend the Coronation of King George VI on 15 May 1937 at Westminster due to poor health.[235] He no longer attended all the large public functions the Kabaka typically would, including the ceremony to open the Lukiiko in 1938 and a ceremony at Makerere when His Royal Highness the Duke of Gloucester came to Uganda to cut the turf for the foundation of the new Higher College and on Empire day.[236] He was also absent on 8 August 1938 at a thanksgiving service held at Namirembe Cathedral to mark his 43rd birthday.

In his sermon, the Bishop of Uganda made reference to his Highness' prolonged illness and asked for prayers for the health of the body of the Kabaka. As a sign of the times, he asked the congregation that they should especially pray that the Kabaka might be granted health of soul.[237]

By July 1939, matters on the Kabaka's defiant stance had reached a crisis, prompting the new Governor, Phillip Mitchell, to write to the Secretary of State at the Colonial Office in London regarding what he called a "very difficult situation." The Governor had no doubt that the Kabaka's behaviour was "intentional rudeness" to which he could "no longer turn a blind eye" or allow him to make a "public fool of the Protectorate Government." He was particularly concerned that the Kabaka

> has completely withdrawn into his lake-shore house where drunken orgies are, I fear, becoming frequent; he very nearly died after one such affair last January, but since, until recently, exercised some sort of control. This once happened before, with a European boon companion, who, on the intervention of old Apolo Kagwa, was deported; the Ministers then insisted on clearing things up. Now it has started again and the Kabaka's boon companions are getting worse and worse.... About three weeks ago the Chief Minister and Treasurer called on the Resident and said they were gravely perturbed at the drinking which is going on at Salama (the lake-side residence). They said they would write with great respect to the Kabaka, pointing out that he was surrounded by people given to drinking and asking him to get rid of them and appoint others.... [T]his letter was sent on July 4th, signed by the above two ministers, who are Protestant; the Omulamuzi, a Catholic, refused to sign. (I mention denominations because religious rows are never far below the surface in Uganda).
>
> There is little doubt in my mind that the two Ministers who have taken the matter up will force an issue soon, compelled by public opinion; I have had them advised privately by Cox that they must be very careful to act constitutionally, and if they mean to go to extremes, to summon the Lukiiko. If the Lukiiko, led by them, presents a petition to me saying that His Highness' health is such that they have [been] driven to decide that he is no longer able to discharge his functions, and praying me to establish a Regency, I shall do so.
>
> I do not now think a crisis can be avoided. I am hopeful that I may be able to keep it within the native government, between the Ruler and Lukiiko; but if the Lukiiko puts its foot down I shall give it my support.[238]

The Secretary of State for the Colonies entirely agreed with Governor Mitchell's above letter. In his view, if the Governor was to establish a Regency, he would have to follow precedent and appoint the three ministers to act as Regents, though he may exclude the Chief Justice who "appears now to be very much in with the Kabaka's present entourage."[239] The Secretary argued that:

> if the Kabaka has to be suspended, it is evident that a strong case can be presented to support such action. The time has gone by when we can allow "indirect rule" to mean the bolstering up by British authority of native

> rulers who are incapable of playing a useful role. If a Regency is appointed, I think the Governor ought to ensure that affairs will be in the hands of persons who will really get on with the job of ruling the country to the best advantage of the people.[240]

The state of Chwa's health and his defiance continued to cause grave concern to his chiefs, who felt compelled to write a letter to Governor Mitchell, dated 31 August 1939, asking him to advise the Kabaka to return to Mengo Palace, to provide him with a government doctor, and to agree to the appointment of some caretakers for the Palace.[241] The chiefs' appeal to the Governor underscored the political void and crisis in Buganda caused by Chwa falling out with his chiefs and the Protectorate Government. Like his father Mwanga before him, at this moment Chwa was on his own. He neither trusted his chiefs nor the colonial administration.

From the colonial perspective, the situation demanded an urgent solution to the "Chwa problem," and pushed the colonial government to take the ultimate decision to depose him. The decision to depose Sir Daudi Chwa as the Kabaka, if need be, also received British royal assent. In a letter from Balmoral Castle, dated 6 August 1939, to one J. J. Paskin at the Colonial Office, a Palace official wrote:

> I have laid before the King your letter to Harding of August 4 with the attached copy of Mitchell's letter to [the Secretary of State at the Colonial Office]. The Kabaka certainly seems to be becoming a hopeless case, and His Majesty agrees that the action proposed by the Governor is the only possible course, should a crisis arise.[242]

Although he was not violently deposed and exiled like his father Mwanga, Chwa's resistance to British colonial rule almost cost him the royal throne. The plot to depose Chwa and replace him with another king perfectly fits a clear pattern of British rule in Uganda and elsewhere of deposing and deporting leaders that it deemed undesirable or harmful to its imperial interests. For such reasons, it deposed Mwanga and Kabalega in Uganda in 1899, Oba Ovonramen of Benin Kingdom in 1897, and the Ashantehene (King of the Ashanti) Agyeman Prempeh in Ghana in 1896.[243] Indeed, as we illustrate ahead, the same fate befell Mutesa, Chwa's son, once he started asking difficult questions on Buganda's independence and refused to sign up to the colonial blueprint for the country's constitutional and political development. Needless to say, in all the above cases, the victims of Britain's deportation orders received no trial whatsoever.

This injustice was obviously contrary to the principles of the Magna Carta, a British instrument passed in 1215 that guaranteed liberties and freedoms for the population, described by Lord Denning as the "greatest constitutional document of all times—the foundation of the freedom of the individual against the arbitrary authority of the despot."[244] The question then is, why did Britain not apply the Magna Carta's rules and its standard of justice in the Empire? The answer lies in the fact that the Magna Carta was actually used to justify colonisation under the guise of spreading civilisation across the world. When asked whether to celebrate the Magna Carta Day through the British Empire, K. W. Blaxter of the Colonial Office in London, rejected the request on the basis that:

> there is a possibility that the celebration of Magna Carta Day in the colonial Empire might be used for purposes very different from those we desire. In some colonies where ill-disposed politicians are ever on the lookout for opportunities to misrepresent our good intentions, its celebration might well cause embarrassment and in general there is a danger that the colonial peoples might be led into an uncritical enthusiasm for a document which they had not read but which they presumed to contain guarantees of every so-called "right" they might be interested at the moment in claiming.[245]

Blaxter's view, as well that of imperial Britain, demonstrates the double standards that founded colonial rule in Africa and in the rest of the Empire.

However, in the case of Buganda and the threatened deposition, there was no chance or need to challenge the colonial government because the situation dramatically changed before Chwa could be removed. In a sudden and fateful twist of events, he collapsed and died on 22 November 1939, three months after the above letters in which the British Government considered his deposition.[246]

Dr O. Sullivan, his attending physician, reported that around 19 November, the Kabaka developed a temperature, and from then until the 21 became steadily worse. Although his condition was serious, Sullivan did not consider there to be any immediate danger. However, the Kabaka suddenly collapsed on the morning of Wednesday 22 November, and died about 7 am due to heart failure. The Namasole (his mother) was with him when he died.[247]

The timing of Sir Daudi Chwa's demise was fortuitous, for the colonial government. It helped defuse a crisis in which he was, in any case, bound to be deposed. On 24 November 1939, two days after his death, a Regency was announced by the Governor stating that the Native Government of

Buganda had unanimously elected Sir Edward Mutesa, son of the late Kabaka Sir Daudi Chwa, to succeed him. As Mutesa was a minor, three Regents were appointed and sworn in by the Governor of Uganda. They were Prime Minister Martin Luther Nsibirwa, Chief Justice Rauli Kiwanuka, and the Treasurer, Sserwano Kulubya. The Regency lasted three years until Edward Mutesa attained majority age and assumed office in 1942.

Notes

[1] David Livingstone, a leading missionary explorer, had previously called for a worldwide crusade to open up Africa for Commerce, Christianity and Civilisation.
[2] Pakenham, *The Scramble for Africa*, p. xxiii.
[3] Ibid., p. xxv.
[4] See Ferguson, Niall (2004) *Empire: The Rise and Demise of the British World Order and the Lessons for Global Power*, Basic Books, New York, USA.
[5] On the rapacity and overlordship of the BEIC in India, see Tharoor, Shashi (2017) *Inglorious Empire: What the British did to India*, London: Hurst & Company, pp.1-36.
[6] Pakenham, *The Scramble for Africa*, p. 414.
[7] See generally, Arne, P. (2004) *Karl Peters and German Imperialism 1856-1918: A political Biography*, Oxford Historical Monograph.
[8] Pakenham, *The Scramble for Africa*, p. 415.
[9] Ibid.
[10] Ibid.
[11] In Kagwa Apolo (1953) *Bassekabaka Ba Buganda*, London: MacMillan & Co. Ltd., p. 156, Kagwa states that Lugard ordered the king to sign the agreement.
[12] Pakenham, *The Scramble for Africa*, p. 416.
[13] Ibid.
[14] Perham, M. and Bull, M. (eds.) (1963), *The Dairies of Lord Lugard*, Volume 2, Evanston, III: Northwestern University Press.
[15] Moyse-Bartlett, *The King's African Rifles*, p. 50.
[16] Pakenham, *The Scramble for Africa*, p. 422.
[17] Ibid., p. 424.
[18] Ibid., p. 425-6.
[19] Ibid., p. 426.
[20] Ibid.
[21] Ibid.
[22] Ibid., p. 427.
[23] The IBEAC withdrew all its agents from Buganda on 31 March 1893.
[24] See Jeal, T. (2007) *Stanley: The Impossible Life of Africa's Greatest Explorer*, London: Yale University Press, p. 428
[25] Pakenham, *The Scramble for Africa*, p. 431-432.
[26] Ibid., p. 432.

[27] Ibid., p. 433.
[28] Ibid., p. 428.
[29] See the Provisional Agreement Between Mwanga and Gerald Portal dated 29 May 1893.
[30] The Black Baby. Mr Bull "What, another!! Well, I suppose I must take it in!!!," *Punch Magazine*, 21 April 1894, http://punch.photoshelter.com/image/I0000WOK.ss5MQmc (accessed 3 July 2017).
[31] Colville commanded the disastrous Bunyoro expedition which resulted in bringing Bunyoro under the Protectorate.
[32] See Article 2 of the 1894 Agreement. Mwanga was not the king of all of Uganda, but the treaty presupposed that all territories adjoining to Buganda were under his control and were thus part of the new Protectorate.
[33] See Lugard, *The Dual Mandate in British Tropical Africa*, p. 203.
[34] Low & Pratt, *Buganda and British Overrule*, p.12.
[35] On the legality of agreements with native rulers, see generally Ibingira S. K. Grace (1973) *The Forging of an African Nation*, New York: The Viking Press, Inc., p. 13-19.
[36] Lugard, *The Dual Mandate*, p. 207.
[37] Low & Pratt, *Buganda and British Overrule*, p. 15.
[38] Samwiri Lwanga-Lunyiigo, in (2007) *The Struggle for Land in Buganda 1888-2005*, pp. 6, 30 and 32, argues that Sir Apolo Kagwa accumulated plenty of land through the settlement under the 1900 Agreement allocations, intimidation, and outright fraud.
[39] According to his will, Kagwa owned 100 square miles of land—16 square miles granted to him under the 1900 Agreement; 26 square miles granted to him by the Lukiiko out of the 8,000 square miles; 20 square miles granted to him from the British Government's shares; and 38 square miles directly purchased by himself.
[40] On the relationship and bitter power rivalry between Kagwa and Kakungulu in Buganda's politics, see Twaddle, Michael (1993) *Kakungulu and the Creation of Uganda*, London: James Currey, pp. 108-129 and Lwanga-Lunyiigo, Samwiri (2011) *Mwanga II: Resistance to Imposition of British Colonial Rule in Buganda* pp. 85-87, 118-119 and 198.
[41] Kagwa, Apolo (1953) *Bassekabaka Ba Buganda*, pp. 261-264.
[42] Ibid, p. 207.
[43] On the making and implementation of the 1900 Uganda Agreement (which was, in fact, an agreement with the kingdom of Buganda alone, and did not include other domains which were to become part of the Uganda Protectorate), see FCO 141/18259-18260.
[44] Catholics fought Protestants and Muslims, while Baganda traditionalists fought both the Catholics and Protestants.
[45] Johnston's letter to Clement Hill, dated 16 January 1901.
[46] Ibid.

[47] The coronation, originally scheduled for 26 June 1902, was postponed at short notice to 9 August 1902 because the king had been taken ill and required immediate surgery.
[48] Johnston's letter to the Marquess of Lansdowne K. G., 24 January 1902.
[49] Low & Pratt, *Buganda and British Overrule*, p. 182.
[50] Original letters from the Regents to Johnston on FCO 141/18259 TNA. The translations are available at the Entebbe Secretariat Archives A6/8 and SMPC. 450, reproduced in Low, D. A. (1971) *The Mind of Buganda, Documents of the Modern History of an African Kingdom*, London: Heinemann, pp. 32-36.
[51] Ibid., p. 33, the Regents' letter to F. J. Jackson, 16 January 1900.
[52] Ibid., pp. 34-35.
[53] Ibid., pp. 35-36.
[54] Bishop Tucker to Fox, 11 January 1900, FO 2/378, reproduced in Low & Pratt, *Buganda and British Overrule*, p. 39.
[55] Letter from Johnston to Jackson, 5 January 1900, E.S.A S.M.P C450, reproduced in ibid., p. 37.
[56] Concerning the Regents' letter of 13 January, in ibid., pp. 43-44.
[57] Low & Pratt, ibid., p. 44.
[58] Johnston to Jackson, 24 January 1900, E.S.A S.M.P C450 in ibid., p. 56.
[59] Johnston's Memorandum dated 13 February 1900, in ibid., p. 366.
[60] Low & Pratt, ibid., p. 81.
[61] Ibid., p. 88.
[62] See notes on the kingdom of Uganda by an Intelligence Officer, dated 12 October, 1901, FO 2/299.
[63] Awarded by the British Government to men and women in high office or who render extraordinary or important non-military service in a foreign country, and can also be conferred for important or loyal service in relation to foreign and Commonwealth affairs.
[64] See Kaizi, M. *His Highness Edward Daudi Fredrick William Walugembe Mutebi Mutesa II, Kabaka we Buganda* (unpublished copy with author).
[65] Low & Pratt, *Buganda and British Overrule*, p. 245.
[66] Lugard, *The Dual Mandate*, p. 586.
[67] For a detailed account on traditional religion in Buganda, see Sekamwa, J. C. (2016) *Enkuluze y'Ediini y'Abaganda ey'Enono*, Lex Africana Ltd.
[68] Pulford, C. (2007) *Casualty of the Empire: Britain's Unpaid Debt to an African Kingdom*, London: Ituri, p. 38.
[69] Ibid., p. 39.
[70] Tucker, Alfred R. (1910) "Mission and the Development of Uganda" in *World Missionary Conference*, Vol. VII, Edinburgh/New York, pp. 73-74.
[71] Griffiths, T. (2001) "Bishop Alfred Tucker and the Establishment of a British Protectorate in Uganda 1890-1894," *The Journal of Religion in Africa*, 31(1), pp. 92-114.
[72] Ibid.
[73] Lwanga-Lunyiigo (2011) *Mwanga II*, pp. 56-58.
[74] Ibid., p. 62.

[75] Tucker to Wigram 24/4/1893 CMSA G3/A5/O1893.241; and Alfred R. Tucker (1908) *Eighteen Years in Uganda and East Africa*, Vol. I, London: Arnold, p. 270.
[76] Tucker to Stock 30/9/1893 CMSA G3/A5/O1893, 232.
[77] See Johnston's letter to the Lord Salisbury, dated 6 April 1900, FCO 141/18259.
[78] See Low, A. D. (2009) *Fabrication of Empire: The British and the Uganda Kingdoms, 1890-1902*, New York: Cambridge University Press, p. 83.
[79] Griffiths, "Bishop Alfred Tucker," p. 110.
[80] See the Criminal Law (Witchcraft) Ordinance, 1912 in the Laws of the Uganda Protectorate.
[81] Alfred R. Tucker (1911) *Eighteen Years in Uganda and East Africa*, New Edition, Connecticut: Negro Universities Press, p. 284.
[82] Ibid., p. 284.
[83] Ibid., p. 286.
[84] Letter dated 12 March 1900, FCO File 141/18259.
[85] Ibid.
[86] Ibid.
[87] Ibid.
[88] Ibid.
[89] Mutesa II (Kabaka), (1967). *The Desecration of My Kingdom*, Constable & Company Ltd.: London, p. 64.
[90] Ibid. See also letter dated 12 March 1900, FCO File 141/18259.
[91] Although kingdoms in Uganda were abolished by the 1967 Constitution, Mutesa, living in exile in the UK, remained the Kabaka of Buganda and was recognised as such by his subjects who refused to elect another person to replace him as the Kabaka.
[92] Mutesa, *The Desecration of My Kingdom*, p. 61.
[93] Ibid., p. 63.
[94] See the Toro Agreement of 1900, signed between Sir Henry Hamilton Johnson, KCB, Her Majesty's Special Commissioner and Commander-in-Chief for the Uganda Protectorate and the Adjoining Territories representing the Government of Her Britannic Majesty the Queen of Great Britain and Ireland and Empress of India on the one part, and the Kabaka and Chiefs of the District of Toro on the other part.
[95] Ibid., Clause 3. This clause stated that "Chief Kasagama is recognised by Her Majesty's Government as the Kabaka or supreme chief."
[96] See James A. Casada (1977) *Sir Harry Hamilton Johnston: A Bio-bibliographical Study*, Basel: Basler Afrika Bibliographien, p. 23.
[97] See *Celebrations of the Fiftieth Anniversary of the Uganda Protectorate*, File CO/536/210/3, "Imperial and Foreign, Uganda Jubilee: Fifty Years a Model Protectorate," 4 April 1943.
[98] The Black Baby. Mr Bull "*What, another!! Well, I suppose I must take it in!!!*," *Punch Magazine*, 21 April 1894,
http://punch.photoshelter.com/image/I0000WOK.ss5MQmc accessed 3 July 2017.

[99] Brian, L., "A Glimpse into How Citizens of Imperial Britain Felt," in *Heart of Darkness: A Research Guide*, www.ryanweberling.com/heartofdarkness/a-glimpse-into-how-citizens-of-imperial-britain-felt.

[100] Buganda's chiefs and administrative systems were in fact exported to other parts of Uganda. This helped create a sense of suspicion and resentment in other parts of Uganda—particularly in Bunyoro—which felt that Buganda was a sub-agent of British imperialism.

[101] In the Congo, colonial administrators were described by Professor Edgerton as "too young and incompetent; they were sent out, without knowing the native language, without serious training, without a probationary period, to a distant place where they are usually alone." See Edgerton, R. B. (2002) *The Troubled Heart of Africa: A History of the Congo*, St Martin's Press, New York., pp. 162-163. Yet, as William Easterly points out, these "raw recruits had to be tax collectors, census takers, policemen, judges, agronomists, sanitationists, doctors and wise counsellors." See Easterly, W. (2006) *The White Man's Burden: Why the West's Efforts to Aid the Rest Have Done So Much Ill and So Little Good*, Penguin Press, New York., p. 274.

[102] Edmund Burke, referring to the East India Company of the eighteenth century, describes how arrogant British officers did immense harm to India when "a few obscure young men, who having obtained, by ways they could not comprehend, a power of which they saw neither the purpose nor the limits, tossed about, subverted, and tore to pieces … the most ancient and most revered institutions and nations." See speech on Mr Fox's East India Bill, December 1783, in Kramnick, I. (1999) *The Portable Edmund Burke*, Viking Portable Library, Penguin Putman., New York., p. 374. See also Shashi Tharoor (2017) *Inglorious Empire: What the British did to India*, Hurst & Company, London.

[103] In northern Nigeria, Fredrick Lugard set out to rule 10 million people with a staff of nine European administrators and a regiment of the West African Frontier Force consisting of 3,000 African troops under the command of European officers. See Meredith, M. (2005) *The State of Africa: A History of the Continent Since Independence*, Simon and Schuster, London., p. 5.

[104] Pakenham, *The Scramble for Africa*, p. xxv.

[105] Low & Pratt, *Buganda and British Overrule*, p. 3.

[106] Lugard, *The Dual Mandate in British Tropical Africa*, p. 17.

[107] Hochschild, A. (1998) *King Leopold's Ghost: A story of Greed, Terror, and Heroism in Colonial Africa*, Houghton Mifflin Company, New York, p. 71.

[108] Ibid.

[109] Memorandum by P. E. Mitchell, *Relations of the Protectorate Government in Uganda with the Native Government of Buganda*, Government House Entebbe, 15 April 1939.

[110] (1926) A.C. 518.

[111] (1956) Q. B., p. 15. Also because of S.4, Foreign Jurisdiction Act, 1890.

[112] Civil Case No. 50 of 1954, reported in 7ULR.

[113] Ibingira, *The Forging of an African Nation*, p. 15.

[114] Ibid.

[115] Ibid.
[116] Memorandum by Mitchell, op. cit., p. 5.
[117] Pulford, C. (2007) *Causality of the Empire: Britain's Unpaid Debt to an African Kingdom*, London: Ituri.
[118] See Lugard, *The Dual Mandate,* p. 36.
[119] Ibid., p. 35.
[120] Ibid., p. 38.
[121] Mamdani, M. (1983) *Imperialism and Fascism in Uganda*, Heinemann Educational Books, Nairobi., p. 6.
[122] Ibid.
[123] Tharoor, Shashi (2017) *Inglorious Empire: What the British did to India.* Hurst & Company: London; Alavi, Hamza (1982) *Capitalism and Colonial Production: Essays on the Rise of Capitalism in Asia*, Croom Helm; Newsinger, John (2010) *The Blood Never Dried: A People's History of the British Empire.* Trentham Books.
[124] See Monbiot, George "For 300 years Britain has outsourced mayhem. Finally, it's coming home" in *The Guardian*, 8 June 2009.
[125] Stiglitz, Joseph (2018) *Globalization and its Discontents Revisited: Anti-Globalisation in the Era of Trump*, W.W. Norton & Co, New York, pp. 58-59.
[126] Lugard, F. D. (1803) *The Rise of Our East African Empire*, pp. I.585-587, II.69-75.
[127] Miller, Charles (2017) *The Lunatic Express: The Magnificent Saga of the Railways Journey into Africa*, Zeus: UK.
[128] Mitchell, P. (1954) *African Afterthoughts*, London: Hutchinson, p. 169 observes that "Sir Apolo Kagwa was such a centralizer of authority in his own hands, that he and the British Government between them had left no place for the Kabaka when he came of age."
[129] Henry W. West (1972) *Land Policy in Buganda*, London: Cambridge University Press, p. 28 states that "the ruling oligarchy of Abakungu consolidated its own position and, to improve its own security, took care that the prerogative rights of the Kabaka were greatly reduced" and on page 43 he argues that "under Kagwa's guidance the Lukiiko acted in forthright fashion to diminish the power of its political rivals, the infant Kabaka and the abataka."
[130] Buell, R. L. (1928) *The Native Problem in Africa*, Vol.1, London: Macmillan, pp. 576-7 wrote in the mid-1920s that: "At present … the Kabaka occupies a position which is tantamount to that of an ordinary Paramount Chief of one of the second-rate native tribes of Africa. He no longer has any power or control over his own Chiefs and all and sundry officers of the Protectorate Government appear to possess the right to have 'direct access' to the Kabaka, which right was exclusively reserved to the Governor alone. This practice is clearly contrary to the old native principles and system of Government of Buganda Kingdom, and is certainly in direct conflict with the terms of the Uganda Agreement of 1900. At present, in matters of the native administration of Buganda Kingdom, the Provincial Commissioner in Charge of Buganda Province appears to occupy the position which was intended for the Kabaka in the Agreement. The Provincial

Commissioner is now the direct ruler of the native Chiefs of Buganda through his District Officers. Any order issued to the Chiefs by the Kabaka or his government has to be countersigned and approved by the Provincial Commissioner before it can be transmitted to the Chiefs concerned with the natural result that the Chiefs now are beginning to lose their sense of loyalty towards the Kabaka, since he has now come to be looked upon by these Chiefs as merely the headman or superior chief of the natives of Buganda on more or less the same level and receiving a salary from the Protectorate Government in the same way as themselves."

[131] See Low, *Fabrication of Empire*, p. 42.

[132] Ibid., p. 42.

[133] Ibid., pp. 42-45.

[134] The oath was made on 8 August 1914 at the Lubiri in Mengo before H. R. Harris, the Acting Governor.

[135] This was done to help mobilise African natives to join the struggling British war effort. Indeed, after he joined the KAR, the number of recruits dramatically increased. See Kaizi, *His Highness Edward Daudi Fredrick William Walugembe Mutebi Mutesa II*, p. 134.

[136] This was on 17 February 1925, on the visit of the Duke and Duchess of York to Buganda.

[137] See Apolo Kagwa and Zakariya Kisingiri's letter to the Provisional Commissioner dated 26 February 1914.

[138] Together these heads are referred to as *bataka*, meaning custodians of *obutaka* or clan land.

[139] See Low & Pratt, *Buganda and British Overrule*, p. 233.

[140] (1966) EA 514.

[141] See Low & Pratt, *Buganda and British Overrule*, p. 233.

[142] Ibid., p. 235.

[143] Ibid.

[144] Ibid.

[145] Ibid.

[146] Dispatch No. 6 in X3807/36.

[147] Low & Pratt, *Buganda and British Overrule*, p. 236. The distortion of land tenure in Buganda it has its roots in the 1900 Agreement. The beneficiaries took over the best land whenever they could find it, without regard to the rights of those in occupation. In 1908, the British Government approved the Lukiiko land law on the tenure of mailo land grants and confirmed the new order and power of chiefs on the land. From then on, the disenfranchised Bataka and peasant occupants have struggled to regain and protect their land rights.

[148] Dispatch No. 6, op. cit.

[149] See Low & Pratt, *Buganda and British Overrule*, p. 233.

[150] Ibid., p. 238.

[151] Bataka letter to Colonel Stanley dated 6 October 1943.

[152] Ibid.

[153] Letter dated 15 October, 1943.

[154] Ibid.

[155] Ibid.
[156] Ibid.
[157] Ibid.
[158] Ibid.
[159] Governor Charles Dundas's letter to Col. Oliver Stanley, Secretary of State for the Colonies dated 12 November 1943.
[160] See Sir Charles Dundas (1955) *African Crossroads*, London: MacMillan, pp. 214-216.
[161] Ibid., p. 209.
[162] See section on Dundas's reforms below.
[163] Miscellaneous Case No. 19 of 1933.
[164] Ibid.
[165] Law Reports, Uganda Protectorate July 1920-July 1929 Vol. III, pp. 101-104.
[166] Law Reports, Uganda Protectorate 1910-1920 Vol. II, pp. 207-213.
[167] Ibid.
[168] See Mutibwa, P. M. (2016) *A History of Uganda: The First 100 Years, 1894-1995*, Kampala: Fountain Publishers, p. 78.
[169] Ibid.
[170] Ibid.
[171] The Ordinance highlighted the difficult working conditions and the prejudices white settlers had about the African workers. It imposed harsh penalties, including imprisonment, for minor offences. For example, for causing loss, damage or risk to an employer's property, a servant could be fined two months' wages or be condemned to two months in prison.
[172] This must have given rise to the Mau Mau rebellion between 1952 and 1960.
[173] (2012) EWHC 2678 (QB).
[174] Mutibwa, *A History of Uganda*, p. 77.
[175] Ibid., p. 78.
[176] Ibid.
[177] Ibid.
[178] See Lord Lugard's Speech in the House of Lords debate of 13 March 1929, vol. 73 cc 458-503.
[179] Ibid.
[180] Letter Ref. No. "S" 531/49/26, dated 8 May 1929.
[181] Mutibwa, *A History of Uganda*, p. 78.
[182] Ibid.
[183] Letter Ref. No. "S" 953/49/26 dated 26 July 1929. The senior ministers were the Katikkiro, Martin Luther Nsibirwa; the Omulamuzi, Rauli Kiwanuka; and the Omuwanika, Sserwano Wokulira Kulubya.
[184] Low & Pratt, *Buganda and British Overrule*, p. 257.
[185] Ibid.
[186] Ibid.
[187] See "Report of the Joint Committee on Closer Union in East Africa," Vol. II Minutes of Evidence, House of Commons Paper 156.
[188] Cited in Mutibwa, *A History of Uganda*, p. 79.

[189] Ibid.
[190] Low & Pratt, *Buganda and British Overrule*, p. 245.
[191] Sir Apolo Kagwa resigned from the post of Katikkiro on 1 August 1926 after serving the kingdom in various capacities from as far back as the early 1890s.
[192] Low & Pratt, *Buganda and British Overrule*, p. 246.
[193] Ibid., pp. 246 and 248.
[194] Ibid.
[195] Commenting on his relationship with Postlethwaite in his petition to the British Colonial Secretary, Kagwa says "our official relationship became somewhat strained, and I had reason to believe that it was due to his personal animosity which he entertained towards me." reproduced in Low, *The Mind of Buganda*, p. 70.
[196] Postlethwaite was described as a "strong willed and forceful administrator" in Low & Pratt, *Buganda and British Overrule*, p. 214.
[197] Mutibwa, *A History of Uganda*, p. 72.
[198] Low & Pratt, *Buganda and British Overrule*, p. 215.
[199] Ibid.
[200] Governor from 4 February 1925 to 27 July 1932. According to M. Kaizi in *His Highness Edward Daudi Fredrick William Walugembe Mutebi Mutesa II*, p. 91, Gower, who served a term of seven years, was a difficult and complicated man with little care for native opinions.
[201] Pratt, R. C. (1965) "Administration and Politics in Uganda, 1919-1945," in Harlow, V. & Chilver, E. M. (eds.) *History of East Africa.* London: Oxford University Press.
[202] Low & Pratt, *Buganda and British Overrule*, p. 217.
[203] Ibid. See also, His Highness the Kabaka, Daudi Chwa (1928), *Lwaki Sir Apolo Kagwa Yawumula*, Kampala.
[204] Low & Pratt, *Buganda and British Overrule*, p. 217.
[205] See Low, *The Mind of Buganda*, op. cit., p.73.
[206] Low & Pratt, *Buganda and British Overrule*, p. 238-9.
[207] Letter by Acting Provincial Commissioner Buganda, J. de Delmege to Chief Secretary, Entebbe dated 28 July 1926.
[208] See letter by P. W. Perryman, AG, Chief Secretary to Kabaka Daudi Chwa dated 28 July 1926.
[209] See the *Uganda Herald*, 6 August 1926.
[210] See pamphlet by Kabaka, Daudi Chwa (1928) *Lwaki Sir Apolo Kagwa Yawumula*, Kampala.
[211] See Medical Certificate of Death dated 21 February 1927, issued by Dr S. D. Karve, the Colony and Protectorate of Kenya.
[212] On 23 February 1927.
[213] In 1922, the Bataka Federation had requested Chwa to sack Apolo Kagwa.
[214] Extracted from *Munyonyozi* of 30 July 1927, pp. 10-11.
[215] See Mutibwa, *A History of Uganda*, p. 73.
[216] Letter dated 25 November 1926.

[217] Letter by the acting Chief Secretary, P. W. Perryman to the Kabaka, dated 6 December 1926.
[218] Letter by the Chief Secretary, E. B. Jarvis, to the Provincial Commissioner, dated 11 February 1927.
[219] See Low & Pratt, *Buganda and British Overrule*, pp. 226-7.
[220] www.nationalarchives.gov.uk/pathways/firstworldwar/aftermath/counting_cost.htm
[221] Ibid.
[222] Ibid.
[223] Information from the Memoral Gates, a war memorial on Hyde Park Corner in London.
[224] See Colonial Annual Report No. 1112 on Uganda for 1920 at http://libsysdigi.library.illinois.edu/ilharvest/Africana/Books2011-05/466563/466563_1920/466563_1920_opt.pdf
[225] www.nationalarchives.gov.uk/pathways/firstworldwar/aftermath/brit_empire_after.htm
[226] Ibid.
[227] Ibid.
[228] Mutibwa, *A History of Uganda*, p. 75-6.
[229] Mutibwa, *A History of Uganda*, p. 80.
[230] Ibid.
[231] Ibid.
[232] Ibid.
[233] Low & Pratt, *Buganda and British Overrule*, p. 247.
[234] Mitchell, *African afterthoughts*, p. 171.
[235] See Kaizi, *His Highness Edward Daudi*, p. 102.
[236] See letter dated 15 July 1939, of Governor Phillip Mitchell to the Secretary of State at Colonial Office in London.
[237] See The Kabaka's Birthday Celebrations, *The Uganda Herald*, 13 August 1939.
[238] See letter dated 15 July 1939, of Governor Phillip Mitchell to the Secretary of State, op. cit
[239] Letter dated 26 July 1939.
[240] Ibid.
[241] Letter to Sir Phillip E. Mitchel, dated 31 August 1939m signed by the three chiefs, namely, Katikkiro M. L. Nsibirwa, together with the Omulamuzi and Omuwanika.
[242] A letter from Balmoral Castle to J. J. Paskin Esq. of the Colonial Office, dated 6 August, 1939.
[243] See Prempeh I (King of Ashanti), and Adu Boahen (2008) *The History of Ashanti Kings and the Whole Country Itself and Other Writings*, Oxford University Press, p. 43
[244] Lord Denning's assessment of the Magna Carta at its 750th Anniversary. See Lee Simon (2015) "Lord Denning, Magna Carta and Magnanimity," *The Denning Law Journal*, Vol. 27.

[245] Letter from K. W. Blaxter to I. A. D. Wilson Young, dated 4 February 1947, FO 371/61073, ff.7-8 TNA.
[246] An account of the death of His Highness Sir Daudi Chwa, Kabaka of Buganda, and the Accession of his Successor, Mutesa II, November 1939. See Buganda Affairs Relations and H. H. the Kabaka, File CO 536/202/2 TNA.
[247] Ibid.

PHASE II

RATTLING THE COLONIAL ORDER AND AFRICAN AGENCY DURING AND AFTER THE SECOND WORLD WAR (1939-1952)

Protecting the Protector?

Kabaka Daudi Chwa, who attained majority age at the start of the First World War in 1914, died at the start of the Second World War in 1939 when, once again, Britain and its Empire were at the centre of a global confrontation.

Nazi Germany and the Soviet Union had attacked Poland, and in order to stop Hitler's aggression, Britain, France, South Africa, India, Australia and New Zealand had all declared war against Germany. As in the First World War, Britain once again called upon its colonies to protect the Empire. Thus Uganda, like all other British colonies, was sucked into the conflict. Before his death, Chwa had, at the behest of the colonial authorities, once again issued a declaration authorising his subjects to register for the war. In fact, his three chiefs volunteered for service either in Uganda or abroad. The Omukama of Bunyoro also volunteered for military service and made a formal offer of the services of his people for the defence of the British Empire.[1]

In June 1941, the British Government introduced a policy to compel all British "dependencies" to make their surplus funds available for British use during the war. Ugandans served as soldiers in Kenya, Ethiopia, Somalia, Madagascar, the Middle East and Burma (now Myanmar).[2] According to Thompson, a total of 77,000 were enlisted in the war, 279 of whom died in battle, while another 1,615 died of "other causes."[3] Besides men and money, Uganda also contributed staple products such as cotton, a range of food products and strategic war materials such as timber.[4] As Governor Phillip Mitchell reported to his superiors in London, the native government of Buganda and native administrations of the eastern and the western provinces "promised" to contribute £17,000 "for every year during which the war may last and for one year after it ends," which he called "evidence of African loyalty and practical cooperation in the national effort."[5] According to Mutibwa, the contributions were initially made as "gifts" from the people of Uganda, but as the war progressed, these were replaced by loans raised by way of taxes.[6] Mutibwa also notes:

> From March 1942 instructions came from London for Uganda to intensify all forms of local production to assist the war effort, which included the export of all available foodstuffs destined for its neighbours, to imperial forces in the Middle East and Britain … these shortages contributed to the cocktail of economic grievances which ultimately exploded in the strikes and disturbances of January 1945.[7]

Although the British Empire and the Commonwealth countries all emerged from the war as victors and the conquered territories were returned to British rule, the costs of the war and the nationalist fervour that it stoked became a catalyst for the decolonisation that took place in the following decades. Like the First World War, the Second World War devastated and diminished Britain's economy and empire, and, consequently, its role and power in the world. Britain borrowed heavily from various sources to purchase military equipment and to finance the war operations. By the end of the war in 1945, it was virtually broke[8] and the country's world military and economic position was fundamentally transformed, creating a huge disproportion between its real and apparent strength.[9]

The end of the war triggered major changes in British colonial policies across the world and resulted in the granting of full independence to India and Pakistan—the most populous and valuable colonies in the Empire—in 1947. In Africa, it marked the beginnings of a process of decolonisation. African colonies (mostly from East and West Africa) contributed over 372,000 men to the Second World War effort.[10] The experience of fighting alongside white troops gave rise to new African perceptions on the invincibility of the white man and the character and objectives of colonialism. Based on the changed perceptions and the rise of African nationalism, the struggle for independence assumed a new momentum that was ultimately behind the winds of change that swept across Africa in the late 1950s and early 1960s. In Buganda, the end of the Second World War found a new Kabaka at the symbolic helm of the kingdom's political and cultural structure. It also found a politically awakening population that posed a challenge not only to colonial rule but also to the misrule of its traditional chiefly elite.

The prosecution and conclusion of the Second World War brought about a fundamental change in world politics that saw, amongst other things, the rise of the United States of America as a leading world power, and the decline of Britain. That decline went hand-in-hand with the weakening of its authority in the colonies in Africa and Asia, as manifested in the rise of resistance against colonial rule and the demand for self-determination. The decline was also accelerated by the post-war shift in international perceptions of colonial rule and imperialism —particularly in the period after the founding of the United Nations in 1945 and the passing of the Universal Declaration of Human Rights in 1948. With these developments, colonial powers lost the prestige and acclaim they once had. Imperialism hence became outmoded and embarrassing, even to the colonial powers.[11] This resulted in the adoption of a decolonisation policy and, ultimately, the scramble out of Africa—particularly in the 1960s.

The political significance of the Second World War in Buganda is well articulated by Summers and Sikanga, who points out that the legacy of the war was "not simply integration into a broader world and a new world class of returned soldiers, but an increasingly widespread—and critical—re-evaluation of Buganda's alliance with Britain."[12] In that sense, and based on our foregoing analysis, the Second World War was important in shaping the character of British rule and the growth of nationalism in Uganda, but also, contemporaneously, in accelerating the changes that the country witnessed between 1945 and 1962. From the end of the war, in order to protect its interests, Britain shifted from policies that were oriented towards plunder to those that were more covert and steeped in patronage.

Edward F. L. Mutesa II ascended the Buganda throne in 1942 at the age of 18. This was a time of dramatic change both in the global and local politics of colonial rule. As many Ugandan ex-servicemen and veterans returned from the War there was an increased agitation by colonised peoples for freedom from the yoke of imperialism. During this period, while the grip of the colonial administrators loosened and the authority of the native chiefs came under increased challenge by a restive population, organisation and agitation by the Bataka and other disgruntled groups grew stronger. With a weakening native administration and an overstretched colonial administration came the crumbling of the model of indirect rule.

In this context, in order to tighten its hold on Uganda, the increasingly unpopular colonial administration resorted to more force and violence in enforcing its rule. But, at the same time, it also sought to reform native administrations so as to make them more representative and democratic. The proposed reforms were formulated without consultation with or input from the native population or its leadership. The reforms were also not always coherent, consistent or free of contradictions. For example, as we show below, while Governor Charles Dundas sought to give more power to native administrations, Governor John Hathorn Hall, who replaced him, sought to reinforce colonial authority and domination.

Several events from this period help to illustrate the political and social contradictions and tensions, as well as the deteriorating relationship between the coloniser and the colonised. Most notable among these are the Namasole affair of 1941, the Budo student rebellion of 1942, the contentious allocation of land to Makerere College that led to the assassination of Katikkiro Nsibirwa in 1945, and the demonstrations of 1945 and 1949. These events and other factors, such as the rise in the cost of living, the domination of Asians in the ginning and marketing of cotton, and the crisis between 1953 and 1955 on the deposition of Mutesa, all contributed to the rise and growth of African nationalism. The seeds of resistance from this period resulted in the growth of nationalist political movements and the emergence of trailblazers who spearheaded the anti-colonialist struggles and the demand for independence in the late 1950s and early 1960s.

The Namasole Affair of 1941

By the start of the 1940s, there had been a number of socio-political and cultural developments which collectively exerted pressure on social and power relations in Buganda. The Second World War raged on, colonial rule faced more criticism and scrutiny in Uganda, Buganda was coming to terms with the demise of Sir Daudi Chwa, and the new Kabaka Mutesa II was still a minor and under a Regency. However, nothing created a bigger political and cultural crisis in Buganda than the daring decision of the widow of Sir Daudi Chwa and mother of Kabaka Sir Edward Mutesa, Namasole Lady Irene Drucilla Namaganda, to remarry.[13]

The Namasole's resolve to remarry represented a bruising three-dimensional contest: it pitted traditional native values against Christian ones, colonial authority against native power, and Buganda's oligarchy of chiefs against the peasantry. The colonial government, the Church, the Kabaka, the Lukiiko and an outraged and shocked population were all sucked into the ensuing mêlée involving opposing sociocultural and political forces.

The remarriage of a Namasole was considered a taboo and an abomination according to Buganda's customs. The Baganda were thus greatly scandalised when the Namasole, who was six months pregnant with her lover's child, applied for a special licence to marry to Simoni Petero Wakiwugulu Gyagenda Kigozi, a commoner and a Grade A master in a primary school, whom many considered "unsuitable."[14] However, notwithstanding the native customs and feelings, the sympathetic Governor Charles Dundas, basing his decision on English law and custom, granted the special licence to the Namasole for the marriage. Like Dundas, the Protestant Church leadership considered the Namasole's decision to remarry to be in order and consistent with Christian beliefs and thus blessed the wedding. Similarly, but contrary to popular native opinion on the matter, the Katikkiro, Martin Luther Nsibirwa, supported the Namasole's move and provided his car to transport the new couple to and from the church.

When the Namasole's request to remarry first came up in the Lukiiko, consent was reluctantly given for the marriage.[15] However, in just ten days, and under intense public pressure, the Lukiiko reconvened and reversed its decision. The Lukiiko reasoned that (a) the Namasole was reckoned to be equivalent to a Kabaka; (b) she was the "mother of Buganda" who could thus not be married to any other man; (c) if the Namasole remarried, it would be derogatory to the prestige of the Kabaka and the nation; and (d) from time immemorial it had never been desired by the Baganda that the Kabaka should have a second father.[16]

The Lukiiko's revised position put it in direct confrontation with the Governor, the Protectorate Government and the church which had approved the wedding. The Protectorate considered the Lukiiko's new position "incompatible with the customs of civilisation of the British Empire."[17] Through A. H. Cox, the Buganda Resident, it asked the Regents how the Lukiiko would prevent her if the Namasole refused to follow its instructions and got married in a manner sanctioned by laws and the church.[18] The Lukiiko quickly retorted that if she

> prefers to be married rather than to serve her race and be the "mother of Buganda" as Namasole … she should be deprived of all official allowances granted her by the Buganda Government, all official houses, the Lubiri [palace] and her official estates. She will not be invited on any official occasions as Namasole. The reason for the above is that all these things are allotted to her as a public servant.[19]

With that, the battle lines were clearly drawn between Christianity on the one hand, and Buganda customs and traditions on the other, as well as between native and colonial authority.

The Namasole was indignant at the Lukiiko's position. On 29 March 1941, she wrote a letter to Governor Dundas in which she protested the Lukiiko's resolutions forbidding her to marry Kigozi, arguing that there was a precedent for a Namasole remarriage.[20] She appealed to the

Governor's British and religious sensibilities, claiming that "when religion and personal freedoms which exist within the British Empire were introduced into the country, the idea of Namasole not getting married became a dead letter." She signed off her letter with an assurance to His Excellency the Governor: "I shall be getting married … and shall not be the first Namasole to get married." Nothing was going to stop her. She was prepared to give up all her privileges as Namasole. She rejected the Resident's proposal to "travel to South Africa for her health and general educational improvement pending the birth of her child."[21]

According to the Resident, not even the pleas and tears of her son, the present Kabaka, could persuade her to depart from her wishes. She insisted that she wished to marry her paramour, the father of her child. In what was a bold statement, given all the controversy surrounding the affair, the young Kabaka lent her his full support.[22] On 1 April 1941, at St Luke's Church in Kibuye, amidst boos and hisses inside the church and flying stones outside of it, with Reverend Canon Yokana K. Bina presiding, the Namasole was married to Petero Kigozi. Katikkiro Nsibirwa's car, lent to the couple for the occasion, was immobilised and some malicious person made off with its ignition keys. After the wedding, the couple retired to the Lubiri of Lusaka (the Namasole's official residence), but within only two days of the wedding they were asked by the Lukiiko to vacate the palace.[23]

The Lukiiko was not pleased by the defiant actions of the Namasole, or by the support she received from the Regents (especially Katikkiro Nsibirwa), the Church and the Governor. It was particularly indignant about the conduct of the couple or what they called the "marriage feast" in the precincts of the traditionally sacrosanct Lubiri of Lusaka. The Lukiiko did not let matters lie. Stripping the Namasole of her privileges and expelling her from the Lubiri did not appease it, hence, on 21 April 1941 it solemnly resolved that,

> as Simoni Petero Wakiwugulu Gyagenda Kigozi has broken the customs of the State of Buganda and has got married in the official Lubiri of Lusaka, and has held there his marriage feast and has there committed a foul act never before done in Buganda, and has slept there with the wife whom he has married, Irene, it is fitting that he should be prosecuted in a court of law…. [N]othing has hitherto happened such as this, which has given such pain to the hearts of all people in the state of Buganda.[24]

Although the Governor expressed some reservations, he did not object to the resolution.[25] A day after the resolution was passed, Katikkiro Nsibirwa tried to rely on the ambiguity of the Governor's decision to block the prosecution but failed, upon which he angrily dismissed the Lukiiko and ordered its members to go home.[26] This incident heralded calls for his resignation by many prominent chiefs claiming that he had lost the confidence and respect of the country.

Kigozi was promptly charged with the offence of committing an abomination contrary to Kiganda customary laws. The offences were first, marrying in the Lubiri of Lusaka at Lukuli, and second, sleeping in the Lubiri with his wife whom he married there. He denied the charges. The Namasole, in her defence, testified that although she took him to the Lubiri after the wedding, there was no marriage feast. In passing judgment against him, Judge J. S. Kasirye held that the accused was guilty of marrying in the Lubiri of Lusaka and sleeping there. He held:

> In this case we do not mind about marriage allowed by religious rites. But according to the customary laws of this country, Buganda, the Namasole is not allowed to marry a man in the Lubiri of Lusaka, nor to bring any man and lodge him there in the house "Lusaka," or anywhere in the Lubiri.[27]

In a sentence banishing Kigozi, the court ordered that he "must go away from the Kibuga [city] of Mengo and live outside a radius of 30 miles from the Lubiri … and is not allowed to return to the Kibuga within the radius mentioned above, for a period of 4 years."[28] On appeal, the colonial Judicial Adviser of Buganda, affirmed the conviction but substituted a fine of 40 shillings for the sentence imposed by the trial court.[29]

With the judgment banishing Kigozi in hand, the Lukiiko turned its guns on Katikkiro Nsibirwa,[30] Sserwano Kulubya and Ham Mukasa, all of whom, in its eyes, were complicit in the Namasole's remarriage affair and were guilty of siding with the Church and the British Government and not with the Lukiiko. Nsibirwa generally lost popularity as Katikkiro, as he was seen as being arrogant towards the Lukiiko and considered to be supportive of an inimical colonial order. Many thought that he was the father of the Namasole's child about to be born.[31] His sponsorship of the Namasole's remarriage did not help matters. Nor did his futile attempt to block the prosecution of Kigozi as demanded by the Lukiiko. The Lukiiko demanded Nsibirwa and Ham Mukasa's resignation. When the time came, neither his appeals to the Governor nor his strenuous and frantic efforts to convince the county chiefs to spare him would save his tenure. Seeing that the situation was untenable and that his only options were to resign or be dismissed, the Katikkiro tendered his resignation on 1 July 1941. He was replaced by his arch-rival Samwiri S. Wamala, an ultra-traditionalist[32] and leader of the anti-Namasole remarriage campaign in the Lukiiko.

Somehow, Ham Mukasa and Kulubya survived the purge.

With the Namasole cut to size, Kigozi banished, and Katikkiro Nsibirwa down and out, the Lukiiko felt unstoppable. To further stamp its new authority, the Lukiiko soon decided that a new Namasole should be named by the Cow Clan, and that Lady Irene would no longer be called Namasole but just "Mrs Kigozi."[33] The Lukiiko also demanded that the Namasole hand over the Crown, the wedding ring and the Bible given to her on her marriage to the late Sir Daudi Chwa. The Namasole's appeal to the Governor protesting the Lukiiko's position was met with a cold reply to the effect that the Protectorate Government was unable to intervene in a matter which was the Lukiiko's concern. The Church was alarmed by the developments, which it considered to have "profoundly stirred the country" and "upset the balance of the Government by allowing the introduction of a thorough reactionary" as the Katikkiro.[34]

The Christian Missionary Society—recalling the difficulties it had experienced with Sir Daudi Chwa—was concerned about the impact of such developments on the balance of powers in the kingdom and felt that it was vitally important that the young Kabaka Mutesa be "supported by the best influences possible during these years before he takes over the responsibilities of Government."[35] For this reason, he stressed the need for a tutor, Captain F. Crittenden, to take care of the Kabaka's upbringing.[36]

Matters were to get worse for the couple following Kigozi's appearance within the Kibuga on the 24 and 25 of October 1941. The Regents made an application to the Governor for the annulment of the judgment of the Judicial Adviser and the reinstatement of the judgment of the Lukiiko banishing Kigozi. They swore an affidavit to the effect that

> the re-appearance of Simoni Petero Wakiwugulu Gyagenda Kigozi in the area from which he had been excluded gave rise to a renewal of public anger and anxiety and to disturbances of the peace … and unless measures are taken to prevent him … [he] will again enter and frequent the said area with consequent grave danger to the public peace.[37]

Granting the Regents' application, Governor Dundas made an Order that Kigozi "be deported from the area within a radius of thirty miles of the Kibuga to that part of the Protectorate outside the said area."[38] In a separate note, the Lukiiko wrote to the Namasole banning her from referring to herself as the "mother of the Kabaka" and notifying her of the appointment of "another mother of the Kabaka, who is a fit person to fill that position."[39] For that matter, she was prohibited from visiting Sir Edward Mutesa at Mengo, and they made life difficult for her when Mutesa fell ill and was admitted at Namirembe where he underwent an operation in April 1943.[40]

As of May 1948, Kigozi's Deportation Order was still in place, three years beyond the time stipulated in the judgement of the Principal Court. In order to save the Kabaka[41] from an embarrassing situation, the colonial government felt that it was the opportune time for Kigozi to be released from deportation. Accordingly, on 13 May 1948, Governor John H. Hall found it expedient to rescind, as he did, the Deportation Order ending both the Namasole's and Kigozi's misery of seven years. A grateful Namasole penned a brief note to the Governor thanking him for his kindness in rescinding the deportation that "took so long a time."[42]

The Namasole affair had a profound effect on political developments in Buganda and in redefining the relationships between the Church and the Lukiiko,[43] between the Lukiiko and the Protectorate Government, and between the traditionalist and Christian elitist chiefs in Mengo. In the end, the traditionalists within the Lukiiko, backed by the largely disgruntled Bataka elements from the past and the *Abazukulu ba Kintu* (an association of young and radical Baganda), appeared to be the victors in the long drawn-out battle.

It must be said that Governor Dundas' indirect or reluctant support of Katikkiro Nsibirwa in the fray, coupled with his failure or refusal to check the Lukiiko in its excesses against the Namasole and her new husband, gave impetus to the traditionalist group, led by Wamala, to assert their newly founded power. Thus the Namasole affair, particularly the humbling of a powerful Katikkiro and the reigning Namasole, revealed to the natives the power of rebellion and helped incite a political storm in the Lukiiko that would change the politics in Buganda and Uganda.

The King's College Budo Affair of 1942

If the Namasole affair was the main act in the political drama that pitted different power centres in Buganda against one another, then the events at King's College Budo (KCB), unfolding a few days before the coronation of Kabaka Mutesa in November 1942, were a powerful and telling side show with a similar theme. As the leading Buganda-owned and Church-run school, KCB was the coveted training ground for the future leaders of Buganda. In the words of Carol Summers, it was "a place for the next generation's leadership to acquire the academic, social, political and intellectual skills they would need to run colonial Buganda with its inter-locked and cooperating hierarchies of Kingdom, Protectorate and Protestant Church."[44] Indeed, Kabaka Mutesa and other leading Baganda political personalities including Abu Mayanja, Amos Sempa, E. M. K.

Mulira and Senteza Kajubi all went through the school.

The crisis at KCB was essentially one where the students and African staff stood up to the domineering and demeaning conduct of the British-style leadership, led by Dennis Herbert, the Headmaster. The crisis started with complaints by KCB's African teachers about a slackness of discipline, especially regarding drinking binges in the school, insufficient consultations with the school's head, and the poor state of sanitation and the teachers' quarters.[45] The headmaster resisted his staff's recommendations and dismissed their complaints as "pre-coronation jitters."[46]

The teachers took this as typical British contempt towards Africans. As the coronation day approached, the students decided that it was time to challenge British domination in the school. They replaced the school's portrait of the King of England with a portrait of the Kabaka. Even when Herbert restored the picture of the English king, it was once again removed. Herbert conceded and moved it to a different wall, leaving that of the Kabaka in its place. The symbolic triumph on the position of the Kabaka's portrait over the English king's was not lost on any of the actors. The defiant student action was soon followed by the stoning of Miss Hammand, a missionary teacher, who confronted some boys near the girls' dormitory after dark.

When summoned to explain the indiscipline, the student leadership instead raised the problems of sex and alcohol that undermined the reputation of Europeans, African teachers, and some students. The Head Prefect alleged that some European teachers were involved in acts of homosexuality with students in their homes. According to Summers, seven European men were implicated, including the Kabaka's tutor, Freddie Crittenden—who was immediately recalled to the army and blacklisted by the Colonial Office.[47]

The students' grievances and anger continued, leading to a boycott of activities organised by the headmaster, including a debate that the Resident of Buganda was to attend. Those who attempted to attend the debate were stoned. The grass-thatched roof of the carpentry workshop was set on fire, while the controversial portrait of the King of England was this time damaged and thrown away. Calls for cooperation between the staff and student leadership failed to make any headway. The situation at the school quickly got out of control as the headmaster, European staff, African staff and student leadership traded blame. Eventually, Herbert called police to restore order. Attempts by Katikkiro Wamala and S. W. Kulubya to restore calm were futile, which forced the Resident and the Protectorate's Director of Education to close the school on 12 November 1942.

The next day, mirroring the actions of the Lukiiko in causing Nsibirwa's resignation, the staff sent a memorandum asking Bishop Stuart to sack Herbert. In response, the Protectorate Government instead set up a Commission to investigate the entire affair. In a critical report, the Commission found Herbert to be as "ludicrously out of place as a headmaster in a school of unruly, oversexed adolescents with love for beer-swilling and stone throwing."[48] Herbert was described as "spineless and incompetent."[49] In spite of these findings, the CMS did not ask him to resign but let him stay as the head of KCB until 1946. The complaining teachers and some of the vocal students were not as lucky: 18 teachers resigned, prefects were stripped of their ranks, and 23 students were sent away.[50]

The Budo affair, just like the Namasole's before it, was significant in bringing to the fore the growing African resistance to oppressive authority, colonial or otherwise. As a microcosm of Buganda, the crisis in Budo mirrored the growing tension between the Protectorate, Buganda's leadership, and its population. It represented a shift, and a growing rift, in the relationship between the coloniser and the colonised. Summers succinctly sums up the situation:

> Baganda, missionaries and Protectorate officials recognised that the events of 1942 marked a new sort of uncertain politics that would not immediately settle down into social peace. Baganda protestors, even those unaffiliated with the school, connected Budo's troubles to their sense of grievance against the Christian Mission and Protectorate's polices and their belief that British paternalism was unreliable.[51]

Although Edward Mutesa is silent about the Budo rebellion in his book, *The Desecration of My Kingdom*, there is no doubt that this episode at his old school would have provided a basis for his political outlook as he ascended Buganda's throne and beyond. It can also be argued that the defiant spirit demonstrated in his relations with British authorities had its roots in this epoch. Building on the rebellious disposition developed in the Namasole and Budo affairs, the political unrest and native hostility towards the colonial state escalated after the coronation of Kabaka Mutesa in 1942.

Mutesa's Coronation and His Pledge of Allegiance to King George VI

Kabaka Edward Mutesa attained majority age in 1942. This marked the end of the Regency and the start of his full assumption of office as the Kabaka of Buganda. The Protectorate at this time was under the governorship of Charles Dundas. On the day of his coronation, Mutesa underwent both traditional and Christian rituals at Budo, the historic hill where all Buganda's kings are installed. Once these important ceremonies were completed, and standing before the tall and imposing Governor Dundas, the Kabaka, who admitted to being more fluent in English than Luganda, took the official and the judicial oaths in a flawless English accent as follows:

> I, Edward Mutesa II, Kabaka of Buganda, do hereby swear that I will well and truly govern the kingdom of Buganda in accordance with the laws and customs heretofore established,
>
> AND THAT I will conform to the laws and regulations instituted for the Government of Uganda by his Majesty's Government,
>
> AND THAT I will cooperate loyally with His Majesty's Government in the organisation and administration of the kingdom of Buganda,
>
> AND THAT I will administer justice in accordance with the laws and usages of my country, so help me God.[52]

While Mutesa's overall *savoir-faire* and accent must have mesmerised his adoring subjects, the fact that he pledged allegiance to and undertook to serve King George VI must have saddened the more discerning Baganda. This is because the oaths he took underscored the reality that his position and rule was largely ceremonial and severely limited by and subject to the will of the British king. With the above oaths signed and witnessed by Governor Dundas and Katikkiro Wamala, two interesting speeches followed. The first was by Dundas, who, with colonial and hegemonic flair, lectured the congregation and the young king as follows:

> I need not remind you of the allegiance you owe to our Sovereign Lord the King, but I can assure you that allegiance will never conflict with your duty to your people. For His Majesty's only desire is that all his subjects shall live according to their own ways, in enjoyment of every benefit their countries can afford them, but also with all advantages of membership in the vast community of His Empire.
>
> No people can have better security for their freedom than this overlordship. In faith thereon, I ask you always to have trust in those

appointed by His Majesty to govern this land, to collaborate wholeheartedly and confidently with us and to regard us as your true friends and advisers…

Your Highness assumes rulership in the midst of war … we have good reason to anticipate that, unlike many a land less fortunately situated, Buganda will emerge from these years of trial unscathed, nay, perhaps even in a better estate than before.

With these thoughts in mind, we feel assured that Your Highness assumes rule of your country with the brightest prospects; that with your accession, there is ushered in a time of unexcelled prosperity, progress and content for your land and people.[53]

Governor Dundas, more than his predecessors, believed in strengthening traditional leadership of Buganda. Thus in 1944, two years following Mutesa's coronation, he proposed reforms aimed at giving Africans more power in the management of their affairs. His proposals, discussed in more detail below, suggest that he was sincere in extending Mutesa the hand of friendship and promising him Buganda's progress under his leadership. Elsewhere, Governor Dundas noted that he found Mutesa always respectful and eager to seek advice, but that he never hesitated to express his own views. Dundas thought that this was a virtue rare among Africans, saying "they are prone to conceal their thoughts and are lacking in the courage of conviction." Because of the confidence he had in this young ruler, Dundas felt it safe to relax administrative control in Buganda.[54]

In the midst of a great war, it was necessary for Britain to be on good terms with all its colonies which, as shown above, were supporting the war effort. In fact, Governor Dundas' speech before the Lukiiko on 2 October 1944, two years after the coronation, as well as his attitude earlier in the Namasole affair were all taken by the Lukiiko as giving in to Buganda's demands for "home rule". According to the Resident of Buganda, native newspapers published in January 1945 were running editorials to the effect that "the Governor had empowered the Kabaka to rule his country for himself."[55] In view of this, it is not surprising that on 28 May 1945, the Kabaka, without any real consultations with or approval by the Protectorate Government, made changes in his government and decreased the number of chiefs by retiring those he considered past their prime.[56]

The Protectorate took the Kabaka's actions as indications of "a deliberate attempt to assert independence and freedom from Protectorate Government's control far beyond the terms of the 1900 Agreement."[57] It was thus felt necessary to bring the Kabaka and the Lukiiko back into line and to reaffirm to them "the correct view of the relations between the

British administration and the Buganda Government."[58] However, as the war ended and Dundas' replacement as Governor took office, the promises to strengthen and progress the Kabakaship were abandoned and the policies granting more authority for African self-rule reversed. The events and actions of the colonial government that followed Mutesa's coronation in the build up to and after independence, including the summary deposition and deportation of Mutesa, thus brought into question Britain's sincerity in asserting that British colonial officials were Buganda's "true friends, protectors and advisers."[59]

The second speech at the coronation was made by Katikkiro Wamala who, in the name of the Kabaka, thanked the Governor for officiating and for a great and impressive speech

> I am confident that this cooperation is going to continue, especially during these very difficult times over which the war has cast its sinister shadows; a war which we are fighting in the cause of liberty and freedom.... In the midst of this joy and happiness, I must recall a similar day as this one in the year 1914 when the British Empire bore arms against our enemy, Germany, and today's circumstances have repeated themselves similar to those when His Late Highness Kabaka Daudi Chwa II was crowned.
>
> Then, as it is now, Germany fought against us in an effort to destroy that liberty and freedom which we all enjoy in the British Empire. I would like to take this opportunity of thanking all those who, in the fulfilment of the obligations of the Kingdom of Buganda, have given their services in this cause and also thank the people of Buganda for giving themselves up and thus providing their loyalty to the great Empire, which is protecting us.
>
> Undoubtedly, this war has caused considerable hardships in various directions, but in spite of such hardships, we are full of confidence that with fortitude and in cooperation with the protecting Government, we shall attain victory.[60]

Coming in the wake of the Namasole crisis and the ouster of Nsibirwa, Wamala's speech, thanking the Baganda for their loyalty to the great Empire in return for its "protection," was laden with sarcasm. Although Britain regarded Buganda as the "gem of the Empire," its relationship with Buganda was by 1943 fast souring. Moreover, Wamala belonged to the faction of anti-colonial traditionalist chiefs in control of the kingdom who were responsible for the ouster of the Nsibirwa group. The Wamala group was vehemently opposed to colonial rule, which is the reason Wamala was later removed as Katikkiro, as detailed below.

It is noteworthy that Wamala's speech twice referred to the notion of "liberty and freedom" and reminded the Governor of Buganda's sacrifices for the Empire in the fight for these ideals. However, reading between the lines, he could have been talking about Buganda's fight for liberty and freedom from colonial rule. Similarly, his optimism that fortitude and cooperation with the protecting government would deliver victory could have been expressed in reference to Buganda's victory against colonial rule rather than Britain's victory in the Second World War. Wamala's stance on the land question and his anti-colonial activities following the coronation offer some useful clues on these issues.

Marking Fifty Years of Colonial Rule in Uganda

On 1 April 1943, as the Second World War raged, the colonial government marked the fiftieth anniversary of British rule in Uganda. The British monarch, King George VI, sent a congratulatory message to the Kabaka and the people of the Protectorate for the "notable progress" in the five decades and took pride "in the fact that this progress has been made with British guidance and help."[61] On its part, the kingdom of Buganda wrote to the British representative in Buganda congratulating the Protectorate Government on the occasion of the fiftieth anniversary of the British flag being hoisted in Uganda, and Uganda being proclaimed a Protectorate.[62]

The chief ministers were particularly thankful to Britain for saving Buganda "from falling into the hands of another nation which, under its leadership, would be totally unable to make a mutual agreement with [Buganda] … an agreement which [was] entirely in good spirit such as the one between Britain and [Buganda]."[63] They also pointed out that:

> Throughout the time of our development we have always received both advice and protection from the British Government. We are very thankful due to the matters which have led our country to make progress, as brought about by both government officials and missionaries, because without these its progress would have been very negligible.[64]

The Protectorate's Ministry of Information published a document in which it declared that far from being a "black foundling" or "squalid derelict" that the British had in 1893 thought it would be, Uganda had turned out to be the "gem of the Empire." The statement read, in part, that:

> Uganda has not been slow or niggardly in answering the call to colours. In the war of 1914-1918 thousands of her men served in the East African Campaign. In 1943, 50,000 are in Khaki, in fighting units, and with medical, pioneer and labour services and hundreds more are enlisted each week that goes by. They have gone far afield, to the Middle East, to

> Ceylon and Madagascar after playing their part in the conquest of Mussolini's African Empire. More than that, for one purpose or another, in gifts or interest free loans from the central government and native authorities, Uganda has already added three quarters of a million pounds to the Imperial war chest; she has thus helped to ease the privations of victims in Great Britain. She has sent money to buy mobile canteens and food vans, including one presented to the City of Liverpool, as the Kabaka's personal gift while public subscriptions raised by the Uganda War Fund, to a present total of over £130,000, have put a Uganda Squadron of the Royal Air Force into the skies, equipped the cruiser MMS "Uganda" and with aircraft, and supported the Charity, Comfort and Welfare Funds of the Services and the Merchant Navy. When her present task is accomplished, we may safely predict that Uganda will resume her onward and upward progress and that the foundling of 1893 will have gained the place and stature of a self-reliant and vigorous member of the British Commonwealth.[65]

The British press carried stories to the effect that Uganda represented the best elements in the polities of the British Empire. It was hailed as "a cardinal example of the principle of the dual mandate and a great testimony to Lord Lugard's foresight and statesmanship."[66] Other commendations were that "the Protectorate had developed into one of the most prosperous and progressive territories in the colonial Empire" and that "the Protectorate had the best roads, the most schools, and, in some parts, the highest standards of living among the African peoples of the East African territories."[67]

The above accounts suggest that after fifty years of colonial rule in Uganda, relations between the "protector" and the leadership of the "protected" peoples were excellent. But there was more that could have been said at this time. Whereas there is no doubt that the "protector" was taking enormous benefit from this relationship and control of the "gem of the Empire," the same could not be said for the "protected" people therein. As subsequent events show, this period was characterised by a growing unease amongst the "protected" masses who bore the ultimate brunt of imperialism and whose grievances regarding the dispossession of land, forced labour, poor wages, high taxes and the high cost of living erupted into deadly riots just two years after the jubilee party.

Notwithstanding the satisfaction and elevated sense of accomplishment after fifty years of colonial rule, the riots which followed soon after took the British by complete surprise. The aftermath of the riots saw a marked shift in the relationship, characterised by a more ruthless colonial policy on the one hand and a more rebellious population on the other. Thus, whereas in 1943 the colonial "protectors" had been in alliance with (B)Uganda's traditional leadership against the "protected" ordinary people, a decade later the traditional leadership had teamed up with the "protected peoples" against their protector.

It is paradoxical that increased hostility to the colonial state in Buganda came against the backdrop of a relatively liberal attitude towards native rule spearheaded by Governor Dundas. According to Low and Pratt, Dundas had a "nearly dogmatic faith in the ability of native authorities to adapt themselves to meet their own needs."[68] For example, it was he who paved the way for Nsibirwa's purge in 1941 and, more importantly, advocated reforms aimed at making Buganda more self-reliant as it prepared itself for self-government. In what are known as the "Dundas reforms," the Governor wanted Buganda to become "an outstanding example and a model of governance of Africans by Africans."[69] It would appear though, based on the protests of 1945, that these efforts at reform were ineffective and unappreciated by the Baganda, since they did not go far enough to address their immediate demands and expectations. As such, Dundas' short-lived regime, far from ameliorating the colonial brunt, emboldened African colonial critics and gave them a chance to organise and mobilise against British rule.

The Land Question and the Assassination of Katikkiro Martin Luther Nsibirwa

Resistance to British colonial rule in Buganda mainly coalesced around the controversy on the ownership and control of land, with its roots in the controversial land allotments under the 1900 Agreement. The land crisis in Buganda became a constant sore spot for the colonial and native governments and a core rallying cry for Bataka activism. Coupled with other political and economic grievances against British rule—high taxes, forced labour, poor wages, economic hardship resulting from the war and low commodity prices, as well as demands for more representation in the Lukiiko—the land injustices metamorphosed the Bataka agitation into an anti-colonial political movement.

Agitation on the land problem, which had started in the 1920s, along with the increased hostility towards colonial rule in Buganda came to the fore once again in 1943 when the Protectorate Government made proposals to acquire land for the expansion of Makerere College and the establishment of an Empire Cotton-Growing Research Station in Kampala. The new Lukiiko—dominated by an ultra-conservative leadership under Wamala—was required to pass a law granting the government permission to acquire land compulsorily for public purposes, but its members were suspicious and strongly opposed to the idea. They felt that the law was intended, as was the case in Kenya, to secure Buganda's land for European settlers. Protests were organised and, in 1944, a pamphlet entitled *Buganda Nyaffe* was published, criticising the Protectorate Government's demand for land in Buganda.[70]

In the Lukiiko, the proposed law was almost solely supported by S. W. Kulubya but was vehemently opposed by the rest of the members. Because of his position on the proposed law, Kulubya, who narrowly survived lynching over the Namasole affair and was considered a British protégé, like Nsibirwa before him, was forced to resign in the protests of January 1945 (described below).[71]

The strong opposition to the proposed law in Buganda forced the colonial government to make changes such that it was the Kabaka and not the Protectorate Government that was to be granted the power to compulsorily purchase land for public purposes.[72] The new Bill was styled as the "Law to Empower the Kabaka to Acquire Land for Purposes Beneficial to the Nation."[73] But even with these changes, the Lukiiko refused to pass it. It took the removal of Katikkiro Wamala from office (deported by the British in a general purge of troublesome elements under the accusation of inciting the January 1945 protests) and the reappointment of M. L. Nsibirwa in his place to get it passed. Thanks to his forceful disposition, Nsibirwa prevailed over a reluctant Lukiiko to pass the land acquisition law on 4 September 1945.

To achieve this goal, a buoyed Nsibirwa spoke for hours in support of the law and, in spite of the stiff resistance of the Lukiiko, he carried the day, but paid the ultimate price as a result.[74] On 5 September 1945, a day after the law was passed, Nsibirwa was assassinated as he arrived for morning prayers at Namirembe Cathedral, as was his daily custom.

Nsibirwa's assassination shocked the country and the colonial government. The new Governor, John H. Hall, was astounded by the tragic news. In a message communicating the death, he said:

> This shameful and cowardly outrage has robbed Buganda of a great and fearless patriot and a great and wise Katikkiro who, answering the call of duty, left his well-earned retirement to help the Kabaka and his country at a critical time.... [I]n that task he has sacrificed his life just as a brave soldier lays down his life for his country.... [F]or the man who committed this foul murder ... there can be nothing but execution. They deserve and will receive no mercy.[75]

The Governor offered a reward of £1,000 for evidence leading to a conviction, and one G. W. Senkatuka was subsequently tried and sentenced to death for the murder. The Governor also quickly signed deportation orders to the Seychelles Islands for 14 persons who he believed were conducting themselves “so as to be dangerous to peace and good order in Uganda.”[76] The application for their deportation was made by D. R. Robertson, Acting Resident of Buganda, who stated that the deportees were “associated with those who planned the political disturbances in Uganda during January 1945, that they are the leading agitators against the acquisition of private lands for public purposes, and that the murder of Martin Luther Nsibirwa on 5 September 1945 was planned by those agitators.”[77]

The Kabaka was equally stunned and saddened by the violent murder of his loyal old man.[78] He said that he had high hopes that Nsibirwa’s leadership would help restore calm after the January protests He was particularly pained by the manner and place of the assassination. He castigated the perpetrators of the dastardly crime and appealed to the public to refrain from such evil acts for the good future of Buganda.[79]

Bishop Stuart’s sermon at the funeral service was equally melancholic. He preached: “this crime did not come on us suddenly. It is the result of months and years of gradual deterioration of the lives of some Baganda.”[80] Nsibirwa was replaced by a son of Sir Apolo Kagwa: Kawalya Kagwa, who was at that time serving in the King’s African Rifles. Paulo Kavuma observes that “like Nsibirwa, Kawalya Kagwa was really appointed by the Protectorate administration, not by the Kabaka, because His Highness, who was still a young man, did what the Governor wanted.”[81] Kavuma’s observation underlines the power vested in the colonial administration *vis-à-vis* the powerlessness of the Kabaka.

The appointment of Kawalya Kagwa as the new Katikkiro could not have come as a surprise. Clearly, after the experiment with Wamala and his traditionalist and radical group, and after the riots of January 1945, the colonial government needed to have a steady hand and a pro-British man of Apolo Kagwa’s pedigree and loyalty at the helm in Buganda. It is for this same reason that the Protectorate Government had returned a reluctant Nsibirwa to office. In the reappointment of Nsibirwa and appointment of Kawalya Kagwa, the colonial government disregarded and was insensitive to the negative public opinion on the old chiefly oligarchy, especially those perceived to be protégés of Apolo Kagwa. As we have shown, this attitude tended to have disastrous consequences for this category of Buganda’s chiefs. Yet, in spite of the tragic death of Nsibirwa, the colonial government was not minded to change the law on the compulsory acquisition of land, or to make serious reforms to address the injustices on the ownership and control of land in Buganda.

The 1945 Protests in Buganda

The hitherto simmering tensions between the colonial state, Buganda's chiefly class and the disgruntled groups in Buganda, such as the Abataka, blew up in January 1945.[82] For the entire month, with the Protectorate Government and police taken by complete surprise, the country was rocked by a series of unprecedented protests and strikes that were misleadingly characterised as mere "disturbances" or else "riots" by the colonial administration.[83] These spread like wildfire across the Protectorate starting from Masaka to Entebbe, Kampala, Mpigi, Mubende, Jinja and Mbarara.[84] They also extended to Lugazi, Iganga, Mbale and Tororo.[85]

With an un-prepared police force, and while both the new Governor Hall and the Kabaka were away (in Karamoja and on a hunting expedition respectively) the situation rapidly became chaotic. The protestors had varied objectives and demands, the prime ones being stirring up popular feeling against the Protectorate Government, securing wage increments for the workers, protesting high prices for goods, agitating for the resignation of S. W. Kulubya as Buganda's Omuwanika (Treasurer), and demanding more representation in the Buganda Lukiiko.[86] The protests were masterminded by I. K. Musaazi and J. M. Kivu and included thousands of "houseboys," tailors, hospital staff, clerks, government labourers, drivers and farmers. They paralysed work in government offices, residences and the private sector.

To bring the situation under control, the Governor and the Kabaka were rushed back to Kampala and the police were reinforced with the army on the streets. The strikes, which were largely peaceful at the start, became more and more violent as the days passed, reaching a climax on 15 January. Governor Hall warned that firearms would be used and that the police and military would direct their fire on the ringleaders. This and other attempts to pacify the protestors were futile.

Between 19 and 23 January, the protestors converged at Mengo, in the Lukiiko courtyard, demanding the Kabaka and his leading chiefs respond to the injustice of the deaths of their members at the hands of the Protectorate forces.[87] On the 19th, they refused to allow Omuwanika Kulubya to address them. However, they listened when the Chief Justice, Omulamuzi Kiwanuka, asked them to return the next day, as the Kabaka was away. As soon as the Kabaka returned to Mengo that day, the protestors held him up for at least half an hour and castigated him for "seeking his own pleasure when his people are suffering."[88] They returned on the 20 January and, in the Kabaka's presence, raised the issue of wages and demanded that he sack Kulubya, who they considered to be "cold, ungenerous and entirely European in outlook."[89]

They were asked to wait as the Kabaka consulted his advisors. The crowds returned on the 23rd to see him and were told that he had appointed a special committee, headed by Kulubya, to look into Buganda's government salaries. Dissatisfied with this measure, they refused to leave, even when they were asked by the Kabaka through a messenger and by the Resident to disperse. They remained peaceful nonetheless.

The protestors' "ceasefire" did not last long. They soon ran out of patience and roughed up Kiwanuka, the Omulamuzi, as he entered the palace. They then started looking for Kulubya who was hiding in the premises. Upon being told that the mob had set the palace on fire (which was false), Kulubya tendered his resignation.[90]

The Kabaka, who described the protests as "serious," was hesitant to accept Kulubya's resignation, having rung to ask the advice of the Resident (who in turn asked the Governor) and been advised not to accept it.[91] But when the menacing crowd delivered to the Kabaka a 30-minute–long ultimatum either to accept the resignation or be deposed, he accepted it.[92] Once the news of Kulubya's resignation was released, the jubilant crowds peacefully dispersed. According to Hanson,

> that evening, Governor Hall made broadcasts by loudspeakers in Kampala claiming that the "misguided," "wicked" strikes and disorders had been carefully planned to achieve a purpose that was "primarily political and not economic." The leaders, who had stayed in the background, had "incited Government labourers to strike" with a "hidden motive" "to bring forcible pressure on the young ruler of Buganda to compel him to carry out certain changes in his Government."[93]

To resolve the crisis and restore order during the protests, the colonial state resorted to brutal force and violence, firing indiscriminately at the protestors with live ammunition and smoke bombs. It also subsequently purged and deported suspected leaders without trial. Unlike the peaceful "talks" the protestors had with the Kabaka over the resignation of S. W. Kulubya, the Governor did not offer the protestors a chance to communicate their grievances, let alone attempt a civic or negotiated settlement, even though the Kulubya matter had shown it was possible to reach a peaceful resolution. The police arrested and prosecuted over 558 strikers, 335 of whom were later convicted. There was no evidence as to whether there was a plot, or who the ringleaders were, so no ringleaders were ever prosecuted.[94]

In the absence of evidence, and because the Governor needed to purge some difficult elements, he resorted to the draconian Deportation Ordinance to detain and later deport the suspects, namely, Katikkiro Samwiri Wamala, Joshua Mavumirizi Ndifiirakumazima Kivu, Fenekansi Musoke, Bulasiyo Kayonga and Ignatius Musaazi. The deportation orders were made without any trials. Samwiri Wamala, who was forced to resign as Katikkiro, died mysteriously while under deportation.[95] He was quickly replaced by the more loyal and trusted M. L. Nsibirwa, who had been removed as Katikkiro in 1941, while Serwano W. Kulubya, was replaced by Michael Kawalya Kagwa, a son of the late Apolo Kagwa, as Omuwanika.

In total, eight unarmed strikers were shot and killed by policemen, special constables and the KAR. Numerous others were wounded. None of the dead were Baganda. Property, including telegraphic communication cables, railway facilities and motor vehicles, was destroyed.[96] A one-man Commission of Inquiry headed by N. H. P. Whitley was set up.[97] In a report dated 14 June 1945, the Commission concluded that the origins of the disturbances were political, not economic, and that the plotters had in "view, amongst other aims, the deposing of the Kabaka … and [to] get rid of Kulubya."[98] Criticising the leadership of Wamala as "unsatisfactory," "vindictive," and filled with "intrigue," the Report stated:

> Buganda seems to be the only part of the Protectorate which is badly infected with the political virus and it may be hoped that these disturbances may prove to have been a blessing in disguise, as having in good time brought to light some of the troubles which require to be remedied.[99]

The Report wholly downplayed the economic factors spurring the strike and stated that "the organisers were not really interested in the wages of the workers at all and that they made use of the wages question as a means to bring the workers out on strike so as to further their own personal ends."[100] On how the Protectorate Government handled the strikes, the Report had nothing but "praise and appreciation of the prompt, firm, efficient and patient manner in which the Protectorate Administration Officers and the police grappled with a sudden emergency."

According to Commissioner Whitley, "the police did magnificently" and "the military also did extremely well" but "the Native Administration Police do not appear to have been of much use—as there can be little doubt that they had been infected by the organisers."[101]

The Report recommended some *ex-gratia* compensation to the family of one Indian who was killed and to an African whose house was burnt.[102] But it made no mention whatsoever of compensation for the deaths of the eight Africans who were killed or the fourteen who were wounded, finding it sufficient to say that, in respect of all other matters, "the Government has disclaimed all responsibility."[103]

A critical review of the Whitley Report shows that the Commissioner was not wholly objective, judicious or thorough in his approach and hence he reached the wrong conclusions. For example, there is no evidence that the strikers aimed to depose the Kabaka or overthrow his government. The strikers were mostly peaceful and specific in their demand for Kulubya's resignation. The Report also ignores the fact that the strikers, coming from different parts of Uganda, were more united in their demands for increased wages than in a common political goal to oust the regime in Mengo. Why would strikers from diverse areas such as Tororo, Mbale, Jinja and Mbarara—all of which are outside the Kingdom of Buganda—be concerned with or participate in a plot to overthrow the Kabaka in Mengo? It would appear that Whitley's mind was made up *a priori* on the causes of the strike and that his report was intended to lend support to Governor Hall's public pronouncements that the purpose of the strikes was primarily political and not economic.

Clearly, the Report obscured and trivialised the economic impact of inflation resulting from the Second World War and made no mention of other economic grievances the strikers had against the Protectorate Government, even though these were readily apparent. This view is shared by Thompson, who argues that while the riots had a political dimension, economic grievances in towns and on plantations lay at the heart of the strikers' interests, namely, in the fall of real wages brought about by wartime conditions, and the government's inability to control imports and prices.[104] Needless to say, the composition of the Commission could have benefited with the addition of one or more Ugandans possessed with a deeper local knowledge of the cultural, political and economic milieu from which the strikes arose.

Whitley's Report and, by implication, the Protectorate Government, missed a wider and more glaring point that informed the January 1945 strikes, namely, the growth of African nationalism in Uganda and the beginnings of a national anti-colonial struggle seeking independence, accountability, democracy and economic freedom. In the interests of justifying and protecting the status quo, the Report ignored or trivialised the build-up and history of grievances against colonial rule in Uganda between 1900 and 1945.

It disregarded the dangers these presented to the future of the colonial state. And, by choosing to forcefully suppress African aspirations and demands for freedom, particularly after the eye-opening experiences of the

Second World War and information on the struggles of decolonisation in other parts of the world, instead of engagement, the Protectorate Government buried its head in the sand and postponed the inevitable. It thus set the stage for the next scene of confrontation four years later, in 1949, when a series of more serious riots took place in Buganda.

The changes in Buganda's leadership initiated by the colonial government that introduced new and more agreeable senior ministers and Ssaza (county) chiefs in Mengo, did little to calm the situation or to address the aspirations of the people. In fact, as the assassination of Nsibirwa in September 1945 demonstrates, the changes may instead have exacerbated matters. Nor did Governor Hall's reversal of colonial policy, the deconstruction of Dundas' reforms,[105] or his iron-fisted style of governance[106] help much. And although, after the 1945 riots, Governor Hall for the first time allowed for three African representatives in the LEGCO, the gesture was not really appreciated, especially in Buganda.[107] This is because Buganda always viewed the LEGCO as a Eurocentric body designed to serve British interests and, at the same time, diminish the authority and influence of the Kabaka and the Lukiiko.

In the aftermath of the 1945 crisis, several actions were taken to help regain colonial control and stabilise the Protectorate. These measures included debunking the reforms proposed by Dundas, purging difficult elements in Buganda's native Government, reining in an ambitious and potentially problematic young Kabaka Mutesa, and a niggardly expansion of the Legislative Council to introduce a few African members for the first time since its creation in 1920. We look at each of these below.

Deconstructing Dundas' Reforms

The 1945 protests shocked and rattled the Protectorate administration, both in their speed and geographical scope. They threw the colonial administration into a crisis and it was felt that something had gone seriously wrong and needed to be fixed quickly. As the Whitley Report shows, the blame was mostly placed on the political intrigue of the Wamala group in Mengo and on the mistaken views the Baganda held on the Dundas reforms.

In a secret memo to the Secretary for the Colonies, written five months after the protests, Governor Hall reported that the political situation in Buganda was "rapidly deteriorating," that "the disloyal elements have now largely recovered from the shock administered to them by the Protectorate Government's unexpectedly firm and speedy suppression of the disturbances," and that "they are now once again busy with plot and intrigue."[108] The

Governor warned London thus:

> if this process of political and administrative deterioration is allowed to continue unchecked until the demobilised soldiers return, a really critical situation will inevitably develop, and the result may well be not merely an isolated outbreak of disturbances, but a prolonged series of civil disorders which may be expected to spread beyond the borders of Uganda.[109]

It was to these problematic areas that Governor Hall immediately gave his attention. On the problems caused by his predecessor's philosophy on "indirect rule," and particularly on his concepts of governance of Africans by Africans, Governor Hall did not hesitate to revert to the old order that had pacified Buganda and served Britain well. Under the old order, especially in the post-Apolo Kagwa period, native authority was clearly under the supervision of colonial administrators and there was little or no pretence as to who was in charge. According to Low and Pratt, "the Administration had never favoured such a relaxation of control and the riots of 1945 were taken as proof that the older pattern of rule should be re-established."[110]

It was felt by the Resident of Buganda that the Dundas reforms had created the mistaken view that Buganda had been granted "home rule" and that "even to some British Officers conversant with native administration, the terms of the announcement and its intention were not wholly clear."[111] As a result, the Resident observed that there was a general feeling that the "Protectorate Government had no jurisdiction over Buganda and that, amongst the Baganda chiefs, there was a new 'keep-off' attitude."[112] It is on this basis that Governor Hall scrapped the Dundas reforms and reverted to the old colonial *modus operandi*, where the assistant Residents renewed their previous supervision of the chiefs' work with even more vigour.

Purges and a Reshuffle at Mengo

On the issue of the disloyal and anti-British elements in Mengo, as seen above, the Governor swiftly moved to "weed out of the administration those Baganda who are really incurably evil and disloyal."[113] Using colonial authority he removed Wamala from the Katikkiroship and had him and others immediately deported without trial. Several unreliable (in the view of the Governor) chiefs were relieved of their duties.[114] This was followed by the reappointment, at his request, of a reluctant and generally unpopular Nsibirwa as the new Katikkiro,[115] and the appointment of Kawalya Kagwa as Kulubya's replacement.

Nsibirwa resumed office with much enthusiasm and immediately got rid of some of the chiefs who had ganged up against him in 1941.[116] These purges, as well as his crucial role in passing the Land Acquisition Act that had stalled for two years, contributed to his brutal murder. However, in Governor Hall's view, cleansing Mengo would be incomplete so long as "the present weak and inexperienced Kabaka is nominally holding the reins of power."[117] He further wrote:

> His enemies are far too strong and cunning for him and he, a mere schoolboy and believed by many to be a bastard, a belief sedulously fostered by his ill-wishers, has at present neither the prestige nor the character to establish his traditional authority.[118]

These were rather harsh statements from someone whom the Kabaka thought he "[got] on well" with and considered a "life-long friend" who gave him "good advice."[119] But what must have informed the Governor's opinion, and what he did not say directly in his memo, is the fact that Kabaka Mutesa was beginning to assert himself as king in Buganda and to talk about topics hitherto considered taboo (to colonial rule)—such as sovereignty for his kingdom. For example, the Kabaka wrote a memo to E. A. Temple Perkins, the Resident of Buganda, in which he set out to "reconstruct" his government and "decrease the number of Ssaza and Gombolola chiefs who appear to have reached the age of sixty years."[120] The memo named the Ssaza chiefs to be affected, namely, the Kago, the Sebwana, the Luwekula and the Lumama. On receipt of the memo, the Resident shot back:

> Such action as you have taken would not be approved by His Excellency the Governor … as your proposal had not received my concurrence and, as you well know, should have been submitted to His Excellency before implementation…. [A]t all events the four chiefs in question must be told at once that their retirements cannot take effect.[121]

In his reply of 9 June, the Kabaka informed the Resident that the withdrawal at this stage of the Kabaka's instructions in connection with the retirement of the four chiefs would have unfavourable and undermining repercussions on his sovereignty. Reporting on the exchange on the matter to his superiors in Entebbe, the Resident stated that the Kabaka's actions showed the tendency to develop independence beyond the limits of the Agreement. He felt, after "making due allowance for incomplete knowledge of English," that the Kabaka's use of the word "sovereignty" was "to say the least, unfortunate" and his suggested line of action, "unsound."[122]

The other reason, buried in the British National Archives, and which the Governor did not disclose, was that during the January protests the Kabaka's loyalty was strongly suspect, as he "sat on the fence" during the protests. An undated secret intelligence report on the character of Kabaka Mutesa states that "in the 1945 disturbances, it was clear that the Kabaka was not playing straight with the government, but he was given a benefit of doubt and arrangements were made to send him to Cambridge for three years to shake off undesirable associations."[123]

The report also points out that the Kabaka strongly opposed a levy of 6 shillings which the Protectorate Government imposed on the inhabitants of the twelve counties in Buganda that had been affected by the disturbances.[124]

Reining in an Ambitious Kabaka Mutesa

To tame an increasingly ambitious and potentially problematic Kabaka, the Governor devised a sly scheme to temporarily remove him from Buganda and to rid him of the bad influences therein. The scheme was also intended to extend British patronage and influence to Mutesa and render him or pliant to the demands of the colonial power. As we show below, in dispatching the Kabaka to Cambridge, the colonial government intended to use his absence from Buganda to uproot disloyalty and carry through certain political, administrative and fiscal reforms in Buganda with the help of a loyal Regency that it would install.

Thus, on 16 June 1945, he met the Kabaka and gave him a piece of his mind. The Governor's record of the conversation merits extensive reproduction:

> I saw the Kabaka on the 16 June and had a long and serious talk with him. I pointed out to him:
>
> (a) that he had made a serious constitutional blunder in calling upon four Chiefs to resign, which was tantamount to dismissing them, without first seeking my approval;
>
> (b) that in failing to have the Mujaguzo drums beaten on V. E. Day he had drawn upon himself and his Government the adverse criticism not only of Europeans and non-Baganda natives, but also of his own people, as well as strengthening the impression left by the disturbances that the people of Buganda—or at any rate a section of them—were disloyal;
>
> I that my officers and I were beginning to get the impression that he was, doubtless as a result of bad advice, playing for popularity with the disloyal and anti-British elements and gradually being drawn into the "opposition camp," possibly from a desire to appease the extremists;
>
> (d) that he was reported to be ignoring his Ministers and seeking advice from other sources such as certain ex-Budo masters, whose reputation in certain unsavoury matters was beginning to attach to him;

(e) that I was very doubtful of the wisdom of his choice of Sempa (an ex-Budo master) for the important post of Secretary of the Lukiiko, and that before making this appointment he would have been better advised to consult the Resident and me;

(f) that unless he was careful he would come into serious conflict with me and thus with the British Government and that certainly offered no future for him. Indeed, he had no future unless he worked with the Protectorate Government in full confidence and cooperation;

(g) that it was no good his attempting to come to terms with the disloyal elements in Buganda and those who engineered the disturbances because (i) they wanted to get rid of him in favour of their own nominee and (ii) I proposed to get rid of them;

(h) that my policy was (i) to root out of his administration the really disloyal elements, leaving in office such of the "waverers" as I thought would come down on the right side of the fence if given a lead (i.e., shown clearly on which side lay their bread and butter); (ii) replace some of the older and less educated Chiefs by younger and better educated men so as to encourage the latter; (iii) increase the representative character of the Lukiiko; and (iv) endeavour to introduce some form of graduated taxation in Buganda. All these measures would be unpopular with some sections of the Baganda and I thought it better that the odium should rest on my shoulders rather than on those of the Kabaka, whose position was already sufficiently precarious;

(i) that I was seriously exercised by the frequent reports reaching me of plots to assassinate the Kabaka. These reports might not in every case be well-founded; but usually where there was smoke there was some flame and the Kabaka would do well to take all possible precautions;

(k) that in my view while the Kabaka continued to attend Makerere [College] and remained in intimate and daily contact with the students there, studying and playing games with them, it was impossible for him to acquire the prestige and detachment necessary for him to fill his high position adequately at a time and in circumstances of especial difficulty. He could not easily detach himself from school and college contacts without seeming ungraciousness, yet many of those contacts were most unsuitable. Moreover, the contrast between the free and easy atmosphere of Makerere and the extreme formality of the Palace at Mengo (where his Ministers had to approach him on all fours) was so great as to be quite unreal. *It would be far better, I suggested, for the* Kabaka *to detach himself from Uganda for a year or two, and then to return with the added prestige of a sojourn in England and a course of study there. He could then resume only such of his previous social contacts as he thought politically desirable. He would, moreover, by this means escape the odium likely to flow from (h) above; and provided a loyal, firm and efficient Regency were set up he would, I hoped, return to find a well ordered and contented Kingdom*; [emphasis mine]

(l) that the course of studies in England from which I considered that

> he would benefit most was the proposed 15-month course for administrative officers; but (i) he would probably need some preliminary coaching and (ii) I had not consulted the Secretary of State and could not therefore guarantee that arrangements could be made for his admission;
>
> (m) that to act as Regents I suggested (i) Martin Luther [Nsibirwa] as Katikkiro, the present Omulamuzi, and Lieutenant Kawalya Kagwa as Finance Minister. The Queen Mother should not, I considered, be brought back to Mengo.
>
> 2. As regards (a), the Kabaka said that he had consulted Mr Temple Perkins on two occasions, and thought that he was acting in accordance with his advice.... He most readily accepted the proposal at (k) and (l) and asked me to write at once to the Secretary of State and ask that the necessary arrangements be made. I impressed on him the need for secrecy".[125]

Once he had warned the young Kabaka that he had "no future unless he worked with the British in full confidence and cooperation" and convinced him of the "prestige of a sojourn in England," Governor Hall wrote a long memo to the secretary of the colonies setting out the real reasons why he needed to urgently dispatch the Kabaka to England. He wrote:

> My advisers and I have been seriously exercised of late by the increasing tendency on [the Kabaka's] part to take action without consulting the Resident and myself. Such action has in almost every case been as to encourage the disloyal and anti-British elements in Buganda and to discourage the loyal elements, with the result that the prestige and power of the former are increasing at the expense of those who are both loyal to the British connection and, unlike the anti-British section, loyal to the Kabaka himself.
>
> I have reason to know that the Kabaka is ignoring his Ministers, who are admittedly men of little force of character, and is seeking advice from persons of undesirable antecedents who were [to a] greater or lesser degree involved in the disturbances.... Among the Kabaka's other associates are several men who were masters at Budo [College] at the time of the outbreak of the indiscipline in 1942 and were then dismissed or forced to resign.... The foregoing may give you an impression that the Kabaka is both evil and anti-British. If so, nothing could be more misleading. He is, I believe, fundamentally a very nice youth, with a genuine liking for and admiration of the British. He is intelligent, well-mannered and possessed of charm and humour. But he is a very frightened, inexperienced and bewildered young man, who knows how precarious is his present position, and doubtless thinks that the safest course for him to pursue is to appease the extremists and thus to show himself independent of British control. He is probably attempting the impossible course of at once keeping with the Protectorate Government and with his own anti-British elements. But he

most certainly has not yet gone too far to be saved; and he is worth saving.... In consequence both of his vacillation and of the absence of any firm native Government, the political situation in Buganda is in my opinion rapidly deteriorating.... If this process of political and administrative deterioration is allowed to continue unchecked until the demobilized soldiers return, a really critical situation will inevitably develop, and the result may well be not merely an isolated outbreak of disturbance, but a prolonged series of civil disorders which may be expected to spread beyond the borders of Buganda….

My advisers and I are convinced that in the interests of the Kabaka himself, who, apart from other considerations, will quite probably be murdered if he remains here, and *in the interests of Buganda and thus of the Protectorate at large, it is essential that he should leave this country for a space of time, and should entrust the Government of Buganda to a loyal, firm and efficient Regency who acting, as I am assured that they will, in full cooperation with the Protectorate Government, will, during his absence, uproot disloyalty and carry through those political, administrative and fiscal reforms that the country so urgently needs in preparation for the return of our demobilised soldiers.... A period of selected study in England, accompanied by the right social contacts and associations, would do much to remedy the Kabaka's present defects of character and would give him the confidence and the prestige in the eyes of his own people that he now lacks.* [italics mine] The need for it would be readily recognized by the Baganda and particularly by the educated classes. As you will see from the attached record, the Kabaka would welcome the proposed arrangement.[126]

The Secretary for Colonies was agreeable to the proposal for the Kabaka to join Cambridge, and the Colonial Office, working through A. B. Cohen, quickly swung into action with arrangements for his admission to a colonial administration course at the university.[127] In his letter to the Registrar of the University, Cohen stated that the admission of the Kabaka was "a matter to which the Colonial Office attaches great importance. The Kabaka is the ruler of the most important native state in Uganda and it is essential that his education should be completed under the best possible circumstances."[128]

On 18 September 1945, a few days after Nsibirwa's murder, the Kabaka, escorted by Yosia Kyazze, set off from Port Bell on his way to Cambridge, where he was admitted in Magdalene College. He left the kingdom in the hands of three Regents, namely, Michael Kawalya Kagwa (the new Katikkiro), Ezekel Walusimbi (the new Omuwanika) and Kigonya (the new Omulamuzi), all nominated by Governor Hall. The Kabaka writes that the news that he was to go to Cambridge came as a "pleasant surprise" and that he was "eager to go to England."[129]

He was, perhaps, oblivious of Governor Hall's hidden imperialist agenda. For although he enjoyed his stay in Cambridge—which lasted until October 1948[130]—his educational sojourn there was far from altruistic on the part of his sponsors. In reality, it was part of a colonial scheme of patronage aimed at regaining loyalty and control in Buganda in his absence.

As part of his tutelage, Mutesa had an audience with King George VI in London.[131] As we have pointed out, after the 1945 protests, Governor Hall's scheme was to remove the radical elements at the centre of Buganda's political structure. To that extent, Hall's claim that the Kabaka's hasty enrolment at Cambridge was in the "interests of the Kabaka himself," to remove the risk of his being murdered if he remained in Buganda, must be read and taken with a pinch of salt. With Mutesa removed from the political scene and with the radical elements sequestered away from power, Hall hoped that the colony would be pacified and thus rendered more manageable. However, as the events of 1949 show, this plan did not work.

Between 1945 and 1949, the Protectorate, under Hall's governorship, and the Regency in Buganda remained outwardly calm. But below the surface, anti-colonial sentiments and struggles continued to simmer. So, when he returned home in October 1948, Kabaka Mutesa did not find a "well-ordered and contented kingdom" as had been hoped by Hall. The Kabaka soon noticed that all was not well, especially in terms of "the anti-European feeling" that was strong but not fully realised by the British.[132] He observed that a "vague wave of resentment had been started by [the] high prices which followed the war" and he developed "an equally uncertain suspicion that the Baganda might be losing the control of their own affairs."[133]

For these and other reasons, his honeymoon following his marriage to Lady Damali Kisosonkole[134] was short-lived. In many ways, the situation had worsened since he was away. His subjects were more disgruntled both with his government at Mengo, which they regarded as nothing but a British proxy,[135] and with the Protectorate Government, which had become more authoritarian. Many of the economic and political troubles that caused the 1945 protests had since been exacerbated. To this was added the unpopular actions of deportation and the incarceration of anti-colonial actors like Ignatius K. Musaazi. The situation had given rise to a more structured opposition, with the rejuvenation of organisations such as the Bataka Party, led in 1946 by James Miti, Festo Kibuka Musoke and C. Semakula Mulumba, and the birth of the Uganda Africa Farmer's Union, led by Musaazi.

In 1948, the Bataka Party started holding regular meetings, attended by large crowds ranging from 1,000 to 8,000 people.[136] The Bataka Party mobilised the population using provocative rhetoric and established an anti-colonial publication, *Gambuze*. In April 1948, the party representative, Semakula Mulumba, working with the Soviet Deputy Foreign Minister and Soviet delegate to the UN, Andrej Gromyko, petitioned the United Nations to look into the Bataka's grievances against British imperialism.[137] The interest of the Soviet delegate to the UN in the Bataka's struggle against British rule may explain Governor Hall's statement that Communist elements were involved in the uprisings against British rule in Buganda. It may also be seen as part of Soviet attempts to widen its sphere of influence in this period, which was characterised by geopolitical jostling between Europe, the USSR and the US in the wake of anti-colonialist nationalist movements. Eventually, a combination of the above matters gave rise to a fresh insurgence.

The 1949 Protests in Buganda

The protests really started on 15 March 1949 when the Bataka Party declared that there would be a massive gathering on 25 March to meet the Kabaka to communicate their grievances. On 21 March, the organisers extended an invitation to all people in Buganda to attend the meeting at 6 am, at which the Kabaka would be informed of "what hurts his people most and what is destroying his kingdom."[138] The people were asked to come with food and money to sustain them for some time. To pre-empt a potentially rowdy meeting, the Kabaka, under pressure from the Resident, wrote a letter informing all and sundry that he was not to meet the crowd except, maybe, for six or eight of its representatives.[139] These representatives were picked at a meeting on 24 March.

On 25 March, while the Kabaka held talks with eight Bataka Party representatives, a large crowd gathered outside his palace. The representatives demanded that (i) the Kabaka democratise his government and allow the people to elect their own chiefs, (ii) the Kabaka increase the number of Lukiiko elected representatives to sixty, (iii) the Kabaka sack his present government, (iv) the people be allowed to gin their cotton, and (v) the people be allowed to sell their own cotton directly to other countries by way of free trade.[140] On the first three points, the Kabaka referred the meeting to the 1900 Agreement that provided for the matters raised in the demands. On the last two points, the Kabaka informed the meeting that he would act once guided by his advisers. With that, he asked the representatives to inform the crowds outside and ask them to go home.

Once outside, the Katikkiro M. Kawalya Kagwa attempted to address the crowd on the outcome of the meeting. Instead, he was booed and not allowed to address the gathering. The crowd refused to disperse even when asked to do so by both the organisers and the police. However, they were not violent.

The next day the police tried to force them to leave the palace grounds. This sparked an angry exchange between the police and the crowd. The crowd was overpowered and it retreated. This was followed by the burning of several chiefs' houses, interspersed with looting and other acts of violence which lasted for two days.[141] Once again, just as in 1945, the riots caught the Protectorate administration and the police flat-footed. Reinforcements from the King's African Rifles were called in. Although order was restored in the vicinity of the capital within a couple of days, incidents continued in Masaka district until 2 May.

Over 1,700 arrests were made, leading to nearly 300 convictions.[142] In total, 8 people were killed by police fire and 33 were wounded.[143] Neither the Kabaka nor the Protectorate Government met any of the Bataka Party's demands. The hard line adopted thus bottled up discussions on democratisation and accountability in the kingdom of Buganda and, conversely, the rest of the country—something both the Kabaka and the colonial government would later regret. The Kabaka subsequently wrote:

> Though [the Batakas'] suspicions and fears were largely unfounded, I was sorry to have to refuse the wishes of the people so flatly. If they had thought I was influenced by the Governor in 1945, I must now have appeared to be dominated by the Lukiiko.[144]

On 27 April, Governor Hall made a public statement castigating the Bataka Party and the African Farmers' Union, calling them "wicked people." Attributing the whole affair to "a comparatively few evil and self-seeking men who have brought great trouble and disgrace upon Buganda," he wrote:

> Acting on Communist inspiration from their so-called representatives in Britain, they are seeking to oppose by violence, intimidation, arson and murderous assault all constituted authority, the authority of [His Highness] the Kabaka's Government, the authority of the Protectorate Government and of the King's force of law and order. In so doing they are following the usual pattern of Communist penetration, with which people in Europe and the Far East are already familiar. Their attempt was prefaced by a long campaign of foul lies and slander aimed at deceiving the people and shaking their confidence in His Highness' Government and the

> Government of the Protectorate. This too follows the usual Communist pattern.[145]

Another one-man investigation dubbed the "Commission of Inquiry into the Riots Which Occurred in Uganda during April, 1949," headed by Commissioner Donald Kingdon, was set up. In its Report, dated 7 December 1949, the Commission concluded that the protests followed "a planned and pre-arranged pattern," and that it was "quite impossible" that the arson committed was "haphazard" or the result of a spasmodic outbreak.[146] It partly attributed the disturbances to the Dundas reforms of October 1944, which it described as "premature and harmful."

It made three key findings. The first was that the disturbances were a planned rebellion against His Highness the Kabaka and the Buganda government organised by the leaders of the so-called Bataka Party and the Uganda African Farmers' Union, and that Semakula Mulumba, more than any other individual, was responsible for the disturbances.[147] The Report found no real evidence of, and thus downplayed, the Communist connections or role alleged by Governor Hall. The second was that, with the possible exception of the fact that a large sum of money derived from the sale of produce was retained by government for the benefit of the people, none of the grievances alleged by Semakula Mulumba and his supporters had any substance.[148] The third was that in suppressing the disturbances, the Protectorate Police Force and the troops used no more force than was necessary and their behaviour was admirable.

Once the Report was completed, the Protectorate Government issued a memo declaring the actions it was taking in view of the recommendations made therein; announcing the ban of the Bataka Party and the Uganda African Farmers' Union, and warning that it would "not be deterred by this attempted rebellion, nor by any other subversive activities by self-seeking malcontents, from pursuing its policy of entrusting African local governments with progressively more responsibility in the administration of their own affairs, and of developing the growth and quality of African Councils on democratic lines."[149] Strangely, in saying he was giving the Africans "more responsibility in the administration of their own affairs," Governor Hall was supporting the Dundas position and contradicting his own policies and practice.

To the extent that it was a one-man affair focused on defending Hall's obdurate views—that the protests were purely political and championed by hooligans intent on ousting the Kabaka's government, not the colonial state—and given that it circumvented or concealed the underlying and often overlapping political and economic issues that engendered the colonial crisis, the Kingdon Report had serious flaws similar to those of the Whitley Report before it. Like its predecessor, it failed to consider the evidence suggesting that the colonial state was once again caught up in a crisis of legitimacy and was implicated in the protests. Similarly, the Report suggested that the Bataka Party was simply a reactionary, self-interested grouping of malcontent, unrepresentative agitators or Communists.[150]

Equally, in using force to suppress Bataka Party dissent and not constructive engagement, the Protectorate Government appears not to have learned any lessons from the 1945 experience. It failed or refused to see and understand the changing political landscape and dynamics in post-Second World War Buganda and Uganda. Yet it had to confront this new anti-colonial nationalism, led by a new educated generation with no ties to the historical and chiefly hierarchy in Mengo.

With the British Empire in decline in India and elsewhere, the colonial administrators in Uganda seemed keen to hold on to the easy and glorious times of imperial control—as epitomised by chiefs like Apolo Kagwa, whose word was as good as law[151]—and to perilously ignore the changing power relations between the people, the Kabaka, and the colonial regime. Indeed, as Low and Pratt point out, the Kingdon Report and Governor Hall's reaction to it "did not suggest that the changing political atmosphere in Uganda necessitated major reforms in the structure of the Buganda Government and in the relationship between Buganda and Uganda. Instead, he demonstrated a marked desire to re-establish the relationship that held before the war."[152] On the effect of the protests and Britain's response to them, Hanson rightly points out that:

> The excessive paranoid response of Governor Hall to the efforts towards accountable governance in 1945 and 1949 substantially hindered Uganda's path towards independence. Uganda lost the insight, vision, and commitment to good governance of [the] true patriots Hall deported, including the important Buganda Royal Prince Suna and the long-serving Ssaza (provincial) Chief S. Wamala, both of whom died in detention. While in other colonies labour activism helped build national coalitions that contributed to vital independence movements, in Uganda the 1945 strike and the 1949 bid for more accountable governance in Buganda taught harsh lessons in keeping quiet and avoiding the public sphere.[153]

Clearly, both in 1945 and 1949, Governor Hall misread the writing on the wall. While the political and economic dynamics within the colonial society had shifted, he was stuck with the old methods of enforcing law and order. Yet, in this new African context, suppression and authoritarian rule had limited potency. A new approach was needed. This, indeed, may explain the entry of a new Governor, Andrew Cohen, who was aggressively, focused on expanding African representation in the governance of the colony and on setting the Protectorate on a path of constitutional development and self-rule.

In dealing with the immediate aftermath of the 1949 riots, however, Hall was not slow in proscribing police the Bataka Party and the African Farmers' Union or prosecuting their leaders. At the same time, he took action to strengthen and equip the native (with the provision of boots to all African ranks) and the Protectorate police, increasing their capacity and improving their readiness to deal with emergencies. The Police Service Unit, as the mobile strike force was known, was expanded to be fully equipped to deal with widespread civil disturbances, and at least 14 new police stations were to be built and manned.[154]

Reforms in the administrative organisation of Buganda, especially in the increase of unofficial elected members, commenced. Addressing the Lukiiko in December 1949, the Kabaka said that the time was ripe for the introduction to the LEGCO of people who would be of great value to the Lukiiko by virtue of their education or by their prominence in various occupations, and that this would involve a slight increase in the total number of unofficial members. In March 1953, changes were made in the composition of the Lukiiko: 60 out of 89 members were directly elected; the number of ministers was increased from three to six and, according to Paulo Kavuma, the Kabaka "got rid of his chief ministers because they were so unpopular."[155] Paulo Kavuma was then introduced as the new Katikkiro in the place of Kawalya Kagwa, and Matayo Mugwanya and L. M. Mpagi were appointed the new ministers for Justice and the Treasury respectively. There were changes in the Protectorate Government as well.

The above analysis shows that the events of the late 1930s and the 1940s, both within and outside the Uganda Protectorate, formed the basis of the growth of African nationalism and resistance to colonial rule and, simultaneously, witnessed the decline of colonial authority resulting from constraints brought about during and after the Second World War.

The protests of 1945 and 1949 pointed to the growing political consciousness of the African population, as well as its increased unease with British rule. They also flagged the urgent need to reform the autocratic governance of the colony to make it more representative and accountable. For these reasons, it was necessary for Britain, whose global economic and political power was declining, to adopt a new colonial policy in Uganda and elsewhere that would ensure the protection of its economic and strategic interests and entrench the system of imperial patronage—through the policies of divide and rule, indirect rule based on pliant agents and within the LEGCO—while at once accommodating the views and aspirations of its colonial subjects.

Notes

[1] See Mutibwa, *A History of Uganda*, p. 89.

[2] See Jorgensen, J. J. (1981) *Uganda: A Modern History*, London: Croom Helm, p. 121.

[3] See Thompson, Gardner (2003) *Governing Uganda: British Colonial Rule and its Legacy*, Fountain Publishers, Kampala, p. 96.

[4] See Mutibwa, *A History of Uganda*, p.91.

[5] In Mitchell's letter to Malcolm MacDonald, the Secretary of State for the Colonies, dated 5 December 1939, Buganda promised to contribute £5,000; the eastern province promised to contribute £7,000, and the western province promised to contribute £5,000.

[6] Mutibwa, *A History of Uganda*, p. 90.

[7] Ibid., p. 92.

[8] Ibid.

[9] See "Report of the Long-Term Study Group" by the Cabinet Defence and Overseas Policy Committee, dated 12 October 1964, on CAB 148/7, ff 270-284.

[10] Information from the Memoral Gates, Hyde Park Corner, London. See also McIntyre, W. D. (1999). "The Commonwealth," in R. Winks (ed.) *The Oxford History of the British Empire: Volume V: Historiography*, Oxford University Press, p. 558.

[11] Neocolonialism became a better imperative because it retained the domination of former colonies without a visible presence of the colonialist.

[12] See Summers, C. and Sikanga, A. A. (2015) "Uganda Politics World War II (1939-1949)," In Judith A. Byfield, Carolyn A. Brown, and Timothy Parsons (eds.) *Africa and World War II*, Cambridge, UK: Cambridge University Press, pp. 480-98.

[13] FCO141/18118 and FCO141/18222 on Lady Irene Drusilla Namaganda, the Namasole (Queen Mother) of Sir Edward Mutesa II of Buganda 1938-48.

[14] Letter of Resident, Buganda, dated 4 March 1941, to the Chief Secretary, FCO 141/18222.

[15] On 1 March, 1941, the Lukiiko passed a resolution to the effect that "in these days of Christianity it is difficult to prevent anyone from marrying if he wishes to do so. We therefore find that the former custom should be altered in the case of a Namasole who desires to marry. We have discussed and agreed that the man who the Namasole marries shall have no official position as the husband of the Namasole, *vis-à-vis* the Government of Buganda." See Lukiiko resolution dated 1 March 1941, FCO 141/18222.

[16] In a Lukiiko resolution taken on 11 March, 1941, FCO 141/18222.

[17] Letter of the Resident, Buganda, A. H. Cox, dated 13 March 1941, to the Regents, FCO 141/18222.

[18] Ibid.

[19] Letter of the three Regents to A. H. Cox, the Resident, Buganda, File No. FCO 141/18222.

[20] Letter of the Namasole to Governor Dundas, dated 29 March 1941, FCO 141/18222. When Kabaka Mutesa I died, Namasole Bagalayaze, Mwanga's mother, was allowed by Kabaka Mwanga and the Lukiiko to remarry one Juma Kabamba.

[21] Resident's letter to the Chief Secretary, dated 4 March 1941.

[22] In the *Desecration of My Kingdom*, p. 84-85, the Kabaka writes "An important decision was required of me in 1941…. My mother was a woman of character and not a traditionalist. She decided to remarry, and gained the support of the Katikkiro. There was great opposition. In such cases the Kabaka alone has the power to allow tradition to be broken—that is to say, to alter tradition. She was determined, so I gave her my support, and the remarriage took place."

[23] When she was expelled from the Lubiri, the Namasole moved to Mukisa Cottage, in Ngogwe in the Ssaza of Kyagwe, 42 miles from Kampala.

[24] Buganda Lukiiko resolutions, dated 21 April 1941, FCO 141/18222, TNA.

[25] According to a note dated 25 July 1941 by A. O. Jenkins, the Resident of Buganda, "the Governor did not withhold his consent" but advised that the "prosecution might be regarded by many as purely vindictive and on this ground, and also because the prosecution might not succeed the proposed action, did not commend itself to him."

[26] Jenkins, above, notes that Nsibirwa's twisting of the Governor's comments to suit the occasion infuriated members and was met with uproar, leading to the Katikkiro's dismissing the assembly using language that "passed the bounds of decency."

[27] Judgement of Judge J. S. Kasirye in Principal Court Criminal Case No. 205/41, *Semioni Katende Njuki, Saza Chief, Kago v. Simon Petero Wakiwugulu Gyagenda Kigozi*, dated 10 June, 1941.

[28] Ibid.

[29] Judgment by Ag. Judicial Adviser, Buganda Criminal Appeal No. 34/41 in Principal Court Criminal Case No. 205/41, *Semioni Katende Njuki, Saza Chief, Kago v. Simon Petero Wakiwugulu Gyagenda Kigozi*, dated 22 July, 1941.

[30] A son of Kiwana from Bugerere, he was brought up in the homestead of Apolo Kagwa. He served Buganda for an uninterrupted period of 41 years, starting as a land clerk and surveyor. He rose to become a Gombolola chief in 1911 and a Ssaza Chief in 1921 (first as Mugerere and later as Mukwenda). He was one of the executors of Sir Apolo Kagwa's will. He was appointed by Sir Daudi Chwa as Omuwanika in 1935. In the same year, he was awarded the Member of the Shield and Spear (MSS). In 1936, he became the Katikkiro of Buganda.

[31] As stated by Katikkiro Nsibirwa in his meeting with Governor Dundas on 21 June at Makindye in the presence of C. M. S. Kisosonkole and the Resident.

[32] It is said by Paulo Kavuma (1979) in *Crisis in Buganda: The Story of the Exile and Return of the Kabaka, Mutesa II*, London: Rex Collings, p. 9 that Wamala did not "know English but he had a lot of support among the old fashioned Baganda

who wanted to restore the old ways of the country and who did not like the innovations the Protectorate Administration wanted to see introduced."

[33] Lukiiko resolution taken in its sessions of 30 to 31 May, 1941, FCO 141/18222, TNA.

[34] H.D. Hooper's letter to C. W. M. Cox, dated 4 March 1942.

[35] Ibid.

[36] Ibid.

[37] Affidavit sworn by Regents, S. S. Wamala, Rawuli S. L. Kiwanuka and Serwano W. Kulubya on 29 August 1942.

[38] Deportation Order dated 23 September 1942.

[39] The Namasole's letter to the Governor, dated 1 February 1944, FCO 141/18222, TNA.

[40] Ibid.

[41] Who was due to return from his studies in Cambridge around this time.

[42] The Namasole's letter of 27 May 1948, FCO 141/18222.

[43] In a letter to the Governor, dated 9 June 1941, Bishop Cyril Stuart wrote in support of the remarriage of the Namasole and asked the Governor to protect Katikkiro Nsibirwa. According to a complaint by the head of the African clergy, Rev. Canon Yokana K. Bina to the Governor, dated 16 June 1941, the Church felt that the Lukiiko had publically despised Christian marriage and persecuted the Namasole because of her Christian beliefs. It also felt that the Protectorate had done little to protect her and the Katikkiro. In a letter of 3 June 1941, members of the Mothers' Union of Buganda, mobilised by the family of Ham Mukasa through Mary Stuart, decried the fate of the Namasole and asked the Governor to intervene. Needless to say, the Protectorate Government disregarded all these appeals.

[44] Summers, Carol. (2006) "Subterranean Evil" and "Tumultuous Riot," in Buganda: Authority and Alienation at King's College, Budo, 1942," *The Journal of African History*, 47(1) p. 95.

[45] See the teachers' memo to Dennis Herbert, dated 6 February 1942 in file, Education: Disturbances at King's College, Budo, CO 536/210/5 TNA.

[46] Summers, "Subterranean Evil," p. 97

[47] Ibid. p. 100.

[48] Ibid.

[49] Ibid.

[50] Ibid.

[51] Ibid., p. 110.

[52] See file on the Coronation of the Kabaka of Buganda, CO 536/208/16. See also, "Coronation of His Highness, Kabaka Mutesa II, Historic Scenes at Mengo and Budo," *The Uganda Herald*, Wednesday 25 November, 1942, p. 9.

[53] Ibid., pp. 1 and 3.

[54] See Sir Charles Dundas, *African Crossroads*, Connecticut: Greenwood Press, p. 212.

[55] In a letter Ref. S.9/6 of 12 June 1943 to the Chief Secretary.

[56] See the Kabaka's letter to E. A. Temple Perkins, Resident of Buganda, dated 28 May 1945, Ref. No. C/20/28/R/S.

[57] In a letter Ref. S.9/6 of 12 June 1943 to the Chief Secretary.
[58] Ibid.
[59] In his speech during Mutesa's coronation, Governor Dundas urged all people to regard the British as "true friends and advisers." See *The Uganda Herald*, "Coronation of His Highness the Kabaka Mutesa II," op. cit.
[60] Ibid.
[61] King George VI's letter of 1 April 1943 in the file *Celebrations of the Fiftieth Anniversary of the Uganda Protectorate*, CO536/210/3.
[62] Letter on behalf of the Kabaka by S. S. Wamala (Katikkiro), R. S. L Kiwanuka (Omulamuzi) and S. W. Kulubya (Omuwanika).
[63] Ibid.
[64] Ibid.
[65] "*Uganda's Fiftieth Anniversary*," by the Information Officer Uganda Ref. M.O.I No. 385 dated 29 March 1943.
[66] *Celebrations of the Fiftieth Anniversary* CO 536/210/3.
[67] See story by a correspondent: *Uganda Jubilee: Fifty Years a Model Protectorate*, CO 536/210/3 TNA.
[68] Low & Pratt, *Buganda and British Overrule*, p. 276.
[69] In his speech to the Lukiiko on 2 October, 1944.
[70] Musoke, D. S. K. (1994) "Buganda Nyaffe" (trans.). Reprinted in Donald Antony Low, comp. (1971) *The Mind of the Baganda: Documents of the Modern History of an African Kingdom*, Berkley. See also file "Bataka agitators and supporters," FCO 141/18185.
[71] See, generally, Kabaka Mutesa II, *The Desecration of My Kingdom*, p.89. A petition by Ssaza chiefs was made for Kulubya to be removed from office in 1943. It is believed that the ongoing desire among to see him removed from office was a key stimulus for the 1945 riots.
[72] Low & Pratt, *Buganda and British Overrule*, p.274
[73] *Laws of Uganda, 1951*, Vol. II (L.N. 219 of 1945).
[74] See files, "Uganda: Assassination of Martin Luther Nsibirwa, Katikkiro (Prime Minister) of Buganda, 5 September 1945 and subsequent deportations," FCO 141/18153, FCO/18155 and FCO/18156 TNA and Mutibwa, *A History of Uganda*, p. 96.
[75] Published in the *Uganda Gazette,* 6 September 1945.
[76] The 14 were Daudi Mukubira Musoke, Simioni Njuki, Alamanze Ganya, Stanley Kitaka Kisingiri, Semu Mukasa Sepuuya, S. Musajjalumbwa, Tito Serwadda, P. Kiyingi, Y. Bamuta, Samsoni Bazongere, Matiya Wamala, Joshua Kamulegeya, Henry Kanyike, and Yusufu Malindwa. The Orders were dated 8 September 1945. See file Uganda: Assassination of Martin Luther Nsibirwa, FCO 141/18153.
[77] Affidavit sworn by Douglas William Robertson, Acting Resident of Buganda, dated 7 September 1945.
[78] In a message published in the Uganda Gazette, 6 September 1945.
[79] Ibid.
[80] See Bishop of Uganda's Sermon, CO 536/211.
[81] Paulo Kavuma, *Crisis in Buganda*, p. 10.

[82] See "Report of the Commission of Inquiry into the Disturbances which occurred in Uganda during January 1945" CO 536/215/9.
[83] Ibid.
[84] Mutibwa, *A History of Uganda*, p. 123.
[85] Ibid.
[86] Ibid.
[87] Holly Hanson, "Rethinking Uganda in the 1940s with New Evidence" (a paper delivered at Makerere University, Kampala, Uganda, on 3 May 2016.
[88] Ibid., p. 6.
[89] Ibid., p. 5.
[90] Ibid., p. 6.
[91] Kabaka Mutesa II, *The Desecration of My Kingdom*, p. 89.
[92] Holly Hanson, "Rethinking Uganda," p. 6.
[93] Ibid., p. 3.
[94] According to the "Report of the Commission of Inquiry into the Disturbances which occurred in Uganda during January, 1945," p. 17, it was "impossible to obtain evidence sufficient for criminal proceedings against the real heads who plotted the whole affair or indeed to ascertain who they were."
[95] See files on Uganda: deportation and detention of Samwiri S. Wamala, Ex-Katikkiro, FCO/141/18159-18161.
[96] "Report of the Commission of Inquiry," ibid., p. 18; and Hanson, "Rethinking Uganda," p.8.
[97] Ibid.
[98] Ibid., p. 9.
[99] Ibid., p. 32.
[100] Ibid., p. 11.
[101] Ibid., pp. 22 and 23.
[102] Ibid., p. 30.
[103] Ibid.
[104] Thompson, B. G. (1992) "Colonialism in Crisis: The Uganda Disturbances of 1945," *African Affairs*, 91(365), p. 91.
[105] There were claims, including in the Whitley Report at p. 5, that the protests were a result of Dundas' relaxed policy on indirect rule, under which it was felt that the "British had withdrawn control and established self-government for the Baganda."
[106] According to Low & Pratt, *Buganda and British Overrule*, at p. 281, under Governor Hall the Protectorate relied on "an increasing use of force and threat of force if it did not initiate sufficient reforms in the systems of local rule to make it more acceptable to local opinion."
[107] Mutibwa, *A History of Uganda*, p. 127 argues that "the manner in which African representation to the LEGCO was decided on did not bring Buganda any closer to the rest of the Protectorate; if anything, it emphasised Buganda's uniqueness and, therefore, probably encouraged the Kingdom's own desire for separation."

[108] Sir John H. Hall's secret memo to the Secretary for Colonies, dated 25 June 1945.
[109] Ibid.
[110] Low & Pratt, *Buganda and British Overrule*, p. 280.
[111]Letter ref. S.9/6, dated 12 June 1945 addressed to the Hon. Chief Secretary by the Ag. Resident of Buganda.
[112] Ibid.
[113] See Sir John H. Hall's secret memo to the Secretary for Colonies, op. cit.
[114] Mutibwa, *A History of Uganda*, p. 125-126.
[115] Mutesa, in *The Desecration of My Kingdom*, p. 90, says Nsibirwa was "reluctant to return and came to see me personally and, as he had promised my father to help me at all times, accepted when I asked him."
[116] According to Mutesa, these were removed at a 24-hour notice. See *The Desecration of My Kingdom*, p. 90.
[117] Sir John H. Hall's secret memo to the Secretary for Colonies, op. cit.
[118] Ibid.
[119] Mutesa, *The Desecration of My Kingdom*, p. 88.
[120] Mutesa's letter to E. A. Temple Perkins, dated 28 May 1945.
[121] The Resident's letter dated 30 May 1945.
[122] Letter ref. S.5/22 dated 14 June 1945, addressed to the Hon. Chief Secretary by the Ag. Resident of Buganda.
[123] Ibid.
[124] Ibid.
[125] A record of a conversation between His Excellency the Governor of Uganda and H. H. The Kabaka on 16 June 1945.
[126] Letter No. 428 dated 26 June 1945 by Governor J. H. Hall, addressed to the Secretary for the Colonies.
[127] Letter to Dr W. W. Grave, Registrar, University of Cambridge, Ref. 40080/1/45, dated 30 July 1945.
[128] Ibid.
[129] Mutesa, *The Desecration of My Kingdom*, p. 91.
[130] Ibid., pp. 75-85.
[131] March 1946.
[132] Mutesa, *The Desecration of My Kingdom*, p. 111.
[133] Ibid.
[134] By Bishop Stuart at Namirembe on 19 November 1948.
[135] Paulo Kavuma (*Crisis in Buganda*, p.11) suggests that Katikkiro Kawalya Kagwa's "strong rule also made people angry. He thought they were backward and needed to be made to do what was good for them, and that made him unpopular. The people claimed that he was not loyal to his country, but only to the British, and they began to ask to have all the chiefs elected instead of their being chosen by the Kabaka and the Protectorate Administration."
[136] "Report of the Commission of Inquiry into the Disturbances that Occurred in Uganda in April 1949." See FCO 141/18130-18133, 18401, 18404.
[137] Ibid.

[138] Ibid., para. 52.
[139] Ibid., para. 68.
[140] Mutibwa, *A History of Uganda*, p. 132.
[141] "Report into the Disturbances that Occurred in Uganda in April 1949," paras. 94-96, 98-99.
[142] Ibid., para. 54.
[143] Ibid., paras. 56-59.
[144] Kabaka Mutesa II, *The Desecration of My Kingdom*, p. 111.
[145] Message from Governor J. Hathorn Hall dated 27 April 1949.
[146] "Report into the Disturbances that Occurred in Uganda in April 1949," p. 72.
[147] Ibid., paras. 311, 370 and 478.
[148] Ibid., paras. 480 and 482.
[149] Memorandum by the Uganda Government on the "Report of the Commission of Inquiry into the Civil Disturbances in Uganda during April, 1949," dated 14 January 1950, p. 15.
[150] Caroline Howell, *Religion and Nationalism: Buganda and the 1949 Bataka Riots.* University of Cambridge Position Paper 147, p. 18.
[151] According to Low & Pratt, *Buganda and British Overrule*, p. 289, on abandoning the Dundas reforms, the Protectorate Government under Governor Hall "returned to the older system of relying on and ruling through the Kabaka and chiefs although, with the rising strength of organised opposition to British rule in general and to the Chiefs in particular, such a policy was less and less effective."
[152] Low & Pratt, *Buganda and British Overrule*, p. 282.
[153] Holly Hanson, "Rethinking Uganda," p. 17.
[154] Memorandum by the Uganda Government on the Report of the Commission of Inquiry, op. cit., p. 6.
[155] Paulo Kavuma, *Crisis in Buganda*, p.12.

PHASE III

DECOLONISATION AND THE RESURGENCE OF BUGANDA (1952-1960)

Governor Andrew Cohen's Constitutional Reforms and the 1953 Coup in Buganda

Following the 1949 protests and the clamp down on its ringleaders, the political climate in the Protectorate cooled somewhat. But while the clamour over the grievances raised in 1949 subsided, political awakening and activism for self-rule increased. Thus, following the banning of the Bataka Party and the Uganda African Farmers' Union, the character and methods of the political actors also started to change. To get around the ban, two new political organisations—the Uganda National Congress (UNC) and the Democratic Party (DP)—were founded in 1952 and 1954 respectively.

The principal objective of the former was to fight colonialism and of the latter to address the religious grievances of the Catholics (who felt marginalised and discriminated against within Buganda's establishment) and the social and economic distortions in the country.[1] Despite these principal missions, both parties also engaged in the anti-colonial struggle for self-rule and agitated for the return of Edward Mutesa from England, following his temporary exile for his opposition to the Protectorate Government in 1953 (described below).

There were also changes in both the Kabaka's administration and the colonial governorship. In Mengo, Paulo Kavuma replaced Kawalya Kagwa as the Katikkiro, and when Governor Hall's tour of duty ended in 1952, he passed on the baton to Sir Andrew Cohen, a former head of the Colonial Africa Office in London. The change was to be of profound significance for the politics of the country. Like Special Commissioner Harry Johnston before him, Governor Cohen arrived with a go-getter mindset and with passionate ideas that he wanted to implement right away. Owen Griffith, a senior British colonial administrator at the time, wrote that "Cohen was a formidable man with outstanding intellectual gifts …

with explosive force and energy … contemptuous of the niceties of colonial etiquette and … lacking in social graces."[2] He added that:

> Cohen's personal idiosyncrasies, his reputation as a radical, his unease with and dislike of the trappings of colonial governorship, all served to jolt the complacencies of colonial society. There was certainly a residue of dislike for his radically pro-African policies, but he found no difficulty in silencing opposition. There was no one to match the force of his intellect, his energy and the power of his personality.[3]

On Cohen's rather eccentric personality, the Kabaka stated that:

> where the ideas and the country did not fit, it was the country that was going to be altered … he was referred to as a bear. Not only his solid figure, but his large face, heavy hands, combined with [an] almost total lack of small talk, make the comparison irresistible.[4]

Little wonder that Cohen did not hit it off with the Kabaka, who felt that the "Baganda like to be slowly persuaded and not bludgeoned."[5] Yet just as the restless Cohen lacked the niceties of colonial etiquette, he also had little time for niceties with the native authority. In his memoirs, the Kabaka notes that Cohen "decided gradually and then swiftly that any influence of mine must be destroyed, perhaps by making me a figurehead, perhaps by discrediting me or perhaps by more drastic means. Under the circumstances, it is not surprising that good fellowship drained away."[6]

Cohen's strategy, consistent with a new policy Britain was applying elsewhere in the Empire, was to develop and broaden representative government before self-governance was granted. However, Buganda, which considered itself as a separate entity from the rest of the Protectorate, was not agreeable to Cohen's constitutional path and agenda. Accordingly, the Kabaka rejected his plans. But Cohen was not prepared to sacrifice the future of Uganda to what he saw as the obstinacy of one hereditary ruler. Instead he opted for those "more drastic means," taking a hasty decision to depose and exile Kabaka Mutesa within a year of his arrival as Governor of the Protectorate. Thus from early 1953, the stage was set for a showdown between Uganda's new domineering and patronising Governor and a firm young Cambridge-educated captain and crown ruler of an old and ambitious kingdom.

Cohen's arrival marked a watershed in the politics of Uganda and, in particular, in the relationship between Britain and Buganda. Unlike his predecessors, Cohen's first priority was to put the country on a path towards political development within a unitary national framework. He thus immediately set off with an ambitious plan "to educate African administrators, increase African participation in the central government, and place local governments on a stable, democratic, and viable basis."[7] However, as we show below, Buganda had other ideas and its priorities were radically different from those of the new Governor. Buganda's priority was independence from Britain and having a strong Kabaka, free from external influence—even if this meant its separation from the rest of the Protectorate.

Within the first two months of his arrival, Governor Cohen engaged the Kabaka and his ministers in closed meetings.[8] Apart from these discussions, Cohen did not have any consultations with the leaders of political parties or anyone else. The discussions resulted in the "Memorandum on Constitutional Development and Reform in Buganda,"[9] which was issued jointly by Cohen and the Kabaka. The Memorandum, which emphasized that the Uganda Protectorate would continue to be developed as a unitary state, essentially aimed to increase the responsibilities of the Buganda Government,[10] increase the number of senior officials in the Buganda Government (three new ministers), increase the number of elected members of the Lukiiko, require the Kabaka to consult the Lukiiko before appointing ministers, and change the system of local government at the Ssaza (provincial) level.[11]

The Memorandum was followed by modifications to the LEGCO, whose membership was increased from sixteen to twenty-eight, fourteen of whom were to be Africans. The changes did not arouse much excitement in Buganda, especially those to the LEGCO. However, the increase in the number of elected representatives in the Lukiiko was welcomed, as it was one of the key issues raised in the 1949 protests. In any event, the Lukiiko refused to appoint representatives to the LEGCO as required under the Memorandum because it considered the LEGCO to be an entity whose objectives were antithetical to its own survival. To break the impasse and avoid embarrassing the new Governor, the Kabaka decided to choose the representatives.[12]

Things appeared to be falling in place for Cohen until Oliver Lyttelton, Secretary of State for the Colonies, at a meeting of the East Africa Dinner Club in London on 30 June 1953, made the following remark: "Nor should we exclude from our minds the evolution, as time goes on, of still larger measures of unification, and possibly still larger measures of federation of the whole of East Africa."[13] This information was published in *The East African Standard* on 3 July, and all hell broke loose. Buganda—always fearful of the idea of the East African Federation—immediately protested to the Governor to the effect that the Kabaka and people of Buganda were deeply disturbed and confused by Secretary Lyttelton's statement, which was "bound not only to shake the foundations of trust amongst our people, but will badly damage the good relations which hitherto obtained between the Baganda and the British."[14]

The Governor responded to the ministers on 27 July, saying that Buganda need have no fear on the matter, as although no one could foresee what would happen in the future, in terms of present intentions, the Secretary's speech "did not indicate any change in policy and … that the future development of Uganda and other East African territories must be largely guided by local public opinion."[15] The Governor repeated this assurance in the LEGCO on 11 August, calling Buganda's fears "groundless" and reiterating that "future developments would take local public opinion fully into account."[16] However, this assurance, insomuch as it was vague on the future and in its reference to public opinion, did not satisfy Buganda. The Kabaka considered that the Governor's assurances were as "disquieting" as they were "mealy-mouthed and half hearted," intended only from "a wish not to make Lyttelton appear foolish by contradicting him."[17]

Given the gravity of the matter, the Kabaka, with the full support of his ministers and the Lukiiko, wrote a long letter to the Governor on 6 August, in which he stated that the Governor's assurances left no shadow of doubt about the intentions of Her Majesty's Government.[18] According to him, the Governor's assurances contrasted with past assurances which were "never limited to the present, but committed to the future too and definitely excluded the kingdom of Buganda from any possibility of any future inclusion into such a union."[19] On the assurance that the future decisions of the Protectorate Government would take public opinion into account, the Kabaka was not convinced: recent developments in Central Africa had illustrated that "however many there may be Africans opposing a proposal, the wishes of the minority who are generally non-Africans must necessarily prevail, no matter what petitions, deputations and representations are sent to the highest authorities by the Africans."[20]

The Kabaka concluded the letter with two new matters. First, that Buganda's immediate and strong desire was that the affairs of the kingdom be managed by the Foreign Office, as was originally the arrangement, rather than the Colonial Office. Second, that Her Majesty's Government should prepare and put into effect a plan designed to enable Buganda to achieve her independence and, if possible, within a short stated period of time.[21] To the Kabaka's letter was appended a Memorandum from the Lukiiko to the Governor on the matter. With a detailed history of the Buganda-British relations outlining agreements and assurances made on several matters, the Lukiiko felt "compelled to take immediate steps to safeguard [Buganda's] future" and thus (i) opposed any form of political union affecting Uganda and her neighbouring territories, (ii) urged that the affairs of Buganda revert to the Foreign Office, and (iii) asked a time limit be set for Buganda's independence within the Commonwealth.[22]

Buganda's new demands, set against Cohen's strategy and agenda for reform, brought the politics of Uganda to a precipice. They also represented a change both in the position and the players in the political sphere. Unlike the situation in 1945 and 1949 where the divide was between the people (represented by the Bataka) against the colonial state and the kingdom's leadership in Mengo, in 1953, the Bataka (agitating for the return of the Kabaka from deportation), the Kabaka and the Lukiiko were all aligned against the colonial state.

Similarly, while the demands in the 1945 to 1949 period were sometimes nebulous, the demands in 1953 were direct and unequivocal. The colonial state could no longer dismiss them as coming from "wicked hooligans" that were bent on overthrowing the Kabaka; this time, they came in the form of clear and well-reasoned petitions demanding for freedom and independence. Because the colonial state had no opportunity to shoot the messengers as it had done before, it was left with two alternatives: to cave in, grant independence and go home, or to resort to other more drastic measures.

Faced with this dilemma, Governor Cohen retreated to London on 7 October 1953 to consult his superiors. He returned to Buganda on 27 October and immediately summoned the Kabaka for a meeting. He handed the Kabaka a letter from the Secretary of State for the Colonies and warned him to "avoid open friction with the Protectorate administration and Her Majesty's Government."[23] Cohen also demanded that he and the Kabaka issue a joint statement to the Lukiiko, communicating the declarations set out in the Secretary of State's letter. The Kabaka declined the request for a joint communication without consulting the Lukiiko first. This was obviously a departure from past conduct on the part of the Kabaka who, when he signed the first joint memorandum with Cohen, did not consult the Lukiiko. It was a sign of new times.

In a subsequent meeting on 29 October 1953, the Governor once again pressed the Kabaka to sign a joint declaration, which, once again, the Kabaka declined. At a third meeting on 3 November, which was also attended by the Kabaka's ministers, the Governor reiterated his demands for a joint communiqué to the effect that "there would be no East African Federation unless the majority of the people wanted it," but also that "HM Government could not make any final statement on the matter because the wishes of the people might change."[24] He wanted the Kabaka to tell his people that he was "satisfied with this assurance from the Secretary of State."[25]

With this, Cohen advised, further consideration for the transfer of Buganda's affairs to the Foreign Office would be unnecessary. He also explained that it was impossible for a timetable to be worked out for the achievement of independence because the attainment of that goal would depend on the development of the country. Once again, the Governor unsuccessfully tried to compel the Kabaka to agree, as the 1900 Agreement bound him to do so. On his part, the Kabaka "felt he was duty-bound to tell his people if they were faced with something unsatisfactory," and that, in a contest of loyalty, if he had to choose between loyalty to the Government and loyalty to his people he would be loyal to his people.[26]

A fourth meeting on the matter was called on 6 November 1953 at which there was an impasse. The Kabaka was told that "Buganda could not stand on its own, separate from the rest of the Protectorate," and that "if he failed to accept the advice of the Governor, Britain would withdraw recognition from him."[27] The reason for denying Buganda a chance to be an independent country, according to Governor Cohen, was always that:

> A separation would break the country into two parts with a frontier between them and would thus hamper the progress of all the people. If the Protectorate were to be split, the whole wealth of the country, its ability to trade, its great plans for the advancement of education and other services, would suffer. Buganda by itself would not be strong enough to make the progress it is now making as part of the Protectorate.[28]

Cohen also argued that Buganda's independence was undesirable because it geographically lies at the centre of the Protectorate and economically and in other ways its affairs are completely bound up with those of the Protectorate as a whole.[29]

When the matter came up for debate in the House of Commons on 3 December 1953, Lyttelton stated that "it was his unshakable belief that the peoples of Uganda could not achieve political, social and economic progress without unity." However, Cohen and Lyttelton's arguments for and justification of a forceful union of Uganda, based on the unfortunate and often cynical imperial methods of creating new countries in Africa, must be seen as self-serving. After all, there was little that the British rulers had done previously to engender the unity of the colonised peoples in Uganda when they were in charge. Conversely, they did everything to undermine the unity of the people of Uganda through a divide-and-rule policy and other colonial measures that saw different parts of the country develop independently and without any consultation or involvement of local leadership in other parts. In the case of Buganda and Bunyoro, as an example, colonial policy propagated division and enmity resulting in the fiasco of the "lost counties" that exploded in 1964.

The Governor, seeing that the Kabaka's delegation was not intimidated or likely to change its position, asked the Kabaka to present the issue to the Lukiiko without letting his [the Kabaka's] personal views on the matter to be known. The Kabaka declined this request as well, insisting that "he must first listen to the views of his people."[30] By 11 November 1953, Governor Cohen had formed the idea to depose the Kabaka and so alerted the colonial security forces to a potential rift with the Kabaka. A telegram dated 11 November with information for security personnel read:

> Constitutional issues in Uganda arising from demands that Buganda Kingdom be transferred from colonial to Foreign Office would be a cause of unrest. Ruler Buganda now identifying himself with Uganda African Congress and may have to be deposed. Fourth Battalion KAR being withdrawn from Kenya operations and move to Uganda.[31]

It was arranged that a press announcement be made upon the KAR's arrival in Uganda on 16 November in preparation for the Presenting of the Colours by the Queen and at the request of the Governor.

A fifth meeting was convened on 27 November 1953, at which the Kabaka's delegation was handed an undertaking in which the Kabaka was required to agree:

(i) That he would accept the decisions of Her Majesty's Government and that he would not make statements opposing these decisions; that he would not by word or deed encourage other persons to oppose them; and that he would inform the Great Lukiiko publicly at its meeting that these decisions must be accepted.

(ii) That he would positively cooperate in the future progress of Buganda as an integral part of the Uganda Protectorate, and reaffirm the statement contained in Paragraph 16 of the Memorandum on the Constitutional Development and Reform in Buganda issued last March; and that he would give a particular undertaking to submit names of Baganda members for appointment to the Legislative Council, and that he would inform the Great Lukiiko publicly at its next meeting that he would submit the names.

(iii) That he would cooperate loyally with Her Majesty's Government and the Protectorate Government in the organization and administration of

Buganda in accordance with the 1900 Agreement.[32]

The delegation declined to accede to the terms of the undertaking demanded by the Governor. To them, signing it "without such consultation would be to ignore [the Kabaka's] role in relation to his people and would in any case be contrary to the democratic principles for which HM's Government was supposed to stand and which [they] had recently been trying to implement in Buganda."[33] With this, the delegation was dismissed and asked to return on 30 November 1953.

On 30 November, at the sixth meeting, the Governor repeated the contentious conditions, reading paragraph by paragraph and asking the Kabaka if he accepted each point. The Kabaka responded "I don't" on each point.[34] At the end, to the utter shock of the Kabaka's delegation, the Governor said: "I am very sorry you are no longer considered to be the Kabaka from today."[35] In what amounted to a *coup d'etat*, he handed him a letter stating in part: "Her Majesty's Government, under the provisions of Article 6 of the Uganda Agreement of 1900, now withdraws recognition from you as native ruler of the Province of Buganda."[36]

There and then, and without any further notice, the Kabaka was arrested, shoved into a waiting military plane and deported to England, where he landed on a chilly winter's day without any money or warm clothing. Such was his anguish and disgust at the point of arrest that the Kabaka had a "hazy feeling" to shoot his captors, which he might have but for Katikkiro Kavuma's restraint.[37]

Such was Cohen's confidence and sense of authority that, once the plane was in flight with his enemy on board, he told the remaining delegation that all was ended as far as the Kabaka was concerned, and that he wanted a new Kabaka to be appointed as quickly as possible.[38] He also demanded that the Kabaka's ministers in the room be appointed as Regents and be sworn in at once. This they declined, suggesting, much to the Governor's dismay, that the Lukiiko needed to be involved in the appointment of a new Kabaka and/or the appointment of the Regents. Not unlike some post-independence African despots, Governor Cohen used power over reason to win a political difference.

The public was both terrified and incensed by the news of the Kabaka's deposition. Nnalinya Zalwango, the Kabaka's sister, collapsed and died on receiving the news.[39] Bishop Stuart attacked Lyttelton's "incredible folly" for the act of deposing the Kabaka and accused him of making a "crassly stupid speech about federation."[40] Strangely, a security report filed on 18 December 1953 claimed that Mutesa was "very glad to go, as he did not like his conditions of life as an African potentate; his domestic affairs were also not at all happy [and] he would prefer to live in Europe with the lady of his choice…. Mutesa may have deliberately got himself deposed in order to secure better financial terms from the British Government than he would have obtained if he had merely abdicated."[41]

To avoid any commotion stemming from the deportation, the Resident asked Katikkiro Kavuma to "tell him the names of any people whom I regarded as being particularly dangerous so that they may be arrested,"[42] adding that he "was prepared to send soldiers through the capital and its suburbs to put fear into the hearts of the people and prevent them from resorting to violence."[43] Thereafter, emergency laws set in and the KAR were asked to be on standby.[44]

Governor Cohen issued a statement entitled "Kabaka Mutesa II has broken the Agreement—A Message to the People of Buganda," in which he accused the Kabaka of unwillingness "to cooperate loyally with Her Majesty's Government by persistently refusing to accept the decisions of Her Majesty's Government on matters of major importance affecting the relations of Buganda with Her Majesty's Government."[45] He outlined the Kabaka's violations as requesting a time limit for the independence of Buganda; the transfer of Buganda's affairs from the Colonial to the Foreign Office; and opposition to the Federation of East African territories, all of which, he claimed, amounted to "impossible and impracticable requests."[46] The Governor made an appeal for the people to

> keep calm in this emergency to continue peacefully with your work and to avoid disturbance. Chiefs should remain at their duties and devote themselves to maintaining peace and order in their areas. Adequate forces are ready to deal with troublemakers. I have declared a state of emergency as a precaution.[47]

This message was amplified in a longer 14-page "Statement by the Governor" in which he stated that "loyal cooperation with HM's Government means of course calm acceptance of the grave decision now taken."[48] The statement was intended to reaffirm Cohen's friendly attitude towards the Baganda and his determination to help them and the rest of the Protectorate in every possible way.

The Governor's drastic measure to forcefully depose and deport the Kabaka without trial for challenging colonial authority was not new in the history of British rule in Buganda. It was the same way the colonial administrators had previously handled dissent in Buganda and elsewhere. Kabaka Mwanga and Katikkiro Wamala, as well as Omukama Kabalega of Bunyoro and many others, had suffered the same fate. The deposition was consistent with the actions of Cohen's predecessors and with the general philosophy of colonial rule, namely, to secure the total allegiance of the traditional ruler, to divide and conquer, and to conceal their absolute control under the fig leaf of indirect rule. Once traditional rulers or their chiefs proved difficult, the solution was to eliminate, depose or deport them and replace them with others more agreeable to British interests. In Mutesa's case, Cohen was convinced that his plans for constitutional change in Uganda were being frustrated by Mutesa and that "the future of Uganda could not be sacrificed to the obstinacy of one hereditary ruler."[49]

Governor Cohen was caught in a contradictory web of colonial policy. He wanted rapid reforms in which the Kabaka and Buganda's power and influence would be reduced in the interest of creating a powerful national government for Uganda.[50] He wanted the Kabaka to cede power to a more democratically elected Lukiiko, yet on the questions of an East African Federation and the demand for Buganda's independence, he wanted him to take a unilateral and undemocratic action to both his personal and national peril. In other words, as Low and Pratt have observed, "faced with a crisis, the Government was asking the Kabaka to pause for a moment on his progress towards being a constitutional monarch and to assert his authority as ruler in support of a Government policy."[51]

Reflecting on this, Low and Pratt further state:

> It was no secret that Sir Andrew [Cohen] believed strongly that Uganda must be developed as a unitary state. He made no public explanation of how the Kabaka and other tribal rulers would find positions of prestige and power in such a unitary Uganda. The inevitable impression is that Sir Andrew was sympathetic to a gradual atrophy of these tribal monarchies. Certainly, if he did succeed in promoting wide African participation and interest in the Legislative Council, if a really united Uganda was the final result and national loyalties replaced tribal ones, then inevitably tribal institutions, including the Kabakaship, would be of declining importance. The Kabaka, in other words, was being pressed, with menaces, to support policies whose unpopularity might increasingly isolate him from his people and which, if successful, would seriously undermine his position.[52]

The Kabaka had similar misgivings and wrote: "we had reached a curious position where Sir Andrew demanded that I should use all my power to help him implement a policy of which I disapproved."[53] The Kabaka wrote that his struggle with Cohen had become personal, with Cohen threatening him: "If you don't agree you'll have to go," to which the Kabaka replied, "if anyone has to go, it will certainly be you." [54] Seen in this context, it is unsurprising that the Kabaka stuck to his guns.

The Aftermath of Mutesa's Deportation

On 2 December 1953, two days after the Kabaka's deportation, the Lukiiko convened. It was an angry and tense gathering. Katikkiro Kavuma was attacked for not preventing the deportation and letting the Kabaka go without as much as a fight. He was asked to resign, but survived the onslaught. The meeting resolved to protest the deportation and send telegrams to Sir Winston Churchill, the British Prime Minister, and to Oliver Lyttelton, the Secretary of State for the Colonies. It also agreed to send a telegram to the Kabaka to reassure him of his people's ongoing support and confidence. A delegation comprising Matayo Mugwanya, Apollo Kironde, Thomas Makumbi, Eridadi M. Mulira and Amos K. Sempa was constituted and immediately dispatched to Britain to fight for the Kabaka's return.[55] The ministers rejected the Governor's request that the Lukiiko appoint regents.

The Lukiiko declared two special days of official mourning for the deposition and deportation of the Kabaka. The days chosen were 8 and 9 February 1954, and it was resolved that from those days all the people of Buganda would remain in "mourning until the return of the Kabaka."[56] It is interesting that, in the face of such colonial aggression, Buganda's official reaction was to mourn endlessly as opposed to outright violence against or resistance to the colonial administration.

To this was added a trade boycott of all foreigners' shops for three months, spearheaded by the Uganda National Congress.[57] Faced with growing anger and resentment among the Baganda, the Protectorate Government responded by banning three newspapers: *The Uganda Post, Uganda Eyogera* and *The Express*.[58]

In addition to mourning, and consistent with its non-violent approach, the Lukiiko subsequently resolved to file a petition in the courts challenging the legality of the Kabaka's deportation, with Alafairi Kasule, Semu K. Mukwaba and Juma Tomusange as plaintiffs, and the Attorney General, Daudi Musoke Mukubira and three others as defendants.[59] The colonial government was not rattled by the threatened legal action; in fact, it believed that the action did not have any chance of success.[60] To further break the spirit of the Baganda and their hope for the return of the Kabaka, the colonial Chief Secretary audaciously addressed the Lukiiko, informing it that the decision to depose and deport Mutesa was taken by Sir Winston Churchill's government in London and that there was no question of the Kabaka's return.[61]

The Women's League of Buganda, acting through Parma Ntanda, also called for the return of the Kabaka and challenged his deposition. It accused the Protectorate Government of planning to get rid of Kabaka Mutesa in order to replace him with a pliable successor.[62] To further illustrate the role of women in the struggle to bring back Mutesa,[63] Owen Griffith, a colonial official working with Cohen, documented a touching scene where a delegation of Baganda ladies presented a petition to Cohen requesting that the Kabaka be returned to his country. Cohen could only express sympathy. Griffith writes:

> [T]he deportation was such a traumatic event that little thought had been given to what should happen when the Kabaka was exiled. It was believed that after the Baganda had gotten over the shock, they would appoint a new Kabaka who would be amenable to changes proposed by the colonial government. This belief was based on the assumption that Mutesa was not personally popular, and that the Baganda would want, above all, to preserve the office of Kabaka, and would sacrifice the person of Mutesa to secure the throne.[64]

In fact, the deposition of Mutesa and the proposal to elect a new Kabaka received the support of some senior Baganda individuals. Surprisingly, these included Kawalya Kagwa, the former Katikkiro under Kabaka Mutesa. Kawalya Kagwa considered the colonial administration to have done the right thing in deposing Mutesa, and believed that the solution to the crisis was to retain Paulo Kavuma as the Katikkiro and to install a new Kabaka "as quickly and as directly as possible," and that Prince Mawanda was the only choice. Kawalya Kagwa's stance was clearly unconventional and suggested a serious personal rift between him and Mutesa, whom he had previously served as Katikkiro.[65] It is surprising that after the deportation debacle, the same Kawalya Kagwa accepted an appointment by Mutesa to Buganda's Civil Service Commission.[66]

In a letter to the Secretary of State for the Colonies, Cohen stated that Britain would achieve its objective if Mutesa relinquished "all claims to the Kabakaship for the rest of his life … and if a new Kabaka were then elected." [67] However, as it turned out, this was a miscalculation on the part of the colonial administration, and one that cost Cohen dearly. Contrary to British expectations, the majority of Baganda men and women remained staunch in their support of Mutesa, as well as to the goal of Buganda's independence on which Mutesa was unwavering.

In England, the deportation of the Kabaka was brought up in the House of Commons,[68] by Labour MP Fenner Brockway who criticised Lyttelton, the Colonial Secretary, for the mistake of regarding Kabaka Mutesa as a recalcitrant king. Other Labour MPs asked the government about the legal basis for deporting a British subject from a British territory. No satisfactory answers were given. They demanded that Lyttelton resign, which he did not.

Instead, Lyttelton told the House about the "extremely painful"[69] but friendly encounter he had with the Kabaka (with whom he had good personal relations) at the Colonial Office following the deportation. He said that the Kabaka's deportation was not brusque, and that everything possible had been done to avoid the drastic steps taken, but that all efforts had failed to persuade the Kabaka to take his "proper part in the development both of his own territory and of Uganda as a whole." He argued that the Kabaka's demand that Buganda be made an independent state would threaten the future of the Protectorate. Adding that it was his "unshakable belief that the peoples of Uganda could not achieve political, social and economic progress without unity … inevitably the proposals of the Kabaka had been a direct contradiction of that aim."[70] For that reason, he emphatically concluded that Buganda would remain a component part of Uganda.

The debate was closed with a statement that "the possibility of the Kabaka being able to return to Uganda must be discounted. The Kabaka had thrown away his opportunity for service through short-sightedness and obstinacy."[71] There was no vote taken on the subject. The Colonial Government offered the Kabaka an ex-gratia award of £8,000 per annum for his maintenance if he would drop all claims to Buganda's throne and "not in any way interfere in the affairs of the Protectorate in the future."[72] Mutesa rejected the bait and declined to yield to the pressure to abdicate and return to Uganda as a private citizen.[73] The four-member delegation that went to Britain to fight for his return issued a statement that the Kabaka was "finding difficulty in getting a financial allowance without agreeing to conditions almost amounting to voluntary abdication."[74] To help Mutesa with his financial difficulties, the Baganda, with the involvement of the *Nnabagereka* (the Kabaka's wife), mobilised and collected money throughout the kingdom.[75]

To justify its decision to deport the Kabaka and to divert attention from the demands made by the kingdom of Buganda, the Colonial Office and the Protectorate Government ran a smear campaign in Britain to discredit the Kabaka and show him as a mean and unreliable personality. However, Cohen was keen that nothing should be done "to lend colour to the suggestion that a smear campaign is being pursued from official sources."[76] As part of the campaign, a secret undated dossier on the Kabaka[77] was published and circulated amongst British MPs in which the Kabaka was described as untruthful, mean, spiteful and vindictive, and as one who sees himself as "the centre of a movement set up in rivalry to the Protectorate

Government."[78]

Cohen was happy to have extracts of this report shown to the Archbishop of Canterbury "provided it [was] made absolutely clear that it [was] secret and personal to him, and that nothing contained in it [would] in any circumstances be divulged to any person."[79] A leading British newspaper reported the "astonishing 'smear' campaign that has been officially but secretively launched against [the Kabaka]."[80] It stated:

> Extraordinary efforts have been made to discredit him as an individual. Officials of the colonial office have lobbied MPs with wild allegations that would plainly be actionable ... the church has also been successfully lobbied.... [T]he Socialist friends of Sir Andrew Cohen, and some of his friends in the press have authoritatively put it about that the Kabaka is a mere nobody, the effete holder of an archaic title, and much too rich as well.[81]

On 23 February 1954, for example, Thomas Reid, a Labour MP, made gross and unfair personal attacks against the Kabaka in the House of Commons.[82] Perturbed by these actions, the Kabaka protested to the Secretary of State for the Colonies, quoting another MP, Clement Davies, who had been approached by officials from the Colonial Office with stories that seriously affected him.[83] He asked the Secretary to prevent his officials from continuing to give currency to harmful reports such as those made to Davies and other MPs. In reply, the Secretary of State said:

> The reasons for which Her Majesty's Government withdrew recognition from you are those set out in the White Paper, but you will no doubt remember that at our interview in December, at which you were prepared to modify the standpoint which you had maintained in your discussions with the Governor, I told you that in making up my mind whether you could go back to Buganda I had to take into account also other matters, such as the advisers with whom you had surrounded yourself in Uganda and your private life. But I deplore the idea of any campaign against your personal character and readily give you my assurance that neither I nor any of the officials under my control will countenance or lend ourselves to such a course.[84]

The assurances given to Mutesa did not, however, bring an end to the nasty campaign waged by the establishment against the "Mutesa problem." Back at home, the state of emergency that had been declared in Buganda on the deportation of the Kabaka was lifted at the end of March 1954.[85] However, before long, Governor Cohen declared another state of emergency in June 1954.[86] In justifying this action, Lyttelton told the House of Commons that the "boycott was being intensified by threats and intimidation to the public in Buganda … people have been forcibly prevented from selling and buying goods … intimidation has greatly increased, and criminal elements have been taking advantage of the situation."[87]

The new state of emergency was roundly criticised by Labour MPs, who felt that it was unnecessary and, in any case, ought to have been "the last step and not the first step."[88] They also argued that it was aimed to pressurise the Baganda and ultimately to pave the way for the election of a new Kabaka. Fenner Brockway specifically argued that the state of emergency was actually motivated by the commercial interests of certain European members of the LEGCO with large commercial interests in the colony, who "had threatened to resign unless the Governor did five things: declared a state of emergency; deported the Congress leaders; dismissed disloyal chiefs; mobilised the police; and suspended the native administration in Buganda."[89] Henry Hopkinson, the Minister of State for Colonial Affairs, denied these allegations, saying that although the British Government would like the Lukiiko to appoint a new Kabaka, it would not bring pressure to bear or to impose a Kabaka upon them.

As Britain grappled with the crisis of the Kabaka's deportation, the trade boycott and the state of emergency in Buganda, it was, at the same time, embroiled in another crisis in neighbouring Kenya, where the Mau Mau rebellion was at its height. In Kenya, during this time, the British, under the command of General Erskine, were engaged in the regular and systematic abuse of detainees in screening centres and detention camps, including beatings, torture and castration of detainees.[90]

With growing hostility in Buganda and the refusal of an obstinate Lukiiko to cooperate in the appointment of regents and a new Kabaka, the Protectorate Government was caught up in a crisis. It had to do something to diffuse the situation and restore order and normality. For this reason, the Secretary of State told the House of Commons that "the long term aim of HM's Government [was] to build the Protectorate into a self-governing state" in which, "when self-government [was] achieved, the government of the country [would] be mainly in the hands of Africans," and that "when the time for self-government eventually came, HM's Government [would] wish to be satisfied that the rights of the minority communities resident in Uganda are properly safeguarded in the constitution, but this [would] not detract from the primarily African character of the country."[91]

Cohen called the statement a "solemn and morally binding pledge that provides a full safeguard for the future."[92] This statement was intended to calm Buganda's nerves on the issue of the East African Federation. Although still vague in some respects, the statement was a better assurance than that given to Buganda prior to the Kabaka's deportation. Further, Cohen requested the Lukiiko to set up a committee, chaired by a constitutional expert, to consider the constitutional restructuring of Buganda. The Lukiiko, with some members hoping that the restructuring would help in the Kabaka's return while others remained sceptical of Cohen's intentions, reluctantly agreed to the proposal and appointed a delegation.[93]

On 1 March 1954, it was announced that Professor William Keith Hancock of the University of London was to head a constitutional committee for Buganda. The committee started its work in June while the state of emergency subsisted in Buganda, and ended in September 1954. It received many petitions and views from Buganda, all of which had to be discussed with Cohen who, in a way, was acting as its clearing house and needed to be informed and approve of what information went before the committee.

Before Hancock could finalise his report, Governor Cohen held a separate meeting with the new Secretary of State for the Colonies, Alan Lennox-Boyd, in mid-August where they agreed to reach a settlement with the committee on specific lines, namely, that the Kabaka would become a constitutional ruler (i.e. removed from the political arena); that Buganda would accept the principle of the Protectorate as a unitary state; that the Protectorate Government would delegate certain powers to Buganda; that a ministerial system would be introduced; and that these arrangements would be subject to review after five years.[94] The meeting underlined the main objective of the Hancock Commission: "that for the first time it would ensure the cooperation and willing participation of the Baganda in the Protectorate Legislative Council and draw them away from their former separatist attitude."[95] It was clear that the return of the Kabaka would only be accepted if the Lukiiko and the people of Buganda accepted these terms.

In this context, the Hancock Commission faced a *fait accompli* and its recommendations[96] (also known as Recommendations of the Namirembe Conference) went along the lines handed down by the Secretary of State for the Colonies and Governor Cohen. The recommendations included, among others, that the Kingdom of Buganda, under the Kabaka's government, should continue to be an integral part of the Protectorate—recognising the final and overriding authority of the Protectorate Government; that the conduct of public affairs in Buganda should be in the hands of Ministers; and that while all the traditional dignities of the Kabaka should be fully safeguarded, Kabakas in the future should be constitutional rulers bound by solemn engagement to observe the conditions of the Agreements regarding the Constitution and not to prejudice the security and welfare of the Buganda people and the Protectorate.[97]

The Hancock Commission also recommended that the government of Buganda become a modern representative democracy and cease to be run on a traditional or tribal basis; that the Governor be granted veto powers over a list of prospective candidates for the Katikkiroship; that ministers should be accountable to the Lukiiko and not to the Kabaka; that a civil service board be established for appointments to the local government; that the judiciary be independent; and that the Kabaka become the "symbol of the unity of the people of Buganda and of the continuity between their past, present and future."[98]

Alongside the Hancock recommendations, Cohen made some others of his own concerning the political structures and developments in the rest of the Protectorate. They included the introduction of a ministerial system; an increase in the number of Africans in the Protectorate government; and the expansion and restructuring of the LEGCO. There is no evidence that these recommendations resulted from consultations or agreements with the leaders or representatives from other parts of Uganda. It is interesting to note that in September 1955, as it concluded the Buganda Agreement, Britain, through Cohen, also signed the Bunyoro Agreement[99] with Sir Tito Gafabusa Winyi IV, the Omukama of Bunyoro, in which the powers of the Omukama were further whittled away and his relationship with the Governor and HMG were redefined.

The discussions between the Governor, the Lukiiko committee and Hancock did little to calm the minds of the Baganda, whose principal concern was the return of the Kabaka. According to Low and Pratt, "interest continued to be concentrated on the Kabaka's return … and the demand was that his return should be granted before any consideration was given to constitutional reform."[100] Buganda's opposition to Queen Elizabeth II's visit to Uganda to open the Owen Falls Dam in 1954 also signified hostility toward the British Government.[101] The support and love for the exiled Kabaka and indignation against the Governor became widespread in Uganda and even extended to Kenya, where the Mau Mau fighters added the release and return of the Kabaka to his throne among the grounds of their struggle against the British.[102]

The hearing of the case, in which three plaintiffs sought declarations on the legality of the Kabaka's deportation, commenced on 27 September 1954.[103] The plaintiffs argued that the Kabaka was wrongly and illegally deposed and deported. Ralph Dreschfield, the Protectorate's Attorney

General, who applied to be joined as a party, argued mainly that the withdrawal of recognition from the Kabaka was done within the terms of the 1900 Agreement. Accordingly, the issue was not justiciable because the matters of the Agreement could only be interpreted, applied or handled by the Protectorate itself and not by courts of law. He argued that "whether just or unjust, politic or impolitic, beneficial or injurious, it was no matter on which a court of law could give an opinion."[104] This line of argument exposed the Protectorate Government as one that acted as if it was above the law and did not really care about the legal, political or other consequences of its actions within the Protectorate.

As the hearing of the case continued, the matter of the Kabaka's deportation continued to be a subject of discussion in the British cabinet. In a meeting of 20 October 1954, the new Secretary of State for the Colonies, Alan Lennox-Boyd, upon his return from Uganda, expressed his conviction against the return of the Kabaka. To him, "the reliable and moderate elements among the Baganda [were] against Mutesa's return."[105] He asked the cabinet to authorise him, in case the judgement was adverse, to talk to the Kabaka, the Governor and the Lukiiko's representatives on the new situation and Hancock's report and, if the decision was pro-government, to announce that the government was right all along and would stand by that decision. On 22 October 1954, he lamented to his colleagues, thus:

> Trouble would have been avoided if the Kabaka had been lectured here and sent back. But the Governor [Cohen] advised to the contrary. Having once deposed him, we are now in a difficult position. During my visit I became satisfied that weight of evidence … is against allowing him to return now that he has been deposed. The Governor meanwhile has turned around to oppose the view. If we were free agents, therefore, I would maintain his exile. But now there is the legal action. The decision should now turn on the result of that action. If we win, his deposition should stand. If we lose, we would have new reason for allowing him to return. The Prime Minister pointed out that "an adverse decision would give us the worst of both worlds: shown to have acted wrongly and get an unfriendly ruler back."[106]

The meeting, however, agreed to take no decision until the judgment was made.

The Chief Justice, Sir John B. Griffin, delivered the judgement on 4 November 1954. He held that the plaintiffs had lost the case, but also that "by declaring withdrawal of recognition under Article 6 of the Agreement the Secretary of State was mistaken."[107] That mistake lay in the fact that although there was a failure by the Kabaka to abide by the decisions of policy, there had not been failure of the kind visualised by Article 6, namely, a failure by the Kabaka, chiefs and people to cooperate loyally in matters of day-to-day administration and organisation of Buganda kingdom. The judgement caused jubilation, followed by demands for the immediate return of the Kabaka. Thousands of people gathered around the Lubiri (palace) to congratulate the Kabaka's wife, the Nnabagereka. The Omukama of Toro declared a public holiday to celebrate the favourable outcome of the Kabaka's case.

The judgment presented a serious dilemma to Cohen and the Protectorate Government. It was a grave indictment on his and Lyttelton's judgement in their harsh decision to depose and deport the Kabaka. Now, all of a sudden, they had to eat humble pie and reverse their position on the return of the Kabaka. The judgement also threatened to torpedo the constitutional reforms proffered by the Hancock Committee—especially the part requiring Buganda to agree to participate in Protectorate affairs, which was the main cause of the dispute leading to the withdrawal of recognition in the first instance.[108]

To avoid humiliation and to redeem both himself and the British Government, Cohen—choosing to see the development as an opportunity for a new approach to the question of the Kabaka's return—came up with a scheme under which the Kabaka would be allowed to return but subject to certain conditions. The scheme aimed at once to justify the original decision to depose the Kabaka and the imposition of stringent conditions on his return. The plot was presented and agreed upon in the British cabinet on 9 November 1954. Under this approach, the British Government would justify the Kabaka's deposition based on the judgment, which found that Mutesa had been disloyal. Secondly, in order that the British Government would be seen as bowing only to the majesty of English law and not any other native pressures, it would allow the Kabaka to return, but subject to certain conditions and after a suitable interval. The conditions were justified as a mechanism to prevent the Kabaka from acting disloyally in future. The plot was that the Lukiiko would be given the opportunity to choose whether a new Kabaka should be elected or whether Kabaka Mutesa II should return as native ruler of Buganda.

The conditions, simultaneously announced both in the Lukiiko and House of Commons, were that:

> (i) The agreed recommendations of the Namirembe Conference [i.e. the Hancock Commission] should be accepted as a whole by the great Lukiiko.
> (ii) Her Majesty's Government and the Lukiiko should agree on the terms of the solemn engagement recommended by the Namirembe

Conference to be entered into by the Kabaka. The amendments and additions to the 1900 Agreement to give effect to the agreed recommendations should also be agreed by Her Majesty's Government and the great Lukiiko and the amending agreement should be formally executed by the Governor on behalf of Her Majesty's Government and by the Regents and representatives of the Lukiiko on behalf of Buganda and be brought into effect.

(iii) In order that the new arrangements may be well established before the Great Lukiiko is called upon to make the decision, its choice whether a new Kabaka should be elected should be made nine months after the new arrangements have been brought into effect. Her Majesty's Government would however be glad to shorten the period if they were convinced before the end of it that the constitutional arrangements had become well established and were working satisfactorily. Her Majesty's Government would make every effort to ensure that they were brought into effect by 31st March next year. When the choice of the Lukiiko has been made, the Kabaka would be required to enter into the solemn engagement and to sign and thereby confirm the amending Agreement before he is recognized by Her Majesty's Government.[109]

Once Cohen mentioned the possibility of electing a new Kabaka, the Lukiiko descended into pandemonium and he was forced to leave the podium and the Lukiiko hall without reading the full conditions he had prepared. Outside the hall, he was greeted with insults and flying stones.[110] Katikkiro Kavuma faced a similar fate.[111] The Lukiiko reconvened a few days later and reconsidered the proposals. Such was its anger that it "rejected almost unanimously the suggestion that it should accept the recommendations of the Hancock Committee even in principle."[112] It was concerned that by pegging the Kabaka's return to the acceptance of the proposals, Cohen was twisting Buganda's arm. Also, the nine-month period given before the Kabaka could return was unacceptable. The Uganda National Congress called the Hancock recommendations a "Lyttelton Constitution" that must be rejected.

The Lukiiko resolved to disband its committee and replace it with a more conservative one headed by Michael Kintu, whose job was to study the Hancock recommendations and report to the Lukiiko. The Resident of Buganda, C. A. L. Richards, was quick to point out that the constitution of a new committee headed by Kintu would delay the possibility of the return of Kabaka Mutesa II, and that the responsibility for postponing that possibility would lie on the Lukiiko. Frustrated by the Lukiiko's position on the Hancock recommendations, Richards separately made an inquiry into the possibility of splitting the new committee from within.[113] It is not clear whether he pursued this option, but Kintu's committee finalised its report and suggested some amendments to the original recommendations which were unanimously passed by the Lukiiko.[114]

After back-and-forth meetings with the colonial government, Buganda yielded to British insistence that the Kabaka's return should be conditional upon the Lukiiko's acceptance of the new Namirembe Agreement. In effect, the Lukiiko was put in a difficult position of either signing up to the new terms that greatly weakened the Kabakaship or having the Kabaka remain in exile. So, just as in 1900, when a major agreement was signed while Kabaka Mwanga was in exile imposed by the British, the situation in 1954 was that a new major agreement was being signed under duress while Kabaka Mutesa was similarly under a British-imposed exile. The Lukiiko passed the provisional agreement on 12 August 1955 and it was signed by the Regents on 14 August 1955. Thereafter, there was a change of guard at Mengo as Katikkiro Kavuma was replaced by Michael Kintu. The date of 17 November 1955 was then set for the Kabaka's return.[115] For the special day, a buoyant Buganda Government ordered for a new state car for the Kabaka—a Rolls Royce convertible.[116] It was a victorious and heroic return for the Kabaka.

Notwithstanding the debacle of Mutesa's deportation, Governor Cohen was gracious and joined the preparations for the Kabaka's return. In fact, he and other Protectorate officials spent a great deal of their time ensuring that the Kabaka received a rousing homecoming. Cohen had fears, though, for the future of some of Buganda's officials: particularly those considered to have been friendly to the Protectorate during the Kabaka's deportation.[117] He thus asked Secretary of State for the Colonies Alan Lennox-Boyd to talk to the Kabaka and discourage him from victimising those that were opposed to his return and to impress upon him the need to cultivate good relations with the Protectorate Government.

He undertook to do everything possible to make the relationship friendly and to help the Kabaka's government in any way. Additionally, he arranged for the Protectorate Government to give new posts to Katikkiro Kavuma and Matayo Mugwanya, who he felt were likely to be victimised.[118] He was also worried about the future of the Ssaza chiefs the Kago (chief) of Kyadondo, the Sekiboobo (chief) of Kyaggwe and the Pokino (chief) of Buddu.[119] The reasons for this patronage are not difficult to fathom: this segment of Buganda's leaders had remained loyal to the colonial officials and did not present much trouble to British rule during the Kabaka's deportation.

On 18 October 1955, Mutesa II signed the 1955 Agreement that made him a constitutional monarch. With that, demands for Buganda's independence subsided and the colony started a new chapter.

A Commentary on the 1953 Crisis

The crisis in Buganda between 1953 and 1955 was seminal in directing the political developments in Uganda and signalling the decline of colonial control and power. For the "protected," it offered an opportunity to galvanise their opposition to colonialism in Uganda. For the "protector," it signalled the need for a policy change aimed at preparing the colony for self-government and the coloniser's inevitable exit. The crisis was the catalyst for the formation and operation of political parties such as the Uganda National Congress, whose focus on the attainment of self-rule became sharper and more urgent.

For Buganda, it was a period of awakening and deep reflection on its relations with the "protector." It helped destroy the myth that Buganda enjoyed, or was entitled to, any special status under Britain. It revealed that the real interest of the "protector" was to make Uganda a unitary state, with Buganda as an equal member therein, even though this was not what Buganda had bargained for. The refusal to move Buganda from the Colonial to the Foreign Office represented another wake up call for the Baganda in terms of Britain's determination to develop Uganda as one country at all costs, despite the fact that it had done little to engender the unity of its constituent parts and, indeed, had arguably negated the possibility of any such unity through its divide and rule policies.

It was during this period that Cohen and his superiors in London drove the final nail into the coffin of Buganda's hopes for independence. Britain's dogmatic belief that Uganda should remain one country, in spite of the complications associated with such a political structure, was based on an *idée fixe* which had been reached without any serious study of local perspectives and without the acquiescence of the people in the colony. It was a colonial imposition, with its roots in the Berlin Conference of 1885 (where the European powers effectively sliced up Africa to suit their own colonial ambitions), and one essentially aimed towards furthering the interests of the "protector" and not those of the "protected." In this way, as it had from the beginning, Britain sought to protect its own interests over and above those of the colonised peoples. Partly because of this self-serving and patronising colonial approach—in the creation of Uganda—the country has suffered instability and struggles to build a national ethos.

For Cohen and Britain, this period presented an unexpected crisis. As it turned out, Mutesa's deportation resulted in a short-term gain but long-term pain for the colonial government because the matter plunged Buganda and the rest of the Protectorate into an unstoppable national political agitation. With the deportation debacle, Cohen's plans for a unitary state with equal constituents, as well as his desire to diminish the role and power of the Kabaka and the Lukiiko, all buckled. Along with these went Britain's long-held strategic desire for a closer union between its territories in East Africa.

Britain's interest in a closer union in East Africa was founded on economic as well as strategic considerations. From a capitalist outlook, a larger territory in East Africa with a large frontage to the Indian Ocean would mean a bigger market, a larger labour reserve, and larger pool of resources and revenue. From a management purview, the economies of scale of administering a large area under single command would help reduce the need to have three Governors for Uganda, Tanganyika and Kenya. It would also help diminish the irritating tribal nationalism from groups like the Baganda in Uganda and the Kikuyu in Kenya.

In the context of Buganda, gone were the days of Mwanga and Kagwa, when a king could be deposed and an infant one installed without so much as a public whimper, as Cohen realised to his cost. He had hoped that by removing the Kabaka and quickly replacing him with another, Britain could swiftly solve the "Mutesa problem." Instead, his removal created an even bigger crisis for the colonial regime. It would appear, however, that Cohen's biggest miscalculation lay in his failure to understand the Baganda and the Kabakaship of the 1950s. His assumption that once he deported the Kabaka it would be easy to impose a replacement, as was done with Mwanga in 1897, was out of step with the times.

In Mutesa—indeed like his predecessors Mwanga and Chwa—Britain failed to build a colonially pliant Kabaka. British benefaction extended to Mutesa through a Cambridge education and other colonial perks, such as his decoration as a Knight Commander of the British Empire (KBE) failed to establish the kind of colonial patronage that would enable Britain to control him and Buganda at will.

Buganda in 1953 was a far different place from the late 1890s. The crisis of 1953 that stretched to 1955 left British colonial authority significantly eroded. Britain needed a different approach in the imposition of its rule and the resolution of disputes, but Cohen was unable to see this. But for his aggressive, impatient strong-arm tactics, the situation could have been different. Indeed, even officials such as Don Marshall —who were involved in the planning and implementation of the constitutional development of the country—believed that Cohen, with Colonial Office approval, "was pushing ahead too quickly and before the people were ready for his sweeping changes."[120] As Cohen's term drew to a close, both he and the Colonial Office realised that they had "gone too far, too fast."[121] For this reason, although at the end of his tour Cohen wished to carry on for a further term as Governor, so as to "retrieve the situation and put things back on an even keel," his request was refused.[122]

The crisis of Mutesa's deportation culminated in the 1955 Agreement, which was intended to diminish the Kabaka's political power and firmly incorporate Buganda into Uganda. In reality, however, the Agreement had only a nominal effect. In fact, the Kabaka returned and operated with even more political clout than before. The Baganda largely disregarded the terms of the 1955 Agreement because of the context and manner in which it was negotiated and executed. With the Kabaka held hostage in Britain, the legitimacy of the Agreement and the freedom with which it was negotiated was always in question. As such, despite the fact that Buganda's leadership participated in the negotiations that preceded the Agreement, it maintained that the Agreement was procured through blackmail; in other words, that it was executed more out of Buganda's desire to get its Kabaka out of captivity than its belief in the need for constitutional change in the kingdom. In fact, as we show ahead, in its Memorandum to the Queen seeking the termination of British protection, the Lukiiko denigrated the 1955 Agreement, saying it had never been freely negotiated, as the Kabaka's return from exile depended on the Agreement being signed by the chiefs. Thus, as far as Buganda is concerned, the Agreement was obtained under duress and was illegitimate and voidable. By the Kabaka's conduct after his return, it is clear that he and the Lukkiko elected to avoid the Agreement.

This argument is particularly relevant in the context of English law that provides that agreements reached under undue influence can be rescinded and those made under duress can be avoided once the duress has been lifted. These principles are applicable in international law relating to the negotiation of treaties between independent nations.[123] But although Buganda was not a sovereign nation in 1955 it is clear that it was not a free party in the negotiations with a controlling colonial authority that placed tough constitutional conditions on the return and reinstatement of the Kabaka who it had wrongfully deported, deposed and held hostage during the Hancock Constitutional negotiations.

The Problematic Enforcement of the 1955 Agreement

As already observed, the return of the Kabaka in 1955 gave a fresh impetus to political activity in Buganda and the rest of the Protectorate. New political organisations headed by youthful leaders with scanty knowledge and experience in governance emerged rapidly. These included the Uganda National Congress (UNC) and the Democratic Party (DP),[124] the Uganda Labour Party, the Uganda Nationalist Party, the Uganda Reform Party, the Uganda Tax Payers' Party and the Progressive Party.[125] The quick growth of political organisations in a wholly traditional population (with little knowledge or appreciation of Western-style political pluralism) and acting against the interests of the colonial government, was a major turning point in the politics of the Protectorate.

In this context the implementation of the 1955 Agreement in Buganda faced great difficulty. In fact, as far as Buganda's leadership was concerned, the Agreement was a dead letter in many ways and was largely disregarded. In particular, little was achieved with regard to the new designation of the Kabaka as a ceremonial or constitutional monarch and the intended emasculation of his power in Buganda's political setup. This was not surprising, given that the new Katikkiro, Michael Kintu, and most of the Lukiiko members were essentially the Kabaka's men, and thus gave much deference to his bidding. On their attitude and behaviour, Governor Crawford noted that

> [T]he first Ministers are [the] Kabaka's yes-men, extravagant and inefficient. I have met them twice and, with the exception of one rat-like little man called Sempa, they are a dull lot.... [It is] difficult to get the Ministers or the Kabaka to accept any advice or to make any impression on them. The Lukiiko is still dominated by the Kabaka's clique.[126]

But not everybody regarded the new Buganda administration in such a negative light. According to Karugire, for example, "the Kabaka, his chiefs and most of his subjects were one and their main object was to protect the institutions of Buganda against all kinds of threat."[127] In view of this, the implementation of the 1955 Agreement faced difficulties right from the beginning and, contrary to the expectation that the Kabaka's power would be diminished, he instead became more popular and more powerful.[128]

To demonstrate his renewed power and influence, the Kabaka intervened and stopped the Lukiiko in its attempts to distribute amongst its own members 154 square miles of land that remained unallocated under the 1900 Agreement as a reward to its members for their role in his return. The Kabaka's influence was also demonstrated by the appointment of the kingdom's Ssaza chiefs without consultation with or the prior approval of the Governor. And, as his veto of Matayo Mugwanya's appointment to the Lukiiko in 1956 showed, the Kabaka wielded more authority in the control of Buganda's politics. Because that veto had considerable significance for events in the run-up to independence, it is the subject of a deeper reflection below.

The Mugwanya Affair and the Waning of Colonial Power in Uganda

Matayo Mugwanya was formerly the Omulamuzi (Minister for Justice) and had been a Regent during Mutesa's infancy. He was the son of Stanislas Mugwanya, who had been a Regent during Daudi Chwa's infancy. He was a staunch Catholic leader and an indomitable political actor in the kingdom of Buganda's structures. However, following the Kabaka's deportation in 1953, he fell out with the Lukiiko and the Kabaka over his alleged views on the replacement of the Kabaka with another prince.[129] He was thus dropped as a Lukiiko member of the Hancock Committee. He also lost an election for the Katikkiroship to Michael Kintu once Paulo Kavuma retired as the Katikkiro. Having lost his position, Mugwanya vied for a position in the Lukiiko.

On 24 July 1956, he was elected to represent the Ssaza of Mawokota. The Lukiiko, however, rejected his election and advised the Kabaka not to appoint him. Although the Kabaka was not bound to follow the Lukiiko's recommendations, he was under a constitutional duty to appoint Mugwanya, who had been duly elected in accordance with Article 5 of the 1955 Agreement. When reminded by the Governor of his solemn undertaking to uphold the Constitution and to appoint Mugwanya, the Kabaka countered that he was less concerned with his reputation in the United Kingdom as with his reputation with the Lukiiko.[130] He felt that his reputation would suffer more if he were to go against the advice given to him by the Lukiiko and less if he defied the Governor and the 1955 Agreement. The Kabaka, who already felt that the 1955 Agreement was due for some alteration, argued:

> We all agree that the law and constitution must be followed, but the Lukiiko has certain things which it cannot avoid from following. The Constitution was made to be followed by the Lukiiko, but on our side there are certain things which we must follow for the good of our country … what we have learned is this, that everything that is done by Mugwanya has the support of the British Government. This makes us doubtful and suspicious.[131]

Mugwanya was incensed by the decision taken by both the Lukiiko and the Kabaka. He decided to defy them and to challenge the decision in court. In addition, he petitioned the Governor saying that the Government of Buganda would never be effective so long as the present Kabaka, ministers and Lukiiko were in office.[132] He went as far as advising the colonial government to suspend the Buganda Constitution and ministers and administer Buganda directly as an ordinary province of the Protectorate. According to him, the Kabaka and Lukiiko's position was made "under the influence of jealousy, envy, fear, hatred and religious bias."[133] He also proclaimed:

> I am ready to stake my life and my all for the sake of good democratic principles. If the Kabaka has unlimited powers in this country this should be clearly stated, otherwise I cannot see why he should be allowed to override the constitution and the laws which are made to bring peace in the land.[134]

However, none of the Governor's directives or Mugwanya's histrionics would move the Kabaka or the Lukiiko and, in the end, Mugwanya was not appointed to the Lukiiko.

The Kabaka's defiance and disregard of the 1955 Agreement and the Governor's instructions set the stage for a showdown and, ultimately, shaped the relations between Buganda and the Protectorate in the subsequent years. It is notable that the colonial administration allowed the Kabaka and the Lukiiko to get away with such disregard of the 1955 Constitution without raising cries of disloyalty or accusing the Kabaka of violating his solemn undertaking. Besides his non-cooperation with Cohen in 1953, this was yet another instance where Mutesa and, by extension, Buganda stood up to an otherwise omnipotent colonial authority.

This may be seen as evidence of both a resurgence of Buganda's power and resistance to British rule, and the waning of colonial authority in general. But it may also be attributed to a reluctance on part of the colonial government to fight another battle with Mutesa following the deportation debacle.

In a way, just as it had abandoned Apolo Kagwa, M. L. Nsibirwa and S. W. Kulubya, the colonial state did not throw its full weight behind Mugwanya. It is probable that the colonial players were still smarting from the Kabaka's deportation and return and did not wish to start another fight with the Kabaka. According to Cohen's replacement, Governor F. Crawford, the refusal to appoint Mugwanya "illustrated that there [was] no real democratic progress, but even retrogression, in Buganda and that the Kabaka [was] still to his people and his ministers and most of the Lukiiko the absolute monarch of yore."[135] But perhaps more importantly, and coming on the heels of the deportation fiasco, this case also illustrated the deepening crisis of the colonial regime in imposing its authority over the Kabaka and his subjects. At the same time, it shows the growing limitations of Buganda's agency in British colonial rule.

Diminished colonial authority was compounded by the difficult financial situation of the Protectorate which, for the first time in 20 years, faced a budget deficit of over £2 million.[136] In a sense, Uganda was quickly becoming not only ungovernable, but also unprofitable to the colonial state, since the revenues had dwindled while the cost of administration and social services had grown significantly.[137] The colonial state was thus caught up in a serious political and financial predicament. Given this precarious context, it was not long before the Lukiiko—led by Amos K. Sempa—started agitating for Buganda's independence. Contemporaneously, bitter over his rejection by Mengo, Mugwanya and other Catholic stalwarts joined the Democratic Party to oppose both British rule and the dominant Protestant oligarchy in Mengo—a development that was to greatly influence political developments in (B)Uganda in the lead-up to and long after independence.

After the Mugwanya affair, Buganda's cooperation with the colonial government went downhill. For instance, going against the wishes of the Protectorate Government, Buganda's leadership opposed the direct elections of Baganda representatives to the LEGCO in 1958 and refused to replace a member who had resigned. To make a political point, Katikkiro Kintu sued the Attorney General of Uganda, challenging the constitution of the LEGCO and Buganda's representation in it.[138] He sought a declaration that the Legislative Council of the Uganda Protectorate as constituted was not the Legislative Council referred to in the 1955 Agreement. This was to justify Buganda's refusal to participate in the elections organised by that Legislative Council.

The Court dismissed the suit, holding that "the words 'the Legislative Council of the Protectorate in the second Schedule' included the Legislative Council after the changes made in 1958." Interestingly, the Court also held that the 1955 Agreement was an Act of State and, as such, was beyond the control of municipal law, and that even if there had been a breach of faith, the matter was outside the purview of the High Court of Uganda, or of the Court of Appeal. This holding reinforced the old colonial view that the courts in Uganda had no jurisdiction in interpreting or determining the legality of the 1955 Agreement and were incapable of making any decision on it. Only the British Courts had such powers.

That notwithstanding, when the case was lost, the Lukiiko rejected the ruling and wrote a memorandum signed by all of its members to the Queen of England in which they stated that "both the 1900 and the 1955 agreements had been imposed upon Buganda against the wishes of the people," and that

> Buganda had been treated simply as one province of Uganda and [her] government had not been respected. Britain was still trying to force

> Buganda to become part of a unitary state whereas it should be left to the Baganda and the other people of the Protectorate to decide for themselves what their future relations should be.[139]

The Lukiiko's standpoint here was really aimed at challenging the validity of the 1955 Agreement and defying its terms, which ultimately aimed to reduce its powers and vest them in the Legislative Council, as well as to trim the powers of the Kabaka.

In response to Buganda's refusal to replace its members on the LEGCO, the Protectorate Government nominated as backbenchers individuals who had either fallen out with Buganda kingdom or were agreeable to the colonial regime. These were Michael Kawalya Kagwa (former Katikkiro), S. W. Kulubya (former Omuwanika) and Matayo Mugwanya (former Omulamuzi).[140] The colonial government thus started a policy that would drive a wedge into Buganda's political class with the debilitating effect of dividing and weakening it. By 1961, it was noted that the Protectorate Government's policy was to "let the Baganda split themselves without any outward sign of action to this end by the central government."[141] Needless to say, Buganda's politics has, since this time, been fractured and, inevitably, the ability of its politicians to speak with one voice on Buganda's issues has been limited.

A Change of Guard—from Cohen to Crawford: Dealing with a Deepening Colonial Crisis in (B)Uganda

Governor Cohen's term of office ended in February 1957 and he was replaced by Sir Fredrick Crawford. Cohen left Uganda a disappointed man because his ambitions of rapid political development of the country under a unitary government and the weakening and removal of the Kabaka from the political scene had not been achieved. In a parting memorandum to the Secretary of State for the Colonies, Cohen listed his achievements in the political, social and economic spheres.[142] He stated how he had helped move the country from "benevolent paternalism" by nominating more African representatives to both the LEGCO and Executive Council, taking pride in his attempts to replace "tribal patriotism" with a strong central government in a united Uganda.[143]

In this regard, he considered that the disparity in size and importance between Buganda and the other parts of the country was a complicating factor. He pointed out that Uganda lacked "ethnological unity" and that virtually all the other tribes feared "Buganda imperialism" in the future and were determined to resist it.[144] He saw the basic political problem of

Uganda as being the "relationship of the country as a whole with its parts, Buganda and the rest."[145] To Cohen, the political solution to this problem was one united country with a strong central government.

Although the majority of the people in Buganda wanted a federated political structure, Cohen strongly felt that the country could not afford one, arguing that

> there would not be sufficient manpower for very many years to come to operate a federal system; nor would a federal system be appropriate to a country of such a relatively small size as Uganda. A series of very small states linked together in a federal system would not have the strength to provide the country with the necessary leadership or to carry through the comprehensive programme of economic and social development which would be needed in increasing measure.[146]

Given the rise of what he called "incipient nationalism" in Buganda,[147] and also informed by the experiences of 1945, 1949 and 1953, Cohen considered that British aims in Uganda would be secured by "advice, persuasion and diplomacy."[148] Compared to his early methods of rapid implementation of his ideas, by the end of his tour, Cohen had realised that securing Bugandas' general acceptance of the central government could "obviously not be done either easily or quickly." It was not, in his opinion, even possible to say whether such a task would succeed, while noting that if it failed, it would be "much more difficult to establish a unitary constitution for the whole country in the future."[149]

Clearly, Cohen understood the limitations of creating a "unitary state" in Uganda and, to allay the public's fears, he avoided the use of the term, choosing instead to refer to his project as building a "strong and united country with a strong central government."[150] At the end of his term, the country was running a deficit budget, and yet the British Government was unable to provide funds for colonial development or loan finance, as it was itself in financial distress.

Oddly, and not withstanding his attempts to Africanise and democratise governance in Uganda, coupled with his various accomplishments, there is no doubt that Cohen left behind a weaker colonial state, both politically and economically, than he had inherited from Governor Hall. Cohen's accomplishments included the building of the Owen Falls Dam, the western extension of the railway, the Kilembe mines in Kasese, a cement factory in Tororo and a textile factory in Jinja, as well as the founding of the Uganda Development Corporation (UDC) in 1952 with £5 million, chaired by Joseph Trevor Simpson, who ran it until 1964. However, much as he succeeded in expanding and inducting more Africans into the

LEGCO and the Executive Council, he miserably failed to coerce or persuade Buganda to embrace either the LEGCO or the idea of a unitary Government. His rushed deposition and deportation of the Kabaka turned out to be his Waterloo. Far from diminishing the stature of Buganda and the Kabaka, it turned out that Cohen's actions at once enhanced the Kabaka's political profile and lowered the authority and esteem of the colonial state in the eyes of the Baganda. The Kabaka's victorious return in 1955 led to a marked upsurge of "tribal pride" in Buganda which, in turn, informed Buganda's renewed push for autonomy and, in particular, its unilateral declaration of independence in December 1960.

At the end of his tour as Governor, and in spite of the Mutesa deportation debacle, Cohen was not given an acrimonious send-off by Buganda. The Governor's non-hostile reception of Mutesa upon his return from exile in 1955, Buganda's generally tolerant and forgiving nature, and the "strange chemistry" of affection by ordinary Africans towards Cohen helped mitigate the anguish that the Baganda felt about his deportation of their king in 1953[151]—so much so that, as stated above, if he'd had his way, Cohen would have chosen to extend his stay as Governor. For the same reason, he was one of the British guests who returned to Uganda to witness the granting of independence in 1962.

When Sir Fredrick Crawford took over office, he found a difficult and fairly delicate situation. He immediately reached out to the Kabaka and his ministers, requesting them to avoid polemics and the adoption of inflexible positions. He urged them instead "by amicable discussion to settle matters locally and not always to resort to petitions to the Queen, or to the Secretary of State, or the costly employment of leading London lawyers."[152] After two months on the job, he found that the political situation was still tense and that the demands for self-government, mostly from the UNC, were persistent. He found the Protectorate government machine in need of reorganisation. Worse still, he inherited a government that was broke: in his own words, "Uganda was no longer rich."[153] The question of elections to the LEGCO was fraught with difficulties, with some parts of the country wanting direct elections and others not. There was a general sense of desperation and urgency to the demands for political freedom.

The crisis of the colonial state can be discerned from Crawford's letter to Alan Lennox-Boyd, the then Secretary of State for the Colonies, in which he observed:

> the need for time is evident everywhere—or to put it in another way, the need to slow things down until we have consolidated recent advances while at the same time keeping up some momentum or at least the

> appearance of it. The politicians, the most likely cause of unrest, will not be diverted, alas, to economic development and "more money for everyone." They press for one thing—breakneck political advance so as to achieve self-government at the earliest [possible moment], regardless of the country's unreadiness for it. Better, they say, bad self-government than British rule.[154]

In confirmation of the issues raised by Crawford, Lennox-Boyd wryly observed that:

> with the political pot boiling on all three rings of the East African stove at once, I find the job of chef (if I may describe my job thus) requires more than normal vigilance and agility…. There comes a time, however, if attenuation goes too far, when the façade becomes transparent … keeping Uganda together is going to be a major problem. I think we should stress the "united country" idea, my predecessor's phrase, without perhaps at this stage saying too much about the exact constitutional structure. It is not so promising to try to create cohesion by imposing a unitary structure which, like the modern constitution of Buganda, fits few of the prevailing facts…. [W]e have a dilemma [in] that moves to promote unity may well arouse the traditional cry from the Baganda that they are being held back because we will not abandon their exploitable compatriots…. I also am conscious of the fact that Uganda's flamboyant prosperity is a thing of the past.[155]

On the complications of creating a unitary state in Uganda, Crawford seems to have touched upon the nub of the problem in a Memorandum to the Secretary of State for the Colonies. He aptly observed that it was the *tribe* and not the idea of the "Ugandan nation" that had the loyalty of the overwhelming proportion of the inhabitants of Uganda. He further noted:

> each tribe [has] a highly developed sense of tribal loyalty … after all, the Protectorate was the creation of British administration, with frontiers to a large extent drawn arbitrarily, and it would be too much to expect a deep sense of loyalty to Uganda, except for a common and often very real feeling of loyalty to the Crown as the protecting power.[156]

This assertion is supported by A. D. Lubowa, a former Buganda Minister of Justice, according to whom the transition from colonial rule to independence was driven more by the colonised people's desire to end colonialism and less by the desire to forge and belong to a united Uganda.[157] As we discuss below, in the last days of imperial rule, there was a marked lack of a common vision for Uganda's political and constitutional future. While kingdom areas like Buganda agitated for separation from, or for federation with, the rest of the Protectorate, others, with the encouragement of Britain, demanded governance under a unitary state.

Yet these differences were not limited to political ideology alone. They extended beyond politics to both ethnicity and religion. Political parties that were founded on either an ethnic or religious base struggled to attain a national character. As a result, to win power some had to make alliances that were shaky and untenable only a few months before independence. Commenting on the task for the new African Government at independence, Douglas Brown noted that welding together a country with twenty or more tribal groups with different languages and different aspirations into a governable entity "was a far more complex assignment than the Governors and administrative officers ever encountered during the Protectorate years."[158]

From Autocracy to Democracy: The Birth Pangs of Electoral Democracy in Colonial Uganda

The long history of an undemocratic colonial hegemony, coupled with the conservativeness of traditional institutions such as the kingdom of Buganda, presented an enormous challenge to the transition from colonial to democratic rule. The reluctance of Buganda to embrace both the LEGCO and the new political parties underlines this point. Fearing a usurpation of its traditional power and structures, the kingdom generally shunned and drove leaders of political parties out of the Lukiiko. For example, E. M. K. Mulira, the leader of the Progressive Party, was dismissed from the Lukiiko in July 1956 for "announcing in public that the Kabaka was a constitutional monarch by the 1955 Agreement and therefore had no power to expel or confirm members of the Great Lukiiko."[159] He was charged in court with an attempt "to treat with disrespect, to bring about discontent among the people, and to cause disrespect to the dignity of the Buganda throne."[160] He was also accused for walking out while a meeting was in progress without, it was alleged, proper salutation of the throne.[161] In reality, Mulira was dismissed from the Lukiiko at Mengo because his views tended to counteract Buganda traditionalism in favour of Uganda nationalism.[162] "Jolly" Joe W. Kiwanuka, a leader in the Uganda National Congress, was dismissed for insulting the Kabaka and was accused of plotting to assassinate him in 1958.[163]

As we have already noted, even though Matayo Mugwanya of the Democratic Party was elected to join the Lukiiko, he was wilfully denied admission to the body, which was dominated by a largely conservative and traditional leadership. The main interest and focus in Buganda at the time was the reversion to the traditional sovereign status it had prior to British colonialism and not experimenting with Western-style democracy and politics. To make the point, in a memorandum to Her Majesty the Queen seeking the termination of British protection under the 1894 Agreement, the Lukiiko categorically refused to entrust the destiny of their country into "the hands of political party leaders whose experience has not been proven by time."[164] To do so "could be extremely risky in the light of recent history, which [had] shown clearly that politicians in emergent countries use parliamentary democracy as a spring board to virtual dictatorship."[165]

With this mindset, and before the ink on the 1955 Agreement had dried, the Lukiiko appointed a Constitutional Committee that met with Governor Crawford in September and November 1957 to discuss major constitutional matters affecting Buganda.[166] The Committee proposed that Buganda should be recognised as a "Protected State" like Zanzibar; that Her Majesty's Government should appoint the Kabaka as the Constitutional Head of Uganda; and that the Lukiiko, not the LEGCO, should be the proper body to negotiate with the Protectorate Government for self-government for the whole of Uganda. However, Crawford postponed the final consideration of these proposals because Buganda was considered to be in breach of the 1955 Agreement by refusing to send representatives to the LEGCO.

During the difficult negotiations for the return of the Kabaka and the 1955 Agreement, the kingdom of Buganda had agreed to remain a part of Uganda as a unitary state and, accordingly, to be represented in the LEGCO by individuals who would form at least one quarter of all African representative members of the Council. However, once the Kabaka was back in charge, Buganda's new leadership had a change of heart. As mentioned above, when the LEGCO elections were held in October 1958, Buganda refused to participate. It instead filed a suit challenging the holding of direct elections. The case was lost. By the time judgment was entered, the elections had been concluded in other parts of Uganda while none were held in Buganda.[167]

Similar to the Mugwanya case, the colonial state chose to ignore Buganda's intransigence once again. Buganda's opposition to the LEGCO generally stemmed from the view that it was a body that was intended to usurp its traditional authority and replace it with a British colonial order. Commenting on the composition and mission of the LEGCO, Tumushabe and Gariyo similarly argue that it was "never established as an institution for the democratic governance of Uganda. Rather it was established as an instrument to further the interests of the colonial regime."[168]

Buganda's stance drew the wrath of politicians such as Abu K. Mayanja who, in a famous letter to the *Uganda Argus*, claimed that he had "crossed the Rubicon setting his face against autocracy whether foreign and imperialist or native and feudal."[169] Mayanja opposed Buganda's sabotage against direct elections for the LEGCO because it amounted to blocking the development of democracy in Buganda and the entrenching of an anti-democratic system by cutting Buganda off from the rest of Uganda. He urged the Protectorate Government not to condone Buganda's non-cooperation and reminded it of "its duty to pursue with vigour those policies calculated to fulfil Britain's mission in her dependencies."[170] Mayanja also assured the Protectorate Government of the "unstinting support of the overwhelming majority of the educated Baganda who struggle tooth and nail to resist the re-imposition of feudal tyranny based on the debasement of human personality and the vagaries of the so called customary law."[171] However, in a dramatic *volte-face,* Mayanja, an ardent critic of British imperialism and the traditionalists at Mengo, was to join the leadership of Buganda as a Minister for Education a few years later.[172]

Buganda's boycott of the LEGCO also attracted the ire of those members from other parts of Uganda that embraced it. For this and other reasons, the new African representatives in the LEGCO soon formed a new party known as the Uganda Peoples' Union (UPU).[173] Unsurprisingly, because of Buganda's reservations about the role, mission and composition of the LEGCO, the UPU was generally anti-Buganda. In fact, the UPU was formed specifically to oppose the concessions that were being extended to Buganda by the British Government.[174]

From this point on, differences between Buganda and the rest of Uganda began to crystallise. Buganda was generally criticised for being insular and parochial in outlook. For its part, Buganda was more inward-looking and focused on the preservation of its heritage, as well as its traditional and cultural identity. The colonial government, in its desire to leave behind a viable and united Uganda, tended to ally with the rest of Uganda against Buganda's isolationist policy. Britain recognised that other tribes in the Protectorate resented the privileged position of Buganda and feared to exchange British imperialism for Buganda's dominance.[175]

On the incompatibility of Buganda's separatism and the pursuit of a government of national unity by the rest of Uganda, Ibingira notes that the rest of Uganda felt there was danger in a British policy to elevate Buganda beyond any reasonable proportion, which in turn made Buganda reassert its superiority and its special position.[176] This, he argues, ultimately drove

Buganda to secession, as it felt that the other tribes were hostile to it.[177] However, as we show ahead, Buganda's separatism was informed more out of a wish for autonomy and the protection of its institutions and less by the fear of the hostility of the rest of the Protectorate.

Once the 1958 elections were out of the way, Governor Crawford appointed a new Constitutional Committee[178] chaired by John V. Wild. The committee comprised ten Africans, two Asians and two Europeans.[179] Its remit was to consider, in addition to the proposal for direct elections in 1961, the size and composition of the legislature and the future form of government for Uganda. The Governor was quick to warn that the Committee's recommendations were to be merely advisory, because the real responsibility in these matters lay directly with Her Majesty's Government and could not be settled in Uganda.

That notwithstanding, the Committee's work represented a major landmark in the governance history of the country, because for the first time, all parts of Uganda were being offered an opportunity to air their views on serious constitutional and political matters that would affect how they would be governed in the future. Unsurprisingly, while the news of the Committee's appointment caused considerable excitement in the rest of the country, it did not move Buganda.

Buganda was stuck on its policy of resisting the LEGCO and being uncooperative with the colonial state. Accordingly, the Lukiiko boycotted and refused to submit any evidence to the Wild Committee, in spite of the Governor's earnest appeals for it to do so.[180] The Wild Committee made several recommendations, including that, unlike in 1958, direct elections should be held in all parts of Uganda on the next occasion and that no option for the alternative of indirect elections should be offered. The Secretary of State for the Colonies accepted this recommendation. Other recommendations regarded the representation of non-Africans in the Legislative Council, the creation of a position for the leader of the opposition, the composition and change in name of the LEGCO to the "National Assembly," the establishment of a Common Roll (Britain was keen to entrench the fundamental interests of the minority communities, especially the Asians[181]) and the clarification of eligibility requirements for voters and candidates.

Governor Crawford—who desired to make special arrangements to ringfence seats for non-Africans in the legislature—was disappointed with the recommendation made against such a measure.[182] Because of his reservations about the Committee's recommendations, he deliberately back-pedalled over adopting and implementing them.[183]

Having boycotted the Wild Committee, as well as the Protectorate's agenda and timing for Independence, Buganda chose to define and set out its own programme and trajectory for the achievement of self-rule. Hence, on 16 December 1958, the Lukiiko dispatched a lengthy Memorandum to the Queen in which it asked Britain to hand over Buganda's sovereignty and bring to an end the agreements that it had with Buganda.[184] The Lukiiko argued *inter alia* that the 1900 Agreement was negotiated and signed under "unsavoury circumstances" and that some of the signatures of the chiefs were "purchased."[185] It recounted the callous exile of the Kabaka in 1953 when he was "kidnapped and unceremoniously bundled into a military aircraft under an escort and flown to England, not being provided with warm clothes … in a severe winter spell."[186] In this connection, it pointed out that the 1955 Agreement was not "freely negotiated" and was signed under duress.[187] Moreover, it questioned how the British-dominated LEGCO membership could, in both fairness and morality, discuss or determine the future position of the Kabaka, who was responsible for the introduction of British protection in Uganda. It castigated the British for reneging on their promise to Buganda, saying "pledges are pledges and they should be honoured," and demanded that the power of protection ought to be "surrendered back" to Buganda.[188] The simple argument, as the Lukiiko saw it, was that since it was Buganda which had asked for British protection, that protection should be terminated at Buganda's pleasure.

However, the Protectorate Government, whose real mission had never been the protection of Buganda or its Kabaka, obviously did not share that view. Britain considered that Buganda's stance was part of its "customary pattern of boycott, intimidation and general defiance of authority." It was thus quick to reject the Memorandum, but, in fear of a recrudescence[189] of the protests of 1945 and 1949, it agreed to hold constitutional discussions with the Kabaka's government—on the condition that Buganda would resume its representation in the LEGCO and that the tensions caused by the UNC-led trade boycott would be eased. Buganda's demands were thus once again put on the back burner.

Notes

[1] Mutibwa, *A History of Uganda*, p. 147-148.

[2] See Griffith, Owen (2006) "Sir Andrew Cohen at Work," in Brown & Brown (eds.), *Looking Back at the Uganda Protectorate: Recollections of District Officers*, Dalkeith, Australia: Douglas Brown, p.109.

[3] Ibid., p. 112.

[4] Mutesa, *The Desecration of My Kingdom*, p. 114.

[5] Ibid.
[6] Ibid., p. 115.
[7] Low & Pratt, *Buganda and British Overrule*, p. 318.
[8] See file "Withdrawal of recognition from the Kabaka of Buganda," CO 822/762.
[9] See "Memorandum on Constitutional Development and Reform in Buganda," dated 17 March 1953, reproduced in Low, *The Mind of Buganda,* pp. 157-160.
[10] These included primary and secondary school education, rural hospitals and health services, and agricultural and veterinary field services.
[11] "Memorandum on Constitutional Development and Reform in Buganda."
[12] Mutesa, *The Desecration of My Kingdom*, p. 117.
[13] See publication on *Withdrawal of Recognition from Kabaka Mutesa ll of Buganda* presented by the Secretary of State for the Colonies to Parliament in December 1953.
[14] Ministers' letter of 6 July 1953.
[15] Sir Andrew Cohen's letter to Kabaka Mutesa II, dated 27 July 1953, reproduced in Low, *The Mind of Buganda*, pp. 161-162.
[16] See part of Sir Andrew Cohen's statement in the LEGCO, dated 11 August 1953, reproduced in Low, ibid., p. 162.
[17] Mutesa, *The Desecration of My Kingdom*, p. 118.
[18] Mutesa's letter to Cohen, dated 6 August 1953, reproduced in Low, *The Mind of Buganda*, p. 163.
[19] Ibid., p. 164.
[20] Ibid., p. 165.
[21] Ibid., pp.165-166
[22] See address by the Chief Secretary to the Great Lukiiko in file "Withdrawal of recognition from the Kabaka of Buganda," CO 822/762.
[23] Paulo Kavuma, *Crisis in Buganda*, p. 25.
[24] Ibid., p. 25.
[25] Ibid.
[26] Mutesa, *The Desecration of My Kingdom*, p. 120. See also, Low & Pratt, *Buganda and British Overrule*, p. 330.
[27] Paulo Kavuma, *Crisis in Buganda*, p. 27.
[28] In a document entitled *The Deportation of Kabaka Mutesa II: Some Questions Answered*, on File with the Author. See also file *Withdrawal of Recognition From the Kabaka of Buganda*, CO 822/762.
[29] These arguments are contained in a report entitled *Withdrawal of Recognition From Kabaka Mutesa II of Buganda* by the Secretary of State for the Colonies to Parliament of December 1953 and in Cohen's statements following the deportation of the Kabaka entitled "Kabaka Mutesa II has broken the Agreement—A Message to the People of Buganda," and "A Statement from the Governor."
[30] Ibid.
[31] Telegram from SLO East Africa Ref. DSO/122 from Macdonald for Sir John Shaw; File SF/East Africa Serial 544a dated 13 November, 1953.
[32] Low & Pratt, *Buganda and British Overrule*, p. 330.
[33] Paulo Kavuma, *Crisis in Buganda*, p. 29.

[34] Oliver Lyttelton states that at this point the Kabaka "had made it crystal clear that nothing could change his attitude on the demand for a timetable for the independence of Buganda and his intended defiance of the decisions by HM's Government on this issue." See publication on *Withdrawal of Recognition from Kabaka Mutesa II of Buganda* presented by the Secretary of State for the Colonies to Parliament in December 1953, p. 13.
[35] Paulo Kavuma, *Crisis in Buganda*, p. 33.
[36] Ibid. See also file on the deportation and deposition of Sir Edward F. W. D. W. M. L. Mutesa II, Kabaka (king) of Buganda, FCO 141/18176.
[37] Ibid. See also, Mutesa, *The Desecration of My Kingdom*, p. 121.
[38] Paulo Kavuma, *Crisis in Buganda*, 35.
[39] Ibid., p. 38.
[40] *The Daily Worker*, Monday 28 December 1953.
[41] "Report on tour to Uganda (2-12) December 1953" by R. E. C Broadbent, Assistant Security Liaison Officer, EA File No. P. F.728883, original file S.F. 205-East Africa.
[42] Paulo Kavuma, *Crisis in Buganda*, p. 40.
[43] Ibid., p. 41.
[44] Under the Emergency Powers Order-in-Council, 1939.
[45] Governor Cohen's undated statement entitled "Kabaka Mutesa II has broken the Agreement—A Message to the People of Buganda."
[46] Ibid.
[47] Ibid.
[48] See Undated 14-page "Statement by the Governor," on file with the author.
[49] See Owen Griffith (2006) "The Governor and the Kabaka," in Brown & Brown (eds.), *Looking Back at the Uganda Protectorate*, p. 65.
[50] Mutesa, in *The Desecration of My Kingdom*, p. 120, called this the "*idée fixe* he had brought from England and nursed still, though it had no support in the country."
[51] Low and Pratt, *Buganda and British Overrule*, p. 331. The Kabaka was being urged to support policies which neither he nor his people trusted.
[52] Ibid., p. 323.
[53] Mutesa, *The Desecration of My Kingdom*, p. 120-121.
[54] Ibid., p. 121.
[55] CO 822/762 TNA.
[56] Resolutions passed by the Lukiiko on 5 and 6 January 1954 and Kavuma, *Crisis in Buganda*, p. 54.
[57] "Uganda National Movement and trade boycott in Buganda," Sessional paper, files FCO/18298 and FCO 141/18256-18257 TNA.
[58] Report "Overview of the State of Media Freedom in Uganda" by George Lugalambi and Bernard Tabaire, African Centre for Media Excellence, September 2010., p.6.
[59] Civil Case No.50 of 1954. On the High Court action challenging the withdrawal of recognition from Mutesa between 1954-56 see FCO 141/18206-18207.

[60] Memorandum on Uganda, from the Foreign Office to Certain of Her Majesty's Representatives, No. 49 INTEL 22 February 1954 on CO 822/762.
[61] Chief Secretary to the Lukiiko on 6 January 1954, on file CO 822/762 TNA.
[62] CO 822/751 TNA and a "Paper Challenging Deposition of H. H. the Kabaka of Buganda" by the Women's League of Buganda, February 1954.
[63] Summers, Carol (2017) "All the Kabaka's Wives: Marital Claims in Buganda's 1953-5 Kabaka Crisis," *Journal of African History*, 58 (1), pp. 107-27.
[64] Griffith, "The Governor and the Kabaka," in Brown & Brown (eds.), *Looking Back at the Uganda Protectorate*, p. 93.
[65] C. H. Thornley, the Chief Secretary, to Andrew Cohen on 16 February 1954, on file CO 822/762 TNA.
[66] Fallers, *The King's Men,* p. 362.
[67] Letter dated 2 March 1954, CO 822/762 TNA.
[68] Hansard, House of Commons Debate on 3 December 1953.
[69] Ibid.
[70] Ibid.
[71] Ibid.
[72] Memorandum on Uganda, from Foreign Office to Certain of Her Majesty's Representatives, No. 49 INTEL 22 February 1954 on CO 822/762 and Kavuma, *Crisis in Buganda*, p. 44. See also, Mutesa, *The Desecration of My Kingdom*, p. 127.
[73] Kavuma, *Crisis in Buganda*, p.44 and Mutesa, *The Desecration of My Kingdom*, p.125, says these manoeuvres had no chance of success.
[74] *The Times* newspaper, 22 April 1954.
[75] Kavuma, *Crisis in Buganda*, p. 56.
[76] Andrew Cohen to the Minister of State for the Colonies 5 February 1954, CO 822/762.
[77] Referred to as a "Secret document for official use" Andrew Cohen to the Secretary of State, 5 February 1954, CO 822/762.
[78] Ibid.
[79] Andrew Cohen to the Minister of State for the Colonies 5 February 1954, CO 822/762.
[80] *The Observer* newspaper, 21 February 1954.
[81] Ibid. *The Observer* published a disclaimer by Canon Max Warren of the Church Missionary Society on 28 February.
[82] Hansard on House of Commons Debate on 23 February 1954.
[83] In a letter to the Rt Hon. Oliver Lyttelton, dated 17 February 1954.
[84] Rt Hon. Oliver Lyttleton [no date is indicated] February 1954 to Mutesa.
[85] House of Commons Debate on Buganda (State of Emergency) on 4 June 1954, Hansard Vol. 528 cc. 1664-91.
[86] Ibid.
[87] House of Commons Debate on Buganda (State of Emergency) on 4 June 1954, *Hansard Parliamentary Debates*, vol. 528 cc. 1664-91.
[88] Ibid.
[89] Ibid.

[90] See *Ndiki Mutua and Four others v. The Foreign and Commonwealth Office* (2012) EWHC 2678 (GB); Caroline Elkins (2005) *Imperial Reckoning: The Untold Story of Britain's Gulag in Kenya*, New York: Henry Holt & Co; and David Anderson (2005) *Histories of the Hanged: Britain's Dirty War in Kenya and the End of Empire*, London: Weidenfeld & Nicolson.
[91] Statement by the Secretary of State for the Colonies to the House of Commons on 23 February 1954.
[92] Presentation on the Uganda Protectorate by the Secretary of State for the Colonies to Parliament, November 1954, p. 20.
[93] Comprising of M. Mugwanya, E. M. K. Mulira, A. Kironde, Ralph Bunche, T. Makumbi and Dr E. Kalibbala.
[94] Cabinet Memorandum by the Secretary of State for the Colonies, 9 September 1954 Ref. C (54) 287.
[95] Ibid.
[96] See FCO 141/18194-18197, 18199-18200, 18208-18210, 18217-18225 and 18229 for the minutes; Commission recommendations and their implementation; reactions on the recommendations, and Sir Andrew B. Cohen's notes.
[97] Presentation on the Uganda Protectorate by the Secretary of State for the Colonies to Parliament, November 1954.
[98] See "Recommendations of the Hancock Committee," p. 1; http://www.buganda.com/hancock.htm (accessed 17 February 2018).
[99] See the Bunyoro Agreement made on 3 September 1955, FCO 141/18410. The Agreement reaffirmed Britain's imperial authority over Bunyoro and its resources. It emphasised that Bunyoro was an integral part of the Protectorate and delimited the powers rights and privileges of the Omukama. It is clear that, by reining in the Omukama under this Agreement, Cohen ensured that Bunyoro did not present the same trouble that Mutesa had in challenging his constitutional reforms.
[100] Low & Pratt, *Buganda and British Overrule*, p. 340.
[101] Kavuma, *Crisis in Buganda*, pp. 60-61. See also, Mutesa, *The Desecration of My Kingdom*, p. 131.
[102] Mutesa, *The Desecration of My Kingdom*, p. 132.
[103] Buganda was represented by W. J. K. Diplock and Ralph Dreschfield for the defence.
[104] *The Times*, 2 November 1954.
[105] In a Memorandum to Cabinet by Secretary of State for the Colonies, Alan Lennox-Boyd dated 20 October 1954, Ref. C (54) 317.
[106] Ibid.
[107] Civil Case No. 50 of 1954.
[108] See Memorandum by the Secretary of State for the Colonies Alan Lennox-Boyd to Cabinet, dated 9 November 1954 Ref. C (54) 336, p. 2.
[109] Presentation on the Uganda Protectorate by the Secretary of State for the Colonies to Parliament, 16 November 1954, p. 5.
[110] Kavuma, *Crisis in Buganda*, pp. 92-93.
[111] The Baganda may have had some misgivings on Katikkiro Kavuma's position on the Kabakaship and his handling of the crisis. Kavuma's views may be

discerned from a letter to the Secretary of the Colonies, dated 13 August 1954, on the private views of leading Baganda citizens on the Kabaka's deportation and possible return, gathered at two sun-downer receptions by Freddie Bennett, an official of the Protectorate Government. Bennett stated that if the British Government "held firm and it was made and re-made abundantly clear that the deposition decision was irrevocable, Katikkiro Kavuma felt that within a year or so, it should be possible to proceed with the enthronement of another Kabaka, and thus achieve the final ending of the crisis. He stated that Katikkiro Kavuma's greatest anxiety was that there was some kind of weakening of HM's Government in this matter". According to Bennett, Katikkiro Kavuma expressed "conviction from first-hand knowledge that the Kabaka had long been looking for a chance to 'retire' with honour prior to his deposition and that only the stimulation of UK and Baganda agitators had caused and were still causing his current recalcitrance". Bennett formed the opinion that Katikkiro Kavuma was inhibited from taking a more forceful pro-government line, partly by a sense of loyalty to the Kabaka, as the man that had appointed him, but mainly through fear of public reaction."

[112] Low & Pratt, *Buganda and British Overrule*, p. 344.

[113] Recorded in a note of his interview with Apollo K. Kironde on 3 January 1955.

[114] There were some disappointments, because there was no definite date set for self-government, the report supported Buganda's participation in the LEGCO, and there was no undertaking excluding Uganda from the East African Federation. Some wanted the report passed so as to secure the early return of the Kabaka; others wanted it deferred until he returned.

[115] Kavuma, *Crisis in Buganda*, p.102.

[116] See special report by the Commissioner of Police (Special Branch) on Edward William Fredrick Walugembe Mutebi Luwangula Kabaka Mutesa II of Buganda Kingdom, SB/ PF2874, January 1957, p. 27.

[117] In his letter to the Secretary of State for the Colonies on 4 October, 1955.

[118] Ibid.

[119] Ibid.

[120] See Don Marshall (2006) "The Deportation of the Kabaka," in Brown & Brown (eds.), *Looking Back at the Uganda Protectorate*, p. 71.

[121] Ibid.

[122] Ibid.

[123] See Thomas Zaccaro, *The Prohibition of the Use of Duress in Treaty Negotiations: Study of the Iranian Hostage Crisis* in the Boston College International and Comparative Law Review., Volume 7, Issue 1, Article 7 dated 12 January 1984.

[124] See, Samwiri Lwanga-Lunyiigo, *A History of the Democratic Party of Uganda*.

[125] See File 141/18263 on the Progressive Party (later the United Federal Party) 1955-1961.

[126] Governor Crawford's letter to Alan Lennox-Boyd, Secretary of State for the Colonies, 23 April 1957.

[127] Karugire, S. R. (1980) A Political History of Uganda, Nairobi: Heinemann Educational Books, p. 163.

[128] See Fallers L.A. (ed.) (1964) *The King's Men: Leadership and Status in Buganda on the Eve of Independence*. London, Oxford University Press, pp. 359-360.
[129]According to Mutibwa, in *A History of Uganda*, p. 145, Mugwanya was believed to be a traitor who approached the royal family to persuade them to select a prince to replace the deposed Mutesa II as the Kabaka.
[130] Secret memo from C. A. L. Richards to H. E. Crawford, dated 29 May 1957.
[131] In a meeting of the Governor and the Kabaka and His Ministers at Makindye on Monday 29 April, 1957.
[132] See Buganda Lukiiko appointments, FCO 141/18188.
[133] In his letter to the Governor, dated 13 May 1957.
[134] Ibid.
[135] Governor Crawford's letter to Alan Lennox-Boyd, Secretary of the Colonies of 23 April 1957.
[136] Ibid., p.5.
[137] Ibid.
[138] *The Katikiro of Buganda v. Attorney General.*, CA No. 2 of 1959.
[139] Cited in Paulo Kavuma, *Crisis in Buganda*, p. 106.
[140] Mutibwa, *A History of Uganda*, p. 161.
[141] W. L. Bell to C. S. Peter Allen, Chief Secretary's Office, 27 April 1961, FCO141/18252.
[142] Memorandum, *Uganda: Political Development and the Problems of the Future*, Ref. EAF 185/96/01, 4 January, 1957.
[143] Ibid., paras. 3 and 4.
[144] Ibid., para. 12.
[145] Ibid., para. 11.
[146] Ibid.
[147] Ibid., para. 13.
[148] Ibid., para. 15.
[149] Ibid.
[150] Ibid., para. 22.
[151] Interview with A. D. Lubowa, former Minister of Justice in the Kabaka's Government, on 1 August 2017.
[152] In his letter to W. L. Gorell Barnes of 14 March 1957.
[153] Letter to Alan Lennox-Boyd, dated 23 April 1957.
[154] Ibid.
[155] Letter Ref. EAF.185/96/01, dated 16 May 1957.
[156] See *Uganda: Problems of Tribalism and Nationalism*, by F. Crawford, CO Ref. EAF 185/96/01, dated 16 August 1957, para. 12.
[157] Interview with A. D. Lubowa, op cit.
[158] See Brown, Douglas (2006) "Afterthoughts," in Brown and Brown (eds), *Looking Back at the Uganda Protectorate: Recollections of District Officers*. Dalkeith: Western Australia p. 344.
[159] Fallers, *The King's Men,* p. 363.
[160] Ibid.

[161] Hansard, House of Commons debate, 01 May 1957, Vol. 569 cc 18-9W.
[162] See *The Daily Monitor*, Thursday 26 July 2012.
[163] Joe Kiwanuka was charged in the Principal Court of Mengo with plotting to murder the Kabaka and other prominent persons. Acting against the advice of the Attorney General, he was charged and convicted by the court at Mengo. His conviction was later quashed by the High Court. See CID report dated 17 May 1961 in file "Buganda Secession Security," FCO 141/18239. See also, Kasozi A. et al. (1994) *Social Origins of violence in Uganda 1964-1985*, McGill-Queen's Press, p. 67.
[164] Memorandum to the Her Majesty Queen Elizabeth II submitted by members of the Lukiiko of the kingdom of Buganda concerning the termination of British protection, 1960. See Appendix IV.
[165] Ibid.
[166] *See Buganda Constitutional Committee*, 1957, FCO141/18214-18216.
[167] Mutibwa, *A History of Uganda*, p. 161.
[168] See Tumushabe, Godber and Gariyo, Zie (2009) *Uganda's Taxpayers Burden: The Financial and Governance Costs of a Bloated Legislature*, Kampala: Acode Policy Research Series, No.28.
[169] Mayanja's letter published in *Uganda Argus*, 6 March 1958.
[170] Ibid.
[171] Ibid.
[172] See Makubuya, Apollo N. "Abu K. Mayanja: A portrait of a pan-Africanist, nationalist and traditionalist," in *The East African*, May 16-22, 2015 and FCO 141/18246 on the education, political activities and career of Abu K. Mayanja.
[173] See Ibingira, *The Forging of an African Nation,* p. 84.
[174] Ibid., p. 85.
[175] See report on "Future constitutional development in the colonies" dated May 1957, CAB 134/1551, CPC (57) 27.
[176] See Ibingira, *The Forging of an African Nation*, p. 140.
[177] Ibid.
[178] Ibid., p. 89
[179] C. J. Obwangor, B.K. Kirya, C. K. Patel, Frank Kalimuzo, Milton Obote, G. Oda, C. B. Katiti, Kenneth Ingham, Erisa Kironde, B. J. Mukasa, W. W. K. Nadiope, H. K. Jaffer, A. A. Baerlein, J. V. Wild, T. B. Bazarrabusa and G. B. K. Magezi.
[180] See file, "Constitutional Committee (Wild Committee)," FCO 141/18276-18293 TNA and Wild, John V. (2006) "The Wild Committee," in Brown & Brown (eds), *Looking Back at the Uganda Protectorate*, p.125.
[181] See report on "Future constitutional development in the colonies" dated May 1957, CAB 134/1551, CPC (57) 27.
[182] See file, "Constitutional Committee (Wild Committee)," op. cit. and Wild, "The Wild Committee," p. 127.
[183] Wild, "The Wild Committee," p. 128.

[184] "A Memorandum from the Buganda Lukiiko for submission to Her Majesty the Queen being the desire for the Baganda to bring the Buganda Treaty of 1894 to an end," dated 16 December 1958.

[185] Ibid.

[186] Ibid.

[187] In law, contracts signed under duress or undue influence are voidable. As such, as we pointed out earlier, the legality of the treaties made between Buganda and the British was questionable both under international and domestic law.

[188] See Memorandum from the Buganda Lukiiko to bring the Buganda Treaty of 1894 to an end, op. cit.

[189] Cabinet Colonial Policy Committee memorandum on "Future policy in East Africa" by Lennox-Boyd on CAB 134/1558, CPC (59)2 , 10 April 1959.

PHASE IV

BRITAIN'S SCRAMBLE OUT OF UGANDA AND THE STRUGGLE FOR POWER IN A NEW UGANDA (1960-1962)

A Change of Wind

The return of the Kabaka in 1955 opened a new chapter both in Anglo-Buganda relations and for the politics of Uganda. On the one hand, it marked the resurgence of nationalism in Buganda and renewed agitation for its separation from the rest of the Protectorate. With Mutesa's triumphant return from what Buganda considered to be an ill-conceived and illegal deportation, the kingdom had now accumulated significant patriotism and political clout with which to challenge British rule and demand independence.

Conversely, because the Protectorate had lost to Buganda in court, the credibility and power of its government was considerably dented. Thus, the mid-to-late fifties marked the diminution of British colonial authority, as well as the further erosion of the goodwill between Buganda and the colonial government. Elsewhere in the Protectorate, the period marked the beginnings of political transition, particularly within the LEGCO, characterised by the intensification of power brokerage and the jostling for power and inheritance of the colonial state.

Globally, the period also coincided with sweeping changes and turmoil in other parts of the Empire precipitated by the granting of independence to India and Pakistan in 1947 and to Ceylon (now Sri Lanka) in 1948. To this was added the growing fervour of nationalism in Africa and the politics of anti-colonialism within the United Nations. Closer to Buganda, Britain was faced with the crisis of the Mau Mau uprising in Kenya, which it suppressed in a manner that left an indelibly inhumane legacy of British rule.

It is in this context that the British Prime Minister, Harold Macmillan, after a tour of British colonies in Africa in 1960, addressed the Parliament of South Africa about "the wind of change" blowing through Africa and the reality of the "growth of national consciousness."[1] Macmillan foresaw that the strong tide against colonialism in Africa and the new anti-colonial outlook of the new world powers were facts that Britain needed to respond to by a change in policy and strategy. He recognized that Britain's role and power in the world had diminished and that, rather than maintain imperial pretentions, it need to have a new outlook that would best safe guard its interests. Imbued with this vision Macmillan worked with Alan Lennox-Boyd (1954-1959), Ian Macleod (1959-1961), Reginald Maudling (1961-1962) and Duncan Sandys (1962-1964), against considerable bureaucratic resistance,[2] to speedily dismantle and wind-up the Empire.

Macmillan's speech was informed by policy studies including one on "Future constitutional development in the colonies" of 1957[3] and a cynical report entitled "Africa: The next ten years" prepared and presented to the British cabinet in July of 1959.[4] The latter report was cynical in that it saw countries in Africa as wholly unstable and lacking in political maturity. It considered that in transferring sovereignty to the local inhabitants of Africa, the West would "in many cases be surrendering power to peoples who are not far removed from primitive savagery."[5]

The paper, formed the basis for the principles that would guide Britain's policy in the context of a rapidly shrinking empire and its ultimate policy aims namely—security from foreign domination or attack; the prosperity of its people and the protection of their freedom and liberty.[6] The other critical principle was Britain's desire to ensure that when African States attained independence they remained actively sympathetic with it and the West and not to succumb to Soviet penetration.

Macmillan's speech was followed by rapid moves to grant independence to many African British colonies. But while Prime Minister Macmillan and Secretary of State to the Colonies Ian MacLeod's rapid exit out of Africa in the 1960s was touted as a move by Britain to give freedom and democracy to Africa, in reality, for Britain, "it was beginning to become clear that staying on in Africa would involve considerable effort and expense, and perhaps fighting, and yet it, like other European colonial powers with the exception of Portugal, did not have the stomach for such effort."[7] But for this pressure Britain understood that, while independence for its African territories was to come, it would come but at a distant date. It is thus misleading to argue, as commentators like Brown do, that decolonisation resulted less from the African struggle for freedom and more from Britain's desire to hastily free itself "from responsibility so as to eliminate the post-war stigma of remaining a colonial power. Liquidation of the empire was a high priority. The pressures in the United Nations and elsewhere were irresistible."[8]

In reality, Britain's scramble out of Africa resulted from a complex web of interacting factors that defy attempts to define one as more significant than the other. The importance of African struggles for independence on the ground, causing flashpoints of conflict which forced the British Government to reassess the situation at the highest level whilst shifting public opinion against imperialism, cannot be dismissed so lightly. However, it can also be argued that the growing strength of the African independence movement was as much influenced by the global shift in attitude as the British were in their gradual acceptance of the need to withdraw.

The growth of African nationalism was bolstered by—and indeed fed into—the growth of similar movements in other colonies such as India and Indonesia (the latter against the Dutch). The emergence of two world superpowers (the USA and the USSR), the passing of the Universal Declaration of Human Rights in 1948, and the signing of the European Convention for the Protection of Human Rights and Fundamental Freedoms in 1950 also had an effect. However, and perhaps more than Britain's obligations under the human rights instruments, was the blow to imperial rule that came with the passing of a Soviet-inspired UN General Assembly Resolution No. 1514, which declared colonialism as a "denial of fundamental human rights" and an "impediment to the promotion of world peace and cooperation."[9] The resolution, which was opposed by nine countries including the United Kingdom, France, USA Spain and Belgium, declared that all peoples have the right to self-determination and that immediate steps should be taken to "transfer all powers to peoples of those territories ... in order to enable them to enjoy complete independence and freedom."[10]

To this was added a meltdown of a colonial civil service structure—particularly in East Africa—where demoralised European colonial administrators, anxious and uncertain about future employment prospects, began to resign and abandon the colonial service.[11] There is no doubt that a combination of these developments rendered colonialism not only less acceptable and morally justifiable within a new world order but also rendered its sustenance extremely problematic and untenable. This reality lent confidence to emergent nationalist and political leaders in Africa and Asia as to the viability of their cause, leading to ever more bold efforts to force the colonisers out as well to an even speedier scramble of Britain out of its African colonies.

With the end of the Empire in sight and with Britain's power greatly reduced, it turned to its alliance with the United States of America (the Atlantic Alliance) which now became the core of its foreign policy and under which it aimed to check Soviet expansion.[12] Ultimately, with decolonisation, Britain's global power and positioning was hinged, no longer on the Empire, but on its partnership with the United States, its relations with the European Union and the new creature of the Commonwealth[13]—which provided an answer to the decline of British prestige, the growing political and economic deterioration of Britain, as well as being a useful tool to propagate British patronage.[14] In addition to the Commonwealth, and in an effort to respond to the growing perceptions of colonial decadence, Harold Macmillan hoped that Britain could use its higher educational institutions and Christianity in keeping Africans oriented towards western ideals[15] as another was to maintain its grip on this part of the world.

Colonial (B)Uganda was caught right in the middle of these gusts of political change. While for Britain the period marked a more rapid disintegration of the Empire, to the colonised people it presented an opportunity to accelerate—and amplify—demands for independence. Yet, in spite of the many signs and predictions of the end of the British Empire, neither Britain nor (B)Uganda was quite prepared for the change of the winds of colonial rule and the turbulence that would follow.

This is because, even with the granting of independence to India in 1947, Britain always knew that the spread of freedom and the granting of independence to African countries like Uganda would be a slow process. According to Anthony Kirk-Greene, by 1947, the Colonial Office in London was redefining Britain's African Policy from one of "trusteeship" in the 1930s and of "partnership" earlier in the 1940s to that of "development" so as to "bring forward the African territories to self-governing responsibility within the Commonwealth."[16]

The new policy focused on the "development of an efficient, democratic system of local government in which indirect rule through native authorities was being replaced by democratic local government councils."[17] In a policy paper discussed by the British Cabinet in 1957, it was argued that Uganda could not be expected, by 1967, to have acquired the skill in government or to have developed the racial harmony, which would satisfy the British Government into relinquishing their authority. Based on this argument, it was suggested that Britain would be obliged to maintain its authority even in the face of opposition and criticism."[18] The justifications given for prolonging colonial rule were, amongst others, economic, defensive[19] and strategic[20] interests. For these reasons, Britain aimed to take every step open to it to ensure that "British standards and methods of business and administration permeate the whole life of the territory"[21] in the knowledge that while there may be alternative sources of raw materials produced in Africa, there was no doubt of the "permanent importance of Africa as a market."[22]

Within this purview, the colonial Chief Secretary in Uganda—somehow disregarding Ghana's independence in 1957—considered it inconceivable that Uganda would be independent within the next twenty-five years.[23] Even Governor Cohen, for all his exuberance and desire to secure rapid progress, believed that Uganda's independence was twenty years or more away.[24] Indeed, many of the low ranking colonial officials like the District Officers were ignorant of the exact policy and were, furthermore, deliberately kept in that state. In what may be described as a crisis of confidence—on colonial rule in general and the future of Uganda in particular—inquiries by District Officers on decolonisation in Uganda solicited vague responses such as "someday," "perhaps," "in the fullness of time," or "who knows?" In fact, according to Ken Gladdish, there was "a deep dilemma in respect of both the question and its possible answer because it was not absolutely clear whether the kingdom of Buganda, as distinct from the Uganda Protectorate, might become a member of the United Nations."[25]

On its part, invigorated by the court victory and the return of the Kabaka, the kingdom of Buganda had as its immediate goal the termination of its agreements with Britain and the restoration of its sovereignty. It had little or no interest in the fate or future of the rest of the British Protectorate. Yet Britain could not contemplate the separation of Buganda from the rest of Uganda. From this point onwards, the real question was whether or not Buganda should be independent of Uganda. This question was the subject of much discussion in the British House of Commons.[26] Little wonder that the period between 1958 to 1962—when Uganda eventually attained independence—was one of anxiety on both sides. It was also a period of intense political activity in which individuals, kingdoms and political parties jostled for position and power in what was to become a brand new country. In this relatively short period, a new legal order uniting the diverse parts of Uganda under a common constitutional framework had to be negotiated and enacted.

As it prepared to exit, Britain was careful not to entirely scuttle the system of patronage that it had constructed and relied upon over the years it was in control. It had to leave behind a political and constitutional structure that would serve its interests beyond the colonial period. To this end, Britain imposed its colonial subjects, for the first time, to the workings of the Westminster model of government,[27] complete with a Speaker, government and opposition benches, an executive Prime Minister, a ceremonial Head of State, and a centralised judicial system headed by a Chief Justice, amongst others. The imposition of parliamentary democracy and the Westminster model of government in Uganda was part of Britain's policy for its African colonies—but one it understood to have serious challenges and limitations in the African context. Indeed, by 1959, it was well known that the Westminster model of parliamentary democracy was not necessarily best suited to African conditions, and that beyond the mere imitation of the British system by the new countries and the extension of British patronage, it was bound to fail.

A report on democracy in the decolonized territories reached the conclusion that the prospects of democracy in backward countries were not encouraging but that this would not materially affect the timing and granting of independence. The same report pointed out that "Westminster Democracy cannot be expected to work well in countries with low standards of living and education. Among other causes of the comparative failure of democratic institutions in backward countries have been abnormal political and economic circumstances, the tradition of authority, the absence of restraint, the lack of maturity and the withdrawal of discipline in a political situation already predisposed to unrest."[28] Equally it was recognized that it was bound to be difficult to build up an effective opposition since prior to independence the main objective of every colony was to obtain independence and that, beyond religion and ethnicity, there was really no distinctive policy between political contenders.[29]

In Uganda, the alien and untested Westminster model of government, that vested ultimate authority in the executive arm of Government, required that the country had to quickly learn the workings of the British parliamentary system and, at once, finding and agreeing on symbols of nationhood, including a new flag, a national anthem, a currency and a coat of arms. The fights on the change of the colours of the national flag[30] from green and white (also the colours of the Democratic Party) chosen under the short rule of Benedicto Kiwanuka of the Democratic Party, to red, black and gold (a close resemblance of the colours of Apollo Milton Obote's ruling Uganda People's Congress) make interesting reading.[31] But as we show below, in spite of all the paraphernalia that came with the Westminster model and with independence, Uganda failed to develop into a stable and credible democracy and, instead, became a failed state that fell under the tyranny of successive dictatorships from the time it attained independence from Britain.

On the whole, the decolonisation process provided a momentous period for a colony consisting of a patchwork of diverse and, in some cases, antagonistic ethnicities which had spent 68 years existing separately but under a common colonial hegemony where the notions of democracy, political freedom and human rights were conspicuous by their absence. For example, there was conflict between the Baganda and the Banyoro, between the Batoro and the Bakonzo, and between the Langi and the Acholi. However, in spite of their historic and cultural differences, the colonised peoples were united in their demand for the end of British rule. For this reason, this period was characterised by agitation and resistance against colonial rule in different parts of the Protectorate including in Buganda, Ankole, Toro, Bunyoro and Bukedi.

For example, in Bukedi district —in the eastern part of the Protectorate —there were serious protests in January 1960 in which the people of the region protested the taxation system imposed by the local government at the behest of the Protectorate.[32] During these riots, fifteen people (including two chiefs) were killed, 23 official brick buildings burnt, and over one thousand chiefs' and councillors' houses destroyed. Many vehicles were also wrecked, livestock killed or mutilated, and crops destroyed.[33] Over 2,000 arrests were made. Unsurprisingly, given the Protectorate's history of dealing with such situations, a Commission of Inquiry into the riots, headed by Justice Bennett, concluded that the blame and "responsibility for the deaths and damage" were to be placed at the door of a local politician, Balaki Kirya,[34] and not the exacting colonial tax regime.[35]

In the north-eastern district of Karamoja, the problems were different for the Protectorate Government. Here, the rush towards independence constrained the Protectorate to hastily initiate and implement a development scheme that would bring this otherwise neglected part of the Protectorate forward "as quickly as possible so that the district could be opened up, play its part in Uganda without special protection and achieve some measure of prosperity."[36] According to John Brasnett, a district colonial official in charge of Karamoja, "until the late fifties, Karamoja remained a backwater in terms of economic and social and political development, well behind the rest of the country. This caused increasing criticism, and the government was accused of neglecting the district and treating it as a 'human zoo'."[37] Unsurprisingly, the integration of Karamoja and Buganda, into Uganda continues to be a problem today.[38]

In Buganda, resistance to British rule in this period culminated in the dramatic declaration of independence in 1960. The build-up to and the ramifications of this hapless declaration are discussed below. Beyond this issue, the colonial government had to deal with other intractable problems such as the ownership of the "lost counties" and the position of Buganda and an obstinate Kabaka in an independent Uganda. With less than two years to Uganda's independence, colonial rule was in a crisis and the situation was described by Macleod as being "extremely complex and difficult" because, amongst other reasons, no national African leader had emerged and the country was embroidered in the struggle between traditional forces led by the Kabaka and the rising power of the political parties.[39] Such was the level of the depth of the crisis that, Buganda's decision to declare independence in December of 1960, almost forced Britain to depose the Kabaka once again and to declare a state of emergence in the colony.[40]

All of these difficulties needed to be resolved quickly because of Britain's accelerated decolonisation policy. Accordingly, even as the last of the British administrators planned their exit, they had to organise elections and initiate a new crop of African administrators and civil servants to take over positions both at the local and central government levels. At independence, Uganda had a dearth of experienced politicians, administrators, doctors, judges and lawyers. Griffith has correctly argued that "a longer period of tutelage might have provided breathing space for a genuine national spirit to emerge and for institutions of government to develop."[41] It is in this context that the rapid arrangements for Uganda's independence and the fragility of its politics—particularly the failure to develop a national political or cultural identity or a credible and sustainable democratic ethos—must be seen and understood.

Events Shaping Uganda's Transition from Colonial Rule to Independence

With only two years left before Uganda's independence, Britain was in a hurry to tidy up its 66-year rule of the Protectorate: it attempted, at once, to unify, democratise and Africanise the politics of Uganda. It must have been a busy time in the Colonial Office in London, considering that many other colonies such as Kenya and the trusteeship of Tanganyika were also clamouring for independence. Thus, as the colonial state hastened its efforts in patching up the administration and constitutional framework for the country before its departure, there was an intensification of political activity through a plethora of political parties, many of whom were without any real constituencies.

It is in this context that the Uganda National Movement (UNM), led by a cobbler, called Augustine Kamya, was started in Buganda in 1959.[42] The UNM was joined by Baganda political veterans like I. K. Musaazi, G. Binaisa and E. M. K. Mulira. The movement promoted the trade boycott of non-African goods, leading to the declaration of Buganda as a disturbed area and the arrest and deportation of six of its leaders.[43] Two major parties in the LEGCO—the Uganda National Congress faction led by Milton Obote, which was opposed to both Buganda's intention to secede from the rest of the country and to the perceived special status accorded to Buganda by the British colonial regime,[44] and the Uganda Peoples' Union—agreed to merge and form a new party called the Uganda People's Congress (UPC).[45] The UPC, which was socialist in ideological terms, aimed to be national in outlook. For this reason, there developed an antithesis between the kingdom of Buganda and the sprouting political parties—particularly the DP and the UPC.

Beyond the desire to preserve its autonomy, Buganda's leaders' reservations towards political activity lay in the possible erosion of its power base once a democratic system of governance was introduced in the kingdom. They viewed the emerging political class as full of disgruntled opportunists who wished to take power away from the Kabakaship using the political party machinery. While Buganda's fears of the emergence of a new political power centre may be understandable, it is difficult to show how this worldview could explain the role of Baganda politicians in the struggle for the return and reinstatement of Mutesa as the Kabaka of Buganda between 1953 and 1955.[46] If these fears were well founded, these politicians would have either been indifferent to or vehemently opposed to the return and reinstatement of the Kabaka.

Buganda's antipathy towards the political class and its failure to nurture its own crop of political actors to advance its interests suggests that the kingdom was not sufficiently strategic, politically speaking, in the build-up to Uganda's independence since, at this point in time, it was focused on a separatist agenda. Buganda's leaders believed that it would have its way, based on the agreements it had with Britain, but failed to read the resolute will of the British to leave it as an integral part of a united Uganda. As we show below, the lack of a clear political fallback strategy in case their bid for separation was unsuccessful may explain the hasty alliance that Buganda's monarchist party, Kabaka Yekka[47] (lit. "King Only"), consummated with Obote's UPC in 1962.

In early 1960, the Lukiiko dispatched a further Memorandum to the Queen in which it expressed anxiety about the position of the Kabaka if Buganda was to remain a part of Uganda.[48] It also made the case that there was no economic justification for Buganda to be a part of Uganda, since most of the Protectorate's revenue was derived from Buganda.[49] For that reason, it concluded that Buganda no longer saw the benefit of remaining in Uganda. At this point, rightly or wrongly, Buganda did not venture to consider whether or not the rest of the Protectorate was economically viable or, indeed, whether it would constitute a feasible nation state. That was not its business.

Buganda's anxiety about the future, and particularly about the Kabaka's position in a new Uganda, was shared by other traditional rulers in Ankole, Bunyoro and Toro, in spite of the fact that these rulers had quite different agreements with the British.[50] Accordingly, as independence rapidly approached, the kingdoms of Ankole, Bunyoro and Toro joined Buganda to secure their positions in a new Uganda, and to ensure that at independence they were on a par with Buganda and that their rulers were on an equal footing with the Kabaka of Buganda.[51]

In a rare show of solidarity, they issued a proclamation in which they invited their ministers to devise means whereby their subjects "may live together in amity and contentment, being secured against exploitation by any individual or minority group." They also stated their intent to "discuss measures to advance the economic and cultural wellbeing of their people" and "safeguard the rights of the people to choose and change their form of government without fear or favour."[52]

The traditional rulers' proclamation was a preamble to their move, the next day, to write to the Secretary of State for the Colonies stating a desire that their positions be defined before independence. This was important because the determination of these positions could not be left "to the tender mercies of the future independent state of Uganda" with which they had "no agreement or relationships at all."[53] They expressed a strong view that their positions could only be safeguarded effectively within a federal and not a unitary constitution. They requested, with justification, that an agreement on their future positions in Uganda be decided before the general elections. They argued:

> Western democracy and parliamentary institutions ought to be based on firm foundations of traditional institutions which our respective subjects still revere and do understand. It would otherwise be too revolutionary to have to sweep away the institutions which we symbolise, or try to render them impotent. In these circumstances western democracy and all it stands for would be in danger, as the stabilising factor would have gone.[54]

The Protectorate Government took the rulers' proclamation as an attempt to sway public opinion against the introduction of any of the recommendations of the Wild Committee. When the Governor met them three days later, he dwelt on the Relationships Commission, which would make recommendations on how best the rulers' positions would be preserved. The rulers were concerned about the future form of government best suited to the known diversities and differences of Uganda and whether it would be federal or unitary. They asked for the full terms of reference of the Commission and requested that direct elections be put off until after the Commission's recommendations had been made public. This request was declined.

Interestingly, however, they agreed that the Commission should be composed of only British nationals because, according to them, impartial African representation on the body was likely to be impossible due to the varying interests of the different parts of Uganda. The Governor assured them that the interests of Buganda and the other three Agreement areas would best be preserved by their constitutions being enshrined, so far as possible, in any new constitutional instruments for Uganda as a whole. This assurance went down well with the rulers.[55]

Based on his assessment of the meeting with the rulers, the Governor appreciated the difficulties of forging a united Uganda and wrote that "it look[ed] as though there might well be a division of interests between the traditional part of the Protectorate and the political or democratic part, indicated roughly by north and south of the Nile and an eastward extension of it to include the populous area of Busoga (which would probably join with Buganda)."[56]

Similarly, the Secretary of State for the Colonies, Iain Macleod (who had taken over from Alan Lennox-Boyd in 1959), considered that the situation in Uganda was potentially highly explosive due to the difficulty of reconciling the position of the rulers of Buganda, Toro, Ankole, Bunyoro and other parts of the country. Macleod recognised that for the traditionalists, led by Buganda, there was a strong fear that constitutional changes aimed to transfer colonial power to democratic elements in Uganda would destroy traditional leadership and institutions.[57] He thus understood that the Kabaka's campaign for self-government was intended to insulate Buganda from these dangers. In this regard, he was cognizant of Britain's past pledge that

> the status and dignity of the rulers would be safeguarded in future constitutional changes … so as to ensure that, after British protection has been withdrawn, the rulers shall be able to maintain their position and, perhaps more important, the country develop in peace and unity.[58]

For this reason, in February of 1960, he invited the cabinet to renew Britain's pledge to ensure the maintenance of the position of the rulers.[59] Britain's pledge to protect the position of traditional rulers even beyond independence was reiterated and reaffirmed when its Cabinet discussed the Wild Report on Uganda's constitution, which stated that:

> Although we [Britain] could not control the course of events after we left,

> our aim as regards the pledge to be given to the Kabaka and other rulers was to ensure their status as constitutional rulers [was] insulated from local politics and safe from deposition.[60]

The preservation of the dignity and prestige of the traditional rulers was also contained in assurances given by HMG to Buganda and other Agreement States, to the effect that they would enjoy a special position under the new system. This was done in order to ensure that Britain gained the cooperation of the various rulers, without which Uganda would face a political dead-end. Perhaps more fundamentally, it was understood by British officials that if the Buganda Government co-operated and honoured the Agreement, they would stand a far greater chance of "this special relationship surviving after independence."[61]

Be that as it may, Macleod formed the view that the Kabaka of Buganda was the main "problem" in forging a united Uganda. In a letter to Prime Minister Harold MacMillan, he claimed that the Kabaka was in fact "a stumbling block to the early attainment of independence for Uganda," and that "if it were not for the existence of the Kabaka, Uganda would have been independent long ago."[62] He explained that it had always proved impossible to negotiate with the Baganda and that the Protectorate Government had been faced over the years with complete non-cooperation from them.[63]

The negotiations seemed impossible not only because the Kabaka chose to opt out of the elections, but also because he did not want to be part of the future development of the country. To stop the Kabaka and his ministers from flouting British authority in Buganda, Macleod toyed with the idea of deporting the Kabaka once again, but quickly dismissed it as it would "make a martyr of him again and almost anything is better than this."[64] He instead advised the Kabaka to run his own political party, or at least give his approval to certain candidates who would stand an excellent chance of election. However, he doubted whether the Kabaka would be "wise enough" to do this.[65] But for the political, geographical and economic centrality of Buganda, Macleod would have considered to let the kingdom go its separate way. He wrote:

> If Buganda was a limb of the Protectorate as Katanga is of the Congo this would be possible although extremely undesirable, but in fact Buganda is the centre and the heart of the Uganda Protectorate and the main centres like Entebbe and Kampala are within it.[66]

Accordingly, everything possible had to be tried in order to bring the country together. Faced with the dilemma of bringing together the disparate peoples of the Protectorate to form a united independent country whilst acting so as to "preserve the position of the traditional rulers,"[67] Secretary of State Macleod decided to ask the Relationships Commission to advise on the best way forward. Even then, he had doubts that the Kabaka would cooperate. In spite of Buganda's refusal to cooperate with the Protectorate's agenda, Macleod announced in June 1960 that direct elections were to be held in Uganda for the LEGCO.[68]

The kingdom of Buganda, having boycotted the Wild Committee, considered that it was not bound by the announcement and refused to participate in the said elections. It requested the resumption of talks on its constitutional proposals made to Governor Crawford in 1957. Although Buganda maintained its refusal to participate in the LEGCO, and although the Governor felt that the proposals made by Buganda went too far and were not acceptable, the Protectorate Government agreed to a resumption of discussions, as the security situation had improved. Macleod invited the Kabaka and his advisers to London for a general exchange of views, including on the forthcoming elections.

With the exception of the rulers of the kingdoms of Toro, Ankole and Bunyoro, Buganda's treatment drew bitterness from other parts of the Protectorate.[69] By this time, the fault lines of the country's political future seemed set. These were based on geographic factors (north versus south), the existence of monarchical institutions (kingdom versus non-kingdom areas), ethnic factors (the Baganda versus the rest of Uganda), and religious factors (the Protestant UPC versus the Catholic DP). These differences were mostly played out in the LEGCO—an institution about which Buganda was apprehensive about—where non-Baganda members felt either that Buganda took itself as *primus inter pares* with other parts of Uganda, or that the British favoured and handled Buganda too leniently.[70] The rest of Uganda thus harboured a generally anti-Buganda outlook. By the same token, in pursuing its independence, Buganda was concerned less with Britain's project of unifying Uganda and more about securing its old monarchy in an autonomous kingdom based on a historic relationship with the British dating back to 1894.

A Square Peg in a Round Hole? Britain Pushes for a United Uganda as Buganda Unilaterally Declares its Independence

As we have noted above, Britain and Buganda were always at cross-purposes insofar as the political and constitutional future of Uganda was concerned. This difference of views was markedly prominent in the years leading up to Uganda's independence. Having failed in its East African unification project, Britain was adamant that it must leave Uganda a unified country with Buganda at the centre. For its part, Buganda, with a long history of autonomy and in the honest belief that the Protectorate government would respect and defend its interests, was bent on an exit from Uganda, or at least joining Uganda as an autonomous federal entity. In this way, Britain's and Buganda's interests were deeply contradictory. Who would prevail and at what cost?

The tug of war in this high stakes political duel between Buganda and Britain formally commenced with the talks headed by Macleod in London. To demonstrate the gravity of the situation, Buganda's delegation to the talks was headed by the Kabaka himself.[71] The talks began on 15 August 1960. The Lukiiko's terms of reference to Buganda's delegation to London were categorical: to terminate the agreements; to ascertain the Kabaka's position in an independent Uganda; to request that the elections be postponed until assurances were obtained on a federal status for Buganda; and to secure a federal form of government for Uganda.[72] However, the negotiations on the above points and for the postponement of voter registration were met with stiff resistance from the British Government and were wholly unsuccessful.

These negotiations were bound to fail because before they had even commenced, Britain, which was always in a more dominant and powerful position than Buganda, had prepared answers to every plausible question that the Buganda delegation might throw at it. The following is a reproduction of a script prepared for Macleod, showing some anticipated subjects, questions and *a priori* responses:[73]

> **1. Agreements:**
> *Question:* Immediate abrogation of [the] present Buganda Agreements and the "return to Buganda of her sovereignty, i.e., withdrawal of British protection.
> *Answer:* The entire abrogation of present Agreements not acceptable, as this infers independence for Buganda now in advance of rest of Protectorate. Any amendment to the agreements is ultimately a matter for negotiation between Her Majesty's Government and the Kabaka's Government. The Secretary of State is setting up a Relationships Commission and final decisions on the best ultimate form of Government will be taken thereafter, probably after a Constitutional Conference at which all shades of opinion in Uganda would be represented.
>
> **2. Legislative Council:**
> *Question:* Buganda is unwilling to resume participation in the Legislative Council, or whatever body may succeed it, until (a) the Kabaka's position

has been clarified vis-à-vis any future Chief Minister, (b) a federal form of constitution has been adopted for Uganda as a whole, and (c) the present discussions regarding a revised constitution for Buganda have been concluded to their satisfaction.

Answer: The question of the Kabaka's position *vis-à-vis* any future Chief Minister and the form of constitution best suited to Uganda must clearly be left for consideration by the Relationships Commission. But an essential condition before any changes in the Buganda Agreements or constitution arising from them is the participation of Buganda in the Central Councils of the Protectorate. Direct elections for the Legislative Council for Buganda, as elsewhere, will be mandatory in 1961 in accordance with Article 7 of the Buganda Agreement of 1955; and any changes in the Buganda Agreement of 1955; and any changes in the Buganda Agreements or Constitution then or before then will be on the strict proviso that Buganda complies with the clear intention of the 1955 Agreement and resumes membership of the Legislative Council.

3. Internal Security and Law and Order:
Question: Buganda should have a small army of its own.

Answer: HMG cannot accept this so long as the Protectorate Government and the Governor remain ultimately responsible to HMG for Uganda's defence and internal security.

Question: There should be a full and efficient Buganda Police Force.

Answer: Agreed, but the Protectorate Police should have access to and operate in Buganda as at present—although there might be a re-arrangement of the powers and activities of the respective Forces later.

Question: Buganda prisons should accommodate all prisoners sentenced by Buganda courts and this would include prisoners of all races.

Answer: HMG cannot agree as Buganda prisons do not at present have suitable accommodation for non-African prisoners or any developed reformative facilities as yet for long-term non-African prisoners; and in any case HMG considers that Buganda courts should not have jurisdiction, as yet, over people of all races in Buganda for the reasons already stated.

4. Land:
Question: All existing crown land should revert to the Kabaka.

Answer: It was agreed at the meeting with the Constitutional Committee on 10 June that a sub-committee should consider the land question with a view to reaching agreement on the future of as much of the Crown land in

Buganda as possible; the remaining areas to be considered by the Relationships Commission (i.e. special areas such as Kampala and Entebbe).

5. Communications:
Question: Buganda should have its own radio station.

Answer: This is for Relationships Commission to consider in the light of the division of powers as between the centre and other parts of Uganda. The power to legislate to control broadcasting is one of the most important prerogatives of the modern state and it would not be right to decide this issue in advance.

Question: Buganda wants railways, aviation and trunk roads and interstate waterways to be administered by the Central Government or "some other body" in Uganda and not by the East Africa High Commission.

Answer: HMG cannot accept the subdivision of the Kenya and Uganda railways into territorial parts.

6. Federalism:
Question: Uganda should have a federal constitution.

Answer: This will be examined by the proposed Relationships Commission: but it would be of assistance to know what powers the Kabaka's government is prepared to give up to a central or federal government.

7. Preservation of the Kabakaship and the Lukiiko:
Question: Preservation of the Kabakaship must embrace the Lukiiko in such a way that the two institutions continue in a functioning and living form.

Answer: Agreed, but HMG would like to see the Lukiiko brought on to a more democratic basis by part at least of its being directly elected.

8. Termination of the Buganda Agreement:
Question: Generally, the Buganda Agreement should be terminated now.

Answer: This is not acceptable to HMG. Furthermore, the termination of the Agreements would not remove Buganda from HMG's protection and would leave the Kabaka's position and the constitution of Buganda without safeguards.

In opening the talks, Macleod, armed with the above responses, reaffirmed Britain's intention for the elections to the new LEGCO to be held throughout Uganda early in 1961, and that voter registration should begin on 22 August 1960. He made it clear that there was no prospect that this position or the postponement of the date of commencement of registration would be reconsidered. He also reaffirmed that a Relationships Commission was to be set up to make recommendations on the final form of government Uganda would have. He was therefore not prepared to discuss matters reserved for consideration by the Commission, including the question of Buganda's demand for a federal constitution. This meant that although Buganda was prepared to send representatives to the LEGCO in exchange for an undertaking that it would have a federal relationship with the rest of the country,[74] the British Government was not prepared to give any such undertaking.

Throughout the negotiations, Macleod, relying on the ready answers prepared for him, insisted that Buganda's demands for a federal form of government should await the Report of the Relationships Commission, which would recommend the final form of government that would be best suited to the needs of an independent Uganda. He advised that the Commission's recommendations would be considered at a conference in the summer of 1961 where all parts of Uganda would be represented. The British Government pressurised Buganda to agree to join the LEGCO, but the delegation refused to budge. Buganda insisted it would only join after the Kabaka's position had been clarified *vis-à-vis* any future chief minister, a federal form of constitution had been adopted for Uganda as a whole, and the discussions on a revised constitution had been concluded. Assurances that Buganda's entry into the LEGCO would not affect its present position and that Britain would maintain its responsibility to safeguard Buganda in accordance with the Agreement were not persuasive.[75]

Britain would not commit itself on a federal constitution and insisted on having direct elections for Buganda's representatives to the LEGCO. Buganda insisted on having a federal constitution and selecting its representatives to the LEGCO, with the Lukiiko acting as an electoral college as a means to have control over them. On this latter point, Buganda was advised that if it wanted to control any representatives directly elected to the LEGCO then it may either support an existing party or form its own.[76] The idea that the Buganda Lukiiko should lead rather than fight democracy was repeated by Lord Perth, who argued that the best method of preserving the position of the traditional rulers in Africa (as once in Britain) lay in their helping democratic trends to go forward. To him, "the best course for the Lukiiko was to take an active part in the forthcoming elections to get representatives of the traditional point of view."[77]

Clearly, Lord Perth's views on the need for a large traditionalist party sympathetic to Buganda's interests were congruent with Macleod's, and there is little doubt that they influenced the formation of the Kabaka Yekka Movement in 1961.[78] As we show ahead, Kabaka Yekka was seen as the antidote to Buganda's foremost dilemma over whether or not to agree to have directly elected politicians—over whom it would have little or no control—to represent its interests in the British-dominated LEGCO which was to ultimately negotiate and determine Uganda's constitutional future. Buganda could not put itself or the Kabaka in a position where it had to depend on directly elected politicians to represent or fight for its interests in the LEGCO.

Moreover, it believed that, unlike other parts of the country, its agreements with Britain placed it in a special position in which it could handle its matters bilaterally and without a need to be a part of the LEGCO machinery. This is why it wished to complete constitutional discussions with Britain before it could contemplate joining the LEGCO, where it had no control or influence and where it could be out-voted by the rest of the country. However, Britain was not agreeable to any proposition aimed at ring-fencing Buganda's interests ahead of the Relationships Commission and the Constitutional Conference. Thus, coaxing the Buganda delegation to change its mind on Buganda's autonomy was particularly difficult. Indeed, it resulted in a stalemate that led Crawford to advise that "if Buganda could not agree with the rest of Uganda on the form of Constitution to be implemented at independence, she might conceivably ask Britain to continue protection under a new agreement."[79]

On 18 August 1960, having made no progress with the Buganda delegation, Macleod and Crawford held a separate meeting with the Kabaka at which he was asked why Buganda was unwilling to cooperate in the elections in spite of assurances Britain had made. Buganda had been assured that the elections and consequent changes would not prejudice Buganda's special position under its Agreement, that the Executive Council would continue to be advisory, and that this would not change until after the constitutional conference in 1961. The Kabaka stated that there was a need for "going through the whole negotiation again next year."[80]

But a determined Macleod was not ready to agree "either to the continuation of the present talks or to the resumption of the constitutional discussions in Entebbe without the Kabaka's government's agreement to Buganda's participation in the elections."[81] He told the Kabaka that he intended the elections to go ahead but equally that he would do all he could to preserve the special position of Buganda. The Kabaka was not persuaded by the reassurances and the meeting ended without making any headway.

Buganda's and the Kabaka's position was not popular with either the British or the rest of the Protectorate. The Kabaka was seen as being recalcitrant and was accused of delaying Uganda's independence.[82] In fact, as mentioned above, Macleod thought the Kabaka was an obstinate and difficult person who was holding back the progress of the wider Ugandan project.[83] In a letter to Prime Minister Macmillan, he felt that because of Buganda's intransigence on this point, Britain was close to where it had been when Oliver Lyttelton had deported Mutesa in 1953.[84]

With this frustration, but with the determination to steer around the rock, the Protectorate Government announced, even before the negotiations were concluded, that voter registration would start in Uganda on 22 August and that the elections would be held in March 1961.[85] To ensure that the exercise happened without trouble, the Protectorate Government passed a law called The Elections 1961 (Prevention of Intimidation) Ordinance in September 1960.[86] The new law was welcomed by the UNC and the DP.[87]

Inevitably, and unsurprisingly, the largely farcical talks ended in a deadlock. It was quite clear now that Britain had an agenda that ran entirely counter to Buganda's, but it needed to string Buganda along as it completed its plans for the elections. From the outset, Britain was not prepared to allow Buganda or anyone else to upset the timing and direction of its plans for Uganda. It would not budge on Buganda's key demands to postpone the date of the elections or guarantee a federal form of government.[88]

Indeed, the delaying tactic was consistent with Britain's policy of "gradualness" in relinquishing control of its East African colonies. This policy, articulated by Lennox-Boyd and supported by Macmillan, aimed amongst other things, at drawing out the period during which HMG could retain control of vital matters in the region, including defence interests, economic interests, and matters of British prestige and influence.[89] In a rather extremist view, Lennox-Boyd, who still by 1959 did not see any prospect of Britain relinquishing control in Kenya in the foreseeable future, and saw the situation in Uganda as complex and threatening, believed that Britain's interests could only be secured "so long as Her Majesty's Government successfully retained ultimate control, i.e., so long as they or their agents are in direct control not only of defence and external relations, but also of law and order—the legal system, the police and the internal security side of the work of provincial Administrations."[90] According to Macleod, Britain's vital interests would be safeguarded even after independence.[91]

Given Britain's standpoint, Buganda's delegation was faced with a *fait accompli* and could not make any more advances. The collapse of the talks set into motion a series of events that drove Buganda and Britain onto a high political precipice.

The Lukiiko was perturbed by the news from London, particularly that the British Government was unable to accede to its requests to postpone voter registration or affirm that Buganda would be a part of Uganda under a federal form of government. To show its disappointment, it boycotted a visit by Macleod who, as if to reconfirm Britain's foremost interests, chose to leave the Buganda delegation behind in London to be in Uganda to open the new LEGCO (the current Uganda Parliament) building.[92] During his visit, Macleod met all the hereditary rulers except the Kabaka, who was still in London, and reiterated Britain's future plans without committing himself to a date for independence or the future form of government for Uganda.

Macleod could not commit to a date or timetable because, at this time, it was difficult for Britain to forecast with any certainty the timescale of constitutional changes in East Africa in general or Uganda in particular. However, at a meeting of East African Governors in London in January 1961, it was suggested that Uganda may be ready for independence late in 1962 or early in 1963 "if the problems associated with the relationships of the four kingdoms could be resolved."[93] On his part, Governor Crawford aimed to have a constitutional conference in 1961 and final negotiations for Uganda's independence in 1964.

Britain's equivocation on the date and the lack of a clear timetable for Uganda's independence in January 1961, shows how ill prepared it was as it rushed to relinquish Uganda in October 1962. This is surprising given the fact that Britain, under Harold Macmillan, had embarked on a decolonisation policy way back in 1959. As suggested above, the crisis that resulted in the grant of independence to Uganda in October 1962, and not a later date as previously envisaged, may only be explained by three key factors, namely, anti-colonial pressure in the UN (UN General Assembly Resolution 1514); the loss of morale and resignations of colonial civil servants in the wake of an uncertain future in a liquidated empire; and the increased pressure by Buganda and other political activists in the Protectorate in their demand for independence.[94]

The Kabaka and his delegation returned on 20 September and, unlike Macleod, received a thunderous welcome from a huge crowd organised by the kingdom and a pro-monarchy group called Sitakange.[95] He immediately addressed the Lukiiko, asking it to be united and to struggle for its country, Buganda. Katikkiro Kintu was left with the task of briefing the meeting on the failed London talks the following day. The disappointed Lukiiko considered Kintu's report and passed three resolutions, namely:

1. **Resolution 10/60** deplored the start of registrations in Buganda when this was one of the points for which the Secretary of State invited the Kabaka and the Lukiiko Constitutional Committee to discuss with a view to arriving at a mutual agreement. The Lukiiko felt that HM's Government "intended to prejudice the Kabaka's subjects" and that the Secretary of State had made up his mind before the discussions in London began.
2. **Resolution 11/60** opposed the Anti-intimidation Bill and accused HM's Government of following communist practices. The Lukiiko felt that the law was targeting Buganda and that the said action would create disunity between Buganda and the rest of Uganda.
3. **Resolution 12/60** declared Buganda's determination to be a separate and autonomous state, and announced that it would not be represented in the future Legislative Council. The resolution further stated that Buganda would not wish to stand in the way of the political development of other parts of Uganda, and would like to make it clear that other parts of Uganda were free to seek the attainment of their autonomy through whatever means they thought fit.[96]

Pursuant to the third resolution, the Lukiiko in its session of 6 October 1960 appointed the Buganda Independence Committee (BIC)[97] to make and communicate plans for the independence of Buganda, including a draft Constitution, to HM the Queen. In taking these decisions, the Lukiiko, buoyed by the support of a packed gallery of mostly Sitakange members, threw caution to the wind and disregarded the Speaker's advice that the resolutions offended the provisions of the 1955 Agreement. Clearly, the Lukiiko had lost its patience and hope in the negotiations and felt that in such an impasse it could and should go it alone.

The Protectorate Government swiftly rejected the Lukiiko's decisions. On September 26, Governor Crawford, through the Chief Secretary, told the LEGCO that there could be no question of any part of the Protectorate seceding from Uganda as long as Her Majesty's Government was the protecting power. The announcement was received with loud applause by the LEGCO members.[98] Elsewhere, Governor Crawford, who considered the Kabaka's subjects as Britain's "problem children" and as "bumptious, beer-swilling, bible-punching, bullying, braggart Baganda,"[99] stated:

> The demand for a separate Buganda is one to which Her Majesty's Government cannot accede to without serious injustice, not only to the people of Buganda themselves but to the remaining four-and-a-half million people in other parts of the Protectorate. During the period of British rule, the economy, the communications system and many other services have been built up by Uganda as a whole and it is abundantly clear that Buganda and the other parts of the Protectorate are interdependent. Her Majesty's Government is opposed to any policy which would result in the disintegration of the country and a legacy of disarticulated kingdoms, provinces and districts.[100]

Similarly, Macleod wrote to the Kabaka warning that there would be no change in the status of Buganda in relation to Her Majesty's Government, at least until after there had been a conference in London involving all interested parties following receipt of the recommendations of the Relationships Commission. He stated:

> if Buganda were to seek to overthrow the Agreements in a mood of impatience at this stage, I do not believe that there would be another. I therefore call upon your Highness to join with me and with His Excellency the Governor in an urgent effort to restore cooperation and good will between us before it is too late.[101]

In sum, Britain was unmoved by Buganda's radical moves, which it deplored as negative and incapable of advancing the interests of its people.

As Uganda's independence appeared imminent and as its British protectors remained unyielding on the reinstatement of its sovereignty, Buganda became more agitated and more anxious about its future. Its anxiety precipitated some rather frantic moves. In apparent defiance, and as a clear rebuff to Macleod's warning, Buganda dispatched another memorandum dated 8 October 1960,[102] in which the Lukiiko made an earnest appeal to the Queen to terminate British protection. The memorandum recounted Buganda's long history as an autonomous kingdom prior to British intrusion, recalled its historic and treaty links with Britain, showed its population and its capacity to raise revenue, expressed the need to safeguard its heritage and the institutions of the Kabaka and the Lukiiko, recalled the failed talks of September 1960, and affirmed its mistrust of political parties as the custodians of Uganda's future. The memorandum set out a detailed plan for an independent Buganda, covering its future relations with Great Britain, international relations, and relations with its neighbours in East Africa. It also set out constitutional plans for its internal government on the legislative, judicial and executive powers, as well as on land, finances, the army, and the cities of Kampala and Entebbe.

More still, it stated that its decision had been made imperative by Her Majesty's failure to recognise the fact that any possible parliamentary democracy ought to be built on the existing institutions of Buganda, that is to say, the Kabaka and the Lukiiko.[103] It added that its decision was taken "in order to avoid another 'Katanga' immediately after independence."[104] Buganda had decided and was determined to go it alone. It proposed that its relationship with Britain be finalised and put into effect by 31 December 1960, after which date Buganda would be independent.[105] In defiance of British imperial power and in disregard of Macleod's warning, with this latest memorandum, Buganda seemed set on a path of confrontation and no return.

Breaking Free of the Protector? Buganda's Unilateral Declaration of Independence[106]

The Buganda Independence Committee (BIC) started its work on 12 October 1960, and in November 1960 published a pamphlet entitled "Buganda's Independence." The pamphlet set out "Buganda's position" and reproduced the Katikkiro's opening speech at the Buganda constitutional talks with the Colonial Secretary in London in August 1960 and the Lukiiko's memorandum. In its report to the Lukiiko,[107] the BIC set out the activity plan for 31 December 1960—the date when Buganda was to declare its independence. It stated that if the Queen responded positively to Buganda's memorandum before 31 December then the door to talks would still be open, but if she refused, the Lukiiko would decide on the way forward. The BIC report set out how Buganda would finance its government with revenues envisaged from taxes on crops such as coffee, cotton, sugar, tea, tobacco, maize and nuts (totalling over £3,589,900); indirect taxes, customs, excise, licences and rents (totalling over £5,025,872); direct taxes of Africans in Buganda (totalling over £1,562,011); and direct taxes of Europeans in Buganda (totalling over £3,000,000).

To these sums would be added grants and loans from external sources.[108] In terms of government operations, the report provided for the law and immigration departments, as well as for a radio station for Buganda's "own propaganda," which it could use "without impediment."[109] It provided for a directly elected Lukiiko as the legislative and deliberative body for Buganda, in which the "fundamental rights of man, and the rule of law as understood in the free world, [would] be strictly observed."[110]

The report also set out a ministry and civil service structure for the new government. In what appeared to be a half-hearted and ill-conceived strategy, it outlined plans for a "strong police force" and military. Remarkably, it stated that "as the police force in Buganda [was] still inadequate, during the handing over, the Protectorate Government police in Buganda [would] be handed over to the Kabaka's government, and [would] be merged with the Buganda police force to become one force for the kingdom of Buganda."[111] Equally remarkable was its rather simplistic plan for the military. The report stated that "there [would] be a department of armed forces led by educated and experienced officers who [would] be trained in the same way as all other independent nations."[112]

These statements suggest several damning things on Buganda's strategy for attaining independence from the British at the time. Foremost was Buganda's assumption that the Protectorate Government would be agreeable to its unilateral declaration of independence to the extent of "handing over" its police personnel (comprising both Africans and Europeans) to the new government. They also suggest that Buganda was naive in its plans for independence, particularly in its failure to plan and provide adequately for a military force to defend its territory and the new government in Buganda. This naivety is also discernible in Buganda's "Plan for Independence," as well as in the memorandum to the Queen of 1960, which both state that Buganda would have its own army, but also that it would form a military alliance with Britain for a specified period, which might be revised from time-to-time.

These elements suggest that the kingdom was ill-prepared to take and hold state power, insofar as it did not appreciate British colonial policy, the mechanics of modern statecraft and the need to hold and control the instruments of coercion. Indeed, it may be said that since the early days of resistance against colonial rule in the 1930s and 40s, Buganda had grossly underestimated British resolve to hold on to the colonial territory in spite of the protected peoples' desire that it let go. Yet, by now Buganda should have known Britain's real and primary mission: exploitative imperialism and not the protection of the colonised peoples.

By 1959 Britain's policy on the future of East Africa was to "retain for a considerable, if not indefinite, period some control in the area in matters of vital concern."[113] By that time Britain had no plans to let Buganda separate from the rest of the Protectorate and, in any case, its bureaucrats believed that it was unlikely that by 1965 Uganda would have achieved full and responsible internal self-government. In its ten-year projections on Africa, made in 1959, it was considered that Uganda would probably attain responsible self-government in 1970.[114] For the reasons we discuss below, this policy quickly became outdated once Britain decided, in 1961, that Uganda would attain independence in 1962.

Clearly Buganda was oblivious to this policy in its struggle for and declaration of independence and thus did not spend more time on devising a more strategic exit. Instead the BIC spent much energy and money on a delegation of four people, including A. K. Sempa, sent abroad to popularize the case of Buganda's independence. The delegation's mission was to explain Buganda's determination to declare independence on 31 December 1960, to seek aid in various forms, and, particularly, to present the case for Buganda's independence to the UN and win support for it. The delegation visited the self-governing countries of Sudan, Morocco and the US.[115] While in Sudan, Buganda's delegation met the Ambassadors of Greece, Yugoslavia, Morocco and Ethiopia.[116] In the US, Sempa visited the UN Headquarters in New York and had talks with Dr Ralph Bunche, the UN Assistant Secretary General.[117] Sempa left a memorandum on Buganda's independence for the attention of the UN Secretary General.[118]

However, in spite of its rather laborious efforts, there is no evidence that the delegation made any effective representations as, in the end, no single country declared its support for or recognition of Buganda's independence. However, it must also be added that Britain intensely lobbied and warned foreign governments, including the Sudanese, Moroccan and Indian and Greek ones, that it would be improper to give any form of official recognition, and still less any moral or material support to Buganda's secession which, according to it, had no legal or practical reality.[119]

There was heightened activity in both the Buganda and British camps as the critical date of 31 December 1960 fast approached. The British camp kept a watchful eye on the political developments in Buganda. It sent out its officials to gather intelligence on the Kabaka, his ministers, his chiefs and other leading figures.[120] In anticipation of the declaration of independence, it planned for rapid responses on the security, legal and political fronts to thwart any such development. Plans were made to tighten the security situation in Buganda,[121] codenamed "Operation Mistletoe."[122] The military were kept east of the Nile to avoid allegations that the Protectorate Government was bringing force to bear on political matters.[123] A total of 2,576 policemen, including six Special Forces units, were deployed in Buganda.[124] The 4th and 5th battalions of the King's African Rifles, under the command of Brigadier Goode, were stationed in Jinja and put on standby. Buganda was declared a gazetted area under the Police Ordinance so that public meetings could be controlled. It was planned that if crowds assembled outside Bulange (the seat of the Lukiiko) and started building up, they should be dispersed forthwith. Private firearms were removed from certain people. Britain was prepared to declare a state of emergency in Buganda if matters got out of control.[125]

On the legal front, the Protectorate Government also sought advice from its Attorney General on the proposed declaration and its possible consequences. It was advised that a resolution declaring Buganda independent would have no legal status because: i) there was no provision for the abrogation of the Agreements by the Kabaka or the Lukiiko; ii) it would require the approval of the Governor before it could have effect; and iii) Buganda had no power to secede even if it chose to break the Agreements.[126] It was thus considered that a proclamation of Buganda's independence would amount to a clear breach of the Agreements and of the Kabaka's solemn undertaking to abide by those Agreements, and perhaps amount to sedition or treason on the part of the person making such a declaration.[127] In this regard, Governor Crawford ordered the police to build up dossiers in respect of Amos K. Sempa, M. Kintu and Dr E. B. S. Lumu with a view to prosecuting and deporting them for their role in the secession.

On the political front, it was agreed that in the event the resolution was passed, the Governor should immediately reject it and make it known that it would have no effect. Further, the Governor should call in the ministers and advise them to take no steps to implement the resolution. If they refused, the Governor was to dismiss them. The meeting also agreed to defer the payment of grants to Buganda until cooperation was restored.[128] In line with the Protectorate's position, Ben Kiwanuka, the Chief Minister, and the Democratic Party (which he led) was also strongly opposed to Buganda's declaration of independence.[129]

One of the key informants of the Protectorate Government on what was happening in Buganda's camp was the Kabaka's former schoolmate and confidant, Daudi Ochieng.[130] According to a record note, on the eve of Christmas 1960, Ochieng met with R. Dreschfield, the Acting Chief Secretary of the Protectorate, and told him that the Baganda groups were "disillusioned with Katikkiro Kintu," and that "more and more [were] prepared to support political parties, especially the UPC."[131] On 28 December, Ochieng spoke to Dreschfield again and informed him that the Kabaka's ministers had decided to put a resolution to the Lukiiko on the 29 December, declaring Buganda's secession on 31 December.[132] He told him that he had impressed upon the Lukiiko the foolishness of the course of action they proposed to adopt, and had suggested they instead press for voter registration in Buganda to be reopened so that they could take an active part in the coming elections.[133]

On the same day, the Resident of Buganda, E. Stone, wrote that Ochieng had that morning asked to see him about an urgent matter, but that he did not want to be seen having discussions with him in the Resident's office.[134] They met at the LEGCO building, where Ochieng told the Resident about the rumours that the Sitakange group were putting up a resolution at the next day's Lukiiko meeting, which was to be signed by all the members of the Lukiiko, to the effect that Buganda had seceded.[135]

He also informed the Resident that he had met Katikkiro Kintu and had spoken in blunt terms, stating that secession was an impossibility for Buganda unless it was done by force of arms; that direct elections would definitely take place in Buganda as elsewhere; that as matters stood at the time, the Democratic Party would have a majority of seats, while no one sympathetic to the traditionalist policies of the Kabaka's government would get in; that a group of African ministers would be in power who would be most unsympathetic to Buganda; and that Kintu's best hope was to try and get as many Lukiiko members as possible on the LEGCO in order to preserve the balance of power and put forth Buganda's case at the forthcoming London conference. Therefore, he had concluded, the best plan for the Kabaka's government and the Lukiiko at this time was to press strongly for the reopening of registration and to pass a resolution to that effect, and that they should thereafter initiate negotiations with the Secretary of State about the reopening of registration.[136]

The Resident mentioned to Ochieng that he would have to work pretty fast and effectively in order to make Kintu and Sempa change their minds in such a short time, and that if the resolution was passed, one of the first steps the Protectorate Government might take would be "to defer payment of the law and order grants, which [were] due on 1 January," hoping that "he may drop an appropriate hint to the ministers later that morning."[137] Ochieng returned to Dreschfield on the same day and told him that he had seen the whole Council of Ministers and that all but three of them were against secession.[138] The three that were in favour were Sempa, Bassude and Musoke. Ochieng said that it was quite clear to him that the Kabaka's government at the time was not ruling Buganda but that it was being ruled by what he described as hooligans in Bwaise and Nakulabye (both suburban strongholds of the radical elements in Buganda at this time).[139]

Based on these records, it is clear that Ochieng was an informant for the Protectorate Government, aiming to advance his own political position and agenda. As we show ahead, Ochieng was highly trusted in Buganda so much so that he, with Abu K. Mayanja, brokered the doomed UPC/

Kabaka Yekka alliance reached between Obote and Mutesa.[140] He was also later appointed as the Secretary General of Buganda's Kabaka Yekka party and as the representative of the kingdom in Uganda's National Assembly. Speaking on the fiftieth anniversary of his demise, Buganda's Katikkiro, Charles Peter Mayiga, described him as a true nationalist who loved Buganda and defended its interests.[141]

Ochieng's information shows that Buganda's camp was not only infiltrated, but was also deeply divided between those who preferred talks before independence and those who wanted talks after independence. Katikkiro Kintu seemed to have retreated in the last days of the campaign for independence and did not appear to be fully in command of the situation. The Kabaka, who generally supported the idea of independence for Buganda, also had reservations on the procedure, timing and execution of the secession project.[142] He wished to avoid a head-on clash with the British and Protectorate Governments. This may also explain why he does not discuss this rather historic and dramatic episode in his book.[143] The members of the BIC were split on the approach. Indeed, some of its members including Fred Mpanga, Abu Mayanja and Godfrey Binaisa resigned from the Committee and submitted a minority report about the issue.[144] Members with the minority view considered that any

> unilateral declaration by the Lukiiko that Buganda was independent on 31 December 1960, without putting her independence into effect would be a mere bluff and positively unwise and would belittle the importance of the Lukiiko in the eyes of the world and the people of Buganda.... [T]he best way would be to negotiate with the Colonial Secretary if we are to achieve the best for Buganda and her throne.[145]

Accordingly, the minority members concluded that "the only way to preserve the throne and the identity of Buganda is not to secede from the rest of Uganda, considering the economics, the politics and the geography of Buganda in relation to the rest of Uganda, and indeed, to the whole of East Africa."[146] Time has vindicated the minority's views in this matter. With the benefit of hindsight, their views were reasonable—especially given that Buganda had not really made sufficient preparations for the declaration of independence. However, given Britain's determination to hold Uganda together as a united country, it is also doubtful that further negotiations would have yielded the autonomy Buganda wanted.

In any event, forces outside Mengo led by the Sitakange group seemed to take lead of the campaign and exert enormous pressure on the Mengo leadership to push for a declaration of independence. Thanks to Ochieng, the British camp knew all about the level of disorganization within the

Buganda camp and planned accordingly.

The equivocation in Buganda's leadership on the planned independence declaration, the lack of a comprehensive strategy, and the absence of widespread public support, combined with Ochieng's leaking of key information to the British, ultimately undermined the declaration for Buganda's independence.

On 31 December 1960, the Protectorate Government held a meeting chaired by Governor Crawford which reached the conclusion that the Kabaka and Katikkiro Kintu were trying to take a more moderate line as far as the declaration of independence was concerned.[147] In fact, from the separate meetings held between the Kabaka and the Resident,[148] and the Kabaka and the Commissioner of Police,[149] it was reported that the Kabaka did not really want secession. It was established that what he wanted was an assurance of a federal form of government. On that basis, it was agreed that the Governor should ring up the Kabaka to express appreciation of his efforts. Otherwise, the meeting agreed that for the time being the policy should be "to sit tight but to deal firmly with any breaches of the law" and if, but only if, the situation demanded, "to declare a state of emergency in order to remove those responsible for the disorders from the scene."[150] The British camp seemed to have the situation under its firm control.

On the same day that the Protectorate Government held its meeting, the Lukiiko also met amidst a packed gallery. A stormy debate ensued. There were principally two views. One was the independence-before-talks (hardliner) view and the other the talks-before-independence (moderate) view. Those for the former view included Kajubi (a member from Kyaggwe) and Dr Emmanuel B. S. Lumu. The latter view was advanced by G. L. Binaisa, and Musoke (the Omulamuzi). Katikkiro Kintu and Sempa, who looked uncomfortable during the debate, did not speak, in spite of demands from the gallery that they do so.[151]

The Kabaka did not address the Lukiiko. According to the records of the Special Branch of the Protectorate Police, based on the reports of their agents in the Lukiiko Hall, the resolutions of the debate were "based on public opinion in the gallery rather than on the opinions of the Lukiiko members."[152] The gallery cheered those who supported independence before the talks and booed those in support of independence after the talks. In the end, the Lukiiko passed a resolution, drafted by Amos Sempa, Yake Kyazze, Dr Lumu and Dr Muwazi, declaring independence before talks.[153] The resolution read:

> In the Name of God and the Nation of Buganda, the Lukiiko of Buganda

> which has met today 31 December 1960, has declared that from this day of 31 December 1960, Buganda has terminated the protection which existed between Her Majesty the Queen and the Kingdom of Buganda, based on the Treaty of 1894 and all subsequent Agreements or where it is derived from any enactment or document which may have been made by Britain alone without the consent of both sides. Buganda asked for British protection. It is only Buganda who may end that protection. Therefore, the Lukiiko has declared that from today, December 31 1960, Buganda is INDEPENDENT. From this Declaration Her Majesty the Queen will hand over to the Kingdom of Buganda all her rights, possessions and powers which she has been protecting. The Lukiiko appeals to all people in the Kingdom of Buganda to keep the laws and the peace.[154]

It was the Lukiiko's honest belief that by making the declaration, they would free Buganda from the clutches of British imperialism.

On the day the Lukiiko passed the above resolution, Governor Crawford issued a counter-statement making it clear that the resolution that purported to declare the end of British protection over Buganda could not and would not be approved by HM's Government.[155] The resolution would therefore be of no effect; after all, it was not within the competence of the Lukiiko. The following day, the Kabaka forwarded the deliberations of the Lukiiko to the Governor in a rather friendly letter that revealed his feelings on the developments. He wrote:

> Dear Fredrick, before you go I thought it proper that you should know the deliberations of the Lukiiko session of yesterday, a copy of which is hereto attached. My compliments to the Earl of Munster that the above-mentioned developments need not frustrate his forthcoming mission. Once more I wish you prosperity and good health. Salutations to all mutual friends. Fredrick Mutesa.[156]

As expected, the Lukiiko declaration of independence caused much smoke but failed to ignite any fire within or beyond Buganda. It was as ineffective as it was underwhelming. This led to calls by the Democratic Party and other groups, such as the pro-monarchy Omwoyo Gw'Eggwanga, for the resignation of Katikkiro Kintu and his colleagues in Mengo.[157] Governor Crawford held a brief meeting with his advisors in Entebbe on 1 January 1961 to assess the situation and agree on how to manage the Katikkiro's team, which had been summoned for a meeting over the declaration later in the day.

The meeting agreed to reject the resolution and, depending on the ministers' attitude, adopt one of the following policies: (a) continue with talks and negotiations with the Kabaka's government, at least until the elections in March, and avoid a real crisis in British relations with Buganda at least until the elections; (b) bring the situation to a head by acting on the assumption that the Lukiiko resolution amounts to an act of distinct disloyalty and an abrogation of the Agreement. It was agreed that the latter policy be pursued. The meeting also noted that since opposition to the present "Mengo Clique" was growing, time was on the British side.

Following the script agreed upon in the British camp, the Governor, in imperial style, summoned the Katikkiro and the ministers to Entebbe to ask them about their plans in view of the Lukiiko's declaration.[158] He asked whether the 1955 Agreement was now abrogated and whether the British Government should now withdraw its recognition from the Kabaka and stop paying the grants to Buganda. He asked the ministers for their views on the way forward. The ministers had no ready or clear answers. There is no evidence that they had envisaged or planned for this kind of confrontation. Abu Mayanja attempted to interpret the intention and meaning of the resolution to the Governor, saying it meant that

> Her Majesty's Government's protection was terminated; that Buganda was now an independent state; that Buganda now wished to negotiate—through peaceful means—a proper handover of the powers which had hitherto been held by Her Majesty's Government in Buganda; that the date for starting discussions should be hastened, so as to provide the best deterrent against worsening relations between the Protectorate Government and the Kabaka's government; and that in the interim period pending talks, the administration of the kingdom, the provision of services, the payment of taxes, normal occupations, etc., would continue.[159]

Mayanja's interpretation was accepted and supported by his colleagues in the room. However, the last part must have been Mayanja's own improvisation because the Lukiiko's declaration was silent on what was to be done in the interim period. With this window, Governor Crawford asked the ministers to make a public clarification as stated by Abu Mayanja on the gist and import of the Lukiiko's declaration. He reiterated that he could not approve the Lukiiko resolution, which was, in any case, beyond his legal jurisdiction.[160] However, he hinted at the possibility of resuming talks and asked the ministers to send him proposals for the terms of reference of any such talks.

In summing up the day's deliberations, the Governor stressed that the agreements Britain had with Buganda could not be terminated without the consent of both parties. He noted the assurance given to him that until further negotiations could be held it was the intention of the Kabaka's government to preserve the status quo, that law and order would be maintained, and that the Katikkiro would issue a statement clarifying the intention behind the Lukiiko's resolution and reassuring the general public. Within less than 24 hours of the passing of the famous declaration of independence, Buganda's leaders had dramatically buckled in the face of British imperialism.

Overnight, Buganda's position changed from talks-after-independence to talks-before-independence. But the notion of independence as understood by the Lukiiko could not have meant, and did not mean, the maintenance of the status quo where Her Majesty's Government remained in charge. In effect, therefore, the meeting was nothing if not a humiliation for the Katikkiro's team and Buganda. It was now clear that Buganda's declaration was both ill-conceived and poorly implemented. It was, inevitably, a still birth.

The Protectorate Government immediately issued a news release to the effect that in their meeting with the Governor, the Kabaka's ministers

> indicated their intention that until further talks, which they desired, had taken place—which they hoped would be as soon as possible—the present basis of administration and relationship with the Protectorate Government would remain unchanged, and services throughout Buganda would continue normally. The ministers gave an undertaking that they would make this position clear to the public, and assured the Governor of their firm intention to maintain law and order and preserve the peace throughout the kingdom of Buganda.[161]

On the same day, the Governor flew to London to brief Macleod over Buganda matters, among other things.

The *Uganda Argus* newspaper headline of 2 January 1961 reading "LUKIIKO DECLARES INDEPENDENCE: Governor Rejects Decision; Ministers Seek New Talks," accurately summed up the situation in Buganda. The paper noted that "relations between the Protectorate Government and the Kabaka's government are to remain unchanged, despite Buganda's secession bid, until the future pattern of relations has been discussed in resumed talks which Buganda wants between its representatives and the British Government."[162] Katikkiro Kintu denied newspaper reports that his government had dropped the idea of Buganda's secession and that he had tendered his resignation.[163] On 3 January, the Kabaka's embattled ministers issued a separate statement on their meeting with the Governor on 1 January saying:

> As some newspapers and people have misinterpreted what the ministers did, stating that the ministers had abandoned the idea of independence, the

> Kabaka's government has found it necessary to issue a full explanation. The Governor invited the ministers in order to get first-hand information on what had taken place in the Lukiiko and what was actually meant by the declaration, which he had not yet received officially. In accordance with the Lukiiko's declaration, the ministers told the Governor that they desired to hold talks; and that these talks should be as soon as possible.
> (a) At these talks Buganda would participate as an independent state.
> (b) The Lukiiko stated in its declaration that "from this declaration of 31 December 1960 Her Majesty the Queen will hand over Buganda's rights which she has been protecting."
>
> The Ministers therefore informed the Governor that the purpose of those talks was to hand over to Buganda the rights which are now being protected by the Queen. In putting forward the purpose for the talks, the ministers felt—as anyone else would also see—that that is the correct procedure. Because if someone wishes to regain rights which [he has] surrendered to someone else, the best thing is to negotiate with him. The Ministers are pursuing that line and they therefore are not at variance with the spirit of the Lukiiko which declared Buganda an independent state.... The Kabaka's government ends by congratulating all the people in Buganda for the exemplary way they have maintained law and order since the declaration. This has proved to the world outside that the Kingdom of Buganda can look after their own affairs in peace.[164]

It is worth noting that this statement was scrupulously couched and silent on the fact that the Governor refused to approve the secession resolution and that the status quo, as far as administration and general relationships between Buganda and Britain were concerned, would remain intact.

On the same day the ministers issued their statement, Crawford met Macleod in London. Macleod was reluctant to resume talks with Buganda and felt that possibly the best way of consuming time would be for Lord Munster, purely as Commissioner, to have talks with them about what they mean by secession and how they would propose to work it, or if it were not agreed, a federation. The two agreed on the following course of action:

> sit tight and deal with any breaches of the law; hold firm on elections throughout Uganda in March; try to keep Buganda stringing along until after the elections; but if this eventually proves impossible, to tell them bluntly that they cannot secede; possibly for Munster to make some statement that will reduce the temperature in Buganda when the elections are held in March; and that if they take any action to implement secession by, for example, usurping Protectorate Government power or levying taxes illegally, then the offenders should be prosecuted under the law.[165]

The general agreement was that Britain should demonstrate that the

Lukiiko resolution meant nothing and that there would be no change unless Her Majesty's Government approved of it. In view of the anticipation and anxiety in Buganda in the wake of the declaration of independence, one would have expected protests and demonstrations at this news. But, surprisingly, Buganda remained calm and peaceful. In fact, in a note to Macleod on 3 January 1961, Acting Governor Cartland said:

> Buganda is unusually quiet. There is no doubt that the presence of the 5th KAR in Jinja together with intensive police patrolling has had a profound effect. Kintu has also instructed his chiefs to ensure that law and order is maintained. There are some signs of public dissatisfaction with the ministers for failure to take any positive action to implement independence and for the tone of their interview with the Governor on Sunday.[166]

Cartland's observations were correct. However, while the KAR and the police patrols under Operation Mistletoe may have intimidated the population to some degree, the real reason Buganda was unusually quiet was that while the Lukiiko had high expectations, the campaign for independence was largely leaderless and weak across the kingdom at all material times. The mobilisation of the public in Buganda in support for independence was taken over by groups like Omwoyo Gw'Eggwanga and Sitakange whose outreach, respectability and authority was limited. Like Buganda's ministers, the public was clueless and mostly confused on the next steps or on their role in getting and defending independence.

There is no evidence that the public was aware of what to do, both when the declaration was made and when it was rejected by the Protectorate Government. The people did not understand the practical and political implications of the declaration. It is thus unsurprising that the population in Buganda gave no support to Mengo once the declaration was rejected by the Governor. It is also plausible that the Kabaka's general detachment and lukewarm attitude towards the declaration of independence further dampened public enthusiasm towards it.

Better still, the absence of violence or outpouring of emotion on the independence debacle may be attributed to the generally non-violent nature of the Baganda who, when faced with adversity, tend to recoil rather that explode with emotions. Their sullen but restrained reaction to Mwanga's deposition and deportation in 1899, as well as to Mutesa's deportation in 1953, are cases in point. But, as they say, to every general rule there are exceptions; in this case, the protests in Buganda in 1945, 1949 and 2009 may have been such exceptions.

A comparison of the levels of mobilisation by Kivu and Musaazi in the 1945 protests and that of Mulumba in the 1949 protests with that of

Katikkiro Kintu and Amos Sempa in 1960 suggests that the architects and champions of Buganda's declaration of independence failed to capture the imagination of the general public in Buganda. In other words, the streetwise activists like I. K. Musaazi and Kivu performed much better at political mobilisation against imperialism than their elite counterparts at the head of the Mengo hierarchy, who were essentially in disarray when their leadership was needed most.

As expected, Omwoyo Gw'Eggwanga started a campaign asking the Kabaka to fire Kintu and his colleagues from office for misleading the people and failing to implement the independence of Buganda. Kintu and his ministers refused to resign and instead pushed for immediate talks with the Governor.[167] In a later statement on the talks, the Kabaka's government stated that it would participate in the talks "not in a subordinate capacity, but that of an equal. Moreover, Buganda [did] not envisage an attitude of dictation from the Colonial Secretary but one of negotiation."[168] As if in response, the Acting Governor felt that it was best to leave the Buganda Government "to stew in their own embarrassment."[169] Once the situation was considered safe and nonviolent, Operation Mistletoe was officially called off on 4 January with praise for "being responsible for the absence of lawlessness" and for proving to be "a most useful and valuable exercise."[170]

The BIC, which had faded into the background in the wake of the declaration, also suffered some battering, especially after some of its members, namely, G. L. Binaisa, Luyimbazi Zake and Fred Mpanga, resigned from it. The discord within the BIC and Mengo is evident from the following records. On 6 January 1961, G. L. Binaisa called on the Resident of Buganda and shared his frustrations in advising the BIC, and Sempa in particular, that secession was a complete impracticability for Buganda.[171] The BIC had made no detailed plans for the implementation of the secession. To him, the campaign for secession had to be fought against and defeated. He asked the Resident for permission to have a public debate with Sempa on this point.[172] Elsewhere, it was said of Binaisa that although he had been sitting on the Committee, he had never supported Buganda's separate independence.[173]

In a meeting with R. N. Posnett, the Judicial Adviser, A. F. Mpanga stated that he was as ardent a supporter of independence for Buganda as anyone, but that he only conceived of it as a result of negotiations, not of a unilateral act.[174] According to Posnett, Mpanga, who he thought to be a close friend to the Kabaka, said that "the Kabaka was much against the resolution for secession and anxious to proceed constitutionally."[175] Posnett further stated:

> [T]he Lukiiko and other members of the Committee had chosen to take unilateral action which in his view was not only wrong but ineffective. He had found in the Committee that he was up against the self-interest of members who wanted to be prime or other ministers of an independent country and who were not therefore open to reason. He could therefore not agree to continue on the Committee.[176]

The BIC report was presented to the Lukiiko on 13 January 1961, thirteen days after the Lukiiko had resolved to declare independence for Buganda. The report was passed with 44 votes in favour, 34 against and 11 abstentions. According to newspaper reports, the general public's reaction to the report was one of confusion and disappointment because it did not have any constructive recommendation for the implementation of Buganda's independence.[177] Writing on the effect of the declaration, the Munster Commission noted:

> it had little practical effect. The Kabaka's ministers assured the Governor of their determination to preserve law and order in Buganda. They continued to collect taxes in Buganda on behalf of the Protectorate Government and to avail themselves of the full range of Protectorate Government services. In return the Protectorate Government refrained from cutting off the grants which account for half of Buganda's revenue. It was a curious fact that day-to-day cooperation between the departments of the two governments actually improved in the period immediately after the declaration of the secession.[178]

Buganda's declaration of independence received little or no attention from other parts of the Protectorate. This may be explained in several ways: there is the fact that the rest of the Protectorate was not really concerned about Buganda's unilateral moves given that they did not have any real legal or political relations with it at the time; also they considered the matter as one between Buganda and the Protectorate government; and generally they chose to wait and see what the outcome and implications of the declaration would be.

By 8 February, when Governor Crawford convened and chaired a meeting with all Buganda's ministers at Entebbe, Buganda's declaration of independence had run out of steam. As such, sticking to the British go-slow plan, the Governor refused the resumption of talks with Buganda until it had given evidence to the Munster Commission and the Commission had made its report. The meeting left the Kabaka's ministers embittered, perplexed and worried about the next moves.

Buganda's failed experiment with the unilateral declaration of Independence in December 1960 is not dissimilar to secession attempts by other peoples on the African continent. In Appendix VI, we highlight two of the more prominent cases involving the Katangese of the Congo and the Igbo of Nigeria, to draw comparisons and understand the commonalities or differences in the causes and effects of the separatist policies adopted by each. In looking at the colonial history of Uganda, Nigeria and the Congo, and the nationalists struggles therein, several conclusions may be drawn.

Firstly, in all cases, colonialism was underpinned by plunder and the protection of colonial commercial interests, as well as political patronage. Secondly, that there exists a causal nexus between Buganda's, Katanga's and Biafra's struggle for autonomy and between Uganda's, the Congo's and Nigeria's historic and contemporary politics. Thirdly, it is demonstrable that the solution to the aspiration for autonomy in all the three cases may be the same—namely, revisiting and reconceptualising the foundations of the colonial state. Fourthly, these cases show the problematic limitations in the realisation of the right of self-determination of indigenous peoples within the context of colonially determined boundaries, both in municipal and international law.

A subdued Buganda picks itself up, dusts up and takes a reluctant plunge into Uganda: The 1961 elections and Buganda's boycott

Although Buganda was subdued with the failed independence declaration, it maintained its notional sense of independence (no Lukiiko resolution was passed reversing the declaration) and continued with its defiance against colonial rule and its struggle for autonomy, albeit this time within the framework of talks with Britain for a united Uganda. Talks with the Governor in 1961 failed to persuade him to either agree to Buganda's separation or to delay the holding of a national general election. Thus, in total disregard of Buganda's position, the Protectorate government proceeded to announce and prepare for general elections throughout the country in March 1961.

Once again, Buganda and Britain, with irreconcilable attitudes and policy positions on the nature and timing of the general elections, were on a collision course, and Buganda chose to boycott the election. According to Mutesa, this decision was informed by the fear that Buganda, without any political machinery, would have a minority position in the LEGCO and yet it was that body that would negotiate the constitutional future of an independent Uganda.[179] It thus preferred that Buganda not be involved in the LEGCO until its position had been negotiated with Britain and its interests entrenched in an agreed constitution.[180]

But while Buganda boycotted the elections, other political actors, with the support of the Protectorate Government, took the opportunity to actively advance their interests. The political parties that participated in the 1961 elections were the Uganda People's Congress (UPC), the Democratic Party (DP), the Uganda National Congress (UNC), the Uganda Hereditary Chieftainship Party (UHCP) and the Uganda African Union (UAU).[181] The campaigns were dominated by the UPC and the DP. While each of the dominant parties had an elaborate manifesto, there was undue influence from religious and ethnic lobbies throughout the campaigns. The DP appealed mostly to Catholic believers, while the UPC reached out to the Protestant faithful.

To frustrate the elections in Buganda, the kingdom forbade its people to register to vote. The boycott was largely effective, because, in spite of a vigorous campaign for registration and voting in Buganda by the DP, with the protection from the Protectorate Government, out of 700,000 eligible voters, only 35,000 (five percent) were actually registered to vote in Buganda.[182] Of this number, only 1,050 (three percent) actually voted.[183] Be that as it may, the DP won the general elections with 43 seats (20 of which were from Buganda), followed by the UPC with 35 seats, the UNC with one seat, and two independents.[184] Ben Kiwanuka, the leader of the DP, was accordingly appointed to head both the first African Government of Uganda and the LEGCO, while the UPC formed the opposition. Thus, the Westminster model of parliamentary democracy was introduced in Uganda a few months before the country's independence.

Uniting a Colony Divided at Birth: How Lord Munster's Relationships Commission Grappled with Uganda's Integration

As Uganda's independence approached, the biggest hurdle for Britain was uniting the different peoples of the Protectorate under one country. This difficulty was exacerbated by Buganda's separatist stance and the quest for special positions by the other kingdoms. Buganda and Britain were following irreconcilable policies.[185] Historically Britain had set different paths for the different parts of the country, and while it promoted a centralised government policy for the country as a whole, at the same time it built up the power of the Lukiiko and the Kabaka's government as if they were a separate entity.

According to Prime Minister Macmillan, the disunity and troublesome situation in Uganda threatened British colonial rule in the entire East Africa region. He believed that failure in Uganda would have a disastrous effect on British policy in Africa and the rest of the world.[186] For this reason, he ordered that a Relationships Commission be set up to advise on the best way the country may be united. According to him, "it was vital that the Relationships Commission should be a success; that it should inspire confidence; and that it should produce sound and workable recommendations in a most complex field."[187] It was therefore crucial that whoever headed the Commission should inspire public confidence and, as advised by Secretary Macleod, be wholly acceptable to the Kabaka. Macleod believed that if the Kabaka's cooperation was secured then Britain would be "sure of avoiding the sort of situation in Uganda that arose in Katanga."[188]

It was not easy to find such a person, as many who were requested—including David Kilmuir, the Duke of Hamilton, and Justice Ronald Roxburgh—declined the job.[189] It was not until the Rt Hon. Earl of Munster,[190] a judge and former British Minister, agreed to take on the task in December 1960 that an entirely British three-man Commission was appointed consisting of Lord Munster, Prof. H. W. R. Wade (a Professor of Law) and Dr A. H. Marshall (an expert on British local government).[191] The Commission's remit was "to consider the future form of government best suited to Uganda and the question of the relationship between the central government and the other authorities in Uganda."[192] This was to be done bearing in mind the need to develop stable institutions, the desire of the people to preserve their existing institutions, and "the special relationship that already exist[ed] between Her Majesty's Government and His Highness the Kabaka's Government and the native governments of Bunyoro, Ankole, and Toro."[193]

The Munster Commission started work in January 1961 but, for the most part, proceeded without Lord Munster, who was taken ill in February and was unable to return to Uganda.[194] Wade and Marshall traversed the country and gathered much evidence from individuals and institutions. They worked throughout the election period in March 1961 and observed the politics and the issues of the day intently. On a few occasions they met the Kabaka, who handed them a copy of the pamphlet "Buganda's Independence."[195] They also met with the Kabaka's ministers on three occasions.[196]

These developments, however, did not stop Buganda from withdrawing its cooperation with the Commission.[197] The Commission submitted its report on 2 June 1961, noting that Uganda had arrived at a turning point in her history and that the colonial regime, accustomed to leisurely development, had to compress a decade of constitutional progress into a few months.[198] It also noted that Uganda had a handicap in the problem of Buganda and the slow Africanisation program, despite which it had to devise a new constitution and make it work instantly.[199] It recommended that "if the changeover [was] to be smooth, a longer rather than a shorter transitional period [was] desirable.[200]

The Commission made a number of recommendations. On the future Constitution, the main recommendations were that Uganda should be a single democratic state with a strong government at the centre and with asymmetrical relationships between different parts of the country; and that Buganda should have federal status and the other three kingdoms semi-federal status, while any other districts should be under the realm of the central government and managed on a unitary basis.[201] The Commission also recommended a directly elected National Assembly to replace the LEGCO[202] and made other recommendations on the legal and judicial system, land tenure, finance, regional and local governments, and boundary disputes.[203] On the question of the lost counties, the Commission noted that "this problem [was] in a class by itself" and that until it was resolved, there was a serious risk of more trouble which might involve other parts of Uganda.[204] On this matter, it recommended that a referendum in the two counties of Buyaga and Bugangazzi and one other county to be chosen by Bunyoro be organised before the end of the Protectorate and that any areas in which Bunyoro was successful should be handed over simultaneously with the end of the Protectorate.[205] In any event, both Buganda and Bunyoro rejected this recommendation.

The Commission went out of its way to ensure that it addressed Buganda's fears and met its interests so that it could drop its separatist agenda. While it ruled out any possibility of secession, the Commission made a number of concessional recommendations. Some of the recommendations included that Buganda should join Uganda in a federal relationship with exclusive powers over the Kabakaship, the Lukiiko and traditional institutions; that the Kabaka should be a genuine constitutional monarch and withdraw from politics; that there should be direct elections to the Lukiiko; that the county chiefs should cease to be members of the Lukiiko; and that Buganda's representatives to the National Assembly should be elected by the Lukiiko acting as an electoral college.[206]

The Commission recommended particularly strong safeguards for the Kabakaship, the Kabaka's government, the Lukiiko and its traditional and cultural institutions. The National Assembly would have no powers to make laws that adversely affected these protected institutions without the consent of Buganda.[207] The Commission emphasised that these safeguards would be absolute legal guarantees. In other words, they were

> altogether unalterable to Buganda's disadvantage without Buganda's own consent. They [would] therefore be markedly stronger than, for example, the guarantees provided by the constitutions of the United States, where the requisite majorities can alter the constitution … these guarantees [would] be legally enforceable, with an ultimate appeal outside Uganda so as to assure complete impartiality.[208]

The Commission pointed out that no such guarantees were given to either the Asantehene in Ghana or the princes in India.[209] However, as it turned out, within less than five years of the Munster report, the said guarantees did not protect the Kabakaship or save Buganda from Obote's dictatorship. And by that time, Britain was no longer available or willing to protect it.

The Commission's key recommendation on the kingdoms of Toro, Ankole and Bunyoro was that they would have a semi-federal status with the same absolute guarantees as proposed for Buganda on their monarchies, legislation, appointments and other ceremonies.[210] There were no specific recommendations on exclusive matters under their jurisdiction, as was the case in Buganda. The Commission felt that these kingdoms should not get full federal status because if they were federal states they would have to equip themselves with a complex government machinery than they currently had, and they lacked resources—both human and financial—for that task. At the same time, the central government would be weakened to the detriment of all.[211]

The recommendation for the rest of the nine districts was that they were unsuitable for development as federal states and that a strong unitary government was required for them.[212] It was recommended that they should be given constitutional rights, such as to maintain their councils and appoint ceremonial heads as part of the ordinary system of local government. It is clear from its recommendations that the Commission concentrated on the goal of uniting Uganda by mostly accommodating Buganda's concerns and providing guarantees for the preservation of its institutions. Ironically, this was to breed further resentment and conflict in the rest of the Protectorate.

For Buganda, the Commission's recommendations on federalism and representation in the LEGCO ought to have been seen as a major breakthrough. After all, short of separation from Uganda, this was Buganda's best hope for self-determination. However, Buganda remained sceptical. It was not pleased, for example, with the idea that the Kabaka should become a genuine constitutional monarch and withdraw from politics; that there should be direct elections to the Lukiiko; that county chiefs should cease to be officials in the Lukiiko; that the present Lukiiko should be dissolved so that direct elections could be held; and that a referendum in the two "lost" counties of Buyaga and Bugangazzi and one other county was to be organised. For these reasons, Buganda rejected the Munster report. The neighbouring kingdom of Bunyoro was also unhappy with the recommendations on the lost counties. The rest of the Protectorate was largely indifferent and did not present strong views for or against the report.

In spite of the reservations of Buganda and Bunyoro, the Munster Commission report paved the way for the Uganda's historic Constitutional Conference in September 1961. The Report provided the colonial government with a blueprint to tackle the seemingly intractable problems of relationships between unequal and diverse parts of the country. In recommending full federal status for Buganda, semi-federal status for the kingdoms of Ankole, Toro and Bunyoro, and a unitary status for the district and territory of Busoga, the Munster Commission performed a delicate balancing act that resulted in an asymmetrical political and constitutional setup that inevitably undermined the future stability of the country. However, given the history and the politics of the country, it is doubtful that a better or more agreeable formula for uniting Uganda could have been found at the time. The fault lines in the Munster recommendations—particularly on the asymmetrical amalgamation of political and ethnic structures and the lost counties problem—extended not just to the Constitutional Conference but beyond into the country's independence.[213]

The Uganda Constitutional Conference in London, September 1961

In setting up a new constitutional order in Uganda, the British Government followed its conventional policy of arranging a constitutional conference in London where it sponsored or hosted delegations from the colony to discuss constitutional matters and reach agreement in an environment far removed from the politics of their localities and perhaps more conducive to obtaining a consensus. Similar conferences were held for Nigeria (in 1957 and 1958), Kenya (in 1960, 1962 and 1963), Somaliland (in 1960), Zanzibar and Tanzania (in 1961), Guyana (in 1963), Basutoland (Lesotho) (in 1964), and Zimbabwe (in 1979). For a country that does not have a written constitution, it is intriguing that Britain insisted on its colonies having written constitutions negotiated only a few months ahead of their independence.

Although the Uganda Constitutional Conference was only advisory in nature and non-binding on the participants, it was hugely significant to the future development of the country. For the first time in the Protectorate's history, and in a politically anxious and expectant environment, the full complexity of issues on relationships, political parties and land were tabled and discussed by all interested parties in the same room. It was expected that in a space of three weeks—and with only a handful of Ugandan representatives at Lancaster House—the country would agree on when and how it would break free from colonialism. The discussions were bound to be difficult given the diversity of interests. For this reason, the meeting witnessed sharp disagreements and walk-outs by disgruntled delegations. In the end, to reach agreement on some points, the colonial master had to prevail and dictate.[214]

In preparation for the Conference, Britain tried to generate as much consensus in the country as was possible. To this end, Governor Crawford held discussions with the Constitutional Committee of the Buganda Lukiiko with a view to reaching agreement on Buganda's lingering concerns. Although the Munster Commission's recommendations for federalism and Britain's pledges of protection had softened Buganda's separatist stance, the kingdom was not yet fully agreeable to joining the rest of the Protectorate on a constitutional path for a united Uganda. This explains why the decision for Buganda to participate in the Conference was taken hesitantly, just one week before it began, and even then only after reaching an agreement to form an alliance between the Kabaka Yekka Movement and the UPC leadership on Buganda's concerns.[215]

The Kabaka Yekka movement, initially organised and led by Latimer Mpagi and S. K. Masembe Kabali, was a political platform from which the kingdom could respond to the political changes in the country ahead of Independence.[216] Ben Kiwanuka was viewed as the arch-enemy of Buganda, and it was hoped that, through Kabaka Yekka, it would be possible to remove him from power.[217] The movement aimed to appeal to the emotions of the kingdom's faithful, mostly located in rural Buganda, so as retain control of the Lukiiko and gain a significant and strategic position in the National Assembly. Its rallying slogan was Kabaka Yekka ("Kabaka Only") and, beyond the retention of the Kabaka's and Buganda's position and power in the new Uganda, it lacked a detailed political or national programme.[218]

The movement attracted most of the leading political actors in Buganda, including J. Luyimbazi Zake, I. K. Musazi, E. M. K. Mulira, Latimer Mpagi, Haji Busungu, Aloni Lubwama, Apollo Kironde and J. Baka.[219] Although it had no formal relations with the Kabaka's government, there was no doubt that it received its support. For this reason, it was commonly referred to as "Kintu's party." It is unsurprising that by November 1961, the Kabaka's government—alongside leaders of Sitakange, the Uganda National Congress and the United Federal Party—had declared its support for Kabaka Yekka.[220]

The alliance between Buganda's political vehicle, Kabaka Yekka, and Obote's UPC was struck on the basis of the mutual interest of Buganda and the UPC in ousting the Democratic Party from power and ensuring that the influence and control of Uganda after independence remained in the hands of their alliance. In many ways the alliance was opportunistic. On the part of the UPC, the goal was to capture the Buganda vote, which would naturally follow the Kabaka and Buganda's leadership. On Buganda's part, it was to ensure that the ousting of the DP and its leader Ben Kiwanuka, so as to be in a position to control the country's post-independence politics. Although Buganda's leadership was persuaded that it would dominate Obote and the UPC, in the end, relying on a host of repressive and extra-legal methods, it was Obote and the UPC that emerged as the dominant force in Uganda's new government.

On his part, to persuade Buganda to drop its plans to boycott the Conference, Secretary Macleod also invited the Kabaka and his advisers to London ahead of the Conference for separate talks, where he gave pledges and assurances on the position of Buganda in the future Uganda.[221] With Macleod's assurances, and with only two days until the Conference, the Kabaka requested the Lukiiko to allow Buganda to participate. In a letter to the Lukiiko, he wrote:

> Considering the assurances which the Colonial Secretary has given me and the Committee after detailed and careful discussions and also after examining what may happen in the future, it appears that Buganda's participation in that Conference will not prejudice Buganda's position at all. Therefore it seems to us to be advisable that the Lukiiko should permit its representatives to take their places in the Conference; this will also enable Buganda to present its case regarding its future relationship with the rest of Uganda.[222]

Based on Macleod's pledges, the Kabaka assured the Lukiiko that his delegation in London was "firm and [would] not relent or falter." With these assurances—particularly those of the Colonial Secretary that Buganda would not lose whatever had been agreed with the Governor, and that outstanding matters would soon be finalised—and with the Kabaka's letter of comfort, the Lukiiko belatedly and reluctantly agreed to

Buganda's participation in the Conference. There is no doubt that the political history of Uganda would be radically different if Mutesa or the Lukiiko had declined to participate in the Conference.

In separate discussions, Secretary Macleod lobbied the hereditary rulers of Toro, Bunyoro, Ankole and Busoga.[223] These discussions, which dwelt on Uganda's future Head of State, future arrangements regarding land, and the demand for full federal status, did not yield much, as Macleod insisted that all these issues were to be considered at the full Constitutional Conference. Macleod also met Ben Kiwanuka of the DP as Chief Minister and Milton Obote of the UPC as the leader of the Opposition before the Conference started.

Following these separate meetings, the Constitutional Conference, under the Chairmanship of Macleod, commenced in Lancaster House, London on 18 September and ran until 9 October 1961.[224] Seventeen plenary sessions were held in total. The Conference was attended by 86 people, inclusive of the delegates, advisers and members of the secretariat. The delegations were from the United Kingdom, the Government of Uganda, the DP, the UPC, Buganda Kingdom, and the District Councils of West Nile, Karamoja, Toro, Kigezi, Ankole, Bukedi, Bunyoro, Madi, Bugisu, Busoga, Teso, Acholi, and Lango. The District Councils were represented by individuals from those areas. Judging from the size of the delegations, the main players at the Conference were the British, Buganda, the DP and the UPC, each of which had at least ten representatives, including advisers. As a sign of the marginal role that women were permitted to play in the constitutional discussions, none of the delegations had a female delegate.

At the opening of the Conference, Secretary of State Macleod stated that it was to be mostly guided by the Munster Commission's Report.[225] On the Agreements of protection Britain had with Buganda and other kingdoms, he stated that these would inevitably end with the independence of the Protectorate. With regard to Buganda, the Secretary reported that Her Majesty's Government felt that "they should do everything in their power to enable Buganda to take its place in the independent state of Uganda upon acceptable terms."[226] He was confident that "the recommendations of the Munster Commission with regard to Buganda provided the best and perhaps the only way of securing the cooperation of the people of Buganda in the creation of an independent Uganda."[227] He reiterated the resolve that Buganda's relationship to Uganda should be federal, that there should be a division of legislative powers, that the Kabakaship and other institutions should be firmly guaranteed, that there should be direct elections for the members of the Lukiiko, and that

Buganda should be represented in the National Assembly. He particularly assured the traditional rulers of his pledge, and Britain's "determination to safeguard their position while the Protectorate continues and to help them to secure safeguards for the future."[228]

In a clearly contradictory statement, Macleod undertook to push forward with the "development of democratic institutions and the centre and transfer the responsibilities of government to elected officials" while at once doing everything within his power to "preserve the position of [traditional] rulers and their special relationships, and to develop and strengthen the administration in the kingdoms."[229] These nebulous and irreconcilable promises meant different things to the politicians and the traditional leaders at the conference, and may explain the difficulties met in gaining a consensus on Uganda's political and constitutional future at the conference and well beyond it.

In their opening statements, the delegations spelt out their goals and expressed their fears. Ben Kiwanuka, the Chief Minister and leader of the DP, in a thinly veiled reference to Buganda's delegation, said the Conference was "a momentous occasion for Uganda, and it was important that an attempt should be made to outgrow tribalism and parochialism and work towards a respected, free, and independent country."[230] He wanted a Constitution that would safeguard the traditions and the positions of the rulers, preserve the oneness of Uganda, respect the rights of individuals and ensure democracy.

He gave an assurance to the Buganda delegation that his delegation was "ready and willing to listen sympathetically to their views."[231] Milton Obote, the Leader of the Opposition, focused on the need to expedite independence and called for a firm date to be declared for the withdrawal of protection. On Buganda's separatist stance, Obote said that the problem needed "comprehensive tolerance and compromise as well as acceptance of the existence of a united Uganda with a viable economy."[232]

Michael Kintu, the Katikkiro of Buganda, observed that Buganda desired a genuine federal relationship with the central government, which seemed the only way of safeguarding its identity as a kingdom, and of ensuring that the Kabakaship and the Lukiiko continued in a living form.[233] To him, "Buganda revered their traditional institutions without which the country would lack both a head and a heart."[234] He supported the desire of the other kingdoms for a firm federal relationship with the centre. The Bunyoro District Council delegate, Z. H. Kwebiiha, congratulated the British Government and the missionaries for what they had done in the past sixty years, and was glad that Britain had "abandoned old fashioned colonial thinking."[235] Speaking for the District Councils, the Hon. C. J.

Obwangor from Teso expressed the Councils' gratitude to Britain.[236]

With such a diverse composition of delegates at the Conference came a host of conflicting and, in many ways, irreconcilable interests. The only common goal was the attainment of Uganda's independence at the nearest date possible. To begin with, as the convenor of the Conference, Britain was at a crossroad. On the one hand, it had an undertaking to push forward with the development of democratic institutions at the centre, and the transfer of the responsibilities of government to elected representatives. On the other, it had a promise to do everything within its power to preserve the position of the traditional rulers and their special relationships, and to develop and strengthen the administration in the kingdoms.

Secretary of State Macleod told the Conference that he saw no clash here, because Britain itself had historically built its democracy around the monarchy. However, given the many years it took Britain to find a balance, it was rather ambitious to expect Uganda in a space of a few months to strike such a balance. Macleod's primary goal was to end Buganda's separatist stance and obtain a quick passage to the independence of a "united" Uganda.

There were other conflicting personal, political, religious[237] and ethnic or regional interests and agendas at the Conference. The key protagonists were Macleod for Britain, Kintu for Buganda, Kiwanuka for the DP, Obote for the UPC and Kwebiiha for Bunyoro. The disagreements played out at different levels. For example, the delegates for other parts of Uganda were suspicious that by offering a full federal status to Buganda and allowing it to avoid direct elections of its representatives to the National Assembly, Britain was favouring it over the other regions.[238] To that extent, there were anti-Buganda sentiments.

On its part, Buganda was determined to retain a special position for the Kabakaship, the Lukiiko and its other traditional cultural institutions in an independent Uganda just as they had existed under its agreement with Britain. It was also ready, in spite of their fundamental ideological and political differences,[239] to team up with Obote's Protestant-leaning UPC in what has been termed an "unholy alliance"[240] to thwart Ben Kiwanuka and the Catholic-leaning DP in the independence elections of 1962. Kiwanuka and the DP were bent on holding onto their minority win in the 1961 elections and were thus strongly opposed to Buganda's plan to avoid direct elections of its representatives to the National Assembly, which would effectively destroy the DP's electability in Buganda. For this reason, and to woo more support outside Buganda, the DP supported Bunyoro over Buganda on the question of the lost counties.[241]

Because of these differences, the Conference witnessed several walk-outs and protests, most notably by Kiwanuka and other DP delegates, Bunyoro's Kwebiiha, Ankole's Kazzora and Acholi's Okenyi.

Beyond the subtle religious tensions between the DP and the UPC, there was no obvious involvement of missionaries or church leadership at the Conference. This was unlike in the negotiations for the 1900 and 1955 Agreements, where the missionaries and the church had played a more overt and pivotal role. However, as we have already discussed above, there were certain behind-the-scenes efforts by Bishop Fisher of the Anglican Church to influence Kiwanuka's DP during the conference.[242]

To steer the conference and emerge with agreement on some of the most contentious issues was not easy and often required a blend of immense diplomatic skills and dictatorship. The most controversial issues at the Conference were the election of Buganda's representatives to the National Assembly; the resolution of boundary disputes, particularly between the kingdoms of Bunyoro and Buganda (the lost counties question); and the date for independence. The Munster Report had recommended that a directly elected Buganda Lukiiko would have a choice to elect Buganda's representatives to the National Assembly either directly or indirectly (i.e. with the Lukiiko acting as an electoral college), a proposition that was fiercely opposed by the Democratic Party.[243]

Its leader, Ben Kiwanuka, argued that "a proposal that one tribe in the country should be treated differently in the matter of choosing representatives to the Legislature did not seem to be a proper foundation on which to build a stable and reliable democratic system of Government."[244] He accused the British Government of favouring Buganda by backtracking on the issue of direct elections agreed upon in the 1955 Agreement and instead supporting indirect elections to the National Assembly in Buganda in return for its support on the other proposals made by the Munster Commission.

But beyond Kiwanuka's arguments on democratic representation, his real fear was that without direct elections in Buganda, the chances of his party winning in Buganda would be greatly diminished. It was no secret that the Buganda Lukiiko was wholly opposed to him and the DP. His only chance of retaining power lay in direct elections to the National Assembly in Buganda. Kiwanuka's views were supported by delegates from Kigezi, West Nile and Acholi, who argued that the recommendation was a sacrifice of democracy for tribal interests and would lead to widespread violence.[245]

To show his displeasure over the prospect of indirect elections, Kiwanuka and his supporters staged a walk-out, but had to return the next day once it was decided that the Conference would proceed without him.[246] Kiwanuka and his group were strongly opposed by Buganda's delegation, as well as by Obote and the UPC, who stood to gain most if indirect elections were organised in Buganda. Obote argued that there would be a greater risk of disorder and intimidation if direct elections were imposed on the Baganda against their will.[247] In his view, since all the parties had a chance to campaign for the direct election of members to the Lukiiko, they would have a chance to be represented in an elected Lukiiko and to influence the decision over whom to choose to represent the Kingdom in the National Assembly. The latter argument was somewhat disingenuous, as Obote knew that the UPC and the Buganda Lukiiko had formed an alliance to effectively lock the DP out of Buganda and out of power.

To resolve the impasse, and to maintain the momentum towards independence, the Chair (Macleod) made an expedient ruling in favour of indirect elections in Buganda. There is no doubt that Macleod sided with Buganda over the rest because he needed to persuade it to stay the course and not to scuttle the Conference. He must have believed that it would be easier for him to persuade the DP and others opposed to this arrangement than to alienate Buganda. In that way, much to the chagrin of Ben Kiwanuka and others, Buganda won the option to hold indirect elections for its representatives to the National Assembly which it could exercise if it so wished.[248] This decision not only settled the question on the mode of election for choosing Buganda's representatives to the National Assembly but also most likely saved the collapse of the talks.

On the lost counties dispute, the conference was faced with a rejection of the Munster recommendations—that there should be a referendum in two counties and possibly in a third—by both Buganda and Bunyoro. Another solution needed to be found. Macleod suggested that the dispute be referred to a Privy Council Commission which would make a final decision binding on the two parties. This view was supported by Buganda, Kiwanuka and Obote, but was roundly rejected by Kwebiiha of Bunyoro, who countered with a proposal that a decision be made at the Conference and that a referendum should be held throughout the disputed areas on a county-by-county basis. He further proposed that the said referendum should be held two months after the Conference and areas which opted to become part of Bunyoro should be transferred to it on 1 February 1962.[249]

The conference was astounded by Bunyoro's revised proposals, as they went well beyond the Munster recommendations and could certainly not be accepted by Buganda. Kwebiiha, convinced that his proposals were most reasonable, walked out of the meeting saying that he considered his tribe "betrayed" and hence unable to participate in future conference proceedings.[250] At this point, once again the Chair had to make another fundamental and difficult ruling. He decided that since his proposals had the general support of the conference, he would invite the British Prime Minister to appoint a Commission composed of Privy Counsellors to investigate and advise urgently on the question of the lost counties.[251]

The ruling was a careful act intended to progress the Conference and with Britain's plans for independence but without alienating either Buganda or Bunyoro over this complex question. In effect, with this ruling, Britain dropped the contentious issue of the lost counties into the independent government's lap when it could have helped Uganda immensely by finding a solution before independence.

Following much debate in the plenary, a number of compromises and concessions were made. Firstly, it was agreed that the relationship between Britain and Buganda, Ankole, Toro and Bunyoro under their respective Agreements would be replaced by new Agreements, which would remain in place during the period before independence. Secondly, the relationship between the Uganda Government and the kingdoms would be given constitutional force in the Constitution of Uganda. Thirdly, Britain's protection over Buganda was to end on the condition that the kingdom of Buganda would be united in a federal relationship with the rest of Uganda in accordance with the Constitutions of Uganda and Buganda. Fourthly, and largely on this basis, Buganda agreed to be represented in the National Assembly by 21 members either directly elected in Buganda or, if the Lukiiko opted to do so, through a system of indirect election. Under the latter alternative, indirect elections would be conducted by secret ballot of the members of the Lukiiko and the members so elected would be drawn from within or outside the Lukiiko.

The conference agreed on matters over which the legislatures of Buganda and Uganda would have exclusive powers and outlined those where they would have concurrent powers. In case of conflict between the laws of Buganda and Uganda, Uganda's laws would prevail. Buganda was to have a High Court to administer justice in the name of the Kabaka and in accordance with the laws of Uganda. It was also to have a police force commanded by its own officers but subject to the authority of the Inspector General of the Uganda Police Force. Although it was denied powers to raise an army, the Buganda Government was required to take reasonable steps within its power to maintain public security in Buganda. Minerals on public lands in Buganda would belong to the Government of Uganda. An agreement was also reached on financial provisions and Buganda's estimates of revenue and expenditure were to be sent to the central government for consideration and observations.

The debate on the dates for self-government and independence was also rather heated. Whereas HMG, as the convenor of the conference, suggested the end of 1962, the delegates pushed for an earlier date. Obote suggested June 1962. There was no consensus and, in the end, Macleod, as Chair, announced the timetable that he felt most suitable. Internal self-government would be attained on 1 March 1962, elections to the National Assembly conducted in mid-April, 1962, and independence for Uganda attained exactly one year from the closure of the conference, on 9 October 1962. It was a one-year crash programme in which to draft and finalise the Constitution, arrange and hold national elections, and prepare a new government before Independence Day.

Overall, to the extent that the constitutional conference was well attended and held together until the end, and that a date for independence was set, it was a significant success. But it was perhaps the British Government and the kingdom of Buganda that emerged with the more satisfactory outcomes. For Britain, the goal of the conference was to obtain a consensus on the future constitutional framework for its hitherto administratively disjointed Protectorate. It aimed to leave behind a united country in which the kingdom areas, particularly Buganda, lived happily with non-kingdom areas and in which traditional and cultural institutions survived in a democratic political environment. It was a tough balance of interests which, nevertheless, was generally achieved. Unfortunately, while all appeared neatly wrapped up, Uganda's postcolonial history has in fact shown that far from a neatly bound package, the British left behind a hornet's nest that tragically unravelled a short two years after their departure from the country.

As it turned out, the conference was a major win for Buganda, whose ultimate goal was to secure a federal status under which the Kabakaship and other traditional institutions would be preserved in a living form. This was achieved, but not without some cost. An otherwise cynical Buganda had to back down on several matters, particularly on its declaration of independence made at the end of 1960, and on its relationship with the rest of Uganda at independence. It had previously refused to send members to the LEGCO, but changed its mind and agreed to send them once they were elected by the Lukiiko acting as an electoral college.

Moreover, and perhaps more significantly, it agreed that the Lukiiko was to be restructured and its members directly elected. The other matter that Buganda dropped was the demand for a standing army for the kingdom.[252] With hindsight, Buganda must regret having dropped this demand, as the lack of an army was later exploited by Obote and Amin to overrun the kingdom in 1966. To this day, Buganda remains vulnerable and incapable of securing itself from aggression or violence emanating from the postcolonial state—a state whose foundation and power base is the military above all. Buganda therefore depends for its existence and survival on the goodwill of the central government that has the monopoly over the coercive machinery of the state. On this point, Thompson explains that

> because [Governor] Cohen did not see the army as important, it was left out of the general process of Africanisation … [and] in turn it had little appeal for [the] ambitious Baganda … [T]heir relative underrepresentation in the army of 1962 was magnified thereafter in an army which soon became the political instrument of northern interest groups … [T]he army was the chosen means by which Milton Obote in 1966 imposed the unitary state which had eluded Cohen's more gentle prompting, in an act of arguably unprecedented "absolutism".[253]

In many ways, the British Government played its hand as a *deus ex machina*, especially in allowing Buganda to have a full federal system, unlike other parts of the country; allowing indirect elections of its representatives to the National Assembly, unlike other parts; and deferring the decision on the lost counties even in the face of obstinate representations from the kingdom of Bunyoro. Little wonder that other parts of the country felt an undue advantage and special status had been granted to Buganda. Together with Buganda, the other winner was Obote and his UPC. The strategic alliance which was forged ahead of the conference between Buganda and the UPC leadership helped to dislodge Ben Kiwanuka and the DP from power.

There is no doubt that the biggest loser at the conference was Ben Kiwanuka and the DP, whose hold onto power was fleeting and who, as a result of the UPC-Buganda alliance, went on to lose the elections in April 1962.[254] Kiwanuka's political star faded pretty much into oblivion thereafter.[255] His political woes did not stop with Mutesa (his former friend and sponsor[256]), the kingdom of Buganda[257] or Obote's UPC. They extended to the colonial government which, during his short tenure as Chief Minister, found him uncooperative, reckless and dictatorial.[258] Others considered him to be an "authoritarian and tactless"[259] leader. For example, Mutesa complained to the Secretary of State, R. Maudling, that Ben Kiwanuka's party was intent on using all "unconstitutional means after 1 March to entrench (itself) in power."[260] In addition, Obote and Kabaka Yekka officials expressed their fears to the Governor on what they saw as Kiwanuka's problematic administration.[261]

On its part, Britain was unhappy with Ben Kiwanuka for not yielding to its patronage. It was particularly displeased because it considered Kiwanuka indebted to it for acts such as refusing to suspend elections to the LEGCO in the face of a boycott by the Kabaka's government; moving troops and police into Buganda for the election (which had enabled him to secure seats in Buganda and a majority in the legislature); and appointing him Chief Minister in a much shorter time after his party had won the election than any other leaders in like circumstances in Africa.[262]

Once he was appointed as Chief Minister, Kiwanuka disappointed his British benefactors by undermining British expatriate civil servants, making public appointments without reference to the Public Service Commission, and refusing to cooperate with the Governor on a number of issues. For these sins, Lord Perth recommended that Kiwanuka be severely reprimanded by Maudling.[263] It is plausible that for these reasons Kiwanuka did not receive much support from the Protectorate Government in the 1962 elections and beyond.

The other loser at the conference was Bunyoro kingdom on the outcome on the lost counties issue. In spite of the spirited fight and walk-outs by its delegation, it failed to get its way. In the end it had no choice but to submit to Macleod's ruling and to defer the resolution of the boundary dispute until another commission was set up. The grant of semi-federal status for the kingdoms of Bunyoro, Ankole and Toro and a promise that new agreements would be signed with the British after the conference were mostly a disappointment for the rulers in these areas. This is because, in effect, they did not win real autonomy or power compared to that granted to Buganda.

Their goal at the conference was to attain full federal status and to be placed on an equal footing with the Kabaka of Buganda. Indeed, after the conference, they continued to demand the full federal relationship that Buganda had been granted.[264] Historically, the three kingdoms had been governed more directly, like the districts elsewhere in the Protectorate, and had no administrative independence. The Conference did not change this materially, because even with a semi-federal status, the administrative Councils in the three kingdoms would remain as before.

The 1961 Separation Agreement: Buganda Exits the British Empire

After the Lancaster House Conference, and once the Lukiiko had approved the positions reached, Buganda wasted no time in concluding another agreement with Britain. This was unlike the kingdoms of Bunyoro, Toro and Ankole, which hesitated to enter into new agreements since they wanted to secure better terms to bring them at par with the kingdom of Buganda.

The Buganda Agreement of 1961 was signed on 31 October 1961 by Sir Fredrick Crawford, on behalf of Her Majesty's Government, and Kabaka E. F. Mutesa II, on behalf of Buganda. This Agreement was significant in two respects. First, it provided the legal framework for the termination of British protection of the kingdom of Buganda, and second, it provided the legal and political basis upon which Buganda agreed to be an integral part of Uganda. In this regard, it provided for a new Constitution under which Uganda would enjoy internal self-governance and Buganda would be united with the rest of Uganda in a federal relationship. Besides this, the Agreement addressed Buganda's concerns including: the election of its representatives to the National Assembly; the exclusive powers of the Lukiiko over the Kabakaship, the Kabaka's ministers, and all traditional and customary matters relating to Buganda; its boundary dispute with Bunyoro (which was to remain ongoing until a new Commission headed by Lord Molson made its report); and the services to be administered by the Kabaka's government.

The Agreement also provided for a new Constitution of Buganda as a kingdom, which was to be incorporated as a schedule into the Constitution of Uganda; an undertaking by Britain to take steps to give the Constitution of Buganda the force of law as part of the Constitution of Uganda; a High Court of Buganda, which was to administer justice in the name of the Kabaka and in accordance with the laws of Uganda; and a police force. Britain undertook to maintain the status quo spelt out in the 1961 Agreement until the independence constitution was promulgated.

The 1961 Buganda Agreement was pivotal to the kingdom of Buganda, because it bound the colonial administration to the terms negotiated and agreed on as a result of the Lancaster House Conference in London and thus enabled Buganda to accept becoming part of Uganda on those terms. It was important that these terms were to be entrenched as a part of the independence constitution. Without this agreement in place, Buganda would not have agreed to join Uganda. But with this agreement Buganda agreed to its incorporation into Uganda and dropped its separatist ambitions.

However, as we will see below, despite this agreement, the guarantees in the 1962 Constitution and the assurances of protection by the colonial government, the agreed terms on the position and powers of the kingdom of Buganda were to be discarded a few years after Uganda attained independence.

The Lost Counties and the Conundrum of Uganda's Integration

Apart from Buganda's separatist agenda, there was nothing as problematic and controversial in the build-up to Uganda's independence as the vexatious sixty-year–old territorial dispute between the kingdoms of Buganda and Bunyoro over the counties of Buyaga, Bugangazzi, Buwekula, Buruli, Bugerere and portions of Ssingo and Bulemeezi. The area in dispute historically belonged to the ancient kingdom of Bunyoro Kitara. However, as Buganda expanded in the 19th century, it began to annex some of this territory through war and conquest. The annexation of Bunyoro's land was increased under the colonial leadership of Colonel Colville, who rewarded Buganda with more of Bunyoro's land for Buganda's military assistance against the anti-colonialist king of Bunyoro, Omukama Kabalega. Once Kabalega was defeated in 1899, the British Foreign Office, acting through E. J. L. Berkeley, confirmed the incorporation within Buganda of all territory south of River Kafu.[265] This annexation was formalised once Buganda signed the 1900 Agreement with British Commissioner Harry Johnston. The Agreement affirmed, in Article 1, that the boundary between Buganda and Bunyoro would be the Nkusi and Kafu Rivers.

From the outset, the Banyoro were aggrieved by the actions of the British and their Baganda allies, because the territory that was ceded to Buganda was not only vast but was also of huge traditional and cultural significance. At least fourteen tombs of Bunyoro's past kings were situated on those lands.[266] It was largely for that reason that in 1921 the Banyoro formed the Mubende-Banyoro Committee, whose purpose was to liberate what was termed as the "lost counties."[267]

This was followed by formal petitions addressed by the Omukama of Bunyoro to the Secretary of State for the Colonies in 1943, 1948, 1949 and 1954 demanding the return of his territory.[268] The Mubende-Banyoro Committee also petitioned the Secretary of State for the Colonies in 1951, 1953 and 1955 on the same matter.[269] The Secretary of State's response to all these petitions was always that he could not alter a decision that had been reaffirmed on many occasions, and that the boundaries laid down in the 1900 Agreement could not be changed in favour of Bunyoro.[270]

Not to give up, the Omukama petitioned Her Majesty the Queen requesting that the dispute be heard by the Judicial Committee of the Privy Council. This too was declined because "there were no legal issues in the dispute which could properly be considered by the Judicial Committee."[271] Commenting on the Omukama's petition to the Queen, the Kabaka of

Buganda was unequivocal. He wrote:

> The inclusion of the six counties in the kingdom of Buganda was clearly recognised in the Uganda Agreement of 1900, which now forms part of the Buganda Agreements 1900 to 1955. I am advised that so long as these Agreements remain in force, they are binding on both parties and cannot be unilaterally varied. I have always understood that this view was shared by Her Majesty's Government, and … I cannot see what purpose the proposed reference would serve, since Her Majesty's Government could not give effect to any recommendations favourable to the Petitioner without a breach of her treaty obligations. If it were decided, largely on historical grounds, to alter boundaries which have remained unchanged for more than sixty years, it would be inequitable that revision should be confined to territories referred to in the Petition. My Government might well decide to put forward claims to any or all of the lands which formed part of the ancient kingdom of Buganda."[272]

Bunyoro was advised to submit its claim to the Munster Committee which, as earlier discussed, recommended that a referendum be held in the counties of Buyaga and Bugangazzi and in one other area chosen by Bunyoro. Both Buganda and Bunyoro rejected this recommendation.

The Commission of Privy Counsellors on a Dispute between Buganda and Bunyoro (Molson Commission)

Upon the failure of Buganda and Bunyoro to reach an agreement on the intractable dispute over the lost counties at the Lancaster House Conference of 1961, Secretary of State for the Colonies Macleod had prevailed over the rulers of these kingdoms to accept the appointment of a Commission of Privy Counsellors to investigate the dispute and make recommendations on the same. While Bunyoro only reluctantly accepted the proposal—for it had wanted the matter to be resolved at the Conference and not later—Buganda was more agreeable.

On that basis, on 20 December 1961, Prime Minister Macmillan announced the appointment of a three-man Commission comprising Lord Molson (Chairman), the Earl of Listowel and Viscount Ward of Witley.[273]

The Molson Commission's terms of reference were rather general. The Commission was asked to investigate allegations of discrimination raised in the Omukama of Bunyoro's petition and other grievances in certain areas of Buganda, namely, the counties of Buyaga, Bugangazzi, Buwekula, Buruli and Bugerere, and portions of Singo and Bulemezi counties. The Commission was also required to receive representations from those concerned and to advise whether any, and if so, what measures should be taken to deal with the situation.[274] In a confidential but controversial letter written after the appointment of the Commission, the Prime Minister stated the above terms of reference and left the Commission free to recommend any solution deemed appropriate, including a transfer of territory."[275]

It is unclear, in view of the rather open-ended terms of reference, why it was necessary for the Prime Minister to emphasise the Commission's power to recommend a transfer of territory and, secondly, why he did not share that letter with all the concerned parties. It is plausible that Buganda would have—as indeed it did when the fact became public—challenged or rejected the Commission's terms extending to making recommendations on transfer of territory. Apparently, Lord Molson himself had doubts about this and took the matter up with the Prime Minister, who wrote another letter confirming that his terms of reference did include possible changes of boundaries.

This letter from the Prime Minister to Lord Molson remained a private matter for many months, until it was suddenly exposed at the Independence Conference in June 1962.[276] However, in explaining the discrepancy, Reginald Maudling, the new Secretary of State for the Colonies, in a rather woolly way, argued that in accepting the terms the Kabaka had made no stipulation that the Commissioners' freedom to recommend any solution that it deemed fit should be restricted in any way; and further that correspondence between Macleod and the Kabaka did not contain either an undertaking by the former that the Commission would be precluded from recommending boundary adjustment or a request by the latter for such an undertaking.[277]

In addressing the dispute, the Molson Commission, like the Munster Commission before it, adopted a rather awkward approach. As its report states, it treated the dispute on "broad lines of equity," taking into account the "happiness and well-being of the people of Uganda."[278] The dispute was also treated as a political problem rather than a juridical one. But given the allegations that the British had violently and illegally annexed and given away Bunyoro lands to Buganda, and to the extent that the colonisers entered into an Agreement with the kingdom of Buganda incorporating the land in 1900 and appropriating some it as "crown land," the dispute could not have been anything but legal and thus justiciable.

It is thus clear that the two Commissions and, by necessary inference, the British Government, deliberately skirted the legality of the issues raised by Bunyoro and Buganda and chose to treat them as political. It is not difficult to see why this was the case. In the first place, if it was handled as a legal problem, the issues of culpability, liability and damages would arise. Secondly, any legal dispute would bring into issue the legality of Britain's Agreements not just with Buganda but also with all the other kingdoms in the Protectorate and beyond.

Such an undertaking would open a Pandora's box, to say the least. Ibingira convincingly argues that the British Government took this route to avoid the embarrassing position of having to return all, and not just some, of the counties to Bunyoro or make a declaration entitling Buganda to the whole of the disputed area.[279] Ibingira also points out that the British Government was reluctant to resolve the matter as it was not ready to hurt the feelings of either Bunyoro or Buganda. In the circumstances, a politically negotiated settlement represented the best option for Britain. This reality also explains why Britain was unable or unwilling to force either side to a resolution before independence: it was too legally and morally conflicted to take a position.

During the inquiry, John Forster QC, who led Bunyoro's case, argued that its claim was based on moral, ethical and legal grounds.[280] He pointed out that if the transfer was made in 1894 by Col. Colville, it was invalid because Colville had no authority to do so. If it was either made or ratified in 1896, there was a Protectorate over Bunyoro at the time, and a protecting power could not take land from a protected state and give it to another protected state. He stated that the existence of a Protectorate did not confer the power to dispose of land.[281]

He asserted further that the Banyoro in the lost counties had been reduced to serfdom. All this stemmed from the initial mistake of the British in being untrue to their duty as a protecting power and putting no real thought into the propriety or consequences of their actions. He accused the Baganda of pursuing a policy of repression in the lost counties, and called upon the British Government to correct the wrongs of the past now that imperial rule was ending.[282] The Commission also received a seven-page Memorandum from the Omukama of Bunyoro in which he stated that the Banyoro would never agree to lose their property, and neither would they accept foreign rule or slavery.[283] The inquiry received cases of violence including the destruction of crops belonging to Baganda chiefs in Mubende.[284] The Commission also heard strong views, including that Bunyoro was ready to fight and die over their counties.

Buganda's case was led by Martin Flegg and others,[285] who argued that the so-called lost counties belonged to the kingdom of Buganda and that they were a subject of a binding treaty with the British Government. They denied any acts of repression by Buganda over the Banyoro in the lost counties. The people of Buganda were equally charged and anxious about the lost counties. For example, a crowd of over 500 people protesting the transfer of the counties to Bunyoro escorted the leaders of the Kabaka Yekka movement when its leaders appeared before the Commission at the National Theatre. These crowds carried placards reading: "Three men cannot change history."[286]

S. W. Kulubya, a member of the LEGCO, told the Commission that one of the major mistakes that Britain had made was to try to impose a form of government that worked in England but might not be suitable elsewhere.[287] Obote, the leader of the Opposition who led the UPC delegation, told the Commission that it was the view of his party that the problem had been created by Britain and that the British must solve it before leaving Uganda. He expressed fears that Britain might "dodge the issue" by not solving it before independence.[288] On 2 February 1962, the Lukiiko passed a resolution that Buganda would never agree to any recommendation of the Privy Council Commission into the lost counties that gave any part of the kingdom to Bunyoro. In the Lukiiko, Katikkiro Michael Kintu said that "not an inch of Buganda soil would ever be given away," and that the Commission was mandated only to inquire into the grievances that the Banyoro in the lost counties were badly treated, but was never asked to inquire into boundaries.[289]

Based on its findings, the Molson Commission was unanimous in recommending that a substantial part of the Bunyoro claim was justified and that a limited transfer of territory was essential to achieve a just and lasting settlement.[290] Unlike the Munster Commission, which had recommended a referendum in two or three of the affected counties, the Molson Commission recommended that the counties of Buyaga and Bugangazzi should be transferred to Bunyoro; that the township and hill of Mubende should be added to the list of towns to be under the control of the central government; and that Buwekula County of Mubende District and the remaining area under dispute to the east of the district should remain a part of Buganda.[291] The Commission also recommended that the transfer of the territory should take place before 9 October while the Governor was still in office. Nothing less drastic would, in their opinion, ensure a peaceful solution. The Commission acquitted Buganda of allegations of discrimination of Banyoro in the areas under dispute.[292]

In view of the hardline positions taken by each party to the dispute, the Commission made an appeal for "a generous act of statesmanship on the part of Buganda," saying that "no other single act would add more to the stature of Buganda or contribute more to the stability of Uganda on the eve of independence."[293] It also called on the Omukama of Bunyoro, for his part, to renounce in the same spirit all claims to the other counties, as this would be an equally valuable contribution on the lasting settlement.

Lord Molson explained his Commission's departure from Lord Munster's recommendation for a referendum: "We thought it unnecessary, and we thought that it was likely to be extremely dangerous, likely to inflame political opinion and likely to lead to intimidation and violence."[294] In any case, he added, the referendum was unnecessary because it was already obvious that the majority of the population in Buyaga and Bugangazzi wanted to return and be a part of Bunyoro. What Lord Molson did not say was that both Buganda and Bunyoro had rejected a referendum during the Lancaster talks and that, more importantly, holding a referendum would have been extremely complicated and impractical when Britain was preparing a hasty exit at the same time as preparing for the national elections in April, the Independence Conference in June, and Uganda's independence in October 1962.

The Molson Commission worked for approximately eight weeks and submitted its report on 2 March 1962, a few weeks ahead of the national elections that were due on 25 April 1962. But it was only made public on 3 May 1962, a few days after the announcement of the election results that saw a shift in power from Ben Kiwanuka's DP to a coalition of the UPC, led by Milton Obote, and Buganda's Kabaka Yekka.[295] Upon the release of the report, Governor Walter Coutts was quick to thank the Commission for "an admirable report … and a detached inquiry into what [was] certainly its most difficult problem."[296]

On the whole, the British Government considered the report accurate and fair and hoped that it would help to bring about an agreed solution to the problem. Unsurprisingly, however, far from convincing and pacifying the two opposing parties, the report was greeted with pandemonium in both Bunyoro and Buganda. There were mild jubilations in Hoima, Bunyoro capital, but these were immediately accompanied by criticism led by Kwebiiha, the Chief Minister of Bunyoro, that not all their demands were met. The Bunyoro delegation in London also criticised the report and maintained its claim for all the six counties. They stated that the report gave them no pleasure, but that "whatever it gives us we shall take."[297] This did not mean, however, that they would stop claiming the other four counties.

The Lukiiko and the Kabaka, in even stronger terms, also roundly rejected the report and accused the Commission of overstepping its terms of reference in recommending a transfer of the kingdom's territory. The Kabaka sent a telegram to the Colonial Secretary, Reginald Maudling, with a sinister message: "darkening of immediate outlook foregone consequence."[298] The Buganda Lukiiko also sent an angry telegram to the

Colonial Secretary rejecting the report and expressing its indignation at the recommendation proffered by the Molson Committee.[299]

Its members were astonished to hear of the British Prime Minister's secret letter to the Commissioners going back on the express terms of reference which were agreed upon by the British Government and the Kabaka. They condemned the "un-agreed dealings" and invited the British Government to back their rejection of the recommendations. Katikkiro Michael Kintu told the Lukiiko that he would resign before agreeing to give away any part of Buganda to Bunyoro. The Lukiiko's views left the Governor "gravely anxious about the future of Uganda and of Buganda."[300]

War drums were sounded by members of the Lukiiko. One member from Nagoje, B. Muwonge, is quoted as having called upon the Baganda to prepare to send out all their men into the counties to fight until they perish, to which he added: "then send out women, boys and girls … only after even the children have perished shall we agree to the return of the counties to Bunyoro."[301] Muwonge accused the Commission of violating the terms of reference and warned that the blood which would be shed by both the Baganda and Banyoro would be the responsibility of the British Government. Another member, E. Mirugwe from Kakuto, said it had been British policy to degrade the Kabaka and reduce Buganda's prestige, then finally give away some of her territory. To him, it was high time Buganda "fought against these intrigues of the British Government."[302] But, perhaps, the most alarming clarion call came from a Ssaza chief, Nelson Ssebugwaawo, who urged anyone in Buganda who had not made his will to do so. According to this chief, the Baganda would "fight to the last drop of blood to retain their counties."[303]

The double rejection of both the Munster and Molson Commissions' recommendations on the lost counties, coupled with Buganda's and Bunyoro's intransigence in the matter, left Britain in a deep political, moral and legal quandary. The political dilemma consisted in its failure to find an acceptable political solution to the dispute, which presented a real risk of jettisoning the set timetable for independence and ruin Britain's plans to leave Uganda a united country. Yet, because of its role and position in the conflict, Britain was able to suggest but was unable to impose a solution. Despite this, for some reason, before coming to Uganda, Molson had understood that his recommendations, whatever they were, would be imposed if need be. But it was quite clear to the bureaucrats in the Colonial Office, who felt that Molson in fact favoured Bunyoro over Buganda in the dispute, that "it would not be possible to impose a solution over Buganda's opposition."[304]

On the moral plane, because the dispute resulted from Britain's actions, and also because under the 1900 Agreement Britain had appropriated and reaped benefits from much of Bunyoro's alienated land,[305] it lacked the moral authority to force a resolution. The moral dilemma was sounded in the House of Commons, where the Government's actions were castigated by G. M. Thomson (Dundee East), a Labour MP, who noted:

> Britain cannot escape a considerable share of the blame for the fact that it has not been possible so far to solve this dispute in advance of independence. The lost counties problem was born in as naked an act of colonial annexation as one will find in the archives, and I am afraid that it is ending in an atmosphere of delay and indecision on the part of the Government which in its way is as deplorable as the excessively arbitrary nature of the original annexation.[306]

Britain found it difficult to deal with the moral dilemma. Yet it could not find a quick and amicable legal resolution to the issue, and we have already pointed out the legal minefield inherent in the lost counties case. In order to avoid legal liability, resultant damages and empire-wide embarrassment, it was not desirable that the conflict be resolved legally but either politically or administratively. It is for this reason that Britain was doubly bent on securing an agreement between Buganda and Bunyoro with the help of local politicians like Obote.

To this end, it set out to persuade the Omukama of Bunyoro that Molson's proposed solution was just, and to assure him that Britain would do all in its power to get the recommendations implemented. However, if the Omukama felt that the proposals did not go far enough, Macleod planned to frankly tell him that "Bunyoro does not have the slightest chance of getting more than the Commission recommended and indeed their chances of getting even two counties are not bright."[307]

But to Macleod, the more intractable problem was how to secure Buganda's acquiescence to even a limited surrender of territory, as he could not contemplate imposing a solution. In his view, the only chance lay "either in sufficient pressure in Uganda being mounted against Buganda to make it seem to them to be worth their while to make a gesture or alternatively in closing a deal with them e.g. the offer of some concession in return for unequivocal agreement to give up these counties."[308] He recognised that such a concession would be substantial in constitutional terms, but also feared the risk that Buganda might end with a major concession without giving up the counties! He also recognised that the possibilities for pressurising Buganda were slim, and thus there was a need to go "gingerly until a political situation in Uganda clarifies."[309]

Britain's man on the ground, Governor Coutts, agreed that a solution could not be imposed. He also doubted that political pressure alone would work against Buganda. Instead, he advised that the first approach should be to the Kabaka, who should be persuaded to be liberal on account of the following facts: that Molson had exonerated Buganda from allegations of discrimination; that Buyaga was useless to Buganda (incidentally, this is the same place substantial volumes of commercial oil and gas are presently being produced); that Bugangazzi was also not of much value; and that the Kabaka's and Buganda's future hinged on a peaceful settlement of the issue.

Additionally, and as a credible indicator of the level of British desperation in the matter, the Governor thought that the central government through Bunyoro might offer Buganda some financial compensation, particularly for such improvements as Buganda might have made in that particular county."[310] Coutts thought that such an offer "might move the avaricious occupiers of office in Buganda rather more quickly than outside pressure."[311]

There is little doubt that in his thinking, the Governor was alive to colonial patronage and the methods used by his distant predecessor, Harry Johnston, who, through bribery and other inducements, got Apolo Kagwa and other Baganda chiefs to sign up to the unfair and problematic 1900 Agreement. In any event, Coutts hoped that Britain would consider assisting financially if this was likely to turn the tide. He also believed that Buganda could be wooed by being allowed to have its own police force, and that the Kabaka, who in Coutts' view was "thinking in terms of his own personal difficulties, might be appeased by the grant of abolition of indirect taxation in respect of himself."[312]

The Uganda Independence Conference in London in June 1962 and How Britain Dithered on the Lost Counties

In keeping with the timetable for terminating British overrule, the Uganda Independence Conference was convened from 12 to 29 June 1962 at Marlborough House in London.[313] It was chaired by the Secretary of State for the Colonies, the Rt Hon. Reginald Maudling MP, and was attended by delegations from Britain and Uganda.[314] On this occasion, the Ugandan Government was led by the 37-year-old Apollo Milton Obote, who had replaced the DP's Ben Kiwanuka as the new prime minister. Obote and his new team had been in office for less than two months. Buganda felt more confident with Obote at the helm than it had done with Ben Kiwanuka.

The Conference agenda focused on the transitional arrangements that would provide for the termination of the protection agreements with the kingdoms of Buganda, Ankole, Toro and Bunyoro, as well as the implementation of the recommendations of the Molson Commission. The Conference sought also to provide for the powers and role of the Governor after independence, and generally for the end of the Protectorate and the attainment of Uganda's independence on 9 October 1962. The Conference constituted three committees, namely, the Constitutional Committee,[315] the Fiscal Committee[316] and the Citizenship Committee.[317] These Committees made recommendations, which were considered in plenary sessions.

Like the Constitutional Conference before it, the Independence Conference was characterized by the usual drama of "main talks, side talks, outside talks, boycotts and returns."[318] However, according to Governor Coutts, the common characteristic that ran through the deliberations was "the determination on the part of Buganda to improve its position and the equal determination on part of the Government, backed by the rest of the conference, to concede nothing."[319] In other words, it was a case of Buganda fighting for its future existence as a politically viable and independent force against a combined front of Britain and the rest of the Protectorate.

As expected, the most controversial subject was that of the lost counties and, once again, no agreement was reached between Bunyoro and Buganda. In spite of all the British manoeuvres, no political or administrative solution had been found to the lost counties problem by the time the conference convened. In fact, the political situation remained strained between Buganda and Bunyoro both during and after the Conference, as none of the belligerents were ready to back down on their stand.

Under these circumstances, and in order to close the matter, the Secretary of State for the Colonies made a decision that there would be no immediate transfer of territory, and that a referendum would be held in the affected areas within two years of independence. As an interim measure, he decided that the administration of the two counties be transferred to the central government. In this way, Secretary of State Maudling married the recommendations of the Munster and Molson Commissions. But even this was rejected by the delegations from Buganda and Bunyoro, who walked out towards the end of the Conference over the issue.[320] To persuade Buganda to participate in the talks, Obote gave a written assurance to the Kabaka and his delegation to the effect that since Kabaka Yekka and the UPC had an alliance, he, as Prime Minister, would not let Buganda down on the lost counties issue.[321]

In a new argument, Buganda disputed the notion that the counties were granted to it by Britain, saying that the British merely confirmed the boundaries over a territory that it had already conquered from Bunyoro. It added that, in fact, Buganda's territory in Busoga and parts of Kavirondo had been taken away by the British.[322] The Conference was reaching breaking point. To salvage the situation, the Kabaka prevailed over his delegation, particularly Michael Kintu, to return to the Conference. The Kabaka's persuasion was based on the assurances he had received from Obote, who promised that the details would be ironed out later in discussions between the relevant Ministers of the Lukiiko and the National Assembly. The Kabaka, with only faint misgivings, felt that he could count on a reassuring and smiling Obote when he said to him: "Trust me."[323] As later events show, Obote's word was not to be trusted

The Toro delegation boycotted the meeting from 12 to 27 June (all but the last two days) over its quest for a full federal status. While agreeing to resume its participation in the Conference, the Toro delegation acknowledged the futility of plunging the whole country into misery and chaos and, in any case, they believed that they had gotten as far as they could go with the means at their disposal.[324] Overall, the Conference was a difficult one to manage, as the participants, especially those from the kingdom areas (except Ankole), had high expectations and were not prepared to concede any ground without a fight.

The foregoing disputes notwithstanding, Britain was determined to close the Conference within the time allocated and to get on with the preparations for independence. In that context, it had to prevail over these many sentiments to reach an agreement. The Marquess of Lansdowne, George Petty-Fitzmaurice, who was then the Minister of Colonial Affairs, considered the most baffling problem of the Conference to be the "welding of the traditional kingdoms of Buganda, Ankole, Bunyoro and Toro into a modern structure of government."[325] He attributed the success of the Conference partly to the confidence which Obote and his ministers were able to inspire among the delegates from all parts of the country.

In sum, the principal conclusions of the Conference were that:

(i) Uganda should attain independence on 9 October, 1962. All the Uganda delegations joined in expressing the wish that on attaining independence Uganda should be accepted as a member country of the Commonwealth.

(ii) The Agreements between Her Majesty and the rulers of the kingdoms would cease to have effect at independence. For Ankole, Bunyoro and Toro, the Conference agreed that a number of additional provisions regarding the relationship between these kingdoms and the central government should be included in the Constitution. Busoga would be treated in the same way as the kingdoms of Ankole, Bunyoro and Toro and would be known as the Territory of Busoga.

(iii) On the lost counties:
   (a) there would be no immediate transfer of territory;
   (b) the administration of the two counties of Buyaga and Bugangazzi would be transferred to the central government;
   (c) after not less than two years from the date of transfer, the National Assembly of Uganda would decide upon a date for a referendum in these two counties in which the electorate would be asked to express their preference between the following choices: to be part of Buganda with the administration of the area reverting to the Kabaka's government; to be part of Bunyoro with the administration of the area passing to the government of Bunyoro; to be a new district, remaining under the administration of the central government;
   (d) the future of the two counties would then finally be determined on the basis of the views expressed in the referendum.[326]

At the end of the Conference, the major concern that remained was the issue of the lost counties. In a last minute effort to achieve a victory, Ivan Majugo, adviser to the Omukama of Bunyoro, rushed to London on 11 July 1962 and, through the Conservative MP Joan Vickers (Plymouth, Devonport), handed a petition signed by 37 people of Bugangazzi and Buyaga to the House of Commons demanding that the Molson Report be implemented before British protection was withdrawn from Uganda. In spite of her passionate speech in support of the petition,[327] Vickers was unable to persuade the House to change the decisions taken at the Independence Conference.

On his return to Uganda, a disappointed Dr Majugo lamented that in the lost counties British imperialism had been replaced by Buganda's imperialism, and that he could not rule out violence. He also stated that Bunyoro would boycott the independence celebrations.[328] On its part, Buganda maintained a hardline stance. In a secret Lukiiko session of 20 July 1962, it passed a resolution confirming that there would be no transfer of the counties and directed the Kabaka's government to engage the central government in talks on the future of the counties of Buyaga and Bugangazzi.[329]

Bunyoro's case found sympathy with some members in the British Parliament, including Lord Molson himself, who strongly believed that the dispute should be settled before independence.[330] It was generally felt that the compromise suggested by the Secretary of State was favourable to Buganda and unfair to Bunyoro. This view was shared by G. M. Thomson (the Labour MP for Dundee East), who said:

> What the government finally put forward at the eleventh hour, in the recent constitutional conference, was the proposal that there should be a minimum cooling-off period of two years in the lost counties, under the central administration, to be followed by a referendum.... The people of Bunyoro have an understandable fear that without some limiting period during which a referendum must take place they might find themselves in the same sort of situation as exists in Kashmir, where the promised referendum has been indefinitely postponed.[331]

Patrick Wall (Conservative MP for Haltemprice) was more critical. He pointed out:

> We are washing our hands off the problem until after independence—a problem that two Commissions have already said could lead to civil war. I believe that we are right in creating a federal setup for Uganda. But I believe that because of expediency and a desire to cut our commitments, we are leaving a position where one part of the federation holds the balance—and perhaps may prove predominant—in the central government. We are also leaving a dispute which has been simmering for sixty years and could break out after independence.[332]

Despite such protests from individual MPs, Britain inevitably kicked the lost counties saga in the long grass, thereby leaving the burden in the hands of the new government led by the youthful Obote. Accordingly, as Uganda attained independence in October 1962, the ticking bomb of the lost counties lay in wait, only to be detonated, as we show ahead, in 1964, with disastrous consequences.

Sailing in Uncharted Waters: The Troubles of Tribalism, Religion and Politics as Uganda Approached Independence

Beyond the issue of the lost counties, regarding which Britain admitted a failure to reach a solution, the conclusion of the Independence Conference was far from the successful and joyous event portrayed by Petty-Fitzmaurice who looked back with pride at the period of British Protection over Uganda. The Minister—who was full of praise for all the

Ugandan delegates, and particularly for Obote—claimed that during the Conference, arrangements which offered a permanent solution to many of the long standing problems Uganda faced had been agreed upon."[333]

In reality, the proceedings and conclusions of the Conference were filled with tensions and anxieties for the future from the perspective of most of the Ugandan delegations—particularly for Bunyoro, Buganda and Toro. If it were not for the patronage of the British Government, the outcomes would have been different and less glamorous. Kabaka Mutesa captures the mood at the end of the Conference thus:

> The Banyoro were not pleased. We were not pleased. Obote, who wanted the difficulty settled without involving him, was not pleased.... Obote assured us that all the details would be ironed out later. We could count on him. "Trust me," he said and smiled reassuringly. With only faint misgivings, we did. So the guarantees were spoken, not written. We could not hold up independence any longer.[334]

What the Conference report did not say—and what Petty-Fitzmaurice was certainly quiet about—were the real anxieties over the fragile political, religious, ethnic and, to a limited extent, racial relations in a new Uganda: a Uganda that Britain was hastily leaving in the hands of a new and inexperienced political class, civil service and partisan army. Thus, without a compass and an experienced captain, Uganda set sail into completely unchartered waters.

On a political level, the shaky coalition between the UPC and Kabaka Yekka was a basis for worry. It was described as a "marriage of convenience." How long would it hold? There were several other questions that remained, for instance: How would the multi-party political and democratic dispensation sit within a deeply traditional and cultural environment in Buganda where the Kabaka and the Lukiiko wielded enormous power? How would the shift in real power from Buganda's traditional institutions to an elected group of youthful political leaders play out? Would Obote manage to maintain a balance between disparate ethnic and regional factions in a novel multi-party political milieu?

On a religious level, the rivalry for power between Catholicism and Protestantism was still alive and was manifested in the power bases of the leading political parties, namely, the DP and the UPC. While the Protestant chiefly oligarchy needed to defend its domination of the politics in Buganda, the Catholics were determined to break that hegemony once and for all. This explains why even though the Protestant-dominated Lukiiko boycotted the elections of March 1961, the Catholic-led DP defied the Kabaka and Mengo and registered its voters, fielded candidates and campaigned in Buganda, leading to their victory and the appointment of Ben Kiwanuka as Chief Minister. Indeed, the coalition between the mostly Protestant Kabaka Yekka and the UPC was seen as one aimed at ousting the Catholics from power. How would this bitter rivalry affect the future political stability and unification of a new Uganda?

Colonial efforts to restrict religious involvement in politics in Uganda were too little and came too late. This aside, the colonial government was faced with the problem of a rapid growth in the number of different Christian sects in Uganda. With an ever-increasing interest from foreign religions wanting to set themselves up in Uganda, the colonial government adopted a policy[335] to restrict new entrants in this field on the basis that "Roman Catholics, Protestants and Moslems, are quite enough!" according to Governor Crawford.[336] The proliferation of Christian sects was thus considered undesirable and their establishment was discouraged. However, in spite of this restrictive policy, the proliferation of religious sects in Uganda increased, as did their interest and participation in its politics.

To put the religious dimension in context, it is worth looking back to the upheavals of the 1950s. When Mutesa was deported by Cohen in 1953, seven weeks after the fact, the Christian Missionary Society issued a mild statement to the effect that it shared public concerns and expressed deep sympathy in the sorrow and perplexity over the withdrawal of recognition from the Kabaka.[337] Perhaps to maintain its credibility and respectability amongst its membership in Buganda, it was quick to dispel rumours that it had been involved in or was consulted on the matter.

The Church of England, led by the Archbishop of Canterbury Lord Geoffrey Fisher, as well the Native Anglican Church also took an active interest in the campaign for the return of Mutesa to Uganda. According to the Archbishop of Canterbury, in spite of what he called Mutesa's deplorable matrimonial situation (in reference to the Kabaka's known extra-marital affairs), "he must be treated purely in his public capacity as the representative of his people and now, whether rightly or wrongly, deservedly or undeservedly, their popular hero."[338]

Bishop Stuart was probably the most outspoken on the matter. He summoned the church to protest against the "monstrous and mad decision of Lyttelton," the then Colonial Secretary, and warned that "there will be bloodshed in the whole of Africa and Lyttelton will be responsible."[339] But Bishop Brown, Stuart's successor as Bishop of Uganda, was lukewarm in his approach. He was reluctant to push Governor Cohen on the matter. The ineffectual involvement of the Church in the matter of Mutesa's deportation suggests that it was itself caught up in a crisis of confidence both with the colonial government and with the native government. Its power over the natives had begun to recede and, under the policy of decolonisation, its influence over the colonial government was also significantly reduced. Another factor may be that the Church was not particularly pleased with Mutesa's lifestyle—particularly concerning his extra-marital affairs, as well as Buganda's handling of the Namasole affair—and as such it did not put up a spirited fight on this matter.

However, once it was announced that Mutesa was due to return, the Church jumped at the opportunity to host the constitutional negotiations headed by Professor Hancock that resulted in the 1955 Agreement. These were conducted under the aegis of the Church and Bishop Brown at Namirembe, the headquarters of the Anglican Church. Just as Bishop Alfred Tucker and Harry Johnston had collaborated in negotiating the 1900 Agreement, Bishop Brown and Governor Cohen worked closely in the negotiations of the 1955 Agreement. And, just like the 1900 Agreement, the 1955 Agreement further whittled away the residual authority or sovereignty left with the Kabaka to render him a nominal ruler whilst, contrary to his wishes, incorporating his kingdom into the wider constitutional framework of Uganda. We discuss the outcomes of the recommendations of the Hancock Commission below.

Religio-political factors provided the foundation of the main political parties in the 1950s and 1960s, and they were driven more by religious considerations than anything else. Given that the Democratic Party was founded and supported by the Catholics, while the Uganda People's Congress and Kabaka Yekka had Protestant leanings and support, on the eve of the country's independence, religious affiliations, beyond political manifestos, were the dominant considerations in determining post-independence politics and leadership. An example to illustrate the influence of religion in Uganda's politics is provided by a sermon by Rev. Ogwal of the Aloi Native African Church (NAC) who, in support of the Uganda National Congress (UNC) in 1958, told his congregation, which included Milton Obote, that it was the UNC that would form the government when self-governance came, and that its leader, I. K. Musaazi, had been "chosen by God to be the prime minister of Uganda as he had chosen Gideon for the Israelites."[340]

On the subject of religion and politics in the 1950s, Governor Crawford was concerned about the dabbling of the Church in politics and warned that political divisions based on purely denominational lines could only lead to "religious fanaticism and intolerance." He threatened to cut support to church schools if this continued[341] and, more profoundly, was pushed to the point of seeking the expeditious departure of the Protestant Bishop Stuart, whom he considered to be too supportive of Buganda politicians such as Michael Kintu and Amos K. Sempa.[342]

But on the question of religious involvement in politics, a defiant Rev. Ogwal would not suffer the patronage and double standards of British rule and reminded the Governor that "during the Second World war [of] 1939-1945, HM the late King George VI anxiously and repeatedly requested the NAC and the CMS to pray for British and enemy armies with a view that God may grant peace and stop the then conflict caused by Satan. Truly God heard our prayers and conflict ceased." He added that "if you have been informed that I preached politics, it must be the work of the Holy Spirit in furthering peace for all in the name of my Lord and not me."[343]

It is important to note that the religio-political foundation constructed in Uganda's political life during the early years of British colonial rule was to remain a constant both during and after colonial rule. The triple alliance between Buganda's oligarchy, the Protectorate Government and the Church was to change as the old generation of chiefs like Kagwa left the scene and were replaced by younger ones, as British colonial policies changed in the wake of the First and Second World Wars, and as the end of imperial rule drew closer—especially once the church sought to be more involved in the politics of the Protectorate, to the chagrin of colonial officials. However, the change in the players did not result in a change in the symbiosis between religion and politics in Uganda. The two remained inseparable.

Lunyiigo has documented the correspondence between the Archbishop of Canterbury, Lord Fisher, and Ben Kiwanuka, in which the former, at the time of Constitutional Conference in 1961, sought to influence the latter to agree to Buganda's demands for electing its own representatives to the National Assembly.[344] Similarly, around the same time, the Catholic Archbishop of Uganda Joseph Kiwanuka, wrote a pointed pastoral letter on the Church and State in which he decried the discrimination against and mistreatment of DP supporters and openly opined on matters of politics and the future of the monarchy in Buganda.[345]

The same letter, which was entitled "Church and State," offers one of the best descriptions of the deep religio-political issues faced by Uganda during that period.[346] It described the sufferings of some DP Catholics and supporters, who faced discrimination and were beaten because they belonged to the DP. It described how the Archbishop himself had been insulted and accused of undermining Buganda's interests in Bulange, the seat of the kingdom of Buganda. The letter explained the source of the religiously-based political antagonism and the fear that Catholics may take over and control power in a new Uganda.

It offered guidance on the separation between the State and the Church, and particularly on why the Kabaka needed to stay outside the political space. The letter critiqued the Kabaka Yekka movement and warned the public to keep away from it, as it would "spoil our royalty by dragging the king in the back-wash of politics."[347] However, this letter did little to ease the tensions that existed between the DP and the coalition of the UPC and Kabaka Yekka during and after the 1962 elections.

Moreover, in spite of the warnings against mixing politics and the Kabakaship, Mutesa agreed to become the first President of Uganda while simultaneously holding onto his position as the Kabaka. In the end, the eventual rupture between the UPC and Kabaka Yekka and the ultimate attack against and ouster of the Kabaka by Obote in 1966 in several ways vindicated the Archbishop and rendered his message uncannily prophetic.

Religious involvement in politics was not limited to Protestants, but extended to Catholics, Muslims and other smaller religious factions.[348] Neither was it limited by the granting of independence. As the above discussion shows, the problems of separation of the church and the state in Uganda, and the influence of religious factors in its unstable and fractured post-independence politics, have roots in the colonial past but continue to the present day. Lunyiigo offers an incisive synopsis on the subject of the church and state in Uganda:

> Both the sword and the bible, those familiar twins of imperialism, were effectively wielded against the precolonial leaderships and people of what emerged as the Uganda Protectorate at the beginning of the century. Bible and sword became weapons of division. The bible plunged a part of Uganda, Buganda, into a civil war in the 1880s which left her divided and weak, destroyed her monarchy in the process and left her an easy prey for incorporation into the British Empire by Captain Lugard and his motley crew in the 1890s. The divisions introduced by the bible soon embraced what became the Protectorate and these divisions still plague independent Uganda and influence her negative politics mightily. These divisions are a solid legacy of colonialism.[349]

The apparent inseparability of religion in the affairs of Uganda's politics somewhat mirrors the situation in Britain. While Britain is a secular state, religion is at the centre of its body politic. For example, its monarch, Queen Elizabeth II, is the Head of State and the Supreme Governor of the Church of England. Its 26 Bishops sit in the House of Lords, which brings together Britain's spiritual and temporal leaders to scrutinise laws passed by the House of Commons.

Until 2009, the House of Lords acted as the supreme court of appeal in the British judicial system. The House of Lords also has powers to receive, consider and pass certain laws called Church Measures, as may be presented by the Spiritual Lords.[350] In these ways, the country's spiritual and temporal leadership intersects and, as a result, religious voices are influential and are often heard by the country's temporal leadership.

Thus the history of, and power relations between, the church and the state in Uganda demonstrates a strong overlap or interplay. It also explains the apparent centrality of religion in its politics. For this reason, it is unsurprising that, like Imperial Britain with the motto "For God and the Empire," at independence Uganda adopted the motto "For God and My Country". Today, the motto of the British monarch reads: "*Dieu et mon droit*"—translated as "God and my right." The words of Uganda's national anthem, "May God uphold thee, we lay our future in thy hand" are not very far from the British Anthem with the words "God Save our Gracious Queen…God Save the Queen." These examples show, if nothing else, the significance of the idea of God and religion in the political ethos of the two countries.

Regional and ethnic antagonism was yet another source of anxiety during and after the Conference. Uganda as a united nation was an abstract notion to many in the Protectorate who, as Governor F. Crawford pointed out in 1957, had loyalty to the tribe and not to the Ugandan nation.[351] Crawford correctly traced the genesis of the problem to the creation of the Protectorate:

> The Protectorate was the creation of British administration, with frontiers to a large extent drawn arbitrarily, and it would be too much to expect a deep sense of loyalty to Uganda, except for a common and often very real feeling of loyalty to the crown as the protecting power.[352]

Andrew Cohen made similar observations in a despatch on the political developments and the problems of the future as he bid farewell to Uganda.[353] The tribal make up and balance in Uganda was seen by Britain as a threat to stability and that the erosion of the problem of tribalism would take a long time.[354]

Uganda has over 50 ethnic groupings. Before British colonial rule, each of these had a separate and sometimes antagonistic existence. During colonial rule, the British maintained a separate existence for each of these groups and accorded them different forms of recognition and powers under various agreements and other political arrangements. The colonial districts were in fact carved out on an ethnic basis. While some were centrally organised in form of kingdoms, many were not as organised and were directly administered as districts. The country was also generally split between Bantu-speaking peoples in the south and the Nilotic Luo-speaking groups in the north and the East. It did not help that the British used the north as a reservoir for recruitment into the armed forces and the south as a reservoir of clerks and administrators, and neither did the economic disparities between the north and the south.

As independence became imminent, the British needed to quickly bring these groups together to constitute a new country under a single Constitution. This was a complex affair, because each of the groups was at a different level of development in both political and economic terms. The larger and more nationalistic entities like Buganda were not interested in being lumped together with the others. According to Governor Crawford, the Baganda entertained a feeling of superiority over other peoples of the Protectorate and took an inordinate amount of pride in their tribal organisation.[355]

As demonstrated in this chapter, for a long time Buganda pursued a separatist policy. To persuade Buganda to join the rest in forming a united Uganda, many concessions had to be given. And, of course, once Buganda got these, the rest of the country, particularly the other kingdom areas, wanted similar concessions. When their demands for parity were not granted, it created resentment within the rest of Uganda against Buganda and *vice-versa.* There was a real fear that independence would mean Buganda's domination of the rest, resulting in the determination in other regions to resist it.

Due to these political and ethnic intricacies, the negotiations for patching Uganda together as one country resulted in a shaky asymmetrical political and constitutional regime. Thus, at independence, Uganda was not quite a federal state, nor was it a unitary country. This rendered it difficult to manage and created a sense of differentiation between groups within the nation, among which some were considered more privileged than others. This was one of the root causes of the political instability and violence that followed only four years after the country's independence.

Racial relations and the question of citizenship in colonial Uganda were never as charged as they were in neighbouring Kenya or in Rhodesia, both of which had a settler class. Those countries were manifestly stratified in racial terms, with the Europeans being the undisputed rulers, followed by the Indian Asians as the business and industrial class, and the Africans who, occupying the lowest ranks in society, were the ruled and chief providers of manual labour to the higher classes.

Nevertheless, tensions, which sometimes escalated into boycotts of European or Indian shops, were present and not always far from the political discourse in colonial Uganda. As independence approached, and the African majority was destined to take political power, the need to make provisions for the protection of minorities—especially the wealthy Asian community—became more urgent. The colonial government needed to ensure that minorities were safeguarded in a new Uganda. However, the idea of providing for adequate representation for non-Africans in the country's constitutional framework was not welcome to the Africans. The Munster Commission recommended that Asians should not have special provisions entrenched in the Constitution but would be entitled to acquire citizenship by birth and by registration.

Thus, although race was not a controversial or emotive subject at the Independence Conference, it remained a latent problem. After independence, under Obote, the Ministry of Internal Affairs revoked the citizenship of many Asians, a large number of whom had to bribe their way to re-acquire citizenship certificates.[356] Afro-Asian racial tensions exploded ten years after independence when, in 1972, General Idi Amin expelled the Indians from Uganda in what he dubbed an economic war. The expulsion resulted in disastrous political and economic consequences.

From the foregoing discussion, it is apparent that in the absence of astute leadership, diplomacy or divine miracles, the political and economic prospects of Uganda after independence were bleak. This was a fact well known to the British Government, and one evident from its turbulent, fragile and often violent postcolonial politics elsewhere. In a secret and "unvarnished account" of the dangers the country faced before independence, colonial officials warned that as Uganda marched to independence, ethnic jealousies and animosities, though to some extent overlaid, had by no means been forgotten, and that the balance of power that had been created after the elections was unstable and none of the parties concerned were satisfied, nor indeed felt safe.[357] The account pointed out that there was a real danger that the various tribes and factions in Uganda, having lost the common overlying purpose of achieving self-determination, would once again split and try to go their own ways after independence. The account noted that the leadership of Prime Minister Obote was weak, especially because in Buganda, with a quarter of the country's population, there was an unwillingness to acknowledge the authority of a commoner and a northerner over the Kabaka.

The account also noted that Obote's government suffered from a lack of direction and policy guidance, and that major policy decisions were often overly influenced by political expediency. It foresaw that Obote was to take a tougher policy with Buganda and predicted the falling-out between Kabaka Yekka and the UPC.[358] Both of these happened soon after independence. It also warned that Obote and the UPC leaders were only paying lip service to democracy, and that they ultimately wanted Uganda to develop along the lines of Ghana and Tanganyika (Tanzania). This, too, turned out to be true: soon after independence, Obote abolished political parties and declared a move to the left and to one-party rule.

But perhaps in a more remarkable and predictive way, the account states that the army would be an important factor in Uganda's future. It pointed out that

> the sympathies of the rank and file of police and the KAR tend to lie with the UPC. They certainly have no love for Buganda. Buganda is aware of this and is trying to build up her own police force, having failed to obtain permission to establish an army. The majority of the police and KAR are still drawn from the Nilotic and Hamitic tribes of the north, that is, from Obote's own area [where] the local officers in both police and the army tend to despise politicians.... [I]t is just possible that eventually the police and army, possibly with the support of the professional civil service, might turn against the politicians and throw them out.[359]

The memorandum further stated that the security forces, unaided, would have the greatest difficulty in holding down Buganda in the event of a major clash between that kingdom and the central government, but neither could Buganda defeat the security forces.[360] The account could not have been more on the mark in predicting the future role of the army in Uganda's politics. Starting from the mutiny in 1964, to the 1966 coup, when Obote ordered the attack of the Kabaka's palace, through Idi Amin's coup of 1971, the Okello and Lutwa coup against Obote in 1985, and the guerrilla war that saw General Yoweri K. Museveni and the National Resistance Army (NRA) capture state power in 1986 until today, the army has been and remains at the centre of the country's politics. On the role of the military in contemporary Uganda, Aili M. Tripp argues that power in Uganda "rests with the security forces, whose main goal is not only to protect the country's citizens from external threats but also to protect those in power from internal threats to their rule by citizens."[361]

A Shredded Legacy: The Disposal and Concealment of Evidence of Colonial Abuses

In the dying days of the British Empire, Britain faced a difficult decision regarding what to do with the tons of secret and potentially incriminating documents accumulated over its many years of colonial rule, in Uganda and elsewhere[362]. So, just as King Léopold's administration had been when exiting the Congo in 1908, when British colonial officials hastily wound up their operations in Uganda between 1961 and 1962, they were extremely careful not to leave behind evidence of colonial plunder, patronage or other iniquities. The shredding and destruction of evidence pertaining to unsavoury colonial deeds was executed under a cryptic and stealth scheme code-named Operation Legacy.

The principal objective of this scheme was to protect Britain from legal or moral condemnation and ensure a clean colonial legacy. A similar scheme was used as Britain exited Tanganyika in 1961 and Kenya in 1963. Operation Legacy involved hundreds of British colonial officials, Special Branch officers, M15 officers, officers of the armed forces and several service men and women, all of whom were required to keep the affair a top secret. The operation lasted until the early 1970s.[363]

In February 1961, a few months before Uganda was granted self-governance, the Protectorate's Chief Secretary outlined the scheme, whose objective was to ensure that no material would be passed to the future government that may:

- prejudice the defence of the Commonwealth in the event of war;
- embarrass Her Majesty's Government, the present Government of Uganda or any other governments;
- lead to the identification of a source and thereby to the possible victimisation of that source; or
- provide information which might be used for the victimisation of any person.[364]

Following consultations with the UK's Ministry of Security and External Relations, Reginald Maudling, the Secretary of State for the Colonies, issued revised instructions to the effect that no material should be handed over that might:

- embarrass Her Majesty's Government or other governments;
- embarrass members of the police, military forces, public servants or others, such as police informers;
- compromise sources of intelligence; or
- be used unethically by Ministers in the successor government.[365]

All files that might defeat the above aims were categorised and marked as "DG" (Deputy Governor) papers. The designation "DG" was only applicable in Uganda. In Tanganyika, where the scheme was first devised before the country obtained independence in 1961, files with dirty material were marked "Guard."[366] According to the Chief Secretary's circular, "DG" papers *automatically* included all papers to or from the Secretary of State in the "personal series;" all papers concerning the propaganda/subversion of the Indian or any other Commonwealth Government; any papers showing religious intolerance on the part of HMG; any papers showing racial discrimination against Africans or Negros on the part of HMG; and all Ugandan intelligence reports.

The files were also classified as either "clean" or "dirty."[367] The files that were considered to be safe or "clean" were marked "Legacy" and were to be handed over to the new Government of Uganda. In some cases, these were to be "doctored" first.[368] Clean papers were to be transferred from the DG files to the Legacy files. All files marked DG were further reviewed and divided into four categories, namely: "D" to be destroyed, "RD" to be retained for the present and reviewed before independence, "L" for legacy files not containing any "dirty" material to be returned to the relevant Ministry, and "CO" to be sent to the Colonial Office for permanent record there.[369]

The selection of the CO files was informed by two factors, namely: the "needs of historical research in the future" and the "possibility of HMG having in the future to defend some past action taken in the Uganda Protectorate."[370] The CO files were to be transported to Mombasa, from where the navy would transport them onwards to the UK. Other files, as we show below, were flown to London by the Royal Air Force.

In May 1961, a new designation, "W" for "WATCH," was introduced to cover papers to be seen only by authorised officers, papers that may safely be seen in the course of duty by persons who may not fit the definition of authorised officer, and papers that may eventually be inherited by the independent government.[371]

For security matters, yet another classification "UK Eyes Only" was devised. This classification was used for files which "must not be disclosed to nationals of any other Commonwealth country or for any foreign country," and which were "subject to an existing risk that they might, if not so marked, be disclosed or distributed in transmission or after receipt to nationals of another Commonwealth country or any foreign country."[372]

The DG papers were to be withdrawn and taken to places where they could only be seen by "authorised officers." In what amounted to a racist policy, authorised officer meant a "civil service officer who is a British subject of European descent employed by the Protectorate Government."[373] It was envisaged that at the handover of government by an authorised officer to an unauthorised officer, the DG papers would "either be destroyed or passed to a higher office under the control of an authorised officer until withdrawn to Government House at Entebbe and finally destroyed or taken to the United Kingdom."[374] The directive required the purging of files under the direct control of authorised officers to begin at once.

Unauthorised officers were not to be aware that Operation Legacy existed. To ensure that the DG papers were only seen and handled by authorised officers, they were to be transmitted in envelopes marked "personal." These were on no account to be seen by any African, by a person of any nationality other than British, or by a non-official. It was for this reason that A. K. Malcolm, the Commissioner for Police, ruled out the question of an African courier carrying DG-classified mail.[375]

A huge quantity of filed "rosters to and from the Secretary of State from the beginning of Uganda time" was also to be destroyed.[376] As such, any pre-1950 papers connected with planning in the Second World War and papers on sources of intelligence or political and connected intelligence were destroyed.[377] Similarly, documents on Britain's East African Defence Scheme were destroyed.[378]

However, R. E. Stone, the Resident of Buganda, was reluctant to destroy the secret files relating to the constitutional and political developments in Buganda between 1958 and 1962 because he felt that the files "would be of immense interest and value to anyone who comes to write about the fascinating events here of recent times."[379] He had locked away many files containing a good deal of "dirty" material which he did not want "to get … into the hands of people who might use the material for improper purposes." He thus felt that the files should be sent to the UK where "in due course they might perhaps be used by some historian for an account of the developments of Uganda during the last few years."[380] However, even with the records that were kept for future reference, there is evidence that some have not been deemed safe enough for public view.

On 14 May 2013, a special category of classified documents under Folio 14 were removed from FCO 141/18409 with instructions that they are to remain closed for 65 years from the date they were written.[381] The UK Public Records Act provides that most documents are declassified after 30 years. While it is not clear why these were removed and excluded from public view for 65 years, it is plausible that they contained damaging material which Britain wished to keep away from the world for an even longer period. Be that as it may, and given the invaluable resource represented by these residual historical records in the UK on which this work has relied, Stone's vision and prophesy could not have been more pointed.

Once the classification of the files was accomplished, the next problem for the Governor's Office was one of disposal of the huge volume of unwanted documents. This challenge is best described in Watson's words:

> The problem is that we have concentrated in this office now most of the dirt of colonial days, much of which will be destroyed but a fair amount of historical interest is to be sent to London for storage in the records there. We think at the moment that the files to be transferred would probably amount to three crates each weighing about 220 lbs or 16cub.ft. Some of the stuff, even though of high security grading, is now relatively harmless, but some is quite hot and I have been trying to think of some really safe way of getting it all home. The ordinary method of having it crated up and sent back by sea is clearly not safe enough unless the files were welded in steel containers. There is rather too much to send home in the personal baggage of some "safe hand" and I have been wondering whether there would be any way of persuading the RAF to take it over and, whenever it is convenient to them, take it home by air. We could without difficulty I think arrange delivery to the Nairobi area and providing that it was kept securely there would be no hurry about getting it home.[382]

Besides the discreet disposal of dirty colonial material, Watson's other worry was how, in the transition from colonial rule to independence, to deal with correspondence from the Colonial Office to the new internal self-government—for example, on anti-communist propaganda, political propaganda, and other material seeking to influence African opinion, amongst other matters.[383] To address this problem, it was decided that "personal" correspondence would be kept to a minimum, while a new category of correspondence was introduced to avoid a breach of security or compromising the confidentiality of the information.

Some of the correspondence was transported to the UK using steel-banded thick plywood boxes lined with chicken wire. For example, on 5 October 1962, four days before Uganda's independence, the Governor wrote to the Secretary of State for the Colonies that he was forwarding, via the Royal Air Force, "four cases of papers of historical or administrative value not considered suitable to be passed on to the successor government." [384] The boxes, measuring 2' x 2' x 2' each and weighing between 150 lb (68 kg) and 200 lb (91 kg), were air lifted to London on a Beverly aircraft that same day.[385] The cases were addressed to B. Cheeseman Esq. of the Colonial Office Library in London.

A number of legacy or clean files were passed on to the British High Commissioner in Uganda.[386] All files labelled D were burnt, shredded or dumped at sea ahead of the handover of the Protectorate.[387] As the incinerator at the Government Press was considered insufficiently secure, the furnace at the Lugazi Sugar Factory was used for this purpose.[388] Other files were packed in weighted crates and dumped in deep, current free waters at maximum practicable distances in the oceans.[389]For the files that were destroyed, a final destruction certificate showing the material destroyed was issued by the Senior Cypher Officer.

When the Ugandan Minister of State heard about the clandestine disposal of historical records, he wrote to the Colonial Administration asking for the destruction to stop and to have the remaining documents preserved. He specifically asked about the status of the files held by the Resident of Buganda. In an obscurant and deliberately misleading response to this inquiry, the official concerned (whose identity is unclear from the file) wrote:

> I apologize for the delay in replying to your undated minute of about a week ago referring to the preservation of government records.
>
> On the more general aspects of this question, it has been the practice in all government offices in the past to destroy certain types of records once they have ceased to have any current value. That policy has, of course, been based on the shortage of storage space for archives, and the need to preserve documents of continuing relevance or historical value. It has been followed conscientiously in my Ministry, against a background of government reorganization and transfers of responsibility for certain subjects during the past year or so.
>
> Turing to the points made in your third paragraph, I at no time took the papers of the Resident of Buganda into my custody. I understand that those in current use were passed either to the government agent, Mengo, or to the Treasury or Ministry immediately concerned, while those dealing with relations with Buganda under the various agreements went to the Governor's office. The papers of this Ministry concerning Buganda were similarly distributed when we relinquished our general responsibility for the affairs of the kingdom on the 1 of March this year.
>
> I am sorry to note that the alleged destruction of records by my Ministry has presented a particular problem, and I should be grateful to learn whether this applies to any areas other than Buganda. I myself am very conscious of the importance of the preservation of historical records, and have borne this firmly in mind when reviewing my papers. If you have been handicapped by lack of information with regard to any specific subject or district, perhaps you would let me know so that I may ascertain whether you have been correctly informed regarding its destruction.[390]

This letter demonstrates the disingenuous methods the colonial government was still pursuing, not only in its dealings with the historical records in question, but also with the new leaders in Uganda. The letter deliberately concealed the existence of Operation Legacy and aimed instead to create the impression that its author and, by extension, the colonial regime, was acting carefully and conscientiously in the preservation of historical records. The author knew full well that by the time he wrote the letter, many documents of historical importance had either been shredded or gone up in smoke in the furnace of the Lugazi Sugar Factory. The author talks of some documents having "ceased to have any current value." This claim itself raises a number of questions: what was the test for the determination of the value of a particular document? Why was the new leadership not consulted or involved in the disposal? If the records had no value, why was their disposal done covertly?

Dealing with Antiquities at the End of the Empire: The Case of the Luzira Head

Related to the story of Operation Legacy is the refusal by Britain to return historic antiquities or archaeological relics that were taken away from different parts of the Empire and kept in certain British museums. The "Luzira Head" is a piece of ancient pottery excavated from an old shrine at Luzira during the construction of a government prison in 1929.[391] According to the Government of Uganda, the piece was sent by E. J. Wayland, Director of the Geological Survey Department, to the British Museum for examination by experts.[392]

However, when Uganda requested the return of the unique piece together with all the associated finds for preservation, the request was declined. According to the Foreign and Commonwealth Office, the Luzira Head, together with the accompanying series of stone implements, had been offered to the Trustees of the British Museum as a gift by E. J. Wayland, and the Trustees had incorporated it into its collection.[393] For that reason, and under the British Museum Act 1963, the Trustees argued that they were precluded from returning it. No question was ever raised as to how or when Wayland had obtained proprietary rights over the Luzira Head, or whether or not he had the legal authority to bequeath it to the British Museum. But in informing the British Museum about Uganda's request to have the piece returned, J. G. Wallace of the Foreign and Commonwealth Office stated:

> I am aware that British Museums, with the concurrence of HMG, have frequently resisted requests for the return of relics, and it may be that in this case, too, the head and the related fragments should not be returned.[394]

Nonetheless, Wallace asked the British Museum whether, if it considered itself to have a good claim on the Luzira Head, it would be prepared to return it for a consideration or to sell it to Uganda at the current market value or some other specified price. Britain's appropriation of relics such as the Luzira Head justifies the view that the retention of vital historical documents and artefacts illicitly taken from its former colonies is part of the colonial legacy of plunder that continues to tarnish its reputation today.

Operation Legacy remained a well-kept secret until the researchers David Anderson and Caroline Elkins published a book called *Imperial Reckoning*, which gave a damning account of Britain's concerted attempts to hide or destroy evidence on the atrocities committed under "Operation Progress" in Kenya.[395] Before the revelations by Anderson and Elkin, the Foreign and Commonwealth Office, in response to inquiries by historians and researchers for information on the Mau Mau, had always stated either that it did not have the files or that they did not exist.[396] It maintained that the British Government's National Archives had plenty of material that showed how the colonial authorities had approached their responsibilities to their prisoners in a largely humane and civilising manner.

Presumably, reference here was being made to the "clean" legacy files. But then the lawyers of the Kenyan claimants discovered a massive cache of secret documents at a high-security government building at Hanslope Park, Buckinghamshire, holding what is referred to as the "migrated archives." Hidden in Hanslope Park were a trove of 8,800 Foreign and Commonwealth Office files, 1,500 of which were records from Kenya that had been declared missing for over 50 years.[397]

Hanslope Park, also used by the UK security organisations M16 and M15, was known as one of the most secure facilities operated by any government, anywhere in the world. It was here that files with evidence on how the British had beaten inmates to death, and even burned them alive, were buried. The evidence at Hanslope, as depicted by Anderson and Elkins, showed "unspeakable barbarity, and a conflict in which the British colonial administrators, police and soldiers—the agents of what was supposed to be a civilising force—had sunk to a moral depth that would be difficult for many members of the British public to comprehend."[398]

The colonial abuses in Kenya were neither unauthorised nor isolated. Cobain has argued that "the torture and murder had been systemic—choreographed, in fact, by colonial administrators and the colony's law officers—while ministers and officials in London had been fully aware of the details of the abuses for which they were responsible: abuses that the British public had repeatedly been assured, throughout the 1950s, were not happening."[399] Eric Griffith-Jones, Britain's Attorney in the Kenyan colony, described the mistreatment of detained Mau Mau suspects as "distressingly reminiscent of conditions in Nazi Germany or Communist

Russia."[400]

To ameliorate the suffering, Griffith-Jones proposed a new law sanctioning a "more lenient" regime of punishment known as the "dilution technique." This technique allowed beatings provided that they were carried out with care and not targeted at the vulnerable parts of the body such as the spleen, liver or kidneys. Anyone who protested would have a foot placed on his throat and mud stuffed in his mouth. In the last resort, the person would be knocked unconscious. In a memo to Governor Evelyn Baring, however, Griffith-Jones cautioned that the introduction of the dilution technique should be shrouded in complete secrecy, adding: "If we are going to sin, we must sin quietly."[401]

In Nigeria, the legacy of Britain's complicity in human rights abuses, particularly during the Biafra civil war in the late 1960s, was exposed with the release of declassified files that show that under Harold Wilson's regime Britain supported the Government of Nigeria in its aggression against Biafra when it tried to secede, in a civil war, in which millions of people died.[402]

In *The History Thieves*, Ian Cobain lays bare Britain's culture of secrecy and, in particular, how under Operation Legacy Britain intended to erase all trace of the darker deeds of its colonial enterprise and sculpt an official—but misleading—narrative of a glorious, gracious, generous and genuine British suzerainty in Africa and elsewhere. It was precisely because the British knew their record to be far from attractive that they created, under Operation Legacy, the aforementioned covert filing and destruction system in which sensitive material was either locked away at Hanslope Park, accessible to security-cleared British officials only, or destroyed.

On the overall objectives and ramifications of the secretive Operation Legacy, Cobain offers a compelling and poignant argument:

> The former colonies had been robbed of the documents that would have mattered most to them at the moment of their independence; they contained evidence of the methods of subjugation that had helped to shape their national identity. And the duplicity and deception of the personal double filing system led to postcolonial governments attempting to conduct their business on the basis of incomplete or bogus records, or no records at all.... Why was it done? The desire to protect British officials from "embarrassment"—or prosecution—is an explanation that can readily be understood. Equally explicable would be an inclination to place at a disadvantage those post-colonial governments whose allegiance may not have been completely assured particularly at a time when Britain, the United States and other Western governments were seeking to manage their cold war objectives.... By the time the greatest of empires was finally

> being dissolved, the most important considerations for those in government, in Whitehall and in the colonies, were that the British way of doing things should come to be recalled with fondness and respect, and that the retreat should be recorded as a dignified affair … a flattering official narrative needed to be established and protected.
>
> Operation Legacy allowed the British to nurture a memory of Empire that was deeply deceptive—a collective confabulation of an imperial mission that had brought nothing but progress and good order to a previously savage world, unlike the French, Italians, Belgians, Germans and Portuguese—those inferior colonial powers whose adventures had been essentially brutal, cynical and exploitative.
>
> As a consequence [of Operation Legacy], some historians would in the future be able to enjoy the smell of the first rains in Kenya and the ripe mangoes, and singing of the Kikuyu women, rather than concern themselves with castrations, and the water-boarding, and the roasting alive.[403]

Indeed, it is the narrative of British graciousness and magnanimity, both during and after colonialism, that Boris Johnson and others like him relish—the narrative that, but for British imperialism and patronage, and left to their own devices, Africans and Africa would be good for nothing.[404] It is with a similar mindset of a glorious British Empire that Gordon Brown, the former Prime Minister of Britain, on a visit to East Africa once declared:

> The days of Britain having to apologise for its colonial history are over. We should move forward; we should celebrate much of our past rather than apologise for it. We should talk … about British values that are enduring, because they stand for some of the greatest ideas in history: tolerance, liberty, civic duty that grew in Britain and influenced the rest of the world.[405]

The discoveries at Hanslope Park prove that the hiding or destruction of incriminating evidence by Britain under Operation Legacy was deliberate and systematic to help perpetuate views that glorify the British Empire while masking its dark machinations. But once the scheme was dragged into the light, the British Government, in April 2011, admitted in the House of Lords that it had hidden over 8,800 sensitive migrated files that might embarrass Britain from 37 former colonies.[406]

There is no doubt that lost or hidden information would be immensely useful in reconstructing and understanding the deeper mechanics of colonial rule and the agreements and commitments that were entered into with entities like Buganda. Much of this secret information may never be seen, as it has been reduced to ashes or lies rotten in weighted wooded crates in the deep seas. While the Mau Mau victims' case managed to squeeze an apology out of Britain for its indiscretions during colonial rule, there remain many questions in places like Uganda regarding its full role as well as its outstanding legal or moral responsibilities. An unequivocal apology, atonement or a full public inquiry would help address these questions.

In the Mau Mau case, Britain offered an "unreserved" apology—more for hiding Britain's colonial past than for the pain and suffering it had caused to millions in its wake—while simultaneously insisting that it bore no legal, moral or other responsibility for colonialism. In seeking to limit the damage and embarrassment arising out of its colonial legacy, Britain engages in chicanery which, ultimately, leaves its imperial legacy and self-described civilising mission in shreds. By delaying or denying justice to its victims by hiding behind the legal defences of immunity, jurisdiction, state succession, time limitation and others, Britain not only prolongs the pain its denials cause, but potentially reduces any financial reparations it may face, as plaintiffs either give up or die before they receive justice.

Notes

[1] See Address by Mr Macmillan to both houses of the parliament of the Union of South Africa, Cape Town on 3 February 1960, in file DO 35/10570 No. 53.

[2] Some British officials resisted speedy decolonisation, arguing that it amounted to premature withdrawal of British rule that would not only create a vacuum which would be filled by Soviet and Communist expansion and but also that British prestige would suffer due to a "moral abdication" in some territories that risked reverting to "a primitive mode or chaos and barbarism" without imperial rule.

[3] In this study, Macmillan sought to understand the costs and benefits or, in his words, the "profit and loss account" for each of Britain's colonial possessions, to enable Britain gauge whether, from the financial and economic point of view it made sense for Britain to hold onto the colony. See a minute of 28 January 1957 by Macmillan to Lord Salisbury, the Chairman of the Cabinet Colonial Policy Committee, on the "Future constitutional development in the colonies, on CAB 134/1555, CPC (57) 6.

[4] Memorandum by the Secretary of State for Foreign Affairs, "1959: Africa: The next ten years," FO 371/137972, No. 24.

[5] Ibid.

[6] Cabinet Memorandum: "Future Policy Study, 1960-1970" dated 24 February 1960 on CAB 129/100, C (60) 35 dated.

[7] Ryrie, Sir William (2006) *Uganda in 1957-58*, in Brown & Brown (eds.), *Looking Back at the Uganda Protectorate*, p. 350.

[8] Douglas Brown (2006) *Afterthoughts* in Brown & Brown (eds.), *Looking Back at the Uganda Protectorate*, p. 344.

[9] Declaration on the Granting of Independence to Colonial Countries and Peoples, UNGA Resolution No. 1514 (XV) passed on 14 December 1960 at meeting No. 15.

[10] Ibid.

[11] Cabinet conclusions on proposals on the reduction in costs of the Overseas Civil Service Scheme, dated 21 July 1960 on CAB 128/34, CC 44 (60)7 and a letter from Macleod to the Prime Minister on the Future of the Commonwealth Relations Office and the Colonial Office, 3 October 1960 on PREM 11/3378, M 37/60.

[12] FO 371/143707, No. 72, dated 22 September 1959.

[13] Policy paper, "Future Policy Study, 1960-1970," on CAB 129/100, C (60) 35, 24 February 1960.

[14] The Commonwealth was thus a postcolonial device under which Britain would generate patronage and preserve its interests once it had relinquished its colonial territory. See Memorandum by the Colonial Office on "The future of British colonial territories" dated 27 September 1963 on FO 371/172610, no.13.

[15] See minutes by Macmillan (M244/59) on "Africa: The next ten years," dated 3 July 1959 on PREM 11/2587, PM/59/72.

[16] Kirk-Greene, A. (2006) *Symbol of Authority: The British District Officer in Africa*, London: I. B. Tauris, p. 208.

[17] Ibid.

[18] See a Memorandum for Cabinet Colonial Policy Committee by Sir N. Brook on "Future constitutional development in the Colonies" dated 6 September 1957 on CAB 134/1556, CPC (57) 30.

[19] The territories of East and West Africa were seen as "the greatest potential sources of military manpower within the Colonial Empire." See a Memorandum for Cabinet Colonial Policy Committee by Sir N. Brook on "Future constitutional development in the Colonies" dated 6 September 1957 on CAB 134/1556, CPC (57) 30.

[20] For example, stationing a strategic reserve in Kenya and the possession of overflying and staging rights in certain territories to safeguard its oil supplies in the Persian Gulf, by use of force if necessary. See minute by F. A. Bishop to Macmillan on "Middle East military plans" dated 8 June 1959 on PREM 11/2753 and Minutes of the Africa (Official) Committee meeting to discuss procedure for study "The next ten years in Africa" on CAB 134/1353, AF 1 (59).

[21] See a Memorandum for Cabinet Colonial Policy Committee by Sir N. Brook on "Future constitutional development in the Colonies" dated 6 September 1957 on CAB 134/1556, CPC (57) 30.

[22] Minutes of the Africa (Official) Committee meeting to discuss procedure for study "The next ten years in Africa" on CAB 134/1353, AF 1 (59).

[23] Ibid., p. 209. See also, B. L. Jacobs (2006) "Postscript," in Brown & Brown (eds.) *Looking Back at the Uganda Protectorate*, p. 58.

[24] Griffith, Owen (2006) "What Went Wrong,?" in Brown & Brown (eds.), *Looking Back*, p. 327.

[25] Ken Gladdish (2006) "A Provincial Honeymoon," in Brown & Brown (eds.), *Looking Back at the Uganda Protectorate*, p. 76.

[26] *Hansard Parliamentary Debates*, House of Commons, 30 November 1953, vol. 524, pp. 779-786; 1238-1283.

[27] By July of 1960, the Colonial Office had decided that Uganda's postcolonial government would be developed as closely as possible along Westminster lines. This was not a subject of debate with the colonised people; it was presented as a *fait accompli* at the Constitutional Conference in 1961. See Minute of F. D. Webber on "Current political problems in Uganda" dated 15 July 1960 on CO 822/2263.

[28] See a report on "Democracy in backward countries," 8 March 1960, FO 371/152113, No.3.

[29]See C. G. Eastwood's comments on the paper "British democracy and the Westminster model," dated 2 January 1961, on CO 1032/242, No. 2.

[30] See despatch from Sir Walter Coutts to Mr Sandys on "Uganda: Future as an independent country," dated 8 October 1962 on CO 822/2266, No. 378.

[31] Clearly the ploy by each party was to associate its colours with the national flag such that the unsuspecting members of the public would confuse the party with the state and *vice versa*. See J. P. Barber (2006) "Flag and Anthem," in Brown & Brown (eds), *Looking Back at the Uganda Protectorate*, p. 255.

[32] See file, "Bukedi disturbances; deportation of ringleaders 1960-61, FCO 141/18268 TNA.

[33] See Ron Roper (2006) "The Bukedi Riot I," in Brown & Brown (eds), *Looking Back at the Uganda Protectorate*, p. 11.

[34] A prominent member of the Uganda National Congress.

[35] See Alan Forward (2006) "The Bukedi Riot II," in Brown & Brown (eds), *Looking Back at the Uganda Protectorate*, p. 18.

[36] See Martin Fleay (2006) "Karamoja's District Team and Development Scheme," in Brown & Brown (eds), *Looking Back*, p. 20.

[37] See John Brasnett (2006) "Karamoja: Basic Administration," in Brown & Brown (eds), *Looking Back at the Uganda Protectorate*, p. 30.

[38] See Nsibambi, Apolo Robin (2014) *National Integration in Uganda 1962-2013* Foundation Publishers, p. 149.

[39] See progress report on colonial policy by Macleod to Macmillan dated 31 May 1960 on PREM 11/3240, PM (60) 33.

[40] See memorandum by Macleod to the Cabinet Colonial Committee, "Colonial problems in 1961," CAB 134/1560, CPC (61)1.

[41] See Owen Griffith (2006) "What Went Wrong?" in Brown & Brown (eds), *Looking Back at the Uganda Protectorate*, p. 330.

[42] Mutibwa, *A History of Uganda*, p. 163.

[43] Ibid.

[44] Ibid., p. 164

[45] Ibid.

[46] Low & Pratt, *Buganda and British Overrule*, p.340.

[47] See file, *Kabaka Yekka Organisation, Monarchist Political Party 1961*, FCO 141/18392 TNA.
[48] Entitled "A Further Memorandum from the Lukiiko to Their Memorandum Petitioning Her Majesty the Queen to terminate the Agreements."
[49] Ibid.
[50] Unlike Buganda, which was treated as a native state with its own system of government, the other three kingdoms were governed directly like the other districts in the Protectorate. As such, these kingdoms did not have administrative independence of the kind Buganda enjoyed.
[51] When they met with Macleod, in the presence of the Kabaka, in September 1961 before the constitutional conference opened, they demanded that the relationship of their kingdoms and of Busoga with the Central Government should be a fully federal relationship and not a semi-federal one.
[52] A proclamation by the rulers of Buganda, Toro and Ankole on 20 February 1960.
[53] On 21 February 1960.
[54] Ibid.
[55] See the Governor's note on the discussions with the four hereditary rulers at Government House, Entebbe, on 24 February 1960, written on 26 February 1960.
[56] Ibid.
[57] See Memorandum for Cabinet Colonial Policy Committee on "Proposals for constitutional reform in Uganda" by Macleod, dated 4 February 1960 on CAB 134/1559, CPC (60)1.
[58] Ibid.
[59] Ibid.
[60] See minutes of the Cabinet Colonial Policy Committee on "Discussions of Wild Report on Uganda constitution" dated 8 February 1960 on CAB 134/1559, CPC 1 (60)1.
[61] See minutes of a meeting of the Colonial office on "Current political problems in Uganda" and a minute by F. D. Webber dated 15 July 1960 on CO 822/2263 Nos. 147 and 151.
[62] Macleod's letter to the Prime Minister, Ref. PM (60) 58, dated 23 September 1960.
[63] Ibid.
[64] Ibid.
[65] Ibid.
[66] Ibid.
[67] Ibid.
[68] Mutibwa, *A History of Uganda*, p. 165.
[69] Ibid.
[70] Ibid.
[71] Others on the delegation were Michael Kintu (Katikkiro), L. N. Bassude, E. W. Kigundu, A. D. Lubowa, Dr E. S. Lumu, H. J. Lutaaya, A. F. Mpanga, and A. K. Sempa.

[72] Reproduced in a letter by Katikkiro Michael Kintu to Iain Macleod, Secretary of State for the Colonies, dated 26 August 1960.
[73] Undated document headed *Points put forward by the Kabaka's Government, or the Buganda Constitutional Committee, or the Lukiiko regarding Buganda's Constitutional advance; and proposed answers*. On file with the author.
[74] In the minutes of discussions with the representatives of His Highness the Kabaka's government held in Room 301 Church House on Thursday, 18 August, 1960. Michael Kintu, the Katikkiro, stated that in exchange for an undertaking that Buganda should be confirmed in a federal relationship with the central government, his delegation were prepared to advise the Lukiiko that Buganda should send representatives to the Protectorate Legislative Council.
[75] See Minutes of discussions with the representatives of His Highness the Kabaka's government held in Room 301 Church House on Thursday 18 August, 1960.
[76] Ibid.
[77] See Minutes of discussions with the Representatives of His Highness the Kabaka's Government held in Room 301 Church House on Monday 19 September, 1960.
[78] On the formation and personalities behind this movement, see file on Kabaka Yekka, FCO141/18392.
[79] Ibid.
[80] See a record of the Secretary of State's first meeting with the Kabaka on 18 August 1960.
[81] Ibid.
[82] Mutesa, *The Desecration of My Kingdom*, p.158.
[83] PREM 11/2586, PM (59)65 29 December, 1959.
[84] Ibid.
[85] As a matter of fact, the voter registration exercise in Buganda was extended by three months.
[86] Under this law, it was an offence for any person to intimidate people involved in the registration exercise.
[87] As if to further aggravate Buganda, the DP strongly condemned it for its disruptive policy of opposing voter registration and went out with full force to campaign for registration in Buganda. Despite Buganda's opposition to the registration of voters in the kingdom, by the end of September 1960, thanks to the DP, at least 15,694 individuals had registered to vote.
[88] See Colonial Office minutes by J. W. Stacpoole dated 11 July 1960 on file "Current political problems in Uganda," CO 822/2263, Nos. 147 & 151 and Minutes of discussions with the representatives of His Highness the Kabaka's Government held in Room 301 Church House on Friday 26 August, 1960.
[89] See Cabinet Colonial Policy Committee memorandum on "Future policy in East Africa" by Alan Lennox-Boyd on CAB 134/1558, CPC (59)2 dated 10 April 1959 and minutes of the Cabinet Colonial Policy Committee meeting on "Future policy in East Africa" dated 17 April 1959 on CAB 134/1558, CPC 1 (59).
[90] Ibid.

[91] See CAB 129/100.
[92] Macleod was in Uganda from 18 to 21 September 1960.
[93] See extract of minutes of the COS Committee meeting of 6 January 1961 on file "Strategic importance of East Africa," DEFE 7 /2033, COS 2 (61) 1A.
[94] See CAB 128/34.
[95] Mutibwa, *A History of Uganda*, p. 167. Sitakange was a radical pro-monarchy group in Baganda.
[96] Resolutions passed at Lukiiko meetings from 21 to 24 September 1960 in file "Buganda Political Intelligence Summary," CO 822/2067.
[97] The membership of the Committee was M. Kintu (Katikkiro & Chairman), A. K. Sempa (Omuwanika), L. N. Bassude, A. D. Lubowa, E. S. Lumu, D. M. Mukubira, M. K. Lwanga, S. Lubega, Dr E. Muwazi, J. Luyimbazi Zake, G. L. Binaisa, W. Kalema and A. F. Mpanga (Secretary).
[98] See Political Intelligence and Security Report for the Month ending 27 September, 1960, dated 29 September 1960 on file CO 822/2067.
[99] File CO 822/1450, no 249, Governor Fredrick Crawford to Turnbull, 25 July 1959.
[100] Quoted by Lord S. T. Oswald in House of Lords Debate on Buganda on 25 October 1960. Hansard Vol. 225 cc 996-9996.
[101] Letter No. EAF/71/6/03.
[102] The 1960 Lukiiko Memorandum to her Majesty Queen Elizabeth II concerning the termination of British protection. The full text of the Memorandum is reproduced at the back of this book as Appendix IV
[103] Ibid.
[104] Ibid. The reference to Katanga here was to the secessionist bid by Katanga province from Congo soon after Congo attained independence from Belgium. For further details on this bid see Appendix VI.
[105] Ibid.
[106] See files on Buganda secession; Constitutional development; Lukiiko and Security, 1960-61. FCO 141/18232-18233 and 18238-18239 TNA.
[107] Report of the Buganda Independence Committee of the Lukiiko (Majority Report), on 13 January 1961.
[108] Ibid., paras. 9-17.
[109] Ibid., para. 27.
[110] Ibid., para 28.
[111] Ibid., para. 22.
[112] Ibid., para. 23.
[113] See Cabinet Colonial Policy Committee memorandum "Future of Policy in East Africa" by Alan Lennox-Boyd on CAB 134/1558, CPC (59)2 dated 10 April 1959.
[114] See Report of the Committee of Officials, "Africa in the next ten years," FO 371/137972 of June 1959.
[115] See file "Buganda Secession Security," FCO 141/18239.
[116] BIC Majority Report, op. cit., para. 30.
[117] BIC Majority Report, op. cit., para. 33.
[118] Ibid.

[119] See file "Buganda Secession Security," FCO 141/18239.
[120] For example, A. G. Riley, the Director of Information, met with A. K. Kironde on 19 December and they discussed Buganda's position and the views of the Kabaka, Kintu and Sempa. Riley reported his findings to the Chief Secretary in a letter, Ref. INF/S.036A, dated 20 December 1960.
[121] See a record of conclusions reached at a meeting held at Police Headquarters Kampala on 29 December 1960. The meeting was chaired by the Ag. Governor Hon. Cartland. See also, Minutes of a meeting chaired by the Governor on 30 December, 1960 at the Chief Secretary's Office in Entebbe, on file "Buganda Secession Security," FCO 141/18239.
[122] Ibid.
[123] Ibid.
[124] Ibid.
[125] See a memorandum by Macleod to the Cabinet Colonial Policy Committee, "Colonial problems in 1961" dated 3 January 1961, CAB 134/1560, CPC (61)1.
[126] Opinion prepared jointly by Ag. A. G, Ag. A. S and S/SER, under Ref. S 10116, addressed to the Chief Secretary's office on 23 December 1960.
[127] Ibid.
[128] Minutes of a meeting chaired by the Governor on 30 December 1960 at the Chief Secretary's Office in Entebbe, on file "Buganda Secession Security," FCO 141/18239.
[129] "No UK support for secession in Uganda—Chief Minister" in *The Argus*, in file "Buganda Secession Security," FCO 141/18239.
[130] Mutesa, *The Desecration of My Kingdom*, pp 160, 182, 183.
[131] He told him that the "Kabaka would not himself declare independence on the 31st," further that the announcement about "the move of the 5th KAR battalion had had a good effect," that "Kintu's Government would collapse on or immediately after 31 December and that Buganda would be leaderless" and that Ochieng was "drumming up political support in order to take advantage of this situation and to fill the political vacuum in Buganda". See Note for Record Ref. 10116/1 by P.S.S.E.R on 24/12/60.
[132] Record note of a telephone conversation with Daudi Ochieng by Mr R. Dreschfield, the Ag. Chief Secretary dated 28 December 1960.
[133] Ibid.
[134] Record note by the Resident of Buganda, 28 December 1960.
[135] Ibid.
[136] Ibid.
[137] Ibid.
[138] A record note by R. Dreschfield, the Ag. Chief Secretary, dictated on 28 December 1960 and signed on 29 December 1960.
[139] Ibid.
[140] See Mutesa, *The Desecration of My Kingdom*, p.160 and Aliker, Martin (2018) *The Bell is Ringing: Martin Aliker's Story*, Fountain Publishers, Kampala, p. 98.
[141] See Makumbi, Cissy, "Daudi Ochieng was a nationalist Katikkiro," *The Daily Monitor*, 3 June 2016.

[142] See Police report "Constitutional Development in Buganda," dated 19 January 1961 on file "Buganda Secession Security," CO141/18239.
[143] Mutesa, *The Desecration of My Kingdom.*
[144] See BIC Minority Report, dated 10 January 1961.
[145] Ibid.
[146] Ibid.
[147] Record note of the conclusions reached by the Uganda Security Committee at a meeting held at Government House on 31 December 1960, para. 1, on file "Buganda Secession Security," FCO 141/18239.
[148] Meeting between the Kabaka and the Resident of Buganda, in the presence of F. Mpanga and Mukasa on 16 December 1960.
[149] Meeting between the Kabaka and the Commissioner of Police M. J. Macoun on 23 December 1960.
[150] Record note of the conclusions reached by the Uganda Security Committee at a meeting held at Government House on 31 December 1960, para. 6., on file "Buganda Secession Security," FCO 141/18239.
[151] A note from the Protectorate's Department of Information, signed by S. S. E. R., at 2.30 pm, 30 December 1960.
[152] A message from the Protectorate's Department of Information, signed by S.S.E.R dated 2.30 pm 30/12/60.
[153] The voting was: 79 votes in favour, 8 against and one abstention.
[154] See Resolution passed by the Buganda Lukiiko on 31 December 1960 on the Declaration of Buganda's Independence.
[155] Crawford's statement on the Lukiiko's Declaration of Buganda's Independence, dated 31 December 1960.
[156] Mutesa to Fredrick Crawford, 1 January 1961.
[157] *The Uganda Argus* of 3 January 1961 reported "The Democratic Party, in a statement yesterday, called on the Kabaka's ministers to resign saying that the ministry had failed in its duty to guide Buganda at a critical time. The statement, signed by Benedicto Kiwanuka, the Party's President General, alleged that within 24 hours of signing a declaration of independence the ministers went to the Governor and assured him that the declaration had not in fact been intended to be proceeded with, but was merely intended to appease the people of Buganda." Further that the declaration was a device "to mislead the innocent people of Buganda because the ministers knew that if there was no declaration the people would demand their resignation." Kiwanuka ended by "appealing to the Baganda to work for the independence of Uganda as a whole."
[158] Buganda's delegation included M. Kintu (Katikkiro), A. K. Sempa, L. N. Bassude, A. K. Mayanja and A. Lubwama.
[159] Record of a meeting between His Excellency the Governor and the ministers of His Highness the Kabaka's Government held at the Government House, Entebbe at 12 noon on Sunday 1 January 1961.
[160] Ibid.
[161] News Release from the Chief Secretary's Office, 1 January 1961, Release authorized at 2 pm on 1 January 1961.

[162] "LUKIIKO DECLARES INDEPENDENCE: Governor Rejects Decision; Ministers Seek New Talks," *Uganda Argus*, 2 January 1961.
[163] See "Resign report denied by Katikkiro," *Uganda Argus*, 3 January 1961.
[164] Statement issued by the Kabaka's ministers on 3 January 1961.
[165] Fredrick Crawford to Cartland, dated 3 January 1961.
[166] Telegram despatched on 3 January 1961. File No.S.10116/1.
[167] In a letter signed by all the six Ministers, addressed to the Governor, Ref S/B.24/III, dated 6 January 1961, they stated that "What the Kabaka's Government and the Lukiiko desire now is to hold immediate talks to discuss and thereafter to handover to Buganda, rights and powers which have been in the hands of Her Majesty the Queen as a result of the terms of the Treaty of 1894 and subsequent Agreements or contracts."
[168] Statement by Kabaka's Government on 9 January 1961.
[169] In a security meeting at Government House Entebbe on 9 January, 1961.
[170] A Memorandum by the Resident of Buganda, R. E. Stone, on *The Political and Security Situation in Buganda* addressed to all holders of the Buganda Internal Security Scheme (BISS) Ref. S.19/00/08/1, dated 4 January 1961.
[171] Record note by the Resident of Buganda of his meeting with Binaisa, dated 6 January 1961.
[172] Ibid.
[173] In a local newspaper *Obugagga*, 9 January 1961.
[174] A confidential record note of a 'long talk' with Fred Mpanga by R. N. Posnett on 6 January, 1961.
[175] Ibid.
[176] Ibid.
[177] See *Uganda Eyogera* newspaper, 14 January 1961.
[178] Report of the Uganda Relationships Commission, p. 26.
[179] Mutesa, *The Desecration of My Kingdom*, p.158.
[180] Ibid.
[181] Ibingira, *Forging of an African Nation*, p. 187.
[182] See FCO 141/18327 for Report of the Uganda Relationships Commission (Munster Report), p. 25-26.
[183] Ibid.
[184] See Barungi, Baganchwera N. I. (2011) *Parliamentary Democracy in Uganda: The Experiment that Failed*, Bloomington: AuthorHouse, p. 71.
[185] The Munster Report p. 42, paragraph 118.
[186] In a letter from Harold Macmillan to Macleod, dated 4 November 1960.
[187] Ibid.
[188] See Appendix VI and Iain MacLeod's letter to the Prime Minister, dated 9 November 1960.
[189] Iain Macleod's letter to the Prime Minister, dated 28 October 1960.
[190] Lord Munster was the Parliamentary Under-Secretary of State at the Colonial Office during the period of the Kabaka's deportation in 1953. He left the Colonial Office in 1954 on his appointment as Minister without a Portfolio.

[191] According to Governor Crawford, in a meeting he had with the four hereditary rulers at Entebbe on 24 February 1960, it was difficult to obtain African representation on such a Commission that would be acceptable to all parts of the Protectorate.
[192] For the Terms of Reference, see Uganda Protectorate (1961) Report of the Relationships Commission, Entebbe: Government Printer.
[193]Ibid.
[194] Lord Munster, however, remained the Commission's Chairman.
[195] See FCO 141/18327 for Report of the Uganda Relationships Commission (the Munster Report).
[196] Ibid.
[197] Ibid., para. 8.
[198] Ibid., para. 472.
[199] Ibid., paras. 474 and 475.
[200] Ibid., para. 475.
[201] Ibid., paras. 150-152.
[202] With the exception of Buganda where, it was recommended, a directly elected Lukiiko, if it so wished, could choose to act as an electoral college to elect the representatives from Buganda to the National Assembly. In this way, the Lukiiko would be free to elect its own members or other people to the central legislature.
[203] See Report of the Relationships Commission, pp. 170-175.
[204] Ibid., p. 173.
[205] Ibid.
[206] Ibid., pp.165-166.
[207] Ibid., p. 167.
[208] Ibid., para. 150.
[209] Ibid.
[210] Ibid., para. 128.
[211] Ibid.
[212] Ibid., p. 167
[213] These problems resulted in several constitutional crises, including the abrogation of Uganda's Independence Constitution and the abolition of the kingdoms in 1966.
[214] See file Uganda Constitutional Conference, 1961, CO 822/2428.
[215] Mutesa, *The Desecration of My Kingdom*, p.160.
[216] See police report to the Permanent Secretary for Security and External Relations on Kabaka Yekka dated 27 June, 1961, FCO141/18392.
[217] Fallers, *The King's Men*, p. 381.
[218] See "The Stand of Kabaka Yekka," in Low, *The Mind of Buganda*, p. 213.
[219] See Memorandum on Kabaka Yekka, dated 18 November 1961, FCO141/18392.
[220] See story, "Parties merge in support of Kabaka Yekka" in *Uganda Argus* 11 November 1961, FCO141/18392.
[221] These were attended by Sir Walter Coutts who wrote that "at separate talks in London at the time of the Conference negotiations with representatives of Buganda

were brought to a satisfactory conclusion…[which] brought to an end the sterile period of the previous two years, in which the leaders in Buganda had increasingly tried to insulate the kingdom from what was going on in the rest of the country." See despatch from Sir Walter Coutts to Mr Sandys on "Uganda: Future as an independent country," dated 8 October 1962 on CO 822/2266. No. 378.

[222] Kabaka Mutesa II's letter to the Lukiiko, dated 16 September 1961, reproduced in Low, *The Mind of Buganda*, p. 210.

[223] See file on Macleod's meeting with rulers, September 1961, FCO 141/18379.

[224] See file Uganda Constitutional Conference, 1961, CO 822/2428.

[225] See statement by Secretary of State Macleod to the delegates at the Uganda Constitutional Conference in Lancaster House, 19 September 1961, CO 822/2428.

[226] Ibid.

[227] See FCO 141/18390-18391 for the Report of the Uganda Constitutional Conference 1961, dated 9 October, 1961.

[228] Statement by Secretary of State Macleod at Constitutional Conference in Lancaster House, CO 822/2428.

[229] Ibid.

[230] See Record of the Second Meeting held in the Music Room, Lancaster House, London, SW1 on Tuesday 19 September 1961 at 3.00 pm.

[231] Ibid., p. 2.

[232] Ibid.

[233] Ibid., p. 3.

[234] Ibid.

[235] Ibid.

[236] Ibid.

[237] Mutibwa, in *A History of Uganda*, p.170, argues that the DP "had been originally formed as a reaction to the Protestant domination of all political affairs in the Protectorate. The party was formed to challenge and, if possible, destroy this Protestant ascendancy and in 1961 it looked as if it was on the brink of achieving this unprecedented objective…. [I]t was a direct challenge to the Protestant interests in the country and all those who wanted to retain and promote these interests had to act…. The DP's potential leadership posed a threat, not only to Mengo; it was also a threat to all Protestant hierarchies in the Protectorate … that had subsisted undisturbed for some sixty years".

[238] See record of the 17th meeting of the Conference held in the Music Room, Lancaster House, on 9 October 1961, on the question of indirect elections in Buganda, CO 822/2428.

[239] The UPC and the Buganda Government lacked any mutual liking for each other and held no common policy interests beyond ousting Ben Kiwanuka and the DP from power and the attainment of independence from Britain as soon as possible. The UPC was a leftist party supported mostly by non-Baganda. The Government of Buganda, on the other hand, was conservative and pursued a separatist agenda with regard to the rest of the Protectorate. The only commonality lay in the fact that both groups had a mostly Protestant following that had been disappointed by

the predominantly Catholic DP's victory in 1961. Both stood to lose politically if they did not deprive the DP of Buganda's seats in the June 1962 elections.

[240] See for example, Thompson, Gardner (2015) *African Democracy: Its origins and Development in Uganda, Kenya and Tanzania*, Kampala: Fountain Publishers, p. 88.

[241] See record of the 17th meeting of the Conference held in the Music room, Lancaster House, on 9 October 1961, on the question of Buganda-Bunyoro boundary dispute, CO 822/2428.

[242] See Lwanga-Lunyiigo, *A History of the Democratic Party of Uganda: The First Thirty Years (1954-1984).* Fountain Publishers: Kampala, Uganda, pp. 184-195.

[243] See record of the 17th meeting of the Conference held in the Music room, Lancaster House, on 9 October 1961, on the question of relationships with the Central Government and representation in the Uganda Legislature, CO 822/2428.

[244] Ibid.

[245] Ibid.

[246] Ibingira, *Forging of an African Nation*, p. 210.

[247] See record of the 17th meeting of the Conference, on the question of relationships with the Central Government and representation in the Uganda Legislature, CO 822/2428.

[248] Ibid.

[249] See record of the 17th meeting of the Conference held in the Music room, Lancaster House, on 9 October 1961, on the question of Buganda-Bunyoro boundary dispute, CO 822/2428.

[250] Ibid.

[251] Ibid.

[252] On 26 October 1961, the Lukiiko endorsed the decisions made at the Lancaster House Conference by 70 votes for and none against. Only two people abstained. With that resolution, Buganda's declaration of independence was effectively set aside. Buganda's views at the conference are best captured by the Kabaka: "The talks were successful for us. With Obote's support, we obtained a great deal of what we wanted and looked to receive the rest later. We were to have our own High Court and bodyguard, which was meant to be 300 strong, but never above 120. Also the Lukiiko could decide whether to hold direct elections for LEGCO, which was to be called the National Assembly, or whether to nominate members; Benedicto Kiwanuka was disturbed by this. Though we had started by asking for an army, we were content. Macleod gave us all sherry and we smiled." See Mutesa, *The Desecration of My Kingdom*, p.161-162

[253] Thompson, G. (2003) *Governing Uganda: British Colonial rule and its Legacy*, Kampala: Fountain Publishers, p. 342.

[254] See Lwanga-Lunyiigo (2015) *A History of the Democratic Party of Uganda*. On the 1962 election procedures and the Uganda Legislative Council Elections, 1961 and 1961-1962 see FCO 141/18396.

[255] See Lwanga-Lunyiigo, *A History of the Democratic Party of Uganda.*

[256] Mutesa, *The Desecration of My Kingdom*, p 159.

[257] The kingdom of Buganda accused Kiwanuka of opposing its struggle for and the declaration of independence; for urging the people of Buganda to register for the 1961 elections against the wishes of the kingdom; walking out of the Constitutional Conference; opposing the interests of Buganda on the question of direct elections to the National Assembly; belittling the Kabaka; and being uncooperative with the kingdom during his tenure as Chief Minister. See Lwanga-Lunyiigo, *A History of the Democratic Party of Uganda*, p.75.
[258] See minutes on "problems" with Chief Minister, Mr Kiwanuka, by W. B. L. Monson and Lord Perth to Maudling dated 2 February 1962 on CO 822/2264 Nos. 256 and 266.
[259] Fallers, *The King's Men,* p. 380.
[260] In a letter to Reginald Maudling dated 7 February, 1962 on FCO 141/18460.
[261] See Governor Coutts' letter to Reginald Maudling dated 5 February 1962 on FCO 141/18460.
[262] See minutes on "problems" with Chief Minister, Mr Kiwanuka, by W. B. L. Monson and Lord Perth to Maudling, dated 2 February 1962, CO 822/2264 Nos. 256 and 266.
[263] Ibid.
[264] The Governor held negotiations on the new agreements with delegations from the three kingdoms between October 1961 and March 1962, and the key demand from all three was for full federal status. Little headway was made on this point. For example, on 9 March 1962, the Omuhikirwa of Toro wrote to the Secretary of State for the Colonies demanding full federal status for Toro, amongst other matters. The Secretary of State wrote back on 29 March 1962 stating that the decisions of the Lancaster House Conference provided the right basis for the relationships in Uganda and that "it is not enough to convince Her Majesty's Government that a federal status is the appropriate one for Toro; but also to convince the representatives of the other parts of Uganda that the safeguards, institutions and powers that Toro seeks can be accommodated within an effective system of government for the country as a whole."
[265] See A. R. Dunbar, *The History of Bunyoro-Kitara*, (1965) Oxford University Press Nairobi, pp. 91,112.
[266] See the Report of a Commission of Privy Counsellors on a Dispute Between Buganda and Bunyoro of May 1962, para. 19, FCO 141/18346.
[267] Ibid.
[268] Ibid., para. 20.
[269] Ibid.
[270] Ibid.
[271] Ibid., para. 21.
[272] In a letter addressed to the Governor, Ref. 420/B, dated 18 June 1960.
[273] See Report of a Commission of Privy Counsellors on a Dispute Between Buganda and Bunyoro of May 1962, para. 19, FCO 141/18346 and file "The Lost Counties of Bunyoro," CO 822/2784. See extracts from the Uganda Argus regarding the lost counties on Bunyoro FCO 141/18416.
[274] Ibid, para.1.

[275] Ibid.
[276] According to G. M. Thomson (Dundee, East), this was an example of the British Government "engaging in what the parties to this dispute are bound to feel to be rather devious dealing, and it is extremely unfortunate that the Government's participation in the matter should at this point have been less successful and less creditable." See House of Commons Debate on 16 July 1962, Vol. 663 cc. 31-66.
[277] A letter from the Secretary of State to the Governor, on the Terms of Reference of the Lost Counties Commission sent on 2 May 1962 and received on 3 May 1962, Personal No. 121 on File CSD S 32/5.
[278] Report of a Commission of Privy Counsellors on a Dispute between Buganda and Bunyoro, para. 3. FCO 141/18346.
[279] Ibingira, *The Forging of an African Nation*, p. 183.
[280] The other members of Bunyoro's legal team were J. J. Pearlman, E. Lauterpacht, J. Nugee, and G. K. Coles.
[281] See *Uganda Argus* of 11 and 12 January 1962.
[282] Ibid.
[283] See *Uganda Argus* of 20 January 1962.
[284] See *Uganda Argus* of 18 January 1962.
[285] Working with E. Gratiaen QC and Fred Mpanga.
[286] See *Uganda Argus*, 26 January 1962.
[287] Ibid.
[288] Ibid.
[289] See *Uganda Argus*, 3 February 1962.
[290] Report of a Commission of Privy Counsellors on a Dispute between Buganda and Bunyoro, para. 82. FCO 141/18346.
[291] Ibid., paras. 84 and 85. The reasons for these recommendations, as stated in the report of the Commission of Privy Counsellors, were mainly that in the two Ssazas of Buyaga and Bugangazzi, the Banyoro formed the overwhelming majority. In addition, that these two areas were in the past an integral part of the kingdom of Bunyoro. The Commission established that the tombs of ten *Abakama* (Banyoro kings) were situated in Buyaga and two in Bugangazzi. For the rest of the counties under dispute, including Buwekula, the Commission established that the population of these areas was predominantly Baganda, and also that in all such areas, including Buwekula, the majority opinion was for remaining in Buganda. On the ownership of Mubende Township and the ancient and sacred "Witch Tree," known as the Nakayima tree, the Commission noted that the powers of the tree were recognized not only by the Banyoro, but by the Baganda, Batoro and Banyankole.
[292] Report of a Commission of Privy Counsellors on a Dispute between Buganda and Bunyoro, FCO 141/18346.
[293] Ibid. para. 107.
[294] See Lord Molson's submission to the House of Commons Debate on the "Uganda Independence Bill," 26 July 1962 vol. 242 cc. 1145-72.
[295] The UPC secured 37 seats and the DP 22 (two subsequent by-elections increased their strength in the National Assembly to 24). Twenty-one

representatives of Buganda were elected by the Buganda Lukiiko, the majority of whose members had themselves been directly elected to the Lukiiko in February. All the Buganda members were members of the Kabaka Yekka movement.

[296] In a letter to Lord Molson, dated 3 May 1962.

[297] See story "Buganda Won't Accept" in *Uganda Argus*, 5 May 1962.

[298] Ibid.

[299] Ibid.

[300] See the Governor's Secret Memo Personal No. 137 to the Secretary of State.

[301] See *Uganda Argus*, 5 May, 1962.

[302] Ibid.

[303] Ibid.

[304] See a Memo by J. W. Stacpoole addressed to Mr W. F. Dawson on the lost counties, dated 24 July 1962.

[305] Under Article 15, waste and uncultivated land measuring 9000 Sq. miles was vested in Her Majesty's Government. The bulk of this land was in the six counties that were taken from the kingdom of Bunyoro.

[306] See House of Commons Debate on 16 July 1962, Vol. 663 cc 31-66.

[307] See Personal Memo No. 118 on File CSD.S.32/5 on the Lost Counties Report from the Secretary of State to the Governor of Uganda, sent on 1 May 1962 and received on 2 May 1962.

[308] Ibid.

[309] Ibid.

[310] See Personal Memo No. 138 on File S.32/5 on the Lost Counties Report from the Governor of Uganda to the Secretary of State, sent on 2 May 1962.

[311] Ibid.

[312] Ibid.

[313]See Independence Conference London, June 1962, report, arrangements and papers on FCO 141/18390-18391.

[314] It was attended by delegations from the UK; the Governor Sir Walter Coutts; the Government of Uganda, led by Prime Minister Apollo Milton Obote; officials of the DP as members of the Opposition; the kingdoms of Buganda, Toro, Ankole, Busoga; the districts of Acholi, Bukedi, Kigezi, Madi, Teso, Bugisu, Karamoja, Lango, Sebei, and West Nile; and the various urban authorities.

[315] The Constitutional Committee dealt with boundary changes, fundamental human rights, head of State, specially elected members of the National Assembly, use of emergency powers, appointment of an Electoral Commission, the prerogative of mercy, the High Court of Uganda, appeals to the Privy Council, the means by which Parliament may amend the Constitution, the civil service and the police force.

[316] The Fiscal Committee handled fiscal relationships between the central government and other authorities in Uganda after independence.

[317] The Citizenship Committee dealt with the subject of citizenship after independence, including persons automatically acquiring Ugandan citizenship on independence; entitlement to citizenship of Uganda by registration; acquisition of

Ugandan citizenship by birth after independence; acquisition of Ugandan citizenship by married women; and dual citizenship. See FCO 141/18419.
[318] See despatch from Sir Walter Coutts to Mr Sandys on "Uganda: Future as an independent country," dated 8 October 1962 on CO 822/2266, No. 378.
[319] Ibid.
[320] On 27 June 1962, the Bunyoro delegation withdrew from the Conference in protest at the Secretary of State's decision. They were not present at the final plenary session when the final Conference Report was adopted. On the same day, the Buganda delegation also walked out of the Conference—See *Uganda Argus* and *Uganda Eyogera* of 28 June 1962. On the last day of the Conference (29 June 1962), the Buganda Delegation stated that it rejected the decision of the Secretary of State.
[321] As told to the author by A. D. Lubowa, a member of the Buganda delegation, in an interview on 23 October 2016. As it turned out, Obote did not keep his promise and, on 1 January 1965, signed off on the transfer of the counties, in spite of the Kabaka's and Lukiiko's protestations. See also, Mutibwa, *A History of Uganda*, p.195.
[322] See statements made by Amos Sempa in *Uganda Eyogerera*, 19 June 1962.
[323] Mutesa, *The Desecration of My Kingdom*, p. 166.
[324] "Toro Ends Boycott—Decision after 12-hour talks with Premier," *Uganda Argus*, 27 June 1962.
[325] House of Lords Debate on the "Uganda Independence Bill," 26 July 1962, vol. 242 cc.1145-72.
[326] See The Report of the Uganda Independence Conference 1962, FCO 141/18390-18391.
[327] See UK Parliament Debates on the "Lost Counties," HC debate, 16 July 1962, vol. 663 ccl-21.
[328] See *Uganda Argus*, 23 July, 1963.
[329] See "No Transfer, Says Lukiiko," *Uganda Argus*, 21 July 1962.
[330] See generally, UK Parliament Debates on the "Lost Counties," HC debate, 16 July 1962, vol. 663 ccl-21.
[331] Ibid.
[332] Ibid.
[333] House of Lords Debate on the "Uganda Independence Bill," 26 July 1962 vol. 242 cc1145-72.
[334] Mutesa, *The Desecration of My Kingdom*, pp. 165-166.
[335] The official policy was laid down in a circular memorandum issued by the Ministry of Social Services in May 1957. See FCO 141/18252.
[336] In his letter to the Chief Secretary of 9 February 1961, FCO 141/18252, TNA.
[337] On 22 January 1954
[338] See his letter to Lyttelton the Colonial Secretary dated 12 December 1953, CO 822/762, TNA.
[339] See Howell Caroline (2004), *Church and State in Crisis: The Deposition of the Kabaka of Buganda,1953-1955*, Chapter 10, in Stanley Brian Ed. *Missions, Nationalism, and the End of Empire*, WM. B. Eerdmans Publishing Co., p. 200.

[340] See meeting report by V. F. G. Stephen O I/C District Special Branch Lango of a meeting on 26 April 1958 at Lira in FCO 141/18252, TNA.
[341] In a letter of 5 June 1958 to the Chief Secretary in FCO 141/18252, TNA.
[342] In a letter of 24 April 1961 to the Chief Secretary in FCO 141/18252, TNA.
[343] In a letter of 1 September 1958 to the Governor in FCO 141/18252, TNA.
[344] Samwiri Lwanga-Lunyiigo (2015), *A History of the Democratic Party of Uganda: The First Thirty years (1954-1984)*, p.71
[345] See Archbishop Joseph Kiwanuka's Pastoral Letter on Church and State, Guiding Principles, November 1961.
[346] Ibid.
[347] Ibid.
[348] See Political Activities of Religious Organisations, FCO141/18252 TNA.
[349] Lwanga-Lunyiigo, Samwiiri, "The Colonial Roots of Internal Conflict in Uganda," MISR Paper No, PAP/017, p. 1. Paper delivered at the International Seminar on Internal Conflict, 21—25 September 1987.
[350] Under the Church of England Assembly (Powers) Act 1919.
[351] *Uganda: political development and the problems of the Future* by Andrew Cohen, op. cit., para. 4.
[352] Crawford, *Uganda: Problems of Tribalism and Nationalism*, para. 12.
[353] See *Uganda: political development and the problems of the Future* by Andrew Cohen, op. cit.
[354] See report "The Tribal Balance in Uganda," by the British High Commissioner D. A. Scott, dated 24 January 1969, in file "Uganda: Social Matters: Tribes of Uganda," FCO 31/495.
[355] *Uganda: Problems of Tribalism and Nationalism* by F. Crawford, op. cit., para. 3.
[356] See Ibingira, *The Forging of an African Nation*, p. 271.
[357] See a Secret Memorandum entitled *Uganda: Prospects Following Independence* by the Colonial Office CO Ref. EAF 185/96/01 Copy 94, dated 23 October 1962.
[358] Ibid.
[359] Ibid., para. 16.
[360] Ibid., para. 18.
[361] Tripp, *Museveni's Uganda,* p.31.
[362] See generally Shohei Sato (2017) "Operation Legacy': Britain's Destruction and Concealment of Colonial Records Worldwide," *The Journal of Imperial and Commonwealth History*, DOI: 10.1080/03086534.2017.1294256.
[363] Cobain, Ian (2016) *The History Thieves: Secrets, Lies and the Shaping of a Modern Nation*. London: Portobello Books, p. 123.
[364] See Circular Memorandum S. 10166 on *Operation Legacy* of 28 February 1961 by the Chief Secretary on file *Constitutional Development: Reorganisation of Classified Files*, FCO 141/ 18408-18409 TNA.
[365] See letter on *Disposal Classified and Accountable Documents and Records Generally* of 9 April 1962 by the Secretary of State for the Colonies to the Officer Administering Uganda in FCO 141/18409 TNA.

[366] Letter from A.S to S/SER, SAS, dated 10 January 1961, on FCO 141/18409 TNA.
[367] See Circular Memorandum S. 10166 *Operation Legacy* of 17 April 1961 by the Chief Secretary on file *Constitutional Development: Reorganisation of Classified Files* FCO 141/18409 TNA.
[368] See story "Revealed: the bonfire of papers at the end of Empire" by Ian Cobain in *The Guardian 29* November 2013.
[369] See Memo *Purging of Files* by C. P. S Allen to S. O. G, dated 3 May 1962, FCO 141/18409 TNA.
[370] Ibid.
[371] See Circular on *Designation "Watch"* by the Ministry of Defence Ref. I&S 137/02 (S), dated 13 May 1961, FCO 141/18409 TNA.
[372] See Memo on *Security: Uganda* by Brigadier Commanding East Africa Command to HQ 70 Inf Bde KAR, dated 2 April 1962, FCO 141/18409 TNA.
[373] Ibid.
[374] Ibid.
[375] See letter by A. K. Malcolm to the PS Ministry of Security and external relations, dated 1 November 1961, FCO 141/18409 TNA.
[376] Letter from S. A. S. to A. S., dated 10 March 1961, FCO 141/18409 TNA.
[377] See Memo by C. P. S Allen to the Permanent Secretary, Office of the Prime Minister, dated 10 April 1962, in FCO 141/18409 TNA.
[378] Letter from A. F. Sagar to A. C. Watson, Office of the Deputy Governor, dated 21 September 1962, FCO 141/18409 TNA.
[379] Letter from R. E. Stone to J. S. Champion, Esq., dated 2 January 1962, FCO 141/18409 TNA.
[380] Ibid.
[381] FCO 141/18409.
[382] A. C. Watson, Office of the D. Governor, to Lt-Col. W. W. Cheyne, OC 4th Battalion of the KAR, dated 7 July 1962, FCO 141/18409 TNA.
[383] A. C. Watson, Office of the D. Governor, to J. W. Stacpoole, Colonial Office, dated 7 July 1962, FCO 141/18409 TNA.
[384] See Governor's letter on *Disposal of Documents* to the Secretary of State for the Colonies, dated 5 October 1961, on FCO 141/18409 TNA.
[385] See letter by H. D. Archer to Watson Office of the Governor, dated 11 September 1962.
[386] See list of documents passed on to the British High Commissioner in Uganda on FCO 141/18409 TNA.
[387] See story "Revealed: the bonfire of papers at the end of Empire" by Ian Cobain in *The Guardian* 29 November 2013.
[388] See Memo *Purging of Files* from C. P. S Allen to S.O.G, dated 3 May 1962, FCO 141/18409 TNA.
[389] Cobain, *The History Thieves*, pp. 105 and 126.
[390] See letter on *Government Records* by the SRA to the Minister of State, dated 4 April 1962, FCO 141/18409 TNA.

[391] See letter from the Ministry of Foreign Affairs of Uganda to the British High Commission, on *Antiquities in Uganda*, dated 22 March 1972, FCO 31/1359 TNA.
[392] Ibid.
[393] See letter from J. G. Wallace EAD, FCO, to Miss H. M. Evans of the BHC in Kampala, dated 13 July 1972, FCO 31/1359 TNA.
[394] See letter by J. G. Wallace EAD, FCO, to the Secretary of the British Museum, dated 1 May 1972, File JE U 9/2 *Antiquities in Uganda*, FCO31/1359 TNA.
[395] Anderson, David and Caroline Elkins (2005) *Imperial Reckoning: The Untold Story of Britain's Gulag in Kenya*, New York: Henry Holt and Company.
[396] Parry, Marc "Uncovering the brutal truth about the British Empire," *The Guardian*, Thursday 18 August 2016, www.theguardian.com/news/2016/aug/18/uncovering-truth-british-empire-caroline-elkins-mau-mau, accessed 15 August 2017.
[397] See letter on *Government Records* by the SRA to the Minister of State, dated 4 April 1962, in FCO 141/18409 TNA.
[398] See Anderson & Elkins, *Imperial Reckoning*.
[399] See Cobain Ian *The History Thieves*, p. 112.
[400] Ibid., p. 110.
[401] Ibid., p. 111.
[402] See story "Britain's Secret File Against Biafra 1966-70 Exposed, Britain's Secret Human Rights Abuses" at http://www.ekwenche.org/britain-secret-file-aganst-biafra-1966-70-exposed.html.
[403] Ibid., pp. 130-132.
[404] See Johnson, Boris "Cancel the Guilt Trip," *The Spectator*, 2 February 2002.
[405] See story "It is time to celebrate the Empire, says Brown" in *The Daily Mail* 15 April 2005.
[406] Anderson, David M. (2011) "Mau Mau in the High Court and the 'Lost' British Empire Archives: Colonial Conspiracy or Bureaucratic Bungle?" *The Journal of Imperial and Commonwealth History*, 39(5), p. 712.

Phase V

Anglo-Uganda Relations in Post-Independence Uganda

We came to find warring kingdoms; we leave a Christian country whose people have learnt from us the benefits of not only our civilisation but of our institutions. Wealth has increased; much has flourished; but above all else, I believe there has emerged a sense of political unity, and aspiration towards a Ugandan nation.

—Hugh Fraser, Under Secretary for the Colonies[1]

[In]dependence?

At the stroke of midnight on 8 October 1962, the dashing red, white and blue British Union Jack was lowered and replaced with the brilliant red, yellow and black Ugandan flag—hoisted to symbolise the end of 68 years of imperial rule and the birth of a new African nation. It was a momentous occasion both for the departing coloniser and the ex-colonial subjects. Independence arrived not only with a new flag, a national anthem, a written constitution, a coat of arms and a national army, but also with a host of responsibilities for statecraft in an ideologically polarised world. The young country, to be led by a 37-year old Prime Minister, faced a new and uncertain future both at home and in its relations abroad.

But the challenges and imponderables of the future did little to diminish or hamper the joy and promise of the moment. The new citizenry—especially the few who understood the English lyrics of the new national anthem—sang their hearts out, heralding a new, free, God-fearing country and a people united in love and liberty, ready to stand together and face the future in friendship and peace.

The Duke and Duchess of Kent, representing Her Majesty Queen Elizabeth at the occasion of severing the colonial cord, were warmly welcomed by the new government and the public. In his maiden speech as Uganda's new leader, Obote thanked those Britons who helped Uganda in the struggle for independence, stressing that Uganda's independence came "without any bitterness."[2] It was a speech markedly different from that of the Congo's Patrice Lumumba, which sharply chastised the Congo's departing colonial masters.[3] Unlike Lumumba, Obote was thankful towards the British and was enthusiastic about the country's independent future which, he told Ugandans and the world, beyond a new flag and anthem, meant great responsibilities for all, without exception. He urged all Ugandans to be responsible, to safeguard their independence, and to ensure that the country enjoyed peace and stability.

For Britain, however, which in the 1890s had set out on a dual mission to civilise and expand its imperial rule, Uganda's independence must have been a bittersweet moment. Bitter because its empire was shrinking further with the loss of yet another territory—one that was considered a gem—in a rapidly changing world where anticolonial pressures were rife. After all, Uganda, once figuratively depicted in Punch as "another black foundling" dropped on the doorstep of 10 Downing Street by the IBEAC in 1894, had turned out not a fiend but a rather handsome child, described by Winston Churchill as "the pearl of Africa" relative to Britain's other imperial possessions.[4]

For these reasons, were it not for the changing world views on colonial rule and the rise in nationalism in Uganda, Britain would have wished to hold onto the Uganda Protectorate indefinitely. It was, however, constrained by circumstances, both at home and in Uganda, to make a hasty exit, leaving behind a problematic constitutional and political order. Nonetheless, for an Empire in crisis and one facing a tirade of international criticism over colonialism, the lowering of the Union Jack in Uganda must have brought some sense of sweet relief as Britain relinquished responsibility over another politically troublesome territory riven with inter-tribal conflicts—which, incidentally, its former policies had played no small role in creating.

The dash to Uganda's Independence Day was filled with much activity. For example, all previous Agreements Britain had with Bunyoro, Buganda, Toro and Ankole were to cease on Independence Day. This meant a series of negotiations had to take place between colonial officials and each of these entities. Also, the Uganda Independence Act of 1962, under which the Uganda Protectorate was to form part of Her Majesty's Dominions under the name "Uganda,"[5] had to be passed in the British Parliament. Under the Act, from 9 October 1962 Her Majesty's Government in the United Kingdom would have no responsibility for the Government of Uganda or any part thereof.[6] Legally, Britain discharged itself of any postcolonial responsibility to Buganda or any part of Uganda. Any claims against it in this regard were left in the realm of morality.

The new Government of Uganda was also caught up in a whirl of activity, ranging from establishing its authority across the entire country, recruiting new administrators, designing a new flag and granting loans to night clubs in preparation for the many anticipated guests on Independence Day.[7] Celebrations for independence lasted an entire week before reaching a climax on 9 October. The changeover of regimes included the granting of city status to Uganda's new capital city, Kampala, on 8 October.[8]

To bring a formal end to the Anglo-Buganda Protectorate relationship, the Duke and Duchess of Kent (Prince Edward and Princess Katherine *née* Worsley) made a courtesy call to the royal seat of the Kingdom of Buganda in Mengo on the eve of Uganda's independence.[9] After inspecting a Guard of Honour mounted by the Buganda Police, they were welcomed into the Lukiiko by the Kabaka and the Katikkiro in the presence of the Omukama of Toro, Governor Sir Walter Coutts, the former Governors Sir Andrew Cohen and Sir John Hathorn Hall (accompanied by Lady Hall), Kenyan politicians Jomo Kenyatta and Tom Mboya and other dignitaries.[10]

The Kabaka said little beyond warmly welcoming the young British royal couple. It was Michael Kintu, the Katikkiro, who made a longer and poignant speech reminding his guests that Buganda sought British protection and that the kingdom was proud of the role it had played in Uganda's progress. He emphasized the point that while the Baganda were determined to embrace and participate in all the new forms of human endeavour that were worthy, they were also determined to safeguard all those institutions that had served them so well in the past.[11] It is clear from Kintu's speech that while Buganda had agreed to form a part of Uganda, it was simultaneously determined not to give up its cultural heritage, power and position.

The Duke of Kent told the Lukiiko that independence should not be the end but the beginning of cooperation between Buganda and Britain. Although the relationship that had existed between the Kabaka, the chiefs and the people of Buganda was officially coming to an end, he was pleased to note that new relationships would be created which would be a source of strength between the peoples of the two kingdoms.[12]

While to some Baganda the visit by the Duke of Kent to the Lukiiko was understood as Buganda regaining her independence on 8 October 1962, the reality is that Britain never granted Buganda independence on that day or at all. This is because when the 1961 agreement was signed, Buganda agreed to form part of Uganda. Once that agreement was signed and, based on it, a new constitution was promulgated in 1962, it was not possible for Britain to grant Buganda independence. Commenting on the mood in Buganda on Uganda's independence, Kabaka Mutesa wrote:

> When independence finally came on 9 October 1962, the Baganda welcomed it confidently as something that had been earned. Veterans of such celebrations have commented on our comparative calm, and it is true that the degree of self-government we have always enjoyed, combined with our long-standing certainty that the struggle would be only over the date, robbed the moment of some of its emotional impact. Neither crowds nor feeling were comparable to the day of my return.[13]

Buganda's lukewarm attitude or apparent lack of enthusiasm on independence may be explained by its frustration and failure to obtain full autonomy as a separate independent state. And, even though it won full federal status under the 1962 Constitution, its leadership and people were unclear about the future of the Kabakaship under the political leadership of Obote, an avowed republican.

A False Start?

Not unlike the Nigerian and the Democratic Republic of the Congo experience, the euphoria of independence in Uganda did not last long. It faded as soon as the new government took charge of the country with limited human and financial resources. Indeed, once the colonial administrators exited the scene, the country started on a slow but sure descent into a political and constitutional crisis. Besides the politics, the challenges of a weak economy constrained the new government and forced it to look to its former colonial master for help.[14]

Uganda's independence and freedom from British colonial rule led neither to the total liberation of its people from imperial rule nor to the end of their exploitation. As in many other former colonies in Africa, and as we show herein, Uganda's independence was only symbolic. Colonial rule was replaced by neocolonialism after independence, as well as new forms of authoritarian rule and corruption by a new political elite. Uganda's post-independence experience validates the view that independence did not represent a clean break from the colonial era but instead steered former colonies firmly towards neocolonialism, particularly through the continued reliance on foreign investments in which transnational corporations dominated the economies and influenced the politics of the new countries.[15]

Given the complex and fragile constitutional and political framework emblematic of Uganda's colonial heritage, cracks soon emerged, not only within the fractious political coalition between Kabaka Yekka and the Uganda People's Congress,[16] but also between Buganda and Uganda. Governor Coutts correctly stated that, the early quarrels within the UPC/

KY alliance revealed the depth of the "conflict between Buganda's aspirations and the emergent Uganda nationalism, and how shallow was the apparent acquiescence of Buganda in the October 1961 and June 1962 settlements."[17] For instance, by August 1963, the governments of Buganda and Uganda were in court over the interpretation of the financial relationships between Buganda and Uganda.

Also, the Government of Buganda had demanded that the Government of Uganda should transfer police stations and police posts in Buganda to the Kabaka's government. But the central government insisted that its obligation to maintain public safety and public order throughout Uganda would not be prejudiced by handing over any police posts or stations to any other authority. It even sought a High Court ruling on this matter. Buganda responded by passing a proposal to build six police stations, in Natete, Kapeka, Kangulumila, Kisoga, Kibibi and Muhororo.[18] Inevitably, these disagreements affected relations between the country's youthful leaders Mutesa and Obote. On his working relationship with the Prime Minister for example, Mutesa lamented:

> I was supposed to be kept informed of affairs by the prime minister, but he gradually ceased to bother to do this. Also, I had certain rights such as appointing and dismissing ministers on the advice of the prime minister. Even when Obote could be sure of my support, he was not interested in honouring such obligations. Later the illegality of his action was clear, but he does not care much for the letter of the law. He cares for power; and this he retained.[19]

However, it is not surprising that the relations between Mutesa, a monarch of an ancient and powerful kingdom, and Obote, a passionate republican, started off poorly. In many ways, the two were strange bedfellows. On the state of Uganda's economy at independence, Governor Coutts wrote that the country, whose budget deficit stood at half a million pounds and whose reserves totalled a paltry £3 million, faced "financial stringency and economic lethargy" and that its capacity to finance development from its own resources was "negligible."[20] In fact, he feared that unless the outside world was sympathetic and granted it financial assistance, Uganda would "relapse into a stagnant, if seemingly lush, equatorial slum."[21]

For these reasons and because of the inexperience of its leaders in economic management, Uganda soon looked to its former colonial master for support soon after independence in continuation of what may be described as economic colonialism. For example, the government sought British support of some £21 million in development aid and was granted

£6 million.[22] Uganda was not alone in suffering an economic slowdown soon after independence. The breakup of the British Empire meant that new nations had to absorb huge administrative and defence costs and seek out help to sustain their economies.[23] The foundations of dependence and economic colonialism in countries like Uganda are best explained by Joseph Stiglitz thus:

> At the end of the colonial period, western powers discovered that they could get many of the economic advantages of colonialism by keeping the developing countries under their thumb through debt. The ex-colonies then suffered from the Washington Consensus, the set of policies based on Western interests and free-market ideology that served corporate interest so well. The West could continue to take resources out of Africa, and impose a set of policies that led to its deindustrialisation. Their indebtedness—and threats about what might happen if they defaulted—enabled the West to impose these onerous conditions on developing countries.[24]

This illustrates how, through bilateral or multilateral aid in the form of debt and grants, Britain and financial agencies like the World Bank and the IMF perpetuate and advance interests of the West in the postcolonial era. It also shows that, for all the official independence ceremonies, many developing countries like Uganda did not become truly free as their former colonial masters continue to dictate their economic—and thus significantly influence their political—destiny.

Alongside the economic doldrums that Uganda found itself in at independence, the lack of a capable civil service to run the affairs of the new country was acute. As in other colonies, the civil service in Uganda was filled mostly with expatriate staff. At independence, little effort had been made to replace these despite an exodus of the expatriates once the date for Uganda's independence was declared. By March 1963, of the 1260 expatriate staff, over 600 had left the country,[25] yet there were an insufficient number of African civil servants to take over their positions. The dire situation was of concern to Governor Coutts, who wondered how so few men, often trained in a hurry and with no real experience of heavier responsibilities of government, would stand up to the strain that Britain had put upon them? On this worrisome note, he rightly predicted that Uganda could expect a kind of modified chaos in 1964.[26]

Regarding the military and defence situation, Coutts warned that "in no [area] will independence bring greater problems to Uganda than in defence and security,"[27] and indeed before long, on 23 January 1964, Prime Minister Obote looked to British forces to help quell a mutiny of 200 troops of the 1st battalion of the Uganda Rifles which broke out in the barracks at Jinja.[28] In seeking British support, the Prime Minister did not consult or inform Mutesa, the President and Commander-in-Chief of the Ugandan Army.[29] Indeed, he "did not admit that English soldiers were in the country for several days after that, and kept a strict censorship of the press and wireless."[30]

The British Government's response to Obote's request for troops was immediate: two companies of the Staffordshire Regiment and one company of the Scots Guards stationed in Kenya were immediately deployed to help restore order and secure Entebbe and other important installations in Kampala. In less than an hour, seven aircraft carrying troops from Nairobi to Entebbe were airborne.[31] They proceeded to Jinja, where they disarmed the mutineers and suppressed the mutiny without firing a single shot.[32] They stayed in the country for three months. In what must have been a carefully calculated move, Obote, having gone behind the back of Mutesa as Commander-in-Chief, had, by July 1964, removed all British officers and appointed Idi Amin to command the battalion at Jinja.[33] There is little doubt that rewarding Amin's with this appointment emboldened him, and the army, to enter into the political arena in later years.

To underline the crisis in the wake of the departure of colonial authority and the ongoing dependence of its East African colonies, around the same period that Britain came to the military aid of Uganda, President Julius Nyerere of Tanganyika also called in British troops to help regain control of the troops of the Tanganyika Army that had also mutinied.[34] Nyerere's request was also acceded to and the mutiny immediately quelled. The Kenyan Government had also called upon British troops to maintain law and order when its soldiers defied authority and attempted to seize the armoury at Lanet, North of Nairobi.[35]

Faced with these challenges, the country got off to a slow and difficult start after independence, and as early as 1963, Obote was moving to tinker with the Constitution, with proposals to amend it in order to grant himself more power. On Obote's thirst for power, Coutts had predicted that the only certainty in Uganda's otherwise uncertain political context was that Obote would "take very vigorous and possibly unpalatable steps to consolidate his position after independence."[36] Obote's subsequent abrogation of the 1962 Constitution and attack against the Lubiri (detailed below), as well as his problematic and unconstitutional political conduct in post-independence Uganda validates Coutts' views, but raises questions as to why Britain, given its official distaste for undemocratic actions and human rights abuses, continued to work with him until he was ousted from power.

The aggregation of various political and economic challenges discussed above problematized Uganda's governance right from the start. These challenges continued long into its future and negated its growth into a peaceful and prosperous country. Notable amongst these challenges were the appointment of a head of state in 1963, the resolution of the lost counties saga in 1964, the gold scandal and the attack against the Lubiri of Mengo in 1966, as well as the costly constitutional crises that followed.

The Queen of Uganda? The Problem of Appointing Uganda's First Head of State

One of the agreements reached at the Uganda Independence Conference in June 1962 was that Uganda would remain part of the British dominions and owe its allegiance to Her Majesty the Queen and thus would not become a republic.[37] It was also agreed that Uganda would become a member of the British Commonwealth.[38] Thus Queen Elizabeth, represented by the Governor General, became the "Queen of Uganda" and Uganda's Head of State at independence.[39] Sir Walter Coutts, the last Governor of the Protectorate, was appointed as the first Governor General of Uganda. This meant that the British Privy Council had the jurisdiction to hear appeals in cases decided by Ugandan courts. Strangely, at least initially, Uganda's Prime Minister had no problem with the Queen being the Head of State in Uganda. When asked at a press conference if he had any plans to make Uganda a Republic he said:

> We have a double monarchy in Uganda. We accept the British Crown as Head of the British Commonwealth today and we accept her as the Queen of Uganda. At the same time, we have Kingdoms here—four of them, so there can be no question of a Republic.[40]

Interestingly, the Democratic Party leadership, now on the opposition benches, shared Obote's views on having the Queen as Uganda's Head of State. It was felt within DP circles that time was not yet ripe for Uganda to have an African as a Head of State. In its election pamphlet of April 1962, the party advocated having the Governor General (representing the Queen) appointed as the Head of State on the advice of the Government of Uganda. But, reflective of the rivalry in the politics of the day, Kabaka Yekka, unlike the DP and UPC, was opposed to the idea of a British Queen or indeed any other African "commoner" as Head of State for Uganda. KY's position was that nobody could ever have a superior position over the Kabaka on Buganda's soil, and that in Buganda no single individual or body of people could ever make laws that the Kabaka must observe, as this would be contrary to Buganda's traditions.

With KY's views in mind, and in less than one year after independence, Obote changed his position on the Queen being the Head of State in Uganda. He thus moved to amend the Constitution to remove the Queen as the Head of State and to make provision for this office to be held by a Ugandan citizen. In a letter to British Prime Minister Harold Macmillan, he proposed to declare Uganda an independent sovereign state which, as of 9 October 1963, while remaining a member of the British Commonwealth, would cease to form part of Her Majesty's Dominions, and Her Majesty would cease to exercise any sovereignty over Uganda. However, Obote maintained that even though Her Majesty would cease being Head of State for Uganda, the country would not become a Republic because the use of the word in a state having monarchical elements (in Buganda, Bunyoro, Toro and Ankole) would be misleading.[41] Macmillan was puzzled by Obote's proposals, given that it was not up to Britain to determine whether constitutional changes were made in what was now an independent country.

In any event, the proposals were passed by the National Assembly through the Constitution of Uganda (First Amendment) Act 1963. On its part, the British Parliament also passed the Uganda Act of 1964, under which Uganda ceased to be a part of Her Majesty's Dominions with effect from 9 October 1963. This paved the way for the election of the 38-year-old Kabaka Mutesa as the first President of Uganda on 4 October 1963.[42] On this point, Mutesa wrote:

> there was little choice either for Obote or me. [Obote] was not in a position to snub the Baganda, who would have been enraged if any other ruler were chosen, as the new President would have precedence over the Kabaka even in Buganda. Similarly, it was difficult for me to refuse.[43]

Mutesa's election and subsequent installation as the President of Uganda followed much political jostling, particularly within UPC and KY circles. While many cautious voices in Buganda, such as Prince Badru Kakungulu, a leader of Uganda's Muslim minority, saw this as a dangerous move, the political actors in KY prevailed and the Kabaka accepted the new role. It was hoped or assumed by the KY leadership that as the President of Uganda and Commander-in-Chief of its armed forces, Mutesa would be at the helm of Uganda's politics and therefore influence policy to best serve and defend Buganda's interests. For Obote and the UPC, Mutesa's acceptance of the position was seen as a victory over Buganda's separatist tendencies. In this regard, Obote made a statement to the effect that "the moment the Kabaka held the bible and took the oath of office I knew he was in."[44] There is no doubt, however, that Mutesa's dual role as King of Buganda and President and Commander-in-Chief of Uganda[45] placed him in a dangerous and controversial spot in terms of conflicts of interest which eventually led to a falling out with Prime Minister Obote on several questions including the lost counties issue, on which Mutesa's partisan interests as the Kabaka of Buganda were primary and generally antithetical to those of Uganda, which he led as President.

Although the news of the Kabaka's election was greeted with much excitement—particularly in Kabaka Yekka circles—in reality the position of President was more titular than substantive. The Kabaka was not oblivious to this fact. He in fact told the press a day after his election that he did not consider the position as the most important in the unification of Uganda, and that "other people [had] more important jobs" than his.[46] It is not difficult to guess who he had in mind. In amending the Constitution, Obote had consolidated power in his office as Prime Minister, including the power to direct the official engagements of the President and the Vice-President.

On the day of his installation as President, Mutesa wore the ceremonial uniform of the British Grenadier Guards (in which he held the rank of Captain) and not his traditional royal regalia[47]—an interesting decision for a king of an ancient and powerful kingdom that had just been liberated from colonial rule and one who had personally suffered a humiliating deposition and deportation at the hands of Britain. More significantly, however, the installation of Sir Edward Mutesa as the Head of State on 9 October 1963 marked a new phase in the local politics of Uganda, particularly in terms of the Kabaka's relations with Obote.

But neither the appointment of an African Head of State nor the departure of the last superintendent of British rule—the Governor General—marked the end of Britain's close and influential involvement in Uganda's affairs. In fact, as we have seen, Uganda's political independence seemed to start a new chapter of its economic, military and financial dependence.

The 1964 Referendum on the Lost Counties

Besides the economic, political and military difficulties facing Uganda's new government, the resolution of the boundary dispute between Buganda and Bunyoro—the lost counties issue—presented another intractable challenge. In fact, this problem, which had been left smouldering in the long dry grass by the departing British in 1962, blew up shortly after independence.[48] Tensions between Buganda and Bunyoro, especially in Buyaga and Bugangazzi counties, remained high throughout 1963. For example, on 9 January 1963, the *Orukurato* (Parliament) of Bunyoro passed a resolution asking the Prime Minister to implement the provisions of the Independence Order-in-Council so as to "relieve the Banyoro in the lost counties from the sufferings and humiliation which are being inflicted upon them by Buganda administrators."[49]

The incidents of violence in the two counties also necessitated the imposition of curfews and a declaration of a state of emergency in Buyaga, which was declared a disturbed area on 7 November 1963. In addition, the collection of graduated or market taxes was opposed and challenged in the High Court in the case of *Joseph Kazairwe vs The Lukiiko*.[50] In this case, Kazairwe was accused of inciting the people of Buyaga and Bugangazzi not to pay taxes to the Kabaka's Government and for obstructing chiefs from carrying out their rightful duties of revenue collection. He was found guilty and was jailed for five years by the Buganda Principal Court.

To deal with the matter once and for all a bill authorising a referendum was passed in the National Assembly in September 1964. Following that, and pursuant to Section 26 of the Uganda Order-in-Council, Obote announced that the referendum would be held in November 1964. Mutesa and the Lukiiko were taken aback by the Prime Minister's actions and timing of the announcement. Buganda expected that the matter would be allowed some time to cool off or be resolved amicably without the need for a plebiscite.[51] It was thought that they had Obote's word not to pursue the matter urgently, especially given that the law did not oblige the government to hold a referendum within the first two years of independence; indeed, it specified that the referendum would be held at least two years after independence. However, Prime Minister Obote must have had other ideas.

It must be recalled that by the time Obote announced the referendum, the ill-fated alliance between Kabaka Yekka and the UPC had all but collapsed and majority of the ministers belonging to the former were out of government.[52] The only KY ministers who remained on the government benches were Luyimbazi Zake and Joash Mayanja Nkangi. On the relations between KY and the UPC at this time, Mutesa writes:

> the alliance between KY and [the] UPC was formally broken. It had long been dead in spirit. In the National Assembly [the] UPC held a handsome majority over both parties. Obote no longer had need of us. Indeed, he was now powerful enough to destroy us as the main obstacle between himself and complete power. The KY ministers were out of Government.[53]

Once the Referendum Bill was passed by the National Assembly, the Kabaka found himself in a conundrum. As the President of Uganda, he was required to sign the Referendum Bill, but his position and interests as the Kabaka of Buganda contradicted such a move. In the end he chose not to sign the Bill, a decision that attracted a political furore and sharp criticism from Obote, who accused him of being difficult and impossible to work with.[54] While Mutesa and Buganda were dismayed and felt let down by the Prime Minister with whom they had an alliance and whom they had expected, at worst, to delay the referendum, the people and leadership in Bunyoro were jubilant over the announcement. On Obote's crafty behaviour in this matter, Ibingira writes that Obote had secretly assured Mutesa that the referendum would never take place, while at the same time telling the Omukama of Bunyoro that he was going to have the counties returned to Bunyoro.[55]

Faced with a looming referendum, Buganda moved quickly to ensure that it did not lose the vote and, by implication, the counties. To hedge its position in the claimed counties of Buyaga and Bugangazzi, from 1962 Buganda arranged to resettle many of its ex-servicemen there, and spent considerable sums on projects aimed to win the hearts and minds of the Banyoro in the affected areas.[56] One such project was the construction of roads, which came with a promise to establish a modern city at Ndaiga.[57] Applications for vacant plots of land in the county were solicited from interested individuals in Buganda.[58] A promise was made to the effect that the government of Buganda would assist the owners of all those allocated plots in the construction of the commercial premises, which they would be allowed to occupy for two years without paying anything.[59] The Kabaka himself spent a lot of effort, time and money at Ndaiga and personally supervised the resettlement programme. He was determined to retain the land that had been part of his kingdom for as long as anyone could remember. He later wrote:

> I hoped to develop the area, persuade many Baganda to live there and, by bringing roads and schools and better prices for their crops, persuade the inhabitants that life as part of Buganda was tolerable—even pleasant…. [M]y plan could have led to a peaceful and prosperous solution if I had had the support of the prime minister.[60]

Not only did Buganda's grand plans fail to receive the support of the Prime Minister, they were also seriously thwarted by a High Court ruling that new settlers (i.e. those who settled after 1960) were ineligible to vote in the referendum.[61] It was clear that on this question, and regardless of his assurances to Mutesa to the contrary, Obote was determined to have the referendum held on his terms. This was in spite of the fact that the counties had been declared a disturbed area and that Buganda's appeal was yet to be determined in the Privy Council in Britain.

In the end, the referendum was held and the results showed that the majority of the inhabitants in the two counties wanted to return to Bunyoro.[62] Buganda thus lost the 70-year–old contest over the ownership of the counties. Once again, Mutesa was required to sign an instrument of transfer handing the said counties to Bunyoro. Unsurprisingly, he refused to sign away the counties. Once Mutesa declined to sign the transfer instrument, Obote gladly and quickly signed the two counties away to Bunyoro with effect from 1 January 1965.

While Bunyoro was ecstatic, the result was catastrophic for Buganda and caused an almighty uproar at Mengo, the seat of the kingdom's administration. The loss of the counties was humiliating both for Mutesa and the kingdom of Buganda. The Lukiiko was roundly blamed for the debacle, with Katikkiro Michael Kintu and his cabinet colleagues being the immediate casualties.[63] They were accused of, and unceremoniously forced to resign for, misleading the Kabaka and the Lukiiko by agreeing to the referendum. They were literally stoned out of Bulange, the Lukiiko parliament building, an act which, given Kintu's position during the independence negotiations and his role in the struggle to retain the said counties, seems overly harsh and unwarranted.

Joash Mayanja Nkangi replaced Kintu, following his election as Katikkiro on 17 August 1964. From this point on, the relationship between Buganda and Uganda, and especially that between the Prime Minister and the President, hit a new low. Britain, relying on the policy of non-interference in internal matters of an independent nation, kept a stoic distance in the process that saw the historically contested lost counties move from Buganda to Bunyoro in 1964.

Following Buganda's loss in the lost counties referendum the army was put on high alert in the kingdom, in fear of some form of insurrection. The tensions, public unease and heavy military deployment in the kingdom precipitated the Nakulabye massacre.[64] On 10 November 1964 at Nakulabye, a suburb in the northwest of Kampala city, government security agents murdered six unarmed civilians. The incident was sparked by a domestic fight between a husband and a wife. When a neighbour called in the police, the gun-wielding officers recklessly and indiscriminately shot into the gathering without so much as an inquiry as to what the brawl was about. No charges were brought against the security officers responsible, nor did the government offer any apology or compensation in the matter.

Unlike the British colonial government that set up commissions of inquiry to investigate the 1945, 1949 and 1960 riots, Obote's regime did not investigate the killings. The callous handling of the incident by the government suggests several things, including the early signs of impunity, intimidation and brutality in Obote's first regime. Obote needed to stamp his political and military authority on Buganda. Coming so soon after the referendum, the Nakulabye incident was intended to forestall uprisings in Buganda over the matter. It was a clear signal to all that Obote was fully in charge.

The Congo Gold Scandal and the 1966 Buganda Crisis

The estrangement between the President and the Prime Minister following the 1964 referendum, the exodus of politicians from the DP and Kabaka Yekka to join the UPC, and the increased militarisation of Uganda's politics after the Nakulabye incident, all plunged the country into a deeper crisis. The situation was exacerbated by accusations that Ugandan troops were looting gold and ivory from the Congo, where they had been sent to support the fight against Moise Tshombe's secessionist regime in Katanga.[65] Leading the accusations were KY's Daudi Ochieng and the DP's Alexander Latim, who informed the National Assembly that the bank account of Idi Amin, the Deputy Commander of the Army, held a sum of US $51,000 whose source was unexplainable.[66]

Amin's immediate response to the allegations was to call Latim on phone and threaten to kill him and Ochieng.[67] On his part, the Minister of Defence, Felix Onama, dismissed the accusations on the floor of Parliament, saying they were the "usual latrine talks which Honourable Members opposite pick up and rush with to everybody beating drums for everybody to come and listen."[68] On the source of the funds on Amin's account, Onama explained that Amin's relatives, who were distributed between Uganda and the Congo, had given them to him or, alternatively, that refugees from the Congo might have given the money to him for safe keeping.[69]

Not intimidated by Amin's threats, Daudi Ochieng brought a motion before Parliament on 4 February 1966, in which he alleged that members of the government, together with a high-ranking army officer (Amin) were involved in a planned coup to overthrow Uganda's Constitution. Ochieng also alleged that three ministers (Obote, the Prime Minister; Onama, the Minister of Defence; and Nekyon, the Minister of Planning and Community Development and a cousin to Obote) had received large sums of money from selling gold and tusks from the Congo. Ochieng's motion called for the suspension of Amin pending the conclusion of police investigations into his bank account.[70] Even though the motion was passed, Amin was not suspended. To justify and explain his government's defiance of the Parliamentary resolution, Obote called a press conference on 13 February 1966 and denied the allegations against him and the other ministers. Separately, Onama, Nekyon and Amin demanded for an apology from Ochieng, but Ochieng was undeterred and largely ignored them. His unwavering stance constrained Obote's Cabinet into setting up a Commission of Inquiry on 15 February to investigate the allegations.

It is puzzling that the inquiry was quickly set up by the Cabinet and not by Parliament, where Ochieng's motion was made. In any event, even before the Commission's work got underway, Obote made a startling announcement, saying:

> In the interest of national stability and public security and tranquillity, I have today, the twenty-second day of February 1966, taken over all the powers of the Government of Uganda.
>
> I shall henceforth be advised by a Council whose members I shall name later. I have taken this course of action independently because of my understanding of the wishes of the people of this country for peace, order and prosperity.
>
> Five former ministers have been put under detention pending investigations into their activities. I call upon the judges and magistrates, civil servants—both Ugandan and expatriate—members of the security forces, and the general public to carry on with their normal duties. I take this opportunity to assure everybody that the whole situation is under control.[71]

With those few words, Obote unilaterally overturned the normative constitutional order of Uganda and usurped all the powers of the government, including those of the president. Mutesa heard about this only after the fact. The country was in shock—not just because of Obote's coup but also due to the hasty, reckless and vicious purge and detention of ministers E. B. S. Lumu, Grace S. K. Ibingira, B. K. K. Kirya, M. M. Ngobi and G. B. K. Magezi.

Evidencing the haste and recklessness of Obote's actions, the warrants for the arrest and detention of the ministers were signed by a magistrate long after these individuals were arrested and deported. The charges against the ministers were for: (i) conducting themselves in a manner dangerous to peace and good order in Uganda, (ii) inciting enmity between the people of Uganda and the government, and (iii) intriguing against the power and authority of the Ugandan Government. Remarkably, the deportation orders against the ministers was executed in a manner similar to those made under British colonial rule, in that they were carried out without any investigation or trial. In this case, the ministers were deported from Entebbe in Buganda to Patiko, a location in northern Uganda.[72]

The ministers were produced in court on 8 March 1966, but were further remanded to Luzira prison. Even though the courts eventually acquitted them of the charges, they were never freed and stayed in illegal incarceration for five years.[73] In a move to secure his coup, Obote promoted Amin and appointed him the Commander-in-Chief of the Ugandan Army, replacing Brigadier Opolot, who was appointed to the newly created position of Military Adviser in the Ministry of Defence.[74] Once the army was safely in the hands of his protégé, Amin, Obote and his Cabinet made another astounding declaration on the next day. It read:

> WHEREAS in the interests of national stability and tranquillity, the prime minister on the twenty-second day of February 1966 took over all the powers of the Government of Uganda as a temporary measure;
>
> AND WHEREAS we the undersigned are desirous that there should be as quickly as possible a return to normality;
>
> NOW THEREFORE in order to maintain national stability, public security and tranquillity, and to ensure a speedy return to normality which existed before the events leading to the action taken by the prime minister on the twenty-second day of February 1966, we the undersigned do hereby declare that any action or actions taken by the prime minister does not affect and shall not affect or be deemed to affect any of the following provisions of the constitution, that is to say:-
>
> (a) The powers, dignities, status and privileges of the rulers of the Federal States and the constitutional heads of the districts;
> (b) The Constitutions of the Federal States and the administrations of the districts and the councils and boards of the municipalities and towns;
> (c) The powers, duties and functions of the courts, the judges and magistrates;
> (d) The national assembly;
> (e) The smooth working of the civil service;
> (f) The armed forces of Uganda, the police and the prisons service.
>
> We hereby further declare that as a temporary measure there is hereby established a Security Council of Uganda, of which the Prime Minister shall be chairman, and a Cabinet of ministers holding portfolios who shall be appointed by the Prime Minister.
>
> We further declare that the suspension of the other parts of the Constitution is only a temporary measure for the promotion of unity, peace and good government of Uganda.[75]

This declaration, although signed by some ministers, was outright illegal and unconstitutional. Obote and his cabinet colleagues—some of who may have signed under fear of arrest—had no powers whatsoever to suspend any part of the Constitution let alone to abolish the positions of President and Vice-President. The declaration was targeted at the Presidency—and at Kabaka Mutesa in particular—with the intent of usurping all his powers and vesting them in the Prime Minister. Indeed, a declaration by the Government on 2 March 1966 achieved this purpose. It stated

> The executive authority of Uganda shall vest in the Prime Minister and shall be exercised by the Prime Minister acting in accordance with the advice and consent of the Cabinet; and
>
> The duties, powers and other functions that were performed or were exercised by the President or the Vice-President immediately before the twenty-second day of February, 1966, shall vest in the Prime Minister and be performed or be exercised by the Prime Minister by and with the advice and consent of the Cabinet.[76]

Unlike the unilateral declaration made on 22 February, this one purported to have been made with the "advice and consent of Cabinet." Tellingly, it was also silent on the Advisory Council that Obote had originally promised to name. He must have changed his mind about the new Council and, in subsequent declarations, aimed to clothe his actions with Cabinet support and approval.

The coup against Mutesa and the Constitution was confirmed in Obote's profound radio broadcast on 3 March 1966. For the first time, Obote publically accused Mutesa of asking ambassadors accredited to Uganda to supply him with troops to invade Uganda; of dereliction of Presidential duties—particularly the failure or refusal to sign the "Lost Counties" Referendum Act of 1964 and the Act setting out the Buganda/Bunyoro boundaries after the referendum; and of failure to open the Session of Parliament on 15 November 1965.[77] Given that Mutesa had not been charged or tried, nor had his conduct been found evidentially unconstitutional by any judicial body, Obote's accusations, made long after the events in question, could only have been a publicity stunt aiming not only to embarrass Mutesa but also to justify the abrogation of the Constitution.

To reinstate constitutional order, an anxious Mutesa wrote letters to the Prime Minister advising that there was no provision in the Constitution for its suspension, either by the National Assembly or by anybody else, and asked him to retract his unconstitutional acts.[78] He also pointed out that Obote's "endeavours to introduce a totalitarian regime" in Uganda had no support from the people and that he would be failing in his duty if he left the Prime Minister "in the slightest doubt" that Ugandans would do anything but reject his unconstitutional measures.[79] However, these letters were ineffective in turning the tide or halting Obote's determination to grab power and defile the Constitution. Equally impotent were the several resolutions, passed by the Buganda Lukiiko, condemning Obote's arbitrary actions and asking him to restore the Constitution.[80]

In the face of these outcries, Obote resorted to even more bizarre conduct, including throwing the President out of the official State House without any notice and stripping him of all the privileges that come with the Presidency. The staff were ordered not to attend to him, personal aides were wantonly dismissed, and his personal property was removed and dumped at the Lubiri in Mengo to create space for Obote and his family, who had already moved in.[81] An agonised Mutesa once again wrote to the Prime Minister:

> You have taken away all my staff including the security officers, thereby exposing my life to maximum danger. The people of this country, and I think in many parts of the world, will find it extremely difficult to appreciate all these reprehensible things which are now being perpetrated in your name, contrary to all known norms. The future is mercifully closed to most of us, but the past, which is the greatest teacher known to man, has shown that desperate measures such as the ones we are now being subjected to by yourself, have the quality of [a] boomerang and they invariably lead to limited or general misery. The verdict will not wait for posterity as the living have now written their judgment regarding your actions.[82]

Obote was not moved by this rather poignant missive and, accordingly, did not honour Mutesa with a reply. Instead, his spokesman issued the following statement

> It must be made clear that with the suspension of the Constitution, the former President cannot expect to use State House or any government property or have the use of central government officials. Anybody working for him must consider himself a personal employee at Sir Edward's [Mutesa] expense. Arrangements have been made to secure government property for safe custody. This opportunity is taken to warn editors of newspapers who are continuing to refer to the offices of President and Vice-President as if they still exist to stop misleading or misinforming the public.[83]

Perplexed at the rapid pace of events and Obote's alarming actions, the Kabaka's government filed a suit against the Government of Uganda in the

High Court of Uganda in which it sought declarations that the usurpation of power by the Prime Minister and the suspension of the Constitution was a contravention of the 1962 Constitution.[84]

To legalise his actions, Obote introduced a new Constitution to the country on 15 April 1966. To menace the MP's, he first surrounded the National Assembly buildings with mean-looking military troops, armed to the teeth. Before a fully packed Assembly, he made a scathing three-hour–long attack on Mutesa, whom he mocked, ridiculed and accused of masterminding the Motion on the Congo gold and ivory scandals on 4 February 1966—a day he termed "the darkest Friday that this country ever witnessed since the creation of [the] Earth."[85]

He accused Mutesa of seeking military assistance from abroad to overthrow the Government and thereby cause chaos in the country, in a bid to turn it into a feudal state. According to Obote, Mutesa wanted to act unconstitutionally to remove the Government of Uganda and, having failed in that attempt, sought military assistance from Britain. To support this, he noted that Mutesa had, on 9 February 1966, sought British military assistance though its High Commissioner Roland C. C. Hunt and excoriated the British High Commission for its failure to notify the Uganda Government of Mutesa's "plot."[86] The British High Commission denied the allegations as being completely unfounded, and recorded that the meeting with Hunt was for a "precautionary" and "hypothetical" request for British military assistance, in case Obote's regime descended into further lawlessness.[87]

Obote also accused Mutesa of attempting to merge the office of the Kabaka with that of the President and of meddling in the office of the Commander-in-Chief.[88] Finally, and perhaps most seriously, he accused Mutesa of treason and claimed that he was part of a sinister plot to kill him. He brazenly told the House that on 4 February 1966 "steps would have been taken to get rid of Obote, who was stopping one man from being the feudal lord of Uganda. Thank God there was that Obote!"[89]

Without batting an eyelid, Obote told a restless Assembly that in order "to stop the President from causing us more headaches and trouble and probably leading us into a dangerous situation," he and his unnamed colleagues had decided to suspend the Constitution.[90] However, in almost the same breath, he told the Assembly that he had acted alone on the night of the 22 February once he received information that troop movements had been made without his or the Defence Minister's knowledge, because he feared that a coup was underway. He told the Assembly that if he had not acted on that day, the country would have been in greater chaos and that "no one would say that anyone of us would be alive today."[91] Inexplicably, given the gravity of the accusations, he did not provide the house with any evidence to back his claims.

Once he had admonished Mutesa, Obote declared: "the Constitution we had from 9 October 1962 is hereby abrogated.... let us recall that the 1962 Constitution was worked out by citizens of Uganda, but in a large measure was also worked out by the British Government."[92] With that, he revoked the Constitution under which he was not only sworn in as Prime Minister but also the very one he swore to defend and uphold. Without allowing debate, he asked the Assembly to immediately approve and pass a new Constitution that they had not seen or read, telling the bewildered members of the House that copies of the new "nationalist" Constitution would be found in their pigeonholes during the recess.[93] No questions were allowed by the Speaker, who said that there was nothing on which he could permit questions at that time.[94] An intimidated and anxious Assembly obliged and hurriedly passed the new Constitution without debate or cheer.[95]

The Speaker then suspended the sitting for a few minutes and, in a grossly legally flawed procedure, returned to dramatically administer oaths for the same members for their new positions as Members of Parliament under the new Constitution. Without an election under the new Constitution, it must have been presumed that no fresh election was desired or necessary.

The main features of Obote's "Pigeonhole" Constitution were: the abolition of the federal status of kingdoms; the abolition of the offices of the President and the Vice-President; the fusion of the office of Prime Minister with that of the President resulting in an all-powerful Executive President in Obote; and the declaration that Uganda was a Republic. The Kabaka and the kingdom of Buganda, which, in the absence of a strong opposition party in the country, appeared as the last bastion against Obote's rising dictatorship, refused to recognize the new Constitution, insisting on the legality of the 1962 Independence Constitution and challenging the illegality of Obote's actions in this connection. Accordingly, in a resolution of Saturday 16 April 1966, the Lukiiko rejected Obote's new Constitution, maintaining that the "Constitution that was made by the people of Uganda with their own consent is the only one that the Lukiiko supports."[96] Two days later, in an extraordinary session, it issued a strong statement opposing the abrogation of the 1962 Constitution and the abolition of the federal system of government, which was done in a way that not only rocked Buganda's power base and identity but also "fossilized" its institutions.[97]

The Lukiiko appealed to all the people in the rest of Uganda, the

United Nations, Britain, and the entire world to support Buganda on its firm stand. Despite their passionate pleas, no support whatsoever was forthcoming from these quarters. The reason for this inaction from abroad, at least in the reasoning of UN Secretary General U Thant, was that the developments in Uganda were internal affairs which did not constitute a threat to international peace and security and, as such, his organization would not interfere.[98] Britain also turned down Buganda's appeal.[99] At home, Buganda's pleas received no support from the rest of the country. This can be explained in two ways. Firstly, the rest of Uganda may have felt that Buganda had been historically privileged and continued to enjoy special status under the 1962 Constitution and, as such, needed to be cut down to size. Secondly, Obote's dramatic arrest of five ministers and his readiness to rely on violence and the army had intimidated the rest of the country into silence.

With the failure of diplomatic, legal and international measures to help resolve the constitutional crisis in Uganda, the desperate Lukiiko resorted to self-help and passed a resolution on 20 May 1966 condemning the abrogation of the 1962 Constitution and asking the Government of Uganda to remove itself from the soil of Buganda. Far from resolving the crisis, the Lukiiko resolution played into Obote's hands and offered him the opportune excuse to ignite a fire that left Buganda and Uganda deeply scarred.

On 23 May 1966, Obote declared a state of emergency over all of Buganda on the basis that, with the Kabaka's support, the Lukiiko had made an open declaration of rebellion.[100] On 24 May 1966 at about 5.30 pm, the Ugandan Army, under the command of Major General Idi Amin and acting on the orders of Obote, attacked the Kabaka's palace in Mengo.[101] The entire perimeter wall of the palace and neighbouring villages were surrounded by the Ugandan Army's Special Forces who were firing in the air, presumably to scare off any crowds that might have come to the Kabaka's rescue. Amin's soldiers rampaged inside the palace, shooting to kill anyone in sight. It is estimated that over 2,000 civilians were killed during the attack.[102] With a scene similar to Mwanga's battle with Lugard in Mengo, the palace grounds were once again a bloody battlefield. Although the Kabaka and his guards put up a brave resistance, they were overrun by Amin's forces.

The Kabaka was lucky to escape by scaling the palace wall, but many who remained in the palace were murdered. The carnage was so extensive that once the battle ended, it took four days to remove the dead bodies from the Lubiri. Once they took over the palace, the soldiers burnt houses, offices and the royal drums. Other soldiers went on a looting spree.

Members of the royal family—including the Nnabagereka Lady Damali (Mutesa's wife), Sarah Nalule Kabejja (the mother of Prince Ronald M. Mutebi who later became the Namasole), Nnaalinya Mpologoma (the Kabaka's sister) and his brother Prince Ssimbwa—were arrested and imprisoned at Luzira.[103] It is estimated that over 2,000 civilians were killed during the attack. No formal inquiry into the killings was commissioned by the government and no prosecutions were ever made in respect of the gross violations that were committed in the Lubiri and elsewhere in Buganda. As such, the cause, the cost and the roles of the individual actors in the execution of this infamy will never be known.

On 25 May 1966, Obote made a statement to the National Assembly justifying the attack on the Lubiri. He claimed that he had documentary evidence—which once again he did not produce—that the Kabaka had decided to mount a full-scale rebellion against the "authority and the oneness of Uganda."[104] He alleged that Mutesa's plan was, first, to appeal to African and other states to secure diplomatic recognition and moral support; second, to mobilise the Lukiiko to pass a resolution to promote a rebellion and the separation of Buganda from Uganda; and, third, to appeal to the Secretary General of the United Nations to support Buganda's rebellion.[105]

For this reason, Obote stated that he had empowered the security forces, under the Emergency Regulations to suppress all manner of lawlessness, intimidation, violence and hooliganism, to stamp out Mengo's rebellion. Obote told the Assembly that his security forces had "brought under their control an effective occupation of all the palaces" where "arms, ammunition and weapons of various makes and calibre were captured."[106] Without providing details on the arms found in the palaces, he claimed that he was "fully satisfied that persons in Mengo, including Sir Edward Mutesa, as their leader, [had] for a long time … been planning for an insurrection and for the control of Uganda as a whole."[107]

To him, that was reason enough to justify the government's full determination to bring under control "all the rebellious elements who [had] brought … misery to innocent people."[108] He wound up his fiery speech by saying he had no regrets because "the midwife of an old society, pregnant with a new one, is force. It is my view that Buganda is an old society pregnant with a new one."[109] Obote made no comment whatsoever on the deaths of hundreds of innocent people in the Lubiri, on the whereabouts or safety of former President Mutesa, on the wanton destruction and looting of the palace, or on the arrests and detention of many blameless others. As on the occasion when Obote introduced the Pigeonhole Constitution, the Speaker informed the House that there would be no permission for anyone to ask the President any questions. Thus, without any debate, the House was adjourned to allow its members to return home in time for the curfew!

Obote's explanations and his actions in abrogating the 1962 Constitution and the wanton attack on the Lubiri are often justified as having been a necessary pre-emptive measures not only to stop Mutesa's plans to overthrow his government, but also to put a problematic Buganda in its rightful place. G. W. Kanyeihamba has argued, for example, that while Obote's actions were unconstitutional, they were politically justified because many outside the kingdom areas felt the actions dealt a death blow to the feudal and traditional elements which had for long been a hindrance to the progress of the country."[110] To Kanyeihamba, Buganda's failure to contain Obote lay in the fact that it had no "foresighted leadership," and that

> its leadership was nothing more than an introvert [sic] oligarchic band of frightened men. The enlightened among themselves were caught in suspended indecision … and lacked the tactical ability to plan any political action.… [W]hile Obote appealed to the masses in the country, and his actions transcended tribal allegiances, the Buganda leadership did not look beyond the Buganda boundaries. Whereas the central government was united behind one man with one purpose, the Buganda leadership was completely divided as to what should be done.[111]

For all that they contain some valid points, Kanyeihamba's arguments cannot pass unchallenged. First of all, they help obfuscate Obote's reckless, violent, unconstitutional and dictatorial conduct. However problematic Buganda or Mutesa was to Uganda or to Obote, nothing could justify Obote's actions in tearing up the 1962 Constitution and killing so many people in his quest for power. Indeed, if Buganda or Mutesa were the problem, why did Obote unilaterally abolish the kingdoms of Toro, Bunyoro, Ankole and the Kyabazingaship of Busoga. What wrongs had the rulers in these kingdoms committed? Were they also guilty of the treasonous activities Mutesa was accused of?

If his concern was with President Mutesa, why did Obote not spare Sir W. Nadiope the Vice-President of Uganda?[112] Was Nadiope also guilty of the treasonous activities Mutesa was accused of? And why did Obote not challenge Mutesa's allegedly treasonous acts in the courts of law? The absence of substantive evidence, a commission of inquiry or a trial for the suspects severely undermines the credibility of Obote's claim to have acted altruistically on behalf of the people of Uganda.

Ironically, Obote accused Mutesa of having contacted foreign missions with requests to bring troops into the country without consulting him in an obvious a case of selective amnesia, since Obote himself had called in British troops to put down the army mutiny of 1964 without consulting President Mutesa.[113] These examples suggest that the real problem was not what Mutesa did or did not do. The tribally minded, dishonest and power-hungry Obote was prepared to destroy anyone who stood in his way to attain absolute power in Uganda. As we show below, Obote's scheming mindset was revealed in his conduct towards Mutesa when he was in exile in Britain between 1966 and 1969, but more revealingly in a public statement he made in Mbale, eastern Uganda, in 1967, where he boasted that he had "made Mutesa President of Uganda in order to trap and eventually destroy him."[114]

The second reason to challenge Kanyeihamba's views is that he unfairly attacks the Lukiiko in its fight to resist Obote's dictatorship. In fact, it was Mutesa and the Buganda Lukiiko that offered the final point of resistance when the rest of the country either looked on or cheered Obote as he mauled the 1962 Constitution. The Lukiiko's stance must be understood within the context of Obote's unconstitutional and dictatorial moves, starting with the suspension of the Constitution and the arrest and detention of his ministers, and ending with the unilateral move to dismiss Mutesa from the Presidency and abolish that office. The Lukiiko's resolutions, taking a stand against Obote and calling him to order, were heroic and indeed laudable in such a context.

Thirdly, Kanyeihamba does not attempt to explain why Obote did not take legal action against the Lukiiko or charge Mutesa with treason instead of arrogating himself the powerful role of witness, prosecutor, judge and executioner. Why, when he introduced the 1966 Constitution under threat of violence, did he not give Members of Parliament a chance to debate it? Why did he not allow the National Assembly to discuss his statement following the unauthorized attack on the Lubiri?

The legality of the Pigeonhole Constitution was challenged by Abu Mayanja in the controversial case of *Uganda v. Commissioner of Prisons ex-parte Matovu.*[115] Oddly enough, among the lawyers who defended Obote's actions were two of Buganda's leading legal minds at the time, namely, Godfrey L. Binaisa Q.C. and Peter James Nkambo-Mugerwa. The case was heard by Chief Justice Sir Udo Udoma (a Nigerian who had taken the oath of allegiance to the 1966 Constitution!) and two British Judges, Justice Sheridan and Justice Jeffrey Jones (who had not taken any such oath on the questionable 1966 Constitution).[116] The British High Commission in Kampala followed the case closely. In a letter on the topic, the High Commissioner stated that the British judges had been "unhappy for some time" about the legal validity of the 1966 Constitution, which "Obote introduced practically at gunpoint."[117] He feared, however, that any attempt by the British judges to question its validity in the *Matovu* case was likely to be an exercise in futility.[118] He summed up his fears thus

> I suppose this is inevitable when a coup is dressed up in pseudo parliamentary legal clothes to try and make it look respectable but, nevertheless, I think there may be doubts as to whether it is wise for the judges to force the issue in this way since, even if they rule that the 1966 Constitution is not legally valid, we shall only be in a position uncomfortably similar to that in Rhodesia where we have a *de facto* Constitution which is not *de jure.*[119]

In fact, the British Government was also aware that Nekyon, Obote's Acting Minister of Defence, had threatened the British judges in the *Matovu* case.[120] The High Commissioner reported that Justices Sheridan and Jones had received threatening letters from Nekyon—copied to President Obote—in which he stated that he "took exception to their making pronouncements on constitutional matters which were not directly concerned in the case they were hearing and that he intended to take some action to prevent similar situations arising in the future."[121] On 14 December 1966, even before the *Matovu* case was determined, Obote addressed the National Assembly confirming that he would not tolerate any questioning of the legal validity of the Constitution. He argued that there was a revolution in Uganda and the 1966 Constitution started an entirely new chapter in the constitutional development of Uganda.[122] The case was thus heard and determined in a context of intimidation and fear by its prosecutors and the members of the bench.

At the hearing of the *Matovu* case, the government adduced evidence in support of the "revolution." Its key witnesses were leading political personalities including Francis Kalimuzo, G. L Binaisa, W. Oryema, Okumu Lutara, V. A. Ovonji, David Oyite Ojok, Z. Bigirwenkya and Alfred Mubanda, all of whom swore affidavits stating that the people of Uganda had accepted the new Constitution. Obviously, they conveniently ignored the protests from the kingdom of Buganda against the new Constitution.

In reaching its verdict, the court sought refuge under the Kelsenian principle of law, and found that the "revolution" in Uganda between February and April 1966 had "destroyed the entire legal order that was superseded by the 1966 Constitution."[123] It further held that the 1962 Constitution had been deprived of its *de facto* and *de jure* validity.

Unsurprisingly, the court did not seriously inquire into, or pronounce any judgement on Obote's illegal actions in suspending the 1962 Constitution or his illegal introduction and adoption of the 1966 Constitution by the National Assembly. Thus, the *Matovu* case not only sealed the fate of the 1962 Constitution and all claims made under it but, by legalizing and legitimizing the use of force to overthrow an established constitutional order, it also set a bad precedent for constitutional law in Uganda.[124]

In comparative terms, Obote's heavy-handed and violent handling of this fabricated rebellion in Buganda went over and beyond anything the British had ever done in terms of suppressing dissent or rebellions in Uganda, particularly in 1945, 1949 and 1960.[125] Moreover, Obote's term of office, between 1962 and 1971, witnessed a breakdown in the rule of law and an increase in violations of human rights. With the controversial return of the lost counties from Buganda to Bunyoro, the abrogation of the 1962 Constitution, Obote's self-elevation and usurpation of all executive powers, the passing of a "nationalist" Constitution, the abolition of the federal system of government, the attack against the palace and the exiling of Mutesa, and the abolition and dismantling of the kingdom of Buganda (which was carved up into four separate districts),[126] Obote completed a grand scheme to break the back of his erstwhile allies, Mutesa and Buganda. From this point onwards, Obote's one-party and one-man rule in Uganda spiralled into an ever-darker void filled with violence, tyranny and despotism.

Choosing not to dabble in the internal affairs of its former colony, the British Government looked on as Obote ripped apart the 1962 constitutional order. Notwithstanding Obote's unconstitutional and violent conduct, Britain remained detached and indifferent. By not inquiring into the legality or morality of Obote's actions against the kingdom of Buganda, for example, Britain's official position was that the Kabaka's government "no longer existed in practice since neither the ministers nor the officials function and their offices remain closed."[127] It thus ceased to have any business with the kingdom or the people who "purported to speak or act on its behalf."[128]

No wonder it looked away and ignored petitions by the people of Buganda following Obote's coup.[129] It remained complicit working with Obote's regime as if it was business-as-usual—complicit because while it understood the illegality of Obote's Pigeonhole Constitution, it did little or nothing to keep him in check. This posture is aptly demonstrated by a memorandum by the British High Commissioner to the Rt Hon. George Thomson MP, stating:

> It is true that the 1966 Constitution, pushed through Parliament without warning and without debate, was little more than a fig-leaf for Dr Obote's February coup which forestalled the ambitions of five rebellious ministers and removed Sir Edward Mutesa from the Presidency.[130]

Clearly, Britain was armed with sufficient information but made no call to rein in Obote. Presumably, this was because at this stage British interests in Uganda were not under direct threat. Once this changed, Britain's attitude towards Obote transformed rather radically.

Harold Wilson, Britain's Labour Prime Minister took the view that his government would not interfere uninvited in the internal affairs of another Commonwealth country.[131] The Commonwealth Office took the view that after independence, the agreements between Her Majesty's Government and the kingdom of Buganda ceased to have effect, and that Britain could not be drawn into the politics of Uganda after that period. In a memorandum on the status of the Government of Buganda, the East African Department of the Commonwealth stated that "the government of Uganda [had] taken over the functions of the Kabaka's Government of Buganda and the latter [had] ceased to exist … there should now be no dealings with people purporting to speak or act for the Government of Buganda."[132] This position did not question the validity or the legality of Obote's actions in overthrowing a constitutional order that was negotiated and put in place by the same British Government, even when it had the means to do so.

Britain's stance must be seen as a broken pledge to the kingdom, which it coaxed to accept the 1962 Constitution and to join Uganda with promises that it would safeguard its interests as enshrined in the agreements reached at the constitutional and independence conferences in London. While Britain's postcolonial responsibility to Buganda is generally denied, there is documentary evidence that suggests the contrary. For example, on 7 February 1962, the Kabaka of Buganda wrote to the Colonial Secretary, Reginald Maudling, on the subject of Buganda's interests in Uganda after independence. Consistent with Britain's past pledges to Buganda on its post-independence protections, on 26 March 1962, acting through the Governor, the British Government wrote to the Kabaka and further reassured him thus:

> Buganda's security and interests are fully safeguarded for the period up to the general election, which are to be held on April 25th 1962 and *indeed beyond it.* I am confident that Your Highness and your government will faithfully perform the obligations which Buganda has undertaken in the Buganda Agreement 1961. Her Majesty's Government for their part will

> be scrupulous in the discharge of their own obligations under that agreement.[133]

However, when Obote abrogated the 1962 Constitution, attacked the Lubiri and abolished the kingdom of Buganda, Britain looked away. In spite of the fact that Buganda had complied with the Agreement of 1961 and the Constitution of 1962, Britain took no action to provide the protections it had promised and on the basis of which Buganda had accepted its incorporation into Uganda.

In view of the abovementioned pledges, and as the architects of the founding Constitution of Uganda, Britain owed Buganda a moral, if not a legal, responsibility to ensure that the agreements that were reached under its watch in the creation of Uganda were adhered to and that Uganda, as a member of the British Commonwealth, did not slide into tyrannical rule. As a bare minimum, given that Uganda was now an independent and sovereign country, Britain could have publically condemned the dictatorship and unconstitutional actions of Milton Obote and desisted from supporting his regime. The fact that it chose to focus more on its economic interests and to ignore the deteriorating political and constitutional situation of its former colony justifies the claim that Britain not only reneged on its promises, but also contributed to the political and economic disorder in post-independence Uganda.

Republicanism and Socialism in Obote's Uganda: The 1967 Constitution and the "Move to the Left"

Within less than a year of passing the Pigeonhole Constitution, Obote introduced proposals for yet another Constitution. The proposals called for the abolition of the kingdoms; abolition of the office of the Director for Public Prosecutions; abolition of the official Opposition; restructuring local government based on districts throughout the country; removing the constitutional requirement that the President needed to act on the advice of Cabinet; and bringing public service and local government service appointments directly under Presidential control. He also proposed to abolish the right to freedom from detention without trial; modify the constitutional provisions on freedom of assembly and association to allow for the introduction of a one party political system and control over trade unions; vest the control of the armed forces and appointments therein in the President; and reserve citizenship rights to persons of the African race. The proposals also sought to grant the President the power to nominate up to one third of the Members of Parliament and wide powers to declare and act in states of emergency.[134]

In presenting the proposals to the National Assembly, which, for the purpose of passing the 1967 Constitution, transformed itself into a Constituent Assembly, Obote claimed that their objective was to create unity, stability and prosperity in Uganda.[135] To justify these draconian proposals, he argued that Ugandans as a whole were as yet incapable of operating a full parliamentary democracy, and that the ancient petty kingdoms had to be abolished as a prerequisite to building an undivided loyalty to Uganda throughout the nation.[136] In defending Obote, the Minister of Defence, Felix Onama, said that the present state of emergency in Buganda was "just for convenience."[137] Onama reminded those who opposed the changes that they did so at risk of their lives; and, in reply to those who said that the President was being given enormous power, he retorted, "too much freedom was dangerous."[138]

The proposals for the new constitution were debated while Buganda was still under a state of emergency. It was also at a time when Buganda's king was still in exile in Britain and the Lukiiko was dispersed. The kingdom's land and properties were expropriated and placed under the control of the Uganda Land Commission, a government entity. As such, the kingdom was denied its principal source of income. Aside from a few lone voices in the National Assembly, such as that of Abu Mayanja,[139] and the voices of Mulira and Boniface Byanyima there was little advocacy for Buganda's or the other kingdoms' interests. When the Constituent Assembly passed the new Constitution on 8 September 1967, Buganda's fate was largely sealed. During the deliberations, Mayanja argued for the retention of Buganda as a separate entity, complete with its king.

In a private conversation with the British High Commissioner, Mayanja pointed out Obote's ruthlessness and the fact that even though he was the UPC's leader, he could not afford to preserve a democratic system on the Westminster model or to allow a semblance of democratic discussion within his own party.[140] Mayanja was not alone in opposing the proposals; others included Adoko Nekyon, C. J. Obwangor and Alexander Latim. However, as already indicated, in a House dominated by Obote's supporters, these voices were unable to turn the tide. For his critical position on the proposals, for example, Obwangor, the leader of government business, was immediately sacked by Obote.[141] And, for his audacious pro-Buganda speeches, Mayanja was expelled from the UPC.[142]

Unlike the situation in April 1966 when the Pigeonhole Constitution was passed, the proposals for the 1967 Republican Constitution were passed by the Constituent Assembly following a lengthy debate in the National Assembly. They were then passed on 8 September and all in the name of all the people of Uganda and generations yet unborn. All the government's amendments were accepted—including one that allowed it to stay in power indefinitely should it feel that there was any likelihood of its being overthrown.[143] All proposals from the opposition were rejected. The passing of the 1967 Constitution thus provided legal cover to Milton Obote's dictatorship.

The British Government followed the constitutional developments in Uganda between 1966 and 1967 closely. On 24 February 1966, Arthur Bottomley, the British Secretary of State for Commonwealth Relations, informed the Cabinet of the coup in which Obote had arrogated to himself most, if not all, of the powers previously exercised by the President. He informed the Cabinet of the chaotic political situation in Uganda and of the occurrence of a military coup in Ghana.[144] However, the Cabinet did not show any interest in these matters. It simply "took note" of the statement before moving on, subsequently spending considerable time on a draft White Paper on *Leisure in the Countryside: England and Wales*.[145] For its part, the British House of Lords was generally concerned, following the attack on the Lubiri, about the safety of British subjects and property in Uganda, and particularly about an incident in which two young British surveyors lost their lives.[146] The House made no comment on the hundreds of Ugandans who had died in the Lubiri and elsewhere at the hands of Obote's soldiers or on the violent, unconstitutional actions of his regime.

By December 1966, the British Government was aware that Obote sought to promulgate another constitution that would "suit Uganda better than the Westminster type arrangements bequeathed by Britain," and that he "intended to stay in power as long as he possibly [could] and [had] no intention of seeking any fresh mandate from the electorate for a long time to come."[147] Indeed, when the new Constitution was adopted in 1967, the British High Commissioner put London on notice, describing the Constitution to be "of the strong presidential kind," because, as he explained, "it provides cover for any action which the present incumbent may care to take and it entrenches him and his party in power as far ahead as can be foreseen."[148] Yet, in technical spite of the fact that Britain fully knew about Obote's despotic rule, it offered him and the country more support in the form of financial aid and assistance. The figures for the amount of overseas aid provided by Britain to Uganda between 1963 and 1968 are as follows:[149]

Year	Amount (£)
1963–64	5.5 million
1964–65	4.4 million

1965–66	4.5 million
1966–67	5.7 million
1967–68	3.6 million

The above figures exclude aid to East African regional organizations. They show that Obote's regime received the most British support in the period his army attacked the Lubiri and when he abrogated the 1962 Constitution. When quizzed over why Britain supported the regime in the face of such an atrocious record, the government responded: "we provide aid for economic and social development and it is not possible, nor, we believe, sensible to attempt to turn it off and on like a tap according to particular political developments within a country."[150] In this regard, it can be said that, notwithstanding its charity, the advancement of democracy and the promotion of human rights in its former colonies was not as important to the British Government as the pursuit of its commercial and other strategic interests.

The destruction of Buganda, together with the kingdoms of Toro, Bunyoro, Ankole and the territory of Busoga, was completed with the adoption of the 1967 Constitution. The move, which was essentially spearheaded by Obote, was mostly supported by politicians from the non-kingdom areas of Uganda, although some prominent former Kabaka Yekka politicians who had earlier crossed the floor also joined in.[151] Neither the leadership of the vanquished kingdoms nor the people therein were consulted before the abolition of their traditional institutions. On this matter, Obote's statement to the National Assembly is quite telling. He claimed that his introduction of the Pigeonhole Constitution followed "wide and extensive consultations" with a "large number" of the people of Uganda.[152] Yet, in the same breath, he said:

> I regret however that from one government it was not possible for me to get their views, that is, the Buganda Government. Perhaps some people one day will say that I did not try, but let me say that this is double edged. If I did not try, the question is that did they try? .... Time has, therefore, now come when we must think very seriously as to how we are going to move ahead, and let me say this to the country: it is simply not possible to do what the Buganda Lukiiko wants. It is simply not possible to do what Sir Edward wants; it is not possible for us to go back and restore the Constitution and restore the position of Presidency to someone who in ordinary language actually committed treason against Uganda; it is simply not possible and we shall stand firm on that ground.[153]

Clearly Obote's mind was made up about entrenching his authority and he was not going to allow himself to be bothered or impeded by consultations with Buganda or anyone else. To consolidate his new power and dictatorship, Obote relied on draconian colonial laws—particularly the Habitual Criminals (Preventive Detention) Act, 1951 and the Emergency Powers Act, 1968. These laws allowed him to detain without trial any person he perceived to be his critic and to keep the whole of Buganda Kingdom under emergency conditions from 1966 until he was overthrown in 1971.

The events of 1966 marked a watershed in both Buganda's and Uganda's political history. For Buganda, the 1966 and 1967 Constitutions were the first major constitutional instruments affecting it that it did not negotiate. This was unlike the situation in 1900, 1955 and 1961 when it concluded agreements with the British, or the making of the 1962 Constitution. Starting from 1966, the position and power of the kingdom of Buganda, as it was historically known, was effectively undermined in Uganda's realpolitik and constitutional discourse.

Indeed, in all subsequent constitutional developments in Uganda, such as the Constituent Assembly of 1993 which negotiated and promulgated the 1995 Constitution, Buganda and the other former kingdoms had no official role and gave no input.[154] This is also true for all subsequent amendments of the Constitution, the only exception being the rather *ad hoc* engagements Buganda had with President Museveni and some government officials that resulted in the Regional Governments law during the Constitutional amendments of 2005.

Given its struggles to survive British colonialism, as well as to secure its place in an independent Uganda, the fate of Buganda kingdom in postcolonial Uganda could not have been more incongruous. D. A. Low captures the irony of this when he observes that "no part of the country had done more to secure its African character against the slings and arrows of the colonial period than Buganda. In the end however, it was the African government that brought it to independence which clove its heart."[155] With the passing of the 1967 Constitution, therefore, Obote's hand was further strengthened to handle Buganda and Uganda as a whole as he pleased. Having weakened the political opposition in the National Assembly between 1962 and 1967, as we show below, Obote later declared Uganda a one-party state and adopted a quasi-socialist manifesto (akin to Julius Nyerere's *Ujaama* or the Arusha Declaration in Tanzania) called the Common Man's Charter under a shift in ideological posture described as the Move-to-the-Left.[156] Suffice to say that none of these political manoeuvres secured unity, stability or prosperity in Uganda.

Mutesa's Struggle against Obote and the British Establishment between 1966 and 1969

When Edward Mutesa, the Kabaka of Buganda and the first President of Uganda, jumped the high perimeter wall of his palace, the Lubiri, in Mengo to escape the killers sent by Obote, he did not know what lay in store for him. Entirely ill-prepared, and accompanied by two ex-police personal guards, Aide-de-Camp George Mallo and Captain Jehoasti Katende, Mutesa began a fateful run from Obote, who had issued orders to his troops for his capture dead or alive.[157] Soldiers in Land Rovers and spotter planes were deployed to hunt him down. Roadblocks were erected everywhere. However, Mutesa, without funds, using false names and disguised in an oversized macintosh, managed to elude them.

The escapees took the western route out of the country and for almost four weeks walked long distances at night through the bush towards the Uganda-Congo border.[158] They spent most days in thickets to avoid their pursuers. Sometimes they hitched rides from strangers. But along the way they met friendly people, including the Catholic White Fathers at Rubaga, who were helpful with food and directions.[159] When they arrived at the Congolese border, they were held by the Congolese army for a night but later released without charge.[160] They then trekked through Goma and Bukavu to the Burundi border. Using fake travel documents, they managed to enter Burundi without incident.

Then followed the problem of the Kabaka's arrival in Burundi and his departure from the country. From the Congolese border, Mutesa and his party arrived in Bujumbura by car on Sunday 19 June 1966 and checked into the Paguidas Hotel.[161] The Government of Burundi, where Mutesa was acquainted with the royal family,[162] and J. S. Bennett, the British High Commissioner were receptive to the fugitives. For the first time in a month, the exhausted, hungry and anxious men looking like "filthy vagabonds" were given a kind welcome, a house and lunch with High Commissioner J. S. Bennett and his wife.[163] In a note on the details of Mutesa's arrival and stay in Burundi and his departure to Britain, Bennett said:

> The Kabaka quickly asked that he and his two aides, Mallo and Katende, should be allowed to go to England as soon as possible…. Sir Frederick was clearly edgy, did not eat anything and said he was suffering from fever. This may have been true. On the other hand, he may have been suffering from a fair intake of gin.[164]

Mutesa, recalling the time, wrote that besides the constant doses of gin and tonic he actually had a "fever and a temperature and felt a very sick man."[165] The High Commissioner made arrangements for the Kabaka to fly to the UK and blocked three seats on the Sabena Flight SN 526 via Brussels. But the flight had to refuel in Cairo, where the Kabaka could have been deplaned and detained as a fugitive. On the other hand, it was not safe to fly via Nairobi or Léopoldville for similar reasons. Left with no options, the High Commissioner and Mutesa were in a fix, because while the Government of Burundi was providing "as good an umbrella as possible"[166] for Mutesa, it was also anxious to get Mutesa and his aides out of the country as soon as possible. This was in order to avoid a diplomatic imbroglio with Obote who, having received the news of Mutesa's presence in Burundi, was already plotting for his repatriation to Uganda to answer for the "serious criminal offences" committed before he "abdicated his position in Buganda and escaped from Uganda."[167]

However, in a rather dramatic turn of events, a "modest" but safe means to Brussels was made available. According to Bennett,

> suddenly out of the blue, during Wednesday 23 June, an American aircraft, with an American crew on charter to Sabena, arrived here from London carrying 13 tons of Lee Enfield rifles. The aircraft was scheduled to return direct to Brussels the following day. This offered us a unique opportunity for moving the party out. Since the aircraft was a freighter it was up to the pilot to decide whether he would carry passengers. At first he said he would take only one passenger as there were no seats, but eventually he was prepared to take all three.[168]

The compromise on the part of the pilot was influenced by the Kabaka's insistence that he could not leave Bujumbura without his two aides. Since there were no seats on the plane, the two aides had to be strapped firmly down in the two toilets and the Kabaka was strapped to the floor for take-off for a flight whose estimated flying time was 13½ hours.[169]

In a friendly and charitable gesture, the British Home Secretary authorised the issue of an entry certificate to the Kabaka as a Commonwealth citizen and thus helped him and his aides to escape the claws of Obote's government.[170] With the Kabaka's guarantees for repayment, as well as undertakings from individuals such as Lord Montagu, Colin Tenant, George Drew and Fredrick Mpanga,[171] arrangements were made for their air tickets, maintenance and reservations in London. The Kabaka mentioned that he could obtain assurances about his finances from Lord Boyd, Anthony Tuke, Lord de la Warr and Sir Dingle Foot.[172] With these assurances, sufficient money was availed through the British High Commissioner in Burundi to pay his hotel bills in Bujumbura. Other British friends, such as

Captain Owen and the solicitor Martin Flegg, were prepared to fly over to join the Kabaka in Bujumbura, but the Kabaka discouraged them, as he considered it unsafe for them to attempt to join him in Burundi.[173]

Since the new exiles had no Belgian visas, the British High Commission was on standby to help and to organise the onward journey from Brussels to London.[174] The Kabaka (under the name of Edward Walugembe) and the two aides were issued with *laissez-passer* visas for the UK and with letters of identification for the UK immigration authorities by the Burundi authorities. Britain's assistance to the Kabaka was made behind the back of Obote's government. The British High Commissioner in Kampala was understandably concerned that Obote should not come to hear about the support given to Mutesa and his party in Burundi. He therefore advised London that the line to be taken with Obote's government was that Mutesa was admitted as a private citizen on humanitarian grounds, and that his entry was conditional upon refraining from political activity in Britain.[175] Thus, the Government of Uganda was only informed once the Kabaka's plane was nearing London, and in the following terms: "Her Majesty's Government saw no grounds for refusing admission given that the Kabaka was able to comply with the normal immigration requirements for commonwealth countries."[176]

Obote and Britain's Handling of Mutesa's Finances and Maintenance in the UK

Upon arrival in England, following their successful escape from Obote's men, Mutesa and his party were now faced with new problems.[177] They were penniless and, far from the grandeur of the royal palaces and the splendour of State House in Uganda, the trio had to put up with a tiny one-bedroom flat offered by a friend, Major Richard Carr-Gomm, in Bermondsey.[178] Other friends, including Lord Boyd of Menton, Ronnie Owen and Martin Flegg, set up a small trust for Mutesa's upkeep.[179]

To make ends meet, Mutesa sought employment in the British Army, where he was a Colonel with the Grenadier Guards. However, mostly for political reasons, the Labour government declined his request. According to the British Ministry of Social Security, no "suitable" employment was available for Mutesa except "if he undertook agricultural or forestry training."[180] Mutesa was not happy with this suggestion. In any case, the British bureaucrats regarded the Mutesa employment as a "dubious prospect."[181] Given that he was unemployed, the British Government put him on unemployment benefits of £8, 1s a week and £7, 6s a week for Katende, his guard. Mallo managed to secure some employment. As a recipient of government benefits, Mutesa was required to declare any gifts donated by his friends, including birthday presents, to the British Government. His request for a pension from the civil contingency fund was turned down.

Living off the dole (as unemployment benefits are colloquially known in the UK) was debilitating for the ex-Kabaka. He and Katende mostly survived on a diet of tea and biscuits. In the circumstances, he relied on the kindness of his friends to pay school fees for his children. His dire condition was exacerbated by the fact that even though he had secured asylum in the UK, he remained a fugitive: on the run from Obote and living in fear for his life. He constantly feared abduction by Obote's Secret Service and/or repatriation to Uganda. According to Lord Boyd, his close friend and benefactor, Mutesa's situation was pathetic, he suffered from delusions and sometimes seemed to be nearing a mental break down.[182]

Britain's goodwill towards Mutesa appeared to have started and ended at granting him asylum. Its relationship with him thereafter was shabby. In dealing with the "Mutesa problem," as the British bureaucrats called it, Britain's Labourite government offered little to help alleviate the wretched life of an erstwhile knighted ally and a leader of one of its best former colonies. Sadly, he was caught up in the middle of political rivalry between his mostly Conservative friends and the bigwigs of the Labour Party in power at the time.[183]

As far as Anglo-Ugandan relations were concerned, Mutesa's arrival in the UK created a diplomatic nightmare. On the one hand, the Labour government did not wish to annoy Obote's government, while on the other, it was under immense pressure from Mutesa's influential Tory friends to take good care of him. Britain understood that President Obote was extremely sensitive on the question of Mutesa and his family. It therefore tried to avoid any action that could conceivably be construed as support for the exiled king. P. M. Foster, the British High Commissioner in Uganda, wrote that on matters concerning Mutesa, Obote's "emotions [were] strongly engaged and his behaviour [tended] to be irrational."[184]

To keep the Uganda Government at bay, Britain treated Mutesa as a private citizen, not as a political refugee. It gave him no more financial assistance than it would any other "destitute resident" and refused to have any official dealings with him. Prime Minister Harold Wilson believed that "any overt grant to the Kabaka could be politically embarrassing."[185] While the Prime Minister pondered discreet support from "secret funds," this idea was rejected because his bureaucrats felt that Her Majesty's Government had "no moral or legal obligation to assist Mutesa."[186] According to this source, it was not easy to see what political interest would be advanced by rescuing the Kabaka from poverty. It was also felt that while the risks of detection would be slight, there was just a possibility that the Ugandans might guess the truth and that this would seriously damage relations with them.[187]

In any case, British officials considered that it would be injudicious to impose any risk, no matter how slight, on the whole complex of relations with the Ugandan Government just because of the impecuniousness of an individual.[188] The Secretary of State argued that Britain could not give any support to Mutesa because it seemed doubtful whether Mutesa would return to Uganda and Her Majesty's Government might be faced with an open-ended commitment lasting up to 40 years.[189] In any event, it was felt that Mutesa's friends, who were only too anxious to promise financial support to enable him get into the UK, should bear the burden of his finances, and that the British Government should not take over the responsibility. Britain's position on Mutesa is best captured by R. G. Tallboys of the Commonwealth Office:

> If we are ever going to be rid of the Mutesa problem, other than simply waiting for him to go away, there are two lines of approach we should adopt. One is to use his friends and sympathisers in this country as a channel for putting heavier pressure on Mutesa to accept the Uganda conditions, rather than having these friends serve as their main purpose to channel to us tales of woe about Mutesa's circumstances. The situation is: (a) His family have been generously treated by the Uganda Government; (b) He has been given assistance by Her Majesty's Government in the form of social benefits; (c) He has assets in Uganda that can be sold; (d) He can almost certainly obtain access to the proceeds, or some of the proceeds, of these assets if he accepts the reality of political conditions in Uganda; (e) There is no case whatever for Her Majesty's Government to do more for him than has and is being done. The second thing is, without waiting for Mutesa to agree to the Uganda conditions, to encourage the realisation of his land in Uganda.... I am writing to Peter Foster suggesting that Mutesa's land should be sold without waiting for prior approval to the effect that the proceeds can be transferred.... Once there is cash in the bank it may be easier to get both Mutesa's agreement to Obote's conditions and/or to get Obote to agree to remission of some of the money—even if only interest earned. Mutesa is not a destitute in the sense that he has no assets—his financial difficulties here are no more than the cost of his personal vanity and pride.[190]

The Ugandan Government's position on Mutesa—and that of Obote in particular—was always clear.[191] The official line was that Mutesa was a wanted man who had abdicated his throne after causing all the political and constitutional chaos in Uganda. He was a criminal on the run. He thus needed to be found, arrested and charged. Furthermore, he needed to concede to the changes brought about under Obote's 1966 "revolution." For this reason, Mutesa needed to be starved of funds so that he succumbed and acknowledged—either privately or publically—the established state of affairs in Uganda. When the British Government raised the subject of Mutesa's finances with Obote, he reacted violently and indicated it was a subject he would prefer not to discuss.[192]

Sam Odaka, Uganda's then Minister of Foreign Affairs, set the conditions for the amelioration of Mutesa's plight. He declared that the Government of Uganda was prepared to consider any proposal to remit funds from Mutesa's assets in Uganda to England, but that such consideration was dependent on Mutesa providing "definite and unequivocal proof that he accepts the changes that have taken place in Uganda, the 1967 Constitution, and the authority of the present government."[193] To make him surrender, Obote left nothing to chance in ensuring that Mutesa was rendered destitute. For example, he actively followed his finances to ensure that the former Kabaka had no access to funds from Uganda. On one occasion, he summoned a Standard Bank official and asked him if he could shed light on the possibility of funds being passed from Uganda to Mutesa. The discussion, at which Obote was described to have been pleasant and amiable, lasted two hours, but the bank official explained that he was unable to help the President on this question.[194]

On another occasion, Obote twice summoned the local manager of Barclays Bank, Mr Woodcock, to establish that the Kabaka had no funds. The bank official confirmed that there was no money available to Mutesa. Despite this, in a meeting Obote held with the British Commonwealth Secretary, he pretended that he did not know whether "the income from the private estates was reaching Mutesa" and also that "the government had done nothing to impede the transfer of money to Britain."[195] In the meeting, Obote ridiculed the idea that Mutesa might be capable of working to earn a living, saying that he had never worked in his life and even if he got a job he would probably be sacked on the first day.[196]

In the meantime, Sam Odaka discussed with the British High Commissioner the possibility of Mutesa's land and property being sold by his sister Princess Victoria Mpologoma. However, as the High Commissioner saw it, even if the land was sold, there was "no reason to think that the Uganda Government [would] allow Mutesa to receive these moneys without paying the political price or eating a full measure of humble pie."[197] In a letter to British State Minister, George Thomson, Sam Odaka reiterated the Ugandan Government's position on Mutesa and his funds: he could access them if he gave definitive and unequivocal proof that he accepted the changes that had taken place in Uganda, the 1967 Constitution and the authority of the present government. "It is on this condition that we, on our part, could consider any proposals he may make concerning the disposal of his property in Uganda and the remittance of the proceeds to him."[198]

Mutesa was caught up in a problematic political and financial maze involving a hostile government and an indifferent one. While Britain's agenda was more obscure than Obote's, it was equally uncharitable. In spite of his plight, some British bureaucrats felt that the government was handling Mutesa with "kid gloves" and that he needed to be told the facts of life. Nevertheless, alongside the Uganda Government, the British High Commission in Kampala maintained an intense search for Mutesa's assets in Uganda.[199] The British High Commissioner hoped that the assets could be sold and the proceeds sent to Mutesa to "keep the wolves away from his door for at least a few months" and, perhaps, more importantly, that Mutesa could cease being a dependant on the British Social Security fund.[200]

Yet in his efforts and hopes, the British High Commissioner was aware that Obote would not let Mutesa access his funds or assets in Uganda unless he abdicated and renounced his official status in Buganda and in Uganda. It was from this perspective that he urged Mutesa, through Lord Boyd, to abdicate so as to secure some reprieve and access to his funds. In this respect, the High Commissioner informed Lord Boyd:

> it should be possible to secure some kind of effective undertaking from the Ugandan Government in exchange for a renunciation of his throne by the ex Kabaka... [I]f he signed a renunciation immediately, this would have some advantage.... [W]ith regard to abdication, it might not be necessary for Mutesa to do more than renounce his own personal interest in the Kabakaship. He could perhaps, for instance, nominate one of his sons as Kabaka-designate, indicating that he was not claiming the throne for him at the present time.... [I]t should not be impossible to reach some kind of effective bargain with the Ugandan Government whereby certain funds would be remitted immediately in exchange for a public statement by Mutesa.[201]

Thus, as Obote pushed Mutesa to the wall to force him to accept the changes in Uganda, the British Government played along and pressured Mutesa to accept these conditions, in disregard of their illegality, immorality or even implications on the historic relationship it had with the kingdom and the people of Buganda. The Baganda were able to see through this, although they could do little because of the fear instilled in them by the emergency laws and Obote's brutal terror regime in Buganda. However, in a brave open letter to the British Prime Minister, dated 21 May 1968, Baganda students in the UK, including Yusuf Nsambu, Joseph Male, M. Nansamba and S. Nansamba, protested the actions of Obote and the British Government. They criticised the British Government for joining hands with the Ugandan authorities in "holding the Kabaka as a hostage until His Highness surrenders"[202]

To complete the humiliation of Mutesa and the Baganda, Obote converted the Kabaka's palace at Mengo into an army barracks. He took over the former Lukiiko building (Buganda's parliament) and made it his new army headquarters. The palace grounds were later to become one of Uganda's most notorious killing fields and torture chambers. Many people, including Abu Mayanja (the former pro-Buganda UPC member) and Prince David Ssimbwa (the Kabaka's brother) were detained without trial.[203]

However, and in spite of the immense difficulties that Mutesa suffered at the hands of his British hosts and Obote, he did not relent or abdicate. Much to their chagrin, Mutesa refused to make the declaration which would have enabled the Uganda Government to permit the transfer of some of his assets to Britain. Mutesa did not seem to be especially concerned about his own plight and gave the British Government the impression that he was lethargic and complacent. Writing in his book, about Obote, he said that Obote was

> behaving much as the British did when they exiled me, and making the same mistakes, though he has added violence and chaos. The army rules ... but just as I was supported by my faith in the loyalty of my people in the dark years of exile, now I believe utterly that the Baganda will show their devotion, though it demands great courage and perseverance. In the end I shall return to the land of my fathers and to my people.[204]

Clearly, in his perseverance Mutesa was inspired by the faith he had in his people. Sadly, he did not return to Uganda alive.

Mutesa's Mysterious Death and Contentious Burial in Britain

Mutesa died suddenly in his London flat on 21 November 1969—a day before he was to attend his 45th birthday party, organised by his friends. According to the post-mortem report, the cause of death was "acute alcohol poisoning." The report's chemical analysis revealed high levels of alcohol present in the specimens examined. His blood was found to contain 408 mg of ethanol per 100ml; the blood in his liver was found to contain 302 mg of ethanol per 100ml.[205] An inquest into the sudden death was conducted by a coroner who, based on the evidence of Henry Dowswell (Detective Sergeant of the Metropolitan Police attached to Southwark Police Station), Jehoasti Katende (bodyguard and servant of the deceased) and Dr Hugh Robert Molesworth Johnson (a pathologist at the London Hospital), concurred that Mutesa died from acute alcohol poisoning.[206]

At the inquest, Detective Dowswell testified that Mutesa had collapsed around 8.30 pm and that he found his lifeless body at about 12.50 am. He found no marks of violence; there were no suspicious circumstances; there were no tablets or other form of drugs or any letters or bottles of drink. He also said:

> As a result of the collapse a call was made to a Doctor Rosser, who was the Kabaka's doctor … [but] he was not available. It was not wished that the collapsed man should be put into an ambulance. At about midnight a doctor arrived and certified life extinct.[207]

Katende testified that the Kabaka's general health had been quite good over the past three years. He could not tell whether the Kabaka was drinking heavily on the day he died. He told the Coroner that he did not know if there were any bottles there or if any had been cleared away. He added that the Kabaka had been drinking dry wine on that day and not spirits.[208]

Ms P. Seymour, who attended the inquest on behalf of Her Majesty's Government, reported that Katende, who arrived and left under the escort of one plain-clothed and two uniformed police men, had difficulty in answering the coroner's questions, particularly on who had cleared away the bottles which must have been in the flat at the time of the Kabaka's death.[209] Dr Johnson, who arrived at the flat around midnight, some three-and-a-half hours after Mutesa had collapsed, testified that he had conducted a post-mortem and found that Mutesa's organs, apart from the congested lungs, were perfectly normal. The only and significant finding was the presence of alcohol, in huge quantities, in the body. He told the coroner: "a blood level of 408 milligrams of ethanol, a urine figure of 444 milligrams of ethanol, and liver blood of 302 milligrams ethanol … in my view he has died of acute alcohol poisoning.… [F]igures of over 350 milligrams in the blood are said to be lethal."[210] The Ugandan Government was represented at the inquest by a European solicitor, who said he was instructed to express condolences to the widow and to reiterate the Uganda Government's offer to assist with the repatriation of the body, as was usual in cases of Ugandan citizens who died abroad.

Based on the records of the inquest, it is curious that the lead counsel at the inquest did not ask any questions whatsoever of the above witnesses, yet it seemed anomalous that, for example, Mutesa remained unattended by any doctor from 8.30pm when he collapsed until midnight when his doctor showed up. It is also curious that he was not taken to a nearby hospital in an ambulance. Equally odd is that in a one-room flat there was no evidence of empty bottles of alcohol, if so much alcohol had been consumed by the deceased. The counsel should have been interested to find out more about the disappearance of the empty bottles. If not Katende, then who else would have cleared away the bottles? When were they cleared, why and to where?

It is known that on that fateful day and the days preceding it, Mutesa met and talked to several people, including his daughter, Sarah Kagere Mutesa.[211] A journalist from the *Daily Telegraph* reported that the Kabaka entertained ten guests in his flat on his birthday, on Wednesday 19 November 1969, two days before he collapsed.[212] They had four bottles of wine and two bottles of brandy. On Thursday night, he dined with Major Carr-Gomm and other guests and they drank a little.[213] According to this journalist, the people he interviewed who had spoken to the Kabaka in his last days said that he was cheerful and not intoxicated. And the journalist's own evidence at the time suggested that the Kabaka was not a "morose or secret drinker."[214]

Another British journalist, John Simpson, was sceptical of the alleged cause of Mutesa's death.[215] He had interviewed Mutesa in his flat only a few hours before his death, and found him sober and in good spirits. Although Simpson reported this to the police the following day, this line of inquiry was not pursued. He wrote: "I tried to tell the British police my story and even though I was the last person to see him they didn't seem to want to interview me, which I have always found very strange and rather disturbing."[216]

It is curious, therefore, that neither of these two journalists were summoned to the inquest to testify about Mutesa's state of health over those last few days. Because the inquiry left a number of questions hanging, many people were left suspicious of the real cause of Mutesa's death, despite the coroner's verdict. Remarkably some British officials, including former Governor John Hall, speculated that he committed suicide[217] while others believed that he was poisoned.[218] Among them, rather extraordinarily, was General Idi Amin himself, who stated that

Obote arranged for Mutesa to be poisoned in London.[219]

Many of the Baganda in London, particularly those who were planning to attend the Kabaka's birthday party on Saturday 21 November, were in a state of shock on the sudden news of his death. Some believed that Mutesa was assassinated using poison administered by a female, suspected to be Obote's agent, who was reported to the British police to have shown a keen interest in getting to know the Kabaka closely.[220] The coroner did not question this girl. In fact, the British police advised her to change her address in order to avoid angry telephone calls from the Kabaka's followers.[221]

These developments added to the suspicions and wild rumours about the real cause of Mutesa's death, both in the UK and in Uganda. Due to the way the British police acted with respect to the female suspect, as well as the gaps left in the inquest, many felt that the coroner's findings did not stand up to scrutiny, especially given the lack of evidence that Mutesa had ingested excessive amounts of alcohol in the preceding days, or on the day of his death. According to the opinion of a specialist on alcohol poisoning cited in *The Telegraph*, the pathologist's findings of 408 mg/dL of ethanol in the blood could indeed have caused death, although it is always difficult to say exactly how much alcohol is required to kill a person. According to him, blood alcohol levels of 408 mg/dL "represents three quarters of a bottle of brandy absorbed in the body or the amount of alcohol that there would be in three bottles of white wine."[222] And according to this specialist, "to absorb that amount, the deceased would have to drink considerably more than that, as the body rids itself of some. The fact that the blood contained only 10% less alcohol than that found in the stomach suggests that the alcohol had been taken over a period."[223]

Speculation of death by poisoning was heightened by the fact that after the coroner had entered a verdict, the Government of Uganda dispatched its own Special Branch detectives to London to make inquiries concerning the death of Mutesa.[224] It is difficult to reconcile the Ugandan Government's sudden apparent concern over Mutesa's demise with its previous attacks on him.

On the day following his death, the Uganda Government, under the direction of President Obote, issued a statement saying that it had instructed its High Commission in London to make immediate arrangements for the return of Mutesa's body to Uganda for burial. The High Commission was also tasked with finding out from the British authorities the cause of Mutesa's death. It sent messages of condolence to Mutesa's widow, Lady Damali, offering to take charge of the funeral arrangements.[225] It stated that it would allow Mutesa's family to select any place, including Kasubi, the ancestral burial ground of the Kabakas, for burial. It also announced the release of Mutesa's sister, Princess Victoria.[226]

The British Government also had a real interest in seeing Mutesa's body quickly returned to Uganda, in order to deal once and for all with the "old irrational suspicion on the part of Obote's government that [the British were] somehow involved in backing the Baganda and Mutesa's family."[227] For this reason, it asked Lord Boyd to use his influence with Lady Damali to persuade her that burial in Uganda would be the wisest course.

However, in spite of the Uganda Government's latest magnanimity and overtures and the covert coaxing by the British Government following Mutesa's death, the Kabaka's family, along with certain Baganda officials (led by F. Mpanga and J. Mayanja Nkangi) and other friends had different ideas. They feared that the Ugandan Government would not only refuse to allow a proper burial ceremony to be conducted, but that it might subject Mutesa's body to a trial for his alleged misdeeds in life. They thus chose to bury the body in Britain, as they felt the conditions for a proper funeral did not exist in Buganda, which was still under a state of emergency.[228] Like Obote's government, British High Commissioner Webber-Smith was obviously disappointed with this decision. Writing to R. M. Purcell of the Foreign and Commonwealth Office, he stated: "clearly the capacity of the Baganda for self-delusion is almost limitless, though one can understand why they are unwilling to expect any good of Obote's regime."[229]

A delicate balancing act had to be achieved regarding the representation of Her Majesty's Government at Mutesa's funeral. On the one hand, the British Government did not want to annoy Obote's government, which had sent a formal note saying they would regard it as an unfriendly act if Mutesa were given a funeral "with full military Honours."[230] On the other hand, it wanted to give Mutesa, his family and friends some respect and representation that would help dispel criticism that it had snubbed him even in death. Moreover, the British Government feared that it would come under more fire for failing to make suitable financial provisions from public funds if they did not show up at all at the funeral.[231] The British High Commissioner in Kampala had other more general and personal fears. He could not rule out either deliberate action by Obote's government against British interests in Uganda such as the Murchison hydroelectric scheme, or a demand for his recall![232]

The Government of Uganda was categorical on the question of its representation at Mutesa's funeral. Through Akena Adoko, it took great exception to reports that Mutesa would be buried in London with full military honours[233] and told the British Government that if the reports were true, it would be regarded as "an unfriendly act incompatible with the relationship between two Commonwealth countries."[234]

In that connection, Akena Adoko added that the British press' use of the title of "Kabaka" in referring to Mutesa, and their use of former titles of Baganda ministers in London was also greatly resented."[235] In a letter to the British High Commissioner, Foreign Affairs Minister Sam Odaka not only objected to the formal representation of Her Majesty the Queen or members of the British Government at the funeral, but also stated that his government would not be represented at the funeral, which it considered to be a private affair.[236]

In addressing the British Government on the matter, the Government of Uganda stated:

> The Government of the Republic of Uganda has been informed through reports reaching it that Sir Edward Mutesa, who died in London last week, is to be buried next Wednesday, 3 December 1969, at Kensal Green with full military honours preceded by a service in the Guards' Chapel at Wellington Barracks. It has also been indicated that this would be so because he was an Honorary Lieutenant Colonel of the Grenadier Guards.
>
> The Government of the Republic of Uganda views this report with great consternation and does not see how the late Sir Edward could possibly have claim to a burial with "Full Military Honours" as reported. Sir Edward was conferred with the honorary title of Lieutenant Colonel of the Grenadier Guards when he was Kabaka of Buganda.
>
> As Her Majesty's Government is well-aware, the institution of Kabakaship ceased to exist in Uganda in 1966, and Sir Edward was no longer Kabaka at the time of his death. It is difficult to believe that Her Majesty's Government can allow forces serving under the Crown to accord "Full Military Honours" at the funeral of a private individual who no longer has any claim whatsoever to such honours. It is equally difficult to imagine that Her Majesty's Government can be blind to the provisions of the Constitution of the Republic of Uganda and to facts, and put itself on [sic] a position where its actions would be construed to mean that it still recognises institutions that have ceased to exist and personalities that symbolised those defunct institutions. The Government of the Republic of Uganda views the implication of this with great exception.
>
> If the report given above is correct, and Her Majesty's Government accords the said "Full Military Honours" at the funeral, the Government of the Republic of Uganda will take it as an unfriendly act and reserves its position to take any necessary measures to re-assert the image of Uganda to Her Majesty's Government and the British public.[237]

Such was the anxiety and seriousness that the Ugandan Government attached to the possibility of Mutesa being accorded a funeral with full military honours, it was said that Uganda's ministers were thinking of little else for two days.[238] Clearly, apart from his mysterious death, Mutesa's funeral had suddenly turned out to be a burning political and diplomatic issue with serious ramifications for Anglo-Ugandan relations.

Britain's response and attitude towards Uganda's position was firm. While it would not accord Mutesa a funeral with full military honours, it would also not be pressured into refusing to show minimum courtesies to a former ruler, with whom and with whose family it had a long historical connection.[239] The British High Commissioner in Uganda was asked to see Obote personally as soon as possible to explain the situation. He was to confirm that Her Majesty's Government had taken the greatest care to avoid any actions that would imply that they were in any way supporting Mutesa against the Government of Uganda. Obote was to be told that the British Government had been subject to bitter criticism for refusing Mutesa any kind of financial support to the extent that he had been living on the most basic form of national assistance; and that there would be bitter and unacceptable criticism if, in order not to offend Obote, Her Majesty's Government persisted in inflicting final and gratuitous humiliation on Mutesa even after his death. He was to be assured that it was not in the interests of both governments to let a contentious situation arise over the funeral service, because once it was over "Sir E. Mutesa would be forgotten by the press and public media."[240]

Once all the politicking was done and the parties had taken their positions, Mutesa's funeral service was held at the Guards Chapel in Wellington Barracks on 3 December 1969 starting at 11.30 am. It was a normal regimental funeral service at which, according to Stewart, an official of the Foreign and Commonwealth Office, nothing was said to which any one would take exception.[241] The Grenadier Guards were the pallbearers. After the private service, Mutesa's body was temporarily buried at a cemetery at Kensal Green in London. Le Tocq, the Head of the East Africa Department at the FCO, who was not a Minister,[242] represented the British Government. However, the Queen, the Queen Mother and Princess Margaret all sent representatives.[243] There were no official messages of condolence save for personal messages to the widow. It is unclear whether the Ugandan Government, although vigorously represented at the inquest, was represented at the funeral by its High Commissioner, Mr Waako.

On the day of the funeral, crowds of mourners in Uganda attempted to mark the occasion but were faced with severe difficulties. To start with, the Government of Uganda, acting out of pique—and in vindication of Buganda's fears—cancelled its approval of a memorial service that was to be held at Namirembe Cathedral.[244] It then unleashed the army on the mourners at the ancestral Kasubi tombs. The army prevented people from approaching and gathering at the burial grounds and in other places, including Makerere University.[245] Such was the sad and bitter end of Mutesa's chapter in the UK. But to this day, speculation remains over the cause of his death. The truth may perhaps never be known.

After the events of 1966, and in total disregard of all the legal and moral questions involved in Obote's coup, Britain chose to all but abandon Mutesa and Buganda in favour of supporting Obote. In so doing, it no doubt considered that its interests—not least the territorial preservation of its former colony—were best served by Obote's more nationalistic outlook than by Mutesa's separatist purview—even though he was instrumental, in 1961, in persuading the Lukiiko to agree to be a part of Uganda. In any event, there had always been a British view that Mutesa's loyalty to Uganda was secondary to his kingdom of Buganda and, therefore, his loyalty to Uganda would always be suspect. He was known to nurse nationalist and separatist ambitions for Buganda.

Yet Britain always knew that Uganda could only survive with Buganda as an integral part of it. Thus, it fully understood that taking sides with Buganda would result not only in the destruction of Uganda but, perhaps more crucially, in a reduction of Britain's territorial, economic and political spheres of influence. Indeed, it is for the latter reasons that Britain pushed for the East African Federation even though the African people of East Africa, particularly in Buganda, were opposed to it at the time. While Buganda could exist without Uganda, the reverse did not follow. It is therefore easy to see why Britain chose to work with Obote, in spite of his irrational and erratic temperament, and not with Mutesa. In any event, Mutesa's defiant personality, beginning in 1953 leading him to act against British policy, did not make him the best custodian of British interests in postcolonial Uganda or, for that matter, for the future of Anglo-Ugandan relations and the Commonwealth.

When Sir Edward Mutesa was removed from the political scene in Uganda and the kingdom of Buganda then abolished, Britain turned to the new power-broker, Milton Obote, to protect its interests. This largely explains why it ignored any moral or other obligation to Mutesa or Buganda beyond the bare or minimum support and courtesies. In all of its actions, it ensured that it did not annoy Obote, even where he or his government were in blatant violation of the constitutional order in Uganda, or even where their actions were inconsistent with Britain's avowed principles of democracy and human rights.

There is no doubt that Britain's attitude contributed to the breakdown of law and order and to the rise of Obote's dictatorship in Uganda, particularly after the 1966 crisis. Britain always conveniently argued that it would not interfere in the internal affairs of a sovereign state and a member of the Commonwealth. However, the reliance on the principle of non-interference in the internal affairs of sovereign states has been used rather selectively by Britain and other big powers in international law.[246] In view of this, it emerges that Britain was driven by one enduring principle: the need to protect British interests at all times and at all costs.

The political situation in Uganda, particularly after Mutesa's demise, went from bad to worse. Obote's government became more dictatorial, repressive and unpopular. Buganda remained under a state of emergency and the ministers who had been arrested in 1966 remained incarcerated. The relationship between Obote and the Baganda also worsened and, within a month of Mutesa's death, an assassin attempted to kill Obote as he left a UPC meeting in Lugogo.[247] Five Baganda suspects were arrested, charged, and sentenced to death, even though there was a paucity of evidence against them.[248] A day after the attempted assassination, the government declared a state of emergency throughout the country and banned the DP for being a "danger to peace and order."[249] Several other political organizations were similarly proscribed, and some of their leaders detained.

With the UPC playing a dominant role, the country veered towards a leftist one-party state. Critics of the regime such as Abu Mayanja, Ben Kiwanuka, Paulo Semwogerere and Rajat Neogy were arrested and detained at various times under the emergency regulations.[250] Following his announcement of an economic policy dubbed the "Move to the Left" in 1968, Obote launched the "Common Man's Charter" followed by the "Nakivubo Pronouncements" in December 1969.[251] In general, these policies aimed at the nationalisation of the economy so as to "place the control of the means of production in the hands of the people as a whole."[252] While these moves were largely intended to endear Obote to the populace, they also targeted rich individuals, traders and land owners in Buganda who "were in a position to stir up ethnic opposition to the Government."[253]

Given their leftist orientation, Obote's pronouncements were not welcome in London and the West in general. They were seen by foreign investors, including British companies such as Shell, Grindlays Bank and Brooke Bond, as outright expropriation. For Anglo-Ugandan relations, Obote's ideological and political manoeuvres, including the nationalization of foreign assets involved in the import and export business and the compulsory acquisition of 60% of the shares of oil companies, manufacturing industries, plantations, banks, credit institutions, insurance companies and transport undertakings without prompt and adequate compensation, hit directly at the heart of British interests in Uganda.[254] This situation was exacerbated by Obote's campaign against Britain's sale of arms to South Africa and his threats to pull Uganda out of the Commonwealth.[255]

The combination of these measures resulted in a reduction in confidence in the economy by the private sector and, consequently, a drop in foreign direct investments.[256] Britain was concerned about Obote's moves not only because they mostly targeted British interests and investments in Uganda, but because they presented a risk that other countries would be tempted to try and get away with similar measures.

Harold Wilson's Government must have been disappointed by Obote's moves after 1966 and particularity with his hostility once he was securely in control and revealed his true quasi-socialist self. At this point, Obote presented a huge threat to Britain's financial, industrial and strategic interests in Uganda in particular, and in the region as a whole. Therefore, as with his comrades Kwame Nkrumah in Ghana and Patrice Lumumba in the Congo, Britain felt it had to deal firmly with Obote. It threatened to cut aid to Uganda unless Obote's government undertook to uphold its obligations under international law.[257]

To address the "deplorable state of affairs" in Anglo-Ugandan relations, the FCO advised the British Government to demonstrate to Obote, now an implacable enemy, its displeasure over his actions.[258] In 1971, when, within two years of his Move to the Left, Obote was violently overthrown and replaced with Idi Amin, Britain (then under Prime Minister James Callaghan) had little cause to shed tears over his unceremonious departure.[259]

Since there were no agreements with Uganda under which Obote could call on Britain for assistance, it was not prepared to offer him any following his deposition.[260] Under these circumstances, it is unsurprising that Britain was not just amongst the first countries to recognise Idi Amin, but went out of its way to anchor and provide military and financial support to his regime—a fact that it would come to bitterly regret.

Britain Embraces Idi Amin Dada and the 1971 Military Coup d'État

General Idi Amin Dada overthrew Obote's government on 25 January 1971 with the support of Israeli intelligence. At the time, Obote was attending a Commonwealth Conference in Singapore. Richard M. K.

Slater, the British High Commissioner in Uganda, reported to London that in the small hours of that morning, the army, under the command of Idi Amin Dada, had started sporadic firing in Kampala.[261] This was followed by massive troop movements into the city. Shops were closed and the national broadcaster was taken off air and surrounded by soldiers. The High Commissioner could not reach anyone in authority and the Ministry of Defence headquarters were deserted. Information was nevertheless received from the Israeli Defence Attaché, Colonel Bar-Lev, that to pre-empt his own arrest on Obote's return from Singapore, General Amin struck first and ordered the arrest of all officers in the armed forces sympathetic to President Obote. According to Bar-Lev, a number of pro-Obote officers were shot to "eliminate potential foci of resistance both up country and in Kampala."[262]

He further reported that Amin was in control of vital points in Kampala and Entebbe Airport and had in fact moved against President Obote, whom (together with a number of those who had gone with him) he intended to shoot[263] on arrival at the airport, should he return.[264] This plan was abandoned "because of the difficulty of synchronising it with the liquidation of pro-Obote elements in the army." [265] Bar-Lev stated that the Inspector General of Police Erinayo Oryema survived death only because he took refuge in Bar-Lev's house.[266]

This information creates an impression that Amin's coup was not premeditated and was more about saving himself and less about saving the country from Obote. It is also clear that, in the days and months following the coup, both the British and Israel governments did their utmost to secure Amin's control of power, including recognizing his regime and providing intelligence, arms and financial aid.[267] What is unclear, though, is how Amin could have managed to mobilise the support of the Ugandan Army as well as Israel's forces[268] to execute a supposedly unplanned mission in such a fast and efficient manner.

Ugandans, and the rest of the world, only learnt of the reasons for Amin's coup much later in the day. The reasons were relayed by Warrant Officer (Class II) Samuel Aswa, who stated that the move to oust Obote was "to save the situation from getting worse."[269] The officer stated that Ugandans were angry, worried and sad about the unwarranted detentions of innocent people without trial, the continuation of a state of emergency for an indefinite period, the frequent loss of life and property, proposals for national service, widespread corruption, the failure to organise elections, unemployment, high taxes, low commodity prices, the expulsion of Kenyan and Tanzanian workers, the failure of the defence council to meet and nepotism in the army.[270]

The statement particularly criticized what it referred to as Obote's Lango masterplan of 1967 under which "all key positions in Uganda, political, commercial, army and industrial life, have to be occupied and controlled by people from Akokoro county in Lango district" and that "nothing of importance must be done for other districts especially Acholi district."[271] For these reasons, the statement read: "the men of the Uganda Armed forces decided to take over power from Obote and to hand it to their fellow soldiers." It concluded by calling upon everybody to "continue work in the normal way" and warning all foreign governments "not to interfere in Uganda's internal affairs," adding that "such interference would be crushed with great force."[272]

The announcement was followed by short broadcasts by General Amin and Erinayo Oryema, the Inspector General of Police, to the effect that it had been agreed that Uganda would be run by the armed forces. Amin stated that he had assumed power reluctantly, as he had "always believed the forces should support the popular elected civil power," adding that his would be a "thoroughly caretaking administration pending return to civilian rule."[273] Amin instantly promised the country free and fair elections, ordered the immediate release of political prisoners held on unspecified and unfounded charges, and assured political exiles that they were free to return.

Following these announcements, Kampala was swept by massive jubilation with crowds of people pouring out onto the streets, perhaps less in support of the army and more in joy at the downfall of Obote's regime. There was minimal resistance from Obote's supporters and casualties were minimal. By 26 January, Kampala was rapidly returning to normal although the mood of celebration was still abundant in many parts of the rest of the country. The troops were cheered as they returned to the barracks.

By this time, Obote had proceeded to Dar es Salaam where he arrived on 27 January 1971. He was put up in the State House where the Ugandan flag was allowed to fly—vainly but falsely suggesting that he still had a hold on power in Uganda. On the same day, he called a press conference to announce to the world that he was in Tanzania for discussions and not asylum, that there was no question of a takeover, and that before he left for Singapore he had demanded explanations from Idi Amin about the disappearance of arms and corruption within the army.[274] He also stated that Amin was implicated in the murder of Brigadier Okoya in the previous year.[275] He correctly accused Israel of supporting the coup. The Tanzanian press supported Obote's stance and accused Britain of supporting the overthrow of progressive African Commonwealth leaders in Ghana, Nigeria and now Uganda. They all questioned the value of the Commonwealth if it could not stand behind Obote.[276]

Though taken by surprise, Britain was pleased with Amin deposing Obote, since he had fallen out of favour with Britain, and particularly with Edward Heath's new Conservative government. Obote's policy shift and his overtures towards the Communist east, his Africanisation of trade, his announcement that British Asians would be asked to leave Uganda, and his opposition to Ian Smith in Rhodesia and to Britain's sale of arms to South Africa all combined to break the longstanding support that Britain had given him. Obote's usefulness to Britain's interests had come to an end. His removal from the political scene and his replacement by a more agreeable personality to better protect British interests in postcolonial Uganda was thus desirable to Britain. General Idi Amin—conscripted, trained and trusted by the British colonial army, the King's African Rifles—perfectly fit this bill.[277]

Only a month before the coup, various British officials had been describing Amin as corrupt and unintelligent,[278] pointing out that he had received little education and was almost illiterate, and highlighting suspicions that he was involved in black market deals in gold with Congolese rebels.[279] The Foreign Office file on him noted that had no experience to prepare him for the role of President and had no idea of how to run the machinery of government.[280]

Yet, when the coup happened, Britain was quick to embrace him, in order to enhance its prospects and interests in Uganda. Indeed, despite all reports to the contrary, Richard Slater, the British High Commissioner to Uganda, informed the Foreign Secretary in London that Amin had the "wherewithal to provide satisfactory administration" and that with him "Anglo-Ugandan relations [could] only take a turn for the better."[281] As subsequent events showed, the High Commissioner's judgement could not have been more wrong.

The Foreign and Commonwealth Office in London was surprised and excited in equal measure at the news of Obote's ouster and Amin's takeover, however unconstitutional. Although it did not sponsor him, Britain supported Amin's coup, unlike the US, which chose to maintain a low profile and adopt a wait-and-see approach.[282] A few days after the coup, for instance, officials at the Foreign and Commonwealth Office concluded:

> [Our] prospects in Uganda have no doubt been considerably enhanced providing we take the opportunities open to us. We now have a thoroughly pro-Western set up in Uganda of which we should take prompt advantage. Amin needs our help.[283]

This optimism came on the heels of the positive evaluation of Amin by British High Commissioner Slater in Kampala. Commenting on Amin's first press conference, the High Commissioner noted that the General gave the impression of a "bluff and honest soldier," and that "despite his limitations, he [had] considerable dignity and more of the air of a leader than Obote."[284] On this basis, the Foreign Office, which had an interest in Amin's survival, sought ways and means by which it could entrench its interests and "discreetly influence Amin's activities in the direction of greater political sense."[285]

The British press was also taken by surprise by Amin's coup. However, the news of the ouster was generally well received across the board as a good riddance to Obote, who was increasingly being seen as a problematic leader. There was a belief that the new regime, with Amin as its new strongman, would be friendlier. Tom Stacey of *The Evening Standard*, for example, opined that Amin would be good for Uganda and good for Britain.[286] *The Daily Telegraph* considered Amin to be the embodiment of the British notion of a reliable native: pro-British and thick enough to be controlled.[287] Britain also considered that its material and political interests were best served by early recognition of Amin's usurpation of power.[288] For these reasons, in extraordinary haste, Britain wanted to recognise Amin right away—on the day of the coup—but was deterred by the fear of being suspected by African governments of having staged it.[289]

In a telegram to Kampala on the day of the coup, London asked its High Commissioner to assess the level of Amin's control and what Obote might attempt to do as it considered the question of recognition. The FCO's thinking was that it "should not lead the way in recognition but be close behind the leaders, provided these included countries of consequence."[290] To hasten the process of international recognition of Amin's regime, the Israelis and the British encouraged Amin to make the right noises. Britain instructed its High Commissioner to ask the Israel Embassy, through Colonel Bar-Lev, to suggest to Amin that "it would be helpful, in the context of recognition, if he would make an on record statement of his intention to observe Uganda's international obligations."[291]

In addition, Amin was told by the Israelis that: (a) given the importance of the UK and the US as sources of public and private funding, he should avoid doing anything "silly" and must try to restore confidence; (b) he should go slow on nationalisation, and if possible de-nationalise; and (c) he should at once bring back those ministers who were not wholly unacceptable. Colonel Bar-Lev told the British that this advice had been well received by Amin and assured them that they now had "a thoroughly pro-western setup in Uganda of which [they] could take prompt advantage."[292]

Amin did not disappoint. On the third day after the coup, and clearly in line with Colonel Bar-Lev's guidance, he made a press statement to the effect that fifty five detainees—including the five ministers arrested by Obote in 1966—would be released; that Uganda would honour all agreements signed by the former government and would maintain good relations with Britain because she ruled Uganda well up to independence; and cautioned celebrating citizens to respect property, to molest no one, and to avoid infringing the law or interfering with work or freedom of movement.[293] In the same statement, Amin said that even though Obote, at a secret meeting on 11 January 1971, had decided to order Amin's murder, he was welcome to return to Uganda as a private citizen but not as President.[294] A few days after the military coup, a London-based group of Baganda, styled as the Uganda Reconstruction Committee, called on the British Prime Minister and urged him to "recognise the new administration, especially now that President Mobutu of [the] Congo Kinshasa has already done so."[295] The group was headed by S. Galabuzi, and Fredrick and Joyce Mpanga, who believed that Idi Amin had the full backing of Buganda and that he would quickly help the country to return to "democracy and tranquillity."[296]

With suitable noises coming from General Amin and from groups like the Uganda Reconstruction Committee, Britain canvassed support from friendly governments, including the USA and other Western European countries, on the question of recognition of the new regime in Uganda. In addition, Britain canvassed the governments of Kenya, Nigeria, Ghana, Ethiopia and the Congo (Kinshasa) and encouraged them to accord recognition quickly, with a view that they take the same step at the same time.[297] Amin was to be discreetly made aware of the efforts Britain was making on his behalf in this regard.[298]

Tanzania was the exception. In a letter to the British Prime Minister, President Nyerere refused to recognise Amin's regime because it constituted a serious threat to the peace and stability of East Africa.[299] He could not have been more prophetic. Nonetheless, Britain pressed on and asked its Commissioner in Uganda to "keep close to Amin on this and other matters."[300] The scene was thus set for Britain to recognise General Amin's new government in Uganda and place its relations with Uganda on a friendly footing, which it did—on 5 February 1971.[301]

Britain's recognition of Amin's government led to a soaring of Anglo-Uganda relations. To extend British patronage and influence, the British Foreign Office ensured that Amin's first official trip abroad as President was to the UK, where officials pulled out all stops to flatter and honour him. During his four-day visit, not only did he lunch with Prime Minister and various high-profile guests (including businessmen and top military personnel)[302] but on 13 July 1971, Amin, his wife Malyam and his young son Moses were hosted as special guests of the Queen at Buckingham Palace.

On this trip, Amin's entourage also visited Sandhurst and Scotland (he flew on the Queen's plane to Edinburgh and with the Royal Air Force back to Heathrow). Beyond such pampering, Britain committed to providing him with an immediate loan on concessionary terms of £10 million in development aid, as well as assistance in the training of his army.[303] Indeed, a team from Sandhurst was quickly dispatched to Uganda to advise on the establishment of an Officers' Training School, with another from Warminster to be sent to advise on a new School of Infantry.[304] At the end of his visit, General Amin was all praise for Britain and the Queen:

> The reason for my visit was to thank Her Majesty the Queen for the assistance that has been given to Uganda by the British government in the fields of education, military training, health, and the like, and also to thank her for allowing the body of Uganda's first President to be returned home. I decided that before I went anywhere else in the world I must come to Britain first to thank the Queen personally.[305]

The Queen, in her own hand, referred to Idi Amin as her "good friend."[306] Amin's other good friend, adviser and close confidant was Bob Astles, a former British colonial and military officer.[307] As we show ahead, Astles played a central role as a factotum in the machinations and tyranny that characterised Amin's eight-year rule.

It is noteworthy that on his way to and from Britain, Amin made brief stopovers in Israel and on both occasions met with Moshe Dayan, the Minister of Defence and the Chief-of-Staff.[308] He promised to open an embassy in Jerusalem as a sign of friendship with Israel and presented a long list of requests for military (to deal with the threat of Tanzania) and economic aid (to deal with Uganda's ailing economy), which Israel undertook to give a sympathetic examination.[309] He visited the Al-Aqsa mosque and the Dome of the Rock, where he contributed $2,000 for their rehabilitation.[310]

Despite the warm reception extended to Amin, Britain did not deliver the goods as swiftly and as generously as he would have wished. Exasperated, he despatched his Minister of Defence, Oboth Ofumbi, to the British Prime Minister Edward Heath with a letter on a matter of "crucial importance" and "extreme urgency," seeking British help to ease Uganda's debt repayments and for military equipment and training. In the letter, he reminded the Prime Minister that when he took over the government, "the financial state of the government as well as the economy of the entire nation were in near chaos … largely due to the misguided economic policies of the last regime … exacerbated by the general corruption which had permeated government machinery."[311]

Britain was hesitant to support Amin's requests for military equipment, precisely because of Uganda's financial difficulties in paying back the debts incurred by Obote's regime. In fact, it feared that Amin would squander the money to buy expensive yet unnecessary military equipment that Uganda could ill afford, recommending that he be "warned against excessive expenditure on sophisticated military equipment (such as Harriers)" to avoid the country getting into "debt beyond her capacity to recover."[312] Yet, at the same time, it needed to protect its interests in Uganda. It was aware that if it did not oblige, Amin was likely to look elsewhere, especially to Libya, for military supplies.

For this reason, it hedged its risks. The Foreign and Commonwealth Office advised the Ministry of Defence of the need to drive the facts home to Amin, while at the same time reassuring him of British willingness to help. In a letter from Patrick Gratton, an FCO official, to R. C. Mottram of the Ministry of Defence, the former said: "we also want to make sure that our financial stake, as by far the biggest creditor, is safeguarded and that our position in Uganda is not pre-empted by foreign suppliers."[313] Britain insisted that Amin should seek help from the International Monetary Fund (IMF) and that only if he did would the UK be willing to help with defence requirements.[314] At this point in time, the IMF and the World Bank—both dominated by the wealthiest industrial countries—were "the new missionary institutions" and the lead agents of these powers in exporting free-market ideology to poor countries which were often desperate for loans and grants. In this role, the IMF approach had "the feel of a colonial ruler" with fixed nostrums of what their "client countries" like Uganda needed.[315]

By February 1972, it was clear that Amin's rule was gaining notoriety, with increased numbers of killings and disappearances and the banning of all political activities. However, when reporting on events in Uganda around this time to FCO, the British High Commissioner in Kampala incredibly stated that he had "no immediate bilateral problems to discuss."[316] This was followed by a visit by Lord Aldington, a special representative of Prime Minister Edward Heath, who was sent to Amin to discuss how Britain would help the regime on economic matters, arms procurement and "to secure those orders for the United Kingdom." [317] Aldington met Amin on 24 March 1972, just a few days after Britain received confirmation from High Commissioner Slater that "up to 400 detainees at Mutukula were put to death in cold blood after appearing before some sort of Kangaroo court" in Amin's Uganda.[318]

However, by June 1972 Britain was beginning to consider reducing its cooperation and support to Amin and it was decided that only a small defence sales team be sent to Uganda. By this point, Amin's relations with Britain were rapidly deteriorating and he was accused of making "wild and irresponsible statements" such as advocating "military action against imperialists, including the liberation of Seychelles and Djibouti."[319] In addition, Anglo-Ugandan relations were rocked by the arrest and interrogation of Martin Meredith, a correspondent with *The Observer* newspaper, as well as allegations of the mistreatment of British nationals in Uganda.[320]

With these developments, and from this point onwards, the relationship between the two countries soured. However, while Britain dithered, Amin set his eyes elsewhere for military and financial support. Indeed, to demonstrate his disenchantment with Britain, in December 1972 Amin made a proclamation on national radio in which he informed the public of his decision to rename Uganda's physical features and roads because those previously used by British colonialists were "insignificant to independent Uganda" and because "it was time Uganda restored its cultural heritage, human dignity and respect, which [had] hitherto been denied to [it] by forces of imperialism and their agents."[321] Under this decree, Queen Elizabeth National Park became Rwenzori National Park, Lake Albert became Lake Idi Amin Dada, Lake Edward became Lake Mubutu Sese Seko, Salisbury Road became Nkrumah Road, Prince Charles Drive became 25 January Avenue and Queen's Road became Lumumba Avenue.

Idi Amin's warm relations with Britain were short-lived primarily (from Amin's perspective) because of Britain's failure or refusal to yield to his pleas for military and financial support. His relations with Buganda followed a similar trajectory, starting with the high point of the return of Mutesa's body for a state funeral in Uganda, and ending in the frustration of Buganda's aspirations on the restoration of its monarchy. Amin did not care much for Buganda; once he had gained national and international recognition and acceptance, he neither needed nor counted on its support.

The Exhumation of Mutesas' body in the UK and its Reburial in Uganda

Two days after the military coup, Amin, who had led the attack on Mutesa's palace in 1966 which led to the Kabaka's exile and death in London, announced that the body of Sir Edward Mutesa would be flown back to Uganda and buried with full military honours. He also promised to build a special house for the late Kabaka's children.[322] Save for a few sceptics, the Baganda, who welcomed Amin and the coup with much enthusiasm, were generally ecstatic at the news of the return of Mutesa's body.[323] Overnight, Amin became the darling of the kingdom. The irony that Amin—the same man who had attacked and killed hundreds of people in the Lubiri—was being showered with praises by Baganda for allowing Mutesa's body back for reburial cannot be overstated.

It was not only Buganda that was pleased with Amin's magnanimity on Mutesa's reburial in Uganda. Britain was also happy with the news and, acting through its Ministry of Defence and the services of Major Paul Cordle of the Grenadier Guards, quickly provided full cooperation before and during the five-day funeral, which lasted from 31 March to 4 April. Britain was fully represented by a high-powered delegation at the funeral. Lord Boyd represented Her Majesty, while Sir William Hayter represented the Queen Mother. The British High Commissioner, R. M. K. Slater, attended the funeral, as did other British guests including five Members of Parliament.[324] The Vice-President of Kenya, Daniel Arap Moi, also attended with a big delegation. Ministers from the Central African Republic, Ethiopia and Malawi also attended.[325]

The Government of Uganda took charge of all the ceremonies and ensured that Mutesa was accorded a dignified reburial. The public turnout to view the body and participate in the ceremony was huge. Indeed, the public display of affection for the late Kabaka—and for Amin, who had made the reburial possible—was overwhelming. In the end, the whole affair put Amin in good light and aptly demonstrated the disdain the people of Buganda felt for Obote and his fallen regime.

But it was not just Amin's star that rose with the reburial. Britain, and more generally Anglo-Ugandan relations, were also on the ascendant. It was felt that the whole affair had a cathartic effect and turned out to the advantage of Her Majesty's Government, which was accorded great honour throughout the proceedings. The British National Anthem was played more often than the British officials could remember. In return for his courtesies, the British delegation presented six silver tankards to the President after the funeral. A full account of Mutesa's reburial is contained in a diplomatic report by the British High Commissioner to the Secretary of State for Foreign and Commonwealth Affairs, dated 13 April 1971, reproduced in Appendix V below.

Following the reburial, Amin held meetings with the British delegation at which he expressed gratitude to Britain for its role in the return of Mutesa's body. At these meetings, he declared that he was against Communism and once again asked for assistance on security and intelligence matters, army medical training, and for VTOL (vertical take-off and landing) aircraft.[326] He also asked for a signed portrait of the Queen. He told his guests that his biggest problem was Buganda and that he hoped that the return of the body of Sir Edward Mutesa would help over this.[327] The delegation was impressed with Amin as an excellent host and was left in no doubt that he was extremely pro-British.[328] They noted all the requests, and were optimistic that with Amin a new and brighter chapter in Anglo-Ugandan relations had started. Lord Boyd was particularly impressed with the warm reception of the British delegation by the leaders of Buganda. He could not understand why this was the case, in view of the shabby treatment the Labour government had given the Kabaka in exile.[329]

From the outset, Amin's motive for returning Mutesa's body was clear, namely: to mollify and win the hearts and minds of the Baganda, whom he knew loathed Obote over the abolition of the kingdom and the exile of their king. It was in the same spirit that he released all political prisoners that had been jailed by Obote and returned Mutesa's motorboat to Mutesa's son, Prince Ronald Mutebi, with much publicity.[330] He saw no problem whatsoever in enacting a symbolic deed of reconciliation with the Baganda.

However, beyond the symbolism, Amin had no intention of restoring the kingdoms in Buganda or any other part of the country. In fact, this had never been one of the 18 reasons that he and the army gave for the overthrow of Obote's regime.[331] On 20 February 1971, Amin endorsed the "Soldiers' Declaration" in which it was stated that there would be no return to the former kingdoms. This, however, did not stop Baganda loyalists from demanding their restoration and hoping for the best. To address these demands, Amin held a large meeting of Baganda elders at the International Conference Centre in Kampala and used the opportunity to criticise Buganda's characteristics such as isolationism, conservatism and arrogance.[332]

Nevertheless, his final remarks left the door open, conceding that the issue was so important that it must be considered more fully at a later date. On another occasion, he warned Baganda Elders against pushing for the

Kabakaship and against confusing Prince Mutebi, accusing them of pretending to work for Mutebi when in fact they were working for their own stomachs.[333]

Once Amin settled into the Presidency, the restoration of the kingdom in Buganda or elsewhere was the least of his concerns. And, like Obote before him, he maintained the military occupation of the Kabaka's palace at Mengo and Buganda's headquarters, later grotesquely turning them into torture and murder chambers. The British High Commission in Uganda held the view that few in Buganda would, in fact, back a return of the Kabakaship and thus seemed cynical about a possible restoration of the kingdom of Buganda, given that it would inevitably allow a push for a separate Buganda identity.[334] For that reason, the High Commission believed that Amin might later regret allowing the Kabakaship issue to be so widely discussed, since it "seemed to increase the head of steam rather than letting it off."[335]

The British High Commission felt that following a pro-Buganda policy would create problems and warned that Amin's government had to "tread warily if it [was] not to further alienate and upset the northern and eastern tribes."[336] Commenting on Buganda's push for the restoration of kingdoms, P. R. G. Redshaw of the High Commission considered that the demand was not supported by the whole of Buganda but by the "poorer, less educated Baganda. The better educated younger elements [saw] the Kabakaship as an irrelevant, expensive and retrogressive institution."[337] As later events have shown, these views could not have been further from the truth; Buganda and her institutions—including the monarchy—have, over the years demonstrated remarkable resilience and survived several adversities and adversaries.

Defining Moments and Personalities in Anglo-Ugandan Relations under General Amin, 1971-1979

By the first anniversary of the coup, it was clear to Amin, the British, and the Baganda that several things were not going to happen as hoped or promised in January 1971. For example, there were not going to be elections and a handover to a civilian government in Uganda. On the prospects of returning Uganda on a democratic path, the FCO held the rather shocking view that:

> too much democracy in a country like Uganda at the present stage can be as fatal as too great a degree of authoritarianism. What would seem to be required for the foreseeable future is a realistic balance between firm and

> indeed authoritarian, government and some degree of democratic expression…. Uganda needs not necessarily democratic government.[338]

In any event, Britain was well aware, by now, that Amin was besotted with power and that his regime was not going to be a puppet of the British or any other power. And, even though it was also aware that Amin's regime was responsible for the killing and disappearances of mostly Acholi and Langi individuals associated with Obote,[339] it felt that the regime had served it well, having removed one of its more bitter critics in Obote, and that although Amin's was not the ideal government, it was, by "African standards as good as could be hoped for."[340] But because Britain saw no credible alternative to Amin, it set out to make the best of a bad situation working with Amin who it now understood to be "unamenable to reason, pathologically suspicious, a liar and a hypocrite."[341] Because of the visible support it had given in recognizing and establishing Amin, Britain felt embarrassed to condemn him and felt that it could not tell him "to stop murdering people" and that "any credible alternative to Amin would be a great deal worse." Thus, mostly to protect its community in Uganda, it adopted a policy of "business as usual" accompanied by the adoption of a low profile."[342] This way, as we show below, Amin's tyranny was allowed to get out-of-hand with Britain's tacit support.

On Amin's part, it was clear by this time that Britain was not going to be forthcoming with military hardware as requested. And for Buganda, it was clear that the Kabakaship was not going to be restored. By this time, Amin was a frustrated and disillusioned man who faced imminent danger from the south, as well as a failing economy. Tanzania, in hosting the ousted Obote, had already not only demonstrated its hostility to the regime in Kampala, but had been involved in border clashes that ultimately cost Amin dearly and embarrassed him and his troops.[343] In June of 1972, Britain received information from Akena Adoko about a plan by Ugandan army elements, led by Lt. Col. Obitre Gama to overthrow Amin and return Obote as the leader.[344] The British High Commissioner, however, did not support the idea of the return of Obote as Uganda's leader, observing that he "has never been and never will be a friend of Britain…. Obote has no hope whatever of staging a comeback. High Commissioner Slater considered informing Amin about the plan but chose to say nothing."[345]

Amin felt insecure because he feared Nyerere was backing Obote to recapture power in Uganda. For this reason, he needed to quickly develop a military capability with hardware such as MiG fighter planes and other destroyers in order to counter the Tanzanian forces. With Britain and Israel dragging their feet on the matter, he started looking to the East for supplies—particularly to the Soviet Union and China, who could come to his rescue without too many questions. This marked the beginning of cooling off his hitherto warm relations with Britain and, as subsequent events show, the revelation of the true colours of General Idi Amin.

Expulsion of British Asians from Uganda

Nothing shook Anglo-Ugandan relations and British interests in Uganda during the first two years of Amin's rule as much as the expulsion of all British Asians from the country. It is claimed that one night Idi Amin had a dream in which Allah spoke to him and ordered him to expel British Asians from Uganda, and that this was one of the ways to retaliate for the British Government's refusal to provide him with arms to defend Uganda against Tanzania.[346] Accordingly, on 4 August 1972, Amin made a declaration giving British Asians, as well as Pakistani and Bangladeshi nationals, ninety days within which to leave Uganda. This was so that ordinary Ugandans could become masters of their destiny, enjoy the wealth of their country, and be in control of Uganda's economy for the first time in the country's history.[347]

This expulsion, which affected the lives of approximately 80,000 Asians, including those who had obtained Ugandan citizenship, shocked the world. The announcement was followed by pandemonium in both British and Indian diplomatic circles and in the affected families. The British Prime Minister wrote to Amin expressing great concern about the imminent expulsion of Asians who held British passports but Amin simply ignored the pleas and proceeded with the expulsion.[348] Britain offered to take up to 27,200 individuals, while 6,000 migrated to Canada, 4,500 to India and 2,500 to Kenya.[349]

Many of the affected number were second- and third-generation offspring of Indian coolies brought to Uganda by Britain to construct the Uganda Railway in the late 1890s while others were came to Uganda as traders. Others had originally come to Uganda under a British colonial policy to create a buffer between Europeans and Africans and to occupy the mid-ranking positions in commercial and administrative roles.[350] For this reason, the British colonial government had invested significantly in the education of Asian minorities in preference to indigenous Ugandans. By the time of Uganda's independence in 1962, the Asians dominated the economy and the middle management jobs. This had contributed to the stratification of Ugandan society along racial and economic lines and nurtured "Indo-phobia": an acute sense of resentment and hostility by Africans towards Indians.

When Obote announced his policy of Africanisation (under which, ironically, 30,000 Kenyans and Tanzanians were also expelled), he aimed to address this very problem.[351] Amin adopted more extreme measures which he justified on the grounds that this group had *inter alia* shown disloyalty to Uganda, was not integrating with Africans, and was guilty of commercial malpractices. For full measure, Amin followed this action by expropriating all the assets of the expelled Asians, including ranches, houses, cars and other property. No compensation was immediately offered to the departing Asians for the expropriated properties. Amin then proceeded to personally hand out these properties on random street walks to individuals, without regard to their ability to run or develop them. No doubt the recipients were grateful but most failed to run the businesses and, in no time, the economy suffered the consequences.

Following the expulsion, Britain decided to cease arms export and training but not to withdraw the British Army Training Team (BATT) because it did not want the differences over the expulsions to broaden. However, as another sign of seriously deteriorated Anglo-Uganda relations, by 13 September 1972, Amin had announced the expulsion of the BATT.[352]

Bob Astles—Amin's Special British Adviser

In his eight-year rule, Amin relied on advice from an improbable source: Robert Astles, an ex-British soldier, veteran of the Second World War and a recipient of the British Empire Medal for his work in the Colonial Office. Astles' military unit had been sent to Uganda to quell the 1949 riots in Buganda. Following that assignment, he remained in the country as a colonial officer in the Ministry of Works. Astles, who later renounced his British citizenship and became a Ugandan citizen, was most notorious for his dealings with Amin, with whom he had a love-hate relationship.[353]

Shortly after Uganda's independence, Astles had used his savings to set up Uganda Aviation Services Ltd (later nationalised by Amin). At that time, he was a close supporter of Milton Obote, but had also kept his options open by cultivating a relationship with the Kabaka, who put him in charge of the camera at Uganda Television Company.[354] However, according to Barbara Kimenye, after Obote had ousted Kabaka Mutesa, Astles was seen on the steps of the Uganda Parliament loudly announcing: "It is time for King Freddie's Kabaka Yekka and the Mengo set to be put against a wall and shot."[355]

Astles worked for Obote's government as a civil servant, pilot and cameraman until the 1971 coup. Although he swiftly transferred his allegiance to Amin, his previous support for Obote brought him under suspicion, and he spent several weeks in Makindye Prison, where he was shackled and brutally interrogated. After denouncing Obote as "almost a madman" on Ugandan television, he was released and almost immediately recruited by Amin as his adviser on British affairs. He was arrested again in 1976, but released after only a week and appointed head of Amin's anti-corruption squad.[356]

Astles was equally feared by Europeans and Africans. When Astles was not in Amin's jails for one misdemeanour or another—such as "confusing" his ministers—he was a member of Amin's much-feared State Research Bureau. His zoo-like home, which hosted a python, an owl, a mongoose, a monkey, a dog and several crested cranes, was equally intimidating.[357] As Amin's spin-doctor, he explained away Anglican Archbishop Janan Luwum's grotesque murder in 1977 as a mere car accident.[358] His notoriety extended to accusations of murder, robbery, and smuggling—charges he denied and of which he was always acquitted. He always insisted that he had no blood on his hands. But he did not deny humiliating European expatriates by forcing them to kneel before Amin, which earned him the name "the white rat."[359] For his anti-corruption work, Amin awarded Astles the Republic Medal. Amin also appointed Astles' wife, a relation of Kawalya Kagwa's family, as a minister in his government.[360]

Such was Astles' loyalty to Amin that he kept in touch with him long after his deposition and until his death in exile in Saudi Arabia in 2003. The British Government, especially following his detention in May 1979, officially distanced itself from Bob Astles, arguing that since he had renounced British citizenship his difficulties were not their problem.[361] Be that as it may, while in Luzira prison, he was visited by a British journalist, Colin Legum, and by a delegation of five British MPs led by David Mudd.[362]

Reporting to the Head of the East Africa Department at the FCO, the British High Commissioner in Uganda explained that none of its officials attended Astles' trial to avoid the public perception that Britain was "taking any interest in the affairs of Astles."[363] Yet in the same letter, the High Commissioner, monitoring Astles through a British special agent within the prisons system whose particulars he asked to be protected, stated that he was informed of Astles' health and general condition whilst in prison.[364]

Astles was acquitted of criminal charges in 1981 during Obote's second administration, but was kept under detention under Section 12 of the colonially-originated Public Order and Security Act No. 20, on the grounds that Obote's government "was in possession of reliable information that he was a member of the State Research Bureau, an organisation which was involved in indiscriminate killing of many Ugandans," and that it "consider[ed] him to be a danger to the public safety and that his continued detention … was essential for the maintenance of law and order."[365] He was freed after Obote was overthrown for a second time. Astles was eventually deported back to Britain, where he settled in Wimbledon in London before his death on 29 December 2012, at the age of 88.

Amin's "Save Britain" Charity Fund[366]

By December 1973, Anglo-Ugandan relations had hit rock bottom. In a sarcastic response to the economic difficulties faced by Britain at the time, Amin set up the Save Britain Charity Fund. In mocking telegrams to Ted Heath, Britain's Conservative Prime Minister, he asserted that the "rapidly deteriorating economic situation in Britain, which is the most senior member of the Commonwealth, is a shame and a great embarrassment not only to Britain, but also to other members of the Commonwealth."[367]

To arrest the situation and stop the suffering of ordinary British citizens, General Amin launched an appeal to all the people of Uganda to come forward to help their former colonial master by contributing part of their abundant foodstuffs to the cause. In the same spirit, he told Heath that he was contributing 10,000 Uganda Shillings from his personal savings to start the fund. Amin hoped that many Ugandans would donate generously to the fund to rescue their innocent friends. He told Heath: "If you will let me know officially, the exact position of the mess into which Britain has been plunged, I will do my best in asking some of Uganda's friends to join us in giving assistance to Britain."[368] He also wrote that he was ready to assist Britain in every way possible, such as advising on how the British economy may recover.

For effect, Amin copied the telegrams to his friends, Presidents Muammar Gaddafi of Libya, Yasser Arafat of Palestine, Yakubu Gowon of Nigeria, Mobutu Sese Seko of Zaire, Jomo Kenyatta of Kenya and the then Commonwealth Secretary-General, Arnold Smith.[369] Britain, which at this time was more concerned with protecting its citizens in Uganda and in securing compensation for the expelled British Asians than indulging Amin, chose to ignore his whimsical offer. When he got no response to his initiative, Amin wrote to Heath again, saying:

> The people of Uganda have responded very favourably ... to help our brothers and sisters in Britain out of their present economic chaos.... [T]he people of Kigezi District donated one lorry load of vegetables and wheat. I am now requesting you to send an aircraft to collect this donation urgently before it goes bad. I could have sent this donation direct but as we do not, at the moment, have facilities for doing so, I hope you will react quickly so as not to discourage Ugandans from donating more.[370]

However, fearing to pique Amin and thereby risk the lives of its citizens in Uganda, Britain chose to make an oral reply through its High Commissioner, who said that the British Government appreciated

> the concern of the people of Kigezi District but, contrary to reports which may have appeared, the British people are not in fact suffering any intolerable hardship and there is no doubt that we shall overcome our present difficulties; we suggest that the produce collected should be sent to refugees or other people in need in Africa; as for relations between Uganda and Britain, these can only be put back on a normal footing when compensation matters have been settled.[371]

Britain's diplomacy with Amin over the Charity Fund did not discourage him from his wayward attitude towards Britain, nor his Ugandan subjects. In fact, as the case of Dennis Hills illustrates, it instead emboldened him and earned him the title of the "Wild Man of Africa."[372]

Bringing Britain to its Knees: The Case of Dennis Hills

Anglo-Ugandan relations were once again soured when Denis Hills, a British writer, ex-soldier and lecturer at Makerere University, described Amin as Uganda's "Black Nero" and a "Village Tyrant" in an unpublished manuscript of his book, *The White Pumpkin.*[373] When Amin got wind of Hills' writings, he ordered his arrest and arraignment before a military tribunal for the offences of espionage and sedition.[374] Following a military-style trial, Hills was found guilty and condemned to death by firing squad. Britain tried but failed to persuade Amin to pardon and release him. After failed diplomatic pleas, and with one day left before his execution, Amin said that since Her Majesty the Queen of Britain was his friend, he would consider sparing Hill's life, but only if she interceded and apologised to him on Hills' behalf.[375]

To save her subject's life, the Queen dispatched two British officers, Lt-Gen. Sir Chandos Blair and Major Ian Grahame (respectively the former company commander and battalion commander of Amin's regiment in the KAR) to plead for Hill. Armed with a letter of clemency signed by the Queen herself and wearing a full-dress uniform, Blair and Grahame were forced to crawl into a hut with a low entrance where Amin and his cameramen were waiting in Arua, West Nile. The pictures taken depict the emissaries grovelling on their knees, begging Amin to save the life of Hills. In spite of this humiliation, their efforts did not move Amin and a reprieve was not obtained.[376]

When this effort failed, and with the intervention of President Mobutu of Zaire, the Queen asked her Prime Minister, Harold Wilson, to write the apology. Wilson then despatched the British Foreign and Commonwealth Secretary, James Callaghan, to Uganda with another personal appeal to Amin to free Hills.[377] Callaghan, with a party of seven senior British officials, travelled first to Zaire and then to Uganda to negotiate Hills' release. In Kinshasa, he met with Mandungu Bula Nyati, Zaire's Commissioner for Foreign Affairs, and President Mobutu—both of whom acted as mediators between Amin and the British Government.

Callaghan emphasised to the mediators that Britain had "gone to the limit over the Hills case," and that because "the wounds [were] too deep," the restoration of normal relations with Uganda would have to wait.[378] On the commercial side, however, there was nothing to prevent normal trade from going ahead. A sceptical Callaghan said that it was difficult to deal with Amin, who on one occasion sent a message to the Queen saying that he would be arriving on a particular date and asking her to ensure that he got enough food and could visit Wales and Scotland whose people he supported in their fight against the English.[379]

President Mobutu told his guest that Amin was still staunchly pro-British and wanted a rapprochement with Britain. He also said that it was a "moral responsibility on the part of Britain to help Uganda."[380] Callaghan's delegation left for Uganda. At the meeting held at his "Command Post" in Kampala, Amin told Callaghan that he had "always been a warm admirer of Britain and everything British," and that the British people had educated him and trained him, and this was why he had been particularly pained by the criticism of the British press and radio, who had mounted a campaign against him since 1972.[381] Following an exchange of views, Amin assured the visitors that he would release Hills to Callaghan and that the lecturer could return to London with him. At this point, a shaken and dazed Hills was shoved into the room and presented to Callaghan as a free man, having survived 102 days in Amin's jails.[382] He flew back to Britain with Callaghan the same day.

The "Hills saga" proved that Amin did not have any pretentions or fear in his dealings with Britain. The humiliation of the British Government seems to have been Amin's payback for their refusal to provide him with the military and other support that he had long yearned for, and that they had indeed promised when he ousted Obote.

Israel's Raid on Entebbe and the Murder of British-Israeli Citizen, Dora Bloch

The breaking point in the Anglo-Ugandan relationship followed Amin's mistreatment and threats towards British nationals, including the expulsion of two members of the British High Commission and, particularly, the ghastly murder of the 74-year-old British-Israeli citizen, Dora Bloch. Mrs Bloch was left behind in hospital after Israeli Commandos, in a daredevil mission codenamed Operation Thunderbolt, rescued 104 hostages held in Uganda by pro-Palestinian hijackers.[383]

The hijackers, who took over an Air France jet on a flight from Tel Aviv to Paris, first landed in Benghazi, Libya and later at Entebbe Airport, Uganda. Although Amin denied complicity with the hijackers and offered himself as a mediator for the release of the hostages, there is evidence that he personally allowed the plane to land at the airport and that his troops assisted the hijackers in securing the hostages in the old terminal of Entebbe airport.[384] He was known to support the Palestinian cause.[385]

In his self-assigned role as mediator, Amin said that although he knew the hostages to be innocent, their release would be made once Israel had met the hijackers' demands. Israel accused Amin of aiding and abetting the hijackers and decided to take the matter into its own hands. Piloted and commanded by Lt-Col. Joshua Shani, the "Yellow Birds," as the Israeli Air Force's 131 Squadron were known, mounted an audacious and surprise mission in which they killed seven of the hijackers and at least 20 Ugandan soldiers.[386] They rescued all hostages except three who were killed in the crossfire, and left the old terminal, along with Amin's Soviet MiG fighter jets, smouldering in ashes. The Israeli commandos also lost four soldiers, including the commander of their ground unit, Yonatan Netanyahu, the brother of Israel's current Prime Minister, Benjamin Netanyahu.[387]

Britain Severs Diplomatic Ties with Uganda as Amin becomes the "Conqueror of the British Empire" (CBE)

Amin was extremely humiliated by Israel's raid on Entebbe. He accused Britain and Kenya of assisting Israel in breaching Uganda's airspace and sovereignty, for the loss of lives, and the destruction of his treasured fighter jets.[388] Kenya was particularly faulted for allowing the Israeli planes to refuel on their return journey. But it was Dora Bloch who paid the ultimate price, and her death, by murder, triggered the end of British diplomatic relations with Uganda. Explaining the momentous decision to cut diplomatic ties with Uganda, the Foreign and Commonwealth Office said:

> The decision to break relations has been a difficult one. It is the first time we have initiated a break since 1946, when we broke relations with Albania. It is also the first time that we have broken relations with a Commonwealth country, although others have done it to us. The immediate cause has been the case of Dora Bloch, the subsequent unwarranted expulsion of our acting High Commissioner and another member of our High Commission in Kampala, and the renewed evidence at this time of the general irrationality and unpredictability of Amin's government. We have come to the conclusion that it is impossible to have a normal relationship with the present Government of Uganda and that it is impossible for the High Commission to fulfil its proper functions.
>
> The decision is, however, also a culmination of events in Uganda since President Amin came to power. Following his declaration of economic war in 1972, Uganda has taken a series of actions hostile to our interests, including the expulsion of the Asians, the expropriation of British companies and Tea plantations in 1972, two threats to expel the entire British community, the reduction to five of the numbers of the High Commission's UK-based staff in 1974, and the attempted blackmail over Denis Hills in 1975. We have given the Ugandans every chance in the past twelve months to show genuine willingness to fulfil their intention of turning over a new leaf after Callaghan's visit there, but the outstanding problems between us have not changed and the Bloch case and the recent deportations are a clear breach of President Amin's undertaking to Callaghan that the Britons in Uganda could live in safety.[389]

Britain's decision to sever ties with Uganda was effective on 28 July 1976. Not to be outdone, in response to this decision, Amin bestowed upon himself a new title, namely, Conqueror of the British Empire (CBE)[390] and, for good measure, offered to take on the role of the King of Scotland to free the Scots from English oppression.[391] By the time Amin left power in 1979, his list of titles and decorations had grown exponentially. He was officially referred to as: "His Excellency, President for Life, Field Marshal, Al Hadji Doctor Idi Amin Dada, VC, DSO, MC and Conqueror of the British Empire (CBE)."[392]

When Britain exited Uganda, it left its interests under the protection of France, whose embassy in Kampala added the British Interests Section

(BIS) for this purpose. The BIS operated smoothly under the wings of the skilful French Ambassador Renard until Britain denied Amin entry to represent Uganda at the Commonwealth Heads of Government Meeting in London.[393] Despite the fact that Britain had severed diplomatic ties with Uganda, Amin insisted that as Head of State of a Commonwealth country he could not be denied entry to the UK for the meeting. He observed that Uganda was to use the platform to "point out the two thousand mistakes made by Britain during her colonial rule," adding that "gone are the days when Britain wielded the powers and authority of an imperial master over the Commonwealth."[394]

Amin described himself as one of "those true nationalist leaders who refuse to be microphones of Great Britain or any other imperialist power and to succumb to their neocolonialist and imperialistic orders that fall the victims of the British Government's manipulation of the Commonwealth."[395] He warned that the British Government's actions were not only interfering in the internal affairs of Uganda but also creating a bad and dangerous precedent for the Commonwealth.[396] However, Britain could not countenance such a visit without attracting international scandal. Accordingly, it discouraged him from exercising his right to attend the meeting and threatened to deny him entry if he insisted on doing so.[397]

Amin did not back off. He actually announced arrangements to travel to London for the meeting in a newly acquired Boeing with a party of about 250 supporters, including traditional dancers and armed body guards. He would stay at St Ermin's Hotel near Scotland Yard, and as if that was not big enough, he hoped he would be accommodated at Buckingham Palace.[398] This announcement alarmed Britain, which immediately launched Operation Bottle to divert Amin's plane to some military airfield and to handle him when he was on the ground. The operation involved various branches of government, the military (including snipers and explosive experts) and the police, and covered all major London airports including Heathrow, Stansted, Gatwick and RAF Brize Norton.[399] All involved were put on a high state of alert from 27 May 1977 until the end of the meeting.

On 6 June 1977, Amin announced on Radio Uganda that he was leaving for the London meeting, which was due to start on 8 June. Official announcements on Radio Uganda repeated that Amin was indeed on his way, although the whereabouts of his plane were not known by anyone. A false alarm was raised suggesting that he had landed in Dublin. By the time the meeting opened, Amin was nowhere to be seen. The mystery, and the bluff, of his whereabouts was only resolved when, on 9 June, Radio Uganda announced that Amin had returned from the Rwanda/Tanzania/

Uganda border where he "had had useful talks with revolutionary leaders from Tanzania and Zambia."[400]

Britain and everyone involved in Operation Bottle were most relieved, but only until Amin played another trump card. As a direct consequence of Britain's refusal to allow him to attend the Commonwealth meeting, Amin banned all Britons from entering Uganda. Furthermore, he claimed that the French Embassy in Uganda was allowing itself to be used by British nationals for subversive activities. As such, he demanded that "in the interests of preserving the excellent relations obtaining [sic] between France and Uganda, the BIS should be told to find another protecting power."[401] Rather than finding another protecting power, however, Britain chose to close the BIS and, correspondingly, the Ugandan Interests Section under the protection of the Saudi Embassy in London was closed in retaliation.

The "Cargo of Shame:" Britain's Covert Dealings with Amin

Remarkably, even after Britain had cut diplomatic ties with Amin's Uganda, it maintained discreet trade dealings with his government. Using non-scheduled Uganda Airlines flights to and from Stansted Airport, Britain continued to import mostly coffee, tea, cocoa and spices from Uganda and would, in exchange, export luxury items to Amin's military supporters. Britain's exports to Uganda included a wide range of merchandise such as whisky and clothes, supplied to the Uganda Army Shop, as well as electrical machinery, vehicles, telecommunications equipment, sugar, furniture, fertilisers, pharmaceuticals and other chemical materials.[402]

Under this arrangement, Britain was doing business with the Uganda Army Shop to the tune of £70,000 a month.[403] Military exports included spares for military equipment for the Ugandan Armed Forces, ammunition, sporting guns and a small number of small arms.[404] In addition, British companies such as Crown Agents and British Leyland were suppliers of Bedford and Leyland trucks, Land Rovers, sophisticated electronic equipment and aircraft parts for the Uganda Police Force.[405] Marshall of Cambridge (Engineering) Ltd was retained to service Uganda's aircraft, and was accused of adapting a C-130 Hercules for military purposes and *ipso facto* of propping up Idi Amin's war machine. Although the company denied the conversion, it accepted that it routinely serviced Uganda's aircrafts.[406] The arrangement was convenient to Britain, given the general lack of foreign exchange (convertible currency) in Uganda, but also because, in the context of the shortage of supplies in the country, the deal helped keep Amin's soldiers happy and loyal to him. Questioned in the House of Commons about the supply of surveillance equipment to Amin, Prime Minister James Callaghan countered: "the devices were intended to track down television licence dodgers."[407]

Britain's dealings with Amin's regime raised concerns both in its Parliament and among the British public. For example, calling for a ban on what he called the "cargo of shame," Bruce George, a British parliamentarian, told the House of Commons:

> It is also well known that cargoes of whisky and brandy are flown out, most likely for the purpose of buying loyalty from Amin's officers and perhaps to give them even less of a conscience when they go around committing genocide on Amin's instructions.... [T]he fact that this is being exported from Britain is to our eternal shame.[408]

He urged the Secretary of Trade, John Smith, to "end the immoral trade in booze and other luxuries which [was] succouring a tyrannical regime."[409] Another concerned individual, Colm Cavanagh, asked David Owen, the Secretary of State for Foreign and Commonwealth Affairs, about Britain's policy on economic support to the grievous government of General Amin.[410] The British Government's response was as follows:

> The Government fully shares your concern at the massive violation of basic human rights in Uganda and has made this clear on many occasions both in Parliament and elsewhere. Britain has played a leading role in bringing the issue of human rights violations in Uganda before International fora, including the United Nations Human Rights Commission. Uganda's record was also discussed, at the UK's instigation, at last year's Commonwealth Heads of Government meeting, which condemned the state of affairs in Uganda in strong and unequivocal terms. The Government believes that such moves may have made some impact on the attitude of the regime in Uganda towards human rights, though its performance is still very bad.
>
> The Government gives no economic support to Uganda. They continue to review the Stansted operations of Uganda Airlines and appreciate the force of the arguments put forward on this subject. However, this issue involves difficult legal questions and due regard must be paid to Britain's international commitments which have a bearing on the question of whether the flights could be terminated.
>
> The policy of British companies towards the trade in civil goods with Uganda is a matter for their own judgment. To impose general trade sanctions would raise very wide issues for commercial policy. The

> Government does not, however, do anything to encourage British trade with Uganda and does not permit the supply of any goods of a military nature. The Government has no power to stop oil supplies to Uganda. We are in close touch with the two British oil companies which supply oil to Uganda through subsidiaries jointly owned with local interests. It is understood that for a number of technical reasons their supply to Uganda is currently running at substantially reduced levels.[411]

Britain's secret trade deals with Uganda during this time are surprising for three reasons. Firstly, they were inconsistent with the stance Britain projected to the world when it broke diplomatic ties with Uganda: that due to the irrationality and unpredictability of Amin's government, it was impossible for Britain to have a normal relationship with it. Secondly, while Britain traded with Amin behind the scenes, the Foreign and Commonwealth Office publically insisted that the resumption of normal relations with Uganda depended on the improvement of the country's human rights situation,[412] and that Britain could not envisage circumstances under which relations could be resumed while Amin was still in power.[413] Thirdly, Amin's hostility to British citizens and business interests was well known, and his reputation as Africa's leading tyrant was notorious.

Britain's approach to trade with Amin's regime contrasts sharply with that taken by the USA when it cut diplomatic ties with Uganda in 1973. The US policy was to consciously distance itself from "human rights violations, [by] denying Uganda US products and facilities" which would "directly contribute to continued human rights violations, and [encourage] more concerted international attention to this situation."[414]

From 1973, the US took serious measures to condemn and act upon Amin's deplorable violations of human rights in Uganda.[415] These included: denying bilateral US assistance to Uganda; opposing and voting against loan applications by Uganda in international development banks; refusal to licence exports to Uganda on the munitions list; and denial of exports that would contribute directly to continued human rights violations by the Ugandan security establishment.[416]

In contrast, Britain, was reluctant to introduce a comprehensive ban on imports from Uganda, which would surely have hurt Uganda's economic and defence interests.[417] To avoid criticism, Britain was prepared to divert the planes to "other airports" in order to prevent the trade deals from going to other countries. The British Government had the power to stop Crown Agents from supplying equipment to Uganda's armed forces, but this question was left to each individual company to decide for itself.[418] And being in the business of profit and not politics, the Crown Agents made what they considered to be the most rational decision: to continue with the lucrative trade.

In 1978, Amin attacked the Kagera Salient in Tanzania (another Commonwealth country) and, in retaliation, Tanzania launched a serious military counter-offensive against Amin. This event led to a shift in Britain's policy on trade with Amin's rogue regime. The Foreign and Commonwealth Office realized that if the Uganda Airlines flights to Stansted were suspended it would weaken Amin's authority over his soldiers, who could be tempted to turn against him. It therefore urged the Prime Minister not "to let slip an opportunity to take action which might tip the scales against Amin," advising that if action against the flights was to have the desired impact, it would be "important to move swiftly to take advantage of the present unrest."[419]

He was advised that "the time was appropriate" and it was "the best opportunity" to suspend the flights because President Amin was "now in more serious trouble than at any time since he seized power."[420] The Prime Minister was eventually agreeable to the suspension of the flights but suggested that this should be done on "technical grounds."[421] The announcement of the suspension would be made in a "fairly low-key manner."[422] In that sense it may be said that Britain remained Amin's friend to the last and the accusations about its complicity in the crimes of his regime are not without foundation.

There is no doubt that Britain's covert support—through trade and the supply of military equipment—helped to sustain Amin's tyranny in Uganda. It offered a lifeline that helped him and his army maintain a stronghold over power in Uganda; but this meant that Britain consciously and conveniently turned a blind eye to the violence and atrocities Amin meted out to his own people. The Stansted Shuttle trade deals illustrate that Britain—just as it had when Obote's rule suited it—placed the protection of its commercial, political and other strategic interests over and above the promotion and/or the protection of the fundamental human rights of Ugandans as well as the stability, peace and development of its former colony.

Britain Joins Tanzania to Fight General Idi Amin

Once Tanzania's military offensive against Amin gathered momentum, Britain seized the opportunity to change its relations both with Amin's Uganda and Nyerere's Tanzania. It will be recalled that when Amin overthrew Obote in January 1971, Nyerere warned Britain, which was in a hurry to embrace the coup, that Amin's regime was bound to cause "serious danger to the peace and stability of East Africa."[423] Nyerere was particularly concerned about Amin's undisciplined army, its attacks on civilians and its sporadic armed attacks against Tanzania at its common border with Uganda. Britain, whose interests at the time were wholly aligned with Amin's staying in power, chose not to heed Nyerere's warning.

In a dismissive reply to Nyerere, Edward Heath, the British Prime Minister, simply stated: "It is our practice to recognise a government which is in control of its territory, regardless of our attitude towards its policies."[424] To protect its interests in Uganda, Britain thereafter threw its full support behind Amin's leadership. But this was not for long; as we have already seen. Once Britain worked it out that in fact Amin threatened, more than protected, its interests in Uganda, it made a *volte-face* and jumped at the earliest opportunity to get rid of him with Nyerere's help.[425]

For Britain, the best opportunity to finally cut ties with Amin came in 1978, when his army invaded Tanzanian territory, seized the Kagera Salient and declared its annexation to Uganda. Tanzania needed help and Britain embraced the opportunity to mend fences with Nyerere, who soon made an urgent appeal for assistance over the supply of defence equipment to the tune of £20 million. The list included communication equipment, vehicles, floating bridges, mine detectors, ammunition and anti-aircraft missiles. Tanzania also asked Britain to help with some credit terms as well as to expedite the delivery of the goods.[426] On its part, in a bid to protect its national interests, Britain needed Nyerere's goodwill over various Southern African problems—not least Rhodesia and Namibia.

In agreeing to Tanzania's request, the Chancellor of the Exchequer stated: "The national interest justifies our making cover available for the arms sales in question immediately, provided that the amount does not exceed £4 million and that normal credit terms for such sale are applied."[427] In addition to military hardware, Britain approved an aid grant of £2.5 million for Tanzanian imports from the UK for developmental purposes and was prepared to consider requests made for relief requirements beyond this sum.[428] Beyond this, Britain—having itself finally stopped supplying goods to Amin's army under the Stansted Shuttle arrangement—agreed, on behalf of Tanzania, to persuade Kenya to reduce or cut off supplies such as oil through Kenya to Uganda, "but without being directly and openly involved in an inter-African dispute."[429] It was understood that a week without supplies would finish Amin.

By 1979, Amin's regime was fast falling to its knees. A combination of the US trade embargo (three US oil companies stopped supplies to Uganda and withdrew their staff), the cessation of British military and other supplies to Amin, the disruption of supplies to Uganda from Kenya, and the boosting of British military and financial support to Tanzania was galvanized by the cooperation and support from Ugandans in exile to sweep Amin off the political scene.[430] Nyerere's resolute stance on defending Tanzania's territory and getting rid of Amin afforded him a leading role in the mobilization of the Ugandan exiles, who were hastily called together in Moshi to form the Uganda National Liberation Front/Army (UNLF/A) and agree on an interim regime after Amin had fallen.[431] Thus, even though Amin's Tanzanian campaign had the support of some 2,000 troops from Libya (equipped with fighter jets, tanks and other hardware), it was boldly repulsed as his regime collapsed on 11 April 1979. Amin fled to Tripoli in a bid to save his life, thus bringing a dramatic end to another tragic chapter in Uganda's political history.

Anglo-Ugandan Relations in Post-Amin Uganda

Just a few days before Amin's government was toppled, Britain was, once again, grappling with the issue of recognition of a new coup and of the UNLF government in Uganda. As it had done with Amin in 1971, it was keen to move fast on recognition. Although the main force behind the UNLF was the Tanzanian army, Britain felt that once Amin was overthrown and off the scene, and once the UNLF had a "reasonable prospect of permanence," it would move with all speed to negotiating terms with the new government.[432] According to the Foreign and Commonwealth Office, the objective was for Britain to re-establish itself politically in order to prepare a basis for the pursuit of its "interests, which include[d] official and private debt and a large number of compensation claims."[433]

Britain was prepared to move ahead of its allies, including the US and its European Economic Community partners, in recognising the new regime. Thus, the moment Amin fled Uganda and Kampala was liberated, Britain was immediately back on Uganda's diplomatic scene. It despatched Richard Posnett to assess the situation on the ground and re-establish its mission. Posnett described the scene he found in Kampala thus:

> The situation there in those first few hectic days was a mixture of ecstasy and chaos. Ugandans returning from exile embraced Ugandans emerging from their farms. Everybody was swept up in the general euphoria and they embraced me with equal enthusiasm. The arrival of a British representative while the battle front was still only 20 miles east of Kampala was welcomed with tremendous warmth after the years of separation. Having acquired a car and a Union Jack I explored the environs of the city, and

> was astonished to encounter clapping and cheering crowds. When I stopped I was pulled from the car to shake a hundred hands. It may be that having suffered so much since independence, the people recalled the days of the British Protectorate as the golden age and forgot the pinpricks. But for whatever reason, Britain now has an important place in the affections of most Ugandans. By the same token, much is expected of us.[434]

Rallying behind the generally pro-British Yusuf Kironde Lule and later Godfrey Lukongwa Binaisa, Britain immediately embraced the UNLF and announced a provision of £2,500,000 to fund the provision of humanitarian relief to the country. A further sum of £5 million in aid (targeting the cotton industry) was negotiated within a year. Britain also commenced discussions on the supply of military equipment and the provision of military training, and provided Land Rovers and trucks as well as training courses to the police. It was also keen to revive its business dealings with Uganda and to settle all of its outstanding business claims (British firms claimed over £100 million for expropriated assets).[435]

The new regime revived hope among the Baganda for the restoration of the Kabakaship. However, this matter did not seem to be a priority for the new government, given the general political and economic instability at the time.[436] This prompted some of the interested Baganda to approach Britain to enlist its support for this endeavour. Britain saw these enthusiasts as "self-styled representatives of the Kabaka's government," who wanted the British High Commissioner "to become involved in the dispute between supporters of the kingdom of Buganda and the Central Government" and considered them time wasters.[437] Its response was thus to stonewall these demands and to strongly deny any responsibility towards Buganda. It insisted that it severed its relations in 1962 and would rather not have anything to do with Prince R. M. Mutebi, whom it called a "pretender to the Kabakaship," or any of his agents.[438]

In light of the highly sensitive nature of the issue, the Foreign and Commonwealth Office advised the High Commission in Kampala to distance itself from the restoration agitators, pointing out that: "we certainly do not wish to become involved with Buganda politics and if possible you should avoid contact with the Kabaka and his family for other than routine business. We will take the same line in London should, for example, we be approached for advice regarding the return of Ronald Mutebe [sic]."[439] On the question of Britain's legal or other responsibilities toward Buganda, the Foreign and Commonwealth Office stated:

> no such responsibilities exist. The Agreements of 1894 and 1900 to which reference has been made, together with various other special agreements between the Crown and the Kingdom of Buganda, were all revoked by Article 1(2) and the First Schedule of the Buganda Agreement of 1961. This Agreement has in turn ceased to have effect by virtue of Section 1(3) of the Uganda Independence Act 1962. Section 1(1) of that Act also states that HMG in the United Kingdom "shall have no responsibility for the Government of Uganda or any part thereof". While the Buganda loyalists may have a case in the context of Uganda politics in claiming that the abolition of the Kabaka's special position in the 1967 Constitution was illegal, HMG is not responsible for maintaining the former constitutional provisions of Uganda.[440]

Thus Britain, oblivious to its past assurances that it would protect the constitutional order negotiated and agreed at Lancaster, was unwilling to take any responsibility for its role in the constitution-making process. As we have shown above, it had, during this process, given the otherwise sceptical Kabaka Mutesa and Buganda its assurances that the position reached in the Buganda Agreement of 1961 would be maintained after independence and beyond, if they signed up to the 1962 Constitution and agreed to be a part of Uganda.[441] On a moral plane, Britain, focusing on the protection of its commercial and strategic interests in Uganda, was prepared to turn away from the long relations it had with Buganda since 1894. It particularly and deliberately closed its memory to the fact that the pre-independence agreements that it had brokered in Lancaster House and Marlborough House—where it had significantly influenced Buganda to drop its separatist aspirations—were unilaterally and violently abrogated by a man to whom it then gave its fullest support.

In its post-Amin dealings with Uganda, Britain insisted that it was not available to meddle in the internal affairs of an independent country. There is evidence to show, however, that behind the scenes, Britain both covertly and overtly influenced political events in the country, including who assumed its highest political office. Although Uganda was headed to elections in 1980, a year after Amin's ouster, it was still unstable. The economy was struggling to recover, and the government was yet to achieve a firm grip on law and order. Without an army—save for a few bands of guerrilla outfits—Uganda depended wholly on Tanzania for its defence. As such, Tanzania's President Nyerere wielded immense influence in the military and political affairs of the country.

Yusuf Lule, the first President of the UNLF Government after the fall of Amin, took office on 13 April 1979 under the 1967 Constitution. According to Binaisa (who was to follow him as President), President Lule had agreed to observe the Moshi Agreements on the UNLA. However, in practice, Lule had ignored this agreement and claimed that he was bound by the 1967 Constitution alone. Also, although he had not been elected, he behaved as if he had a full popular mandate under the Constitution, for example, appointing senior officials without seeking the approval of the National Consultative Council. For this reason and others, he was deposed on 20 June 1979 after only 68 days in power.[442]

This coup saw G. L. Binaisa assume the presidency.[443] At the same time, with elections coming up in a little over a year, Milton Obote, Paulo Muwanga (a far from popular figure and with little ability but who, like Obote, had the backing of Tanzania) and Yoweri Museveni were all jostling for power ahead of the elections.[444] More than Obote,[445] Binaisa was particularly wary of Museveni who "thought himself qualified to join the club of extreme leftists and under 40-year-olds who were the Presidents of Angola, Mozambique and Ethiopia."[446] Only a few years later, Binaisa's fears turned out to have been well-founded.

President Binaisa looked to Britain for financial aid and the supply of military equipment. In January 1980, he sent Defence Minister Col. William Omaria to London to discuss this issue with the British Government. He also held a meeting with the British High Commissioner in Uganda, in which he discussed his fear of a coup and asked whether Britain would assist him and whether it would engage with Kenya to provide military support on request in the event of such a coup. He even asked whether Britain would enter into a Memorandum of Understanding on defence matters, including setting up a training facility for British troops in Uganda.[447]

While Britain made no commitments on a defence pact, when the possibility of a coup increased with Obote's imminent return to Uganda, it felt that it needed to help Binaisa, who would in turn protect its interests. Britain believed that because most of the UNLA commanders were supporters of Obote, and because Obote could not win in a fair election, he would use his friends in the army to overthrow Binaisa.[448] It also believed that since Nyerere wanted to see Obote back in power, it would follow that "if there was a pro-Obote coup the Tanzanians would merely look the other way and no other force could prevent the coup from succeeding."[449]

According to its High Commissioner in Uganda, Britain was also concerned that Obote's return would have implications for, among other things, the internal political situation in the country; the security situation and the growing levels of violence; and British policy towards selling arms to, or training, the UNLA.[450] The High Commissioner thus advised the British Government to be prepared to do what it could to "help Binaisa, who [was] more friendly to Britain, to the West and to [British] commercial interests than Obote or any other alternative could be expected to prove."[451] The only dependable alternative in the circumstances would be Lule coming back to power in the general elections "on the backs of the DP," but such an alliance was not distinctly possible.[452]

Like Britain, Kenya was circumspect about Obote's second coming. President Daniel Arap Moi told Britain's Margret Thatcher that he was deeply concerned about Uganda and hoped that Lule would be given a chance to rule again following a free and fair election.[453] Yet at the same time, he knew that Obote would "definitely take over from Binaisa before too long," and was uncomfortable about the precedent set by Tanzania where a president in one country could remove a fellow head of state with the acquiescence of the Organisation of African Unity (OAU).[454]

British interests in Uganda were almost a do-or-die matter, and it was not long before Britain turned to Yoweri K. Museveni, Binaisa's Minister of Defence. Although it considered his views as "radical," Britain considered Museveni not to be anti-British and as the man to watch.[455] Posnett, the British representative in Uganda, had created a good working friendship with him and, to extend British patronage and influence over Museveni, soon recommended that he and his wife be invited on an official visit to Britain.[456] Posnett told his superiors in London that "it would be invaluable if Museveni could be invited to visit the UK as soon as possible as a guest of HMG."[457] On such a visit, Museveni "could be influenced in the right direction, both politically and in defence matters, if we caught him in time."[458] Museveni had already expressed a keen interest visiting the UK to see military training systems and establishments.[459]

The Foreign and Commonwealth Office was persuaded by Posnett's proposal and believed that there were good political grounds, in terms of Britain's relations with Uganda, for offering an official visit to Museveni. Since the purpose and nature of the visit was essentially political, the invitation would be from the Foreign Minister.[460] However, the Secretary of State for Defence, having considered the political and military case for the invitation, was hesitant and expressed doubts about the value of such a visit, fearing that Museveni would only seek additional aid and free defence equipment—neither of which Britain could offer.

The matter was eventually left open for the new High Commissioner Designate to reconsider.[461] Around this time, seeking to secure his hold onto the presidency, Binaisa announced a ministerial reshuffle where Museveni was dropped as Minister of Defence and appointed as Minister of Regional Cooperation.[462] Binaisa's hold on power was all but lost once he demoted the powerful Army Chief-of-Staff, Oyite Ojok, by appointing him Uganda's Ambassador to Algeria.

Following the unexpected reshuffle, Britain put Museveni's invitation on hold and decided to watch his next steps, since his new posting was, in many ways, viewed as a demotion. Unsurprisingly, Oyite Ojok, Muwanga and Museveni were not happy with the reshuffle. They both turned down their new appointments. Binaisa was subsequently removed from power by the Military Council in May 1980. The Military Council was headed by Muwanga, with Museveni as his Deputy. British officials believed that with the removal of Binaisa, Museveni was virtually unassailable.[463] For that reason, and to ensure that he was friendly to Britain, the government prepared to invite him for an official visit.

Since the UNLF's rule was only a transitional arrangement, a General Election was held on 10 and 11 December 1980 under a multiparty system. Three parties contested the poll: the newly created Uganda Patriotic Movement (UPM) led by Museveni, the DP led by Kawanga Ssemogerere, and the UPC led by Milton Obote. The election was, for all intents and purposes, a political fiasco. Although it was widely believed that the DP's Ssemogerere won the ballot, Muwanga hijacked the role of the Electoral Commission at the ballot-counting stage and helped Obote steal the election.[464]

From 1980 to 1985, Obote was once again at the helm of Uganda's politics. His second administration was, unsurprisingly, worse than his first one. With a stolen election as the grounds to fight Obote, Museveni and others launched a five-year guerrilla bush war in which thousands lost their lives. Even though Britain was uncomfortable with Obote's second regime,[465] it supported him militarily. In 1984, as his war with Museveni intensified, Britain entered into a Memorandum of Understanding with Obote for a British Military Advisory Training Team (BMATT) to assist his army.[466] In spite of Britain's assistance, Obote's second regime remained unstable to the end thanks to a bad economy, insurgencies by Museveni's National Resistance Army (NRA) and a host of other guerrilla outfits, and a lack of internal cohesion among his allies. During this period, British interests in Uganda were damaged and its primary objective became "damage limitation, and the preservation of some ability to influence events when the situation took a turn for the better."[467]

On 2 December 1983, a senior and influential officer in Obote's army, Brig. David Oyite-Ojok, was killed in a suspicious helicopter crash in Luwero District.[468] Upon his death, the army developed split loyalties and insecurity in the country increased. This eventually led to another coup on 27 July 1985, led by Brigadier Bazilio Olara-Okello (a KAR veteran), in which Obote was once again overthrown. Olara-Okello later handed over power to his fellow Acholi tribesman, General Tito Okello, who at the time chaired the powerful Military Council. The coup, however, did not stop the fighting between the NRA and the Military Council; instead, it gave Museveni's guerrillas a new impetus to remove a regime dominated by the northern tribes of the Langi and Acholi, who had steered Uganda's politics since independence.

President Moi of Kenya brokered peace talks in Nairobi between Tito Okello's military government and Museveni's NRA. These talks initially provided some hope of an amicable resolution to the war, and they brought some respite through occasional ceasefires. With time, however, neither party gave serious regard to the talks, so they faltered and later collapsed. It appears, as Britain had suspected all along, that throughout the entire process the NRA had been intending to seek a decisive military victory rather than share power with Okello's Military Council.[469] For this reason, the talks and the peace agreement that was reached in Nairobi on 17 December 1985 are often referred to as "peace-jokes." Museveni exploited the weakness of Okello's army to make a final military offensive which helped him capture state power on 26 January 1986.[470]

It is worth noting that on the morning of 26 January, the British High Commissioner, C. McLean, called on Museveni "to make early contact and seek NRA assistance … in protecting the British community" and to assure him that the messages that Museveni had the previous night given to Major General Commander A. J. G. Pollard, the Head of the BMATT, about the capture of Kampala were passed on to Presidents Moi of Kenya and Mwinyi of Tanzania.[471] The proximity and ease with which these senior British officials accessed Museveni, as well as the trust that Museveni had in them before and immediately after the capture of power, suggests that there were longer and deeper but covert dealings between Museveni's NRA and Britain.

The cosiness between Museveni and Britain at this time may be explained by the fact that in November 1985, while the peace talks between Museveni and Okello dragged on, Britain, under Operation RAHU, deployed to Nairobi a contingent of soldiers led by Pollard as an advance party of the British Military Mission to the Government of Uganda to cover the intelligence and the fighting in the country.[472] The soldiers were officially there to help with the peace process. While in Nairobi, Britain's Sir Len Allinson and Pollard made contact with Museveni and his senior officers. On 19 December 1985, Britain announced a grant of £5 million to help resettle former soldiers pending the resumption of normal British aid. In backing the peace process and appearing to support both factions, Britain was placed in a good and apparently neutral position and, in its own assessments, the immediate outcome of these interventions was that both Okello's and Museveni's sides "regarded British policies as helpful and in Uganda's interests."[473]

Although information on Operation RAHU is scanty, the deployment of British forces to Nairobi where there were ongoing talks, and later to Kampala in February 1986 after Museveni had captured power, suggests that Britain's intention was to assess the military and political weight of the actors and, perhaps more importantly, to leverage the outcome of the talks. In a report to his superiors in London, Pollard wrote:

> The failure of the peace agreement prevented our carrying out the mission you originally gave us. We were however able to advise the NRM regime when they took power on the reorganisation and training of their guerrilla army and to offer and provide British training assistance.[474]

Commenting on Britain's relations in the early days of Museveni's rule, the British High Commissioner noted that Pollard and Allinson's links with the NRA in Nairobi and in Kampala "paid off handsomely when Museveni captured power" and helped Britain once again to be in a position to promote its prestige and interests.[475] To this end, the British Foreign and Commonwealth Office allocated an additional sum of £1,100,000 as a military training package for Uganda so as to "further British interests in East Africa."[476] This account makes it abundantly clear how and why Pollard emerged as a central player and a handy adviser to Museveni in the immediate aftermath of the capture of Kampala, and how he helped advance Britain's agenda in Uganda.

Anglo-Uganda Relations under General Yoweri Museveni's Rule, 1986—2018

Museveni's capture of state power was legalised before a rapturous crowd in a dramatic and momentous swearing-in ceremony held on the steps of Uganda's Parliament on 29 January 1986. Clutching the Bible with a raised right hand, the youthful 40-year-old former "rebel," Yoweri K. Museveni,[477] clad in military dress and surrounded by eagle-eyed guerrilla soldiers, was sworn in by the country's British Chief Justice, Peter Allen, as Uganda's ninth President. After the oath, the confident President told jubilant Ugandans, and the world, that this was

> not a mere change of guards, it is a fundamental change in the politics of our country.… [A]ny individual, any group or person who threatens the security of our people must be smashed without mercy.... The people of

> Uganda should only die from natural causes which are not under our control but not from fellow human beings.[478]

His immediate focus was stated to be the restoration of democracy and the protection of individuals and their property. He castigated corrupt African leaders who were unable to meet the needs of their citizens and those that overstayed in power. He counselled that democracy was the right of the people of Africa, and that governments must not be the masters but the servants of the population.[479] With such a rousing opening speech, many felt that with a young, charismatic and revolutionary leader they could trust, the country was set on a new journey to a democratic, peaceful and prosperous destiny. This journey has so far lasted 32 years with an almost imperial General Museveni riding at the helm of Uganda's politics.

With over three decades in power to cover, a full discussion of Anglo-Uganda relations during Museveni's tenure deserves a separate book. However, for our purposes and using a broad brush, we attempt a sketch of what, in general terms, appears to be stable and good relations between Uganda and Britain. As we have shown, Britain was, through General Pollard, to a limited extent involved in Museveni's final takeover of power. Britain's close association at inception meant that its relations with Museveni and his regime were mutually beneficial from the start. And although Museveni started off as a radical left-leaning revolutionary whose closest allies were Nyerere of Tanzania, Gaddafi of Libya, Chissano of Mozambique, Zenawi of Ethiopia and Fidel Castro of Cuba, Britain did all that was possible to wean him over from those quarters and influenced him to embrace and rely on a more Western-oriented economic and political outlook.

As we show below, this was not easy because, ever mindful of its acts or omissions in Uganda's past, Museveni had little penchant for the West and its capitalist ideology. Indeed, to counteract capitalistic orthodoxy, his policies—including on barter trade, *mchaka mchaka* (National Service for youth, civil servants, and the army), village committees, and frugal public expenditure—came closer to the socialist, and sometimes Communist, ideology he originally espoused. He was critical of the West in general and of the policies of the Bretton Woods institutions (the International Monetary Fund and the World Bank) in particular—notwithstanding that, as early as 1987, with Britain's encouragement, he took a rightist pro-World Bank position.[480] At his first speech at the Heads of State meeting at the Organization of African Unity (OAU) Summit, Museveni broke with protocol and castigated African leaders for looking on as thousands of Ugandans either died or suffered under the tyrannies of Milton Obote and General Idi Amin.[481] In another long speech at the United Nations

General Assembly, Museveni critiqued the world economic order and argued that Western countries, out of morality if nothing else, "ought to compensate for [the] transfer of resources from present day third world countries to themselves."[482]

It is thus not surprising that on his first official visit to the UK, in a discursive speech on precolonial and colonial African history—described by an FCO official as "rambling" and "fairly disastrous"[483]—the President attributed Africa's and Uganda's ills to the intervention of external powers as well as the unjust and oppressive role played by the existing economic world order. Because of his ideological outlook and revolutionary attributes, the West—with the exception of Britain—was slow to warm up to him and *vice versa.*

Faced with an unconventional politician and a former guerrilla leader with a radical streak, Britain based its tentative agenda during Museveni's first years in power on policy guidelines published in June 1986. The policy, *inter alia*, aimed to maintain and extend British and Western influence in Uganda; to encourage good relations with its neighbours and not to give support to dissident movements, e.g. in the Sudan; to seek by all means possible to limit the spread of Libyan influence, and to promote a clearer perception of the threat of Libyan activities; to explain British policy on South Africa and Libya, the advisability of agreement with the International Monetary Fund (IMF) and the need for settlement of claims; to encourage Western colleagues, particularly the US and EC partners, to exert influence along the same lines and to coordinate policies with those of Uganda's neighbours, especially Kenya; and seek the views and assistance of those who may have influence on Museveni, e.g. Daniel Arap Moi (then President of Kenya) and Samora Moises Machel (then President of Mozambique).[484] To achieve these policy objectives, Britain was to use the political connections established by Lynda Chalker and General Pollard. It was planned that David March, the new British High Commissioner, should win the confidence of Museveni and his leading ministers as well as the "emerging kitchen cabinet" of NRA and NRM members. In addition, visits of UK ministers to Uganda and Ugandan ministers to London were to be encouraged. A private visit to London for Museveni was to be arranged.

Under the said policy guidelines, and "in order to maintain British influence in Uganda,"[485] Britain undertook to quickly train 200 NRA instructors, train police officers, assist the Ugandan civil service, assist in the education sector, support agriculture and rehabilitate the Owen Falls power station. Other urgent measures included the promotion of constructive dialogue with the IMF and the International Bank for

Reconstruction and Development (IBRD); encouraging UK business in the rehabilitation of the economy by "keeping it informed in particular of the likely aid projects and taking its interests into account in the pattern of aid;"[486] encouraging Uganda to become a party to the main human rights instruments, i.e., the two international Conventions on Human Rights; and assisting the judiciary and the Ministry of Justice. However, all this assistance was conditional on the Ugandan Government's implementation of economic reforms on the basis advocated by the IMF and, unlike in its previous dealings with Obote's and Amin's regimes, on the government's human rights record.

In spite of his ideological leanings and his misgivings about the West, Museveni took these conditions seriously. He needed all the help he could get, given that his government took over an almost failed state whose economy was on its knees and whose politics were characterised by civil conflict. For that reason, he adopted a pragmatic approach for his regime's survival. To start with, he ensured that Uganda quickly ratified a raft of international human rights instruments including the Convention Against Torture and Other Forms of Cruel, Inhuman and Degrading Treatment (CAT) in 1986, the African Charter on Human and Peoples' Rights (ACHPR) in 1986, the International Covenant on Economic, Social and Cultural Rights (ICESCR) in 1987, the International Convention on the Rights of the Child (CRC) in 1990, and the International Covenant on Civil and Political Rights (ICCPR) in 1995.

In addition, in May 1986, Museveni set up a Commission of Inquiry into the Violations of Human Rights,[487] headed by Justice Arthur Oder, which operated between 1986 and 1994. Its work was hampered by financial problems, and the recommendations in its report were never fully implemented. According to the Institute of Peace, a US-based institution involved in conflict analysis across the globe, the Commission lacked political support and "only served as a political strategy to provide legitimacy to the new government."[488]

Uganda's poor record of, respect for and compliance with international human rights instruments suggests that it signed them more out of expedience than a genuine will to respect or enforce them. Certainly, Uganda's reporting on the implementation of its obligations under these treaties has been both delayed and problematic.[489] Furthermore, in pursuance of the pragmatic politics of survival, but essentially at the behest of Britain and other Western governments, Museveni embraced the IMF Structural Adjustment Programme (SAP) and Uganda adopted various austerity measures that helped its economy recover from the regression it suffered in the 1970s and 1980s.[490]

Once Britain sensed that Museveni would be useful in advancing its interests, it embraced him and his regime. And, to rebuild its patronage machine in Uganda, Her Majesty's Government, through Major General Pollard, delivered a message to Museveni stating that Britain wanted to see a peaceful and united Uganda in which there was full respect for human rights and fair processes of law. He was cautioned not to include people with unacceptable past records in his government. Two days after being sworn in, Museveni responded to Margret Thatcher's letter saying that his government was committed to human rights and the due process of law, and would bring criminals who had committed atrocities and violated human rights to book. He said that he looked forward to working with Thatcher "to consolidate and strengthen further the traditional ties of friendship and all-round cooperation that happily exists between our two countries and peoples."[491]

This was followed by a visit by Lynda Chalker (now Baroness Chalker), Minister of State at the Foreign and Commonwealth Office with Special Responsibilities for Africa on, 12 February 1986. Chalker's visit to Uganda, coming a little over a fortnight after Museveni captured power, was used to consolidate the ties developed by Pollard with Museveni and to create new inroads into his regime. It was the first high-level ministerial visit from another country to Museveni's government and signalled the unequivocal intention of the UK to forge close ties with the new regime. During this visit, Chalker more or less presented Museveni with a *carte blanche* to ask for whatever assistance he needed from the UK. Museveni's priorities were security, including military training, and economic rehabilitation. Britain quickly responded with a grant of £5 million for rehabilitation, plus £22 million from the ODA and the Commonwealth Development Corporation for the rehabilitation of the Owen Falls power station.

Within three months of the Museveni administration, the British High Commissioner felt that Britain was once again in a position to promote its interests and influence in Uganda. By June 1986, Chalker, who was greatly impressed with Museveni during her visit, felt that he would emerge as a major African political figure.[492] Pollard was similarly persuaded that Museveni, though inflexible and touchy,[493] was the best man to stabilize Uganda and re-establish its economy—which Museveni insisted was to be done "outside the democratic process."[494] Thus, the foundation for a follow-up visit by Museveni to the UK was set, and eventually arranged for November 1986.

But even as the UK organised this visit, two matters bothered it about Uganda's new leader. The first was his economic policy, and the second, his "injudicious relations" with Libya. Museveni's economic policy was aimed at building an independent, integrated and self-sustaining national economy,[495] which seemed socialist oriented and suspicious of the West in general and of the UK in particular.[496] Britain felt that this economic policy was wrongly structured and that obtaining decisions from the government was difficult. This was compounded by the fact that "even minor matters apparently have to be decided by President Museveni."[497]

For these reasons, Britain felt that after eight months in power, Museveni's government was losing its way, particularly on the economic side of things. His international relations were also problematic to the UK,[498] which felt he had to be encouraged to regain the initiative, and ensure that he was not "prematurely written off by western donors."[499] On relations with Libya, Britain considered that, with regards to Gaddafi, Museveni was "dining with the wrong spoon" and that he needed to be watched closely in view of Britain's position and interests.[500] Commenting on Gaddafi and Museveni's relations, the Foreign and Commonwealth Office noted:

> Museveni is also developing a worryingly close relationship with Colonel Gaddafi (who visited Uganda in early September and from whom the NRA is receiving training and reputedly equipment). Other reports suggest that he is actively contemplating arms deals with the USSR, Cuba and Yugoslavia…. It is clearly important for our interests in Uganda, and in East Africa more generally, that we seek to disengage Museveni from these hostile influences and steer him in directions which we should regard as positive and sensible. A call to the Prime Minister would be a valuable opportunity to contribute to this process.[501]

In view of this, Britain could have been harder on Museveni. But because the NRM's record on Libya and African socialism was inchoate, rather than upset Museveni, Pollard advocated a "suck it and see" policy.[502] Indeed, Britain's nervousness about Museveni was eased once, under the influence of Thatcher,[503] Chalker[504] and British aid, Museveni became more pliant.[505] He opened up Uganda's economy and later embraced the economic orthodoxy advanced by the IMF and the World Bank, whilst easing his restrictions on political pluralism.

Museveni's visit was used by his hosts to effectively put across its views on a number of issues, including economic policy, aid, military assistance and Uganda's foreign policy. An elaborate programme for the visit (which was originally intended to have been private) was developed to involve an audience with Her Majesty the Queen, the Prime Minister, the Foreign Secretary, the Archbishop of Canterbury (on account of the fact that Museveni was an Anglican) and the leaders of the Opposition parties. It was also felt by the FCO that an invitation to attend the State Opening of Parliament would be "a very good way of flattering Museveni and showing that we take Uganda seriously."[506] On her part, to get Museveni's allegiance to Britain, Prime Minister Thatcher advised:

> Museveni should leave London feeling that Britain is friendly and reliable; the areas in which we should assist him should be defined and we should get credit for our help; we should encourage Museveni to persevere in his commitment to human rights but warn him that we think his economic policies are adding to his problems and will not encourage UK investors; we should encourage him to reach an agreement with the IMF and creditors; we should continue to express concern about contacts with Libya and the Soviet Union.[507]

Based on this, Britain's interests and involvement in Uganda were agreed upon ahead of Museveni's visit, namely: to work with President Moi to influence Museveni towards a stable Uganda that does not injure neighbouring countries, especially Kenya, where Britain had substantial direct interests; to ensure that Ugandans look to Britain for support in the first instance by making sure the UK has a closer relationship and greater potential for influence than any other country; to eliminate the risk of Libya and/or Soviet influence replacing that of UK and the West; to maintain substantial contacts within Uganda for the benefit of the UK public (especially churches, voluntary organisations, and universities); to maintain a substantial share of a growing market (17.3% in 1985); and to ensure that Uganda pays its arrears to the ECGD.[508]

Britain's High Commissioner in Kampala cautioned the Foreign and Commonwealth Office that it needed to be clear about "the primary purpose of [its] financed military training in Uganda, which [was] surely to develop friendly relations with senior NRA officers and not to enhance the military capability of the NRA itself;" and that "military training should not be regarded as the only plank in our programme for developing bilateral relations with the NRM Government."[509] These views show how Britain aimed to utilise Museveni's visit to entrench its patronage.

Museveni visited the UK between 15 and 18 November 1986. His hosts had an elaborate program arranged for him. In a major speech to a large audience at the Royal Commonwealth Society, Museveni remarked extensively—to the embarrassment of his hosts—about African precolonial and colonial history and how this related to Africa's present backwardness. Wilcox, Museveni's escorting officer on the trip, reported that in his view, Museveni's anti-colonial rhetoric at the Royal Commonwealth Society was "lamentable and did nothing ... to indicate the possession of a clear, logical mind." Otherwise, Wilcox found Museveni to be presidential in outlook and manner but one who "did not appear to be conscious of any limitation to his power."[510]

His ill-received speech at the Royal Commonwealth Society notwithstanding, Museveni was articulate and impressive in all his other meetings, where he honed his ability to express the ideology of the NRA and the opportunities available in Uganda as well as his advocacy for international barter trade. On the Libyan connections, Museveni conceded that he was a friend to Gaddafi. He agreed with Britain, though, that Gaddafi had made some mistakes on foreign policy. He argued that the US and the UK's actions attacking Libya strengthened Gaddafi's position and that if they wanted to weaken him they should isolate him.[511] Museveni was asked about Uganda's abstention on a vote on Afghanistan in the United Nations. Not pleased with his response, Secretary of State Howe stated that he hoped the vote could be reviewed the following year.[512]

During this visit, Museveni had an audience with Her Majesty the Queen. He also met with Prime Minister Margaret Thatcher who, while urging the President to negotiate with the IMF, made an additional offer of £10 million as a grant of aid to Uganda.[513] Museveni's statement—that he did not wish to be dependent on aid, whilst asking Thatcher for additional help for a line of credit to enable Uganda buy vehicles and spare parts—was considered graceless. During the visit, Tiny Rowland of Lonrho promised 100 MAN trucks to be paid for in barter trade with Ugandan cotton.[514]

For Britain, Museveni's visit went excellently and met its objectives. Museveni was particularly made aware of the need not only to review and change his economic policies and engage with the IMF and the IBRD, but also to reconsider his dealings with Libya if he was to get additional UK support. On his part, Museveni was pleased with the warm reception and support from the British Government and for the assurances of ongoing support. In a letter to Chalker, Ernest Rusita, the Ugandan High Commissioner to the UK, reaffirming the traditional and historical cordial relations between Uganda and Great Britain, conveyed Museveni's gratitude for his audience with the Queen and the additional economic assistance from the UK.[515]

Museveni used this same trip to meet the Pope in Italy, King Baudouin in Belgium, and the leaders of the European Community. On what was clearly a triumphant maiden presidential trip for Museveni, the European Community signed up to two road contracts and a grant of $125 million under the Lomé Convention (III); the Belgian Government offered Uganda $30 million; while Italy offered 40 trucks and 100 tractors.[516] By November 1986, less than a year after Museveni captured power, Britain's overall economic aid commitments to Uganda totalled £30 million.[517]

With international recognition and support, Museveni was well on his way to becoming an influential international actor in Africa and beyond. Indeed, by 1996, Museveni had charmed the West and become one of its star African leaders. He, together with President Paul Kagame of Rwanda, Isaias Afwerki of Eritrea and Meles Zenawi of Ethiopia, was dubbed by US President Bill Clinton, during his African tour in March 1998, as one of the "new breed of African leaders" in what many, particularly President Thabo Mbeki of South Africa, saw as Africa's renaissance.[518] Museveni and Lt Jerry John Rawlings of Ghana soon became elite African leaders in the eyes of the IMF and World Bank. Uganda and Ghana's economic policies became the standard benchmarks for IMF and World Bank support across Africa.[519]

Under Museveni's new political and economic direction, Anglo-Ugandan relations improved remarkably. Britain increased aid and other financial support, the supply of military wares, and police and military training. This was not withstanding the disturbing findings, by the United Nations in 2003[520] and by the International Court of Justice (ICJ) in 2005,[521] that officers and soldiers of the Uganda Peoples' Defence Force including its most high-ranking officers, were involved in the looting, plundering and exploitation of the DRC's natural resources and that Uganda's military authorities did not take any measures to put an end to these acts while it effectively occupied the Ituri District in the Congo.

The Court also found that Uganda's army "committed acts of killing, torture and other forms of inhumane treatment of the Congolese civilian population, destroyed villages and civilian buildings, failed to distinguish between civilian and military targets and to protect the civilian population in fighting with other combatants, trained child soldiers, incited ethnic conflict and failed to take measures to put an end to such conflict; as well as by its failure, as an occupying Power, to take measures to respect and ensure respect for human rights and international humanitarian law in Ituri district."[522] Uganda was condemned to pay reparations to the DRC for the five-year occupation of its eastern regions. Congo's unpaid claim stands at $10 billion.

Uganda's plunder of Congo's resources didn't deter the UK from signing a 10-year £700m development aid deal with Uganda in 2007. The aid was to help in Uganda's reconstruction. In 2009, it provided £70m to Uganda through the Department for International Development (DfID), making it the second largest bilateral donor to Uganda after the US.[523]

Furthermore, many senior military officers, including Museveni's son, Major General Muhoozi Kainerugaba, have been trained at Sandhurst and other Staff Colleges in Britain. It must be pointed out that the mellowing of Anglo-Ugandan relations was facilitated a great deal by Museveni's close friendship with Baroness Lynda Chalker, the British Minister for Overseas Development and Africa from 1989 to 1997, who had interests in the British firms of Unilever and Lafarge.[524] After ending her political career, Chalker resurfaced as a consultant for Uganda's Presidential Investors' Round Table and a close adviser on how to improve Uganda's investment climate and competitiveness.

With the support and influence of Baroness Chalker, Museveni hosted Queen Elizabeth II at the Commonwealth Heads of Government Meeting (CHOGM) in Kampala in 2007. In a rare and major show of support to the regime, the meeting was attended by the Queen together with Prince Phillip, the Duke of Edinburgh, and their son Prince Charles. The Prime Minister, Gordon Brown, led a big delegation of British bureaucrats and business moguls at the meeting, which was attended by 48 Heads of State and Government. In many ways, the CHOGM meeting was a success that further cemented Anglo-Ugandan relations.

At a special sitting of the Ugandan Parliament, the Queen, in a short speech, spoke on Parliament's duty to protect democracy and the rule of law. She hailed Uganda for its role in establishing peace in the region, and paid tribute to Ugandan soldiers for serving in the African Union peacekeeping force in Somalia. At the opening of the CHOGM plenary, the Queen expressed her delight at being in Kampala and spoke on the CHOGM theme of "transforming societies." In what seemed a veiled message to the Ugandan leadership, however, she said:

> Our Commonwealth theme over the whole of this year is "Respecting Difference, Promoting Understanding." Recognising that each one of us is made up of layer upon layer of identity and that each of our unique personalities has ties to culture, religion, community, country and beyond, is the essence of open and tolerant communities. I hope that, in your discussion about transforming societies you will consider this abiding principle: that we should treat those around us as we would wish to be treated ourselves.[525]

The Queen also spoke about the importance of dialogue; the need to listen to voices in society and to respect fundamental human rights. Is it possible that the Queen's speech was a veiled attack on Museveni? This is plausible given that everyone was not particularly pleased with Britain's support to the CHOGM meeting in general and to the Museveni regime in particular. A cross-section of people both in Uganda and abroad saw CHOGM as a missed opportunity to deal with what they considered as Britain's support for the entrenchment of Museveni's dictatorship and his harassment of members of the Opposition—in particular of Dr Kizza Besigye, his closest rival for the presidency in 2006 and later in 2011 and 2016. In an open letter to the President, Mahmood Mamdani, a respected professor of political science, called on him to shift the contest for power in a divided Uganda from the military to the political field and thus to demilitarise political competition.[526]

Another cause of concern was the attack on the independence of the judiciary. In November 2005, the special forces known as the "Black Mamba" prevented the release on bail of Opposition politicians.[527] In March 2007, a few months before the CHOGM meeting, the same Black Mambas stormed the High Court to re-arrest five men that had been granted bail after 15 months of detention. The men had, together with Besigye, been charged with treason. The judiciary went on strike to protest what they called the defilement of the Temple of Justice.[528] Spontaneous demonstrations on the streets were met and quelled heavy-handedly using tear gas and the notorious Kiboko Squad, who used big sticks to indiscriminately beat anyone in their way.

These blatant acts by the army to intimidate and interfere with the independence of the judiciary, coupled with government attempts to thwart and harass leaders of the Opposition ahead of elections, crowned with the runaway corruption in government, did not bode well in terms of the principles of the Commonwealth. The conduct of the army and the impunity it enjoyed confirmed fears that the army—particularly the NRA High Command—was the core of the state and the country's power structure.[529]

Before the 2006 elections, the UK announced that it would withhold £20 million in aid money. Museveni reacted angrily and wrote to Hillary Benn, the Minister in charge of aid, accusing the UK and other donors of interfering in Uganda's domestic politics. In the letter, leaked to the press, an angry Museveni wrote that it was unacceptable for the UK

> to think, and even say, that because of the modest sums [it had given] a country like Uganda, [it was] entitled to exercise suzerainty over [Uganda's] sovereign issues (foreign affairs, politics and defence).... Does a freedom fighter like myself have [the] ability to know what good governance is or is it a monopoly of British ministers and the British High Commissioner in Kampala?[530]

Britain's threats to withdraw aid stopped neither the harassment of the Opposition nor the flaws in the 2006 election.[531] The Opposition hoped that Britain would take a tougher stance on Uganda's leader, particularly on the questions of democracy and human rights, but that did not happen.[532] Museveni's critics had hoped that such gross abuses, rather than earning him the honour of hosting the CHOGM, would have been reason enough for its cancellation and calling Museveni to order.[533] As it turned out, however, none of these excesses proved sufficient for the Queen to cancel her visit to Uganda or for CHOGM to be relocated to another country. Allowing such a high profile meeting to be held in Uganda attracted criticism of Britain's policy towards Museveni's regime. This raised questions about Britain's—and the Commonwealth's—double standards in the promotion of democracy and human rights, as noted in the Guardian newspaper:

> By holding CHOGM in Kampala, the Commonwealth is rewarding Museveni's authoritarianism, social injustice and human rights abuses. It is a sick betrayal of the Ugandan people. If the Commonwealth won't defend its democratic and humanitarian principles against autocratic leaders like Museveni, what is the point of the Commonwealth?[534]

But while the real value of the Commonwealth may be questioned by some, there is no doubt that Britain derives prestige and patronage for the body's continued existence with its monarch perched at its top.[535]

Beyond the Kampala 2007 CHOGM controversy, General Museveni's star continued to rise in the context of Anglo-Ugandan relations. He remained a close British ally and was considered a go-to person on questions of peace and security in the Great Lakes region. In 2007, the UK signed a 10-year £700m development partnership deal with Uganda.[536] For that reason, despite his questionable democratic credentials,[537] and aid cuts over corruption in 2012[538] and over his position on homosexuality in 2014[539] notwithstanding, Museveni has remained a close UK ally and a pivotal figure in the East and Central African region. Particularly on the question of peace and security in South Sudan, Somalia and the Democratic Republic of the Congo (DRC), he is highly regarded and often consulted by Britain and the US, who have strategic and other interests in the region.

The British Foreign Secretary, Boris Johnson—who is known to view the African continent through a racist, paternalistic and neo-imperialist lens[540]—was in Uganda on 15 March 2017 to discuss trade deals with Uganda and security issues in Somalia, the DRC and South Sudan. He also needed to secure the personal attendance of President Museveni at the

London Conference on Somalia on 11 May 2017. During the discussions with Museveni, Johnson acknowledged that the UK-Uganda relationship was now more important than ever[541] and lauded the existing close political dialogue, strong trade relations, and excellent defence and cultural links between the two countries. He expressed Britain's wish to grow this relationship in the future. Needless to say, Britain's generous support to Museveni's regime occurred in spite of criticisms of his democratic and human rights credentials.[542]

Boris Johnson's high profile visit to Uganda was followed immediately by visits from Lord Dolar Popat, a trade envoy of the British Prime Minister, and Baroness Aneley, the Foreign and Commonwealth Minister; and later by the UK's Department for International Development (DFID) Minister, James Wharton, who visited Uganda in early 2017 in a search of markets and opportunities for Britain outside the European Union.[543] The visits by these senior British officials all point to two things: namely, that in spite of all the other political, constitutional and governance problems of the country,[544] Anglo-Ugandan relations are alive well and, perhaps more importantly, that Britain, now wary of the effects of its looming exit from the European Union, continues to focus more on its trade and commercial interests in Uganda and in the region and less on human rights and governance issues with its trading partners. As in the past, it will do all it can to secure these interests under the Museveni presidency and, certainly, beyond it. Thus, through neocolonial patronage (arms sales, trade, aid and covert support to pro-British or pro-Western leaders), Britain has played an influential role with all the country's postcolonial regimes—including those of Obote, Idi Amin and Yoweri Museveni.

Museveni and Buganda

Between 1967, when Obote abolished kingdoms in Uganda, and 1993, when Museveni restored the institution of traditional and cultural leaders, the kingdom of Buganda was in hibernation and had vanished off Uganda's political landscape. As we have shown, the struggle to restore the kingdom during and immediately after Amin's regime was futile. And, once Obote returned to power in 1980, hopes for its restoration seemed lost, considering that it was he who had abolished the kingdoms in the first place.

However, with the degeneration of Obote's second regime and the rise of military opposition to his rule came a renewed fervour from the Baganda to fight for the restoration of their kingship.[545] Military groups formed by Baganda nationalists—most notably the Uganda Freedom

Fighters (UFF) led by Yusuf Lule, the Uganda Freedom Movement (UFM) led by Andrew Kayiira, and the Federal Democratic Movement FEDEMU led by Lawrence Semakula—took up arms to fight Obote's dictatorship and also to advance Buganda's traditional and political interests. These forces fought alongside others like Museveni's Popular Resistance Army (PRA), the Uganda Rescue Front (URF) and, later, the Uganda National Liberation Front (UNLF). With the killing of the leaders of the UFM and FEDEMU, Buganda's cause in the liberation struggle was sidelined in the interests of national liberation.[546]

Yusuf Lule and Museveni joined ranks to form the NRA, which fought Obote's government in a five-year guerrilla war. During this war, the then Prince Ronald Muwenda Mutebi (currently the Kabaka of Buganda) was called upon to mobilise and increase the morale of the NRA fighters in the bush.[547] According to Nadduli, a bush war veteran and currently a Minister without a Portfolio, Mutebi was secretly flown from London to Nairobi and driven to the "Luwero triangle," not only to witness how the war was advancing towards Kampala, but also to prove to the population that Museveni was keeping his promise to restore the kingdom of Buganda if he gained power.[548] Not long after Prince Mutebi's visit, the NRA successfully captured power in 1986. It is estimated that 300,000 mainly Baganda civilians were killed and over 500,000 were displaced from their homes during the war.[549] Because of the support and sacrifice rendered by the Baganda to Museveni's bush war, as soon as the war ended, the question of Buganda and the restoration of the Kabakaship re-emerged.

However, in spite of the fact that he fought the war against Obote on Buganda soil and with the support of the Baganda and Prince Ronald Mutebi, Museveni denies ever having agreed to, or promised anyone that he would restore the Kabakaship. Although there is talk that an agreement was struck in Kikunyu Makulubita in the Luwero bush for the restoration of the kingdom, this remains unsubstantiated. In fact, President Museveni has vehemently denied the existence of such an agreement.[550] He has frequently maintained that he never fought the war to restore kingdoms in Uganda. In what may lend credence to this view, according to Sam Kalega Njuba, a former Museveni confidant and senior member of the UPM and later the NRM, asserts that Museveni "does not like the Kabaka as an institution let alone Mutebi as Kabaka ... because they are extremely popular in Buganda."[551]

Whatever the case, given his revolutionary antecedents, General Museveni and his leftist guerrilla comrades in the NRA were not too keen on the restoration of the Kabakaship when they captured power in 1986. Perhaps it is for this reason that the NRA bush war manifesto, the Ten-

Point Programme, is silent on the issue, although it may be argued that the matter fits under point No. 8 that promises to redress errors that resulted in the dislocation of sections of the population and the impoverishment of others.[552]

It took seven years from the end of the bush war for Museveni's government to allow the restoration of traditional leadership in Uganda, but even then, it was done in the face of stiff resistance among sections of the army. According to Major General Kahinda Otafiire, in April 1992, the army told Museveni "not to return these obsolete institutions and he did not listen to us. He begged, he pleaded, he went on his knees and the army grudgingly accepted to return these things."[553] Their resistance was based on the view within the NRA junta that traditional leadership was the cause of the 1966 Buganda crisis and the resultant political chaos in the country. However, after a heated debate over the restoration of the Buganda monarchy, President Museveni prevailed upon the army commanders to accept the restoration.[554]

Like Obote and Idi Amin before him, Museveni was aware of the political capital to be gained in Buganda on anything that promoted the Kabakaship. He knew that to consolidate his power and rule effectively he needed its support.[555] Motivated thus, he ensured that the institution of traditional and cultural leaders was grudgingly restored in 1993.[556] In order to control and own the process of the restoration of the Kabakaship, Museveni did not wait for a national debate on the issue within the Constituent Assembly. For that reason, the restoration took place before the Assembly had concluded its deliberations (including on the possibility of restoring the federal system of Government, loosely called "federo"). The legislation necessary for the restoration was steamrolled through the National Resistance Council (NRC) by Museveni, despite some opposition in the form of a court case filed by Kenneth Kakuru, a prominent lawyer (and now Judge of the Court of Appeal Constitutional Court), and public statements by the then President of the Uganda Law Society, Solome Balungi Bbosa.[557]

With Museveni's resolve to restore traditional leadership in Uganda against the wishes of the army and other actors, many in Buganda saw the sun rising on the horizon and looked up to him as their hero and saviour.[558] When the Constitutional Commission headed by Justice Benjamin Odoki was set up to seek citizens' views on a new Constitution, Buganda overwhelmingly demanded the return of the kingdoms as well as the restoration of a federal system of government. Indeed, the draft constitution made some reference to these issues. These two issues also had overwhelming support across the country. However, the power politics around the making of the new Constitution of 1995 helped to sideline Buganda's demands for a federal system of government and the restoration of the kingdoms as they had existed before the 1966 Crisis.

Instead, the new Constitution provided for the existence of the institution of traditional or cultural leaders whose roles and powers were restricted to matters cultural. These leaders were prevented from exercising any administrative, legislative or executive powers of government or local government. Their survival was left to the mercy of the central government handouts and the charity of their subjects. In the place of the federal system of governance that the Baganda yearned for, the new Constitution, under Article 178, offered the districts of Buganda, and others that so wished, the option to cooperate by way of a charter. The charter was to be a loose instrument of cooperation between the districts but one where the kingdom and its traditional structures had no power or role.

The new Constitution was promulgated in October 1995, much to the disappointment of the Baganda, who felt that what was restored was not the envisaged political kingdom but merely a powerless cultural entity. Consequently, the Buganda Lukiiko passed a resolution rejecting the new instrument. Interestingly, the resolution has never been rescinded, yet the Lukiiko continues to operate under the Constitution and often relies on it to defend its positions on matters such as land, the legal status of the Kabaka and other cultural rights. The Lukiiko's behaviour in 1995—to say one thing and do another or conduct itself differently—is similar to how it dealt with its declaration of independence from British rule in 1960. The Lukiiko's apparent payment of lip-service to these issues suggests either a lack of clear strategic thought before the resolutions are taken or the absence of the willpower or firmness needed to stick to difficult positions in the face of a government authority.

From the late 1990s, relations between Buganda and the central government became even more problematic. The Kabaka and the leadership in the kingdom of Buganda were perceived to grow political wings, following their persistent demands for federalism and the return of Buganda's assets expropriated by Obote's regime after the 1966 Crisis. These demands irritated Museveni and his government, and set the two sides on a collision course. Buganda's leaders came under attack from Museveni as liars and opportunists.[559]

In 2004-5, a decade after its promulgation, the Constitution was to be reviewed and revised to cater for any changes or omissions. The task was handed to a Constitutional Review Commission headed by Professor Edward Fredrick Ssempebwa. This development offered Buganda and other parts of Uganda the chance for a second bite of the constitutional cherry. Buganda's leadership, headed by Katikkiro J. G. Mulwanyamuli Semwogerere, marshalled over 200,000 Baganda who peacefully marched to the Nile Conference Centre in Kampala to tender Buganda's demands for federalism and other constitutional changes.[560] Although the delegation was well received by the Commission, and its arguments well presented to it, once again, Buganda's efforts yielded none of the desired fruits. In spite of the popularity of Buganda's views, the Commission never recommended the adoption of a federal system of government for Uganda. Instead, it recommended the introduction of a less autonomous form of regional government in the country.

Parallel to the process of the Constitutional Review Commission, President Museveni set up a separate *ad hoc* process in which he engaged with Buganda's leadership on the question of federalism. This convoluted process, which was chaired by the President, was essentially outside the public sphere. On one occasion the kingdom's officials walked out on the President upon his insistence that the kingdom should have two centres of power: one being a cultural council headed by the Kabaka and the other being a political council headed by an elected individual. Once the president dropped this proposition, the meetings resumed but under the chairmanship of John Patrick Amama-Mbabazi, Museveni's trusted ideologue and the country's Attorney General at the time.

The outcome of the *ad hoc* negotiations was a half-hearted plan to grant limited autonomy in the form of a regional government to the kingdom of Buganda, but one that was fraught with political and other structural problems. And, although the kingdom initially embraced the regional government idea, it later roundly rejected it following closer scrutiny and a public criticism.[561] The behind-the-scenes negotiations between Buganda and the President were frowned upon by other parts of the country and Buganda was accused, once again, of seeking special status over and above other parts of the country. For his role in the affair, Museveni was accused by his political opponents of being opportunistic in trying to reach a hush-hush settlement to win Buganda's support ahead of the 2006 elections.

By 2007, the general political environment in Uganda had soured and the strain in the Buganda/Uganda relationship had reached breaking point. The tension was manifest in a number of anti-Buganda policies advanced by the government, prominent among which was the controversial Land Bill of 2007 which Buganda strongly opposed. As the kingdom's Attorney General at the time, I was at the forefront of its opposition to this Bill.[562] Increased tensions around the Land Bill resulted in the arrest and detention of three Buganda kingdom officials for several days and without trial.[563] In reacting to Buganda's stance, Museveni accused Buganda of demonising him and the NRM, in a scathing speech to Members of Parliament from Buganda. He bitterly complained about the Kabaka's refusal to answer his telephone calls and warned that he would not tolerate Mengo's "unconstitutional behaviour."[564]

In a move, similar to the colonial divide-and-rule policy, to undermine the Kabaka's authority, Museveni recognised and funded rival 'kings' called Ssabaruli and Ssabanyala in the counties of Buruli and Bugerere respectively, both of which are within the jurisdiction of Buganda kingdom. The Government prohibited the Kabaka from visiting these two counties. This resulted in extensive and deadly demonstrations across the kingdom in 2009.[565] A police station was burnt at Natete and over 30 people killed by government soldiers. Fearing that the demonstrations might spread to other parts of the country, the government closed the Central Broadcasting Service (CBS) Buganda kingdom's radio station. To date, no serious investigations have been made and no public report has ever been issued on these riots.

Over 500 people were arrested and detained on charges ranging from assault to terrorism, but all were acquitted once the Directorate of Public Prosecutions failed to prove the offences.[566] Unfortunately, those charged for terrorism spent three years in detention for crimes they never committed. No apologies or compensation have been forthcoming. By creating and funding competing centres of power within Buganda, the Government intended to challenge, divide and hence weaken the Kabaka and the kingdom of Buganda. These machinations resulted in the worst demonstrations under Museveni's long reign.

The tension between the central government and the kingdom of Buganda was only eased when the Kabaka met the president in 2009 at State House in Entebbe. But, in what appeared as another affront to the Kabaka, this was followed by the introduction of the controversial Institution of Traditional or Cultural Leaders Act of 2011 which aimed to operationalise Article 246 of the Constitution and sought, amongst other matters, to forbid traditional or cultural leaders from participating in partisan politics. Partisan politics was defined as:

(a) promoting, or supporting a political party or political organisation or an individual in respect of political activities;
(b) making statements against Government or opposition policies or programmes;
(c) making statements or comments on Bills or motions under consideration by Parliament with a view to influencing their outcome.

When an opinion was sought on the legality of the proposed Bill, Dr Khiddu Makubuya, the Attorney General of Uganda, advised that it was a major addition to the substance of Article 246 of the Constitution, which would attract questions on its constitutionality.[567] He envisaged that the Bill would attract costly litigation and, to avoid this, proposed that non-legislative measures "may have to be devised to deal with the rather provocative stances of some of the traditional or cultural leaders."[568] Clearly the aim of this Act was to gag traditional leaders and prevent them from criticising government policies or in any way expressing political opinions. The kingdom of Buganda opposed the Act and some of its subjects filed a petition challenging its constitutionality.[569] However, the case has not been heard or determined by the Constitutional Court for over five years. One can only speculate why the court has been so inordinately tardy in this case.

The relations between the central government and Buganda kingdom, which had hit rock bottom by the end of 2009, only improved when the President, perhaps with his eyes on the 2016 elections, invited the Kabaka, out of the blue, to discuss the return of some assets that were expropriated way back in 1967. Following brief negotiations, the Kabaka signed an agreement with the President on the return of the assets in 2013.[570] This paved the way to the President receiving an invitation to the Kabaka's 20th Coronation Anniversary; however, the President, in spite of the return of the assets, was heckled in the middle of his speech and was constrained to leave unceremoniously.

Since then, relations have thawed and the animosity between the two entities has reduced greatly. But in spite of these developments, there still remains a deep mutual suspicion and mistrust. In particular, the kingdom does not trust the central government's intentions, but neither does the central government trust or support Buganda in its pursuit of self-determination. The contradiction essentially lies in the historical desire for the kingdom to assert its political power on the one hand, and the central government's desire to confine it to the cultural realm, on the other. Nelson Kasfir, a leading political scientist on African matters, discusses the fissures and collisions between the kingdom of Buganda and the central government arising out of the former's desire to obtain political power and the latter's rejection of the same.[571] Buganda's resolve to fight for federalism has grown over the years. But as this resolve grew so did the reluctance on the part of the central government to listen, let alone give in to its demands for autonomy. A congruence of minds on a civic resolution of the Buganda question remains elusive. We discuss this matter in some detail below.

Relations between Britain, Buganda and other Kingdom's in Museveni's Uganda

As it had under Obote and Amin's regimes, in Museveni's Uganda, Britain maintained a policy of detachment from the kingdoms with which it had had agreements until independence. In February 1986, a few weeks after Museveni had captured power, the Foreign and Commonwealth Office expressed concern that Museveni's ideas and practices would alienate traditional elements in Uganda. It was particularly feared that "as ever, the parochialism and intrigue of the Baganda could prove a major obstacle to national unity."[572]

Yet as we have seen, the artificiality and fragility of nationhood in Uganda lies in how Britain, in the dying days of its colonial rule, hurriedly patched together a constitutional framework in London that saw, for the first time, the people from Kisoro to Karamoja, from Bunyoro to Bugisu, from Toro to Teso, from Arua to Ankole, and from Buganda to Bundibugyo talking to each other about how to weld themselves together for a future in a new country constructed on a Western and adversarial political system. This accounts demonstrates that from the days of Sir Harry Johnson in 1900 to the days of Boris Johnson in 2018, and from Lord Lugard to Lord Popat today, Britain's core objective was, and remains, the protection of its national interests in Uganda—sometimes in a manner inimical to the interests of the people of Uganda. We have seen how, on its exit, Britain left behind a nominally independent country with an alien and fragile political system in the hands of a young and inexperienced political elite riven with sharply contradicting worldviews and political outlooks. At the same time, Britain left it with several unresolved and intricate political questions at play, such as the problem of constitutional relationships and internal administrative boundaries (e.g. the lost counties issue). This, coupled with a small and inexperienced African civil service—incapable of managing institutions in a modern state and dependent on a few British expatriates—signaled a bleak future for the country.

It is unsurprising however that Britain's attitude towards Buganda had not changed by 1986—even though its kingdom had been abolished for over 19 years. This attitude, where Buganda is seen by Britain as parochial and an obstacle to Uganda's unity has continued during the Museveni era. Pursuant to this policy, and particularly since the restoration of the Kabakaship in 1993, save for sponsoring a four-day trip[573] for Buganda's Attorney General John W. Katende and myself, as the Minister for *Nkuluze* (Privy Purse) to experience devolution at work in Northern

Ireland, Scotland, and Wales, Britain has had little official contact with the kingdom of Buganda or any other kingdom in Uganda.

Unlike other foreign governments such as the US, whose Ambassador, Jerry Lanier, once paid a courtesy call on the Kabaka in February 2010,[574] Britain has maintained an arm's length relationship with the Kabaka and the kingdom of Buganda. While this may be justified on the policy of non-interference in domestic affairs of sovereign nations, it could equally be that Britain does not want to stir past expectations and (dis)agreements. For that reason, it made no public statements about the tensions that have gripped the kingdom of Buganda and the central government, even after the 2009 disturbances. During the CHOGM meeting that was held in Uganda in 2007, a request for a private meeting between the Kabaka and the Queen was declined by its officials in Kampala. On the whole, Britain's detached stance towards the kingdoms with which it had colonial relations in the past does not removed questions about its responsibilities arising from its 68-year of rule in Uganda.

One such question was the subject of a legal suit filed in the Ugandan courts by the kingdom of Bunyoro against Britain. In 2004, acting through a ten-member Bunyoro-Mubende Committee, the reigning king, Omukama Solomon Gafabusa Iguru, filed a suit accusing Britain—and the kingdom of Buganda as its accomplice—of deposing his grandfather, Kabalega; killing hundreds of people in Bunyoro; and stealing livestock, land and ivory during an imperial expedition to overpower his kingdom carried out in the early 1890s. Kabalega's resistance to British rule attracted the wrath and full force of the British, with disastrous consequences for the kingdom and its people.[575] It has been said that "nowhere in Uganda was the coming of the colonialists felt more strongly than in Bunyoro, with its violent conquest and subsequent denigration of the old order."[576]

Bunyoro's claim was in excess of £3 billion and was founded on the evidence obtained from military field notes, diaries and dispatches by colonial officers in Uganda at the height of the colonial conquest and rule.[577] Some of the evidence showed that the British were responsible for plundering the kingdom.[578] Britain denied the claims but, interestingly, sought an out-of-court settlement of the dispute.

By 2012, because no settlement was forthcoming, the claimants filed a new notice of intention to sue Britain, claiming that "during the CHOGM meeting held in Kampala in 2007 the UK Government offered to settle out of court and paid £700 million through the Government of Uganda."[579] President Museveni was said to have confirmed that £700 million had been received from Her Majesty's Government but that he had "forgotten to give directions to the Ministry of Finance" to pay out the compensation to Bunyoro.[580] However, in an apparently contradictory response to the notice of intention to sue, British Foreign Secretary, William Hague, informed the claimants:

> All liabilities and obligations relating to the colonial administration passed to the Uganda Government at Independence. We have in the past asked that the Government of Uganda speaks directly with your Majesty [Omukama Solomon Gafabusa Iguru] to address any concerns.[581]

In an evasive and diversionary manner, Hague told the claimants that Britain had a strong development partnership with Uganda, and that UK development assistance to Uganda had increased from £63.5 million in 2007 to a commitment to provide £356 million between 2011 and 2015.[582] No doubt this letter did not placate the claimants, who chose to pursue the same in the Constitutional Court. Bunyoro's case is still before the Constitutional court awaiting a full hearing and final verdict.

At the time Bunyoro sued it for the atrocities committed by its colonial agents in Uganda, Britain was also entangled in another suit by the Mau Mau survivors of torture and other violations in neighbouring Kenya.[583] However, rather than confront its former subjects in court and stand the graphic details of their wrenching testimony, Britain reached out with a quick settlement. The British Foreign Secretary, William Hague, in announcing the settlement expressed "sincere regret" for the torture and abuse committed by British colonial officers against Kenyans in the 1950s and announced a compensation package of £19.8 million to be divided between 5,200 victims. But in spite of the pay out and statement of regret, Hague was quick to add that Britain continued "to deny liability… for the actions of the colonial administration and … [did] not believe that this settlement establish[ed] a precedent."[584]

Hague's caution sounded hollow and at risk of flying in the face of new evidence of atrocities committed by Britain during its colonial heyday. The Mau Mau victims' case opened a Pandora's Box and exposed what has been called a "deliciously dramatic, if damning tale of missing archives, clandestine purge operations, and high level state cover-ups."[585] While denials of negative attributes of colonialism by British officials such as Boris Johnson and William Hague may persist, the Mau Mau victims' case, as well as recent document-based research, paints a vivid picture of a Janus-faced Britain.

Research on Operation Legacy and the messy liquidation of the British Empire in Africa and elsewhere shows that Britain had a lot to hide—and perhaps to account or apologise for—regarding certain aspects of its imperial record. This is why, over 50 years after the end of Empire, there are earnest calls for Britain to apologise for UK's historic wrongs. For example, at the Commonwealth Heads of Governments Meeting (CHOGM) in London in April 2018, there were calls for the British Prime Minister to apologise to Commonwealth leaders for past failures by the British Government, and for its inhumane, exploitative record overseas.[586]

In response to these demands, Prime Minister Theresa May avoided a full apology, but could not escape voicing regret on the Windrush deportation scandal affecting immigrants from Caribbean members of the Commonwealth.[587] In showing limited contrition, she obviously missed both the opportunity and the point which is, as these cases suggest, that Britain needs to come to terms with its past squarely once and for all. Piecemeal and half-hearted apologies have not worked in the past and will not serve in the future, because as more and more hidden embarrassing history comes to light, many more blots on the country's moral conscience will emerge, generating even more scandals and prolonged odium.

Justice and Accountability for Colonial Wrongs

We have shown that many wrongs were committed against the people of Uganda during colonial rule—often in repudiation of Britain's own legal and normative standards on human dignity and fundamental rights. However, to understand the full scope and nature of these wrongs, it would be necessary to obtain evidence through a full-scale public and international investigation into Britain's actions and/or the actions of its agents, similar to the inquiry conducted by the UN in the case of Uganda's plunder of the resources of the DRC. The investigation would entail an inquiry into, *inter alia*:

a) The massacre by Lord Fredrick Lugard and other British agents of hundreds of innocent people on Bulingugwe Island in Lake Victoria and elsewhere in the establishment and entrenchment of the British rule in Uganda.
b) An account of the deposition and deportation of Kabaka Mwanga and Omukama Kabalega to Seychelles in 1899, including a full account of how Britain prosecuted the war against Kabalega, and the claims that it tortured and killed hundreds of people in Bunyoro under the command of Samuel Baker, Henry Edward Colville and other colonial administrators.
c) The negotiations of the 1900 Buganda Agreement where, through

bribery, lies and intimidation, the British Crown secured over 50% of Buganda's land for the British crown under the banner of "protection" and without any valuable consideration.

d) The killing of protestors in the 1945 and 1949 demonstrations in Buganda and the wrongful deportation of several people under Governor J. Hall's watch.
e) The deposition and deportation without trial of Sir Edward Mutesa in 1953, as well as the deportation of several other Ugandans without trial.
f) The killing of protestors in the 1960 Bukedi demonstrations.
g) A full account of revenues including money raised as taxes, like hut tax, gun tax, poll tax and taxes on produce throughout the Protectorate.
h) The execution of Operation Legacy and a full disclosure of details of documents that were destroyed and that those that were hidden away.

An inquiry into historical injustices of British colonial rule in Uganda, and elsewhere, would aim to secure and promote accountability, justice, rule of law and to help end a culture of impunity and double-standards regarding state and personal responsibility for acts of aggression, plunder, mistreatment and human rights violations during the colonial era. It would also help in the verification of the facts and in obtaining a full and public disclosure of the truth.

The need to redress past wrongs and violations is recognised in international law. Soon after the Second World War, the UN Charter was adopted by nations, including Britain, with the principal objective of respecting the principle of equal rights and self-determination of peoples as well as promoting peace and human rights without distinction. In 1960, at the height of decolonization in Africa, the UN, under Resolution 1514, required member states to bring to a speedy and unconditional end of colonialism in all its forms and manifestations and pronounced that the subjection of peoples to alien subjugation, domination and exploitation constitutes a denial of fundamental human rights.[588] Since then, the UN has passed several other resolutions on the subject of colonialism and the right to self-determination.[589] Thus, within the realm of international law, there is a recognition that: colonial rule constitutes a violation of human rights; it has impeded development in former colonies; and that all former colonial powers are responsible for restitution and full compensation for the exploitation, depletion and damage of natural resources in postcolonial states.[590]

In 2005, the UN General Assembly adopted the Basic Principles and Guidelines on the Right to a Remedy and Reparation for Victims of Gross Violations of International Human Rights Law.[591] These guidelines require states to investigate violations effectively, promptly, thoroughly and impartially and, where appropriate, take action against those allegedly responsible in accordance with domestic and international law. International law recognises a right to a remedy for victims of human rights violations.[592] The remedies, which aim to promote justice and redress, include the provision of adequate, effective and prompt reparation, restitution, compensation and access to relevant information concerning violations. Other non-material remedies include a full public apology acknowledging the facts and accepting responsibility. Commemorations, tributes to the victims and the inclusion of an accurate account of the violations in school curricula are also considered helpful.[593]

The work of the UN on the question of accountability and redress for injustices of colonial rule has, however, had limited success because the UN recommendations on these issues are not supported by former colonial powers and they are generally non-binding. In any case, Britain and other former colonial powers often vote against, or abstain from voting on these resolutions.[594] And even though in 2013 Britain recognised, apologized and paid a sum of £19.9 million for acts of torture and other forms of ill-treatment against certain Kenyans in the Mau Mau protests—and despite the fact that it agreed to compensate the Bunyoro claimants—it continues to deny liability for claims over injustices because these incidents "occurred overseas outside direct British jurisdiction more than fifty years ago" and because the "testimony of key witnesses is no longer available."[595] Given the vastness of the British Empire and the potential claims against HMG that would arise from the deeds of its officials, in far-flung places such as Cyprus, India and Malaya, it is not difficult to see why these denials are made. It is also the case that with the passage of time it becomes more difficult to sustain such claims or to obtain witnesses against the injustices. So the aim of repeated denials could well be to delay and ultimately defeat claims for colonial injustices.

Beyond political limitations, the demands for justice for colonial abuses face a myriad of legal complications. Fundamental amongst these is the paucity of evidence for specific cases of violations, some of which happened more than one hundred years ago. In the absence of documented personal testimonies, there can be no fair trial. Another point related to the passage of time is the question of who the proper victims or claimants, defendants or beneficiaries would be. It is often argued that because of the legal principle of retroactivity, postcolonial regimes—which by definition did not exist at the time the atrocities were committed—lack the legal capacity or basis to sustain claims against the perpetrators or their successor governments. It is also argued that actions taken under colonial rule were not explicitly illegal at the time they were committed and therefore cannot be judged by today's legal standards, and that decades have passed since these crimes were committed so current governments and their people cannot be held accountable for the actions taken by governments during the colonial era. To these are added the usual legal technicalities of sovereign immunity and statutes of limitation that would render many of the actions time-barred. However, the UN guidelines provide that statutes of limitations shall not apply to gross violations of international human rights law and serious violations of international humanitarian law which constitute crimes under international law.[596]

Because of these technicalities, the success of political actions (within the UN and other international organizations) and legal actions (in courts of law and other judicial bodies) has been limited. The challenges of realising remedies for colonial injustices should not, however, stop the pursuit of justice and accountability for colonial wrongs. Britain's acknowledgment, apologies and settlements for wrongs in the Mau Mau and Bunyoro cases show that there is still work to be done to bring colonial injustices to the fore and to seek redress. To achieve this requires the collection and analysis of available evidence and demands for action to end impunity. In this regard, a public inquiry would be a good start.

But outside legal action, bilateral engagements with Britain would help to secure material and non-material remedies, such as recognition of the wrongs committed and appropriate apologies. The establishment of a "truth and reconciliation" commission to uncover the true extent of the crimes committed—followed with a public apology, including acknowledgement of the facts and acceptance of responsibility—would help to heal and restore the dignity of the victims. To these would be added symbolic gestures and support, to be agreed upon with the affected peoples. The argument, presented by William Hague and others, that bilateral or multilateral development aid to Uganda and other former colonies should be seen as part of the remedies for colonialism cannot be accepted in the absence of clear recognition and acceptance of responsibility for these injustices on the part of the former colonial powers.

Reflections on Buganda's Rediscovery and the Future

This account shows how British imperialism worked to disempower and reduce the kingdom of Buganda—whose traditional authority and systems were greatly admired by the first British explorers and administrators—to fit within its imperial objectives. To achieve this, Britain occupied it and disempowered its leadership including through the deposition and deportation of its leaders like Mwanga in 1899 and Mutesa in 1953.

It also shows how, Buganda resisted British rule and unsuccessfully attempted to break free from British occupation in December 1960. Following this we have seen how Britain cajoled the kingdom into the 1961 Agreement where it agreed to form part of Uganda, based on non-binding guarantees that Britain would protect its special status at independence and—in vague terms—beyond it. Indeed, it is the use of these vague "guarantees" that had no real legal standing that represents the true scandal, laying the ground for Britain's subsequent abandonment of the kingdom when Obote seized power. The unravelling of the constitutional order from 1966 left the kingdom in political doldrums and an occupation of a new kind.

But in spite of the odds against it, Buganda has demonstrated resilience and continues to fight for autonomy under a federal system of governance. There is evidence that today it is on a path of rediscovery and its ability to mobilize its population for cultural or for economic reasons remains strong. However, history shows that from the time it lost out to colonialism, the kingdom has been handicapped and thus unable to translate or convert its popularity into political power. Mamdani has observed that Baganda are a majority that is held back by a mindset of a political minority or victimhood:

> If you look around the world, you will find that the largest groups usually vie for political leadership in a country: the English in the United Kingdom, the Prussians in Germany, the Kikuyu and the Luo in Kenya. But in Uganda, this has not been true. Not that the Baganda are unable to lead; the Baganda have simply been unwilling to lead. The great political riddle of Uganda politics is that the largest nationality in the country is gripped by a minority psychology.[597]

But as we have seen, in efforts to regain its political clout and fortify its interests, Buganda has continually sought to enter political and military alliances with forces that, in the end, have let it down. Its alliances—for example, with Britain, Obote, Amin and Museveni—have ended in frustration. While these former allies consolidated their own power, Buganda lost out and, in all these cases, has felt betrayed and been left in a weaker position. This reality underlines one of the principal weaknesses in Buganda's approach to politics in a modern Uganda: the lack of a coherent long-term political strategy for addressing its position, power and relationships with the rest of Uganda. We have shown how a lack of a well-defined strategy cost Buganda in 1960 once it declared itself independent from Britain; how it was side-lined by Obote between 1962 and 1966; how it was abused by Amin and, more recently, how its interests remain thwarted under Museveni's regime.

These examples underline the need for the leaders of the kingdom of Buganda to reflect on how they may take charge of its destiny within a new Uganda by relying on the support of its subjects. In doing so, it will need to revisit the relations between its political class—those within and outside Buganda—and its traditional and cultural structures. This relationship did not get off to a good start during the birth of most political parties in the late 1950s. We have seen how, historically, the kingdom's leadership did not embrace political parties out of fear that they would undermine or usurp its authority.

For their part, members of the political class have been reluctant to embrace Mengo for fear that they would be marginalized, either because they are not part of the old system or the Establishment, or because they have limited prospects owing to their religious faiths. There thus appears a continuing dichotomy, and a struggle, between the interests of the traditional setup and those of the political actors. The lack of political unanimity or convergence of purpose between the political class and the traditional and cultural leadership in Buganda explains Buganda's perennial paradox: namely, wielding popular support but lacking political power.

Some of the issues Buganda needs to address are: what powers will the Kabaka have and what role and powers will the Katikkiro, the Lukiiko and the county chiefs wield in contemporary times? Will Buganda be prepared to once again have a constitutional monarchy? For how long will it remain a cultural or traditional institution without political power? How will Buganda, an entity without any armed forces, survive and succeed in Uganda's political milieu, which is underpinned and greatly influenced by the army? We have seen how, historically, the lack of a defensive arm meant that Buganda lost out to Lugard and to Obote in 1966. Also, in spite of the fact that the war of liberation was mostly fought and won in Buganda, the kingdom's lack of a central role in fighting the war meant that it was not in a position to effectively bargain for its post-war interests such as the restoration of the federal system of government. As such, given the centrality of the army in the politics of postcolonial Uganda, the defenceless kingdom has remained vulnerable. Unless there is a change, Buganda will remain at the mercy of its adversaries.

Notes

[1] Statement by Hugh Fraser, Under Secretary for the Colonies, in the House of Commons on Uganda's Independence Bill. HC Deb 16 July 1962, Vol. 663 cc3 hansard.millbanksystems.com/commons/1962/jul/16/uganda-independence-bill.

[2] "Remember our British friends," *Uganda Argus*, Tuesday 9 October 1962, p.4.

[3] See Meredith, *The State of Africa*, p. 101-102 and African Yearbook of Rhetoric 2, 3, 2011, ISSN 2220-2188: Patrice Lumumba, "The Congo Independence speech," pp. 41-43.

[4] Churchill, Winston S. (1908) *My African Journey*, London: Hodder and Stoughton.

[5] A Dominion was an autonomous entity which was part of the British Empire and retained the British monarch as its own Head of State, but was self-governed by locally elected officials. Canada, Australia and New Zealand are still Dominions today, but in the former colonies of Africa the designation tended to be short-lived, with the new self-ruling governments of Uganda, Nigeria, Tanganyika, Kenya and Malawi all declaring themselves republics shortly after independence.

[6] With the passing of this Act Britain's promises of a special postcolonial relationship with Buganda or its pledges to maintain and safeguard the status of the Kabaka and other rulers from deposition evaporated.

[7] Minutes of the 36th Cabinet meeting held on 11 September 1962.

[8] See "Kampala becomes a City," *Uganda Argus*, Tuesday 9 October 1962, p. 4.

[9] *Uganda Argus*, Tuesday 9 October 1962

[10] Ibid.

[11] Ibid.

[12] However, as post-independence events show, from this point on, the relations between Buganda and Britain weakened rather than strengthened.

[13] Mutesa, *The Desecration of My Kingdom*, p. 167.

[14] See, for example, Mutibwa, *A History of Uganda*, pp. 190, 198-204.

[15] See generally Nabudere, Dan Wadada (1980) "Imperialism and Revolution in Uganda," Onyx Press Ltd London, and Fenwick, Laura (2009), "British and French Styles of Influence in Colonial and Independent Africa: A Comparative Study of Kenya and Senegal." SIS 419 002: Honors Capstone, 23 April, 2009.

[16] The full text of the pamphlet is reproduced in D. A. Low, *The Mind of Buganda*, p. 215.

[17] See despatch from Sir Walter Coutts to Mr Sandys on "Uganda: Future as an independent country," dated 8 October 1962 on CO 822/2266, No. 378.

[18] See story "Uganda Cannot Accept Buganda's Claim" in *The Uganda Argus*, 12 August 1963. Also, while Buganda wished to join the East Africa Federation as a constituent member, Uganda insisted that this was not possible as Uganda was one independent sovereign state, which could contract with another country. See

"Buganda's Position in EA Federal Set-up: Only Uganda Can Decide" in *Uganda Argus*, 23 August 1963.

[19] Mutesa, *The Desecration of My Kingdom*, p. 174.

[20] See despatch from Sir Walter Coutts to Mr Sandys on "Uganda: Future as an independent country," dated 8 October 1962 on CO 822/2266, No. 378.

[21] Ibid.

[22] FCO file "UK Aid to Uganda" (copy with author but reference unclear).

[23] Mutibwa, *A History of Uganda*, pp.198-204. Also see generally, Leigh, Gardner (2012) *Taxing Colonial Africa: The Political Economy of British Imperialism*, Oxford, OUP, p. 226.

[24] Stiglitz, *Globalization and its Discontents*, p. 59.

[25] See despatch from Sir Walter Coutts to Mr Sandys on "Uganda: Future as an independent country," 8 October 1962, CO 822/2266, No. 378.

[26] Ibid.

[27] Ibid.

[28] See file, "Request by Uganda Government for British troops to be sent there," DO 213/250 and records from the British Ministry of Defence East African Situation Report No. 20 covering the situation up to 0600Z 24 January 1964.

[29] Mutesa, *The Desecration of My Kingdom*, p. 179.

[30] Ibid. p. 179.

[31] A Statement issued by the Commonwealth Relations Office, dated 23 January 1964. See file, "Request by Uganda Government for British troops to be sent there," DO 213/250.

[32] See file, "Request by Uganda Government for British troops to be sent there," DO 213/250 and Mutibwa, *A History of Uganda*, p. 190.

[33] Ibid.

[34] See See file, "Request by Uganda Government for British troops to be sent there," DO 213/250 and story "British troops move into three East African countries to restore order," and *The Telegraph*, 26 January 1964.

[35] Ibid.

[36] See despatch from Sir Walter Coutts to Mr Sandys on "Uganda: Future as an independent country," dated 8 October 1962 on CO 822/2266. No. 378.

[37] This decision was not reached easily because on the one hand the British were wary that the Queen's position would become a political issue after independence (as indeed it did) while on the other, there was no general agreement in Uganda on any alternatives to the Queen as the Head of State.

[38] Its application to become a member of the Commonwealth was approved on 10 September 1962.

[39] In the Independence conference report, this was recorded as follows: "Uganda's representatives were united in desiring that after independence Uganda should continue in allegiance to Her Majesty the Queen as the Queen of Uganda."

[40] Extract from Obote's Press Conference at Uganda's Independence on 9 October 1962.

[41] See Obote's letter to MacMillan, dated 9 September 1963.

[42] The Kabaka polled 62 votes and the Kyabazinga of Busoga (William W. W. Nadiope) only 27. The Kyabazinga was chosen as the Vice-President.
[43] Mutesa, *Desecration of My Kingdom*, p. 172.
[44] See *Uganda Argus*, 1 March 1967.
[45] He was installed in a military barracks in Jinja as the Commander-in-Chief of the Uganda army and given the rank of Major-General on 20 December 1963.
[46] See "Not the Most Important Job in Uganda," *Uganda Argus*, 5 October 1963.
[47] "Thousands see Kabaka and Kyabazinga installed," *Uganda Argus*, 10 October 1963.
[48] See *Uganda Argus*, 4 July 1963.
[49] See Resolution of the Orukurato of Bunyoro passed on 9 January 1963.
[50] (1963) EA 472.
[51] Mutibwa, *A History of Uganda*, p. 195
[52] Ibid. pp. 194-5.
[53] Mutesa, *The Desecration of My Kingdom*, p. 179.
[54] Ibid., p.174.
[55] Ibingira, *The Forging of an African Nation*, p. 273.
[56] Mutibwa, *A History of Uganda*, p. 195.
[57] See *Taifa Uganda Empya* newspaper, 13 July 1963.
[58] Ibid.
[59] Ibid.
[60] Mutesa, *The Desecration of My Kingdom*, p. 177.
[61] Mutibwa, *A History of Uganda*, p. 195.
[62] Ibid.
[63] Ibid. p. 195.
[64] Mutibwa, *A History of Uganda*, p. 191.
[65] See Baganchwera, op. cit., pp. 125-135.
[66] See Sir Edward Mutesa II's Appeal to the Secretary General of the United Nations (UN) on Uganda's Constitutional Crisis, p. 12 and Mutibwa, *A History of Uganda*, p. 205.
[67] Ibid. p. 12. See also, Kabaka Mutesa II, *The Desecration of My Kingdom*, pp. 182-3.
[68] Sir Edward Mutesa II's Appeal to the Secretary General of UN, p. 13.
[69] Ibid.
[70] Ibid., p. 13.
[71] Ibid., p. 15.
[72] Ibid.
[73] Paradoxically, they were only released by Idi Amin following his coup against Obote in January 1971.
[74] Sir Edward Mutesa II's Appeal to the Secretary General of UN, p. 14.
[75] On 24 February, the prime minister and thirteen cabinet ministers signed the declaration, which, unsurprisingly, made no mention of their five colleagues who were under detention.
[76] See Declaration by the Government, dated 2 March 1966, extracted from Sir Edward Mutesa II's appeal to the UN, op. cit., p. 26.

[77] Section 67 of the Independence Constitution provided that if the President declines to perform an act as required by the constitution, the Prime Minister may himself perform that act. The Prime Minister was alive to this provision when he used the procedure to sign the Acts in question. On the opening of Parliament, the constitution envisaged a situation where the Vice-President could perform functions should the President himself be unable to do so. Indeed, it was agreed between the President and Prime Minister that the Vice-President should perform the ceremony in question.

[78] 28 February 1966 and on 3 March, 1966.

[79] Ibid.

[80] Resolutions No.3 of 26 February 1966; No. 4 of 1 March 1966; No. 5 of 5 March 1966; No. 6 of 12 March 1966 and No.7 of 13 April 1966.

[81] See statement issued by the spokesman of the Prime Minister's office on 10 March 1966, reproduced in *Uganda Argus* of 11 March 1966.

[82] In a letter dated 8 March, 1966.

[83] Statement issued on 10 March, 1966.

[84] See Sir Edward's Appeal to the Secretary General of the UNO on Uganda's Constitutional Crisis.

[85] Uganda Parliamentary Debates, Hansard 2 Series, Volume 59 on the emergency meeting held on 15 April 1966, p.1.

[86]See letter from P. M. Foster, the British High Commissioner in Kampala, to the Commonwealth Office, dated 4 March 1967, on UK-Uganda Relations, FCO 31/193.

[87] Ibid.

[88] Mutesa was accused of using his position as Commander-in-Chief to request the army dance band play at Mengo Palace on the occasion of his birthday on 19 November 1965. The request was rejected because, according to the Prime Minister, in a letter to the President dated 17 November 1965, the office of the Kabaka was not the same as the office of the President of Uganda, and that if the request was accepted it could develop into a serious constitutional and political issue.

[89] Uganda Parliamentary Debates Hansard 2 Series, Volume 59, p. 10.

[90] Ibid., p.10.

[91] Ibid., p.13. However, the account offered to the Assembly was significantly different from the one Obote gave the country on 22 February 1965.

[92] Ibid., p. 14.

[93] For this reason, this constitution was referred to as the Pigeonhole Constitution.

[94] See Uganda Parliamentary Debates Hansard 2 Series, Volume 59 on the Emergency Meeting held on 15 April 1966, p. 19.

[95] Fifty-five members voted for the resolution and four against it. Obote's actions in surrounding the Assembly with armed soldiers, his arrest of the five ministers, and his shabby treatment of Mutesa must have cowed the members into passing the Constitution without any debate.

[96] Resolution 8 of the Buganda Lukiiko, dated 16 April 1966.

[97] See Statement of the Buganda Lukiiko, dated 18 April 1966.

[98] Ogenga Otunnu, 2016. *Crisis of Legitimacy and Political Violence in Uganda: 1890 to 1979.* Springer pp.187-188.
[99] Ibid.
[100] See Obote's statement to the Parliament of Uganda in the Official Report of the Proceedings of the National Assembly, Wednesday 25 May 1966.
[101] Uncannily, this attack was not unlike the vicious attack led by Brigadier Peter Elwelu of the Uganda Peoples' Defence Forces on the palace of Omusinga wa Rwenzururu Charles W. Mumbere in Kasese in 2016, where many people were killed. See *New Vision*, 27 November 2016.
[102] Tripp, *Museveni's Uganda,* p.45.
[103] Mutesa, *The Desecration of My Kingdom*, p. 193.
[104] See statement by HE the President in Uganda Parliamentary Debates, Hansard, 25 May 1966, p. 53.
[105] Ibid., pp. 52-60.
[106] Ibid., p. 59
[107] Ibid.
[108] Ibid.
[109] Ibid., p. 60.
[110] G. W. Kanyeihamba (2002) *Constitutional and Political History of Uganda—From 1894 to the Present*, Centenary Publishing House Ltd., p. 107.
[111] Ibid., pp. 107-108.
[112] Nadiope was the Kyabazinga (King) of Busoga kingdom, and in 1963 he was elected Vice-President of Uganda. He, along with Mutesa, was unilaterally and illegally removed from his office by Obote.
[113] See file, "Request by Uganda Government for British troops to be sent there," DO 213/250.
[114] Ibingira, *The Forging of an African Nation*, p. 288.
[115] (1966) EA 514.
[116] For details on the dramatis personae in this case see Oloka-Onyango, J. (2015) "Ghosts and the Law" (an inaugural lecture presented at Makerere University, 12 November 2015).
[117] See letter on the 1966 Constitution by M. P. Preston of the British High Commission to L. Reid of the East Africa Department, Commonwealth Office, Ref. 2-72/23/4, dated 14 November 1966.
[118] Ibid.
[119] Ibid.
[120] See letter from M. P. Preston of the British High Commission to L. Reid of the East African Department, Foreign and Commonwealth Office, Ref. 2-72/23/4, dated 21 November 1966 on the 1966 Constitution.
[121] Ibid.
[122] See Hansard of the Uganda National Assembly of 14 December 1966.
[123] Ibid.; judgement (1966) EA 514
[124] See generally, Oloka-Onyango, J. "Ghosts and the Law," an inaugural lecture presented at Makerere University, 12 November 2015.

[125] With the exception of Lugard's massacres at Bulingugwe and the massive killings in Bunyoro.
[126] From 10 June 1966, the new districts of East Mengo, West Mengo, Masaka and Mubende were governed directly by the Central Government.
[127] See letter by R. N. Posnett to W. G. Lamarque, Ref. 2 EA 179/23/1, dated 29 July 1966 on the Status of Buganda after the 1966 coup.
[128] Ibid.
[129] Several petitions were made to Her Majesty the Queen, the British Prime Minister and the British High Commissioner in Uganda by individuals and groups including M. K. L. Kabugo, the Monarchist League, the Buganda Mothers Association, the Buganda Central Ancestral Sovereign State and D. K. Sekkuma. See File 2, EA K/17, DO 213/237 in the National Archives TNA on petitions concerning the aftermath of Obote's coup.
[130] Despatch No. 6 dated 29 September 1967.
[131] See letter dated 6 June 1966 from 10 Downing Street signed by A. M. Palliser in response to a petition made by M. K. L. Kabugo, dated 24 May 1966.
[132] See a memorandum Ref. EAD220/183/01 by M. de N. Ensor, dated 2 August 1966.
[133] See statement entitled *Uganda: Discussions with the Kabaka and His Government Prior to Independence*, issued by the Commonwealth Office, dated 10 October 1966 (emphasis mine).
[134] See Uganda Government, *The Government Proposals for New Constitution*, 9 June 1967.
[135] Ibid.
[136] Obote's speech to the National Assembly on 22 June 1967.
[137] See confidential report, telegram no. 15, dated 1 July 1967, on the 1967 constitutional proposals by Foster of the British High Commission to the Commonwealth Office in FCO31/185, *Uganda Political Affairs (Internal) New Constitution.*
[138] Ibid.
[139] See letter by P. M. Foster to Michael Scott of the East African Department of the Foreign and Commonwealth Office, dated 1 July 1967, FCO31/185, *Uganda Political Affairs (Internal) New Constitution.*
[140] Ibid.
[141] When Obwangor gave way to another speaker on a point of order, Obote, who was sitting next to him, told him to resign and Obwangor immediately crossed the floor to join the opposition benches. See letter by Foster to the Commonwealth Office dated 11 July 1967, FCO31/185.
[142] See despatch No. 6 by D. A Scott to George Thomson dated 29 September 1967, FCO31/185.
[143] Section 61(4).
[144] See minutes of the British Cabinet meeting held at 10 Downing Street, on Thursday 24 February 1966 at 10.30 am.
[145] Ibid.
[146] See House of Commons debate 25 May 1966, Hansard Vol. 729 cc 474-5.

[147] See letter on the Internal Situation and the Constitution by M. P. Preston of the British High Commission, to L. Reid of the East Africa Department, Commonwealth Office, Ref. 2-72/23/4, dated 15 December 1966, FCO31/185, *Uganda Political Affairs (Internal) New Constitution.*
[148] See letter by D. A. Scott, British High Commission to The Rt Hon. George Thomson MP, Despatch No. 6, dated 29 September 1967.
[149] According to Prentice, the Minister of Overseas Development, House of Commons Debate, 21 January 1969, Vol. 776 cc59-60W59W.
[150] House of Commons Debate, 16 March 1967, Vol. 743 cc 699-700, §24.
[151] Among the prominent Baganda politicians who remained loyal and active in UPC were W. W. Kalema, L. Kalule Settala and Paulo Muwanga.
[152] The fact is that no consultations were made about the new constitution, which was essentially drafted within a few days by a few men unknown to the members of the National Assembly and the country at large, except Godfrey L. Binaisa. Indeed, no records can be found of any "wide and extensive consultations"!
[153] See Uganda Parliamentary Debates Hansard 2 Series, Volume 59 on the Emergency Meeting held on 15 April, 1966, p. 14.
[154] See generally, Odoki, Benjamin J. (2005), *The Search for a National Consensus: The Making of the 1995 Uganda Constitution.* Fountain Publishers, Kampala.
[155] See Low, *Buganda in Modern History*, p. 239.
[156] Mutibwa, *A History of Uganda*, p. 218.
[157] Mutesa, *The Desecration of My Kingdom*, pp. 14-16.
[158] Ibid, p. 16
[159] Ibid, p. 16
[160] Ibid, p. 20
[161] See letter by High Commissioner J. S. Bennett to G. A. Duggan, Head of the West and Central African Department, Commonwealth Office, dated 28 June 1968, FO 371/187871 TNA.
[162] In fact, the *Mwami* (Burundian king) telephoned the Kabaka and the Burundi Government from Spain telling the government to look after the party and put a house at the Kabaka's disposal. See file *The Problem of the Kabaka's Asylum in Burundi and His Departure for Britain*, FO 371/187871 TNA.
[163] The British High Commissioner proposed to the British Foreign Office to "offer informal hospitality to the Kabaka and his party and to give them what assistance I can to make their stay here friendly." See telegram No. 121 from Bujumbura to Foreign Office, dated 20 June 1966. Given the support accorded to Mutesa while in Burundi, there is no doubt that the British Government accepted this proposal. FO 371/187871 TNA.
[164] Written to G. A. Duggan, Head of the West and Central African Department, Commonwealth Office, dated 28 June 1968, FO 371/187871 TNA.
[165] In *The Desecration of My Kingdom*, p. 21, Mutesa writes that "This was not malaria, but a protest from an exhausted body, keyed up to withstand too much pain and too little sleep and food for a month."

[166] In Mutesa's words to the British High Commissioner. See Telegram No. 126 of June 21 1966 from Bujumbura to Foreign Office. FO 371/187871 TNA.
[167] See story in the *Uganda Argus* of 21 June 1966. Telegram No. 646 of June 1966 from Kampala to the Commonwealth Relations Office refers to a statement by Obote suggesting that the Uganda Government would do its best to get Mutesa back to Uganda. FO 371/187871 TNA.
[168] The British Government had decided that the Kabaka himself should be admitted at once but that his two companions must remain in Burundi until he had been able to satisfy the authorities that they could be adequately supported. But the Kabaka refused to agree to this arrangement. Because of this, and the fact that the flight had to land in Cairo, the booking on Sabena Flight SN 526 had to be cancelled. Subsequently, the Kabaka confirmed that he would take full financial responsibility for his aides and he was sure that Lord Boyd would underwrite him. See Telegram No. 128 of 22 June 1966 from Bujumbura to Foreign Office, FO 371/187871 TNA.
[169] See letter from High Commissioner J. S. Bennett to G. A. Duggan, Head of the West and Central African Department, Commonwealth Office, dated 28 June 1968, FO 371/187871 TNA, and Mutesa, *The Desecration of My Kingdom*, p. 22.
[170] See telegram No. 683 22/6 from the Commonwealth Office to Kampala, dated 22 June 1966. FO 371/187871 TNA.
[171] See telegram No. 1372 from Nairobi to Commonwealth Relations Office on the Kabaka, dated 21 June 1966, FO 371/187871 TNA.
[172] See telegram No. 124 from Bujumbura to Foreign Office, dated 21 June 1966, FO 371/187871 TNA.
[173] See telegram No.125 from Bujumbura to Foreign Office, dated 21 June 1966, FO 371/187871 TNA.
[174] See telegram No.132 from Bujumbura to Foreign Office, dated 23 June 1966, FO 371/187871 TNA.
[175] See telegram No. 644 from Kampala to Commonwealth Relations Office on the Kabaka, dated 20 June 1966, FO 371/187871 TNA.
[176] See telegram No. 652 from Kampala to the Commonwealth Relations Office on the Kabaka, dated 22 June 1966, FO 371/187871 TNA.
[177] See generally files on Uganda: Political Affairs (Internal) Ex-Kabaka of Uganda: Sir Edward Mutesa, FCO 141/18197, FCO31/475 and FCO31/178.
[178] See notes of meeting between the Minister of State George Thomas, Lord Boyd of Merton and the Rt Hon. Hugh Fraser MP, on 28 February 1967 in FCO 31/178.
[179] Ibid.
[180] See letter by L. Reid of the East African Department written to M. P. Preston, at the British High Commission in Kampala, dated 3 March 1967.
[181] Ibid.
[182] At a meeting with the Secretary of State on 10 May 1968.
[183] On Her Majesty Government's refusal to find suitable employment for Mutesa in the military or in the Ministry of Defence for fear that it would be accused by the Uganda Government of supporting him, an indignant Alan Lennox-Boyd (Conservative) wrote to George Thomas (Labour), the Minister of State at the

Commonwealth Office, on 25 May 1967, saying: "some people in Government circles have said the only people interesting themselves in Mutesa were former Conservative Ministers; even if this were so I trust it would not be thought an adequate reason to turn down an appeal … it is very important indeed that the Commonwealth Office should now take active steps to implement their promise that no obstacles will be placed in his path."

[184] See letter by P. M. Foster, the British High Commissioner to Richard G. Tallboys of East African Department dated 19 October 1968.

[185] According to a letter from 10 Downing Street to O. G. Forster at the Commonwealth Office February 1967.

[186] See memorandum on Sir Edward Mutesa by the FCO, East African Department, dated 5 June 1969.

[187] According to a memorandum from 10 Downing Street, dated 6 February 1967. See also, a memorandum addressed to Mr Norris Ref PS 1/1 by M. Scott of the East African Department, dated 23 February 1967.

[188] According to a secret memorandum on Sir E. Mutesa: Payment from secret funds by L. Reid to Mr Scott.

[189] See notes dated 1 March 1967 of a meeting between the Minister of State (Mr George Thomas), Lord Boyd of Merton and the Rt Hon. Hugh Fraser MP, on 28 February 1967, taken by Mr M. Scott.

[190] See Memorandum dated 24 June 1968 by R. G. Tallboys of the Commonwealth Office (East Africa Department) to Mr Scott at the British High Commission in Kampala, Uganda.

[191] In *The Desecration of My Kingdom*, p .192, Mutesa writes that by 1966 "Obote [had] already put me as President squarely in his sights and having obtained the range by mere pointing out at me publicly, he is now pressing firmly at the trigger."

[192] According to a secret memorandum on *Sir Edward Mutesa: Payment from secret funds*, by L. Reid to Scott, it is stated that this subject was raised by Mrs Hart, the Minister of State, with Obote when he was in the UK at the time of the Commonwealth Prime Ministers' Conference.

[193] See letter by Sam Odaka, Minister for Foreign Affairs Uganda, to George Minister of State dated 15 January 1968.

[194] According to a memorandum from the British High Commission in Uganda, dated 4 January 1967.

[195] See letter from P. M. Foster, British High Commissioner in Uganda, to R. G. Tallboys of the East African Department on Mutesa's financial affairs, dated 19 October 1968.

[196] Notes on a discussion between the Commonwealth Secretary of State and the President of Uganda on 27 October 1967.

[197] See letter from P. M. Foster, British High Commissioner in Uganda, to R. G. Tallboys of the East African Department on Mutesa's financial affairs, dated 19 October 1968.

[198] Dated 15 January 1968.

[199] See letter by P. M. Foster, British High Commissioner in Uganda, to R. G. Tallboys of the East African Department on Mutesa's financial affairs, dated 19 October 1968.

[200] The wolves were not only at Mutesa's door, they were in fact already in Princess Victoria Mpologoma's house! Indeed, according to the *Daily Telegraph* of 18 February 1969, she and 15 others were arrested and detained under the emergency laws. She was to be charged with high treason. It was believed by Bataringaya, the Minister of Internal Affairs, that she supplied money for an abortive army mutiny in an attempt to overthrow the Ugandan Government and secure the return of the Kabaka. When Mutesa's friends asked the British Government to intercede in Princess Victoria's long detention without trial, HMG's response was that it could "do nothing about the detention of Victoria since she is a Ugandan citizen." To them, her detention was "a matter for the Uganda Government and any approach by Her Majesty's Government would be taken by President Obote as interference in the internal affairs of Uganda."

[201] See notes contained in a letter by D. A. Scott to Le Tocq of the FCO, East African Department, dated 15 November 1968 on the future of Sir Edward Mutesa.

[202] See open letter from Yusuf Nsambu, Joseph Male, M. Nansamba and S. Nansamba to the British Prime Minister, dated 21 May 1968.

[203] Mutesa, *The Desecration of My Kingdom*, pp 193-194.

[204] Ibid., p.194.

[205] See file "Sir Edward Mutesa, ex-Kabaka of Buganda," January 1968—December 1969, FCO 31/475 for Mutesa's postmortem examination report, dated 24 November 1969, signed by Dr A. E. Robinson of the Department of Forensic Medicine, London Hospital Medical College. Blood alcohol levels greater than 300-400 mg/dL can be fatal due to respiratory depression (https://emedicine.medscape.com/article/2090019-overview, accessed 1 March 2018).

[206] Conducted by Arthur Gordon Davies, Her Majesty's Coroner, at the Coroner's Court Southwark on 28 November 1969, FCO 31/475.

[207] See notes of evidence taken at the inquest of Mutesa by Arthur Gordon Davies, HM's Coroner, at the Coroner's Court, Southwark on 28 November 1969, FCO 31/475.

[208] Ibid.

[209] In her letter of 2 December 1969 to W. N. Weban-Smith of the British High Commission in Kampala, FCO 31/475.

[210] Ibid.

[211] As told to the author by Princess Sarah Kagere.

[212] See Colvin, Ian, "Police File Still Open on Kabaka," *The Daily Telegraph*, 6 December 1969.

[213] Ibid.

[214] Ibid.

[215] Makubuya, Apollo N., "The last days of Kabaka Edward Mutesa" in *The Daily Monitor*, 24 November 2011 and Kasozi, A. B. K. (2013) *The Bitter Bread of*

Exile; The Financial Problems of Sir Edward Muteesa II During his Final Exile, 1966-1969., p.244.
[216] Ibid.
[217] In a note dated 15 December 1969 addressed to Counsel Le Tocq and copied to W. N. Wenban-Smith, the British High Commissioner in Kampala, R. M. Purcell of the East Africa Department, FCO, wrote that "Sir John Hall, a formidable and distinguished Governor of Uganda under whom I served prior to Sir Andrew Cohen ... said that in his view there was no doubt whatsoever that he quite deliberately committed suicide since he couldn't face the thanksgiving service laid on the following day. As he said, 'what had the poor fellow to give thanks for!' Personally, I believe that this bizarre theory of suicide by alcohol is right." On the future of Buganda without Mutesa, Sir John Hall was of the view that "the Baganda were not only subdued but would probably stay that way for the foreseeable future.... [T]hey are good at talking when up against it but will seldom act.... [T]he Baganda have always been effective enough when on top but they are not, and never have been, fighters in any real sense of the word, " FCO 31/475.
[218] According to Colvin's article, "Kabaka File for Lawyers," in *The Daily Telegraph*, 15 December 1969, Mutesa suspected an attempt to poison him a month before his death, and there were several witnesses who recalled this.
[219] In a document with Amin's comments on Obote's letter written in the name of "Secret Council 777," sent to Uganda secretly after Amin's coup of January 1971. Amin's motives, though, must be questioned given his own role in deposing Mutesa.
[220] See Colvin, "Kabaka File for Lawyers" and Kasozi, *The Bitter Bread of Exile*, p. 244.
[221] See Colvin, "Kabaka File for Lawyers."
[222] Ibid.
[223] Ibid.
[224] See story Colvin, Ian, "King Freddie Inquiry by Uganda Police," *The Daily Telegraph*, 9 December 1969.
[225] In a letter from F. K. Kalimuzo to Lady Damali, dated 22 November 1969.
[226] See "The Government Sends Instructions to London: Sir Edward Will be Buried in Uganda," in the *Uganda Argus*, 24 November 1969.
[227] See telegram No. 805 from Booth at the British High Commission in Kampala to the Foreign and Commonwealth Office on the Burial of Mutesa in Uganda, dated 25 November 1969.
[228] This was announced in a statement issued in London on 24 November by Fred Mpanga.
[229] Letter by British High Commissioner, Weber-Smith, to R. M. Purcell of the FCO, East African Department on "Sir Edward Mutesa's Death: Reaction among the Baganda," dated 2 December 1969.
[230] See telegram 832 from The British High Commission in Kampala to FCO dated 28 November 1969, FCO 31/475.
[231] Note from E. G. Le Tocq of the East Africa Department on the Late Sir Fredrick Mutesa to Tebbit, dated 27 November 1969. Le Tocq feared that if the

British Government was not represented it would be further criticised for snubbing him even in death.

[232] Telegram No. 834 from Scott at the British High Commission in Kampala to the FCO on Mutesa's funeral, dated 29 November 1969.

[233] *The Times of London* on 29 November reported that the Kabaka would be given a full-scale military funeral service at the Guards' Chapel. It noted that when the Kabaka was exiled to Britain in 1966, the Grenadier Guards—unlike the Government—had rallied to his support, even setting up a fund for him. It was thus fitting that they should also perform the funeral rites.

[234] Telegram No. 830 from Scott at the British High Commission in Kampala to the Foreign and Commonwealth Office on Mutesa Kabaka, 28 November 1969.

[235] Ibid.

[236] In a letter to David A. Scott, 2 December 1969.

[237] See telegram No. 832 from Scott at the British High Commission in Kampala to the Foreign and Commonwealth Office on Mutesa, 28 November 1969, FCO 31/475.

[238] See telegram No. 836 from Scott at the British High Commission in Kampala to the Foreign and Commonwealth Office on Mutesa, 29 November 1969, FCO 31/475.

[239] Kabaka Mutesa KBE had been made an honorary Captain in the Household division of the Grenadier Guards by King George VI and promoted to the honorary rank of Lieutenant Colonel by Queen Elizabeth II.

[240] See telegram No. 711 from Stewart of the Foreign and Commonwealth Office to the British High Commission in Kampala on Mutesa's funeral, dated 29 November 1969.

[241] See telegram No. 728 from Stewart of the Foreign and Commonwealth Office to the British High Commission in Kampala on Mutesa's funeral, 4 December 1969.

[242] The official line was that because Mutesa had been deposed and he had lived as a private citizen in the UK, it was not considered appropriate that Her Majesty's Government would be represented at his funeral.

[243] The Queen was represented by Colonel Prescott, commanding the Grenadier Guards.

[244] In a letter from F. K. Kalimuzo, Permanent Secretary in the Office of the President and Secretary to the Cabinet, to Bishop Nsubuga.

[245] See "Burial marked in Uganda" in the *Uganda Argus*, 4 December 1969.

[246] The UK's more recent roles in the wars in Iraq and in Libya provides cases in point.

[247] Mutibwa, *A History of Uganda*, p.226.

[248] Ibid., p.227.

[249] Ibid., p. 227.

[250] Mutibwa, *A History of Uganda*, p. 225.

[251] Ibid., p. 218.

[252] Ibid., p. 219.

[253] Ibid.

[254] See paper on "Uganda Nationalisation" by the FCO to the "Commonwealth Finance Minister's Conferenvce-1970, on FCO 31/727 and Memorandum by Richard Slater, "Uganda: Annual Review for 1970," dated 14 January 1971, FCO 31/1022.

[255] Richard Slater to FCO, 27 July 1970, FCO 45/687 and Malcom Macdonald, Kampala, to FCO 5 December 1970, FCO 45/687.

[256] Mutibwa, *A History of Uganda*, p. 220.

[257] Ibid.

[258] R. Purcell, FCO notes, 17 December 1970, on file "Nationalisation in Uganda, FCO 31/728.

[259] See note from Harold Smedley, Assistant Under-Secretary of State at the Foreign Office, dated 27 January 1971, FCO 31/1028.

[260] See letter from E. Counsell, EAD, FCO to Sir Stewart Crawford, 26 January 1971, on FCO 31/1023.

[261] See telegram No. 56 from Slater at the British High Commission in Kampala to the Foreign and Commonwealth Office, 25 January 1971 in file "Coup d'etat in Uganda" on FCO 31/1023.

[262] See telegram No. 67 from Slater at the British High Commission in Kampala to the Foreign and Commonwealth Office, 26 January 1971, FCO 31/1023.

[263] See telegram No. 67, ibid.

[264] See telegram No. 57 from Slater at the British High Commission in Kampala to the Foreign and Commonwealth Office, 25 January 1971, FCO 31/1023.

[265] See telegram No. 67, ibid.

[266] Ibid.

[267] The UK supported Amin through its early recognition, help over the funeral of the ex-Kabaka, military and police training, and loans despite its knowledge that Amin was a tyrant with a muddled political philosophy. See file "Coup d'etat in Uganda," FCO 31/1023 and letter from Slater at the British High Commission in Kampala to Alec Douglas Home, Foreign Secretary, "The first six months of General Amin's government,' 6 August 1971, FCO 31/1017.

[268] According to Hutton, P. and J. Bloch (2012) "Uganda: How the West brought Idi Amin to Power," in *Links International Journal of Socialist Renewal*, http://links.org.au/node/2784 accessed on 1 March 2018, the main Israeli objective in supporting Amin was to ensure that the rebellion in Southern Sudan kept simmering for as long as possible, distracting the military forces involved from aligning with Egypt in the Arab-Israeli conflict. Since Amin was central to Israel's operations in the 1960s in supplying arms to the South Sudanese Anya-nya rebel group in fighting the Arab/Muslim government in Khartoum, Israel felt that they were better off with Amin than Obote as President in Uganda. This article states that the Anya-nya troops formed a core of the forces in the Amin coup and that many joined the Ugandan Army thereafter.

[269] See telegram No. 61 from Slater at the British High Commission in Kampala to the FCO, dated 25 January 1971.

[270] See FCO, East Africa Department, 'Note for Secretary of State: Cabinet on 28 March 1971,' 27 January 1971, FCO 31/1023.

[271] Ibid. For more on the Lango masterplan, see file "Tribalism in Uganda," FCO 31/1067.
[272] Ibid.
[273] See telegram No.50 from Douglas-Home of the FCO to the British High Commission in Kampala, dated 25 January 1971, FCO 31/1023.
[274] See telegram No. 51 from Phillips at the British High Commission in Dar-es-Salaam to the Foreign and Commonwealth Office, dated 27 January 1971, FCO 31/1023.
[275] On Okoya's death, see British High Commission's memorandum, "Survey of Events in 1970," dated 10 April 1970, on FCO 31/710.
[276] Ibid.
[277] Amin started his career in the British Colonial Army, the King's African Rifles, and later served on the British side in suppressing the Mau Mau rebellion in Kenya in the 1950s and the Bukedi riots in 1960. Britain knew that Amin was intensely pro-British and easy to manipulate given his general illiteracy. For a biography of Major General Idi Amin, see A. Fabian, IRD to R. Purcell, EAD, 27 January 1971, FCO 31/1024.
[278] Harold Smedley, FCO, Note, 27 January 1971, FCO 31/1028.
[279] A. Fabian, IRD, to Purcell, EAD, 27 January 1971, FCO 31/1024.
[280] See FCO file on "Leading Personalities in Uganda, 1971," FCO 31/1026.
[281] Richard Slater to Sir Alec Douglas Home, Foreign Secretary, "Military Coup in Uganda, 15 February 1971," FCO 31/1024.
[282] The US was inclined to avoid a formal act of recognition but sought to maintain continuous contact with the authorities in power on routine matters while monitoring how the situation developed. See telegram No. 300 from Millard of the Foreign and Commonwealth Office to the British High Commission in Kampala, dated 26 January 1971, FCO 31/1023.
[283]See Article *Documents on Idi Amin's 1971 Coup Released*, accessed at http://www.afrol.com/news2002/uga004_amin_uk.htm
[284] See telegram No. 78 from Slater at the British High Commission in Kampala to the Foreign and Commonwealth Office, dated 27 January 1971, FCO 31/1023.
[285] Harold Smedley, FCO, to Richard Slater, 25 February 1971, FCO 31/1024.
[286] For a roundup of British press coverage of the coup, see telegram No. 81 from Douglas-Home of the FCO to the British High Commission in Kampala, dated 27 January 1971, FCO 31/1023.
[287] See "Idi Amin" in *The Daily Telegraph*, 18 August 2003.
[288] E. G. Le Tocq, EAD to Smedley, Parliamentary Unit, on 1 February, 1971. FCO 31/1023.
[289] See "Afterword: Idi Amin" by John Fairhall in *The Guardian*, 18 August 2003 and letter by Eric Le Tocq, EAD, to Smedley, FCO, 1 February 1971 on FCO 31/1023.
[290] See telegram No.50 from Douglas-Home of the FCO to the British High Commission in Kampala, dated 25 January 1971, FCO31/1023.
[291] See letter to Smedley by Le Toqc, FCO, East Africa Department, 27 January 1971, FCO 31/1023.

[292] See telegram No. 66 from Slater at the British High Commission in Kampala to the FCO, dated 26 January 1971, FCO 31/1023.
[293] See telegram No. 90 from Slater at the British High Commission in Kampala to the FCO, dated 28 January 1971.
[294] Ibid.
[295] In a letter dated 31 January 1971.
[296] Ibid.
[297] See FCO brief, "Uganda: Note for the Secretary of State," 3 February 1971, FCO 31/1024.
[298] Ibid.
[299] On 4 September 1971, President Nyerere wrote to the Rt Hon. Edward Heath, warning him of the dangers that Amin posed to East Africa's peace and stability. As it turned out, in 1979, Tanzania was to play a leading role in ousting Amin from power and, eventually, in the return of Obote as Uganda's President in 1980.
[300] See letter from the FCO to Peter J. S. Moon at 10 Downing Street, dated 3 February 1971.
[301] See Richard Slater to FCO, 3 February 1971, FCO 31/1028.
[302] Peter Moon, No.10, to N. Barrington, FCO, 6 July 1971, FCO 31/1072.
[303] Amin made requests for equipment for the air force, infantry, airborne troops and sophisticated long-range aircraft like Harrier jets, which could operate from Entebbe and Gulu over Rwanda and deep into Tanzania. Britain made no commitments on these because Uganda's economy could not afford such wares. See FCO brief for the Prime Minister, "Uganda," 9 July 1971, FCO 31/1071 (1) and (2).
[304] Ibid.
[305] See brief from East African Department to Guidance Department, FCO, entitled "President Amin in Scotland," dated 16 July 1971.
[306] In reply to President Amin's invitation of 10 January 1972 to attend the tenth anniversary of Uganda's independence in October of the same year, the Queen stated that she was "most disappointed" that her commitments prevented her from accepting the invitation and wished him, Uganda and its people all success with the celebrations. She signed off "I am your good friend, Elizabeth R." A copy of the said letter is reproduced in *The Mail on Sunday*, 27 December 2014.
[307] On Amin's special relations with Bob Astles see section titled "*Meet Bob Astles—Amin's Special British Adviser*" below.
[308] See story "Israeli Asserts He Helped Amin Achieve Rule in '71" by Moshe Brilliant in *The New York Times,* 17 July 1976.
[309] Telegram No. 581 on "Visit of General Amin," dated 20 July 1971 on FCO 31/1072.
[310] Ibid.
[311] Letter from Idi Amin to Edward Heath, dated 10 January 1972.
[312] See letter from Le Tocq, EAD, to Smeldley, dated 9 July 1971, (copied to Hale, D. E. Young and A. D. Steven).
[313] Letter from Patrick Gratton, FCO, to R. C. Mottram Esq., Ministry of Defence, dated 6 March 1972.

[314] Patrick Grattan, FCO to Lord Bridges, No. 10, 6 March 1972, PREM 15/1257.
[315] Stiglitz, *Globalization and its Discontents*, pp. 111, 137.
[316] Richard Slater to Simon Dawbarn, FCO, 8 February 1972. FCO 31/1324.
[317] See Lord Aldington to Amin, 25 March 1972 and enclosure to Lord Aldington's letter, "Report on visit to Uganda," 5 April 1972, both in PREM 15/1257.
[318] According to Simon Dawbarn, FCO, to Le Quesne, 20 March 1972, FCO 31/1327, Slater confirmed that anything up to 400 mainly Acholi and Langi soldiers were killed at Mutukula.
[319] In a letter from Patrick Gratton to Lord Bridges, dated 2 June 1972.
[320] Letter by Patrick Gratton, FCO to R. C. Lord Bridges, and Prime Minister's Office at 10 Downing Street, dated 2 June 1972.
[321] See Decree passed on 17 December 1972 and a story by Faustin Mugabe headed "Amin renames lakes, roads and mountains to 'decolonise' Uganda" in *The Sunday Monitor* 26 November 2017, pp. 16, 31.
[322] See letter from P. R. G. Redshaw of the British High Commission Kampala, to R. M. Purcell, East Africa Department of the Foreign and Commonwealth Office, dated 2 March 1971. See File "Exhumation in UK and re Burial in Uganda of body of ex-Kabaka of Buganda and first President of Uganda, Sir Edward Mutesa," FCO 31/1074 and 1075.
[323] See open letter headed *If No Recognition of Kabakaship—No Return of Kabaka's Body* by Joseph G. Serubyale, dated 24 February 1971, arguing that there can never be peace and stability in Buganda unless there is a Kabakaship. Also, see letters by Buganda's clan leaders Lwomwa, Kasujja and Mugalula to Her Majesty Queen Elizabeth II, demanding the restoration of the Kabakaship, FCO FCO 31/1074 and 1075.
[324] Including Keith Speed, Lt-Col. Colin Mitchel, Michael Cocks and George Cunningham. See memorandum "Funeral ceremonies of Sir Edward Mutesa" by Richard Slater, the British High Commissioner in Kampala, to the Secretary of State for Foreign and Commonwealth Affairs, dated 13 April 1971, FCO 31/1075.
[325] Ibid.
[326] See notes on talks between Lord Boyd and General Idi Amin on 1 April (in Kampala) and 3 April 1971 in Entebbe, written by Lord Boyd, on FCO 31/1075.
[327] Ibid.
[328] See letter from the delegation of MPs by Hon. Martin to the Foreign Secretary, dated 7 April 1971, FCO 31/1075.
[329] See note by H. Smedley to Le Tocq, dated 6 April 1971, FCO 31/1075.
[330] On 7 September 1971, FCO 31/1075.
[331] For a full list of the reasons for Amin's coup, see Ibingira, *The Forging of an African Nation*, p. 289.
[332] In a speech on 7 September 1971 on the occasion of handing over Sir Edward Mutesa's motor boat to Ronald Mutebi, FCO 31/1075.
[333] Ibid.
[334] See letter headed *Buganda and the Kabakaship* from Robin A. C. Byatt to A. A. Joy of the EAD, FCO, London, dated 10 September 1971.
[335] Ibid.

[336] See letter headed "General Amin and the Baganda," from P. R. G. Redshaw to R. M. Purcel of the EAD, FCO, dated 3 March 1971, FCO 31/1075.
[337] In a letter dated 24 August 1971 to G. A. Duggan of the East African Department Foreign and Commonwealth Office headed "Amin and the Baganda," FCO 31/1075.
[338] R. Purcell, FCO, to Peter Redshaw, Kampala, 30 March 1971, FCO 31/1017.
[339] See G. Duggan, EAD to E. Counsell, FCO, *Deaths in Uganda*, 14 February 1972, FCO 31/1327 and Richard Slater to Simon Dawbarn, 29 February 1972, FCO 31/1327 on 400 mainly Acholi and Langi soldiers that were killed at Mutukula.
[340] Charles Booth, Kampala to D. Brinson, FCO, 6 July 1971, FCO 26/747.
[341] Richard Slater to Simon Dawbarn, FCO, 30 May 1972, FCO 31/1328.
[342] Ibid.
[343] On the Uganda- Tanzania clashes, see Roberts, George (2014) "The Uganda–Tanzania War, the fall of Idi Amin, and the failure of African diplomacy, 1978–1979," *The Journal of Eastern African Studies* 8(4).
[344] Campbell, High Commission, Ethiopia to FCO, 8 June 1972, FCO 31/1328.
[345] Richard Slater to Simon Dawbarn, 13 June 1972, FCO 31/1328.
[346] See generally file, "Expulsion of Ugandan Asians," FCO 89/10.
[347] See file, PREM 15/1258.
[348] Prime Minister James Callaghan to Amin, 8 August 1972, PREM 15/1258.
[349] Jørgensen, J. J. (1981) *Uganda: A Modern History*, London: Taylor & Francis, p. 288.
[350] Op. cit., p. 286.
[351] Ibid.
[352] FCO to Kampala, 9 September 1972, PREM 15/1258.
[353] Amin had dealings with Astles even before he took power in 1971; see file "Defence Attaché reports on Ugandan Army: discussions with Brig. Amin and Bob Astles," FCO 16/131 and Bob Astles' obituary in *The Daily Telegraph*, 15 February 2013.
[354] Bob Astles' obituary in *The Daily Telegraph,* ibid.
[355] Kimenye, Barbara "Bob Astles is Rejected by Kabaka, Hangs onto Obote, Amin," *The Daily Monitor*, 8 November 2015.
[356] Astles' obituary, *The Daily Telegraph*, 15 February 2013.
[357] Kimenye, "Bob Astles is Rejected by Kabaka," *The Daily Monitor*, 8 November 2015.
[358] Astles' obituary, *The Daily Telegraph*, 15 February 2013.
[359] Ibid.
[360] Ibid.
[361] See letter by R. Kershaw, Head, EAD, FCO to A. J. Wilkes Esq., dated 4 March 1983, in file *Uganda: Trial of Bob Astles*, FCO31/4128, TNA.
[362] Ibid.
[363] See letter from R. P. Smith of the British High Commission in Kampala to R. Kershaw, Head of the EAD, FCO, dated 15 February 1983, in file *Uganda: Trial of Bob Astles*, FCO31/4128, TNA.

[364] Ibid.
[365] See letter by T. V. Edwards & Company to FCO, dated 15 April 1983, in file *Uganda: Trial of Bob Astles*, FCO 31/4128, TNA.
[366] See, generally, file *General Amin's 'Save Britain Charity Fund,'* PREM 15/2230, TNA.
[367] See General Amin's telegrams to the British Prime Minister, dated 14 December 1973 and 18 January 1974, PREM 15/2230.
[368] Ibid., 18 January 1974.
[369] According to a letter from A. A. Acland of the FCO to Lord Bridges, dated 23 January 1974, PREM 15/2230.
[370] See General Amin's letter to the Prime Minister of United Kingdom, dated 21 January 1974, PREM 15/2230.
[371] Letter from A. A. Acland of the FCO to Lord Bridges, dated 23 January 1974, PREM 15/2230.
[372] See story "Uganda: Amin, the Wild Man of Africa" in *Time Magazine*, 7 March 1977.
[373] See file "Visit of the Foreign Secretary to Kampala July 1975," PREM 16/1480.
[374] Otunnu, O. (2016) *Crises of Legitimacy and Political Violence in Colonial Uganda, 1890-1962*, Palgrave Macmillan, Cham, p. 282.
[375] "Denis Hills," *The Guardian*, Tuesday, 4 May 2004, www.theguardian.com/news/2004/may/04/guardianobituaries.booksobituaries, accessed 2 March 2018.
[376] See story on Lt-Gen. Sir Chandos Blair, *The Telegraph*, 24 January 2011.
[377] "Denis Hills," *The Guardian*, Tuesday, 4 May 2004, op. cit.
[378] See PREM 16/1480 and a report Ref. PS/75/2, No. 2 by the office of the Secretary of State for Foreign and Commonwealth Affairs on the *Visit of the Foreign and Commonwealth Secretary to Zaire and Uganda 8-10 July 1975*.
[379] Ibid., p. 7.
[380] Ibid., p. 9.
[381] Ibid., p. 15.
[382] Ibid.
[383] See file "Hijack of Air France plane at Entebbe Airport, Uganda, 27 June 1976, FCO 93/913 and PREM 16/2285 "Uganda: UK/Uganda diplomatic relations; internal situation after Air France hijacking and Israeli rescue operation; fate of Dora Bloch."
[384] Ben Alexander, Operation Thunderbolt: Daring and Luck. www.cija.ca/operation-thunderbolt/ accessed 2 March 2018.
[385] For example, in his earlier communication to Edward Heath, leader of the Conservative Party, during the election campaign in 1974, Amin stated that any victorious party should "strongly support the Palestine cause and stand firmly against the Zionist policies of the Israeli Government in the Middle East." See Amin's letter to Heath, HC 47 12.20 London Telex 254, stamped 20 February 1974. Later, in March 1974, Amin wrote to Queen Elizabeth II urging her to use all her influence to ensure, among other things, "that the new [British] Government gives unswerving and genuine support to the African and the Palestinian

Liberation Movements," adding that were this so, "Her Majesty's Government will be guaranteed … my personal support, that of [my] Government and the entire People of Uganda." See telegram No. 216 of 1 March 1974 from Idi Amin to Her Majesty Queen Elizabeth II.

[386] See David, Saul (2016) *Operation Thunderbolt* Flight *139 and the raid on Entebbe Airport: The Most Audacious Hostage Rescue Mission in History*, reviewed by Alan Furst in The *New York Times*, 22 January 2016.

[387] "How Israel planned 90-minute raid on Entebbe airport," *Daily Monitor*, 3 July 2016.

[388] McManus, James and Eric Silver, "Israelis jubilant as Amin laments," *The Guardian*, Sunday 4 July 1976.

[389] See "British Interests Section (BIS) in French Embassy in Kampala," FCO 31/2063; Telegram 149 of 27 July 1976 to Certain Missions and Dependent Territories on termination of Anglo/Uganda diplomatic relations; and British Cabinet office releases concerning Idi Amin, President of Uganda.

[390] No doubt in ironic reference to the British honours system's CBE: Commander of the Order of the British Empire.

[391] Keatley, Patrick, "Idi Amin" (obituary), *The Guardian*, 18 August 2003.

[392] Ibid.

[393] See Berridge, "The British Interests Section in Kampala."

[394] See Amin's letter to Dr E. Shridath Rumphal, Secretary General of the Commonwealth, sent via telegram, dated 31 May 1977.

[395] Ibid.

[396] Ibid.

[397] In May 1977, Prime Minister Jim Callaghan sent Amin a message via Prince Fahd of Saudi Arabia warning him that he would not be permitted in Britain.

[398] See story "Armed Welcome Was Prepared When Amin Threatened to Visit" in *The Daily Telegraph*, 5 February 2007.

[399] Ibid.

[400] See telegram 130 dated 9 June 1977 from Glasby, British High Commission in Kampala, to the Foreign and Commonwealth Office and, G. Berridge, (2012) "The British Interests Section in Kampala," p. 16.

[401] Ibid., Berridge, "The British Interests Section in Kampala," p. 16. See also telegram No. 130 of 9 June 1977 from Glasby, British High Commission, to FCO.

[402] See file "Uganda Airline Flights to and from UK," FCO 31/2414, 1978 and PREM 16/2285 "UK/Uganda diplomatic relations; Uganda Airlines flights into Stansted ('whisky run')".

[403] See letter by J. Tomlinson, FCO, to John Gilbert, the Minister of State Ministry of Defence on NAAFI Trade with Uganda Armed Forces, dated 5 July 1977.

[404] See file FCO 31/2414.

[405] See background note in response to a parliamentary question by Greville Janner (Labour) to Dr John Gilbert Minister of State for Defence Ref. PQ 6867B, dated 29 June 1977. According to the Sunday Times, in June 1977, Ugandan planes in Stansted picked up 28 Land Rovers, one of them specially converted with

sophisticated equipment for monitoring broadcasts, jamming and so on (cited in Hutton and Bloch, "Uganda: How the West brought Idi Amin to Power.")

[406] See letter from A. G. Munro, EAD, dated 6 December 1978, to Day (copied to Rowlands) on Repairs to Uganda Airlines Hercules Aircraft. Also, see article by Peter Deley, "Dispute over Amin's Jet," *The Observer*, 19 November 1978.

[407] Hutton and Bloch, "Uganda: How the West brought Idi Amin to Power."

[408] Ban Cargo of Shame, Says MP, FCO31/2414.

[409] Ibid.

[410] Colm Cavanagh's letter to David Owen, dated 2 December 1978.

[411] See letter of K. Q. F. Manning, EAD, dated 12 December 1978, to Cavanagh.

[412] See letter by J. S. Wall, FCO, to N. Sanders of the Prime Minister's office, dated 11 August 1978.

[413] See a memorandum of A. C. Hunt, Head of EAD, FCO, to A. I. Glasby of the British High Commission in Kampala, dated 10 September 1976.

[414] See statement by William N. Harrop, Acting Assistant Secretary of State for African Affairs, before the Subcommittee on International Economic Policy and Trade and the Subcommittee on International Organisations of the House International Relations Committee, 2 February 1978 at https://archive.org/stream/IdiAmin/British%20Cabinet%20Office%20-%20Foreign%20Office_djvu.txt accessed 4 May 2018.

[415] Ibid.

[416] Ibid.

[417] See the *Tribune* magazine, 17 June, 1977.

[418] See Memorandum to the Prime Minister on supplies for Uganda, Ref. PM/77/64, dated 22 June 1977.

[419] See letter by from David Owen, Secretary of State for the FCO, to the Prime Minister, Ref. PM /78/119, dated 13 November, 1978.

[420] See letter from David Owen to the Prime Minister, Ref. PM /79/24, dated 27 February 1979.

[421] See letter from B. G. Cartledge, Private Secretary of the Prime Minister, to J. S. Wall of the Foreign and Commonwealth Office, dated 15 November 1978.

[422] See letter from T. G. Harris, Private Secretary Department of Trade to Bryan Cartledge in the Prime Minister's office.

[423] See President Nyerere's letter to Prime Minister Edward Heath, dated 4 September 1971.

[424] See Prime Minister Edward Heath's letter to President Nyerere, dated 28 September 1971.

[425] See "Tanzania. Relations with Uganda; Ugandan incursion and Tanzanian counter- attack; request for UK military assistance" PREM 16/2268, and "Relations between Uganda and Tanzania: Uganda-Tanzania War," FCO 31/2680-2685.

[426] See letter from David Owen Secretary of State for the Foreign and Commonwealth Office, to the Secretary of State for Trade Ref. FCS/78/206, dated 4 December, 1978.

[427] See letter from Joel Barnett, Treasury Chambers, to Hon. David Owen Secretary of State for Foreign Affairs, FCO, dated 12 December, 1978.
[428] See letter from R. M. Graham-Harrison, Ministry of Overseas Development, to J. S. Wall, FCO, dated 22 November 1978.
[429] See letter from J. S. Wall, FCO, to Bryan Cartledge Prime Minister's Office, dated 19 March 1979.
[430] On the disruption of oil and other supplies to Uganda from Kenya, see "Energy matters in Uganda: Oil and Uganda's invasion of Tanzania," FCO 96/789.
[431] See Mutibwa, *A History of Uganda*, pp. 294-296.
[432] See Memorandum on "Uganda: Possible Recognition of a New Government" from J. A. Robson of the EAD, FCO to Day, dated 5 April 1979.
[433] Ibid.
[434] See paper *Uganda After Amin* by Sir Richard Posnett when he addressed the Royal African Society.
[435] Ibid.
[436] Buganda's fortunes did not improve in the first six years after Amin was overthrown in 1979. This is because the successive regimes of Dr Obote (in reincarnation), Tito Okello Lutwa, Basilio Okello, Paulo Muwanga, Prof. Yusuf Lule and Godfrey Binaisa had no time or power to ponder the restoration of kingdoms in Uganda. It was only when armed rebellion started against Dr Obote that talk of the restoration of kingdoms took on a more serious turn.
[437] See letter from J. P. Nason, British High Commission, Kampala to A. J. Longrigg, East Africa Department, FCO, dated 14 April 1980.
[438] Ibid.
[439] See letter from A. J. Longrigg of the East Africa Department, FCO, to J. P. Nason, British High Commission, Kampala, dated 6 May 1980, Ref. GRS 265 in File JEU 014/1.
[440] Ibid.
[441] See letter by Governor W. F. Coutts to Kabaka Fredrick Mutesa, dated 26 March 1962, in file *Personal Correspondence with Colonial Office*, FCO 141/18460 TNA.
[442] See Womakuyu, Fredrick, "Lule, the President for 68 days" in *The New Vision*, 19 January 2012 and a note of a conversation between Prime Minister Margaret Thatcher and President G. L. Binaisa at the Ugandan Villa in Lumumbashi Village, Lusaka Zambia, at a CHOGM meeting, 3 August 1979 in file "Prime Ministers Bi-lateral Meetings at the CHOGM in Lusaka 1979," PREM 19/10.xxx
[443] Notes on Binaisa's early history made by R. N. Posnett in Kampala to J. A. Robson, EAD, FCO, dated 29 June 1979, state that he was born around 1924 and educated at King's College Budo and Makerere University where he became a medical student. He flunked out after a year or two and had a mental breakdown which required psychiatric treatment. He is known to have been held in poor regard by the then Kabaka's Government in Buganda. He declined to join the Kabaka Yekka Party in 1961 and instead joined the Uganda People's Congress. He did not stand for election in the 1961 general election but was later appointed by Obote to be Attorney General, an office which carried with it ex-officio

membership of the assembly. Thus, he never held elective office. At the time in 1966, when Obote imprisoned without trial five members of his cabinet, Binaisa, who had no prior knowledge of this event, was asked to draft the Government statement explaining and justifying Obote's action. This he agreed to do. It was only a year or two later that he was forced into resignation by Obote's further proposals to permit imprisonment without trial. He served as a short time as Attorney General under Amin. He later practiced law in New York. In June 1979, he succeeded Yusuf Lule, who headed the first provisional Government which assumed office following the liberation of Kampala in April 1979.

444 See telegram No. 78 of 11 February from B. A. Flack, British High Commission, Kampala to the Foreign and Commonwealth Office.

445 See note of a conversation between British Prime Minister Margaret Thatcher and the President of Uganda Binaisa op. cit., Binaisa told the Prime Minister that Britain should not be taken in by the current scare about Obote's activities because he "would not play any role in Uganda and would not return to the country."

446 See telegram No. 95 from B. A. Flack, British High Commission, Kampala, to FCO, *Call on President Binaisa: Uganda Internal Affairs*, 18 February 1980.

447 Ibid.

448 B. A Flack, dated 28 April 1980, to EAD, FCO.

449 B. A. Flack, on "Possibility of a Coup," to J. A. Robson East Africa Department, FCO, dated 28 April 1980.

450 B. A. Flack, "Uganda: Return of Obote," to the East Africa Department, FCO, dated 23 April 1980.

451 See telegram from B. A. Flack on "Possibility of a Coup," op. cit.

452 Ibid.

453 See note of a conversation between Margaret Thatcher British Prime Minister and the President of Kenya, Daniel Arap Moi at President Moi's bungalow in Lumumbashi Village, Lusaka Zambia on 3 August 1979 at a CHOGM meeting, 3 August 1979. See file, Prime Ministers Bi-lateral Meetings at the CHOGM in Lusaka 1979, PREM 19/10.

454 Ibid.

455 See telegram No. 535 from Posnett, British High Commission, Kampala on "Uganda: Minister's visit," to the East Africa Department, FCO, dated 16 October 1979.

456 Ibid.

457 Ibid.

458 Ibid.

459 See memorandum "Ref. Possible Visit to UK of Ugandan Defence Minister" from J. A. Robson, EAD, to Aspin, Defence Department, dated 29 October 1979 and file 5 in "Visit to UK by Ugandan Defence Minister," CO 31/2698, 1979.

460 Ibid.

461 See telegram No. 342 of 16 November 1979 from Carrington, FCO, to British High Commission, Kampala.

462 Mutibwa, *A History of Uganda*, pp. 314-315.

[463] See generally FCO 31/2698, 1979 File No. JEU 026/5 on *Visit to UK by Ugandan Defence Minister.*
[464] See Mutibwa, *A History of Uganda*, p. 328-329.
[465] According to W. Marsden, FCO in his letter to C. McLean, British High Commissioner at Kampala, dated 16 April 1986, in FCO 31/4943, Ref. JEU 014/2, TNA.
[466] Ibid.
[467] See a diplomatic despatch JEU 014/2 *Uganda: Annual Review 1985* from the British High Commissioner at Kampala to the Secretary of State for Commonwealth Affairs, dated 8 January 1986, in FCO 31/4943 TNA.
[468] See Mutibwa, *A History of Uganda*, pp. 365-365.
[469] See a diplomatic despatch JEU 014/2 *Uganda: Museveni's Assumption of Power* from the British High Commissioner at Kampala to the Secretary of State for Commonwealth Affairs, dated 30 April 1986 in FCO 31/4943 TNA.
[470] See generally, Museveni, Yoweri Kaguta (1997) *Sowing the Mustard Seed: The Struggle for Freedom and Democracy in Uganda*, London: Macmillan.
[471] See letter by A. J. G. Pollard to Admiral of the Fleet Sir John Fieldhouse GCB GBE, Chief of Staff of the Defence Staff, DA/13/1/NBO on "Uganda—Operation RAHU," dated 7 June 1986, FCO 31/4962 TNA.
[472] Ibid.
[473] See a diplomatic despatch JEU 014/2 *Uganda: Annual Review, 1985*, op. cit, p. 4.
[474] Letter by A. J. G. Pollard to Admiral of the Fleet Sir John Fieldhouse, op. cit.
[475] See a diplomatic despatch JEU 014/2 *Uganda: Museveni's Assumption of Power*, op. cit, p. 3.
[476] Letter by A. J. G. Pollard to Admiral of the Fleet Sir John Fieldhouse, op. cit.
[477] According to notes on file FCO 31/4954, prepared ahead of his visit to the UK in November 1986, Yoweri Museveni (b. 1946, Munyankole tribe, southwest Uganda) attended Makerere University and University College, Dar es Salaam where he was Chairman of Students Revolutionary Front 1968). He led a student delegation to liberated areas of Mozambique in 1969 and became a member of President Obote's Research Department 1969-70. In 1972 he formed the Front for National Salvation (FRONASA), a Ugandan guerrilla group based in Tanzania., He commanded his own exile military force in the UNLA/Tanzania invasion of Uganda in 1979-80. Appointed Minister of Defence in April 1979 in President Lule's government, he later became Minister for Regional Cooperation in 1979 under President Binaisa and also Vice-Chairman of the Military Commission. He formed the Uganda Patriotic Movement to fight the 1980 elections and, in 1981, the Movement for the Struggle for Political Rights (MOSPOR) and its military wing, the People's Revolutionary Army or Popular Resistance Army (PRA). He joined Lule to form the National Resistance Movement (NRM) in 1981 and subsequently in January 1982 the Uganda Popular Front. He negotiated a compromise agreement with the Military Council Government after the fall of President Obote in June 1985, but in January 1986 took Kampala by force.

[478] President Museveni's swearing-in address, 29 January 1986, quoted from Richard J. Reid (2017) *A History of Modern Uganda*, Cambridge: Cambridge University Press, p. 79.
[479] See Rule, Sheila, "Rebel Sworn in as Ugandan President," *The New York Times,* 30 January 1896.
[480] See, for example, Museveni's speech at the Woodrow Wilson International Centre for Scholars on 14 May 2002, where he accused the World Bank of double standards and Mallaby Sebastian (2004) *The World's Banker* Penguin Press, Chapter 8.
[481] See Mays, Terry M. and Delancey, Mark W. (2002) *Historical Dictionary of International Organisations in Sub-Saharan Africa*, Rowman & Littlefield, p. 1645.
[482] See address by Yoweri Kaguta Museveni, President of the Republic of Uganda on 21 October 1887 at the UN Headquarters, New York. UNGA Provisional, A/42/PV.45, 23 October 1987.
[483] See letter by J. Jenkin of the East Africa Department of the FCO on *President Museveni's Speech at the Royal Commonwealth Society on 18 November 1986*, addressed to Marsden at the British High Commission in Kampala, dated 22 December 1986, in FCO 31/4954 TNA.
[484] See Guidelines for UK Policy Towards Uganda in 1986 by the EAD, FCO, dated 5 June 1986, in FCO 31/4962 TNA.
[485] Ibid.
[486] Ibid.
[487] See Legal Notice No. 5 of 16 May 1986.
[488] The Truth Commission: Uganda 86, www.UAIP.org
[489] See publication by the Office of the High Commissioner for Human Rights *Uganda and the United Nations Human Rights Mechanisms—A Compilation on the Occasion of the 60th Anniversary of the Universal Declaration of Human Rights*, pp. 13-25.
[490] For details, see Warnock, Frank and Patrick Conway (1999) *Post-Conflict Recovery in Uganda*, Washington DC: World Bank Institute.
[491] See letter from President Yoweri K. Museveni to Prime Minister Margaret Thatcher, dated 31 January 1986, FCO 31/4949 TNA.
[492] See notes of a meeting between Pollard and Chalker on 12 June 1986, FCO 31/4962.
[493] See notes of a meeting between Pollard, Reeve and Johnson on 12 June 1986, FCO 31/4962.
[494] In a letter from A. J. G. Pollard to Admiral of the Fleet Sir John Fieldhouse, op. cit.
[495] See point No. 5 of Museveni's 1986 ten-point manifesto.
[496] In a brief dated 13 November 1986 to Prime Minister Thatcher ahead of Museveni's visit to UK in November 1986. See file, *Visit of President Museveni of Uganda to the UK*, FCO31/4954 TNA.
[497] Ibid.

[498] In a brief dated 13 November 1986 to Prime Minister Thatcher ahead of Museveni's visit to UK in November 1986, the FCO advised that "Museveni's international relationships are alienating his potential Western and other friends. He wants oil, money, arms and military funds from Libya and argues that he needs a reasonable relationship with Libya to prevent Gaddafi from supporting enemies in the north. There is some justification for this but Museveni is taking too many risks. There are reports that he is shopping for substantial arms supplies from the Soviet Union. The Kenyans are very worried by these developments."
[499] In a letter by William Marsden, EAD, FCO to Reeve, dated 13 October 1986. See file, *Visit of President Museveni of Uganda to the UK*, FCO 31/4954 TNA.
[500] See notes of a meeting between Pollard and Chalker on 12 June 1986 in FCO 31/4962 TNA, op. cit.
[501] Letter by C. R. Budd to Charles Powell, 10 Downing Street, dated 15 October 1986, FCO 31/4954 TNA.
[502] Letter by A. J. G. Pollard to Admiral of the Fleet Sir John Fieldhouse, op. cit.
[503] In a meeting with President Museveni on 17 November 1986, Margret Thatcher "strongly urged President Museveni to negotiate with the IMF" because it was "the key to further aid and debt rescheduling." See letter from C. D. Powell of 10 Downing Street to Collin Budd, FCO, dated 17 November 1986, FCO 31/4954 TNA.
[504] In a meeting with President Museveni on 17 November 1986, Lynda Chalker "expressed concern at Uganda's relations with the IMF." Citing the examples of Tanzania and Ghana, she hoped that "the IMF's economic advice could be accepted on its economic merits." She assured her guest that Britain "would not support IMF terms which were contrary to Uganda's interests." See notes by R. J. Sawers to Marsden EAD, FCO, dated 17 November 1986, in file *Visit of President Museveni of Uganda to the UK*, FCO 31/4954 TNA.
[505] In a brief dated 13 November 1986 to Prime Minister Thatcher ahead of Museveni's visit to UK in November 1986, the FCO advised that "it would be inappropriate to provide general balance of payments support until agreement is reached with the IMF." See file, *Visit of President Museveni of Uganda to the UK*, FCO 31/4954 TNA.
[506] In a letter from William Marsden, EAD, FCO, to Reeve, dated 13 October 1986, op. cit.
[507] In a brief dated 13 November 1986 to Prime Minister Thatcher ahead of Museveni's visit to UK in November 1986, in file, *Visit of President Museveni of Uganda to the UK*, FCO 31/4954 TNA.
[508] Ibid.
[509] See telegram 557 stamped 13 October 1986 from David March, British High Commission, Kampala, to the FCO.
[510] See report on a visit by President Yoweri Museveni, President of Uganda, 15-18 November 1986, by C. Wilcox, dated 24 November 1986. FCO31/4954 TNA.
[511] See telegram 523 from FCO to Kampala by Howe on Uganda: President Museveni's visit to the UK, 16-18 November, 1986, FCO31/4954 TNA.
[512] Ibid.

[513] See telegram No. 667 of November 1986 from Pefold in Kampala to FCO on President Museveni's visit to the UK.

[514] Ibid.

[515] Letter dated 27 November 1986 on File FCO31/4954 TNA.

[516] Telegram No. 667 of November 1986 from Pefold in Kampala to FCO, op. cit.

[517] See Speech by Lynda Chalker at a Luncheon for President Museveni at Lancaster House on 17 November 1986, in FCO 31/4954.

[518] See speech *The African Renaissance, South Africa and the World* by South Africa's Deputy President Thabo Mbeki made at the United Nations University on 9 April 1998 and Malagapuru, William (ed.) (1999) *African Renaissance*, Sandton and Capetown.

[519] See Suhuyini and Weijagye Justis, *World View: Ghana, Indonesia, Uganda* in Socialist Standard No. 1167 Published by the Socialist Party of Great Britain, 1 October 2001.

[520]See Report of the Panel of Experts on the Illegal Exploitation of Natural Resources and Other Forms of Wealth of the Democratic Republic of the Congo, UN Doc. S/2003/1027 (28 October 2003).

[521]See judgement of the International Court of Justice in the case: *The Democratic Republic of the Congo v. Uganda (Armed Activities Case),2005.* http://www.icj-cij.org/files/case-related/116/10457.pdf, accessed on 19th May 2018.

[522] Ibid.

[523] See Kelly, Annie and Ford, Liz "Aid to Uganda: How the UK Government is supporting the country," *The Guardian*, 29 January 2009.

[524] See profile of Baroness Chalker of Wallasey at www.parliament.uk.

[525] See *Speech by the Queen at CHOGM, Uganda, 2007*, accessed at www.royal.uk

[526] See story "Professor Mamdani calls for reconciliation" in *The New Vision*, 5 December 2006.

[527] See Kalinaki, Daniel K. (2014) *Kizza Besigye and Uganda's Unfinished Revolution*, Kampala: Dominant Seven Publishers, p. 255.

[528] Ibid., p. 281 and "Uganda's judges strike over raid," *BBC News*, 5 March 2007, http://news.bbc.co.uk/1/hi/world/africa/6418943.stm, accessed 3 March 2018.

[529] Tripp, *Museveni's Uganda,* pp.52,72.

[530] See story "Budget cuts: Museveni writes to UK," *The New Vision*, 23 December 2005.

[531] Although Museveni was declared winner of the 2006 presidential election, the result of the poll was controversial. In a Presidential Election Petition No.1 of 2006 [2007] UGSC (30 January 2007), *Rtd. Col. Dr Kizza Besigye vs. Electoral Commission and Yoweri Kaguta Museveni*, the Supreme Court found several irregularities and illegalities in the poll. It held that there was noncompliance with the provisions of the Constitution, the Presidential Elections Act and the Electoral Commission Act, especially in the disenfranchisement of voters and denying them the right to vote, in the counting and tallying of results, and by acts of violence, bribery, intimidation and multiple voting, all of which undermined the principle of free and fair elections. However, this this notwithstanding, the Court found that the

petitioner had failed to prove that these irregularities had a substantial effect on the results. It thus upheld the Museveni's victory.

[532] See Tatchell, Peter, "Uganda's Tyrant," *The Guardian*, 22 November 2007.

[533] Ibid.

[534] Ibid.

[535] On the value and the future of the Commonwealth see generally Murphy, Phillip (2018) *The Empire's New Clothes: The Myth of the Commonwealth.* C. Hurst (Publishers) Ltd; *The Economist,* "Is the Commonwealth a plausible substitute for the EU? 12 April 2018 and the 2018 Commonwealth Trade Review entitled "Strengthening the Commonwealth Advantage."

[536] See Kelly, Annie and Liz Ford "Aid to Uganda: How the UK Government is supporting the country," *The Guardian*, 29 January 2009.

[537] Commenting on the 2016 Presidential elections, the Commonwealth Observer Group and the European Union Election Observer Mission said the ballot that President Museveni won for his fifth term of office fell short of key democratic benchmarks. See "Yoweri Museveni Wins Ugandan Election as Observers Cry Foul" in *The Daily Telegraph*, 20 February 2016.

[538] The UK's Department for International Development (DFID) suspended £11m to Uganda Government over corruption cases. See story "UK cuts aid to Uganda government" at www.bbc.com, 16 November 2012 and Tran, Mark and Liz Ford, "UK suspends aid to Uganda as concern grows over misuse of funds," *The Guardian*, 16 November 2012.

[539] See Plaut, Martin "Uganda donors cut aid, while others including US review budgets over law imposing harsh penalties for homosexuality," *The Guardian*, 25 February 2014.

[540] See Hirsch, Afua, "It's right for Britain to reach out to Africa—wrong to send Boris Johnson," *The Guardian*, 16 March 2017. On British colonialism in Africa, Boris Johnson has asserted that "Africa is a mess, but it is simply not credible to blame colonialism.... the Continent (Africa) may be a blot, but it is not a blot upon our conscience. The problem is not that we were once in charge, but that we are not in charge any more.... [T]he best fate for Africa would be if the old colonial powers, or their citizens, scrambled once again in her direction on the understanding that this time they will not be asked to feel guilty". See Johnson, Boris, "Cancel the Guilt Trip," *The Spectator*, 2 February 2002, p. 14.

[541] See news article by the British High Commission, Kampala, "Foreign Secretary Visits Uganda," dated 16 March 2017, accessed at www.gov.uk.

[542] See "Britain pours aid into autocratic Uganda despite pleas of democratic opposition" in *The Telegraph*, 21 July 2012.

[543] See Hirsch, "It's right for Britain to reach out to Africa" op. cit.

[544] Including the controversial presidential elections in 2016 and the political fiasco surrounding the amendment of the constitution to remove presidential age limits. See Townsend, Mark "Uganda election victory extends Yoweri Museveni's grip on power," *The Guardian*, 20 February 2016,

www.theguardian.com/world/2016/feb/20/ugandan-election-yoweri-museveni-wins-arrests-opposition-leader-besigye; and "Uganda MPs brawl during presidential age-limit debate," BBC news website, 26 September 2017, www.bbc.com/news/world-africa-41398849.

[545] See Kasfir, Nelson (2017) *Kingdom, State and Civil Society in Africa: Conceptual and Political Collisions*, Basler Afrika Bibliographien, p.13.

[546] See Kalyegira, Timothy, "NRA government's purge of UFM and FEDEMU soldiers," *The Daily Monitor*, 7 December 2012.

[547] See Mugabe, Faustin, "Mutebi arrives in Luwero to drum up support for NRA fighters," *The Daily Monitor*, 4 September 2016.

[548] Ibid.

[549] Tripp, *Museveni's Uganda,* p.47.

[550] See Matsiko, P. and Bichachi, Odoobo C. "Museveni-Buganda bush war deal: Who is telling the truth?" *The Independent*, 29 September 2009.

[551] See Njuba, Samuel Kalega (2003) *The betrayal as Ugandan's are taken for a ride again*, a self-published book, p. 301.

[552] The points were on democracy; security; consolidation of national security and elimination of all forms of sectarianism; defending and consolidating national independence; building an independent, integrated and self-sustaining national economy; restoration and improvement of social services and the rehabilitation of the war-ravaged areas; elimination of corruption and misuse of power; redressing errors that have resulted in the dislocation of sections of the population and improvement of others; cooperation with other African countries in defending human and democratic rights in other parts of Africa; and following an economic strategy of a mixed economy.

[553] See Nalugo Mercy, Yassin Mugerwa & Shiela Naturinda "Uganda: Otafiire—Museveni to Blame for Buganda Mess," in *The Monitor*, 10 September, 2009.

[554] See Mugabe, Faustin "Baganda put pressure on NRA to have Mutebi crowned," *Daily Monitor*, 11 September 2016.

[555] See Kasfir, *Kingdom, State and Civil Society in Africa*, p.14.

[556] For a fuller account on the restoration of Buganda kingdom in 1993, see Charles Peter Mayiga (2009) *King on the Throne: The story of the restoration of the kingdom of Buganda*, Prime Time Communications.

[557]See unpublished paper by Nelson Kasfir, *The Buganda Kingdom Government in Uganda Politics 1986-2014: Culture, contingencies and constraints on organizational success.* p. 11

[558] Ibid. p. 12.

[559] See statement by President Museveni to the Buganda Parliamentary Caucus on 10th September 2009 at Entebbe State House. The statement was published in *The New Vision* of 11 September 2009.

[560] Mayiga, *King on the Throne,* p.222.

[561] See generally Mayiga, *King on the Throne*, pp. 227-256

[562] See Nsibambi, *National Integration in Uganda*, p. 88.

[563] See Mayiga, *King on the Throne*, p.394

[564] Statement by President Museveni to the Buganda Parliamentary Caucus on 10 September 2009, op cit.
[565] See reports by the Human Rights Watch "Uganda: Investigate Use of Lethal Force During Riots," 1 October 2009 and "Uganda: Investigate 2009 Kampala Riot Killings," 10 September 2010.
[566] See ruling by Justice Ralph Ochan in *Uganda vs. Robert Sekabira and 10 others*, Case No. 85 of 2010 where working with Hon. Medard Lubega Ssegona and other lawyers I was the lead defence counsel.
[567] See letter headed "Whether the Institution of Traditional or Cultural Leaders Bill, 2010 is in Conformity with The Constitution" from Edward Khiddu Makubuya, Attorney General and Minister of Justice and Constitutional Affairs, to President Y. Kaguta Museveni of 17 November 2010, Ref. MJ/AG/12.
[568] Ibid.
[569] See *Joseph B. M. Balikudembe vs. The Attorney General of Uganda*, Constitutional Petition No. 33 of 2012.
[570] See Statement from State House on Memorandum of Understanding to return Buganda Kingdom Properties of 3 August 2013 and Makubuya, Apollo N., "Buganda-Government deal is real" in *The Monitor*, 25 August 2013
[571] See generally Kasfir, *Kingdom, State and Civil Society in Africa.*
[572] See document *Uganda's New Government: Ancient and Modern* by EAD, FCO, February 1986, in File FCO31/4939 TNA.
[573] Between 24 and 28 May 2004.
[574] Jerry Lanier, the US Ambassador to Uganda, met the Kabaka at Banda Palace on 18 February 2010. See Musinguzi, Bamuturaki "East Africa: What future for Buganda?" *The East African*, 25 September 2011.
[575] See generally Pulford, *Causality of the Empire.*
[576] Ibid p. 101.
[577] Ibid p. 121.
[578] See Blomfield, Adrian, "African King Aims to Bankrupt Britain" in *The Daily Telegraph*, 13 March 2004.
[579] See story "Bunyoro in Fresh Push for Compensation Amid Claims UK paid £700m," *The East African*, Saturday 13 May 2013, http://www.theeastafrican.co.ke/news/Bunyoro-in-fresh-push-for-compensation/2558-1856358-cmx7t9/index.html accessed 15 March 2018
[580] Ibid.
[581] Ibid.
[582] Ibid.
[583] The victims, who survived severe beatings, rape, castration and other forms of torture, accused Britain of vicarious liability for their suffering. In a suit filed in 2009, survivors of this ignominious episode of colonial rule in Kenya, including Wambugu wa Nyingi, Jane Muthoni Mara and Paulo Muoka Nzili, narrated their gruesome experiences and the grisly murder of their friends and relatives at the orders of British colonial officials. According to the plaintiffs, colonial authorities arrested Jane Muthoni Mara in 1954 when she was 15 and detained her in the Gatithi screening camp. While there she was surrounded by four guards who

pinned her on the ground. One man pushed her thighs apart and held them down with "his spiky army boots." While she screamed, another kicked a glass of soda bottle filled with hot water up her vagina. She endured daily beatings for three months. Wambugu Wa Nyingi was clubbed on the head and left for dead amid a pile of corpses. Paulo Muoka Nzili was castrated in front of other detainees with large pliers used to castrate bulls. But these individuals were lucky to stay alive. It has been reported that over 150,000 Kikuyu were detained without trial, and that tens of thousands died in the camps known as "the pipeline," which were constructed by British colonial officials as part of what was code-named Operation Progress. Britain's legal defence was multi-pronged. Its lawyers argued that the claim should be struck out because the claimants, under the law of state succession, should have sued the Kenyan Government, and not Britain. Under this principle, all legal liabilities for the actions of the British colonial authorities had been inherited by the post-independence Government of Kenya. When this argument failed, the lawyers argued that the claim was time barred, as it should have been brought many years earlier. See *Nditi Mutua and Four Others v. The Foreign and Commonwealth Office*, op. cit.

[584] The UK Foreign Secretary, Willian Hague, made a statement to Parliament on the settlement of claims of Kenyan citizens relating to events during the period 1952- 1963. See statement at https://www.gov.uk/government/news/statement-to-parliament-on-settlement-of-mau-mau-claims .

[585] Ibid.

[586] See story "May urged to apologise to Commonwealth for UK's 'historic wrongs'," *The Guardian*, 13 April 2018.

[587] See story by AFP, "British prime minister apologises to Caribbean leaders over deportation row," *The Guardian*, 17 April 2018.

[588] Declaration on the Granting of Independence to Colonial Countries and Peoples adopted by General Assembly Resolution 1514 (XV) of 14 December 1960.

[589] Declaration on the Granting of Independence to Colonial Countries and Peoples, UNGA Resolution 1514 (XV); Resolution defining the three options for Self-determination, UNGA Resolution 1514 (XV) and Resolution establishing the Special Committee on Decolonisation, UNGA Resolution 1654 (XVI).

[590] Article 16 of General Assembly resolution on the Charter or Economic Rights and Duties of States [A/RES/29/3281] 12 December 1974.

[591] Basic Principles and Guidelines on the Right to a Remedy and Reparation for Victims of Gross Violations of International Human Rights Law and Serious Violations of International Humanitarian Law. Adopted and proclaimed by General Assembly Resolution 60/147 on 16 December 2005.

[592] Provisions on a right to a remedy for victims of violations of international human rights law include article 8 of the Universal Declaration of Human Rights, article 2 of the International Covenant on Civil and Political Rights, article 6 of the International Convention on the Elimination of All Forms of Racial Discrimination, article 14 of the Convention against Torture and Other Cruel, Inhuman or Degrading Treatment or Punishment, and article 39 of the Convention on the Rights of the Child, and of international humanitarian law as found in article

3 of the Hague Convention respecting the Laws and Customs of War on Land of 18 October 1907 (Convention IV), article 91 of the Protocol Additional to the Geneva Conventions of 12 August 1949, and relating to the Protection of Victims of International Armed Conflicts (Protocol I) of 8 June 1977, and articles 68 and 75 of the Rome Statute of the International Criminal Court.

[593]See UN Basic Principles and Guidelines on the Right to a Remedy.

[594] For example Australia, Belgium, Dominican Republic, France, Portugal, Spain, Union of South Africa, United Kingdom and United States abstained from the vote on Resolution No. 1514 (XV).

[595] See Statement to the House of Commons https://www.gov.uk/government/news/statement-to-parliament-on-settlement-of-mau-mau-claims.

[596] UN Basic Principles and Guidelines on the Right to a Remedy and Reparation, Article 7.

[597] Mamdani, Mahmood (2011) *Okugenda Mu Maaso: The Link Between Tradition, Reform and Development*, MISR Working Paper No. 5 November 2011, p.8.

CONCLUSION

THE LEGACY OF BRITISH RULE ON UGANDA'S INTEGRATION AND THE FUTURE

This account, stretching from when Lugard first established the IBEAC in Uganda to the present times, illustrates how the British Empire descended upon, occupied and exited (B)Uganda in 1962 with a grant of nominal independence. It also shows how, thereafter, Britain related with the country both directly and through the Commonwealth. It calls for a deeper investigation and accountability for past wrongs within the realms of morality and public international law. The narrative leads to several conclusions. Principal among these is that Uganda's contemporary politics and development is significantly defined, if not impeded, by a problematic colonial past and that its future is critically influenced by a neocolonial order where Britain plays a dominant role. Nowhere is this more manifest than in Uganda's political instability and the unending struggle for self-determination by the kingdom of Buganda—and conversely, with the resistance and apprehension with which the rest of Uganda responds to its ambitions.

In this context, the legacy of British rule is most evident in the challenges Uganda faces in developing a stable democratic and constitutional framework as well as national ethos. This legacy underpins the challenges of national integration that remain long after the end of colonial rule. As predicated by colonial administrators such as Andrew Cohen, Fredrick Crawford and Walter Coutts, the difficulties of political and ethnic integration are as alive today as they were at the time the Munster Relationships Commission grappled with the issue a few years before independence. Then, just as now, the struggle is about how to fit Buganda's traditional and monarchical power structure into a democratic and unitary postcolonial Uganda.[1]

In this connection, studies of colonial and postcolonial history of Uganda throw up a common cyclical question on the constitutional position and power of both the kingdom of Buganda and its Kabaka within Uganda. This account has demonstrated that this problem, sometimes referred to as "the Buganda Question" or "the Buganda Factor,"[2] is innately a legacy of British colonial rule.

In addressing this question, some of the crucial—and recurrent - concerns are: Is Buganda kingdom a cultural or political entity? Is it a hybrid institution that fuses politics and culture? Should the Kabaka wield political power or should his role be limited to the defence and diffusion of Buganda's culture? Can a strong monarchy exist and survive in a largely republican country? Would a federal system of government mean that Buganda becomes a state within a state in Uganda? Would federalism work in the context of a country with uneven development and resources? Can Uganda survive as a nation without Buganda and *vice-versa*?

All these questions relate not just to Buganda but to the wider challenge of the political and ethnic integration of Uganda which, due to a colonial legacy, has a population that connects more with its sub-national or ethnic base than it does to the nation state. Thus, in a granulated sense, this problem is more of a Ugandan question than a Buganda one. In this regard, it has been correctly argued that "Uganda's larger politics today is a bundle of questions; the Buganda question, the northern question, the Karamojong question and the Asian question and that none of these should be seen as a special question, isolated from the rest."[3]

Nowhere in Uganda has the sense of ethnic identity and nationalism been as alive as in the kingdom of Buganda, whose history predates that of Uganda by many centuries and whose traditional and cultural structures are inherently political. But a sense of sub-nationalism and separatism exists in other parts of the country as well, particularly in northern Uganda.[4] The people of Rwenzururu in the western district of Kasese have also pursued a long struggle in defence of their ethnic identity.[5]

The colonial policy of divide and rule which the British pursued in Uganda ensured that different tribes were administered separately from the rest, with the intention that there would be no common or joint interests from which to resist imperial aggression.

This policy promoted tribal balkanisation and segregation, which led to a strong sense of tribal patriotism in the country.[6] But tribal identity was also a basis for discrimination,[7] and every institution of the state developed an ethnic and regional flavour. So while the army and the police was drawn from the north, the bureaucracy and professional majority was predominantly southern. The merchant class was mainly Asian."[8] These discriminative colonial policies thus divided more than united the country.

In this context, and given the historical relations between Buganda and Britain *vis-a-vis* those of Britain and the rest of Uganda, it was felt by the non-Baganda population that Buganda was given undue privilege and a special status during colonial rule. On this point Governor Andrew Cohen foresaw that the basic political problem in Uganda's future would be "the relationship of the country as a whole with its parts, Buganda and the rest."[9] He attributed this to the "disparity in size and importance between Buganda and the other parts of the country"[10] and to the view that "virtually all the other tribes fear Buganda['s] domination in the future and are determined to resist it."[11]

To incorporate Buganda into Uganda and thus achieve 'national unity,' Governor Cohen pursued a policy aimed at cutting Buganda down to size, starting with the deposition and exile of its Kabaka in 1953. However, although this got Buganda into signing the 1955 Agreement, it did not deter its separatist ambitions or diminish the Kabaka's authority. In fact, it had the reverse effect. On his part, Governor Coutts, on the eve of independence argued that "the growth of a sense of oneness is, without question, Uganda's most pressing need, exceeding even the urgent economic difficulties that face every emergent African State."[12]

The account given in this book shows that from the beginning of the British Protectorate in 1894, Buganda struggled to retain its political and traditional structures and, with Britain's encouragement, held itself out as an autonomous entity. It believed that it would emerge from the colonial era as an independent nation, not unlike Lesotho or Swaziland. Its attempts to lead a separate existence from the rest of Uganda were, however, thwarted because they were contrary to the colonial policy that aimed to maintain the Protectorate of Uganda as a viable and united country. The contradictions and tensions between Buganda and Britain on this policy objective created a major quandary in the lead-up to independence, and therein lies the foundation of the Buganda Question.

As Uganda started its journey of independence, Governor Coutts opined that Buganda, through its isolationist policies, had missed its chance of dominating and perhaps swallowing the rest of the country, and that as the rest of Uganda gained a greater feeling of unity, it would instead swallow Buganda.[13] This analysis, however interesting, has not been validated: as things stand, 56 years after independence, neither Buganda has swallowed the rest of Uganda nor, as Kasfir demonstrates,[14] has the rest of Uganda managed to swallow it.

In the constitutional talks that preceded independence, Britain needed to strike a delicate balance and choose between leaving behind a viable united country and a weak Buganda, or a strong and viable Buganda in an unviable, weak and disjointed Uganda. Buganda was opposed to both scenarios and needed a separate existence. Unsurprisingly, the rest of Uganda was equally opposed to having a dominant and controlling

Buganda in Uganda. These positions were irreconcilable, yet there was not sufficient time to negotiate an agreeable and workable formula before independence. Indeed, even to the colonial administrators in Uganda at the time independence was granted, the future of Uganda was bound to be problematic and none was willing to guess how

> this fragile collection of wildly disparate tribes would fare. Under the surface of the Pax Britannica, violent tribal and political rivalries and antipathies were gathering strength. In the south and west, the four tribal monarchs with their exotic titles were dreaming of establishing for mini-states semi-independent from the new Uganda[15]

As a result, and bearing in mind its broader interests, Britain opted to have a viable and united Uganda with a weak and unviable Buganda, rather than a strong Buganda in a weak Uganda. To ensure that it carried Buganda along into the new Uganda, it devised an asymmetrical constitutional framework where Buganda would be granted special status compared to the rest of Uganda. At the time when the Independence Constitution was made, Buganda accepted the arrangements made at Marlborough House, in spite of its overall concerns and fears over the lost counties issue. Buganda's negotiated settlement attracted resentment from other parts of the country, all of which predicted difficult relations and problems of national integration in the future.

For this reason, non-Baganda political commentators like Yoga Adhola have attributed Buganda's past and present demands for autonomy to "ganda chauvinism."[16] Adhola considers that there was a "feeling among Buganda chauvinists that they were destined to rule the rest of Ugandan's [sic] after independence.... [V]iewing the rest of the country as no more than an appendage to Buganda, the neo-traditionalists assumed power was to be passed on to them at independence."[17] Like Yoga Adhola, President Museveni has weighed in on the Buganda Question and has similarly accused the kingdom of Buganda of promoting chauvinism, feudalism and meddling in politics.[18]

Such views underscore the crisis of Uganda's integration. The mind-sets of either Buganda swallowing the rest or the rest swallowing Buganda persist. These views derive from a colonial history of divide and rule as well as from a colonial *idée fixe* of a united country called Uganda. Yet the unity of Uganda could never have been guaranteed *a priori*. The integration of post-independence Uganda was a job that Uganda's postcolonial leaders needed to do, but have not done. Just like it is wrong to accuse Buganda of promoting chauvinism or feudalism, it is false to claim that Buganda's declaration of independence in December 1960 was aimed at enabling Buganda to "rule the rest" of the Ugandans either before or after independence.

As this account demonstrates, Buganda had no issues with other parts of Uganda doing whatever they wanted once the British had left. In any case by the end of 1961, Buganda had abandoned its separatist aspirations and agreed to become an integral part of Uganda, provided the rest of Uganda agreed to its having a federal government within Uganda. The fact that it insisted and obtained this form of government in its negotiations with Britain and the rest of Uganda should not be used against it. The world has many examples of countries, such as the United Kingdom, with asymmetrical constitutional systems. These systems are reflective of the power relations pertaining to a polity at a particular time.

Do Buganda's aspirations for autonomy represent an opportunistic bid for special status, derived from historic colonial favouritism? This account shows that this is not the case and, far from favouring it, Britain actually undermined Buganda's right to self-determination after using it as a foothold to advance its agenda over the rest of Uganda. In this process its political and military power were greatly emasculated by Britain.

If Britain had really favoured Buganda, it would have granted it independence along the lines it did with Swaziland or Lesotho in southern Africa. Far from British favouritism, the reality is that the historical, cultural and ethnic diversities of the different parts of Uganda, combined with a colonial divide-and-rule policy, ensured that there was an ominous gap between Buganda and the rest of the country. Britain had to deal with Buganda and tried to bring it to the same level as the rest of the Protectorate—at least politically. This new policy objective meant undermining the Kabakaship and other traditional institutions such as the Lukiiko. The colonial plan, with Cohen as its champion, was to replace all indigenous traditional institutions with colonial ones such as the LEGCO and to quickly unite all the diverse tribes in order to leave behind a unitary state. This can hardly be seen as favouritism to Buganda.

Cohen's belated attempt to develop the country as a unitary state failed. The efforts were half-hearted and did not result in the rapid integration of Africans into the central colonial administration. Thus the gap was never seriously addressed before independence. Instead, Uganda was left with an unworkable hodgepodge of constitutional arrangements hastily drawn up at the Lancaster and Marlborough Conferences.

As a result in 1962, when the country attained independence, a sense of Ugandan nationalism was non-existent. Tribal patriotism was predominant in Buganda and elsewhere. It is, therefore, unsurprising that the gaps, as well as the mutual suspicions based on these factors, gave rise to political discord between Buganda and the rest of the country. This explains why Buganda is often accused of harbouring a parochial, feudalistic and chauvinistic outlook by politicians outside Buganda. It is also why, in order to understand the nature and history of Uganda's integration, and thereby find a solution to the problems it has thrown up, the focus should shift from accusations of chauvinism and colonial favouritism to other political and constitutional realities.

Various leaders in postcolonial Uganda have grappled with the Buganda Factor. Unfortunately, some, to gain popularity, have perpetuated the divisive politics of "the rest of Uganda vs Buganda" where, starting in the days of the LEGCO, the other tribes tended "to gang up on the Baganda,"[19] in the words of Governor F. Crawford. On this point, Mamdani has stated that "whenever post-independence governments in Uganda have faltered in building majority support around implementing a positive programme … the tendency has been to demonise a minority and a national threat against which to scare the majority into silent submission."[20]

The politics of using Buganda's separatism to discredit Buganda kingdom and the Kabaka in order to gain the support of the rest of the country has been used by Britain, Obote and others in an attempt to shore up a sense of national identity and unity in a historically and tribally divided country. Obote abolished the kingdoms of Uganda in 1967. In justifying this action, he told the National Assembly that "the ancient petty kingdoms had to be abolished as a prerequisite to building up an undivided loyalty to Uganda throughout the nation."[21] This also did not work. For eight years, beyond the return of Mutesa's body for reburial in Uganda, Amin at best ignored and at worst trampled on Buganda's interests.

But over the years, there has been plenty of evidence showing that the suppression of Buganda nationalism has, in fact, not yielded to or advanced Ugandan nationalism. To tackle the issue, other political leaders like Museveni have sought to accommodate the Kabakaship as a cultural rather than a political entity,[22] but this, too, has fallen short of the aspirations of the Baganda, who continue to agitate for self-determination. And, even though he has sponsored national programmes to promote national patriotism, these are yet to achieve tangible results. Yet, without much effort, Buganda's identity and the popularity of its Kabaka and traditional institutions have grown.

Is Buganda a political or an apolitical kingdom? We have demonstrated that historically, the kingdom of Buganda was always a political entity steeped in tradition and culture. However, following Obote's abolition of the kingdoms in 1967, Buganda's political existence was ostensibly terminated. The (il)legality of this action has already been discussed. And when traditional institutions were restored in Uganda in 1993, it was on the condition that they were to remain cultural and not political. Museveni, in relation to the Buganda Question, states that "the real issue is whether we should have political kings—kings wielding political power." In his view, weak kingdoms and weak traditional leaders were responsible for the colonisation of Africa,[23] and today they should have only a cultural role dealing with languages and customs "compatible with the modern way of life."[24]

But can it be argued that Buganda has shed its political past and embraced a purely cultural status? While this matter has not been a subject of exhaustive debate within or outside Buganda, the assertion that Buganda should be apolitical cannot be justified. Why? As many scholars, including Oloka-Onyango, have rightly pointed out "the insistence on a purely cultural entity when the institution is totally immersed in the politics of kingdom and country, is simply blinding ourselves to reality."[25] Oloka-Onyango rightly observes that because Buganda will remain of paramount importance in the politics of Uganda for many years to come, there needs to be a "frank, democratic and non-conflictual discussion of the parameters of a fully recognized political Kabaka."[26]

Similarly, Gooloba-Mutebi argues that the Baganda were "never going to stop simply at asking for the monarchy to be restored as a cultural institution…. Buganda had a well-developed sense of nationhood by the time colonial rule was introduced, and this pride was never fully undermined by it."[27]

Mutibwa argues that for the Baganda, a non-political Kabaka was the same as *ebyoya bye nswa* [useless remains of white ants' wings] because "the position of the Kabaka as a political ruler rather than a purely cultural ruler"[28] was what Buganda demanded.

In demonstrating the difficulty of separating the Kabakaship from politics, Nsibambi states that although cultural leaders are forbidden from participating in partisan politics, because the Kabaka is so influential in Buganda, the Government tends to involve him in seeking solutions to constitutional and political disputes when they emerge.[29]

On Buganda's political identity within Uganda, Sjogren Anders points out that "it is an axiom of Ugandan politics that the relations between the central government and Buganda constitute a defining parameter, and something that other regions constantly need to relate to."[30] On this point, Catherine Johannessen argues that:

> Since the restoration of traditional leaders in Uganda in 1993, the consent of the Buganda kingdom has served as an important support-base for politicians running for office both in the 1996 and 2001 presidential

> elections. In this sense, the Buganda kingdom has managed to influence national politics despite its cultural character, and has re-entered the political arena as a significant pressure group more than thirty years after its abolition.[31]

The above views point to the reality that Buganda is central to Uganda's politics just like Uganda's politics is crucial to Buganda's existence. There is no doubt that the future of Uganda and Buganda are uniquely, even inextricably, interlinked. Further, that Buganda's demands for a federal system of government are not demands for cultural freedoms[32] but demands that need political solutions. This explains why Buganda kingdom may not be easily relegated to an exclusively cultural domain.

The failure to find a solution to the Buganda Question has meant that even after fifty-six years of Uganda's independence, the problem of integration is still with us. What needs to be done? We believe that the solution to problem lies in a national dialogue on the Buganda, or indeed the Uganda Question of national integration. From the historical evidence presented herein, the country can draw lessons to help address this question.

The lack of constructive engagement on constitutional matters—such as a system of governance suitable for the whole country—is also attributable to a tendency, whose roots lie in Uganda's colonial and precolonial past, to concentrate political and economic power at the centre. This is in spite of the government's rhetoric on its commitment to decentralized governance.

The fixation on a united Uganda—based on an entirely colonial construct—has for the most part also blinded the political class from recognizing the artificiality and fragility of the country, and hence the need to engage in a dialogue that recognizes and respects the diversity of its peoples and history. The future of Uganda's economic and political stability hinges on a workable and acceptable alliance between its constituent parts. National unity, as envisaged under the colonial rule and by later political actors, has not been realised in the past and will not be attainable in the future unless a consensus is reached by Ugandans on an acceptable constitutional and governance framework.

As Buganda and Uganda look to the future and as they search for solutions for enduring peace, progress and prosperity, they need to address not only the challenges of constitutional relationships, integration, and governance within the country but, equally, the complex colonial legacy and continuing influence that Britain holds over Uganda's economy and politics.

Notes

[1] Golooba-Mutebi Frederick (2011) "Settling the Buganda Question: A Peek into the Future," in *Transition* No. 106, Indiana University Press, p.23.

[2] Phares Mutibwa, in (2008) *The Buganda Factor in Uganda Politics*, Fountain Publishers: Kampala, Uganda, discusses how Buganda remains a major factor in the constitutional, political and economic development of Uganda.

[3]Mamdani Mahmood, "50th Anniversary of Uganda's State Independence: A View from Society," *The New Vision*, 23 July 2013, p.10.

[4] Apolo Robin Nsibambi, *National Integration in Uganda*, pp. 205-230.

[5] Syahuka-Muhindo and Kristof Titeca, "The Rwenzururu Movement and the Struggle for the Rwenzururu Kingdom in Uganda," Discussion Paper, 2016.01 ISSN 2294-8651.

[6] Andrew Cohen, *Uganda: Political Development and the Problems of the Future*, p. 1.

[7] Mamdani, Mahmood, "Buganda and Uganda at Crossroads," *The New Vision*, 7 August 2009.

[8] Mamdani, Mahmood, "50th Anniversary of Uganda's State Independence: A View from Society," *The New Vision*, 23 July 2013.

[9] See Cohen, *Uganda*, p. 5.

[10] Ibid.

[11] Ibid.

[12] Walter Coutts to Sandys on "Uganda: Future as an Independent Country," 8 October 1962 on CO 822/2266. No. 378 TNA.

[13] Ibid.

[14] Kasfir, Nelson (2017) *Kingdom, State and Civil Society in Africa: Conceptual and Political Collisions*, Basler, and *The Buganda Kingdom Government in Uganda Politics 1986-2014: Culture, contingencies and constraints on organizational success,* unpublished paper.

[15] See Purcell, R. M., "A turning point" in Brown & Brown (eds), *Looking Back at the Uganda Protectorate*, p.264

[16] See unpublished paper with the author by Adhola, Yoga, "The Buganda Question and the Forging of a Nation State in Uganda," October 2007.

[17] Ibid.

[18] See President Yoweri Museveni's statement to the Members of Parliament on the city riots at Parliament, on 15 September 2009.

[19] See Crawford F., *Uganda: Problems of Tribalism and Nationalism*, EAF 185/96/01, dated 6 September 1957, Op. cit.

[20] See Mamdani, *Buganda and Uganda at Crossroads* a paper delivered at the Abu Mayanja Annual Lecture on 7 August 2009 at the Kampala International Conference Centre.

[21] On 22 June 1967 when he presented proposals for a draft new constitution.

[22] See Yoweri Museveni's statement to the Members of Parliament on the city riots at Parliament, on 15 September 2009.

---

[23] Ibid. In seeking to delimit the power and involvement of the kingdom of Buganda in national politics, he argues that "the colonization of Africa was a vote of no confidence in tribalism and the precolonial kings ... modern Africa must transcend and discard tribal organization." The view that Africa was colonized because its kings failed to defend its sovereignty is debatable. History shows that Africa, and other parts of the world, including America, Canada and India, were colonized regardless of whether kings existed in a particular place or not. There is no doubt that given the technological, organizational, military and financial disparities between the West and Africa at the time, the ability of Africa to successfully resist colonialism was negligible. Thus, precolonial African kings cannot be blamed for the success of the colonial aggression. As a matter of fact, a postcolonial and politically independent Africa remains caught up in a binding neocolonial order that it consistently fails to shake off. This has little or nothing to do with African traditional kings.

[24] Ibid.

[25] Oloka-Onyango, J. (1997) "The Question of Buganda in Contemporary Ugandan Politics," *Journal of Contemporary African Studies*, 15(2).

[26] Ibid.

[27] Golooba-Mutebi, *Settling the Buganda Question*, p.22.

[28] Mutibwa, *The Buganda Factor in Uganda Politics*, p. 235.

[29] Nsibambi, *National Integration in Uganda*, p.329.

[30] Anders Sjogren (2015) "Battles over boundaries: The politics of territory, identity and authority in three Uganda Regions," *Journal of Contemporary African Studies*, 33, (2), p. 280.

[31] See Johannessen, Catherine (2006) *Kingship in Uganda: The Role of the Buganda Kingdom in Ugandan Politics*, CMI (CHR. Michelsen Institute) Working Paper, p. 1.

[32] See generally, Abunuwasi, Mwami and Godfrey Muriuki (2012) *The Federo Question of Buganda in Uganda Within the Context of the East African Political Federation*, Fountain Publishers: Kampala.

APPENDIX I

UGANDA'S COLONIAL AND POSTCOLONIAL LEADERS

Military Administrator

Sir Frederick John Daltry Lugard	1890-1892

Colonial Commissioners:

Sir Gerald Portal	1893
Colonel H. E. Colville	1893
E. J. Berkley	1895
Sir Harry Johnston	1899
Colonel Sir J. Hayes Sadler	1902

Governors:

Sir Hesketh Bell	1905
Sir Frederick Jackson	1911
Sir Robert Thorne Cryndon	1917
Sir William Gowers	1925
Sir Bernard Bourdillon	1932
Sir Phillip Mitchell	1935
Sir Charles Dundas	1940
Sir John Hathorn Hall	1945
Sir Andrew Cohen	1952
Sir Fredrick Crawford	1957
Sir Walter Coutts	1961

Governor General:

Sir Walter Coutts	1962

Presidents:

Sir Edward Mutesa	1963-1966
Dr Milton Obote	1966-1971
Gen. Idi Amin	1971-1979
Prof. Yusuf K. Lule	1979
Godfrey L. Binaisa, Q.C.	1979-1980[1]
Dr Milton Obote	1980-1985
Gen. Tito Okello	1985-1986
Gen. Yoweri K. Museveni	1986 to date.

Buganda's Kabakas in the 19th and 20th Centuries:

Daniel B. Mwanga II	1890-1897
Sir Daudi Chwa II	1897-1939
Sir Edward F. L. Mutesa II	1939-1969
Ronald M. Mutebi II	1969-1993 (as Ssabataka while kingdom was abolished and from 1993 to date as Kabaka)

Buganda's Katikkiros in Colonial and Postcolonial Times:

Sir Apolo Gulemye Kalibbala Kagwa	1897-1926
Tefiro Ssekuuma Kisosonkole	1927-1929
Martin Luther Nsibirwa	1929-1941, 1945 [Jul–Sept]
Samuel Wamala	1942-1945
Michael E. Kawalya Kagwa	1945-1950
Paulo N. Kavuma	1951-1955
Micheal Kintu	1955-1964
Joash Mayanja Nkangi	1964-1993
Joseph Mmulwanyamuli Semwogerere	1994-2006
Daniel Muliika	2006
Emmanuel Sendawula (in acting capacity)	2007
John Baptist Walusimbi	2008-2013
Charles Peter Mayiga	2013 to date

Note

[1] The Military Commission was the 'leader' in second half of 1980 until December

Appendix II

Extract from *The Rise of Our East African Empire: Early Efforts in Nyasaland and Uganda* by Captain Frederick John Dealtry Lugard

"It is sufficient to reiterate here that, as long as our policy is one of free trade, we are compelled to seek new markets; for old ones are being closed to us by hostile tariffs, and our great dependencies, which formerly were the consumers of our goods, are now becoming our commercial rivals. It is inherent in a great colonial and commercial empire like ours that we go forward or go backward. To allow other nations to develop new fields, and to refuse to do so ourselves, is to go backward; and this is the more deplorable, seeing that we have proved ourselves notably capable of dealing with native races and of developing new countries at a less expense than other nations. We owe to the instincts of colonial expansion of our ancestors those vast and noble dependencies which are our pride and the outlets of our trade today; and we are accountable to posterity that opportunities which now present themselves of extending the sphere of our industrial enterprise are not neglected, for the opportunities now offered will never recur again. Lord Rosebery in his speech at the Royal Colonial Institute expressed this in emphatic language: 'We are engaged in 'pegging out claims' for the future. We have to consider, not what we want now, but what we shall want in the future. We have to consider what countries must be developed either by ourselves or some other nation …. Remember that the task of the statesman is not merely with the present, but with the future. We have to look forward beyond the chatter of platforms, and the passions of party, to the future of the race of which we are at present the trustees, and we should, in my opinion, grossly fail in the task that has been laid upon us did we shrink from responsibilities, and decline to take our share in a partition of the world which we have not forced on [ourselves], but which has been forced upon us."[1]

Note

[1] F. D. Lugard, (1893) *The Rise of Our East African Empire: Early Efforts in Nyasaland and Uganda*, W. Blackwood and Sons Edinburgh, I.585-587, II.69-75.

APPENDIX III

MEMORANDUM BY THE SECRETARY OF STATE FOR THE COLONIES

TOP SECRET—Copy No 38 C. (53) 324 18 November, 1953, CABINET, UGANDA PROTECTORATE: THE PROVINCE OF BUGANDA.

Memorandum by the Secretary of State for the Colonies

1. Buganda is one of the four Provinces of the Protectorate of Uganda and economically as well as geographically it is the keystone of the whole country. Its African inhabitants—the Baganda—numbering about one million, are the richest and most advanced tribe in the Protectorate and have long been intensely nationalist. Their hereditary Ruler is called the Kabaka. He is assisted in his local Government of the Province by a Council (the Lukiiko) and three Ministers—the Prime Minister, Treasurer and Chief Justice.

2. The relations of Her Majesty's Government with the Kabaka are governed by an Agreement made in 1900. The relevant articles of this Agreement are:
   a) Article 3, which provides that Buganda "shall rank as Province of equal rank with any other Province into which the Protectorate shall be divided".
   b) Article 6 which reads in part as follows: "So long as the Kabaka … shall cooperate loyally with Her Majesty's Government in the organization and administration of the said Kingdom of Uganda, Her Majesty's Government agrees to recognize the Kabaka of Uganda "as Ruler of the Province."
   c) Article 20 which reads in part "Should the Kabaka, Chief or people of Uganda pursue at any time a policy which is distinctly disloyal to the British Protectorate, Her Majesty's Government will no longer consider themselves bound by the terms of this Agreement".

3. Recently the Kabaka addressed a letter to me in which he made three requests:-
   i. An assurance that there would never be Federation of East African territories.
   ii. Transfer of Buganda affairs to the Foreign Office (they were handed over to the Colonial Office in 1902 after the pacification of the county).
   iii. "Independence" for Buganda.

   On my authority he was given a reply by the Governor at an interview to the following effect:
   i. A detailed assurance that no plan of [an] East African federation is at present contemplated and that for the distant future all organs of local opinion will be fully taken into account.
   ii. A transfer of Buganda affairs to the Foreign Office would be constitutionally inappropriate.
   iii. The request for independence was refused on the grounds that it would be neither in the interests of the Buganda themselves nor of the inhabitants of the rest of the Protectorate. The accepted policy of Her Majesty's Government is to promote the self-Government of Uganda as a unitary state. (This policy was endorsed by the Kabaka himself as recently as March this year when, in connection with certain reforms which confer considerable local autonomy on the Provincial Government in such spheres as education, health and agriculture, he publicly affirmed Article 3 of the Agreement on the future of Buganda as a component part of the Protectorate.)

4. The Kabaka has expressed himself satisfied with (i), agreed to drop (ii) for the time being but refused to accept the reply on (iii). Similar requests have been put forward by the Lukiiko and made public. They have been and are still the subject of considerable Press comment in the territory and public discussion in which the issue of independence for Buganda is much confused with that of self-Government for Uganda. The Kabaka has expressed his intention, if the above reply is given to the Lukiiko on point (iii), of opposing this decision of Her Majesty's Government publicly in the Lukiiko. Despite the best effort of the Governor and his advisers at long interviews he has remained obdurate in this determination.

5. In the Governor's view, if the Kabaka were permitted to voice this public opposition to Her Majesty's Government's policy it would almost certainly precipitate riots and bloodshed which might require

sizeable forces to subdue. In 1945 and in 1949 riots broke out among the Baganda more suddenly than anyone expected or anticipated. These were organized against the Kabaka's authority. If he himself were to instigate the trouble the results might be much more serious.

6. The Attorney General has advised that the declared intention of the Kabaka amounts to a clear breach of the 1900 Agreement.

   The Governor has recommended the following course of action. He would summon the Kabaka and inform him of my re-affirmation of my reply on point (iii). He would ask him whether he is prepared to accept it and loyally abide but it; if the Kabaka says no he would inform him that this refusal must be referred back to me. Not more than four days later he would summon the Kabaka again and hand him a note with my authority withdrawing recognition from him. Immediately afterwards the Kabaka would be served with a notice of deportation from Uganda and escorted to an aeroplane, previous arrangements having been made for his journey to the United Kingdom. Thereafter, the Lukiiko, when the time was judged ripe, would be invited in accordance with custom to elect a successor. The Governor would expect that, when this *coup d'état* became known, trouble would break out among the Baganda which might need limited military action in support of the Police but nothing like the scale on which it might be needed if the Kabaka were permitted to embark on an open trial of strength with Her Majesty's Government.

7. General Erskine has agreed to make available one battalion of the King's African Rifles which is now moving into Uganda ostensibly as a routine transfer. He has also agreed to have a reserve battalion standing by at three days' notice but if this or any further reinforcements were called upon he might have to ask additional assistance from the United Kingdom.

8. There are three reasons why firm and prompt action is desirable:
   i. The Kabaka is already suborning the other three minor Rulers whose districts comprise the Western Province to follow his example of non-cooperation with the Protectorate Government. If the Kabaka is handled firmly it is expected they will promptly back down.
   ii. Elections to new Lukiiko take place at the end of this month. On the recommendation of the new Lukiiko, the Kabaka will choose

new Ministers. The present ones are believed not to be in favour of his defiance of Her Majesty's Government in this matter and its hoped to retain their loyalty even in the face of his deportation.

iii. The longer confused public discussion of the issue is allowed to continue the greater the local tension which may develop.

9. I do not consider, however, that this extreme action should be taken without a personal attempt by myself to bring the Kabaka to his senses. I therefore propose to summon the Kabaka to London early next week for discussion "on grave matters affecting his treaty relationship with Her Majesty's Government". At the interview I shall require the Kabaka, in accordance with his treaty obligations, to give certain assurances regarding his acceptance of my decision and of his future cooperation with the Protectorate Government. If after a suitable interval for reflection he refuses to comply, he will be notified of Her Majesty's Government's withdrawal of recognition under the Treaty, informed that he will not be permitted to reside in Uganda and assured of an appropriate financial settlement to enable him to live elsewhere.

10. If the Kabaka refuses to come to this country to see me, then I propose to authorize the Governor to put into operation the plan described in paragraph 6 above.

11. A timetable of the pertinent dates and a map of Uganda are attached.

12. I invite my colleagues:
    a. To endorse the action which I propose;
    b. To note the possibility of the need for further reinforcements from Kenya as this might lead to a request for their replacement.

Colonial Office, S.W.1.
17 November, 1953.

APPENDIX IV

A MEMORANDUM TO HER MAJESTY QUEEN ELIZABETH II

Submitted by Members of the Lukiiko of the Kingdom of Buganda Concerning the Termination of British Protection.[1]

Here below is the resolution passed by the Lukiiko which has called into being this Memorandum:

> The Buganda Lukiiko, sitting from the 21 to the 24 September, 1960, has heard the report of the Katikkiro in respect of the talks held in London between His Highness the Kabaka, the Lukiiko Constitutional Committee and the Secretary of State concerning the Buganda Constitutional matters.
>
> In that report the Lukiiko was told that the talks ended in deadlock. In view of this deadlock the Lukiiko has resolved that Buganda is determined to be a separate autonomous State and, consequent upon that, Buganda will not be represented in the future Legislative Council.
>
> As Buganda has always stated that while dealing with her constitutional matters it is not her desire to stand in the way of the development of the other parts of Uganda and would like [it] in this connection to be clearly understood that other parts of Uganda are absolutely free to seek the attainment of their autonomy through whatever means they think fit.
>
> The Lukiiko's Memorandum which explains in detail the constitutional plan for an independent Buganda is being prepared and will shortly be forwarded to Her Majesty the Queen of the United Kingdom.'

We intend to divide this Memorandum into three main parts:

(a) Geographical and Historical background of Buganda;
(b) Buganda's reasons for going it alone; and
(c) the Constitutional Plan.

The boundaries of Buganda are defined in Article 1 of the Agreement of 1900. Within those boundaries, Buganda has an area of 25,390 square miles, which is well over a quarter of the size of Uganda, whose neighbours are: the Republic of Sudan in the North, Kenya Colony in the East, the Republic of the Congo in the West, and Tanganyika in the South. Buganda has a population of approximately two million, which [is] about a third of Uganda's six-and-a-quarter million peoples. Buganda is the wealthiest of the four Provinces into which Uganda is divided, with cotton and coffee as the main cash crops. Buganda contributes nearly sixty percent to the total revenue of the Uganda Protectorate, which total amounted to more than £26 million in 1957/58. Of this contribution from Buganda, which on that figure amounted to nearly £16 million, Buganda received back only £1⅓ million by way of grants from the Central Government.

Buganda is an ancient Kingdom with a long history and her dynasty exceeds thirty-seven Kings in an unbroken line. The history of Buganda begins with a King, and continues throughout the centuries with Kingship, right up to the present day. There is not a single period in our history when the Baganda had no King ruling over them. The Baganda have a system of clans and by means of royal marriages among women of various clans, and since by customs members of the royal family belong to the clan on their mother's side, a situation has arisen in passage of time, whereby most clans have had a ruling Monarch or an outstanding prince as a member of their clan. This custom has had [a] profound effect on the Kiganda society. Buganda Kings are unique in that they play two big roles in the tenure of their office as Monarchs, namely that they are rulers as well as being superheads of all heads of Clans in the Kingdom. As a result, the King of Buganda, bears a personal relationship to every single Kiganda family in the Kingdom. In other words it is inconceivable for a Kiganda society to exist without a King.

As far back as imagination can stretch the Baganda have had a system of an organized form of government consisting of The King, a Parliament and Prime Minister. They also had an army and a navy. When the British first came to the country they found this system of government in operation, whose fundamental concepts they have preserved, enriching it as far as possible with their own democratic principles.

There is a wealth of evidence to be found in the writings of the early travelers and discoverers of what was then known as the "Dark

Continent," and H. M. Stanley's remarks on Buganda are eloquent enough. Stanley was one of the great Explorers in Africa in the nineteenth century and he speaks of Mutesa I, who was ruling Buganda at the time as a "powerful Emperor, with great influence over his neighbours." He goes on to say: "I saw about 3,000 soldiers of Mutesa nearly civilized.... I saw about a hundred Chiefs who might be classed in the same scale as the men in Zanzibar and Omman, clad in rich robes and armed in the same fashion; and have witnessed with astonishment much order and law as is obtainable in semi-civilized countries."

Stanley thought Mutesa would "do more for central Africa than fifty years of gospel teaching, unaided by such authority, could do. I think I saw him in the light that shall lighten the darkness of this benighted region, a Prince well worthy of the most sympathies that Europe can give him."

It was Mutesa I who requested Stanley to write to the British people in Great Britain that he and his people were like blind men groping in the dark and that he was anxious to invite the British to come and give him the light. This request shall ever stand to all future generations as a sign of greatness of this far-sighted King Mutesa I. As a result of this request the British Missionaries arrived in Buganda in 1877 to be followed by the French Catholic Missionaries in 1879.

This was the period of the "Scramble for Africa," and, in Buganda, there appeared on the scene the British, the French, the Germans and the Arabs, each group scrambling for power over the country. The confusion into which the mind of King Mwanga was thrown by this scramble can [better] be imagined than stated. To make the long story short, the Baganda picked the British as their Protectors and a Treaty of Protection was signed between the Queen's Representative on behalf of the Queen and the King of Buganda, in 1894. In 1897 an incident happened. The British army in Uganda at the time consisted mainly of Nubians under a British Commander. The Nubians mutinied and the British were proposing to ask for troops from India when the Baganda, under the leadership of Sir Apolo, the then Prime Minister of Buganda, volunteered to fight the Nubians, whom he defeated in the battle of Bukaleba in Busoga, thus redeeming British prestige in Uganda.

Two significant articles stand out in the 1894 Treaty between the Queen and the King of Buganda. The first is Article 2, which reads:

> And whereas Her Britannic Majesty has been graciously pleased to bestow on the said Mwanga, King of Uganda, the Protection which he requested in that Agreement….

This article clearly shows that the Kingdom of Buganda was not conquered or ceded by the British, and that British Protection was requested and so graciously bestowed. The second important article in that Treaty is Article 14 which provides:

> The foreign relations of Uganda and its dependences are hereby placed unreservedly in the hands of Her Majesty's Representative.

This article indicates that Buganda was a real sovereign state before and at the time the British bestowed their protection.

The Agreement of 1900, which followed the 1894 Treaty, has no connection with, and bears no relationship to, the Treaty of 1894, and yet its conclusion was the first move by the British in an attempt to reduce the sovereignty of the Lukiiko, as may be gathered from the official documents between Her Majesty's Representative in Uganda and the Foreign Office in London.

In 1902 an Order-in-Council was passed in the United Kingdom which self-justified the British to rule over Uganda as "a Colony, and as if it was one of our possessions". The propriety of this Order-in-Council, which changed the status of Buganda without the knowledge or consent of the Baganda, will ever be regarded by them as the first classic example of the breach of good intentions on the part of the British. This Order-in-Council, unrelated to the 1894 Treaty, was one of the first major causes of Buganda's misfortunes, and from the time it was launched to the present day the British have been following a policy designed to whittle down Buganda's powers.

The annals of history should never brush aside the important part which the Baganda have played in both [the] administrative and social development of the Uganda Protectorate. Let it be remembered that it is upon the Kiganda system of government that all tribal governments in the Protectorate have been based; this system has been imported to the other tribes by the Baganda themselves, on request. The same is true in the sphere of education and evangelism.

Since the advent of [the] Pax Britannica, at the end of the last century, Buganda has stood in [a] special relationship as regards Her Majesty's Government and the rest of Uganda. This relationship is exemplified by the provisions of the Treaty of 1894 and the subsequent Constitutional Agreements 1900-1955. As an illustration, Article 14 of the 1894 Treaty, already referred to above, could only be enacted in relation to a people who had a well-organized government run on systematic principles as recognized by Sir Gerald Portal, "Her Britannic Majesty's Commissioner" in 1894.

By the Treaty of 1894, British protection was subsequently conferred upon the rest of Uganda.

A further illustration of this special relationship is provided by Article 5 of 1900 Agreement which reads:

> The Laws made for the general governance of Uganda Protectorate by Her Majesty's Government will be equally applicable to the Kingdom of Buganda, except in so far as they may in any particular way conflict with the terms of this Agreement, in which case the terms of this Agreement will constitute a special exception in regard to the Kingdom of Buganda.'

Buganda's Treaty and constitutional Agreements have been made between the Kabaka, Chiefs and people of Buganda on the one hand and Her Majesty the Queen on the other, [w]hereas in other parts of Uganda similar Agreements have been concluded as between the Protectorate Government on the one hand and any Native Government on the other. The Protectorate Government is subordinate to Her Majesty's Government.

The 1955 Agreement has once again stressed Buganda's position by the fact that part of this Agreement is embodied in an Order-in-Council and forms part of the Laws of Uganda. No such provision obtains in any other Agreements found in the rest of Uganda.

Our ancient institutions of the Kabakaship and the Lukiiko have adopted themselves to change in order to fit themselves into the modern world. Since the 1900 Agreement the tendency of the Lukiiko has been to democratize itself. Today, of the ninety-two members of the Lukiiko, sixty are elected by the people, through electoral colleges, a method which has so far proved itself as democratic as any other.

By the 1955 Agreement, the Kabaka is a constitutional monarch, who rules the country on the advice of his Ministers. The Lukiiko, the Parliament of Buganda, and the Kabaka's Government, consisting of six Ministers, operate on a Provincial basis, whereas in the rest of Uganda all Native Governments operate on a District level and they are Local Government units.

It is that special position which Buganda enjoys now that she wants to maintain even after Uganda's independence. The Baganda believe that they can safeguard their prestige only through the survival in a living and functioning form of the Kabakaship and the Lukiiko. The Kabaka is the spirit and motivating power of political, economic, and social activities and the Lukiiko is the legislative forum of the Baganda. That is why anything, either extrinsic or intrinsic, that tends to weaken our institutions is bound to be resisted in Buganda. One of the extrinsic forces that has tried to weaken our institutions is the Legislative Council, which was introduced in Uganda in 1921. This body, which was introduced mainly as a forum for the European planters and traders at that time, has never gained popularity in Buganda since its inception because it was regarded as foreign both in origin and composition. Secondly and more significantly, this Council has been viewed with suspicion as a possible agent to sap the strength of the Lukiiko and lower Buganda's prestige. Part of the 1953 Crisis, whereby the Kabaka was exiled by the British Government for two years, revolved around the controversy of Buganda's representation on the Legislative Council. This Council has failed to win the confidence of the Baganda.

That is the crucial point. Her Majesty's Government have declared that Buganda shall be represented on the Legislative Council as the only means of Uganda's unity. The Lukiiko and the Kabaka's Government on the other hand have said that before Buganda reconsiders her attitude to the Legislative Council her Treaty and constitutional Agreements must be terminated first and Her Majesty's Government should declare now that at least Buganda will be in a federal relationship *vis-à-vis* the future Central Government of Uganda. The Lukiiko Memorandum of 1958, expressing their wish to terminate the Agreements, resulted in constitutional talks held between the Lukiiko Constitutional Committee and Her Majesty's Representative from September 1959 until they ended in deadlock in London this September. The sole purpose of these talks had been for Buganda to receive back the powers exercised by Her Majesty's Representative under the Agreements before Uganda attained independence. The Treaty relationship between Buganda and Britain demanded that Her Majesty's Government could not surrender its powers under the Agreements to a new Government with which Buganda had not concluded an Agreement. Satisfactory conclusion of the constitutional talks would further determine Buganda's federal relationship with the future Central Government.

While these talks were going on, Her Majesty's Government formulated a constitutional plan for the whole of Uganda. This was:

(a) Registration of voters throughout Uganda.
(b) Before the General Elections there would be appointed a Relationships Commission by the Secretary of State for the Colonies to make recommendations as to the form of Government most suitable to Uganda.
(c) General Elections early next year for the Legislative Council, 1961.
(d) After the General Elections there would be a Constitutional Conference, to be held in London in the Summer of 1961, representative of all parts of Uganda, including Buganda, to consider the recommendations of the Commission. This Conference would be attended by the elected members of the New Legislative Council.

Although this plan affects Buganda's Constitutional position fundamentally, Buganda's proposals as to how it should apply to their Kingdom have been brushed aside. For example, during the recent London talks, the Kabaka's delegation suggested that the Relationships Commission should submit its report before these fundamental changes took place. The Secretary of State rejected this suggestion out of hand but declined to answer the relevant question as to what Her Majesty's Government would do should the Relationships Commission recommend a form of government that was contrary to Buganda's desires.

The Secretary of State has declared that he cannot deviate from that plan, whatever Buganda's representations for some modifications, hence the deadlock in the London talks.

Buganda has found it extremely difficult to cooperate in these un-negotiated orders emanating from Whitehall, which … completely disregard the Kabaka's, his Government's and the Lukiiko's representations. There cannot be any other body of opinion more representative of public opinion in Buganda other than the Kabaka's Government and the Lukiiko. This disregard, on the part of Her Majesty's Government, comes as a great shock to the Lukiiko and the people of Buganda.

The Secretary of State has indicated that public opinion in Buganda and Uganda is that expressed by political leaders in this country. Nothing could be more erroneous and misleading. In Buganda there has been a move to form political parties since the early twenties. But Her Majesty's Government's policy has been to suppress them by either proscribing them or deporting and putting political leaders into prison. The result of this repressive policy has been that political parties have failed to establish themselves firmly and win the confidence of the Baganda, whose loyalty has always been towards their Kabaka and the Lukiiko.

It will be recalled that during the 1953-1955 crisis, when political party leaders tried to see the Secretary of State concerning the return of the Kabaka from exile, the Secretary of State said that he could only negotiate with members of the Lukiiko. He did not recognize political party leaders as the right persons to treat with in constitutional matters affecting Buganda.

In these circumstances, it would be asking too much of the Baganda to trust the destiny of their country into the hands of political party leaders whose experience has not been proved by time. This could be extremely risky in the light of recent history, which has shown clearly that politicians in emergent countries use parliamentary democracy as a springboard to virtual dictatorship. Buganda has asked Her Majesty's Government to hand back its powers to the Kabaka who, under the Treaty and constitutional Agreements, entrusted them to that Government. Her Majesty's Government's refusal to do this and instead prefer political party leaders is not only discourteous in the extreme, but also a complete oversight of the facts.

When the Secretary of State recently said at the opening of the new Legislative Council building that he had firm intention to act vigorously under the law in order to carry out his plan, he sounded a warning note that he would use all means to impose the British type of parliamentary democracy which he said the people of Buganda demanded. It is difficult to know what is meant by the "people of Buganda" in this context. The "Special Powers Ordinance" hurried through the Legislative Council immediately after the Secretary of State's visit, which Ordinance gives the

Police unlimited powers to arrest and detain anyone on suspicion that he may intimidate people who want to register or vote, shows that Her Majesty's Government is determined to introduce the British type of parliamentary democracy even by decree.

If Buganda's legitimate constitutional demands have caused all these most unlikely reactions while the Treaty relations are even still existing between Buganda and Her Majesty's Government, the Lukiiko's apprehensions as to what the future of [the] Uganda Government's attitude towards Buganda will be, are greatly intensified. We cannot expect that Government to do much better than Her Majesty's Government as they are going to inherit this form of disguised dictatorship. Public pronouncements made on various occasions by peoples likely to be leaders of a future Uganda are not conducive to unity as Her Majesty's Government envisages it. In order to avoid another "Katanga" in this country immediately after Uganda's independence, Buganda has decided and is determined to go it alone.As a result of this decision, Buganda proposes to establish cordial relationship between Her Majesty's Government and herself for a number of reasons: mainly because the British are monarchists like the Baganda and the special relationship that has existed between the two countries has been a paternalistic one, which has been found to be unsatisfactory in the present circumstances. Since neither Britain nor Buganda desire that this superior-inferior relationship should continue beyond what is absolutely necessary, there ought to be a new Anglo-Buganda Cordial Relationship. **That proposed relationship should be finalized and put into effect by 31 December, 1960, after which date Buganda will be independent.** In the meantime negotiations will be held between representatives of the Lukiiko and Her Majesty's Government with a view to formulating a scheme within which that Anglo-Buganda Cordial Relationship will operate.

Plan for an Independent Buganda

1. Relationship with Great Britain
There shall be established a friendly relationship between an Independent Buganda and Her Majesty's Government on the following lines:

(i) Defence: In this connection, Buganda will have her own Army, but she will form a Military Alliance with Britain for a specified period of time which may be revised from time to time.
(ii) Foreign Affairs: Buganda will establish Foreign Relations by herself where possible, otherwise, in conjunction with Great Britain for a specified period of time.
(iii) Economic Aid: Buganda will seek economic aid from Britain in her economic and technical development.

A Five-Year Development Plan will be drawn up by Buganda following the attainment of her Independence, so as to give the Kingdom an orderly economic development.

In her economic development, Buganda will encourage free enterprise and make conditions favourable for foreign investment. The Kabaka's Government's Policy as to State Ownership is that such ownership should be restricted to those essential services which cannot be beneficially run by Private Enterprise.

2. Relationship with Neighbouring Countries in East Africa
(a) Customs: Buganda will join the Common Customs of East Africa.
(b) Communications: (This includes Road, Rail, Water and Air services.) There shall be joint negotiations as to the membership of Buganda on the bodies controlling those services.
(c) Higher Education:
  (i) All existing institutions of learning will automatically fall under the jurisdiction of Buganda.
  (ii) This position will however not alter the present status of Makerere University College, nor will it change its legal and administrative position as an Inter-State Institution.
  (iii) Buganda will have her full share in the management of Makerere, and shall be fully represented on those bodies which control and administer its activities.
(d) Judicial: Buganda shall have her own High Court and District Courts. Appeals from the High Court shall lie to the Eastern Africa Court of

Appeal and finally to the Privy Council.

(e) Inter-State Trade in East Africa:

(i) Any manufacturing and/or secondary industries operating in Buganda will have to be licenced in Buganda, and all Excise Duty will go to the Buganda Kingdom Treasury.

(ii) There will be free movement of trade between Buganda and the States of East Africa.

(f) Monetary System: Buganda will remain in the Sterling Area.

(g) Immigration: This will apply to non-Africans as defined by the existing Uganda Protectorate Ordinance.

Movement of Persons, however, between Buganda and other neighbouring countries in East Africa will be free and unrestricted.

3. International Relationships

(i) The fundamental rights of man, and the rule of law as understood in the free world, will be strictly observed.

Thus, there will be freedom of worship, freedom of speech, and freedom of assembly in Buganda regardless of race, colour, or creed.

(ii) On her attainment of Independence, Buganda will be associated with the great family of nations— the Commonwealth, and like any other independent nations in the Commonwealth, Buganda will seek admission to the United Nations General Assembly.

(iii) *Posts and Telecommunication* being services conducted on International level, such services will continue to be run as at present in Buganda. The control of those services in Buganda, however, will fall under the Kabaka's Government, and as such, Buganda will make her own postal stamps.

4. Internal Re-Arrangement of Services

(a) The Lukiiko will continue to be the Legislative and deliberate body for Buganda.

(b) All powers now exercised by Her Majesty's Representative under the Treaty and constitutional Agreements of Buganda shall vest in the Kabaka and His Government, e.g., all laws and Buganda's Budget shall be effective after the approval of the Kabaka, who is the Supreme Head of Buganda.

(c) Buganda will have an army of which the Kabaka will be the Commander-in-Chief.

(d) Buganda will have her own Police Force for the purposes of maintaining law and order. In this connection, the present Uganda Police Force responsible for the Buganda province should immediately come under the Kabaka's Government's jurisdiction.

(e) There will be a High Court and District courts for Buganda with a Bench of trained, qualified and experienced lawyers. Parties will be legally represented therein.

(f) Kampala, Entebbe, Masaka, Mubende and all Townships and Trading Centres, as well as Entebbe Airport, without prejudice to its international status, will immediately be brought under the jurisdiction of the Kabaka's Government.

(g) All lands vested in Her Majesty under the provisions of all Buganda Agreements shall revert to the Kabaka of Buganda for the use and benefit of all.

The Lukiiko is fully conscious of the important fact that in order to realize the scheme as outlined above, Buganda will need technicians, doctors, lawyers and many people trained in various professions and trades. She will need a strong Civil Service. Buganda therefore intends to award as many scholarships as possible for long and short courses here and abroad to candidates who are most likely to make the maximum use of the facilities for the benefit of their country in the long run. In the meantime, Buganda will meet the shortage in personnel by employing expatriates on contract.

As to the financing of the whole scheme as outlined above, Buganda intends to use:- (a) The existing resources which will be greatly increased by the change over from British control and (b) by raising local as well as overseas loan; and (c) by inviting outside capital.

In conclusion, this Lukiiko's decision has been made imperative by Her Majesty's Government's failure to recognize the fact that any possible parliamentary democracy ought to be built on the existing institutions in Buganda, that is to say, the Kabakaship and the Lukiiko. Her Majesty's Government's oversight of the Kabaka's, his Government's, and the Lukiiko's representations to that effect can only result in hard feelings unnecessarily. The only possible way out of these difficulties is for Buganda to go it alone and establish the "Anglo-Buganda Cordial Relationship" as outlined above.

The Lukiiko would like to stress the fact that it is not opposed to parliamentary democracy as such, but it views with apprehension any induced democracy which is only strengthened by the desire for independence. To the Lukiiko, parliamentary democracy ought to suit the local conditions, because there cannot be such a thing as international parliamentary democracy. Independence should be a means to an end and not an end in itself. Buganda cannot sell all her heritage for the purchase of Uganda's Independence. That heritage is much more precious in the long run. Nor is Buganda willing to sacrifice everything at the altar of Uganda's unity.

The foregoing does not mean, in the least, that we are not appreciative and actively conscious of the benefits Buganda has derived from Her Majesty's protection for the last seventy years. There cannot be a better way of expressing that gratitude than the proposed Anglo-Buganda Cordial Relationship.

Note

[1] The Lukiiko Memorandum, 1960 reproduced in Low, *The Mind of Buganda*, p.200.

APPENDIX V

FUNERAL CEREMONIES OF SIR EDWARD MUTESA

CONFIDENTIAL: FOREIGN AND COMMONWEALTH OFFICE DIPLOMATIC REPORT NO. 253/71[1]

British High Commissioner at Kampala to the
Secretary of State for Foreign and Commonwealth Affairs

Kampala, 13 April, 1971.

Sir,

1. Sir Edward Mutesa, first President of Uganda and deposed Kabaka of Buganda, was laid to rest in his own country on Sunday, 4 April, some 16 months after his death as an exile in London. In addition to the religious observances and military ceremonial characteristic of a State funeral, traditional tribal rites were performed. The interplay of these elements was complex and in some respects dangerous. It is to the lasting credit of the Government and people of Uganda that the vent passed off harmoniously, with dignity and (more or less) as planned.

2. It is unnecessary for the purposes of this dispatch to recall in any detail the circumstances in which Sir Edward Mutesa was expelled from Uganda by Dr Obote in May 1966 and sought refuge in Britain. As a President of his country who was also king of the historically dominant Buganda tribe and concerned to do justice to both, Sir Edward Mutesa stood in the way of Dr Obote's plans for suppressing tribalism and creating a united nation over which himself would exercise supreme power. Having arrogated to himself the powers of President as well as Prime Minister, Obote ordered an attack on the Kabaka's Palace, as a result of which the latter was forced to flee. For this, as they regard it, impious act Dr Obote will never be forgiven by the Baganda.

3. Sir Edward Mutesa died of alcoholic poisoning in his Bermondsey flat in November 1969. Dr Obote promptly offered an "honourable" (though not a State) funeral in Uganda, but for a variety of reasons, including distrust of the President, Mutesa's family opted instead for a "temporary" burial in Britain. No representative of the Uganda Government attended this event.

4. How long the temporary burial would have lasted had it not been for General Idi Amin is anybody's guess. General Amin seized power on 25 January last. On the following day he announced at a Press Conference that the body of Sir Edward Mutesa would be flown back to Uganda and buried with full military honours. This gave rise to much public rejoicing among the Baganda, but it soon became clear that not all elders of the tribe nor all members of the royal family, whether in Uganda or Britain, were ready to give the idea their blessing. They felt, that coming from a West Niler who could not be expected to have any particular affection for the Baganda, the decision was too blatantly inspired by political expediency. Moreover, it was believed (though the evidence is vague) that Mutesa had expressed a wish not to be buried in Uganda unless and until the Kingdom had been restored; and Amin had made it abundantly clear that this was not the intention. There were other questions to be answered. Would not reburial open a lot of old wounds, quite apart from resurrecting the question of the succession? Prince Ronald Mutebi, Mutesa's son by his wife's sister, had been recognized as heir by his father, but there were other pretenders.

5. These were all tenable objections and Amin did not ride roughshod over them. Legally, all that he needed was the widow's signature on a request for exhumation of the body, but he set out to obtain at least the acquiescence of all concerned. In this he seems to have succeeded. I do not know what arguments ultimately prevailed with whom, but all the critics must have shared reluctance to obstruct the man who had delivered Uganda from Obote.

6. Meanwhile, preparations had been going ahead on the assumption that the political difficulties would be overcome. Thanks to the cooperation of the Ministry of Defence, the services of Major Paul Cordle of the Grenadier Guards, an expert on ceremonial drill, were placed at General Amin's disposal about 10 days before the funeral. Major Cordle was to prove a key figure in the organization of the ceremonies

and his tactful handling of Amin contributed much to the Anglo-Ugandan euphoria of which I shall have more to say later.

7. As the programme for the five-day funeral (period 31 March to 4 April) began to take shape, fears that it would stretch Uganda's resources to breaking point were reinforced. It emerged, for instance, that invitations to foreign guests had been extended not only to those directly concerned (in which category The Queen and Her Majesty's Government, as well as the faithful British friends of Sir Edward Mutesa, were naturally included), but also to Heads of all States with which Uganda is in relations. The prospect of an influx of VIPs focused attention even more closely than before on the security problem.

8. This problem was already exercising a large number of Ugandans and foreigners. The risks appeared to be manifold: mass hysteria leading to violence; ritual murder ("the Kabaka does not die alone"); clashes between Baganda factions; victimization of Acholi and Langi; the paying off of old scores against the political supporters of Obote; attempts by Obote's agents to disrupt the ceremonies—assassination not excluded. Such risks were debated publicly and with remarkable freedom, but at the back of many minds lurked the fear that Amin might not really be in control of his army. The United States Embassy discreetly advised Americans to leave Kampala if they conveniently could. We in the High Commission did not feel justified in giving similar advice (I had been assured that security precautions would be on the massive scale of those taken at the time of the Pope's visit in 1969), but we made it clear that nobody should feel inhibited from taking a holiday away from Kampala if he wished and that the community should not move about unnecessarily.

9. It was this atmosphere of excited but rather apprehensive expectation that the chartered plane carrying the body of Sir Edward Mutesa landed at Entebbe on the morning of Wednesday, 31 March, escorted by fighter planes of the Ugandan Air Force. It carried also some 100 passengers, including the Uganda Foreign Minister who had taken formal delivery of the coffin in London, relatives of Mutesa and other émigrés, many of his British friends, journalists and a detachment of 10 Grenadier Guardsmen who were later to escort though not to carry the bier. As a hatch in the side of the aircraft was lifted to reveal the coffin within, draped in the Ugandan flag and surmounted by military

cap, sword and medals, the traditional drums took over from the army band and a faint ululation from the crowd, the first of many to be heard over the next few days, was borne on the breeze. The coffin was carried to a catafalque opposite the saluting dais, the Guard of Honour presented arms, [and] the band played the Uganda National Anthem followed by God Save the Queen. Sir Edward Mutesa was home again among his people; but the country of his exile was not forgotten.

10. From Entebbe, following a last minute change of plan, the coffin was flown by helicopter to Lubiri where it was exhibited to the Mechanised Battalion stationed there—a gesture to the soldiers who had played a crucial part in the coup. From Lubiri, again by helicopter, the body was flown to Kololo Airstrip, [a] traditional scene of national celebrations. Here the military ceremonial of Entebbe was repeated on a large scale and Amin made a brief speech appealing for unity. A gun-carriage then took the coffin to Parliament Building where it was placed in the Chamber of the assembly and Amin spoke again, emphasizing his role as conciliator and his desire to create conditions in which it would be possible to restore Parliamentary democracy. The final procession that day was from Parliament Building to the Anglican Cathedral at Namirembe. After a brief service, the coffin was placed in the Hannington Chapel. A perspex top was fitted and Sir Edward Mutesa (of whose death many had yet to be convinced) was revealed to his people, dressed in the uniform of a Major-General of the Ugandan Army.

11. For the next three days and nights huge crowds climbed the hill to the Cathedral in an orderly queue and filed past the body. It was a slow and tiring business, particularly in the heat of the day, and tempers could easily have become frayed. The evidence is all to the contrary. Many people have testified to the patience, discipline and reverence displayed by the mourners.

12. On Saturday afternoon, again following a change of plan, the body was flown to Bamunanika, about 30 miles from Kampala, to spend the last night lying in state at the Royal Palace there. It was returned to the Cathedral the following morning. After an extremely impressive service, the funeral procession moved to Kasubi Royal Tombs, a thatched bee-hive structure where wreaths were laid by foreign representatives and Mutebi exercised his prerogative as heir by placing the traditional bark-cloth over the body before it was finally lowered

into the grave. He later returned to Bamunanika where I understand the traditional ceremonies relating to the succession stopped short only of declaring him to be the Kabaka.

13. I believe that the reburial of Sir Edward Mutesa had had a cathartic effect and that Uganda is a better and happier place for the events I have described. It can no doubt be argued that what we witnessed was nothing but an elaborate piece of political stage-craft. This view is not widely held; and I believe it to be wrong. Certainly Amin needs the support of the Baganda. Certainly the honour done to the memory of Mutesa will have helped him to secure it. But cynical opportunism is not a characteristic of the new President—however marked his talent for survival. He is a simple man. As a soldier, it offended against his code that a President of Uganda and Commander-in-Chief of the Armed Forces should have died and been buried in the obscurity of exile; in his speech at Kololo he insisted that this must never be allowed to happen again. And even if Mutesa had not held these high offices, Amin would still, I believe have thought it right to make restitution to the great tribe over which he once ruled.

14. At the final service in Namirembe Cathedral, Bishop Stuart, who had long been associated with Sir Edward Mutesa, praised General Amin for his generosity and courage. He had reason to do so. In staking his prestige on the success of the occasion and in committing to it, in the fullest possible measure, his own energies and resources of his Government, Amin had indeed shown both qualities—and a sense of history too. Government spokesmen have referred to it as an act of national reconciliation. I believe that it was genuinely so viewed by the President and that in the short term at least it will have some such effect.

15. As for the longer-term prospects, a note of caution is called for. It certainly cannot be said that the Baganda are wholly reconciled to the loss of their Kingdom. There are some hard-liners among them who make no secret of their view that the reburial is only a beginning; there can, they say, be no stability in Uganda until the monarchy has been restored. But with the present ban on political activity, there is not much they can do about it; and they will not in any case wish to cause difficulties for the present regime lest it be succeeded by something worse. There is also a very practical problem. Ronald Mutebi is an extremely sensible young man whose only ambitions for the immediate

future are to complete his studies at Bradfield and gain admission to his father's college, Magdalene, Cambridge. A rival claimant could no doubt find supporters, but this would only split the tribe. Faced with these difficulties, the monarchists are likely to be quiescent for a while, comforted by the thought that honour has been restored to the tribe and by the hope that, with another turn or two of the political wheel, power may one day be restored also. I believe this is a vain hope and certainly the present Government have done nothing to encourage it. But if it persists for a time, so much the better: it will have tranquilising effect. Meanwhile the Baganda at least have a titular head of clan.

16. It only remains to record the nature of British participation in this event. As I reported by telegram, Amin went to almost embarrassing lengths to make it an Anglo-Ugandan occasion. His primary motive was, I think, quite simply gratitude to Britain. He had, of course good reason to be grateful to Her Majesty's Government, but he had also become conscious of the debt owed to private citizens in Britain—to Captain Ronald Owen, once aide-de-camp to the Kabaka and now guardian of Mutebi, to Major Carr-Gomm, the guardian of Mutebi's brother, to Lord Boyd and to many other friends of Mutesa who had done much, financially and otherwise, to mitigate the ignominy and poverty of his exile. To the guardians of the children he owed a more specific debt; their agreement to the attendance of their wards at the ceremonies had been given only after much heart searching. But behind all these conscious considerations, Amin was, I think, moved, however dimly, by a sense of history, an awareness of the linking of the destinies of the two countries symbolized by the return of Mutesa from British soil.

17. Whatever his motives, the General's salute to Britain was unequivocal. As The Queen's Special Representative, I was singled out (without warning, incidentally) to accompany Amin to the aircraft when it landed at Entebbe and to stand by the dais for the Presidential Salute. I alone of foreign representatives accompanied the body, first to Lubiri and then to Kololo. The British National Anthem, never previously heard here since Independence, was played more often than I can remember. At the Cathedral Service, the front pew was reserved for myself, Sir William Hayter representing the Queen Mother, and Lord Boyd representing Her Majesty's Government. In less formal ways Britain was equally well served. British guests included a group of five members of Parliament, numerous friends of Mutesa (among them

Lord Montagu of Beaulieu, who also represented Lord Mountbatten) and a particularly pleasant touch, the charlady who had looked after him in Bermondsey. All were most hospitably entertained by the Uganda Government; and Amin somehow found time to attend an informal party which we gave for the British visitors and their Ugandan friends. Lord Boyd, whose choice as representative of Her Majesty's Government gave great pleasure to the Ugandans, received special attention. He had long talks with the President (on which I have reported separately) and lunched informally at State House. At the State Banquet on the evening following the interment he was the only speaker and scored a resounding success. To round it all off, the President gave a luncheon next day for the British Parliamentary delegation at which he expressed his appreciation of all that Britain had done for Uganda and declared categorically that Uganda would not leave the Commonwealth. Replying as leader of the delegation, Mr Speed admirably reflected the mood of the occasion.

18. Thus ended six hectic days which, whatever their consequences domestically, may be said to mark the opening of a new chapter in Anglo-Ugandan relations. I would only add that, in extending the hand of friendship to Britain, General Amin has not overlooked the importance of his most influential neighbour. The strong delegation from Kenya led by Vice-President Moi, though they attended only for the final day, were treated with great respect; the Vice-President sat next to General Amin at the Cathedral Service and the delegation was given a pride of place at Kasubi. Suitable attentions were also paid to the Special Envoys from the Central African Republic, Ethiopia and Malawi—all of Ministerial rank. So long as Amin realizes that to be accepted in Africa is his first priority, his overtures to Britain can only be welcome.

19. I am sending copies of this dispatch to Her Majesty's Representatives in Nairobi, Dar-es-Salaam, Lusaka and Addis Ababa.

R. M. K. SLATER

Note

[1] *Re-burial of Ex-Kabaka of Buganda in Uganda*, 13 April 1971. File No. JEU 26/1 (Part B), FCO 31/1075.

APPENDIX VI

PROBLEMS OF COLONIAL BOUNDARIES, STATES AND SEPARATISM IN AFRICA: COMPARING BUGANDA, KATANGA AND BIAFRA'S STRUGGLE FOR INDEPENDENCE

Within the wider context of colonial machinery in Africa, Buganda was not alone in its struggle to retain its identity and sovereignty in the face of British imperialism. Its separatist tendencies are akin to those of many other African nations—including those outside the former British Empire—who have struggled in the past, or continue to fight today, for autonomy. And, while it failed to achieve independence in 1960, due to several endogenous limiting factors, its aspirations towards some kind of autonomy are still alive today. Indeed, and for similar reasons, its aspirations are shared with other peoples across Africa. For example, the Katangese in the former Republic of Zaire (presently the Democratic Republic of Congo), the Igbo in Eastern Nigeria and the Nuer in South Sudan are all involved in one form or another of a struggle to break free from colonially determined political and territorial structures.

These struggles all point to the deep-rooted constitutional and political problems emanating from colonial rule that have undermined the stability, peace and prosperity of many of the new nations. Needless to say, the fight for autonomy has been extremely costly and has resulted in profound human suffering. Sadly, the response by both the colonial and postcolonial states to the crises caused by demands for autonomy have been met more by repression and violence and less by dialogue and democratic means. Accordingly, many separatist bids have been brutally crushed militarily so as to maintain the colonial order and boundaries. But, while some groups have surrendered to militarism or authoritarian rule within the old colonial borders, many continue to fight for their liberation from imposed boundaries and imposed unity.

These include independence struggles by the Biafra in Nigeria and the Katangese in Congo. The history of these struggles shows that Biafra's fight for an independent existence, like Katanga's before it, differs in many ways from that of Buganda. Because while Biafra's struggle came after Nigeria's independence and was armed, Buganda's came before Uganda's independence and was non-violent. Furthermore, while Biafra's independence was recognised by some states attracted much international support and attention, Buganda's was not. Also, while the Biafrans had vast resources of oil, Buganda had limited resources.

Nevertheless, as in the case of Katanga, there are commonalities that make Buganda's and Biafra's struggle for independence equally interesting in the study of colonial history and politics in Africa. As we have pointed above, both Nigeria and Uganda were the colonial creations of the British, who used administrative structures and policies that divided ethnicities and promoted the independent and often unequal development of each. Through indirect rule, the British used the leaders of these strong ethnic groups to perpetuate a semblance of traditional authority, whereas in reality this authority had been severely eroded. In both cases, colonial rule was focused more on the exploitation of the territories and the protection of British interests than on the promotion or securing of their economic and political advance.

For this reason, in both countries, during and after independence, Britain insisted on the existence of a unified country and disregarded or suppressed voices that sought a separate or independent existence. In both countries, the constitutional framework and political setup bequeathed by the British soon crumbled, with disastrous consequences. Both countries have experienced civil wars, military coups and counter-coups that have undermined their political stability, resulting in a reliance on authoritarian military rule to keep them together. Yet, in spite of this history, the people of Buganda, Katanga and Biafra still harbor the desire for a truly autonomous existence.

PHOTOGRAPHS

Punch cartoon depicting Uganda personified as a White elephant that the East Africa Company is attempting to sell to Britain (1892).

THE BLÂCK BABY.

MR. BULL. "WHAT, ANOTHER!!—WELL, I SUPPOSE I MUST TAKE IT IN!!!"

PHOTO SWAINE, LONDON

Sir Harry Johnston
1922

Fredrick Lugard

Kabaka Daniel B. Mwanga II

Winston Churchill with the young Daudi Chwa in Uganda

Kabaka Daudi Chwa

Apolo Kagwa (right) and Ham Mukasa

Hesketh Bell (fourth from right) with Kabaka Daudi Chwa (centre) in 1903

Poster urging men from countries of the British Empire to join and support the British Army in World War II

Fredrick Crawford, Governor of Uganda, accompanying John Griffith, former Chief Justice of Uganda, into the Council Chamber of the Town Hall, Kampala, where Griffith was sworn in as the first Speaker of Uganda Legislative Council on 13 January 1958. On the right is A. L. Pennington, Clerk to the Council.

Mengo Palace, 1955

Governor Hall and Kabaka Mutesa

Kabaka Mutesa inspects a parade at Mengo

Governor John Hall and Kabaka Mutesa

Edward Mutesa with Governor Andrew Cohen at Mengo palace

Kabaka Mutesa arrives at the Colonial Office in London to meet the Secretary of State for the Colonies Oliver Lyttleton following his deportation in 1953

Signing of the 1955 Agreement by the Kabaka and Governor of Uganda, Andrew Cohen, in the Lukiiko, October 1955

The Kabaka and Governor Andrew Cohen, October 1955

Buganda Kingdom Headquaters, Bulange Mengo, 1959

Lancaster House, London, 2018

Prime Minister Obote addresses the Duke Kent and other guests at Kololo on Independence Day, October 1962

Prime Minister Obote, the Duke Kent and other guests at Kololo on Independence Day, October 1962

Prime Minister Obote and Kabaka Mutesa, 1962

Attack on the Lubiri, 1966

Attack on the Lubiri, 1966

Dr A. Milton Obote and British Prime Minister Harold Wilson at Marlborough House, London, 6 September 1966

Mutesa's body returned to Uganda, 1971

Mutesa's body returned to Uganda, 1971

Britons kneel to swear allegiance to Amin and Uganda

Britons carry Amin in 1975. He referred to himself as the conqueror of the British Empire

President Idi Amin and President Mobutu Sese Sekop speaking to journalists

Amin and Bob Astles, 1978

One of the victims of Amin's reign of terror at a public execution, 1972

Yoweri Museveni swearing-in as President, 1986

Kabaka Mutebi's coronation at Nagalabi Budo, 1993

President Museveni returns the land title for the Lubiri Palace at Mengo

Protests following the refusal of Kabaka Mutebi to travel to Kayunga, 2009

Army armoured personnel carriers at Wandegeya-Bwaise Road during Kayunga protests, 2009

A Police post torched during Kayunga protests, 2009

Buganda's Kasubi tombs on fire March 2010

President Museveni, Kabaka Ronald Mutebi and Katikkiro C. P. Mayiga, 2013

Kabaka Mutebi opens the Buganda Lukiiko, August 2015

President Museveni hands some of Buganda's land titles to C.P. Mayiga, Katikkiro, 2015

Buckingham Palace, London.

President Museveni with Queen Elizabeth II at Uganda's Parliament, 2007

British Foreign Secretary Boris Johnson and British High Commissioner Peter West with State Minister for Foreign Affairs, Okello Oryem in Uganda, 2017

President Museveni with Queen Elizabeth II at State House Entebbe, 2007

President Yoweri Museveni meeting Boris Johnson, UK Foreign Minister, at State House, Entebbe

President Yoweri Museveni meeting Theresa May, UK Prime Minister, at Lancaster House in London

Kabaka Ronald Muwenda Mutebi II

BIBLIOGRAPHY

Adhola, Yoga, "The Buganda Question and the Forging of a Nation State in Uganda," October 2007.

Aliker, Martin. 2018. "The Bell is Ringing: Martin Aliker's Story," Fountain Publishers, Kampala.

Alavi, Hamza. 1982. *Capitalism and Colonial Production: Essays on the Rise of Capitalism in Asia*, Croom Helm;

Amone, Charles. 2014. "The Creation of Acholi Military Ethnocracy in Uganda, 1882 to 1962." *International Journal of Liberal Arts and Social Science.* Vol. 2, No. 3.

Anderson, David M. 2011. "Mau Mau in the High Court and the 'Lost' British Empire Archives: Colonial Conspiracy or Bureaucratic Bungle?" *The Journal of Imperial and Commonwealth History*, 39(5).

—. 2005. *Histories of the Hanged: Britain's Dirty War in Kenya and the End of Empire.* Weidenfeld & Nicolson: London.

Azikiwe, Ifeoha. 2013. *Nigeria: Echoes of a Century, 1914-1999.* AuthorHouse: Bloomington.

Bland-Sutton, John, 1933. *Men and Creatures in Uganda*, London: Hutchison & Co.

Barungi, Baganchwera N. I. 2011. *Parliamentary Democracy in Uganda: The Experiment that Failed.* Author House: Bloomington.

Barber, J. P. 2006. "Flag and Anthem." In Brown, D. & Brown, M. V. (eds.) *Looking Back at the Uganda Protectorate: Recollections of District Officers.* D. Brown: Dalkeith, Western Australia.

Berridge, G. R., "The British Interests Section in Kampala," 1976-7, January 2012, http://grberridge.diplomacy.edu/

Brasnet, John. 2006. "Karamoja—Basic Administration." In Brown, Douglas & Brown, Marcelle V. (eds.), *Looking Back at the Uganda Protectorate: Recollections of District Officers.* D. Brown: Dalkeith, Western Australia.

Brian, L. (n.d) "A Glimpse into How Citizens of Imperial Britain Felt." In *Heart of Darkness: A Research Guide.* http://www.ryanweberling.com/heartofdarkness/a-glimpse-into-how-citizens-of-imperial-Britain-felt, accessed 7 March 2018.

Brown, Douglas. 2006. "Afterthoughts." In Brown, Douglas & Brown, Marcelle V. (eds.), *Looking Back at the Uganda Protectorate: Recollections of District Officers.* D. Brown: Dalkeith, Western

Australia.

Buell, R. Leslie. 1928. *The Native Problem in Africa.* Vol. 1. Macmillan: New York.

Churchill, Winston S. 1908. *My African Journey.* Hodder & Stoughton: London.

Chwa, Daudi (Kabaka). 1928. *Lwaki Sir Apolo Kagwa Yawumula,* Kampala.

Cobain, Ian. 2016. *The History Thieves: Secrets, Lies and the Shaping of a Modern Nation.* Portobello Books: London.

Crawford, Young. 1965. *Politics in the Congo: Decolonization and Independence.* Princeton University Press: London.

Dunbar, A. R. 1965. *The History of Bunyoro-Kitara.* Oxford University Press, Nairobi.

Dundas, Charles. 1955. *African Crossroads.* MacMillan: London.

De Roche, Andrew. 2003. "Relations with Africa since 1900." In Robert D. Schulzinger (ed.) *A Companion to American Foreign Relations.* Blackwell Publishing: Malden, MA.

Easterly, W. 2006. *The White Man's Burden: Why the West's Efforts to Aid the Rest Have Done So Much Ill and So Little Good.* Penguin Press, New York.

Edgerton, R. B. 2002. *The troubled Heart of Africa: A History of the Congo.* St Martin's Press: New York.

Ekon, E. E. 2014. "Christian Missions and Colonial Rule in Africa: Objective and Contemporary Analysis." *European Scientific Journal,* 10(17).

Elaigwu, Isawa, J. 1977. "The Nigerian Civil War and the Angolan Civil War: Linkages between Domestic Tensions and International Alignments." In Ali A. Mazrui (ed.) *The Warrior Tradition in Modern Africa.* E. J. Brill: Leiden.

Elkins, Caroline. 2005. *Imperial Reckoning: The Untold Story of Britain's Gulag in Kenya.* Henry Holt & Co: New York.

Fallers, L.A. (ed.). 1964. *The King's Men: Leadership and Status in Buganda on the Eve of Independence.* Oxford University Press, London.

Falola, T. and Oyebade, A. 2010. *Hot Spot: Sub-Saharan Africa.* GreenWood: Westport, CT.

Felkin, Robert William *Notes on Labor in Central Africa,* Edinburgh Medical Journal, Volume 20, April 1884, pp. 922-30.

Fenwick, Laura. 2009. "British and French Styles of Influence in Colonial and Independent Africa: A Comparative Study of Kenya and Senegal." SIS 419 002, Honors Capstone.

Ferguson, Niall, 2004. *Empire: The Rise and Demise of the British World Order and the Lessons for Global Power*. New York.
Fleay, Martin. 2006. "Karamoja's District Team and Development Scheme." In Brown, Douglas & Brown, Marcelle V. (eds.), *Looking Back at the Uganda Protectorate: Recollections of District Officers.* D. Brown: Dalkeith, Western Australia.
Forward, Alan. 2006. "The Bukedi Riot II." In Brown, Douglas & Brown, Marcelle V. (eds.), *Looking Back at the Uganda Protectorate: Recollections of District Officers,* D. Brown: Dalkeith, Western Australia.
Frank, Mclynn. 2004. *Stanley: Dark Genius of African Exploration.* Pimlico: London.
Gladdish, Ken. 2006. "A Provincial Honeymoon." In Brown, Douglas & Brown, Marcelle V. (eds.), *Looking Back at the Uganda Protectorate: Recollections of District Officers.* D. Brown: Dalkeith, Western Australia.
Golooba-Mutebi, F. 2011. "Settling the Buganda Question: A Peek into the Future." *Transition*, Issue 106.
Grant, J. A. 1863. *A Walk across Africa, or Domestic Scenes from my Nile Journal.* W. Blackwood & Sons: Edinburgh/London.
Johnston, Harry (1902) *The Uganda Protectorate*, London: Hutchison & Co. Paternoster Row.
Griffith, Owen. 2006. "The Governor and the Kabaka." In Brown, Douglas & Brown, Marcelle V. (eds.), *Looking Back at the Uganda Protectorate: Recollections of District Officers.* D. Brown: Dalkeith, Western Australia.
—. 2006. "What Went Wrong?" In Brown, Douglas & Brown, Marcelle V. (eds.), *Looking Back at the Uganda Protectorate: Recollections of District Officers.* D. Brown: Dalkeith, Western Australia.
Griffiths, Ieuan L. I. 1995. *The African Inheritance.* Routledge: London.
Griffiths, T. 2001. "Bishop Alfred Tucker and the Establishment of a British Protectorate in Uganda 1890-1894." *The Journal of Religion in Africa*, 31(1).
Hanson, Holly. 2016. "Rethinking Uganda in the 1940s with New Evidence" (paper delivered at Makerere University, 3 May 2016).
Howell, Caroline. 2001. "Religion and Nationalism: Buganda and the 1949 Bataka Riots." University of Cambridge Position Paper 147.
Hochschild, A. 1998. *King Leopold's Ghost: A story of Greed, Terror, and Heroism in Colonial Africa.* Houghton Mifflin Co.: New York.
Hutton, P. and Bloch, J. 2012. "Uganda: How the West brought Idi Amin to Power," *Links International Journal of Socialist Renewal*,

http://links.org.au/node/2784, accessed 1 March 2018.

Ibingira, Grace S. K. 1973. *The Forging of an African Nation.* The Viking Press, Inc.: New York.

Jacobs, B. L. 2006. "Postscript." In Brown, Douglas & Brown, Marcelle V. (eds.), *Looking Back at the Uganda Protectorate: Recollections of District Officers.* D. Brown: Dalkeith, Western Australia.

James A. Casada. 1977. *Sir Harry Hamilton Johnston: A Bio-bibliographical Study.* Basler Afrika Bibliographien: Basel, Switzerland.

Jeal, T. 2007. *Stanley: The impossible life of Africa's greatest explorer.* Yale University Press: London.

Johannessen, Catherine. 2006. "Kingship in Uganda: The Role of the Buganda Kingdom in Ugandan Politics." CMI Working Paper 8, CHR. Michelsen Institute: Bergen.

Jorgensen, J. J. 1981. *Uganda: A Modern History.* Croom Helm: London.

Kagwa, Apolo. 1953. *Bassekabaka Ba Buganda*. MacMillan & Co. Ltd.: London.

Kaizi, M. (n.d) *His Highness Edward Daudi Fredrick William Walugembe Mutebi Muteesa II, Kabaka we Buganda* (Unpublished).

Kanyeihamba, G. W. 2002. *Constitutional and Political History of Uganda—From 1894 to the Present.* Centenary Publishing House Ltd.: Kampala, Uganda.

Karugire, S. R. 1980. *A Political History of Uganda.* Heinemann Educational Books: Nairobi.

Kasfir, N. 2017. *Kingdom, State and Civil Society in Africa: Conceptual and Political Collisions*. Basler Afrika Bibliographien: Basel, Switzerland.

Kasozi, A. B. K. 2013. *The Bitter Bread of Exile: The Financial Problems of Sir Edward Muteesa II during his final exile,* 1966-1969. Progressive Publishing House, Kampala Uganda.

Kasozi A, Nakanyike Musisi, James Mukooza Sejjengo. 1994. *Social Origins of Violence in Uganda 1964-1985*. McGill-Queen's Press.

Katjavivi, P. H. 1988. *A History of Resistance in Namibia.* James Currey: Oxford.

Kavuma, Paulo. 1979. *Crisis in Buganda: The Story of the Exile and Return of the Kabaka, Mutesa II.* Rex Collings: London.

Kim, Kwang-Su. 2016. "The Historical Contextualisation of the Kongo Kingdom in the Democratic Republic of the Congo's History." In Julien Bobineau and Philipp Gieg (eds.). *The Democratic Republic of the Congo: Problems, Progress and Prospects.* Lit. Verlag: Berlin.

Kirk-Greene, A. 2006. *Symbol of Authority: The British District Officer in*

Africa. I. B. Tauris: London.
Kiwanuka, M. S. M. Semakula. 1972. *A history of Buganda, from the foundation of the Kingdom to 1900*, Longman: London.
Kramnick, I. 1999. *The Portable Edmund Burke, Viking Portable Library.* Penguin Putman: New York.
Laidlaw, Z. 2015. "Empire and After." In Breay, C. & Harrison, J. (eds.). *Magna Carta: Law, Liberty, Legacy*. The British Library: London.
Larmer, Miles and Kennes, Erik. 2014. "Rethinking the Kantangese Secession," *Journal of Imperial and Commonwealth History*, 42(4).
Low, D. A. 2009. *Fabrication of Empire: The British and the Uganda Kingdoms, 1890-1902.* Cambridge University Press: New York.
—. 1971. *The Mind of Buganda, Documents of the Modern History of an African Kingdom.* Heinemann: London.
Low, D. A. and Pratt, R. C. 1960. *Buganda and British Overrule 1900-1955.* Oxford University Press: London.
Lugard, F. D. 1893. *The Rise of our East African Empire: Early Efforts in Nyasaland and Uganda.* William Blackwood & Sons: London.
—. 1922. *The Dual Mandate in British Tropical Africa.* William Blackwood & Sons: London.
Lule, Joseph, 2006. *The Hidden Wisdom of the Baganda,* Humbolt & Hartman, Inc: Arlington, Virginia.
Lwanga-Lunyiigo, Samwiri. 2015. *A History of the Democratic Party of Uganda: The First Thirty Years (1954-1984).*, Fountain Publishers: Kampala, Uganda.
—. 2011. *Mwanga II: Resistance to Imposition of British Colonial Rule in Buganda 1884-1899.* Wavah Books Ltd.: Kampala, Uganda:
—. 2007. *The Struggle for Land in Buganda 1888-2005.* Wavah Books: Kampala, Uganda.
—. 1987. The Colonial Roots of Internal Conflict in Uganda, MISR Paper No, PAP/017 (Paper delivered at the International Seminar on Internal Conflict, 21-25 September).
Mallaby Sebastian. 2004. *The World's Banker* Penguin Press: New York.
Mamdani, Mahmood 1983. *Imperialism and Fascism in Uganda.* Heinemann Educational Books: Nairobi.
—. 2011. *Okugenda Mu Maaso: The Link Between Tradition, Reform and Development*, MISR Working Paper No. 5 November 2011.
Marshall, Don. 2006. "The Deportation of the Kabaka." In Brown, Douglas & Brown, Marcelle V. (eds.), *Looking Back at the Uganda Protectorate: Recollections of District Officers.* D. Brown, Dalkeith, Western Australia.
Mayiga, Charles Peter. 2009. *King on the Throne: The Story of the*

Restoration of the Kingdom of Buganda. Prime Time Communication: Kampala, Uganda.

McIntyre, W. D. 1999. "The Commonwealth." In R. Winks (ed.). *The Oxford History of the British Empire: Volume V.* Oxford University Press, New York & Oxford.

Meredith, M. 2005. *The State of Africa: A History of the Continent Since Independence.* Simon & Schuster: London.

Miller, Charles. 2017. *The Lunatic Express: The Magnificent Saga of the Railways Journey into Africa.* Zeus: UK.

Mitchell, P. 1954. *African Afterthoughts.* Hutchinson: London.

Moyse-Bartlett, H. 1956. *The King's African Rifles: A study in the Military History of East and Central Africa, 1890-1945.* Volume 1. Gal & Polden: Aldershot.

Mulinge, M. M. & Lesetedi, G.N. 1998. "Interrogating Our Past: Colonialism and Corruption in Sub-Saharan Africa." *African Journal of Political Science.* 3(2).

Musoke, D. S. K. 1944. "Buganda Nyaffe" (trans.) reprinted in Donald Antony Low, comp., 1971. *The Mind of the Baganda: Documents of the Modern History of an African Kingdom*, Berkley.

Mutibwa, P. M. 2016. *A History of Uganda: The First 100 Years, 1894-1995.* Fountain Publishers: Kampala, Uganda.

—. 2008. *The Buganda Factor in Uganda Politics.* Fountain Publishers: Kampala, Uganda.

Murphy, Phillip. 2018. *The Empire's New Clothes: The Myth of the Commonwealth.* C. Hurst (Publishers) Ltd.

Museveni, Yoweri Kaguta. 1997. *Sowing the Mustard Seed: The Struggle for Freedom and Democracy in Uganda.* Macmillan, London.

Mutesa II (Kabaka). 1967. *Desecration of My Kingdom.* Constable & Company Ltd.: London.

Mwakikagile, G. 2001. *Ethnic Politics in Kenya and Nigeria.* Nova Science Publishers: New York.

Mwami, Abunuwasi and Muriuki, Godfrey. 2012. *The Federo Question of Buganda in Uganda within the Context of the East African Political Federation.* Fountain publishers: Kampala, Uganda.

Nabudere, Dan Wadada. 1980. *Imperialism and Revolution in Uganda.* Onyx Press Ltd., London.

Newsinger John. 2010. *The Blood Never Dried: A Peoples History of the British Empire.* Trentham Books.

Njuba, Samuel Kalega 2003. *The betrayal as Ugandan's are taken for a ride again*, a self-published book.

Nsibambi, Apolo. 2014. *National Integration in Uganda 1962-2013.*

Fountain Publishers: Kampala, Uganda.
Odoki, Benjamin J. 2005. *The Search for a National Consensus: The Making of the 1995 Uganda Constitution*. Fountain Publishers, Kampala.
Ojeleye, Olukunle. 2016. *The Politics of Post-War Demobilisation and Reintegration in Nigeria.* Routledge: London.
Oloka-Onyango, J. 2015. Ghosts and the Law (Inaugural lecture presented at Makerere University, November 12).
—. 1997. "The Question of Buganda in Contemporary Ugandan Politics." *The Journal of Contemporary African Studies*, 15(2).
Olusoga, D. 2016. *Black and British: A forgotten history.* Pan Macmillan: Basingstoke, UK.
O'Neill, T. J. and Rees, N. 2005. *United Nations Peacekeeping in the Post-Cold War Era.* Routledge: Abingdon.
Otunnu, O. 2016. "Crises of Legitimacy and Political Violence in Colonial Uganda, 1890–1962." In O. Otunnu (ed.). *Crisis of Legitimacy and Political Violence in Uganda, 1890 to 1979.* Palgrave Macmillan: London.
Pakenham, T. 1999. *The Scramble for Africa 1876–1912.* Abacus: London.
Perham, M. 1959. *The Diaries of Lord Lugard: East Africa 1889-1892.* Vols 1-3, Evanston: Northwestern University Press.
Perham, M. and Bull, M. (eds). 1963. *The Dairies of Lord Lugard*, Volume 2, Evanston, III: Northwestern University Press.
Perras, Arne. 2004. *Karl Peters and German Imperialism 1856-1918—A political Biography.* Oxford Historical Monograph. Clarendon Press: Oxford.
Pratt, R. C. 1965. "Administration and Politics in Uganda, 1919-1945." In Harlow, V. & Chilver, E. M. (eds), *History of East Africa.* Oxford University Press: London.
Rodney, W. 1972. *How Europe Underdeveloped Africa.* L'ouverture: London.
Roper, Ron. 2006. "The Bukedi Riot I" In Brown, Douglas & Brown, Marcelle V. (eds.), *Looking Back at the Uganda Protectorate: Recollections of District Officers.* D. Brown: Dalkeith, Western Australia.
Roscoe, John. 1911. *The Baganda: An Account of their Native Customs and Beliefs*, London: Macmillan and Co., Limited St Martins Street, London.
Ryrie, William. 2006. "Uganda in 1957-58." In Brown, Douglas & Brown, Marcelle V. (eds.), *Looking Back at the Uganda Protectorate:*

Recollections of District Officers. D. Brown: Dalkeith, Western Australia.

Sato, Shohei .2017. "'Operation Legacy': Britain's Destruction and Concealment of Colonial Records Worldwide," *The Journal of Imperial and Commonwealth History*, DOI: 10.1080/03086534.2017.1294256.

Sekamwa, J. C. 2016. *Enkuluze y'ediini y'Abaganda ey'enono.* Lex Africana Ltd: Kampala, Uganda.

Sjogren, Anders. 2015. "Battles over boundaries: The politics of territory, identity and authority in three Uganda Regions." *Journal of Contemporary African Studies*, 33(2).

Speke, J. H. 1863. *Journal of the Discovery of the Source of the Nile.* W. Blackwood & Sons: Edinburgh/London.

Stiglitz, Joseph (2018) *Globalization and its Discontents Revisited: Anti Globalisation in the Era of Trump*, W.W. Norton & Co, New York Summers, Carol. 2017. "All the Kabaka's Wives: Marital Claims in Buganda's 1953-5 Kabaka Crisis" in *Journal of African History*, 58(1).

—. 2006. "'Subterranean Evil' and 'Tumultuous Riot' in Buganda: Authority and Alienation at King's College, Budo, 1942." *The Journal of African History*, 47(1).

Summers, C. and Sikanga, A. A. 2015. "Uganda Politics World War II (1939-1949)". In Byfield, J. A. et al. (eds), *Africa and World War II.* Cambridge University Press: Cambridge.

Syahuka-Muhindo and Kristof Titeca. 2016. "The Rwenzururu Movement and the Struggle for the Rwenzururu Kingdom in Uganda." Discussion Paper /2016.01 ISSN 2294-8651.

Tharoor, Shashi. 2017. *Inglorious Empire: What the British did to India.* Hurst & Company: London.

Thompson, Gardener. 2015. *African Democracy: Its origins and Development in Uganda, Kenya and Tanzania*, Fountain Publishers: Kampala, Uganda.

—. 2003. *Governing Uganda: British Colonial Rule and its Legacy*, Kampala: Fountain Publishers.

—. 1992. "Colonialism in Crisis: The Uganda Disturbances of 1945," African Affairs, 91(365).

Tripp, Mari Aili, 2010, *Museveni's Uganda: Paradoxes of Power in a Hybrid Regime*, Lynne Rienner Publishers, London.

Tucker, Alfred R. 1908. *Eighteen Years in Uganda and East Africa.* Vol. I. Edward Arnold: London.

—. 1910. "Mission and the Development of Uganda." In *World Missionary Conference*, Vol. VII, Edinburgh/New York.

—. 1911. *Eighteen Years in Uganda and East Africa.* Negroes University Press: Connecticut.

Tumushabe, G. and Gariyo, Z. 2009. *Uganda's Taxpayers Burden: The Financial and Governance Costs of a Bloated Legislature.* ACODE Policy Research Series, No.28.

Twaddle, Michael. 1993. *Kakungulu & the Creation of Uganda.* James Currey, London.

Villafana, Frank R. 2009. *Cold War in the Congo: The Confrontation of Cuban Military Forces, 1960-1967.* Transaction Publishers, New Jersey.

West, Henry W. 1972. *Land Policy in Buganda.* Cambridge University Press: London.

Wild, J. V. 2006. "The Wild Committee." In Brown, Douglas & Brown, Marcelle V. (eds.), *Looking Back at the Uganda Protectorate: Recollections of District Officers.* Dalkeith: Douglas Brown.

Wright, Michael, 1971. *Buganda in the Heroic Age*, Oxford University Press: Oxford.

Reports

Report of a Commission of Privy Counsellors on a Dispute Between Buganda and Bunyoro of May 1962.

Report of the Commission of Inquiry into the Disturbances in Uganda during April, 1949

Report of the Commission of Inquiry into the Disturbances which occurred in Uganda during January, 1945.

Report of the Joint Committee on Closer Union in East Africa, Vol. II Minutes of Evidence, House of Commons Paper 156.

Report of the Uganda Constitutional Conference 1961, dated 9 October, 1961.

Report of the Uganda Independence Conference 1962.

Report of the Uganda Relationships Commission.

Report on tour to Uganda (2-12) December 1953 by R. E. C Broadbent, Assistant Security Liaison Officer, EA File No. P. F.728883, original file S.F. 205- East Africa.

Newspaper Articles

Blomfield, Adrian, "African King Aims to Bankrupt Britain," *Daily Telegraph*, 13 March 2004.

"British troops move into three East African countries to restore order," *The Telegraph*, 26 January 1964.

"Buganda's Position in EA Federal Set-up: Only Uganda Can Decide," *Uganda Argus,* 23 August 1963.

"Bunyoro in Fresh Push for Compensation Amid Claims UK paid £700m," *The East African,* Saturday 13 May 2013, accessed at www.theeastafrican.co.ke/news/Bunyoro-in-fresh-push-for-compesation-/255-1856358.

"Coronation of His Highness The Kabaka Mutesa II, Historic Scenes at Mengo and Budo," *The Uganda Herald,* Wednesday 25 November, 1942.

"Denis Hills," *The Guardian*, Tuesday 4 May 2004.

"For 300 years Britain has outsourced mayhem. Finally, it's coming home," *The Guardian*, 8 June, 2009.

"How Israel planned a 90-minute raid on Entebbe airport," *Daily Monitor,* 3 July, 2016.

"Is the Commonwealth a plausible substitute for the EU? *The Economist,* 12 April, 2018.

"Kampala Becomes a City," *Uganda Argus*, Tuesday 9 October, 1962.

"No Transfer, Says Lukiiko," *Uganda Argus*, 21 July, 1962.

"Not the Most Important Job," *Uganda Argus*, 5 October, 1963.

"Bob Astles" (obituary), *The Daily Telegraph*, 15 February, 2013.

"Remember our British friends." *Uganda Argus*, Tuesday, 9 October, 1962.

"The Government Sends Instructions to London: Sir Edward Will be Buried in Uganda," *Uganda Argus*, 24 November 1969.

"Thousands see Kabaka and Kyabazinga installed," *Uganda Argus*, 10 October, 1963.

"Toro Ends Boycott—Decision after 12-hour talks with Premier," *Uganda Argus*, 27 June, 1962.

"Uganda Cannot Accept Buganda's Claim in Uganda," *Uganda Argus*, 12 August, 1963.

Hirsch, Afua. "It's right for Britain to reach out to Africa—wrong to send Boris Johnson," *The Guardian*, 16March, 2017.

Kimenye, Barbara "Bob Astles is Rejected by Kabaka, Hangs onto Obote, Amin," *The Daily Monitor* Newspaper, 8 November, 2015.

Colvin, Ian, "Kabaka File for Lawyers," *Daily Telegraph*, 15 December,

1969.
—. "King Freddie Inquiry by Uganda Police," *Daily Telegraph*, 9 December, 1969.
Fairhall, J. "Afterword: Idi Amin," *The Guardian*, 18 August, 2003.
Faustin, Mugabe, "Baganda put pressure on NRA to have Mutebi crowned," *Daily Monitor*, 11 September, 2016.
Freeman, Colin, "The Man Fighting for Independence of the West African Nation of Biafra…From a Flat in Peckham," *The Telegraph*, 21 January, 2017.
Keatley, Patrick, "Idi Amin" (Obituary), *The Guardian*, 18 August, 2003.
Mamdani, Mahmood "50th Anniversary of Uganda's State Independence: A View from Society," *The New Vision*, 23 July, 2013.
—. "Buganda and Uganda at Crossroads," *The New Vision*, 7 August, 2009.
McManus, James and Eric Silver, "Israelis jubilant as Amin laments," *The Guardian*, Sunday, 4 July 1976.
Obugagga newspaper, 9 January, 1961.
"UK to compensate Kenya's Mau Mau torture victims," *The Guardian*, Thursday 6 June, 2013.
"Resign Report Denied by Katikiro," *Uganda Argus*, 3 January 1961.

"The Black Baby. Mr Bull "What, another!! Well, I suppose I must take it in!!!,"" *Punch Magazine*, 21 April 1894. Retrieved from http://punch.photoshelter.com/image/I0000WOK.ss5MQmc accessed 3 July, 2017.
Taifa Uganda Empya newspaper, 13 July, 1963.
The Daily Worker, Monday, 28 December, 1953.
The Mail on Sunday, 27 December, 2014.
The Observer, 21 February, 1954.
The Telegraph, 18 August, 2003.
The Telegraph, 24 January, 2011.
The Times, 22 April, 1954.
The Times, 2 November, 1954.
Tribune magazine, 17 June, 1977.
Uganda Argus, 6 March, 1958.
Uganda Argus, 11 January, 1962.
Uganda Argus, 12 January, 1962.
Uganda Argus, 18 January, 1962.
Uganda Argus, 20 January, 1962.
Uganda Argus, 26 January, 1962.
Uganda Argus, 3 February, 1962.

Uganda Argus, 5 May, 1962.
Uganda Argus, 28 June, 1962.
Uganda Eyogera, 28 June, 1962.
Uganda Argus, 4 July, 1963.
Uganda Argus, Monday 23 July, 1963.
Uganda Eyogerera, 19 June, 1962.

List of Cases

Alafairi Kasule, Semu K. Mukwaba & Juma Tamusange v. Daudi Musoke Mukubira vs. Attorney General & Three Others, Civil Case No.50 of 1954

*Democratic Republic of the Congo v. Uganda (*Armed Activities Case), 2005. http://www.icj-cij.org/files/case-related/116/10457.pdf, accessed on 19th May 2018.

Fazaldin Miraneux v. Simoni Lule, Civil Case No. 50 of 1954, reported in 7.U.L.R.

The Katikiro of Buganda v. Attorney General Mwenge v. Migade, Miscellaneous Case No. 19 of 1933

Nditi Mutua and Four Others v. The Foreign and Commonwealth Office (2012) EWHC 2678 (QB).

Nyali Ltd. v. Attorney General of Kenya (1956) Q.B.

Sobhuza II v. Miller and Others (1926) A.C. 518

Stanislas Mugwanya v. Lui Sensuwa

Uganda v. Commissioner of Prisons ex-parte Matovu (1966) EA 514

GLOSSARY OF NON-ENGLISH TERMS

Ab'amasiga	sub-clan heads
Abakama	ancient name for Bunyoro and Toro kings
Abakulu b'obusolya	clan heads
Abalangira	princes
Abataka	clan heads or senior citizens in an area
Abasomi	"readers" or Christian converts
Abasamize	high priests or practitioners of traditional religion
Abazukulu ba Kintu	an association of young and radical Baganda
Amasaabo	shrines
Amasaza	counties
Askari	colonial guards/ regiments
Bakopi	commoners
Bakungu	non-hereditary chiefs
Banyoro	the people of Bunyoro kingdom
Busulu	dues, taxes
Bataka	clan chiefs
Eddiini	traditional religion/spirituality
Ekipande	identification passes
Emisambwa	deities
Envujjo	rent or tribute in kind from produce from one's land
Kabaka	king
Kasanvu	compulsory labour
Katikkiro	Buganda's prime minister
Katonda	God
Kibuga	capital city

Lubiri	royal enclosure
Luganda	the language of the Baganda people
Lukiiko	Royal Assembly
Luwalo	public works
Mailo	land tenure granted under the 1900 Agreement
Mchaka mchaka	National Service
Mwami	the Burundian king
Namasole	the mother of the Kabaka (king)
Obutaka	clan lands
Obutaka bw'akasolya	major clan estates
Obutaka bw'amasiga	sub-clan estates
Omuhikirwa	prime minister of the kingdom of Toro
Omujasi	head general
Omukago	a sacred rite of blood brotherhood
Omukulu W'ekibuga	chief in charge of the capital city
Omulamuzi	chief justice
Omutaka	clan leader
Omuwanika	treasurer
Orukurato	the parliament of Bunyoro
Ssaza	county
Wafaransa	local name for the Catholic White Fathers of France
Wangeleza	local name for the Christian Missionary Society

INDEX